AF516486

DUTCH SOURCES ON SOUTH ASIA
c. 1600-1825

DUTCH SOURCES ON SOUTH ASIA
c. 1600-1825

VOLUME 1

Bibliography and
Archival Guide to the
National Archives at The Hague
(The Netherlands)

JOS GOMMANS, LENNART BES, GIJS KRUIJTZER

MANOHAR
2001

This publication has been financed by the Gonda Foundation of the Royal Netherlands Academy of Arts and Sciences (KNAW) and facilitated by the Algemeen Rijksarchief.

Algemeen Rijksarchief (National Archives)

Prins Willem-Alexanderhof 20
2595 BE The Hague
P.O. Box 90520
2509 LM The Hague
http://www.archief.nl/rad
e-mail: ara@rad.archief.nl

First published 2001

ISBN 81-7304-370-1 (Set)
ISBN 81-7304-384-1 (Vol. 1)

Published by
Ajay Kumar Jain for
Manohar Publishers & Distributors
4753/23 Ansari Road, Daryaganj
New Delhi 110002

Printed at
Replika Press Pvt. Ltd.
A 229, DSIDC Narela Indl Park
Delhi 110040

Contents

APPENDICES

Maps

Abbreviations

ARA	Algemeen Rijksarchief (National Archives).
CDNI	*Corpus diplomaticum Neerlando-Indicum* (see Bibliography, no. 10).
EIC	(English) East India Company.
GG&C	Governor-General and Council (at Batavia).
IGG	*Ingekomen stukken van Gouverneur-Generaal en Raden bij de Heren XVII en de Kamer Zeeland* (papers received from Governor-General and Council by the Gentlemen XVII and the Zeeland Chamber).
IKI	*Ingekomen stukken van de kantoren in Indië bij de Heren XVII en de Kamer Zeeland* (papers received from the establishments in the Indies by the Gentlemen XVII and the Zeeland Chamber).
IRAA	*Inventarissen van Rijks- en Andere Archieven.*
KHGU	*Kroniek* (or *Kronijk*) *van het Historisch Genootschap gevestigd te Utrecht.*
Meilink-Roelofsz	M.A.P. Meilink-Roelofsz and others, *De archieven van de Verenigde Oostindische Compagnie/The Archives of the Dutch East India Company* (see Bibliography, no. 82).
OBP	*Overgekomen brieven en papieren* (letters and papers received).
VOC	Verenigde Oostindische Compagnie (Dutch East India Company); VOC series.
VROA	*Verslagen omtrent 's Rijks Oude Archieven.*

Note on Orthography

Archival collections and specific administrative functions are given in Dutch with an English translation when used for the first time. Abbreviations also refer mostly to current Dutch usage. Hence, you find *OBP* (*overgekomen brieven en papieren*) and not *LPR* (*letters and papers received*). Only well-known administrative functions such as *Heren XVII* and *Gouverneur(-Generaal) en Raden* are translated as Gentlemen XVII and Governor(-General) and Council. Dutch and English usage of archival terms and collections are based on Meilink-Roelofsz's *The Archives of the Dutch East India Company (1602-1795)* (The Hague, 1992). In general, geographical, personal and technical terms are given in modern transliteration without the use of diacritical marks and according to their current usage. Where the latter is uncertain we have preserved the Dutch form between inverted commas. In the end, dealing with a myriad of different language traditions, a degree of inconsistency cannot be avoided. To facilitate the use of the guide and the archives, Appendix III offers an Indo-Dutch spelling list which gives various Dutch forms of the more common South Asian names and terms.

Geographical Terms

The geographical scope of the volume comprises the modern states of India, Sri Lanka, Bangladesh, Pakistan and the Maldives. Whenever the expression India is used it is in its wider, pre-modern meaning of the Indian subcontinent including Sri Lanka. Other geographical names are often given according to their historical context and relevance: e.g. Ceylon instead of Sri Lanka and Malabar instead of Kerala. The geographical division of both the bibliography and the archival guide is based on the administrative organization of the VOC in South Asia. Thus, we will employ the five regional divisions which at that time were usually labelled as Surat, Malabar, Ceylon, Coromandel and Bengal. Surat included not only Gujarat but also the western parts of Hindustan (e.g. Agra), Malwa (e.g. Burhanpur) and Sind. Although the VOC settlement on the Konkan (Vengurla) had a direct link with Batavia it will be dealt with under Malabar which term refers to the Kanara Coast as well. The settlements on the Fishery Coast and the contacts with the Maldives will be treated under Ceylon since they were administered from Colombo. Although Coromandel refers to most of the Indian east coast, the settlements of northern Orissa (Balasore and Pipli) belonged to Bengal. Bengal also included Patna in Bihar. More details on the administrative division of the VOC in South Asia as well as on the Indian powers surrounding the Dutch factories are to be found under the regional headings of the Archival Guide in Part II.

Preface

This volume is meant as an introduction and guide to the use of Dutch sources for the late-medieval or early-modern history of South Asia. More specifically, it provides a bibliography of published primary and secondary sources (Part I) as well as a descriptive guide to the archival resources of the Dutch East India Company (VOC) at the *Algemeen Rijksarchief* (ARA) in The Hague (Part II). Apart from the VOC archives, the latter will include closely related archives and collections such as various private and family papers. As such, the guide aims at stimulating and facilitating the use of this material by both historians and social scientists, in particular those from South Asia.

This volume dispenses with giving an overall description of the VOC archives as this has been done by others. For an introduction to the history of the VOC and its The Hague archives in general, one should consult the recently published general inventory of M.A.P. Meilink-Roelofsz and others, *The Archives of the Dutch East India Company (1602-1795)* which also provides essential information on the organization and the decision-making process of the Company (see Bibliography, no. 82). The present guide will serve as a more descriptive, regional extension of this inventory which remains essential reading for every new researcher in the field. The Appendices provide a description of the sources in Indian languages at The Hague, a list of Dutch chiefs in Batavia and South Asia and an Indo-Dutch spelling list. In the future we hope to produce a second volume which will deal with Dutch archives beyond the *Algemeen Rijksarchief*.

In order to facilitate the use of both bibliography and archival guide, a brief survey of the history and the historiography of Indo-Dutch interaction during the VOC period will be presented. For mere convenience the latter will be referred to as Indo-Dutch studies although it should neither be considered a separate discipline nor do we wish to create such a discipline. Our purpose is merely to present a survey of the various ways historians of South Asia in the past have used the Dutch archives. For a detailed account of Dutch relations with South Asia readers should take note of the excellent recent surveys, *The Merchant Warrior Pacified* by G.D. Winius and M.P.M. Vink (no. 132) and the New Cambridge History of India volume *European Commercial Enterprise in Pre-colonial India* by O. Prakash (no. 124). A descriptive treatise of the most eye-catching seventeenth-century Dutch travel accounts on South Asia is provided by D.F. Lach and E.J. van Kley's *Asia in the Making of Europe*, vol. 3, book 1 and 2 (no. 270).

Finally, we would like to thank those institutions and people which made the whole project both possible and worthwhile. First of all we would like to thank the Gonda Foundation of the Royal Netherlands Academy of Arts and Sciences (KNAW) for the indispensable financial backing of the whole project. The Algemeen Rijksarchief and its staff turned out to be very cooperative, not only by providing easy access to the various archival depots and excellent working facilities but also by their expert advice at times of utter desperation. In particular we should mention Pieter Koenders, Trix van Hoof, Max Beekhuis, Paul van Royen, Louisa Balk, Iris Heidebrink, Ron Guleij, René Haubourdin, Eric Ooievaar, Diederick Kortlang, Peter Wijnmaalen and Richard Bakx. As early as 1997 Jan Fernhout was already working at the ARA to produce a research guide on South Asia but due to lack of time and financial assistance, the project never really took off. Nevertheless, in about two months time, he produced the initial framework of the guide which was of great help to Jos Gommans of Leiden University who took over the project in 1998. Two of his students, Lennart Bes and Gijs Kruijtzer, became involved in the project during 1999 and conducted all the necessary archival research in about nine months time. The latter also produced Appendix I, the Dutch sources in Indian languages for which he received expert help from Dr A.G. Menon, Zareena Parveen and Mr Armèn Joseph. Very important was the timely assistance of Lizette de Koning who, almost single-handedly, generated the inventory of the map collections. Perhaps not always aware of this themselves, Femme Gaastra and Om Prakash have been generous in sharing with us their rich experience of the archives as well as with various colleagues in the field. As a result of the research for his M.A. thesis, Tycho Wallaardt provided us with valuable information about Vengurla. Martine Gosselink of the Atlas Mutual Heritage project allowed us to utilize the data available with her on VOC settlements. Last but not least, we are much obliged to Peter Rietbergen and Hugo s'Jacob for their incisive and detailed comments on the introduction to this volume. Needless to say that the responsibility for the end product is entirely ours.

At the advent of the VOC's fourth centenary in 2002, this publication is not meant as another tribute to its colourful history but rather as a reminder that it is a unique manifestation of a massive information-gathering institution that created more than 1,200 metres of The Hague files relating to almost all the regions surrounding the Indian Ocean. Hopefully, this volume will make part of this fascinating early-modern database more accessible and stimulate a new generation of scholars the world over to use it more often and more effectively than ever before. Even in the third millennium, there is still much to be explored.

Introduction

The neglect of Dutch sources for this period is all the more to be regretted, because in some respects they are definitely superior to the English. The Dutch merchants were careful to set down in black and white many things which the English were content to take for granted: their more extensive operations gave them wider views; and the discipline enforced by the authorities at Batavia produced detailed and precise records of transactions carried out in distant places. English-reading students will naturally continue to rely mainly on the English sources, but they are likely to form inaccurate or distorted views on many important questions, if they fail to take account also of the information furnished by the Dutch.

W.H. Moreland in 1923[1]

THE DUTCH IN INDIA

It is often forgotten that for about two centuries the Dutch were closely involved with the Indian subcontinent and Ceylon. For the Dutch East India Company (Verenigde Oostindische Compagnie, VOC), this whole area used to be a part of its so-called *westerkwartieren* or *buitencomptoiren*, in other words, its western or exterior provinces, a term that reflects the rather eccentric location from the point of view of the VOC headquarters in Batavia, now Jakarta. Its peripheral position was partly the result of an early Dutch cupidity for the fine spices of the Indonesian Archipelago, especially pepper, cloves, nutmeg and mace, all of which found excellent outlets in Amsterdam and the other bustling markets of western Europe. Moreover, the production of the latter three commodities could be fairly easily monopolized through military intervention or full conquest. Hence, in due course, the spice-monopoly of the VOC became the mainstay of Dutch policy in the East and conditioned its expansionist drive towards the Indonesian islands.

Initially, Dutch stakes in India were closely tied in to their operations in the Spice Islands. Since India produced first-rate textiles for the Indonesian market, it possessed an indispensable key to the spice trade. Not surprisingly, the first Company traders in India arrived not directly from western Europe, but indirectly from Aceh and Bantam, two of the foremost commercial entrepôts of the eastern 'lands below the winds'. Long before Dutch involvement in the area, these towns had been part of a flourishing, inter-regional trading system embracing the entire Indian Ocean from Mombasa in eastern Africa to Manila in the Philippines. Like their Asian and Portuguese predecessors, the Dutch gratefully exploited the opportunities of this system. For them, Indian textiles, apart from giving easy access to the spice market, also considerably reduced the need to carry huge quantities of American bullion to Asia. Hence, India played a pivotal role in the

[1] Cited from the preface of his book, *From Akbar to Aurangzeb: A Study in Indian Economic History* (London, 1923).

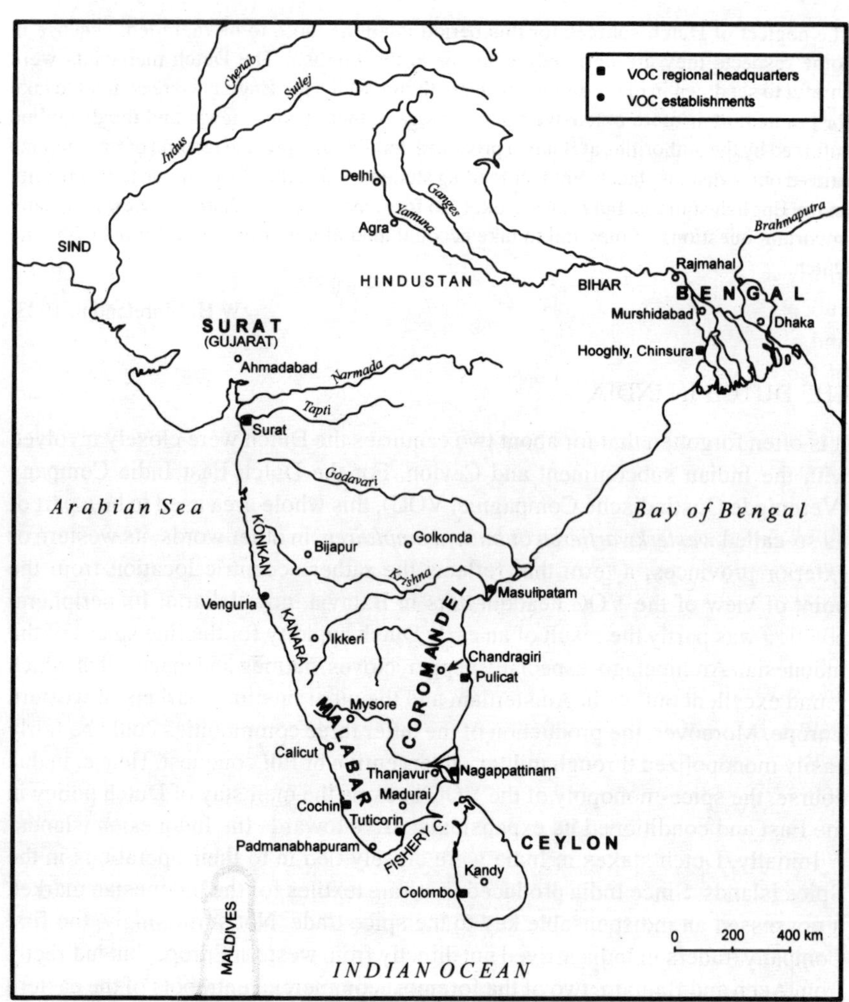

Map 1: The VOC in South Asia

intricate intra-Asiatic network of exchange in which the VOC bartered Indian textiles for Indonesian spices, Indonesian spices for Chinese silk, Chinese silk for Japanese bullion, and Japanese bullion for Indian textiles.

Although situated at the periphery of Dutch Batavia, in macroeconomic terms, India at large was a global superpower. Since Mauryan and Roman times it had been a major producer of a huge variety of raw and manufactured goods which created an almost structural trade surplus with the outside world. In consequence, India repeatedly served as a reservoir of the world's gold and silver resources. Far from being buried in the soil, as the old oriental cliché has it, this bullion often flowed directly into urban and agrarian expansion. Indeed, India boasted a longstanding reputation for providing endless opportunities for rapid enrichment and careers. The result was a permanent inflow of talented and ambitious merchants, warriors and intellectuals, mostly from West and Central Asia, taking their share of India's proverbial fortune. To a substantial degree, this ongoing influx of bullion and manpower fuelled the process of state-formation on the subcontinent. Hence, from the very start, the Dutch encountered various dynamic and powerful Indian states like the Mughal Empire in the north or the sultanates of Golkonda and Bijapur in the Deccan, all propped up by numerous Iranian, Turkish, Afghan and African immigrants, mostly serving as bureaucrats and warriors. Later, during the seventeenth century, the political crisis of the Mughal Empire stimulated the rise of new regional successor states such as Hyderabad, Arcot, Mysore and that of the Marathas. Also in the south, the small but vigorous Hindu states of Travancore, Ikkeri, Madurai, Thanjavur (Tanjore) and Ramnad similarly built their rising fortunes on the imperial legacy of the decaying Vijayanagara empire. Obviously, for these assertive new rulers, the Dutch could be very attractive business partners, who offered interesting outlets for their much sought after commodities, mainly textiles, pepper, cinnamon, indigo and saltpetre.

In a way, early Dutch commercial interests in the subcontinent were in tune with the *longue durée* pattern in which merchants, both Asians and Europeans, could hardly dispense with the precious goods of India. Therefore, from the early-seventeenth century onwards, the VOC began to establish several trade factories which gradually developed into five regional headquarters: Surat, Malabar, Ceylon, Coromandel and Bengal. Being the foremost producer of both common and more luxurious textiles, the Indian east coast or Coromandel was rightly considered the left arm of the Spice Islands. To a lesser extent, Surat and Bengal provided textiles, the latter becoming increasingly important during the second half of the seventeenth century. Besides, both gave access to the markets of the interior of Hindustan, such as Burhanpur, Lahore, Delhi, Agra and Benares. Surat developed as a major sales-office providing the VOC with additional silver. During the early eighteenth century, Bengal became the foremost exporter of various commodities that were earmarked for Europe and China. Apart from textiles, it produced saltpetre, opium and the world's cheapest raw silk. The rationale of the Dutch establishments in Malabar and Ceylon was, however, different and was more in accordance with Dutch policy in Java and the Spice Islands. Here the Dutch were primarily concerned with procuring spices: in particular pepper on the Malabar Coast and cinnamon in Ceylon. The Company spent a great deal of time and money to secure its monopoly over these products, however, it was a policy which only bore fruit in Ceylon. As a result, like Batavia, Colombo grew into an administrative centre overseeing large agrarian estates whereas the other Indian establishments always remained mere trading factories.

While the VOC increasingly focused on Java, the Spice Islands and Ceylon, India's economic weight increased even further during the eighteenth century. Now the emerging craze for calicoes in Europe produced an even more booming trade in Indian textiles. The latter replaced spices as the prime commodity of Asian trade with Europe. At the same time, shifting markets and trade routes had favoured the rise of several regional states as mentioned above. At this stage, it was not the rigid and monopolistic VOC but the more flexible English East India Company (EIC) which managed to rise to the occasion. While the English investments in India had started as a second-best option ever since the Dutch had thrown them out of the Spice Islands, now these turned out to be their crucial asset. Partly driven by the increasing competition with independent English country-traders, who enjoyed much more leeway than their Dutch counterparts or *vrijburgers*, the EIC not only gained the commercial edge but also became far more readily drawn into Indian politics. By contrast, Dutch trade was hamstrung by an exhaustive apparatus of rigid rules and regulations which considerably hampered private initiative. The policy of the Gentlemen XVII was aimed at keeping everyone and everything in place, often at tremendous costs, or to use the words of the Malabar chief Hendrik Adriaan van Reede: 'The indigenes ridiculed us for our lost labours'.[2] Another illustration of this attitude is provided by Georges Roques, who served the French East India Company in Gujarat between 1676 and 1693. According to his account, every month the Dutch factors in Ahmadabad sent an account to Surat, to be finally passed into the General Books in Batavia.

> This is how it is regulated in all the factories. They thus know definitely the amount needed to maintain each of them and, maintaining the sound system, they clearly see their profits and losses every year so that they can withdraw from places which prove to be unprofitable. This is what they do not do although they have several posts too many of which bring them no profit but a lot of expenses; even so they do not give them up. They are there, and there they want to stay, whatever be the cost. Those who have but a light job, endeavour to inform the head factory about what the others are doing, and about whatever happens there and all around down to the smallest detail. The Council takes its resolution on it, in order to go forward. By this excellent policy, they know everything that happens in India, by sea and land, in order to profit from it.[3]

In the end, the bureaucratic supervision on the basis of purely commercial objectives, explains the fact that, whereas the Dutch became notorious imperialists in Southeast Asia and Ceylon, they persisted as prudent emporialists in India to the very bitter end. After the 1750s and in particular after the fourth Dutch-British

[2] Cited in G.D. Winius & M.P.M. Vink, *The Merchant-Warrior Pacified. The VOC (the Dutch East India Company) and its Changing Political Economy in India* (Delhi, 1991), p. 39.

[3] Translated by Indrani Ray in L. Subramaniam (ed.), *The French East India Company and the Trade of the Indian Ocean: A Collection of Essays by Indrani Ray* (Delhi, 1999), p. 73.

war (1780-4), the VOC's fortunes in India were clearly in decline; its last ailing factories being easily confiscated as a result of the war between the British and the Batavian Republic in the Netherlands (1795-1802).

Although this Dutch predilection for rules and regulations was hardly conducive to the private trader, after two centuries it clearly turns out to be a blessing in disguise for the modern historian. Indeed, the Dutch zeal to produce endless reports about the way these rules and regulations were observed or ignored, makes their records by far the richest and, perhaps, best accessible source of pre-colonial Indian history.[4] To what extent have historians in the past exploited these archival riches?

INDO-DUTCH STUDIES

Three quarters of a century ago, the well-known English civil servant and historian W.H. Moreland wrote a brief article about 'Dutch sources for Indian history: 1590-1650'. Moreland, known to be a pioneer in the field of economic history of Mughal India, considered the VOC sources indispensable for any student seriously interested in the Mughal period. According to Moreland, there were several reasons for this. First of all, following Dutch supremacy in the seaborne trade, the VOC records contained an enormous amount of information relating to Indian commerce and standards of consumption. Dutch accounts on the working of Indian markets in cities like Agra or Golkonda were far superior to anything he had found in English so far. Even students interested in political and administrative themes, contemporary public opinion or social life in India, were well advised to consult these neglected records. Often, as Moreland continued, these Dutch sources delineated the day-to-day working of institutions too familiar for indigenous chroniclers to describe: administrative procedures, types of punishment, methods of levying local taxes, and a great variety of detailed information which the historian must take seriously into account.[5]

At the time Moreland wrote these lines, hardly any scholar had used Dutch records as a source for Indian history and even for a very long time since, Moreland's appeal was ignored. Fortunately, 75 years later, the picture has changed dramatically. To give just one indication of this, Moreland in his 1923 article could count only 17 relevant contributions for the first 60 years of Indo-Dutch interaction whereas the bibliography in the present volume contains more than 800 titles, admittedly for the VOC period as a whole.[6] For example, since Moreland's time, a great deal has been achieved in the publication of source

[4] It is only from about the second-half of the eighteenth century that the records of the English and French East India Companies become more informative on the indigenous situation in India.

[5] W.H. Moreland, 'Dutch Sources for Indian History: 1590 to 1650', *Journal of Indian History*, 2 (1923), pp. 222-5.

[6] Besides, commenting on the few available published sources at that time, Moreland had to apologize to his readers that they were written in Dutch and were not to be found in Indian libraries. At present, the subject has become far more accessible since numerous, primary as well as secondary, publications have appeared in English although their availability in Indian libraries has not much improved. Despite the translations of a few Dutch sources in English, Dutch language skills still remain indispensable.

materials. The publication of the *Batavia daghregister* (up until 1683) started as early as 1887 and was completed in 1931. From 1907 onwards, Dutch-Asiatic contracts and treaties were being published in the *Corpus diplomaticum Neerlando-Indicum* and completed in 1955. Thanks to the Linschoten Vereniging—the Dutch counterpart of the Hackluyt Society—several important travel accounts were published. The State Committee for Fatherlandic History has included in its series of the *Rijks Geschiedkundige Publicatiën* (RGP) several official VOC records such as the extensive and very informative report by the Company's Chief Secretary Pieter van Dam, and the general reports (*generale missiven*) of the Batavia government to the *Heren XVII* in the Dutch Republic (1610-1750). Of particular importance for Ceylon was the 1991 publication of the Dutch-period edicts in the *Ceylonees plakkaatboek.*

Apart from this exponential growth in the production of source publications, what about the historiographical achievements since Moreland's article? Here the story becomes more complex since we need to make a distinction between two tendencies within the wider field of Indo-Dutch studies. Indeed, one group of scholars, mainly from India and Sri Lanka, following Moreland's footsteps, used Dutch sources for tracing information on the economic history of South Asia proper. Another, much older variety of Indo-Dutch studies concerns historians, mainly from the Netherlands writing in Dutch, who remain firmly embedded in the field of so-called 'fatherlandic' history, i.e. the history of the Netherlands and its overseas expansion. Both this Hollando-centric tradition and the more recent Indo-centric approach developed against heavy odds since Dutch historians tended to be primarily concerned with Indonesia whereas their South Asian colleagues were mostly preoccupied with the British colonial legacy. Nonetheless, Indo-Dutch studies survived, partly also because during the last two decades, Hollando-centric and Indo-centric scholars have moved towards each other, both showing a growing interest in the impact of Dutch trade on the various regional economies of South Asia. Nowadays, scholars from both traditions meet regularly, presenting and exchanging their research in an ever wider historiographical context. It remains to be seen whether a new generation of historians will continue the two existing historiographical traditions and to what extent they will be able to find new ways and challenges for the future.

THE HOLLANDO-CENTRIC TRADITION

The Hollando-centric tradition evolved slowly during the nineteenth century. In 1825, the Netherlands finally lost its last, moribund possessions in India which had been briefly re-established after the Napoleonic wars. But Dutch colonial circles retained a detached interest—more as a hobby—in what was now increasingly considered the dead past of a defunct institution. Articles on India rarely appeared in *De Indische Gids* and other colonial journals because the prime focus of interest remained those Indies that became increasingly dominated by Dutch colonial rule. The colloquial expression *Indië* which was formerly used to refer vaguely to everything beyond the Cape of Good Hope, came to refer to Indonesia only. Moreover, historical studies on Dutch overseas history were considerably hampered by the persisting policy of secrecy and censorship regarding the Company's archives.[7] In the Netherlands, it was only at the very end of the nineteenth century that various source publications began to mark a renewed interest in the Company's history. We mentioned already the *Batavia daghregister* and the *Corpus diplomaticum Neerlando-Indicum*. At about the same time, there was a remarkable revival of historical studies on Dutch Ceylon. To a large extent, this was part of a growing awareness among the so-called *burghers* of Ceylon of their Dutch descent. This growing sense of Dutchness was reflected in the establishment of the Dutch Burgher Union in 1911. As a consequence, Dutch sources in Colombo more and more attracted the attention of energetic archivists like S. Anthonisz-Pieters and later E. Reimers. Other interested individuals like D. Fergusson, F.H. de Vos, R.G. Anthonisz, J.P. Lewis and P.E. Pieris wrote numerous, at times very nostalgic articles on various aspects of Ceylon's Dutch heritage. Interestingly, at about the same time, the British civil servant A. Galetti, assisted by Dutch and Belgian Catholic priests like A.J.M. Heyligers, P. Groot, A.J. van der Burg and J. Fruijtier, started their pioneering work on the Dutch records in Madras. Meanwhile, in the Netherlands, the simmering interest in Indo-Dutch relations also focused on Ceylon as indicated by the work of W. van Geer, G. Nypels and W. Zwier. However, apart from scattered contributions by A.K.A. Gijsberti Hodenpijl and N. MacLeod, the Indian mainland hardly attracted serious attention. Others, like S. Kalff and the well-known traveller and novelist M. Wagenvoort, turned a more romantic eye to the Indo-Dutch past, using such evocative titles as *In het voetspoor der vaderen* (In the footsteps of the fathers). As with earlier romantic authors like Jacob Haafner, they emphasized the theme of personal adventure in an increasingly orientalized context. Obviously, at this time of vibrant European nationalism, all history meant fatherlandic history whereas overseas history referred to the colonial history of the Dutch East Indies. India very much remained a paradise lost to the British.

During the nineteenth century, almost all research of the VOC records was conducted by archivists. The pioneering work of Anthonisz-Pieters and Groot in Colombo and Madras has already been mentioned. At the *Algemeen Rijksarchief*, the National Archives in The Hague, a few enterprising archivists like P.A. Leupe and P.A.S. van Limburg Brouwer incidentally worked on India.[8] Later, from the early 1930s onwards, it was one of their successors at the ARA, Mrs. M.A.P. Meilink(-Roelofsz) who stood at the beginning of a more thorough, and scholarly interest in the overseas history of the VOC. Meilink closely cooperated with Heert Terpstra, at that time a teacher at the *Gymnasium* (Dutch grammar school) in Hilversum. Influenced by the famous indologist-*cum*-historian Johan Huizinga at Groningen, Terpstra was pathbreaking in ridding Dutch overseas history from

[7] M.A.P. Meilink-Roelofsz, *Van geheim tot openbaar: Een historiografische verkenning* (Leiden, 1970).

[8] Van Limburg Brouwer's fascination with India is shown in his numerous indological articles in e.g. *De Gids* and *De Nederlandsche Spectator*, and also in his novel *Akbar* which appeared in 1872 in which he attacks the rigid and intolerant rules of the Christian Church by idealising Akbar's open, contemplative, Indian mind. For his archival work on the early history of the South Asian VOC factories, see ARA, *losse aanwinsten*, inv. no. 151.

its overwhelmingly Hollando- and Indonesia-centric bias. Perhaps, his work may be considered the first modern scholarly contribution to the early history of Indo-Dutch relations. It was Meilink-Roelofsz, inspired by Terpstra and influenced by renowned colonial revisionists like Van Leur, Schrieke and Romein, who continued Terpstra's work into the 1960s.[9] Nevertheless, Dutch historical research on South Asia remained at a very low ebb during this period.[10]

Obviously, decolonization marks an important caesura in the writing on Dutch overseas history. In the Netherlands only Utrecht managed to retain its chair in Dutch overseas history into the early 1970s.[11] Moreover, the colonial trauma after Indonesian independence (1947) only served to strengthen the earlier proclivity to neglect Dutch entanglements with India. Fortunately, this general lack of Dutch scholarly attention was to some extent compensated by a renewed interest from the newly independent states of India and Sri Lanka. This is indicated, for example, by the studies of T.I. Poonen on Malabar and K.K. Datta on Bengal. Both historians, however, hardly used unpublished sources and mainly reworked earlier Dutch contributions. As such they could not escape the prevalent Hollando-centric approach. Again Ceylon was more or less exceptional in this respect as scholars like R. Raven-Hart, J.H.O. Paulusz and S.G. Perera continued to translate and work on VOC-related sources, both written in Dutch and in German.

Equally important in keeping Indo-Dutch history alive during these years were the pioneering studies of C.R. Boxer and H. Furber. Of course, these remarkable historians were only partly interested in Indo-Dutch history but their refreshing approach clearly paved the way for the upsurge of Indo-Dutch studies during the 1960s and 1970s. Boxer's work mainly focused on the various social and cultural aspects of Dutch life in the Tropics. Furber also paid tribute to the more unofficial and informal side of the VOC by paying a great deal of attention to its existence as a kind of shadow empire consisting of numerous transnational and personal networks. From about this time, two exceptional Danish historians, K. Glamann and N. Steensgaard, became fascinated by the VOC as the first modern commercial joint-stock company. Steensgaard even presented the Company as the prime carrier of an Asian trade revolution. Clearly, these international scholars did much to liberate Dutch historians from their colonial trauma and created an atmosphere in which scholarly interest for Dutch overseas history could re-emerge.[12] As mentioned already, this happened during the late 1960s and 1970s, mainly at the instigation of Leiden University where in 1970 good-old Meilink-

[9] See the 1977 interview with Meilink-Roelofsz in L. Blussé and others (eds), *Pilgrims to the Past: Private Conversations with Historians of European Expansion* (Leiden, 1996), pp. 21-33.

[10] Exceptional, however, is Van Lohuizen's study on Mysore: *The Dutch East India Company and Mysore* (The Hague, 1961).

[11] After Coolhaas (to 1967) and Van der Wal, Utrecht discontinued the chair in 1972. Immediately after WW II, Leiden had exchanged its chair in colonial history (Heeres-Colenbrander-Krom) for a chair in maritime history (Milo).

[12] Nevertheless, the colonial trauma still lives on in the latest controversies about Indonesia between historians from Leiden and social scientists from Amsterdam. As with the earlier animosity between the liberal Leiden and conservative Utrecht academics, these discussions have had hardly any influence on either the VOC or South Asian studies in the Netherlands.

Roelofsz was installed as professor for the history of Western-European expansion overseas. Four years later, also in Leiden—the centre for the history of overseas expansion and as a result of the increasing interest in the subject—was launched under the guidance of H.L. Wesseling. This renewed interest into the phenomenon of overseas expansion also reverberated towards the field of Indo-Dutch studies. For example, one of Meilink-Roelofsz's PhD students, H.K. s'Jacob, took a closer look at Dutch relations with Kerala. Another of her students, F. Lequin, extensively studied the Company's huge staff files relating to Bengal. From the fatherlandic-history section at Leiden, F.S. Gaastra enhanced our understanding of the Company's organization, especially with regard to its shipping, bookkeeping and other financial operations.[13] At the University of Utrecht, J. van Goor continued the Utrecht tradition of colonial history by showing a marked interest in Ceylon. Like Boxer taking advantage of his grasp of the Portuguese overseas history, the American but Leiden-based scholar G.D. Winius, with another Leiden student M.P.M. Vink, wrote an excellent survey of the VOC's history in India. Recently, the IGEER at Leiden produced several dissertations pertaining to the activities of the Dutch East India Company in Ceylon and South India.[14] Although many of these studies tend to give up the Hollando-centric approach, the latter remains prominent, the more so as it links up very well with the renewed popularity of all kinds of VOC representations among the general public.[15]

THE INDO-CENTRIC TRADITION

As pointed out earlier, it was the historian Moreland who first drew attention to the importance of Dutch sources for the history of Mughal India. Moreland himself used mainly published Dutch sources in which he was assisted by the well-known Dutch historian P. Geyl.[16] In the 1930s and 1940s, the iconoclastic Dutch civil servant-*cum*-scholar J.C. van Leur also appealed to his colleagues to be more sensitive to the Asian context of what was still widely known as the colonial history of the Dutch East Indies. Moreland's and Van Leur's calls for a more Asia-centric perspective were taken seriously in the direct aftermath of decolonization; historians from the newly independent states of South Asia playing an ever more prominent part in it. To name the most important among them:

[13] See especially his project with J.R. Bruijn, *Dutch-Asiatic Shipping in the 17th and 18th Centuries*, which enables a more quantitative analysis of Dutch-Asian trade.

[14] See the work of L. Wagenaar on Galle, the comparative approach of R. Raben on Colombo and Batavia, and M. de Lannoy on Travancore.

[15] See, for example, the VOC-mania as described in the Dutch magazine *Elsevier* of 17 June 1995. At present, this "Disneyland version" of the VOC not only sells very well in the Netherlands but also in Japan and, to a lesser extent, in Sri Lanka. There appears to be no such enthusiasm in India. Nonetheless, at the instigation of the Dutch Embassy in India, a first inventory of the remaining Dutch monuments in Bihar, Gujarat, West Bengal, Andhra Pradesh and Cochin has been produced by F.F. Ambachtsheer and L.B. Wevers in 1997.

[16] See, for example, the comments of Ashin Das Gupta in his 'Moreland Hypothesis', in K.S. Mathew (ed.), *Mariners, Merchants and Oceans: Studies in Maritime History* (Delhi, 1995), pp. 19-25.

H.A.I. Goonetileke and S. Arasaratnam on Ceylon, the latter and T. Raychaudhuri on Coromandel, A. Das Gupta on Malabar, and Gujarat and O. Prakash and S. Chaudhuri on Bengal. These scholars—some from a more or less Marxist or nationalist perspective—were primarily interested in the economic history of India as gleaned from Dutch sources. Hence, they were particularly concerned with the impact of the VOC as it had massively exported raw and manufactured goods in exchange for ever growing quantities of bullion. For example, they focused on the way the VOC engendered new demand which may have stimulated inflation or, as others would have it, led to growing production levels in India. There is still a lively discussion going on about the way the VOC influenced and anticipated the inner dynamics of India's regional economies in which the validity of quantitative methods based on VOC data are all part of the debate.[17] In any case, by highlighting the sophistication and rationality of Indian rulers and merchants, these historians succeeded in revising earlier stereotypes such as those of 'hoarding' oriental despots or petty Asian pedlars. Most of them worked extensively with published and unpublished VOC records and, by pronouncing the so-far ignored indigenous side of the picture, tremendously enhanced our understanding of Dutch commercial operations in South Asia.

In spite of the growing awareness of the Indian viewpoint, the scope of these economic studies remained very much within the limited reach of the VOC, in other words, it remained confined to the coast.[18] Like their Dutch colleagues, scholars from South Asia mainly relied on Dutch and other European source material. Being mostly economic historians, the European material, full of all kinds of facts and figures, was far more attractive than the more narrative-oriented sources in Indian languages. As a result, there continued to exist a huge gap between, on the one hand, the historical research directed towards the European companies and the littoral economies, and, on the other hand, the discussions on, for example, state-formation in the Indian interior. This is illustrated by the fact that the recent wave of revisionist historians working on eighteenth-century India—mainly from Delhi, Cambridge and Leiden—have hardly found any response from VOC historians or vice versa.[19] Recently, one Indian scholar, S. Subrahmanyam, has successfully and almost single-handedly attempted to bridge the gap by paying more attention to the political and commercial connections between coastal regions and hinterland. Playing down the innovative commercial impact of the VOC, he underscores its so-far neglected political and military role. As such, the ambivalence of the Dutch merchant-*cum*-warrior comes very

[17] For a summary of these debates, see S. Subrahmanyam, *The Political Economy of Commerce: Southern India 1500-1650* (Cambridge, 1990), pp. 1-8. See also the debate between O. Prakash and S. Chaudhuri in *Modern Asian Studies*, 27, 2 (1993) and the recent review by L. Subramanian, 'Alternate Approaches to Maritime India', *The Indian Economic and Social History Review*, 33, 2 (1996), pp. 209-17.

[18] Most of the mentioned authors were perfectly aware of this. A. Das Gupta, in particular, attempted to examine the nexus between maritime trade and hinterland politics (A. Das Gupta, 'Trade and Politics in Eighteenth-Century India', in D.S. Richards (ed.), *Islam and the Trade of Asia: A Colloquium* (Oxford/Philadelphia, 1970), pp. 181-214).

[19] For a balanced evaluation, see D.A. Washbrook, 'Progress and Problems: South Asian Economic and Social History c.1720-1860', *Modern Asian Studies*, 22, 1 (1988), pp. 57-96.

near to his model of the Indian *portfolio-capitalist*, both thriving at the interface of commerce and politics.[20]

An approach more or less similar to Subrahmanyam's is offered by the PhD thesis on Surat by the Dutch indologist H. van Santen in which a great deal of information is gathered on the working of the Mughal state. Interestingly, the Indo-centric stance of Van Santen is part of the much older tradition of Dutch classical indology. Early indologists like H. Kern, W. Caland and J.Ph. Vogel felt attracted to the informative Dutch travel accounts which they made more accessible by editing those of Linschoten, Geleynssen de Jongh and Ketelaar. Besides, orientalists like Van Ronkel and Vogel drew linguistic attention to some forgotten early Dutch grammars and glossaries of Indian languages. With a little good will one may even recognize in the theological works of clergymen like Rogerius and Baldaeus or in the chronicles of Pelsaert, De Laet, Van Twist, Valentijn and Mossel the earliest antecedents of Dutch indology. But oddly enough, Dutch indology started relatively late during the second-half of the nineteenth century, mainly stimulated and strengthened by its connections with Dutch, Indonesian and classical studies, and hardly at all by the impressive knowledge of India accumulated during the VOC period of intense contact.[21] It is only recently that indologists have started to exploit the VOC sources, mainly in the context of newly emerging historical studies which were forcefully stimulated, especially during the 1980s and 1990s, by J.C. Heesterman at the Kern Institute in Leiden.[22]

CHALLENGES AHEAD

Both Hollando-centric and Indo-centric approaches have greatly contributed to our understanding of Indo-Dutch interaction during the early-modern period. Especially the economic dimensions of Dutch activities have been very well discussed, in particular by Indian historians. Dutch and Danish historians have considerably improved our understanding of the working of the VOC as a huge, 'multinational' trading company with commercial stakes all over the Indian Ocean.

[20] Subrahmanyam's close cooperation with other South Asianists working mainly with Indian-language sources like V. Narayana Rao, D. Shulman and M. Alam has already shown the enormous potential of combining Indian with Dutch source material. See, e.g. *Symbols of Substance: Court and State in Nayaka Period Tamilnadu* (Delhi, 1992). Also successful in 'exploring the hinterland' are the contributions by B. Bhattacharya and, again, Subrahmanyam and Alam in A. Das Gupta's *festschrift*: R. Mukherjee and L. Subramanian (eds), *Politics and Trade in the Indian Ocean World* (Delhi, 1998).

[21] J.C. Heesterman, 'The Precarious Rise and Survival of Sanskrit and Indian Studies', in W. Otterspeer (ed.), *Leiden Oriental Connections 1850-1940* (Leiden, 1989), pp. 115-25.

[22] Apart from Van Santen, Heesterman supervised R.J. Barendse's 1991 dissertation on the Arabian Seas which builds extensively on VOC sources. See his unpublished 'Koningen, compagnieën en kapers: de Arabische zeeën 1640-1700' and also its revised English version *The Arabian Seas 1640-1700* (Leiden, 1998). For the 'revisionist' historical work of some of Heesterman's other students, see A. Wink, *Land and Sovereignty in India: Agrarian Society and Politics under the Eighteenth-Century Maratha Svarajya* (Cambridge, 1986), D.H.A. Kolff, *Naukar, Rajput and Sepoy: The Ethnohistory of the Military Labour Market in Hindustan, 1450-1850* (Cambridge, 1990), J.J.L. Gommans, *The Rise of the Indo-Afghan Empire, c.1710-1780* (Leiden, 1995; 2nd ed.: Delhi, 1999).

But how should we proceed from here? What are the challenges for the future?

It would be useful to continue the earlier, economy-oriented, fact-and-file approaches since much of the source material is still left unexplored. Following the course set out by Moreland, the economic historian still has numerous opportunities to investigate the material for new information, for example, on trade volumes, commercial networks, shifting patterns of trade, and perhaps most important for the highly monetized economy of India, on monetary policy and banking. But also in terms of state-formation and political chronology the VOC archives still have much to offer. For example, Dutch sources have as yet been insufficiently consulted for the political history of the Deccan sultanates of Bijapur and Golkonda, or hardly at all for the eighteenth-century Coromandel states of Arcot and Thanjavur. Although Ceylon appears to be very well covered by the existing historiography, no serious study has been made of eighteenth-century Kandy.[23] Even the economic history of the VOC in India still has scope for further study, especially with respect to the eighteenth century. Apart from focusing on the regional polities of South Asia, we should not forget to keep an eye open to the very extensive Indian connections overseas. Following the *Annales*-like approach of K.N. Chaudhuri, we should look for trans-regional economic systems based on 'inner seas' like the Bay of Bengal or the Arabian Sea. The global perspective of the VOC managers should remind us of the fact that these geographical categories are mostly far more relevant than the more current concepts of modern nation-states or continents. Here VOC-based studies may help to break through the still prevalent boundaries of area studies.

We may also take up Boxer's earlier example by paying closer attention to the still much ignored realm of mentalities. This would mean that we should investigate the VOC material for its potential to reveal the categories created by their being written as ever so many forms of European cultural discourse. For example, we are still at a loss to understand what really happened to people, both high and low, when they passed the Cape of Good Hope to be temporarily settled in a world which required different skills and rules of conduct. Dutch sources may tell us a great deal about the world view of individual VOC servants who extensively travelled between so many disparate subcultures. Here emerges an entirely new field for historians keen to embrace anthropological and psychological methodology. Studies into the *mentalités* of overseas Dutchmen may direct our attention to those rare intellectual figures like Hendrik Adriaan van Reede or Herbert de Jager, who had a deep interest in the cultural and scientific dimensions of India, and in writing down their findings, created the categories which helped them to master the unknown. Perhaps it will also disclose all kinds of affective liaisons with Indian society, for example through local marriage, patronage or military service.[24] It may stimulate renewed attention to such well-

[23] Recently, M. Vink at Minnesota finished his dissertation on seventeenth-century Madurai. The Leiden PhD student S. van Galen is presently working on the connection between Arakan and eastern Bengal.

[24] Interesting examples in this respect are the eighteenth-century Dutch military adventurers Johannes Hessing and his son Joris alias *Jorus Sahib,* who both served in the army of the Maratha chief Madhoji Sindhia (H. Compton, *European Military Adventurers of Hindustan from 1784 to 1803* (Karachi, 1976), pp. 363-4).

known Dutch issues like corruption and other forms of public or private misconduct.[25] As Holden Furber has shown already, even the most scrupulous among Dutch traders proved human after all and once in a while gave in to the Indian laws of gravitation offering rapid careers and easy money. Indeed, through the cracks in the official correspondence, at times there emerges a cosmopolitan network of private interests and patronage that penetrated deeply into the informal circles of Indian political and social systems. For example, apart from making them obey the orders of their superiors in Batavia, the VOC servants in Golkonda could not be restrained from smuggling copper and elephants to the Mughal court, making use of the military might of the Company to protect their private interests.[26] It is very well possible that on closer scrutiny, even the official correspondence will reveal numerous other examples of illicit and informal networks that could overarch the apparent rigidness of the divide between Europeans and Indians.[27]

Keeping these cultural and psychological aspects in view, it would be fascinating to set out from Boxer's and Holden Furber's concept of an Indo-European frontier. According to Furber the Europeans lived in a frontier society that was characterized both by the omnipresence of danger and by an untrammelled scramble for wealth. Such a society presented opportunities to build new careers which combined with a freedom to shift from one occupation to another and to associate with people of differing social and ethnic origins.[28] From hindsight we know that the English, especially the free-wheeling country-traders, were most successful in bridging this frontier by increasingly infiltrating the political, commercial and affective networks of the so-called hinterland.[29] By contrast, the Directors of the VOC did not allow any of their servants to be drawn into what they considered the far too dangerous and opaque imbroglios of Indian society. Even Dutch *vrijburgers* were hardly given any leeway since the Company wanted to cling to its various trade monopolies. Hence, despite numerous incentives to be torn into the fluid politics of Indian states, the VOC very much remained a trading institution more at home at sea than on land. As mentioned already, only in Ceylon the Dutch managed to cross this frontier as they became increasingly engaged in controlling the production of another of their monopoly spices: cinnamon.

[25] It appears the VOC was very early in scrutinizing the behaviour of their overseas servants. For example, one may claim that the moral indignation which led to the late-eighteenth-century impeachment of Warren Hastings had a late-seventeenth century predecessor in the VOC's 'commissie van redres' which was set up by the visionary Directors Joannes Hudde and Coenraad van Beuningen, both members of the so-called *Collegianten* movement which, apart from various regents, also included Spinoza and other freethinkers of the Republic.

[26] G. Kruijtzer, '"De blode Brahminees": Madanna, Akanna en het politieke systeem van Golkonda 1660-1687' (Unpublished M.A. thesis, Leiden University, 1997).

[27] Apart from taking account of the fashionable but perhaps somewhat overrated 'deconstructivist' approach *à la* Michel Foucault and Edward Said, it would be useful to connect with German scholarship on early-modern Eurasian *Kulturgeschichte*. See, e.g. J. Osterhammel, *Die Entzauberung Asiens: Europa und die asiatischen Reiche im 18. Jahrhundert* (Munich, 1998).

[28] H. Furber, *Rival Empires of Trade in the Orient, 1600-1800* (Minneapolis, 1976), pp. 336-7.

[29] Apart from Furber, see e.g. the more recent study by C.A. Bayly, *Empire and Information: Intelligence gathering and Social Communication in India, 1780-1870* (Cambridge, 1996).

The concept of an Indo-European frontier also enables us to bring the operations of the VOC more clearly within the South Asian historiographical build-up. As mentioned earlier, this frontier was situated at the junction of the coast and the interior; the first characterized by a large degree of mobility facilitated by large amounts of mobile resources, the latter more focused on settled, agrarian investment. In this view, the essential dichotomy is not that between Indian and European but that between the mobile society of the sea and the sedentary society of the mainland.[30] Here we come across a familiar theme in Asian history where state building does not proceed from the centre to periphery, but revolves around an *inner* frontier between settled and nomadic societies.[31] Hence, by elaborating on the concept of an Indo-European frontier, we may find new ways to incorporate the history of the VOC into the complex, pre-existent fabric of South Asian history.

[30] One recent example of this approach is the unpublished Leiden M.A. thesis of L. Bes, 'Friendship as long as the sun and moon shine: Ramnad and its perception of the Dutch East India Company, 1725-1750' (1997).

[31] This idea derives from J.C. Heesterman. See, e.g. his 'Littoral et intérieur de l'Inde', in L. Blussé, H.L. Wesseling and G.D. Winius (eds), *History and Underdevelopment: Essays on Underdevelopment and European Expansion in Asia and Africa* (Leiden, 1980), pp. 87-92.

Part I: Bibliography

INTRODUCTION

This bibliography relates to published primary and secondary sources pertaining to the history of Indo-Dutch interaction from *c.* 1600 to 1825. The list of primary sources comprises works that were produced around this time and are generally given in their first edition although recent editions or translations have been added. The scholar who cannot read Dutch should take note of the fact that most Dutch travel accounts have numerous contemporary translations in various European languages, although these are often incomplete or inaccurate. The scattered and mostly anonymous reports in contemporary Dutch newsletters such as *Hollandsche Mercurius*, the *Europische Mercurius*, *Maandelijkse Nederlandsche Mercurius* and *Staatkundige Historie van Holland*, or yearbooks such as the *(Nieuw) Nederlandsche Jaarboeken* have not been included in the bibliography.

The list of secondary sources embraces titles that were produced from about 1825 to 2000. Some titles which at first sight appear to bear no direct relevance have been included when they substantially relate to the theme of Indo-Dutch interaction or to the study of Dutch sources on South Asia. The list covers not only titles concerning the Dutch presence in South Asia but also, vice versa, titles that relate to South Asian influences on Dutch society or culture. Furthermore it comprises non-Dutch works as far as these are produced by servants of the VOC such as the numerous travelogues by German soldiers.

The titles have been ordered according to the administrative regions of the VOC (e.g. information on Madurai and the Fishery Coast is found under 'Ceylon'). Works pertaining to more than one region are to be found under General. In order to trace titles on a certain region one should both check the general (1) and relevant regional lists (2-6). At the end an author index has been added referring to title nos. Obviously, although covering more than 800 titles, the bibliography is not exhaustive. It is strong on titles in Dutch, English, German and French but rather weak on titles in other European languages. Besides, it contains only two works in an Asian language (nos 340, 385). Most of the titles were taken from other bibliographies, footnotes and catalogues which means that their relevance could not always be checked and that mistakes are unavoidable. Following Dutch rule, authors with a prefix such as 'van' or 'de' are to be found under their full second name.

1. GENERAL

1.1. Primary Sources

1 Allard, Carel, *Orbis habitabilis oppida et vestitus* (Amsterdam, *c.*1695); reprint with introduction by R.A. Skelton (Amsterdam, 1966).

2 Baldaeus, Philippus, *Nauwkeurige beschryvinge van Malabar en Choromandel, derhalver aangrenzende ryken, en het machtige eyland Ceylon. Nevens een omstandige en grondigh doorzochte ontdekking en wederlegginge van de afgoderye der Oost-Indische heydenen*, 3 vols (Amsterdam, 1672); part. ed. A.J. de Jong (The Hague, 1917).

3 Broecke, Pieter van den, *Korte historiael ende journaelsche aenteyckeninghe* (Haarlem, 1634).

4 Broecke, Pieter van den, *Pieter van den Broecke in Azië*, 2 vols, ed. W.Ph. Coolhaas (Werken Linschoten Vereniging, 63-4) (The Hague, 1962-3).

5 Bry, Johann Theodor de, and Johann Israel de Bry (comps), *India orientalis*, 12 vols (Frankfurt, 1598-1628).

6 Carmona, Don G., 'De godsdienstige toestand in Voor-Indië onder Hollandsch bestuur', ed. J. Kleyntjens S.J., *Tijdschrift voor Indische Taal-, Land- en Volkenkunde van het Koninklijk Bataviaasch Genootschap van Kunsten en Wetenschappen*, 76 (1936).

7 Carolinus, Godefridus, *Het hedendaagsche heidendom, of beschrijving van den godsdienst der heidenen* (Amsterdam, 1661).

8 Coen, Jan Pieterszoon, *Bescheiden omtrent zijn bedrijf in Indië*, 7 vols, eds H.T. Colenbrander and W.Ph. Coolhaas (The Hague, 1919-53).

9 Commelin, Isaac (comp.), *Begin ende voortgangh van de Vereenighde Nederlantsche Geoctroyeerde Oost-Indische Compagnie*, 2 vols (Amsterdam, 1645); fasc. ed. by C.R. Boxer (Amsterdam, 1969).

10 *Corpus diplomaticum Neerlando-Indicum. Verzameling van politieke contracten en verdere verdragen door de Nederlanders in het oosten gesloten, van privilegebrieven aan hen verleend, enz.*, 6 vols (1596-1650, 1650-75, 1676-91, 1691-1725, 1726-52, 1753-99) eds J.E. Heeres and F.W. Stapel (The Hague, 1907-55); vols I-V in *Bijdragen van het Koninklijk Instituut voor Taal-, Land- en Volkenkunde*, vols 57, 87, 91, 93, 96.

11 *Daghregisters gehouden int Casteel Batavia vant passerende daer ter plaetse als over geheel Nederlandts-India (1628-1682)*, 31 vols, eds J.A. van der Chijs and others (Batavia and The Hague, 1888-1931).

12 Dam, Pieter van, *Beschrijvinge van de Oostindische Compagnie*, 4 vols, 7 parts, eds F.W. Stapel and C.W.Th. van Boetzelaer (Rijksgeschiedkundige Publikatiën, Grote Serie, 63, 68, 74, 76, 83, 87, 96) (The Hague, 1927-54).

13 *De oudste reizen van de Zeeuwen naar Oost-Indië, 1598-1604*, ed. W.S. Unger (Werken Linschoten Vereniging, 51) (The Hague, 1948).

14 Dubois, J.P.L., *Vies des Gouverneurs Généraux de la Compagnie des Indes avec l'abrégé de l'histoire des établissements hollandois aux Indes orientales* (The Hague, 1763).

15 *Dutch-Asiatic Shipping in the 17th and 18th Centuries*, eds J.R. Bruijn, F.S. Gaastra and I. Schöffer (Rijksgeschiedkundige Publikatiën, Grote Serie, 165-7) (The Hague, 1979-87).

16 'Eerste sprokkeling uit de papieren van eenen Bewindhebber der O.-Indische Compagnie', *Kroniek van het Historisch Genootschap gevestigd te Utrecht*, vol. 28 (1872) [relating to Jacob van Ghesel].

17 Frick, Christoph, *Ost-indianische Räysen und Kriegesdienste* (Ulm, 1692); ed. J. Kirchner (Berlin, 1926); trans. C.E. Fayle, *Voyages to the East*

Indies by Christopher Fryke and Christopher Schweitzer (London, 1929).

18 *Generale missiven van Gouverneurs-Generaal en Raden aan Heren XVII der VOC*, 10 vols, eds W.Ph. Coolhaas (vols 1-8), J. van Goor (vol. 9) and J.E. Schooneveld-Oosterling (vol.11) (Rijksgeschiedkundige Publikatiën, Grote Serie, 104, 112, 125, 134, 150, 159, 164, 193, 205, 232) (The Hague, 1960-97).

19 Haafner, Jacob, 'Dichterlijke beschrijving van den regenmoesson, op de kusten van Malabaar en Coromandel', *Algemeene Vaderlandsche Letteroefeningen* (1801).

20 Haafner, Jacob, *Lotgevallen op eene reize van Madras over Tranquebaar naar het eiland Ceilon* (Haarlem, 1806).

21 Haafner, Jacob, *Onderzoek naar het nut der zendelingen en zendelingsgenootschappen* (Haarlem, 1807); eds J.A. de Moor and P.G.E.I.J. van der Velde (Hilversum, 1993).

22 Haafner, Jacob, *Reize in eenen palanquin* or *Lotgevallen en merkwaardige aanteekeningen op een reize langs de kusten Orixa en Choromandel*, 2 vols (Amsterdam, 1808).

23 Haafner, Jacob, *Lotgevallen en vroegere zeereizen van Jacob Haafner*, ed. C.M. Haafner (Amsterdam, 1820).

24 Haafner, Jacob, *Reize naar Bengalen en terugreize naar Europa*, ed. C.M. Haafner (Amsterdam, 1822).

25 Haafner, Jacob, *Proeve van Indische dichtkunde volgens den Ramaijon*, ed. C.M. Haafner (Amsterdam, 1823).

26 Haafner, Jacob, *De werken van Jacob Haafner*, 3 vols, eds J.A. de Moor and P.G.E.I.J. van der Velde (Werken Linschoten Vereniging, 91, 94, 96) (Zutphen, 1992-7).

27 Hagen, Steven van der, *Korte ende warachtig verhael* (Rotterdam, 1606) [see also Commelin].

28 Hartgers, Joost (comp.), *Oost-Indische voyagien door dien begin en voortgangh, van de Vereenighde Nederlandtsche Geoctroyeerde Oost-Indische Compagnie* (Amsterdam, 1648) [for similar collections, see: Gillis Joosten Saegman (comp.), *Verscheyde Oost-Indische Voyagien: met de beschrijvingen van Indien* (Amsterdam, 1663); P. Conradi and V. van der Plaats (comps), *Nederlandse reizen ter bevordering van den koophandel, na de meest afgelegene gewesten des aardkloots* (Amsterdam and Harlingen, 1784-7)].

29 *Historisch verhaal van het begin, voortgang en tegenwoordigen staat des koophandels van de generale Nederlandsche Geoctroyeerde O.I. Compagnie*, 2 vols (Arnhem, 1768-72).

30 Hogendorp, Dirk van, *Mémoires du Général Dirk van Hogendorp, Comte de l'Empire, etc.*, ed. D.C.A. van Hogendorp (The Hague, 1887).

31 Hulsius, Levinus (comp.), *Sammlung von sechs und zwanzig Schiffahrten in verschiedene fremde Länder durch Levinus Hulsius und einige andere aus dem Holländischen ins Deutsche übersetzt und mit allerhand Anmerkungen versehen*, 26 vols (Nuremberg, Frankfurt and Hannover, 1598-1660).

32 Langhansz, Christoph, *Neue ost-indische Reise* (Leipzig, 1705).

33 Leeuwenson, Joannes, 'Daghregister van de landreijs, gedaen bij mij Joannes Leeuwenson, secretaris van de Ed. Heer Ryckloff van Goens, Raed Ordinaris

van India, Super-Intendent, Admirael, Krijgs- en Veldoverste, soo te water als te lande; dienende tot bescherming van 't eiland Ceylon, de custen van Cormandel, Mallebaer, Madure, etc. beginnende Ao. 1674', ed. P.A. Leupe, *Bijdragen tot de Taal-, Land- en Volkenkunde van Nederlandsch Indië* (1863).

34 Linschoten, Jan Huygen van, *Reysgeschrift van de navigatiën der Portugaloysers* (Amsterdam, 1595).

35 Linschoten, Jan Huygen van, *Itinerario. Voyage ofte schipvaert* (Amsterdam, 1596)

36 Linschoten, Jan Huygen van, *Itinerario. Voyage ofte schipvaert van J.H. van Linschoten naer Oost ofte Portugaels Indiën, 1579-1592*, vols 1-2: ed. H. Kern (Werken Linschoten Vereniging, 2) (The Hague, 1910) and rev. ed. H. Terpstra (Werken Linschoten Vereniging, 57-8) (The Hague, 1955-6); vol.3: eds C.P. Burger and F.W.T. Hunger (Werken Linschoten Vereniging, 39) (The Hague, 1934); vols 4-5: ed. J.C.M. Warnsinck (Werken Linschoten Vereniging, 43) (The Hague, 1939).

37 Luzac, E., *Hollands rijkdom. Uit het Fransch vertaald, vervolgens overzien, merkelijk veranderd, vermeerderd en van verscheiden misslagen gezuiverd*, 4 vols (Leiden, 1780-3).

38 Merklein, Johann Jacob, *Ost-indianische Reise* (Nuremberg, 1663) [see also *Reisebeschreibungen*; ed. A. Estermann (Munich, 1985)].

39 Mossel, Jacobus, *Beknopte historie van het Mogolsche keyzerryk en de zuydelyke aangrensende ryken* (Batavia, 1758).

40 *Naamlyst van de respective gouverneurs, directeurs, commandeurs item verdere opperhoofden en mindere bediendens op de buyten comptoiren van Nederlands India zoo als derzelve in wezen zyn geweest in den jaare ...* (Amsterdam, n.d.) [published in the annual '*Herenboekjes*' of the eighteenth century].

41 *Nederlands-Indisch placaatboek 1602-1811*, 17 vols, ed. J.A. van der Chijs (Batavia and The Hague), 1907-55).

42 Poser und Gross Nedlitz, Heinrich von, *Lebens und Todes Geschichte, worinnen das Tage Buch seiner Reise von Constantinople aus durch die Bulgarey, Armenien, Persien und Indien* (Jena, 1675); part. trans. G. Dharampal, 'Heinrich von Poser's Travelogue of the Deccan', *Quarterly Journal of the Mythic Society*, 73 (1982).

43 Purchas, Samual (ed.), *Hakluytus Posthumus, or Purchas his Pilgrimes*, 4 vols (London, 1625); reprint in 20 vols (Glasgow, 1905-7).

44 Radermacher, J.C.M., 'Schets van het Hindostansche rijk en het half-eiland bewesten de Ganges (1783)', *Verhandelingen van het Koninklijk Bataviaasch Genootschap voor Kunsten en Wetenschappen* (1824).

45 Radermacher, J.C.M., 'Schets van den tegenwoordigen staat van het half-eiland beoosten de Ganges (1783)', *Verhandelingen van het Koninklijk Bataviaasch Genootschap voor Kunsten en Wetenschappen*, 4 (1824).

46 *Reisebeschreibungen von deutschen Beamten und Kriegsleuten im Dienst der niederländischen West- und Ost-Indischen Kompagnien*, 13 vols, ed. S.P. l'Honoré Naber (The Hague, 1930) [vol. 4: Johann von der Behr; vol. 5: Albrecht Herport; vol. 3: Johann Jacob Merklein; vol. 6: Johann Jacob

Saar; vol. 11: Christoph Schweitzer; vols 12-13: Martin Wintergerst; vols 8-9: Johann Sigmund Wurffbain].

47 Saar, Johann Jacob, *Ost-indianische fünfzehen-jährige Kriegs-Dienst* (Nuremberg, 1662) [see also *Reisebeschreibungen*].

48 Schouten, Wouter, *Oost-Indische voyagie*, 2 vols in 1 (Amsterdam, 1676).

49 Schröder, Johann Heinrich, *Der Seefahrer* (Leipzig and Gotha, 1749).

50 Stavorinus, Johan Splinter, *Reize van Zeeland over de Kaap de Goede Hoop en Batavia, naar Samarang, Macassar, Amboina, Suratte enz. in 1774-1778* (Leiden, 1793).

51 Tappe, David, *Fünfzehen jährige curiöse und denckwürdige auch sehr gefährliche ost- indianische Reise-beschreibung* (Hannover and Wolfenbüttel, 1704).

52 *The Dutch Factories in India 1617-1623. A Collection of Dutch East India Company Documents pertaining to India*, ed. O. Prakash (Delhi, 1984).

53 *The Private Correspondence of Isaac Titsingh*, 2 vols (Japonica Neerlandica, vols 4 and 5), ed. F. Lequin (Amsterdam, 1990-2).

54 'Tweede sprokkeling uit de papieren van eenen Bewindhebber der O.-Indische Compagnie', *Kroniek van het Historisch Genootschap gevestigd te Utrecht*, vol. 29 (1873), vol. 30 (1874) [relating to Jacob van Ghesel].

55 Twist, Johan van, *Generale beschrijvinge van Indiën. Ende in 't besonder kort verhaal van 't koninckrijck van Gusuratten* (Amsterdam, 1647-8) [i.e. the account on Gujarat only, for the full account, see Commelin].

56 Valentijn, Francois, *Oud en nieuw Oost-Indiën*, 5 vols in 8 parts (Dordrecht, 1724-26).

57 *Verzameling van instructiën, ordonnanciën en reglementen voor de regering van Nederlandsch-Indië*, ed. P. Mijer (Batavia, 1848).

1.2. Secondary Sources

1.2.1. *Archives, bibliographies and historiography*

58 Arasaratnam, S., 'Some Comments on the Use of the Records of the Dutch East India Company as Sources for the Writing of History', *Journal of Southeast Asian History*, 3,1 (1962).

59 Arasaratnam, S., 'Recent Trends in the Historiography of the Indian Ocean 1500-1800', *Journal of World History*, 1, 2 (1990).

60 Bos-Rops, J.A.M.Y. and others (eds), *De archieven van het Algemeen Rijksarchief* (Alphen aan de Rijn, 1982).

61 Bracht, J. van (ed.), *Atlas van kaarten en aanzichten van de VOC en WIC, genoemd Atlas Vingboons, in het Algemeen Rijksarchief 's-Gravenhage* (Haarlem, 1981).

62 Buur, D., *Alfabetisch persoonsnamenregister behorende bij J.C. Hooykaas 'Repertorium of de koloniale literatuur in mengelwerken en tijdschriften van 1595-1865 uitgegeven in Nederland en zijn overzeesche bezittingen'* (Leiden, 1981).

63 Charpentier, J., 'The British Museum Manuscript Sloane 3290, the Common

Source of Baldaeus and Dapper', *Bulletin of the School of Oriental Studies*, 2 (1923-5).

64 Chijs, J.A. van der, *Proeve eener Nederlandsch-Indische bibliografie (1659-1870)* (Batavia, 1875).

65 Chijs, J.A. van der, *Inventaris van 's Lands Archief te Batavia (1602-1816)* (Batavia, 1882).

66 Chijs, J.A. van der, *Realia. Register of the generale resolutiën van het kasteel Batavia, 1632-1805*, 3 vols (The Hague and Batavia, 1882-5).

67 Coolhaas, W.Ph., *A Critical Survey of Studies on Dutch Colonial History* (The Hague, 1960; 2nd rev.ed. by G.J. Schutte, The Hague, 1980).

68 Dharampal-Frick, G., 'Frühe deutsche Indien-Berichte (1477-1750). Bibliographie', *Zeitschrift der Deutschen Morgenländischen Gesellschaft*, 134 (1984).

69 Goonewardena, K.W., 'Dutch Historical Writing on South Asia', in C.H. Philips (ed.), *Historians of India, Pakistan, and Ceylon* (London, 1961).

70 Hair, P.E.H., 'Bibliography. Dutch Voyage Accounts in English Translation 1580-1625, a Checklist', *Itinerario*, 14, 2 (1990).

71 Hartman, J., *Repertorium op de literatuur betreffende de Nederlandse koloniën voor zoover zij verspreid is in periodieken, serie- en mengelwerken*, 9 vols (The Hague, 1895-1934).

72 Hooykaas, J.C., *Repertorium op de kolonial literatuur in mengelwerken en tijdschriften van 1595 to 1865*, 2 vols (Amsterdam, 1874-80).

73 s'Jacob, H.K., 'De Europese expansie', in H. Baudet and H. van der Meulen (eds), *Kernproblemen der economische geschiedenis* (Groningen, 1978).

74 Jaquet, F.G.P., *Sources of the History of Asia and Oceania in the Netherlands, Vol. 2: Sources 1796-1949* (Munich, 1983).

75 Kan, J. van, *Compagniesbescheiden en aanverwante archivalia in Britisch Indië en op Ceylon* (Batavia, 1931).

76 Landwehr, J. and P. van der Krogt (eds), *VOC: A Bibliography of Publications relating to the Dutch East India Company, 1602-1800* (Utrecht, 1991).

77 Lindeman, R., Y. Scherf and R. Dekker, *Reisverslagen van Noord-Nederlanders van de zestiende tot begin negentiende eeuw. Een chronologische lijst* (Haarlem, 1994).

78 *List of Volumes of Dutch and Danish Records preserved in the Madras Record Office* (Madras, 1916).

79 Meilink-Roelofsz, M.A.P., 'Aspects of Dutch Colonial Development in Asia in the Seventeenth Century', in J.S. Bromley and E.H. Kossmann (eds), *Britain and the Netherlands in Europe and Asia* (London, 1968).

80 Meilink-Roelofsz, M.A.P., 'Enige opmerkingen over een nieuwe benadering van de Nederlandse expansie geschiedenis', *Kleio*, 18 (1976).

81 Meilink-Roelofsz, M.A.P. and others, *Dutch Authors on Asian History. A Selection of Dutch Historiography on the Vereenigde Oostindische Compagnie* (Dordrecht and Providence, 1988).

82 Meilink-Roelofsz, M.A.P., R. Raben and H. Spijkerman (eds), *De archieven van de Verenigde Oostindische Compagnie/The Archives of the Dutch East India Company (1602-1795)* (The Hague, 1992).

83 Moreland, W.H., 'Dutch Sources for Indian History from 1590 to 1650', *Journal of Indian History*, 2 (1923).

84 Prakash, O., 'Dutch Source Material on Indian Maritime History in the Early Modern Period - An Evaluation', *Indian Historical Review*, 8 (1981-2).

85 Prakash, O., 'The Dutch East India Company Documents as Source Materials on Indian History in the Seventeenth- and Eighteenth Centuries', *Itinerario*, 7, 2 (1983).

86 Prakash, O., 'The Best of Two Worlds: An Interview with Om Prakash', *Itinerario*, 22, 2 (1998).

87 Roessingh, M.P.H., *Sources of the History of Asia and Oceania in the Netherlands, Vol.1: Sources up to 1796* (Munich, 1982).

88 Sareen, T.R., 'Nature of the Archival Sources for the Study of Modern Indian History', *Indica*, 28, 2 (1991).

89 Schutte, G.J., 'De koloniale geschiedschrijving', in W.W. Mijnhardt (ed.), *Kantelend geschiedbeeld: Nederlandse historiografie sinds 1945* (Utrecht and Antwerpen, 1983).

90 *Supplementary Catalogue of Dutch Records* (ed. J. Fruytier) (Madras, 1952) [pertaining to the records from Surat and Bengal kept in Madras].

91 Terpstra, H., 'Koloniale Geschiedenis', in *Geesteswetenschappelijk Onderzoek in Nederland* (Amsterdam, 1948).

92 Terpstra, H., 'Inheemse stemmen over het Compagnies-beleid in Voor-Indië en Ceylon', *Tijdschrift voor Geschiedenis*, 77 (1964).

93 Tiele, P.A., *Mémoire bibliographique sur les journaux des navigateurs néerlandais réimprimés dans les collections de De Bry et de Hulsius, et dans les collections hollandaises du xviie siècle, et sur les anciennes éditions hollandaises des journaux de navigateurs étrangers; la plupart en la possession de Frederik Muller* (Amsterdam, 1867; reprint 1960).

94 Tiele, P.A., *Nederlandsche bibliographie van land- en volkenkunde* (Amsterdam, 1884).

95 Vogel, J.Ph., *De beoefening van de studie der Oud-Indische literatuur in Nederland* (Amsterdam, 1898).

96 Vogel, J.Ph., 'Nederlandsche documenten betreffende de geschiedenis van Voor-Indië in de 17de en 18de eeuw', *Mededeelingen Koninklijke Akademie van Wetenschappen, Afdeling Letterkunde*, 73 (1932).

97 Wesseling, H.L., 'Dutch Historiography on European Expansion since 1945', in P.C. Emmer and H.L. Wesseling (eds), *Reappraisals in Overseas History. Essays on Post-War Historiography about European Expansion* (Leiden, 1979).

98 Wesseling, H.L., 'De overzeese studies in Nederland. Historische ontwikkeling en hedendaags perspectief', *Universiteit en Hogeschool*, 31, 4 (1985).

99 Wesseling, H.L., 'De overzeese geschiedenis in Nederland na de Tweede Wereldoorlog. Historische achtergronden, moderne ontwikkelingen, hedendaagse situatie', in *Koninklijke Academie voor Overzeese Wetenschappen/Academie Royale des Sciences d'Outre-Mer, Mededelingen der zittingen/Bulletin des séances*, 37, 4 (1991).

100 Wesseling, H.L., 'Overseas History in the Netherlands after the Second World War. Historical Backgrounds, Modern Developments, Present-Day Situation', *Itinerario*, 18, 2 (1994).

1.2.2. *General surveys*

101 Balkrishna, 'The Rise and Fall of the Dutch in India', *Indian Historical Records Commission, Proceedings of Meetings*, 15 (1938).

102 Blussé, L. and J.A. de Moor, *Nederlanders overzee. De eerste vijftig jaar 1600-1650* (Franeker, 1983).

103 Boxer, C.R., *The Dutch Seaborne Empire, 1600-1800* (London, 1965).

104 Boxer, C.R., *Jan Compagnie in oorlog en vrede. Beknopte geschiedenis van de VOC* (Bussum, 1977); trans. *Jan Compagnie in War and Peace 1602-1799. A Short History of the Dutch East India Company* (Hong Kong, 1979).

105 Boxer, C.R., *Dutch Merchants and Mariners in Asia, 1602-1795* (Aldershot, Variorum Reprints, 1988).

106 Chaudhuri, K.N., *Trade and Civilization in the Indian Ocean. An Economic History from the Rise of Islam to 1750* (Cambridge, 1985).

107 Colenbrander, H.T., *Koloniale geschiedenis*, 3 vols (The Hague, 1925-6).

108 Das Gupta, A. and M.N. Pearson (eds), *India and the Indian Ocean 1500-1800* (Delhi, 1987).

109 Davies, D.W., *A Primer of Dutch Seventeenth Century Overseas Trade* (The Hague, 1961).

110 *Encyclopaedie van Nederlandsch-Indië*, 4 vols, 3 suppls, eds D.G. Stibbe and others (The Hague, 1917-32).

111 Furber, H., *Rival Empires of Trade in the Orient, 1600-1800* (Minneapolis, 1976).

112 Gaastra, F.S., *De geschiedenis van de VOC* (Zutphen, 1991).

113 Geyl, P., 'The Dutch in India', in H.H. Dodwell (ed.), *Cambridge History of India*, 5 (reprint New Delhi, 1968).

114 Glamann, K., *Dutch-Asiatic Trade, 1620-1740* (Copenhagen, 1958).

115 Goor, J. van, *De Nederlandse koloniën. Geschiedenis van de Nederlandse expansie 1600-1975* (The Hague, 1993).

116 Goor, J. van, 'Dutch Factories in Asia (1600-1800): Bridgeheads of Political, Economic and Cultural Interaction', in J. Everaert and J. Parmentier (eds), *Shipping, Factories and Colonization* (Brussels, 1996).

117 Henige, D.P., *Colonial Governors from the Fifteenth Century to the Present. A Comprehensive List* (Madison, 1970).

118 Israel, J., *Dutch Primacy in World Trade 1585-1740* (Oxford, 1989).

119 Jacobs, E.M., *The Verenigde Oostindische Compagnie, VOC* (Utrecht, 1997).

120 Jonge, J.K.J. de (ed.), *De opkomst van het Nederlandsch gezag in Oost Indië*, 13 vols (The Hague, 1862-1909).

121 Kail, O.C., *The Dutch in India* (Delhi, 1981).

122 Mauro, F., *L'expansion européenne (1600-1870)* (Paris, 1964).

123 Parker, G., *The Military Revolution. Military Innovation and the Rise of the West, 1500-1800* (Cambridge, 1988).

124 Prakash, O., *European Commercial Enterprise in Pre-colonial India (New Cambridge History of India*, V, 5) (Cambridge, 1998).

125 Reinhard, W., *Geschichte der europäischen Expansion*, 4 vols (Stuttgart, 1983-90).

126 Schmitt, E. and Th. Schleich (eds), *Kaufleute als Kolonialherren. Die Handelswelt der Niederlanden von Kap der Guten Hoffnung bis Nagasaki 1600-1800* (Bamberg, 1988).

127 Schwartzberg, J.E., *A Historical Atlas of South Asia* (New York and London, 1992).

128 Stapel, F.W. (ed.), *Geschiedenis van Nederlandsch-Indië*, 5 vols (Amsterdam, 1938-40).

129 Steensgaard, N., *The Asian Trade Revolution of the Seventeenth Century. The East India Companies and the Decline of the Caravan Trade* (Chicago, 1974).

130 Terpstra, H., *De Nederlanders in Voor-Indië* (Amsterdam, 1947).

131 Wijnaendts van Resandt, W., *De gezaghebbers der Oost-Indische Compagnie op hare buitencomptoiren in Azië* (Amsterdam, 1944).

132 Winius, G.D. and M.P.M. Vink, *The Merchant-Warrior Pacified. The VOC (the Dutch East India Company) and its Changing Political Economy in India* (Delhi, 1991).

1.2.3. *Commerce*

133 Alam, Ishrat, 'Gujarat and Coromandel as Rival Exporters in Seventeenth Century. A Study of Dutch Document', *Proceeding of the Indian History Congress* (1989-90).

134 Alam, Ishrat, 'A Dutch Memoir of 1603 on Indian Textiles', in I. Habib (ed.), *Akbar and his India* (Delhi, 1997).

135 Arasaratnam, S., 'Indian Traders and their Trading Methods, Circa 1700', *Indian Economic and Social History Review*, 3, 1 (1966).

136 Arasaratnam, S., 'Aspects of the Role and Activities of South Indian Merchant Communities 1650-1700', *Proceedings of the First International Conference Seminar of Tamil Studies*, Vol.1 (Kuala Lumpur, 1967).

137 Arasaratnam, S., 'Monopoly and Free Trade in Dutch-Asian Commercial Policy. Debate and Controversy within the VOC', *Journal of Southeast Asian Studies*, 4, 1 (1973).

138 Arasaratnam, S., 'De VOC in Ceylon en Coromandel in de 17de en 18de eeuw', in M.A.P. Meilink-Roelofsz (ed.), *De VOC in Azië* (Bussum, 1976).

139 Arasaratnam, S., 'Indian Commercial Groups and European Traders 1600-1800. Changing Relationships in Southeastern Asia', *South Asia*, 1, 2 (1978).

140 Arasaratnam, S., 'Trade and Political Dominion in South India 1750-1790', *Modern Asian Studies*, 13, 1 (1979).

141 Arasaratnam, S., 'Mare Clausum, the Dutch and Regional Trade in the Indian Ocean 1650-1740', *Journal of Indian History*, 61 (1983).

142 Arasaratnam, S., 'Merchants, Commerce and the State in South India', *Revista de Cultura* (Special Number) (1991).

143 Arasaratnam, S. and A. Ray, *Masulipatnam and Cambay. A History of Two Port Towns 1500-1800* (Delhi, 1994).

144 Arasaratnam, S., *Maritime India in the Seventeenth Century* (New Delhi, 1994).

145 Arasaratnam, S., 'Slave Trade in the Indian Ocean in the Seventeenth Century', in K.S. Mathew (ed.), *Mariners, Merchants and Oceans: Studies in Maritime History* (Delhi, 1995).

146 Arasaratnam, S., *Maritime Trade, Society and European Influence in Southern Asia 1600-1800* (Aldershot, Variorum Reprints, 1995).

147 Arasaratnam, S., 'The Eastward Trade of India in the Eighteenth Century', in R. Mukherjee and L. Subramanian (eds), *Politics and Trade in the Indian Ocean World: Essays in Honour of Ashin Das Gupta* (Delhi, 1998).

148 Attman, A., *Dutch Enterprise in the World Bullion Trade 1550-1800* (Göteborg, 1983).

149 Attman, A., 'The Flow of Precious Metals along the Trade Routes between Europe and Asia up to 1800', in K.R. Haellquist, (ed.), *Asian Trade Routes. Continental and Maritime* (London and Copenhagen, 1991).

150 Barendse, R.J., 'Koningen, compagnieën en kapers: de Arabische zeeën 1640-1700' (Unpublished PhD-thesis, Leiden University, 1991).

151 Barendse, R.J., *The Arabian Seas 1640-1700* (Leiden, 1998).

152 Boomgaard, P., 'Geld, krediet, rente en Europeanen in Zuid- en Zuidoost Azië in de zeventiende eeuw', in C.A. Davids, W. Fritschy and L.A. van der Valk (eds), *Kapitaal, ondernemerschap en beleid. Afscheidsbundel voor professor dr P.W. Klein* (Amsterdam, 1996).

153 Bruijn, J.R. and F.S. Gaastra, 'The Dutch East-India Company's Shipping, 1602-1795 in a Comparative Perspective', in J.R. Bruijn and F.S. Gaastra (eds), *Ships, Sailors and Spices. East-India Companies and their Shipping in the 16th, 17th and 18th Centuries* (Amsterdam, 1993).

154 Das Gupta, A., *Merchants of Maritime India, 1500-1800* (Aldershot, Variorum Reprints, 1994).

155 Emmer, P.C. and F.S. Gaastra (eds), *The Organization of Interoceanic Trade in European Expansion 1450-1800* (Aldershot, Variorum Reprints, 1996).

156 Everaert, J., 'Willem Bolts; India Regained and Lost: Indiamen, Imperial Factories and Country Trade (1775-1785)', in K.S. Mathew (ed.), *Mariners, Merchants and Oceans: Studies in Maritime History* (Delhi, 1995).

157 Furber, H., *John Company at Work. A Study of European Expansion in India in the Late Eighteenth Century* (Cambridge, 1951).

158 Furber, H., *Private Fortunes and Company Profits in the India Trade in the Eighteenth Century*, ed. R. Rocher (Aldershot, Variorum Reprints, 1997).

159 Gaastra, F.S., 'Geld tegen goederen. Een structurele verandering in het Nederlands-Aziatische handelsverkeer', *Bijdragen en Mededelingen betreffende de Geschiedenis der Nederlanden*, 89 (1976).

160 Gaastra, F.S., 'The Shifting Balance of Trade of the Dutch East India

Company', in L. Blussé and F.S. Gaastra (eds), *Companies and Trade. Essays on Overseas Trading Companies during the Ancien Régime* (Leiden, 1981).

161 Gaastra, F.S., 'The Export of Precious Metals from Europe to Asia by the Dutch East India Company 1602-1795', in J.F. Richards (ed.), *Precious Metals in the Late Medieval and Early Modern Worlds* (Durham, 1983).

162 Gaastra, F.S., 'The Independent Fiscaals of the VOC, 1689-1719', *Itinerario*, 9, 2 (1985).

163 Gaastra, F.S., 'The Dutch East India Company and its Intra-Asiatic Trade in Precious Metals', in W. Fischer (ed.), *The Emergence of a World Economy 1500-1914. Papers of the IX International Congress of Economic History* (Wiesbaden, 1986).

164 Gaastra, F.S., *Bewind en beleid bij de VOC. De financiële en commerciële politiek van de Bewindhebbers, 1672-1702* (Zutphen, 1989).

165 Gaastra, F.S., 'Private Money for Company Trade. The Role of the Bills of Exchange in Financing the Return Cargoes of the VOC', *Itinerario*, 18, 1 (1994).

166 Gaastra, F.S., 'The Textile Trade of the VOC. The Dutch Response to the English Challenge', *South Asia*, 19 (Special Issue) (1996).

167 Gaastra, F.S., 'Competition or Collaboration? Relations between the Dutch East India Company and Indian Merchants around 1680', in S. Chaudhury and M. Morineau (eds), *Merchants, Companies and Trade* (Cambridge, 1999).

168 Jacobs, E.M., *Varen om peper en thee. Korte geschiedenis van de Verenigde Oostindische Compagnie* (Zutphen, 1991); trans. *In Pursuit of Pepper and Tea. The Story of the Dutch East India Company* (Zutphen, 1996).

169 Meilink-Roelofsz, M.A.P., 'The Dutch East India Company's Ports of Call', *Receuils Société Jean Bodin*, 33 (1972).

170 Mukherjee, R. and L. Subramanian (eds), *Politics and Trade in the Indian Ocean World: Essays in Honour of Ashin Das Gupta* (Delhi, 1998).

171 Parmentier, J., 'De handelaars en supercargo's in de Oostendse Moka- en Indiahandel (1714-1735)', *Handelingen van het Genootschap voor Geschiedenis*, 22, 3-4 (1985).

172 Parmentier, J., 'The Ostend Trade to Moka and India (1714-1735). The Merchants and Supercargos', *The Mariner's Mirror*, 73, 2 (1987).

173 Parmentier, J., 'Factories and Country Trade. The Role of the European Factories in the Intra-Asian Trade during the First Half of the 18th Century', in J. Everaert and J. Parmentier (eds), *Shipping, Factories and Colonization* (Brussels, 1996).

174 Pearson, M.N., *Spices in the Indian Ocean World* (Aldershot, Variorum Reprints, 1996).

175 Pearson, M.N. and I.B. Watson (eds), *Asia and Europe. Commerce, Colonialism and Cultures. Essays in Honour of Sinappah Arasaratnam* (=*South Asia,* 19 (Special Issue) (1996)).

176 Pol, A., '"Tot gerief van India". Geldexport door de VOC en de muntproductie in Nederland 1720-1740', *Jaarboek voor Munt- en Penningkunde*, 72 (1985).

177 Pol, A., 'For the Convenience of the Indies. Coin Production in 18th-Century Holland for Internal Circulation and for Exportation', *Proceedings of the 10th International Congress of Numismatics* (London, 1986).

178 Pol, A., 'Baren voor Bengalen. De productie van staafzilver ten behoeve van de VOC', *De Beeldenaar. Tweemaandelijks Tijdschrift voor Numismatiek*, 11, 6 (1987).

179 Pol, A., *Schepen met geld. De handelsmunten van de Verenigde Oostindische Compagnie, 1602-1799* (The Hague and Leiden, 1989).

180 Prakash, O., 'European Trade and South Asian Economies. Some Regional Contrasts, 1600-1800', in L. Blussé and F.S. Gaastra (eds), *Companies and Trade. Essays on Overseas Trading Companies during the Ancien Régime* (Leiden, 1981).

181 Prakash, O., 'Portugiesen und Niederländer im asiatischen Seehandel, 1500-1700', *Periplus. Jahrbuch für aussereuropäische Geschichte*, 1 (1991).

182 Prakash, O., *Precious Metals and Commerce. The Dutch East India Company in the Indian Ocean* (Aldershot, Variorum Reprints, 1994).

183 Prakash, O., 'Europeans, India and the Indian Ocean in the Early Modern Period', *South Asia*, 19 (Special Issue) (1996).

184 Prakash, O., 'The European Factories in India: A Blessing or a Curse?', in J. Everaert and J. Parmentier (eds), *Shipping, Factories and Colonization* (Brussels, 1996).

185 Prakash, O. (ed.), *European Commercial Expansion in Early Modern Asia* (Aldershot, Variorum Reprints, 1997).

186 Prakash, O., 'European Corporate Enterprise and the Politics of Trade in India, 1600-1800', in R. Mukherjee and L. Subramanian (eds), *Politics and Trade in the Indian Ocean World: Essays in Honour of Ashin Das Gupta* (Delhi, 1998).

187 Prakash, O., 'The Portuguese and the Dutch in Asian Maritime Trade. A Comparative Analysis', in S. Chaudhury and M. Morineau (eds), *Merchants, Companies and Trade* (Cambridge, 1999).

188 Prakash, O. and D. Lombard (eds), *Commerce and Culture in the Bay of Bengal, 1500-1800* (Delhi, 1999).

189 Scholten, C., *The Coins of the Dutch Overseas Territories 1601-1948* (Amsterdam, 1953).

190 Subrahmanyam, S., *The Political Economy of Commerce. Southern India 1500-1650* (Cambridge, 1990).

1.2.4. *Politics and law*

191 Aalbers, J., *Rijcklof van Goens, Commissaris en Veldoverste der O.I.C. en zijn arbeidsveld 1653/54 en 1657/8* (Groningen, 1916).

192 Alexandrowics, C.H., 'Treaty and Diplomatic Relations between European and South Asian Powers in the Seventeenth and Eighteenth Centuries', *Recueil des cours de l'académie de droit international de la Haye*, 100 (1966).

193 Blussé, L., and G.D. Winius, 'The Origin and Rhythm of Dutch Aggression against the Estado da India, 1601-1661', in T. de Souza (ed.), *Indo-Portuguese History. Old Issues, New Questions* (Delhi, 1985).

194 Boxer, C.R., 'Portuguese and Dutch Colonial Rivalry, 1641-1661', *Studia* (Lisboa), 2 (1958).

195 Fisch, J., 'Law as a Means and as an End. Some Remarks on the Function of European and Non-European Law in the Process of European Expansion', in W.J. Mommsen and J.A. de Moor (eds), *European Expansion and Law. The Encounter of European and Indigenous Law in 19th- and 20th-Century Africa and Asia* (Oxford and New York, 1992).

196 Fisch, J., *Die europäische Expansion und das Völkerrecht. Die Auseinandersetzungen um den Status der überseeischen Gebiete vom 15. Jahrhundert bis zur Gegenwart* (Stuttgart, 1984).

197 Heesterman, J.C., 'Was there an Indian Reaction? Western Expansion in Indian Perspective', in H.L. Wesseling (ed.), *Expansion and Reaction. Essays on European Expansion and Reactions in Asia and Africa* (Leiden, 1978).

198 Heesterman, J.C., 'Littoral et intérieur de l'Inde', in L. Blussé, H.L. Wesseling and G.D. Winius (eds), *History and Underdevelopment. Essays on Underdevelopment and European Expansion in Asia and Africa* (= *Itinerario*, 4, 1 (1980) (Leiden, 1980)).

199 Heesterman, J.C., 'Warriors and Merchants', *Itinerario*, 15, 1 (1991).

200 Kail, O.C., 'Dutch Commercial and Territorial Influence in India', *Journal of the Asiatic Society of Bombay*, 43/44 (1968-9).

201 Kalff, S., 'De O.I. Compagnie in Hindostan', *Indische Verlofganger* (1929-30).

202 Kemp, P.H. van der, 'De teruggave der Nederlandsche factorijen in Hindostan krachtens het Londensch traktaat van 13 Augustus 1814', *Bijdragen tot de Taal-, Land- en Volkenkunde van Nederlandsch-Indië*, 50 (1899).

203 Kemp, P.H. van der, 'De Nederlandse factorijen in Voor-Indië in den aanvang der 19e eeuw', *Bijdragen tot de Taal-, Land- en Volkenkunde van Nederlands-Indië*, 53 (1901).

204 Kemp, P.H. van der, 'De jaren 1817-1825 der Nederlandsche factorijen van Hindostans Oostkust. Naar onuitgegeven stukken', *Bijdragen tot de Taal-, Land- en Volkenkunde van Nederlandsch-Indië*, 74 (1918).

205 Leue, H.J., 'Legal Expansion in the Age of the Companies. Aspects of the Administration of Justice in the English and Dutch Settlements of Maritime Asia, *c.*1600-1750', in W.J. Mommsen and J.A. de Moor (eds), *European Expansion and Law. The Encounter of European and Indigenous Law in 19th- and 20th-Century Africa and Asia* (Oxford and New York, 1992).

206 MacLeod, N., 'De machtsuitbreiding der OIC op het vasteland van Azië van 1683-97', *De Indische Gids*, 23 (1901), 24 (1902).

207 MacLeod, N., 'De OIC op het vasteland van Azië in de laatste jaren der 17e eeuw', *De Indische Gids*, 24 (1902).

208 MacLeod, N., *De VOC als zeemogendheid in Azië*, 2 vols (Rijswijk, 1927).

209 Meilink-Roelofsz, M.A.P., 'Een vergelijkend onderzoek van bestuur en handel der Nederlandse en Engelse handelscompagnieën op Azië in de eerste helft van de zeventiende eeuw', *Bijdragen en Mededelingen betreffende de Geschiedenis der Nederlanden*, 91 (1976).

210 Niel, R. van, 'Dutch Views and Uses of British Policy in India around 1800', in G.D. Winius, P.C. Emmer and D.H.A. Kolff (eds), *The Ancien Regime in India and Indonesia* (Leiden, 1988).

211 Ottow, W.M., *Rijkloff Volkertsz van Goens. De carrière van een diplomaat 1619-1655* (Utrecht, 1954).

212 Ottow, W.M., *Rijkloff Volkertsz van Goens. Krijgsman, commissaris en regent in dienst der VOC* (The Hague, 1995).

213 Ottow, W.M., *Rijkloff Volkertsz van Goens. Krijgsman, commissaris en regent in dienst der VOC. Archiefstudie over het Europese verlof (1655-57) en de eerste grote Ceylon periode* (Leiden, 1997).

214 Poonen, T.I., 'Anglo-Dutch Relations in India Proper', *Journal of Indian History*, 28 (1950).

215 Renny, C.A., 'Dutch Possessions in Southern India', *Inter-Ocean* (1929).

216 Srinivasan, V., 'The Dutch in India', *Journal of Indian History*, 9 (1932).

217 Stapel, F.W., 'Zeeroovers in dienst van de Oostindische Compagnie', *Bijdragen tot de Taal-, Land- en Volkenkunde van Nederlandsch-Indië*, 86 (1930).

218 Temminck Groll, C.L., 'Vijf-vier-drie-twee-een. Vanuit Nederland gestichte forten in andere werelddelen', in *Stichting Menno van Coehoorn. Jaarboek 1989/1990* (Zutphen, 1990).

1.2.5. *Art, intellectual life, religion, travel*

219 Arasaratnam, S., 'Protestant Christianity and South Indian Hinduism. Some Confrontations in Society and Ideology', *Indian Church History Review*, 15, 1 (1981).

220 Bakker, H., 'De culturele ontdekking van India', in H. Bakker and M. Gosman (eds), *De Oriënt, droom of dreiging. Het Oosten in westers perspectief* (Kampen, 1988).

221 Balen, W.J. van, *Naar de Indische wonderwereld met Jan Huyghen van Linschoten* (Amsterdam, 1946).

222 Barend-Van Haeften, M.L., 'Wouter Schoutens "Papiere wicht". De Oost-Indische voyagie (1676)', *Indische Letteren*, 6 (1991).

223 Baudet, H., *Het paradijs op aarde, gedachten over de verhouding van de Europese tot de buiten-Europese mens* (Assen, 1959).

224 Beekman, E.M., *Troubled Pleasures. Dutch Colonial Literature from the East Indies 1600-1950* (Oxford, 1996).

225 Bergvelt, E. and R. Kistemaker (eds), *De wereld binnen handbereik. Nederlandse kunst- en rariteitenverzamelingen, 1585-1735* (Zwolle, 1992).

226 Bernet Kempers, A.J., 'Oud-Hollandsche grafdichten uit Voor-Indië', *Indische Gids*, 59 (1937).

227 Bethlehem, J. and A.C. Meijer (eds), *VOC en cultuur. Wetenschappelijke en culturele relaties tussen Europa en Azië ten tijde van de Verenigde Oostindische Compagnie* (Amsterdam, 1993).

228 Boogaart, E. van den, 'In Portugese dienst: Van Linschoten in Goa en op Terceira', in R. van Gelder, J. Parmentier and V. Roeper (eds), *Souffrir pour parvenir* (Haarlem, 1998).

229 Boot, J.A.P.G., 'Over Aziatische katoenen garens en de 18de eeuwse Achterhoek', *Textielhistorische Bijdragen*, 4 (1963).

230 Brans, P.H., *350 Jahre Arzneimittelversorgung in Niederländisch-Indien* (Vienna, 1952).

231 Busken Huet, C., 'Literarisch-critische studie over Francois Valentyn', in A.W. Stellwagen (ed.), *Van en naar Indië, Valentyns 1ste en 2de thuisreis* (The Hague, 1882).

232 Das Gupta, J., *India in the Seventeenth Century as depicted by European Travellers* (Calcutta, 1916).

233 Davids, C.A., 'Navigeren in Azië. De uitwisseling van kennis tussen Aziaten en navigatiepersoneel bij de voorcompagnieën en de VOC, 1596-1795', *Tijdschrift voor Zeegeschiedenis*, 9, 1 (1990).

234 Dharampal-Frick, G., ''Irdisches Paradies' und 'Veritable europäische Schatzkammer'. Kontouren und Entwicklungen des deutschen Indienbildes im Zeitalter der Entdeckungen', *Pickheimer-Jahrbuch 1986*, 2 (1987).

235 Dharampal-Frick, G., 'Zwischen Utopie und Empirie. Indien im Spiegel deutscher Reisebeschreibungen der Frühen Neuzeit', *Zeitschrift für Kulturaustausch*, 37 (1987).

236 Dharampal-Frick, G., 'Die Faszination des Exotischen. Deutsch Indien-Berichte der frühen Neuzeit (1500-1750)', in U. Bitterli and E. Schmitt (eds), *Die Kenntnis beider 'Indien' im frühneuzeitlichen Europa* (Munich, 1991).

237 Dharampal-Frick, G., *Indien im Spiegel deutscher Quellen der Frühen Neuzeit (1500-1750). Studien zu einer interkulturellen Konstellation* (Tübingen, 1994).

238 Dibbits, H. and G. Rooijakkers, 'Materiële cultuur tussen zee en vasteland. De diffusie en receptie van Asiatica in de Republiek', in K. Davids and others (eds), *De Republiek tussen zee en vasteland. Buitenlandse invloeden op cultuur, economie en politiek in Nederland, 1580-1800* (Leuven and Apeldoorn, 1995).

239 Eeghen, I.H. van, 'De familie Vickboons of Vingboons', *Oud Holland*, 2 (1952).

240 Feith, J.A., 'De Bengaalse Sichterman', *Groningse Volksalmanak 1914* (1913).

241 Fisch, J., *Hollands Ruhm in Asien. Francois Valentijn's Vision des niederländischen Imperiums in 18. Jahrhundert* (Stuttgart, 1986).

242 Gelder, R. van, 'Pitzliputzli aan de Ossemarkt', *Kunstschrift*, 36, 6 (1992).

243 Gelder, R. van, 'Noodzaak of nieuwsgierigheid. Reismotieven van Oostindiëgangers in de zeventiende en achttiende eeuw', *Indische Letteren*, 8, 2 (1993).

244 Gelder, R. van, 'Azië in Duitse ogen', *Tijdschrift voor Geschiedenis*, 109 (1996)

245 Gelder, R. van, *Het Oost-Indisch avontuur. Duitsers in dienst van de VOC 1600-1800* (Nijmegen, 1997).

246 Goetz, H., 'Holländische Wandfliesen in einem altindischen Königspalast', *Oud Holland*, 66 (1951).

247 Goor, J. van, *Kooplieden, predikanten en bestuurders overzee* (Utrecht, 1982).

248 Goor, J. van, 'Dutch Calvinists on the Coromandel Coast and in Sri Lanka', *South Asia*, 19 (Special Issue) (1996).

249 Haeger, A., 'Duitschers in Indië', *Tijdschrift voor Nederlandsch Indië*, 2 (1888).

250 Harbsmeier, M., *Wilde Völkerkunde. Andere Welten in deutschen Reiseberichten der frühen Neuzeit* (Frankfurt and New York, 1994).

251 Hartkamp-Jonxis, E. and others, *Sits. Oost-west relaties in textiel* (Zwolle, 1987).

252 Hartkamp-Jonxis, E., *Sitsen uit India/Indian Chintz* (Zwolle and Amsterdam, 1994).

253 Heesterman, J.C., 'De Oriënt, droom en werkelijkheid', in H. Bakker and M. Gosman (eds), *De Oriënt, droom of dreiging. Het Oosten in Westers Perspectief* (Kampen, 1988).

254 Heniger, J., 'Der wissenschaftliche Nachlass von Paul Hermann', *Wissenschaftliche Zeitschrift der Martin-Luther-Universität Halle Wittenberg*, 18 (1969).

255 Hulshof, A., 'Duitschers in dienst der Oost-Indische Compagnie', *Haagsch Maandblad*, 34 (1940).

256 Itscherenska, I., 'Deutsche Reiseberichte über Indien vom 16. bis 18. Jh. Bemerkungen zu ihren Aussagen in Bezug auf das ökonomische und soziale Leben in Indien', in H. Krüger (ed.), *Neue Indienkunde/New Indology. Festschrift Walter Ruben zum 70. Geburtstag* (Berlijn, 1970).

257 Jabukowski, Manfred, 'Die 'Orientalische Reisebeschreibung' des Jürgen Andersen aus Tondern', *Nordfriesisches Jahrbuch*, 15 (1979).

258 Jacobs S.J., H., 'Een Culemborger in India, die de Hollanders voor was. Lambert Ruysch, 1549-1611', *Bijdragen en Mededelingen der Vereniging Gelre*, 70 (1978-9).

259 Jörg, C.J.A., 'Jan Albert Sichterman. A Groninger Nabob and Artcollector', *Itinerario*, 9, 2 (1985).

260 Kalff, S., 'Francois Valentijn', *De Indische Gids*, 22 (1900).

261 Kalff, S., 'Duitschers in Indië', *Koloniaal Tijdschrift*, 15 (1926).

262 Keunig, J. 'Johannes Vingboons, teekenaar, graveur en kartograaf', *Het Boek*, 22 (1933-34).

263 Kirsch, P., 'Deutsche Reiseberichte des 17. Jahrhunderts als Quelle für die Niederländische Ostindienfahrt', *Deutsches Schiffahrtsarchiv, Zeitschrift des Deutschen Schiffahtsmuseum*, 13 (1990).

264 Kirsch, P., 'VOC-Trade without Ethics', in K.A. Sprengard and R. Ptak (eds), *Maritime Asia. Profit Maximisation, Ethics and Trade Structure* (Wiesbaden, 1994).

265 Kirsch, P., *Die Reise nach Batavia. Deutsche Abenteuer in Ostasien 1609 bis 1695* (Hamburg, 1994).

266 Kühne-Van Diggelen, W., *Jan Albert Sichterman. VOC-dienaar en 'koning' van Groningen* (Groningen, 1995).

267 'Kurze Lebensbeschreibung von Deutschen, die sich in der Vergangenheit um die Kolonie verdient gemacht haben', in F.A. Schöppel (ed.), *Deutsches Jahrbuch für Niederländisch-Indien* (Batavia and Leiden, 1925).

268 Lach, D.F., *Asia in the Making of Europe, Vol. 1: The Century of Discovery*, 2 books (Chicago and London, 1965).

269 Lach, D.F., *Asia in the Making of Europe, Vol. 2: A Century of Wonder*, 3 books (Chicago and London 1970-77).

270 Lach, D.F. and E.J. van Kley, *Asia in the Making of Europe, Vol. 3: A Century of Advance, Book 1: Trade, Missions, Literature; Book 2: South Asia* (Chicago and London, 1993).

271 Lahrkamp, H., 'Münsterische Ostindienfahrer des 17. und 18. Jahrhunderts', *Westfählische Forschungen*, 16 (1966).

272 Lequin, F., 'A 'Mandarin' from Vlissingen in Lhasa and Peking. The Hidden Life of Samuel van de Putte (1690-1745)', *Itinerario*, 9, 2 (1985).

273 Lequin, F. and A. Meijer, *Samuel van de Putte. Een Mandarijn uit Vlissingen (1670-1745)* (Middelburg, 1989).

274 Leupe, P.A., 'Nederlandse schilders in Perzië en Hindoestan in de eerste helft van de 17e eeuw', *De Nederlandse Spectator* (1873).

275 Lunsingh Scheurleer, P., 'Hoe een etser in Nederland geïnspireerd werd door een miniatuur in India', *Antiek*, 12, 10 (1978).

276 Lunsingh Scheurleer, P., 'Mogolminiaturen door Rembrandt nagetekend', in *De Kroniek van het Rembrandthuis*, 32, 1 (1980).

277 Lunsingh Scheurleer, P., 'De Mogol miniaturen van Rembrandt', in *Museum Magazine Vitrine*, 4, 1 (1991).

278 Lunsingh Scheurleer, P., 'Jewels for the Stadholder', in S. Strong (ed.), *The Jewels of India* (Bombay, 1995).

279 Lunsingh Scheurleer, P., 'Twee oosterse sieraden uit de stadhouderlijke verzameling', *Bulletin van het Rijksmuseum*, 44, 1 (1996).

280 Lunsingh Scheurleer, P., 'Rich Remains from Social Anthropological Fieldwork in Eighteenth-Century India', *Journal of the History of Collections*, 8, 1 (1996).

281 Lunsingh Scheurleer, P., 'Het Witsenalbum. Zeventiende-eeuwse Indiase portretten op bestelling', *Bulletin van het Rijksmuseum*, 44, 3 (1996).

282 Moor, J.A. de, and P.G.E.I.J. van der Velde, 'In het rasphuis van Europa. De reisverhalen van Jacob Haafner (1755-1809)', *Indische Letteren*, 5, 3 (1990).

283 Moor, J.A. de, and P.G.E.I.J. van der Velde, ''De heilige tale des lands'. Jacob Haafner als voorloper van de studie van het Sanskrit in Nederland', in H.J. 't Hart-van den Muijzenberg (ed.), *Waarom Sanskrit? Honderdvijfentwintig jaar Sanskrit in Nederland* (Leiden, 1991).

284 Moor, J.A. de, and P.G.E.I.J. van der Velde, 'Jacob Haafner. Travels through the Island of Ceylon in 1783', *Journal of the Dutch Burgher Union of Ceylon*, 86 (1991).

285 Moreland, W.H., 'Johan van Twist's Description of India', *Journal of Indian History*, 16 (1937).
286 'Niederländische Künstler und der Orient im 16. und 17.Jahrhundert', in G. Sievernich and H. Budde (eds), *Europa und der Orient 800-1900* (München, 1989).
287 Overvoorde, J.C., *Verslag van het onderzoek naar de monumenten van Nederlandschen oorsprong of onder Nederlandschen invloed ontstaan in de vroegere nederzettingen buiten Europa* (Leiden, 1912).
288 Parmentier, J., 'In het kielzog van Van Linschoten: Het Itinerario en het Reys-gheschrift in de praktijk', in R. van Gelder, J. Parmentier and V. Roeper (eds), *Souffrir pour parvenir* (Haarlem, 1998).
289 Pott, P.H., 'Willem Verstegen, een Raad van Indië als avonturier in India in 1659', *Bijdragen tot de Taal-, Land- en Volkenkunde*, 112 (1956).
290 Pott, P.H., *Naar wijder horizon. Kaleidoscoop op ons beeld van de buitenwereld* (The Hague, 1962).
291 Prakash, O., 'The Transfer of Science and Technology between Asia and Europe', *Itinerario*, 14, 2 (1990).
292 Roeper, V.D. and G.J.D. Wildeman, *Reizen op papier. Journalen, reisverslagen van Nederlandse ontdekkingsreizigers, kooplieden en avonturiers* (Amsterdam, 1996).
293 Rose, H.D., *Die Arbeit deutscher Ärtzte im Dienste der Niederlandisch-Ostindischen Kompagnie (1602-1797), dargestellt am Beispiel des Ulmer Wundartztes Christoph Frick* (Dortmund, 1982).
294 Rouffaer, G.P., 'Een curieus Duitsch boekje over onze Oost uit 1646', *Bijdragen tot de Taal-, Land- en Volkenkunde van Nederlandsch-Indië*, 69 (1913) [about Wurffbain].
295 Salverda, M., *Uit menschlievendheid zoude ik barbaar kunnen worden. Reizen in Azië 1770-1830* (Amsterdam, 1992).
296 Schmidlin, W., 'Ulmer im fernen Osten während des 17. Jahrhunderts', *Ulm Oberschwaben. Mitteilungen des Vereins für Kunst und Altertum in Ulm und Oberschwaben*, 29 (1934).
297 Sirks, J., *Indisch natuuronderzoek* (Amsterdam, 1915).
298 Teensma, B.N., 'Neerlandofobia en Goa a principios del siglo XVII', *Foro Hispánico, revista hispánica de los Países Bajos*, 3 (1992).
299 Terpstra, H., *Buitenlandse getuigen van onze koloniale expansie* (Amsterdam, 1940).
300 Terpstra, H., 'Jacob Haafner en zijn denkbeelden over het kolonialisme', *Tijdschrift voor Geschiedenis*, 75 (1962).
301 Toussaint, J.R., 'Jacob Haafner, a Sketch of his Life', *Journal of the Dutch Burgher Union of Ceylon*, 17 (1928).
302 Übleis, F., 'Deutsche in Indien 1600-1700. Entstehung, Struktur und Funktion des Indienbildes der deutschen Reiseberichte des 17. Jahrhunderts', *Zeitschrift für Religion und Geistesgeschichte*, 32 (1980).
303 Veenendaal, J., *Furniture from Indonesia, Sri Lanka and India during the Dutch Period* (Delft, 1985).

304 Velde, P.G.E.I.J. van der, 'The Orientalist, Artist and Writer J.G. Haafner (1755-1809)', *Dutch Crossing*, 39 (1989).

305 Veth, P.J., 'De Nederlandse reiziger Samuel van der Putte', *Tijdschrift van het Aardrijkskundig Genootschap*, 2 (1877).

306 Veth, P.J., 'Samuel van der Putte', in P.J. Veth, *Ontdekkers en onderzoekers* (Leiden, 1884).

307 Veth, P.J., 'Philippus Baldaeus', in P.J. Veth, *Ontdekkers en onderzoekers* (Leiden, 1884).

308 Veth, P.J., 'Hendrik Adriaan van Reede tot Drakestein', *De Gids* (1887).

309 Vogel, J.Ph., 'Jacob Haafner. Schets uit de laatste jaren der O.I. Compagnie (Bengalen en Ceylon)', *De Indische Gids*, 22 (1900).

310 Wagenvoort, M., 'Zoekende het voetspoor der vaderen', *Neerlandia*, 11 (1907).

311 Wagenvoort, M., *In het voetspoor der vaderen. Indrukken van modern Hindoestan* (Santpoort, 1929).

312 Wennekes, W., *Gouden handel. De eerste Nederlanders overzee* (Amsterdam, 1996).

313 Wichmann, A., *Dirck Gerritsz. Ein Beitrag zur Entdeckungsgeschichte des 16ten und 17ten Jahrhunderts* (Groningen, 1899).

314 Wolff, M.P. and R. Wassing-Visser (eds), *Met andere ogen. 400 Jaar afbeeldingen van Europeanen door verre volken* (Delft, 1986).

315 Wunder, G., 'Johann Jacob Merklein (1620-1700), ein fränkischer Weltreisender', in G. Wunder (ed.), *Lebensläufe, Bauer, Bürger, Edelmann, vol.2* (Sigmaringen, 1988)

316 Ydema, O., 'Zeldzame herinneringen aan de hoftapijten van de Groot-Moghul uit Lahore', *Bulletin van het Rijksmuseum*, 34, 3 (1986).

317 Ydema, O., 'Carpets in 17th-Century Dutch and Flemish Painting', in *The European Fine Art Fair Maastricht. Special Exhibition. Carpets in 17th-Century Dutch Painting* (Den Bosch, 1988).

318 Zadoks, A.N. and J. Jitta, 'De lotgevallen van den grooten Camee in het Koninklijk Penningkabinet', *Oud Holland*, 66 (1951).

2. SURAT (including Sind and Hindustan)

2.1. Primary Sources

319 Adrichem, Dircq van, *Journaal van Dircq van Adrichem's hofreis naar den Groot Mogol Aurangzeb 1662*, ed. A.J. Bernet Kempers (Werken Linschoten Vereniging, 45) (The Hague, 1941).

320 Andersen, Jürgen and Volquard Iversen, *Orientalische Reisebeschreibunge Jürgen Andersen aus Schleszwig der An. Christi 1644 ausgezogen und 1650 wieder kommen. Und Volquard Iversen aus Holstein so An. 1655 ausgezogen und 1688 wieder angelanget* (Sleeswijk, 1669); ed. D. Lohmeier (Tübingen, 1980); for Dutch edition, see Georg Andriesz, *De beschrijving der reizen*

van Georg Andriesz deur Oostindien en d'eilanden, deur Sina, Tartarijen, Persien etc. sedert 1644, ed. A. Olearius, ed. J.H. Glazemaker (Amsterdam, 1670).

321 *Beschryvinge van eenige voorname kusten in Oost- en West-Indiën: als Zueriname, Nieuw-Nederland, Florida, van 't Eyland Kuba, Brazil, Suratte, Madgascar, Batavia, Peru en Mexico: van haar gelegentheid, aart en gewoonte dier volkeren; hun koophandel, gods-dienst, en zelzaame voorvallen* (Leeuwarden, 1716).

322 Dapper, Olfert, *Asia, of nauwkeurige beschrijving van het rijk des grooten Mogols en de groot gedeelt van Indien* (Amsterdam, 1672).

323 *Extract uyt seeckere missive, geschreven in 't Nederlants comptoir der stad Agra* [20-8-1653] (n.p., n.d.).

324 Geleynssen de Jongh, Wollebrandt, 'Reis van den opperkoopman Wollebrandt Geleynsz. de Jongh van Soeratte naar Agra, 1636-1637', ed. P.A. Leupe, in *Tijdschrift van het Koninklijk Nederlandsch Aardrijkskundig Genootschap*, 6 (1882).

325 Geleynssen de Jongh, Wollebrandt, *De remonstrantie van W. Geleynssen de Jongh*, ed. W. Caland (Werken Linschoten Vereniging, 31) (The Hague, 1929).

326 'Instructie voor den Oppercoopman Marcus Oldenburgh, gecommitteert aen den Grooten Mogol Chasean', ed. P.A. Leupe, *Kronijk van het Historisch Genootschap gevestigd te Utrecht*, vol. 9 (1853).

327 Ketelaar, J.J., 'De lingua Hindustanica', in: David Mill(ius) (ed. and trans.), *Miscellanea Orientalia*, 1 (Dissertationes Selectae, Lugduni Batavorum, 1743).

328 Ketelaar, J.J., *Journaal van J.J. Ketelaar's hofreis naar den Groot Mogol te Lahore 1711-1713*, ed. J.Ph. Vogel (Werken Linschoten Vereniging, 41) (The Hague, 1937); part. trans. D. Kuenen-Wicksteed, 'Embassy of Mr. Johan Josua Ketelaar', *Journal of the Panjab Historical Society*, 10 (1929).

329 Laet, Joannes de, *De imperio magni mogolis sive India vera commentarius e variis auctoribus congestus* (Leiden, 1631); eds J.S. Hoyland and S.N. Banerjee, *The Empire of the Great Mogol. A Translation of de Laet's 'Description of India and a Fragment of Indian History'* (Bombay, 1928).

330 Pelsaert, Franscisco, *De geschriften van Franscisco Pelsaert over Mughal Indië, 1627. Kroniek en remonstrantie*, eds D.H.A. Kolff and H.W. van Santen (Werken Linschoten Vereniging, 81) (The Hague, 1979); part. trans. W. Moreland and P. Geyl, *Jahangir's India. The Remonstrantie of Fransisco Pelsaert* (Cambridge, 1925); part. trans. B. Narain and S.R. Sharma, *A Contemporary Dutch Chronicle of Moghul India* (Calcutta, 1957).

331 Rheeden, D. van, 'Souratte. Radicale beschrijving anno 1758', *Bijdragen en Mededeelingen Historisch Genootschap*, 6 (1883).

332 Wurffbain, Johann Sigmund, *Reißbeschreibung* (Nuremberg, 1646).

333 Wurffbain, Johann Sigmund, *Vierzehen jährige ost-indianische Krieg- und Ober-Kauffmanns-Dienste* (Sultzbach, 1686) [see also General, Primary Publication, *Reisebeschreibungen*].

2.2. Secondary Sources

334 Akhtar, Jawaid, 'Trade and Society in Gujarat. A Dutch Account, *c.* 1617', *Proceeding of the Indian History Congress* (1994).

335 Akhtar, Jawaid, 'Gujarati Merchants and the VOC', *Proceeding of the Indian History Congress* (1995).

336 Alam, Ishrat, 'Trade at Surat, 1648 - Dutch Memoir', *Proceeding of the Indian History Congress* (1994).

337 Bautze, J., 'Maharana Sangram Singh of Udaipur entertaining Members of the Dutch East India Company led by Johan Josua Ketelaar', *Bulletin van het Rijksmuseum*, 36, 2 (1988).

338 Bernet Kempers, A.J., 'Een Hollandsch gezantschap naar den Groot-Mogol in 1662', *De Gids* (February and March, 1936).

339 Bernet Kempers, A.J., 'Hollandsche grafmonumenten te Surat', *Tijdschrift voor Indische Taal-, Land- en Volkenkunde van het Koninklijk Bataviaasch Genootschap van Kunsten en Wetenschappen*, 78 (1938).

340 Chatterji, S.K., 'Hindustānī kā sab-se prācīn vyākaran' [= The oldest grammar of Hindustani], in *Dvivedi Abhinandan Granth* (Benares, 1990) [= AD 1933].

341 Compton, H., *A Particular Account of the European Adventurers of Hindustan from 1784-1803* (London, 1892).

342 Das Gupta, A., 'De VOC en Suratte in de 17de en 18de eeuw', in M.A.P. Meilink-Roelofsz (ed.), *De VOC in Azië* (Bussum, 1976).

343 Das Gupta, A., *Indian Merchants and the Decline of Surat c.1700-1750* (Wiesbaden, 1979).

344 Das Gupta, A., 'Pieter Phoonsen of Surat, ca.1730-1740', *Modern Asian Studies*, 22, 3 (1988).

345 Fisher, K., 'The Beginning of Dutch Trade with Gujarat', *Proceedings of the Indian History Congress* (1965).

346 Floor, W.M., 'The Dutch East India Company's Trade with Sind in the 17th and 18th Centuries', *Moyen Orient et Océan Indien*, 3 (1986).

347 Floor, W.M., *The Dutch East India Company (VOC) and Dewel-Sind (Pakistan) in the 17th and 18th Centuries (based on Original Dutch Records)* (Karachi, 1994).

348 Floor, W.M., 'New Facts on Nadir Shah's Campaign in India', in Kambiz Eslami (ed.), *Iran and Iranian Studies: Essays in Honor of Iraj Afshar* (Princeton, 1998).

349 Gaastra, F.S. and W. Seybel, 'Een Kollumer koopman in de Oost. Eyso de Wendt (1718-1780)', *De Vrije Fries*, 74 (1994).

350 Gelder, H.E. van, 'Wollebrandt Geleynsz. de Jongh, 'De Alkmaarder Wees'', *Oud Holland*, 33 (1915).

351 Greshoff, M., 'De grafstede van H.A. van Rheeden te Surat', *Eigen Haard* (1906).

352 Grierson, G., 'The First Hindostani Grammar', *Proceedings of the Asiatic Society of Bengal* (May, 1895).

353 Grierson, G., 'The First Hindostani Grammar', *Linguistic Survey of India*, 9, 1 (Calcutta, 1916).

354 Hasan, Farhat, 'Mughal Officials at Surat and their Relations with the English and the Dutch Merchants based on a Collection of Persian Documents of the Reigns of Jahangir and Shahjahan', *Proceeding of the Indian History Congress* (1989-90).

355 Heyligers, A.J.M., *Résumé of the Contents of the Dutch Diaries in the Agency Records of the Surat District, Bombay* (Madras, n.d.).

356 Hullu, J. de, 'Beschrijving eener verzameling stukken, afkomstig van Wollebrand Geleynssen de Jongh', *Verslagen omtrent 's Rijks Oude Archieven*, 35 (1912), 36 (1913).

357 Kalff, S., 'Een voormalige Hollandsche factorij (Suratte)', *Indische Verlofganger* (1927-8).

358 Kolff, D.H.A., 'La nation chrétienne à Surat au début du XVIIe siècle', in R, Goutalier (ed.), *La femme dans les sociétés coloniales* (Aix en Provence, 1984).

359 Kondo, O., 'Japan and the Indian Ocean at the Time of the Mughal Empire with Special Reference to Gujarat', in Satish Chandra, *The Indian Ocean. Explorations in History, Commerce and Politics* (Delhi, 1987).

360 Kownatzki, H., 'Johann Josua Kettler, Elbings grösster Abenteurer', *Elbinger Jahrbuch*, 12-3 (1936).

361 Moreland, W.H., 'A Dutch Account of Mogul Administrative Methods', *Journal of Indian History*, 4 (1925), 5 (1926).

362 Moreland, W.H., 'Pieter van den Broeke at Surat (1620-29)', *Journal of Indian History* (1931-2).

363 Radwan, A. Bos, *The Dutch in Western India, 1601-1632. A Study of Mutual Accommodation* (Calcutta, 1978).

364 Santen, H.W. van, *De Verenigde Oost-Indische Compagnie in Gujarat en Hindustan 1620-1660* (Meppel, 1982).

365 Santen, H.W. van, 'Trade between Mughal India and the Middle East, and Mughal Monetary Policy, *c.*1600-1660', in K.R. Haellquist, (ed.), *Asian Trade Routes. Continental and Maritime* (London and Copenhagen, 1991).

366 Singh, O.P., *Surat and its Trade in the Second Half of the 17th Century*, (Delhi, 1977).

367 Terpstra, H., *De opkomst der westerkwartieren van de VOC. Suratte, Arabië en Perzië* (The Hague, 1918).

368 Tracy, James, 'Asian Despotism? Mughal Government as seen from the Dutch East India Company Factory in Surat', *Journal of Early Modern History*, 3, 3 (1999).

369 Vogel, J.Ph., 'The Author of the First Grammar of Hindustani', *Mahāmahopādhyāya Gauriśankar Hīrācand ke sammān men samarpit Bhāratīya-anuśīlangranth*, 4 (Delhi-Prayag, 1990) [= AD 1934].

370 Vogel, J.Ph., 'Joan Josua Ketelaar of Elbing, Author of the First Hindustani Grammar', *Bulletin of the School of Oriental Studies*, 8 (1935).

371 Vogel, J.Ph., 'De eerste 'grammatica' van het Hindoestansch', *Mededeelingen van de Koninklijke Nederlandsche Akademie van Wetenschappen, Afdeling Letterkunde*, n.s., 4 (1941).

3. MALABAR (including Kanara and Konkan)

3.1. PRIMARY SOURCES

372 *Afbeeldinge van de Oost-Indise cust van Malabare* (Amsterdam, 1663).

373 *Catalogus van Hollandsche handschriften, brieven en officieele stukken*, ed. P. Groot (Selections from the Records of the Madras Government, Dutch Records, 6) (Madras, 1909).

374 *Dagboek der gebeurtenissen gedurende den oorlog met den Zammorijn 1716-1717*, ed. P. Groot (Selections from the Records of the Madras Government, Dutch Records, 8) (Madras, 1910).

375 *De Nederlanders in Kerala, 1663-1701. De memories en instructies betreffende het commandement Malabar van de VOC*, ed. H.K. s'Jacob (Rijks Geschiedkundige Publicatiën, Kleine Serie, 43) (The Hague, 1976).

376 Enkele extracten uit archiefstukken betreffende de VOC en het Katholicisme op de kust van Malabar', ed. J. Notermans, *Tijdschrift voor Indische Taal-, Land- en Volkenkunde van het Koninklijk Bataviaasch Genootschap van Kunsten en Wetenschappen*, 76 (1936).

377 Gravezande, A.'s, 'Geschiedkundige narichten betreffende de blanke en zwarte Jooden te Cochin, op de kust van Malabar', *Verhandelingen Zeeuwsch Genootschap der Wetenschappen Vlissingen*, 6 (1778), 9 (1782).

378 Hackert, Johannes, *Dagregister gehouden door Capitain Johannes Hackert geduurende den train tegen den koning van Trevancoor 1739-1740*, ed. P. Groot (Selections from the Records of the Madras Government, Dutch Records, vol. 10) (Madras, 1909).

379 Hesse, Elias, *Ost-Indische Reise-Beschreibung oder Diarium* (Leipzig, 1690).

380 *Kort verhael van 't veroveren van de stercke stadt Cochin* (Amsterdam, 1663).

381 *Letters from Cochin Rajas to Batavia* (Ernakalam, 1946).

382 *Malabaarse brieven*, ed. J. Canter Visscher (Leeuwarden, 1743); trans. *Letters from Malabar* (Madras, 1862).

383 [*Memoirs of*] *Commandeurs* [*of Malabar*], in *Selections from the Records of the Madras Government, Dutch Records*:
- 1677: Hendrik Adriaan van Reede tot Drakestein, ed. P. Groot (vol. 14) (Madras, 1911)
- 1743: J.V. Stein van Gollenesse, ed. A.J. van der Burg (vol. 1) (Madras, 1908)*
- 1756: Frederik Cunes, ed. P. Groot (vol. 3) (Madras, 1908)
- 1761: Casparus de Jong, ed. P. Groot (vol. 11) (Madras, 1910)
- 1765: Godefridus Weyerman, ed. P. Groot (vol. 12) (Madras, 1910)
- 1769: Cornelis Breekpot, ed. J. Fruytier (vol. 7) (Madras, 1909)
- 1781: Adriaan Moens, ed. P. Groot (vol. 2) (Madras, 1908)*

* for English translations, see *The Dutch in Malabar*, eds I.C.S. Galletti, A.J. van der Burg and P. Groot (Selections from the Records of the Madras Government, Dutch Records, 13) (Madras, 1911).

1793: Johan Gerard van Angelbeek, ed. P. Groot (vol. 4) (Madras, 1908)

384 Nieuhof, Johann, *Gedenkwaerdige zee- en lant-reize door verscheide gewesten van Oost-Indien* (Amsterdam, 1682).

385 *Patappattu*, ed. S. Paramesvara Aiyar (Sri Mulam Malayalam Library, 4) (Trivandrum, 1924).

386 Reede tot Drakestein, Hendrik Adriaan van, *Hortus Indicus Malabaricus*, 12 vols (Amsterdam, 1678-1703); part. trans. A. van Poot, *Malabaarse kruidhof, vervattende het raarste slag van allerlei soort van planten die in het koningrijk van Malabar worden gevonden*, 2 vols (The Hague, 1720).

387 *Selections from the Records of Fort St.George. Papers relating to Cochin with Special Reference to the Dutch Possessions and Claims to the British Rights arising therefrom* (Madras, 1915).

388 *Uitreksels uit de algemeene transports in de jaren 1743, 1761 en 1780*, ed. P. Groot (Selections from the Records of the Madras Government, Dutch Records, 9) (Madras, 1909).

389 *Verhaal van den Nabab Aider Alij Chan van 1763*, ed. P. Groot (Selections from the Records of the Madras Government, Dutch Records, 5) (Madras 1908).

3.2. Secondary Sources

390 Alexander, P.C., *The Dutch in Malabar* (Annamalai Nagar, 1946).

391 Ambachtsheer, F.F. and L.B. Wevers, 'De VOC loge van Wingurla. Een prachtig gebouw, het schoonste dat in India te vinden is', *Bulletin van de Koninklijke Nederlandse Oudheidkundige Bond*, 5 (1996).

392 Das Gupta, A., *Malabar in Asian Trade 1740-1800* (Cambridge, 1967).

393 Das Gupta, A., 'De VOC en de Malabarkust in de 18de eeuw', in M.A.P. Meilink-Roelofsz (ed.), *De VOC in Azië* (Bussum, 1976).

394 Day, F., *Land of the Perumals* (Madras, 1863).

395 Fischel, W.J., 'The Rotenburgh Family in Dutch Cochin of the 18th Century', *Studia Rosenthaliana*, 2 (1967).

396 Fischel, W.J., 'The Jewish Merchant-Diplomat Isaac Surgun and the Dutch-Mysore Conflict (1765-1791)', *Revue des études juives* (1967).

397 Fournier, M., 'H.A. van Reede tot Drakestein en de Hortus Malabaricus', *Spiegel Historiael*, 13, 9 (1978).

398 Fournier, M., 'Hortus Malabaricus of Hendrik Adriaan van Reede tot Drakestein', in K.S. Manilal, *Botany and History of Hortus Malabaricus* (Delhi, 1980).

399 Govindankutty, A., 'Some Observations on Seventeenth-Century Malayalam', *Indo-Iranian Journal*, 25 (1983).

400 Grove, R., 'Conserving Eden. The (European) East-India Companies and their Environmental Policies on St. Helena, Mauritius and in Western India, 1660 to 1854', *Comparative Studies in Society and History*, 35, 2 (1993).

401 Grove, R., 'Indigenous Knowledge and the Significance of South-West India for Portuguese and Dutch Constructions of Tropical Nature', in R.H.

Grove and others (eds), *Nature and the Orient: The Environmental History of South and Southeast Asia* (Delhi, 1998).

402 Heijmering, G., 'Inhoud van den brief door den Gouv. Gen. J. Mossel dd. 15 jan. 1753 aan den Onderkoning van Goa', *Tijdschrift voor Neerland's Indië*, 9 (1847).

403 Heniger, J., *Hendrik Adriaan van Reede tot Drakestein (1636-1691) and Hortus Malabaricus. A Contribution to the History of Dutch Colonial Botany* (Rotterdam, 1987).

404 Heyligers, A.J.M., *Press List of Ancient Dutch Records from 1657 to 1825* [pertaining to the records from Cochin kept at Madras] (Madras, n.d.).

405 Horst, W.A., 'De peperhandel der VOC', *Bijdragen voor Vaderlandsche Geschiedenis en Oudheidkunde*, 8, 3 (1941).

406 Iyer, S. Krishna, 'The Diary of Captain Hackert', *Journal of Kerala Studies*, 7 (1980).

407 Iyer, S. Krishna, 'Travancore-Dutch Tussle', *Journal of Kerala Studies*, 13 (1986).

408 Iyer, S. Krishna, *Travancore Dutch Relations* (Trivandrum, 1995).

409 s'Jacob, H.K., 'De VOC en de Malabarkust in de 17de eeuw', in M.A.P. Meilink-Roelofsz (ed.), *De VOC in Azië* (Bussum, 1976).

410 s'Jacob, H.K., 'Babba Prabhu. The Dutch and a Konkani Merchant in Kerala', *Itinerario*, 9, 2 (1985).

411 s'Jacob, H.K., 'Dutch Memoirs and Instructions on Kerala', *Journal of Kerala Studies*, 13, 1-4 (1986).

412 s'Jacob, H.K., 'Een staat in Kerala-India', in H.J.M. Claessen and A.H. Huusen jr. and E.Ch.L. van der Vliet (eds), *Kolonisatie en staatsvorming buiten Europa* (Groningen, 1993).

413 s'Jacob, H.K., 'State Formation and the Role of the Portfolio Investors in Cochin, 1663-1700', *Itinerario*, 18, 2 (1994).

414 Joseph, M.O., *Valiya Kappittan, the Maker of Modern Travancore* (Alleppey, 1947).

415 Joshi, P.M., 'Johan van Twist's Mission to Bijapur, 1637', *Journal of Indian History*, 34 (1956).

416 Kalff, S., 'Een verloren buiten-comtoir der O.I. Compagnie (Cochin op de kust van Malabar)', *De Indische Gids*, 24 (1902).

417 Kalff, S., 'De Maecenas van Malabar', *Elsevier's Geillustreerd Maandschrift*, 29 (1905).

418 Kienewicz, J., 'The Stationary System in Kerala', *Hemispheres, Studies on Cultures and Societies*, Contributions 1984, no. 1 (Warsaw, 1984).

419 Koshy, M.O., 'Dutch Impact on Kerala Society and Culture', *Journal of Kerala Studies*, 4 (1977).

420 Koshy, M.O., 'The De Lannoys and Travancore', *Journal of Kerala Studies*, 8 (1981).

421 Koshy, M.O., 'The Dutch in the East. A Case Study of their Relations with the Zamorin of Calicut 1604-63', *Journal of Indian History*, 63 (1985).

422 Koshy, M.O., *The Dutch Power in Kerala, 1729-1758* (Delhi, 1989).

423 Koshy, M.O., 'Native Assistance in the Foundation of Dutch Power in

Kerala', *Proceeding of the Indian History Congress* (1989).

424 Koshy, M.O., 'The Deserters of the Dutch East India Company in Kerala', *Indica*, 27, 1 (1990).

425 Koshy, M.O., 'The Expedition of Captain Johannes Hackert against Travancore from 18 October 1739 to 8 June 1740', *Proceeding of the Indian History Congress* (1990).

426 Koshy, M.O., 'The Relations between the Dutch EIC and the Kingdom of Purakkad from 1642 to 1663', *Proceeding of the Indian History Congress* (1991-2).

427 Lannoy, M. de, 'A 'Dutchman' in the Service of the Raja of Travancore. Eustache Benoit de Lannoy (1715-1777)', *Journal of Kerala Studies*, 13 (1986).

428 Lannoy, M. de, 'Een Zuidnederlander in dienst van de radja van Travancore. Eustache Benoit de Lannoy (1715-1777), in C. Koninckx (ed.), *Collectanea Maritima VI. Vlamingen Overzee, Flamands en Outre-Mer, Flemings Overseas* (Brussels, 1995).

429 Lannoy, M. de, 'European Soldiers in the Service of Travancore in the Eighteenth Century', in J. Everaert and J. Parmentier (eds), *Shipping, Factories and Colonization* (Brussels, 1996).

430 Lannoy, M. de, *The Kulasekhara Perumals of Travancore. History and State Formation in Travancore from 1671 to 1758* (Leiden, 1997).

431 Lohuizen, J. van, *The Dutch East India Company and Mysore* (= *Verhandelingen van het Koninklijk Instituut voor Taal-, Land- en Volkenkunde*, 31) (The Hague, 1961).

432 Manilal, K.S. (ed.), *Botany and History of Hortus Malabaricus* (Delhi, 1980).

433 Meilink-Roelofsz, M.A.P., 'Een Nederlander in Engelschen dienst op de Voor-Indische kust', *Tijdschrift voor Geschiedenis*, 57 (1942).

434 Meilink-Roelofsz, M.A.P., *De vestiging der Nederlanders ter kuste Malabar* (The Hague, 1943).

435 Padmanabha Menon, K.P., 'Udayagirifort and the Valia Kappithan', *The Educational Review* (1940).

436 Panikkar, K.M., *Malabar and the Dutch* (Bombay, 1931).

437 Poonen, T.I., *A Survey of the Rise of the Dutch Power in Malabar, 1603-1678* (Trichinopoly, 1948).

438 Poonen, T.I., *Dutch Hegemony in Malabar and its Collapse A.D. 1663-1795* (Trivandrum, 1978).

439 Prakash, O., 'The Dutch Factory at Vengurla in the Seventeenth Century', in A.R. Kulkarni and others (eds), *Medieval Deccan History Commemorative Volume of P.M. Joshi* (Bombay, 1996).

440 Ramachandram, N.P., 'The Dutch Expedition against Kulaccal', *Journal of Kerala Studies*, 5 (1978).

441 Ronkel, Ph.S. van, 'Old Dutch Settlements in British-India. Cochin on the Malabar Coast', *Sluyters' Monthly* (1922).

442 Ronkel, Ph.S. van, 'De eerste Europeesche Tamilspraakkunst en het eerste Malabaarsche glossarium', *Mededeelingen van de Koninklijke*

Nederlandsche Akademie van Wetenschappen, Afd. Letterkunde, n.s., 5 (1942).
443 Scholberg, H., 'European Cartography of the West Coast of India', *Indica*, 27, 1 (1990).
444 Suranad Kunjan Pillai, P.N., 'The Defeat of the Dutch in Travancore', *Indian Historical Records Commission. Proceedings of Meetings*, 21 (1945).
445 Valette, J. de la, 'Het Hollandsche tijdperk in Malabar', *Koloniaal Tijdschrift*, 21 (1932).
446 Vink, M.P.M., 'The Dutch East India Company and the Pepper Trade between Kerala and Tamilnad, 1663-1795: A Geo-historical Analysis', in K.S. Mathew (ed.), *Mariners, Merchants and Oceans: Studies in Maritime History* (Delhi, 1995).
447 Wagenvoort, M., 'De Hollanders aan de Malebaarkust', *Weekblad voor Indië*, 5 (1908).
448 Wetering, H.C.M. van de, 'De VOC en de kapers van Angria. Een expeditie naar de westkust van India in 1739', *Tijdschrift voor Zeegeschiedenis* 10, 2 (1991).

4. CEYLON (including Fishery Coast and Maldives)

4.1. Primary Sources

449 Andriesz, Georg, 'Ceylon and the Sinhalese, 1676 translated from Dutch by J.H.O. Paulusz', *Journal of the Ceylon Branch of the Royal Asiatic Society*, 38 (1948).
450 Baldaeus, Philippus, 'A True and Exact Description of the Great Island of Ceylon by Phillipus Baldaeus', trans. P. Brohier, *Ceylon Historical Journal*, 8, 1-4 (1958-9).
451 Behr, J. von der, *Diarium, oder Tagebuch* (Jena, 1668) [see also General, Primary Sources, *Reisebeschreibungen*].
452 'Beknopte historie van de voornaamste gebeurtenissen op Ceilon sedert de komst van de Nederlanders aldaar in den jare 1602 en vervolgens van het etablissement der edele maatschappij ten zelven eilande to den jare 1757', ed. P.A. Leupe, *Berigten van het Historisch Genootschap gevestigd te Utrecht*, 7, 2 (1862) [see also ed. F.H. de Ves in *Journal of the Ceylon Branch of the Royal Asiatic Society*, 11 (1889-90)].
453 Burckhardt, Christian, *Ost-indianische Reise-Beschreibung* (Halle and Leipzig, 1693).
454 Burmannus, Johannes, *Thesaurus Zeylanicus* (Amsterdam, 1737).
455 *Cartas de Raja Singa II, Rei de Candia, aos hollandeses (1636-1660)* (Do Boletim da Sociedade de Geographia de Lisboa), ed. D. Ferguson (n.p., 1907).
456 *Ceylonees plakkaatboek. Plakkaten en andere wetten uitgevaardigd door het Nederlands bestuur op Ceylon, 1638-1796*, 2 vols, ed. L. Hovy (Hilversum, 1991).

457 'Concept contract voor den koning van Ceylon en Candia, geconcipieerd in Rade van Ceylon op 12 Julij 1688', *Berigten van het Historisch Genootschap*, 7, 2 (1863).

458 *Constantine de Sa's Maps and Plans of Ceylon (1624-1628)*, ed. E. Reimers (Selections from the Dutch Records of Ceylon Governement/Government of Sri Lanka, 2) (Colombo, 1929).

459 'Correspondence between Raja Sinha II and the Dutch', trans. D.W. Ferguson, *Journal of the Ceylon Branch of the Royal Asiatic Society*, 18 (1904).

460 'Correspondentie betreffende Raja Singa' *Berigten van het Historisch Genootschap*, 7, 2 (1863).

461 *Germans in Dutch Ceylon* [Behr, Herport, Schweitzer, Frick], trans. R. Raven-Hart (Colombo, 1953).

462 Haafner, Jacob, 'Iets over het eiland Ceilon. Geschiedkundig overzigt tot 1796', *Vaderlandsche Letteroefeningen*, (1801), (1802).

463 Haafner, Jacob, *Reize te voet door het eiland Ceilon* (Amsterdam, 1810).

464 Heere, Gerrit de, *Diary of Occurrences during the Tour of Gerrit de Heere, Governor of Ceylon, from Colombo to Jaffna, July 9 to Sept. 3, 1697*, trans. S. Anthonisz-Pieters (Colombo, 1914).

465 Herport, Albrecht, *Eine kurze ost-indianische Reißbeschreibung* (Bern, 1669) [see also General, Primary Sources, *Reisebeschreibungen*], trans. R. Raven-Hart, 'A Short Description of a 9-Year East Indian Journey', in *National Museum of Ceylon Translation Series*, 1 (1953).

466 Heydt, J.W., *Allerneuster geographisch-topographischer Schauplatz von Africa und Ost-Asien*, (Wilhermsdorff, 1744); *Heydt's Ceylon being the Relevant Sections of the Allerneuester geographisch- und topographischer Schauplatz*, trans. R. Raven- Hart (Colombo, 1952).

467 *Instructions from the Governor-General and Council of India to the Governor of Ceylon, 1656 to 1665. To which is appended the Memoir left by Anthony Paviljoen, Commandeur of Jaffnapatam 1665*, trans. S. Anthonisz-Pieters (Colombo, 1908).

468 'Letters from Raja Sinha II to the Dutch', trans. D.W. Ferguson, *Journal of the Ceylon Branch of the Royal Asiatic Society*, 21 (1910).

469 'Lijste van alle de familien ... remoreerende binnen dese stede Jaffanapatnam ... 1694', ed. H.A.E. de Vos tot Nederveen Cappel, *Gens Nostra*, 33 (1978).

470 'Major Medeler's Relief Expedition, 1765', trans. R. Raven-Hart, *Journal of the Ceylon Branch of the Royal Asiatic Society*, n.s., 5 (1958).

471 Memoirs of *Commandeurs* of Jaffnapatam:
1665: Anthony Paviljoen [see *Instructions*].
1697: Hendrick Zwaardecroon, trans. S. Anthonisz-Pieters (Colombo, 1911).
1766: Anthony Mooyaart, trans. S. Anthonisz-Pieters (Colombo, 1910).

472 Memoirs of Governors of Ceylon:
1650: Joan Maetsuyker, trans. E. Reimers (Selections from the Dutch

Records of Ceylon Government/Government of Sri Lanka, 1) (Colombo, 1927).

1663/75: Rijcklof van Goens and Rijcklof van Goens (jr), trans. E. Reimers (Selections from the Dutch Records of Ceylon Government/Government of Sri Lanka, 3) (Colombo, 1932).

1679: Rycklof van Goens, trans. S. Anthonisz-Pieters (Colombo, 1910) [Dutch text in *Berigten van het Historisch Genootschap te Utrecht*, 5, 2 (1856)].

1697: Thomas van Rhee, trans. S. Anthonisz-Pieters (Colombo, 1915).

1707: Cornelis Joan Simons, trans. S. Anthonisz-Pieters (Colombo, 1914).

1716: Hendrik Becker, trans. S. Anthonisz-Pieters (Colombo, 1914).

1734: Jacob Christiaan Pielat, trans. S. Anthonisz-Pieters (Colombo, 1905).

1740: Gustaaf Willem Baron van Imhoff, trans. S. Anthonisz-Pieters (Colombo, 1911).

1751: Julius Stein van Gollenesse, trans. S. Arasaratnam (Colombo, 1974).

1757: Joan Gideon Loten, trans. E. Reimers (Selections from the Dutch Records of Ceylon Government/Government of Sri Lanka, 4) (Colombo, 1935).

1762: Jan Schreuder, trans. E. Reimers (Selections from the Dutch Records of Ceylon Government/Government of Sri Lanka, 5) (Colombo, 1946).

473 Parthey, Daniel, *Ost-indianische und persianische neun-jährige Kriegs-Dienste* (Nuremberg, 1687).

474 Queyroz, Fernao de, *The Temporal and Spiritual Conquest of Ceylon*, trans. S.G. Perera, 3 vols (Colombo, 1930).

475 Saar, Johann Jacob, 'Saar's Account of Ceylon, translated by Ph. Freudenberg with Introduction by D. Ferguson, *Journal of the Ceylon Branch of the Royal Asiatic Society*, 2 (1889).

476 Schouten, Wouter, 'Wouter Schouten's Account of Ceylon', trans. Ph. Freudenberg, *Journal of the Ceylon Branch of the Royal Asiatic Society*, 11 (1889-90).

477 Schweitzer, Christoph, *Journal- und Tagebuch* (Tübingen, 1688) [see also General, Primary Sources, *Reisebeschreibungen* and Frick], trans. R. Raven-Hart, 'Journal and Diary of his Six Years East Indian Journey', in *National Museums of Ceylon Translation Series*, 1 (1953).

478 *Secret Minutes of the Dutch Political Council, 1762*, trans. J.H.O. Paulusz. (Colombo, 1954).

479 *Some Documents relating to the Rise of the Dutch Power in Ceylon, 1602-1670, from the Translations at the India Office*, ed. P.E. Pieris (London, 1973).

480 Spilbergen, Joris van, *De reis van Joris van Spilbergen naar Ceylon, Atjeh*

en Bantam, 1601-1604, ed. F.C. Wieder (Werken Linschoten Vereniging, 38) (The Hague, 1933).

481 *The Dutch Wars with Kandy, 1764-1766*, trans. R. Raven-Hart (Colombo, 1964).

482 *The Pybus Embassy to Kandy, 1762*, trans. R. Raven-Hart (Colombo, 1958).

483 *Travels in Ceylon 1700-1800 by Wintergerst (1712) Ives (1773) Guyard (1763) Falck (1767) de Jonville (1800)*, trans. R. Raven-Hart (Colombo, 1963).

484 Valentijn, Francois, *Francois Valentijn's Description of Ceylon* (Hakluyt Society, 2nd Series, 149), trans. S. Arasaratnam (London, 1978).

485 Vennip, Cornelis Janszoon, *'t Historiael journael van tghene ghepasseert in van weghen dry schepen, den Ram, Schaep, ende't Lam* (Delft, 1604); reprint in *De reis van Joris van Spilbergen naar Ceylon, Atjeh en Bantam, 1601-1604*, eds W. Nijhoff and S.P. l'Honoré Naber, F.W. Stapel and F.C. Wieder (Werken Linschoten Vereniging, 38) (The Hague, 1933); part. trans. D. Ferguson, 'The Visit of Spilbergen to Ceylon, translated from Admiral Joris van Spilbergen's 'Relation'', *Journal of the Ceylon Branch of the Royal Asiatic Society*, 30 (1927); part. trans. K.D. Paranavitana, *Journal of Spilbergen. The First Dutch Envoy to Ceylon 1602* (Dehiwala, 1997).

486 Vries, S. de, *'t Eiland Ceylon in sijn binneste, of 't koninkrijk Candy, geopent en nauwkeuriger dan ooit te vooren ontdekt door Robert Knox, scheepskapitein der Engelse Oost-Indische Compagnie ... behelsende een eigentlijcke beschrijvingh, soo van 't landschap in zich selven als der inwoonderen politie, regeeringh, godsdienst, zeden, konsten, en meenigerley seldsame gewoonten* (Utrecht, 1692).

487 Wintergerst, Martin, *Reisebeschreibung* (Memmingen, 1712) [see also General, Primary Sources, *Reisebeschreibungen*].

488 Wolf, Johann Christoph, *Reise nach Zeilan* (Berlijn and Stettin, 1782-4).

4.2. Secondary Sources

489 Abeydeera, A., 'Mapping as a Vital Element of Administration in the Dutch Colonial Government of Maritime Sri Lanka 1658-1796', *Imago Mundi*, 45 (1993).

490 Abeysinghe, T.B.H., 'Embassies as Instruments of Diplomacy. A Casestudy from Sri Lanka in the First Half of the Eighteenth Century', *Journal of the Royal Asiatic Society, Sri Lanka Branch*, 30 (1985/6).

491 Anthonisz, R.G., *Catalogue of the Records of the Province of Galle under the Rule of the Netherlands East India Company, A.D. 1640 - A.D. 1796* (Colombo, 1906).

492 Anthonisz, R.G., *Report on the Dutch Records in the Government Archives at Colombo* (Colombo, 1907).

493 Anthonisz, R.G., 'Governor Falck's Audience to the Kandyan Ambassador in 1772', *Journal of the Dutch Burgher Union*, 2 (1909).

494 Anthonisz, R.G., 'The Dutch in Ceylon. Glimpses of their Life and Times', *The Ceylon Antiquary and Literary Register*, 1, 3 (1916).

495 Anthonisz, R.G., *The Dutch in Ceylon. Early Visits and Settlement in the Island* (Colombo, 1929).

496 Anthonisz, R.G., 'The Dutch Occupation of Kandy in 1765', *Journal of the Dutch Burgher Union*, 21 (1932).

497 Arasaratnam, S., 'Oratorians and Predikants. Catholic Church in Ceylon under Dutch Rule', *Ceylon Journal of Historical and Social Studies*, 1 (1958).

498 Arasaratnam, S., 'Dutch Sovereignty in Ceylon. A Historical Survey of its Problems', *The Ceylon Journal of Historical and Social Studies*, 1 (1958).

499 Arasaratnam, S., *Dutch Power in Ceylon, 1658-1687* (Amsterdam, 1958).

500 Arasaratnam, S., 'The Kandyan Kingdom. Aspects of its External Relations and Commerce 1658-1710', *The Ceylon Journal of Historical and Social Studies*, 2 (1959).

501 Arasaratnam, S., 'Reverend Philippus Baldaeus - his Pastoral Work in Ceylon, 1656-1665', *Nederlands Theologisch Tijdschrift*, 14 (1960).

502 Arasaratnam, S., 'Trade and Agricultural Economy of the Tamils of Jaffna 1660-1690', *Tamil Culture*, 9, 4 (1961).

503 Arasaratnam, S., 'Baron van Imhoff and Dutch Policy in Ceylon (1736-1740)', *Bijdragen tot de Taal-, Land en Volkenkunde*, 118 (1962).

504 Arasaratnam, S., 'Historical Survey of Ceylon 1650-1800', *United Asia* (Special Number of Ceylon Today), 15, 2 (1962).

505 Arasaratnam, S., 'The Dutch East India Company and the Kingdom of Madura 1650-1700', *Tamil Culture*, 10, 1 (1963).

506 Arasaratnam, S., 'Vimala Dharma Surya II (1687-1707) and his Relations with the Dutch', *Ceylon Journal for Historical and Social Studies*, 6 (1963).

507 Arasaratnam, S., 'A Note on Periathamby Marikkar - a 17th-Century Commercial Magnate', *Tamil Culture*, 11, 1 (1964).

508 Arasaratnam, S., 'The Administrative Organization of the Dutch East India Company in Ceylon', *Ceylon Journal of Historical and Social Studies*, 8 (1965).

509 Arasaratnam, S., 'Dutch Commercial Policies in Ceylon and its Effects on the Indo-Ceylon Trade (1690-1750)', *Indian Economic and Social History Review*, 4, 2 (1967).

510 Arasaratnam, S., 'Commercial Policies of the Sethupathis of Ramanathapuram 1660-1690', *Proceedings of the Second International Conference Seminar of Tamil Studies*, 2 (1968).

511 Arasaratnam, S., 'The Vanniar of North Ceylon. A Study of Feudal Power and Central Authority', *Ceylon Journal of Historical and Social Studies*, 10 (1969).

512 Arasaratnam, S., 'The Indigenous Ruling Class in Dutch Maritime Ceylon', *The Indian Economic and Social History Review*, 8, 1 (1971).

513 Arasaratnam, S., 'J.H.O. Paulusz on the 1638 Westerwolt Treaty in Ceylon. A Rejoinder', *Bijdragen tot de Taal-, Land- en Volkenkunde*, 138 (1982).

514 Arasaratnam, S., 'Social History of a Dominant Caste Society. The Vellalas of North Ceylon in the 18th Century', *Indian Economic and Social History Review*, 18, 3-4 (1982).

515 Arasaratnam, S., 'Elements of Social and Economic Change in Dutch Maritime Ceylon (Sri Lanka)', *Indian Economic and Social History Review*, 19, 1 (1985).

516 Arasaratnam, S., 'The First Century of Protestant Christianity in Jaffna 1658-1750', *Indian Church History Review*, 29, 1 (1985).

517 Arasaratnam, S., 'The Dutch Administrative Structure in Sri Lanka', *Modern Sri Lanka Studies*, 2, 1-2 (1987).

518 Arasaratnam, S., *Ceylon and the Dutch, 1600-1800. External Influences and Internal Change in Early Modern Sri Lanka* (Aldershot, Variorum Reprints, 1996).

519 B.[?], H., 'Uit vroeger tijd (over het aan het Daghregister ontleende relaas van het verhaal van in 1639 uit Ceylon teruggekeerde Compagnie's soldaten)', *De Indische Gids*, 28 (1906).

520 Balbian Verster, J.F.L. de, 'Adam Westerwolt', *Journal of the Dutch Burgher Union*, 14 (1924).

521 Balbian Verster, J.F.L. de, 'Gerard Hulst 1621-1656', *Jaarboek van het Genootschap Amstelodamum* (1932).

522 'Baldaeus' Tree: Vanishing Landmarks which made Dutch History', *Journal of the Dutch Burgher Union*, 43 (1953).

523 Blaze, L.E., 'Robert Knox and the Dutch', *Journal of the Dutch Burgher Union*, 4 (1911).

524 Blussé, L., 'The National Archives of Sri Lanka', *Itinerario*, 6, 1 (1982).

525 Boelen, H.J., 'Iets over Ceylon', *De Indische Gids*, 36 (1914).

526 Boudens, R.O.M.I., 'Attempts of Catholic Missionaries to enter Ceylon in 1661-83', *Journal of the Ceylon Branch of the Royal Asiatic Society*, n.s., 4 (1955).

527 Boudens, R.O.M.I., *The Catholic Church in Ceylon under Dutch Rule* (Rome, 1957).

528 Brascamp, E.H.B., 'Over djaticulturen in de memorie van overgave van den Gouverneur van Ceylon W.J. van de Graaff aan C. van Angelbeek in 1794', *Tectona* (1921).

529 Brohier, R.L., 'Land, Maps and Surveys, in Maritime Ceylon during the Dutch Administration', *Journal of the Ceylon Branch of the Royal Asiatic Society*, 38, 3-4 (1949).

530 Brohier, R.L., *Furniture of the Dutch Period in Ceylon* (Colombo, 1969).

531 Brohier, R.L., *A Book of Dutch Ceylon. Links between Sri Lanka and the Netherlands; a Book of Dutch Ceylon* (Colombo, 1978).

532 Brohier, R.L., *De Wolvendaalsche kerk* (Colombo, 1980).

533 'Ceremonieel voor den afgaanden Gouverneur van Ceilon, 18 maart 1757', *Kronijk van het Historisch Genootschap gevestigd te Utrecht*, vol. 16 (1860).

534 *Ceylon - Nederland in het verleden, 1602-1706* (The Hague, 1965).

535 Codrington, H.W., *Ceylon Coins and Currency* (*Memoirs of the Colombo Museum*, Series A, no. 3) (Colombo, 1924).

536 Cohen Stuart, A.B., 'De Hollandsche 'Burgerij' van Ceylon', *Neerlandia* (1921).

537 Colin-Thome, P., 'Governor Van Angelbeek and the Capitulation of Dutch

Settlements in Ceylon to the British (1796)', *Journal of the Royal Asiatic Society, Sri Lanka Branch*, 24 (1978-9).

538 D.[?], A., 'Ceylon in 't begin van onze koloniale geschiedenis', *Indologenblad*, 7 (1915-6).

539 Daalmans, A., 'A Belgian Physician's Notes on Ceylon in 1687-89, translated by Donald Ferguson', *Journal of the Ceylon Branch of the Royal Asiatic Society*, 10 (1887).

540 Dewaraja, L.S., *The Kandyan Kingdom of Ceylon 1707-1782* (Colombo, 1988).

541 Diehl, K.S., 'The Dutch Press in Ceylon', *The Library Quarterly*, 42 (1972).

542 Diehl, K.S. (ed.), *Historical Essays. Primary Printed and Manuscript Sources for Sixteenth to Nineteenth Century available in Sri Lanka* (Colombo, 1976).

543 Diessen, J.R. van, *Sri Lanka. De Singhalese koninkrijken en de Nederlandse kolonisatie. Geschiedenis, kunst en cultuur* (De Bilt, 1986).

544 Diessen, J.R. van, and A. van der Belt (eds), 'Een toelichting op zes topografische aquarellen van Ceylon in het Prentenkabinet', *Bulletin van het Rijksmuseum*, 35 (1987).

545 Dissanaike, A., 'A Dutch Thombo Register (of 1753)', *The Ceylon Antiquary and Literary Register*, 6, 2 (1920).

546 *The Dutch Reformed Church in Ceylon. 1642-1942* (Colombo, 1942).

547 Ferguson, D., 'Haafner's Account of Ceylon', *Ceylon Literary Register*, 5 (1890-1).

548 Ferguson, D., 'The Reverend Phillipus Baldaeus and his Book on Ceylon', *Monthly Literary Register (Colombo)*, 3 (1895).

549 Ferguson, D., 'Joan Gideon Loten, the Naturalist Governor of Ceylon (1752-57) and the Ceylonese Artist De Bevere', *Journal of the Ceylon Branch of the Royal Asiatic Society*, 18 (1904).

550 Ferguson, D., 'The Earliest Dutch Visits to Ceylon', *Journal of the Ceylon Branch of the Royal Asiatic Society*, 30-1 (1927-30); reprint in 1 volume (New Delhi, 1998).

551 Fitzler, M.A.H., *Ceilão e Portugal. O cêrco de Columbo. Últimos dias do dóminio português em Ceilão. Rompimento das hostilidades pelos holandeses até à rendição de Columbo (1652-1656)* (Coimbra, 1928).

552 Franciscus, S.D. (ed.), *Faith of our Fathers. History of the Dutch Reformed Church in Sri Lanka (Ceylon)* (Colombo, 1983).

553 Geer, W. van, *De opkomst van het Nederlandsch gezag over Ceilon* (Leiden, 1895).

554 Geer, W. van, 'De Nederlanders op Ceilon', *Gedenkboek Algemeen Nederlandsch Verbond 1893-1923* (Amsterdam, 1923).

555 Gijsberti Hodenpijl, A.K.A., 'Het buitengewone gezantschap naar het hof van Kandia te Ceylon in November 1736', *De Indische Gids*, 41 (1919).

556 Gijsberti Hodenpijl, A.K.A., 'De overgang van het bestuur van Ceylon van Gouverneur Stephanus Versluys in handen van Mr. Diderik van Domburgh, 1732-1733', *Bijdragen Vaderlandsche Geschiedenis en Oudheidkunde*, 6, 4 (1919).

557 Gijsberti Hodenpijl, A.K.A., 'Gustaaf Willem Baron van Imhoff als Gouverneur van Ceylon, 1736-1740', *Bijdragen tot de Taal-, Land- en Volkenkunde*, 75 (1919).
558 Gijsberti Hodenpijl, A.K.A., 'De inkomsten van een rechtschapen Gouverneur van Ceylon in den Compagniestijd', *De Indische Gids*, 42 (1920).
559 Godée Molsbergen, E.C., 'The Dutch Burgers in Ceylon', *De Indische Gids*, 51 (1929).
560 Goonesekere, S.W.E., 'Colonial Legislation and Sri Lankan Family Law. The Legacy of History', in K.M. de Silva, S. Kiribamune and C.R. de Silva (eds), *Asian Panorama. Essays in Asian History, Past and Present* (Delhi, 1990).
561 Goonetileke, H.A.I., *A Bibliography of Ceylon (Sri Lanka). A Systematic Guide to the Literature on the Land, People, History and Culture published in Western Languages from the Sixteenth Century to the Present Day*, 5 vols (Zug, 1970-83).
562 Goonewardena, K.W., *The Foundation of Dutch Power in Ceylon 1638-1658* (Amsterdam, 1958).
563 Goonewardena, K.W., 'A New Netherlands in Ceylon. Dutch Attempts to found a Colony during the First Quarter Century of their Power in Ceylon', *Ceylon Journal of Historical and Social Studies*, 2 (1959).
564 Goonewardena, K.W., 'Ayutthia in the Twilight Years and its Triangular Relations with the VOC and Sri Lanka', *Sri Lanka Journal of the Humanities*, 6, 1-2 (1980).
565 Goonewardena, K.W., 'Dutch Policy towards Buddhism in Sri Lanka and some Aspects of its Impact, ca.1640-ca.1740', in K.M. de Silva, S. Kiribamune and C.R. de Silva (eds), *Asian Panorama. Essays in Asian History, Past and Present* (Delhi, 1990).
566 Goor, J. van, 'De Nederlandse invloed op Ceylon', *Spiegel Historiael*, April (1980).
567 Goor, J. van, 'Ceylon en de Nederlanders', *Kleio*, 17 (1976).
568 Goor, J. van, *Jan Kompenie as Schoolmaster. Dutch Education in Ceylon 1690-1795* (Groningen, 1978).
569 'Governor Falck's Audience to the Kandyan Ambassadors in 1772', *Journal of the Dutch Burgher Union*, 2 (1909).
570 Grenier, J., 'The Portuguese and Dutch in Ceylon', *Journal of the Dutch Burgher Union'*, 7 (1914).
571 Handy, J.C. (and others), *The Kruyskerk of Jaffnapatnam* (Jaffnapatnam, 1966).
572 Horst, M.J.H., van der, *Het Rooms-Hollands Recht in Sri Lanka* (Deventer, 1984); trans. *The Roman Dutch Law in Sri Lanka* (Amsterdam, 1985).
573 Houten, P.J. van, 'Twee Indische natuurliefhebbers uit de XVIIe eeuw', *Indische Mercuur*, 28 (1905), 29 (1906), 31 (1908).
574 Hovy, L. and C. Streefkerk, *'Zoo is't dat wij daarin nader willende voorzien'. Prolegomena voor een Ceylonees plakkaatboek* (Amsterdam, 1985).
575 'In the Days of the Dutch in Ceylon', *Ceylon Observer Annual* (1934).

576 Jongens, E., *De Nederlandse erfenis in Ceylon* (The Hague, 1980).
577 Jongens, E., *Gecharmeerd van Colombo. Publicatie naar aanleiding van het 15-jarig bestaan van de Stichting Nederland-Sri Lanka* (The Hague, 1991).
578 Jongens, E., *Gefascineerd door Galle. Publicatie naar aanleiding van het 15-jarig bestaan van de stedenband tussen Velsen en Galle* (The Hague, 1991).
579 Juriaanse, M.W., *Catalogue of the Archives of the Dutch Central Government of Coastal Ceylon 1640-1796* (Colombo, 1943).
580 K.[?], R. van de, 'Het wapen van Colombo', *De Navorscher*, 60 (1911).
581 Kalff, S., 'A Lost Dutch Colony (Ceylon)', *Inter-Ocean* (1926).
582 Kan, J. van, 'Uit de Ceilonsche rechtsgeschiedenis', *Bijdragen tot de Taal-, Land- en Volkenkunde van Nederlandsch-Indië*, 102 (1943).
583 Kanapathypillai, V., 'Helen or Castly Bride. The VOC and the Cinnamon Trade of Sri Lanka 1766-1796', *Modern Sri Lanka Studies*, 2, 1-2 (1987).
584 Keuneman, H., 'Galle. Something to crow about through a (Reversed) Telescope', *Journal of the Dutch Burgher Union of Ceylon*, 60 (1982).
585 Kleinschmidt, A., 'De zendingsonderneming der Broedergemeente naar Ceylon (1738-1741)', *Nederlandsch Zendingstijdschrift*, 8 (1896).
586 Knaap, G., 'Europeans, Mestizos and Slaves. The Population of Colombo at the End of the Seventeenth Century', *Itinerario*, 5, 2 (1981).
587 Kotelawele, D.A., 'Agrarian Policies of the Dutch in South-West Ceylon, 1743-1767', *Afdeling Agrarische Geschiedenis (Wageningen) Bijdragen*, 14 (1967).
588 Kotelawele, D.A., 'Realms of Law. Judicial Procedures of the Low Country Sinhalese during Dutch Rule in Sri Lanka', *Modern Sri Lanka Studies*, 2, 1-2 (1987).
589 Kromhout, R. (ed.), *Het machtige eyland. Ceylon en de VOC* (The Hague, 1988).
590 Kularatne, T., 'Introduction of Print to Sri Lanka (Ceylon). The Dutch Press in Ceylon (1736-1796)', *Libri*, 45, 2 (1995).
591 Lauchner, J., 'Itur procul atque reditur. Martin Wintergerst 1670-1728', *Memminger Geschichtsblätter* (1985-6).
592 Leeuwrik, J.H.J., 'Zilver op Ceylon en in de Zuidindiase kustgebieden in de tijd van de Verenigde Oostindische Compagnie', in *Antiek*, 31, 5 (1996).
593 Lewis, J.P., 'Dutch Architecture in Ceylon', *Architectural Review* (1902), (1904).
594 Lewis, J.P., 'List of the Dutch Civil Servants at Jaffna in October 1796', *Journal of the Dutch Burgher Union*, 1 (1908).
595 Lewis, J.P., 'Dutch Extracts and the Dutch Company in the Matara District', *Journal of the Dutch Burgher Union*, 1 (1908), 2 (1909).
596 Lewis, J.P., 'Old Dutch Customs at Batticaloa', *The Ceylon Antiquary and Literary Register*, 5, 2 (1919).
597 Lewis, J.P., 'Dutch Cannon in Ceylon', *The Ceylon Antiquary and Literary Register*, 6, 1 (1920).

598 Lewis, J.P., 'Glimpses of Ceylon in Dutch Times', *Ceylon Antiquary and Literary Register*, 7, 1 (1921).

599 Lohuizen, J. van, *Langs Hollandsche oudheden in Sri Lanka* (Amsterdam, 1976).

600 Loos-Haaxman, J. de, 'Het portret van Stephanus Versluys, Gouverneur en Directeur van Ceylon', *Tijdschrift van het Bataviaas Genootschap*, 83 (1949).

601 Ludovici, L., *Lapidarium Zeylanicum, being a Collection of Monumental Inscriptions of the Dutch Churches and Churchyards of Ceylon* (Colombo, 1877).

602 Lutgert, W.H., 'Pieter Macaré, Independent Fiscaal van Ceylon, 1702-1711', *Archief. Mededelingen van het Koninklijk Zeeuwsch Genootschap der Wetenschappen*, 1988.

603 Lutterveld, R. van, 'Jan Brandes, predikant, landeigenaar en tekenaar', *Bulletin van de Koninklijke Nederlandse Oudheidkundige Bond*, 15 (1958).

604 M.[?], 'Nog iets over 't Katholicisme onder de O.I. Compagnie op Ceylon', *De Java-Post* (1912).

605 M.[?], 'De O.I. Compagnie op Ceilon', *De Java-Post* (1912).

606 M.[?], 'Een en ander over het Compagniesch Protestantisme op Ceilon', *De Java-Post* (1912).

607 MacLeod, N., 'Eerste ontmoetingen van de Franschen en Hollanders in Indië (Ceylon) 1672-74', *De Indische Gids*, 22 (1900).

608 MacLeod, N., 'Uit de geschiedenis der Oost-Indische Compagnie in de tweede helft der 18e eeuw', *De Indische Gids*, 33 (1911), 34 (1912).

609 Mahroof, M.M.M., 'The Muslims under Portuguese and Dutch Occupation 1505-1796', *An Ethnological Survey of the Muslims of Sri Lanka from Earliest Times to Independence* (Colombo, 1986).

610 Marck, J.P.C. van der, 'Lijst der Nederlandsche landvoogden van Ceylon', *Tijdschrift voor Indische Taal-, Land- en Volkenkunde van het Koninklijk Bataviaasch Genootschap van Kunsten en Wetenschappen*, 14 (1865).

611 McGilvray, D., 'Dutch Burghers and Portuguese Mechanics. Eurasian Ethnicity in Sri Lanka', *Comparative Studies in Society and History*, 24 (1982).

612 Meilink-Roelofsz, M.A.P., 'Een tentoonstelling Nederland - Ceylon in het verleden, 1602-1796', *Bulletin van de Koninklijke Nederlandse Oudheidkundige Bond* (1966).

613 Mendis, V.L.B., *The Advent of the British to Ceylon 1762-1803* (Dehiwale, 1971).

614 Mengerink, A.H., 'De landmeterij op Ceijlon in de achttiende eeuw', in P. van Mil and M. Scharloo (eds), *De VOC in de kaart gekeken. Cartografie en navigatie van de Verenigde Oostindische Compagnie 1602-1799* (The Hague, 1988).

615 Mottau, S.A.W., 'Education under the Dutch', *Education in Ceylon, a Centenary Volume* (Colombo, 1969).

616 Mottau, S.A.W., *Inventory of the Archives of the Dutch Government in the Divisions of Galle (Matara) and Jaffnapatam 1640-1796* (The Hague, 1975).

617 Mottau, S.A.W., 'Archival Collections for Studies of the Dutch in Ceylon', *Journal of the Dutch Burgher Union of Ceylon*, 60 (1982).

618 Mottau, S.A.W., 'Glossary of Terms used in Official Correspondence of the Governement of Sri Lanka, compiled from Records at the National Archives', *The Sri Lanka Archives*, 3 (1985-6).

619 Nadaraja, T., *The Roman-Dutch Law as applied in Ceylon and South Africa* (Colombo, 1949).

620 Nadaraja, T., *The Administration of Justice in Ceylon under the Dutch Governement, 1650-1796* (n.p., 1952).

621 Nadaraja, T., *The Legal System of Ceylon in its Historical Setting* (Leiden, 1972).

622 Nelson, W.A., *The Dutch Forts of Sri Lanka. the Military Monuments of Ceylon* (Edinburgh, 1984).

623 Nilakanti Sastri, K.A., 'Tirumala Naik, the Portuguese and the Dutch', *Indian Historical Record Commission, Proceedings of Meetings*, 16 (1940).

624 Nypels, G., *Hoe Nederland Ceylon verloor* (The Hague, 1908).

625 Ondaatje, M.P.J., 'A Tabular List of Original Works and Translations published by the Late Dutch Government of Ceylon at the Printing Press at Colombo', *Journal of the Royal Asiatic Society of Great Britain and Ireland*, n.s. 1 (1865).

626 'Onze betrekkingen met Colombo', *De Indische Gids*, 30 (1908).

627 Pabbruwe, H.J., *Dr Robertus Padtbrugge (Parijs 1637 - Amersfoort 1703). Dienaar van de Verenigde Oost-Indische Compagnie* (Kloosterzande, n.d.).

628 Palm, J.D., 'The Educational Establishment of the Dutch in Ceylon', *Journal of the Ceylon Branch of the Royal Asiatic Society*, 2 (1846-7).

629 Palm, J.D., 'An Account of the Dutch Church in Ceylon collected from the Local Records deposited in the Wolfendahl Church, Colombo', *Journal of the Ceylon Branch of the Royal Asiatic Society*, 3 (1847-8).

630 Paranavitana, K.D., 'A Report from the Archives of Sri Lanka', *Itinerario*, 6, 1 (1982).

631 Paranavitana, K.D., 'The Archives of the 'Waare Christelijke Gereformeerde Kerk' (True Christian Reformed Church in Sri Lanka)', *The Sri Lanka Archives*, 1 (1983).

632 Paranavitana, K.D., *An Inventory of Sri Lanka Maps in the General State Archives in the Netherlands* (Colombo, 1984).

633 Paranavitana, K.D., 'Medical Establishment in Sri Lanka during the Dutch Period', *Journal of the Royal Asiatic Society, Sri Lanka Branch*, 33 (1988-9).

634 Paranavitana, K.D., 'The Archives of the Dutch East India Company: Administration in Ceylon 1640-1796' (Unpublished PhD-thesis, University of New South Wales, Sydney, 1994).

635 Pathmanathan, S., 'Religion and Social Change in Northern Sri Lanka, 1796-1875. Protestant Missionary Activity and the Hindus Response', *Modern Sri Lanka Studies*, 1, 1 (1986).

636 Paulusz, J.H.O. (ed.), *Historical Maps of Ceylon* (Colombo, 1951).

637 Paulusz, J.H.O., 'Dutch Painting of the Kandyan Embassy', *Journal of the Ceylon Branch of the Royal Asiatic Society*, n.s., 3 (1953)

638 Paulusz, J.H.O., 'Ambanwela Appuhamy's Rebellion in 1665', *Journal of the Ceylon Branch of the Royal Asiatic Society*, n.s., 7 (1960).

639 Paulusz, J.H.O., 'The 1638 Westerwolt Treaty in Ceylon. Charges of Dutch Deceit disproved', *Bijdragen tot de Taal-, Land- en Volkenkunde*, 136 (1980).

640 Paulusz, J.H.O., 'Professor Arasaratnam's Rejoinder? Some Comments', *Bijdragen tot de Taal-, Land- en Volkenkunde*, 138 (1982)

641 Pearson, J., 'European Chairs in Ceylon in the Seventeenth and Eighteenth Centuries', *Journal of the Ceylon Branch of the Royal Asiatic Society*, 31, 81, 1-4 (1928).

642 Perera, S.G., 'Historical Records of the Society of Jesus III. The Portuguese and the Dutch in Galle', *The Ceylon Antiquary and Literary Register*, 3, 3 (1918).

643 Perera, S.G., 'Catholic Agitations in Dutch Times as described by a Catholic Priest in 1707', *Ceylon Antiquary and Literary Register*, 6, 3 (1921).

644 Perera, S.G., *A History of Ceylon I: The Portuguese and the Dutch Periods 1505-1796* (Colombo, 1955).

645 Perniola, V., *The Catholic Church in Sri Lanka. The Dutch Period 1747 to 1795* (Dehiwala, 1985).

646 Pieris, P.E., 'The Dutch Embassy to Kandy in 1731-32 translated from the Sinhalese', *Journal of the Ceylon Branch of the Royal Asiatic Society*, 21 (1910).

647 Pieris, P.E., *Ceylon. The Portuguese Era 1505-1658*, 2 vols (Colombo, 1913).

648 Pieris, P.E., *Ceylon and the Hollanders, 1658-1796* (Tellipalai, 1918).

649 Pieris, P.E., *The Dutch Power of Ceylon* (n.p., 1929; reprint 1973).

650 Pieris, P.E., 'A Dutch Painting', *Journal of the Ceylon Branch of the Royal Asiatic Society*, 38 (1948).

651 Raat, A.J.P., 'Enige voorwerpen uit de nalatenschap van Joan Gideon Loten (1710-1789)', *Tijdschrift voor de Geschiedenis van de Geneeskunde, natuurwetenschappen, Wiskunde en Techniek*, 2 (1979).

652 Raben, R., 'Facing the Crowd: The Urban Ethnic Policy of the Dutch East India Company 1600-1800', in K.S. Mathew (ed.), *Mariners, Merchants and Oceans: Studies in Maritime History* (Delhi, 1995).

653 Raben, R., 'Batavia and Colombo. The Ethnic and Spatial Order of Two Colonial Cities 1600-1800' (Unpublished PhD thesis, Leiden University, 1996).

654 Raben, R., 'European Periphery in the Heart of the Ocean: The Maldives, 17th-18th Centuries', in J. Everaert and J. Parmentier (eds), *Shipping, Factories and Colonization* (Brussels, 1996).

655 Raheem, I., 'Catalogue for the Dutch Period Museum' (Colombo, 1982).

656 Raheem, I., 'Views of Colombo 1518-1900', in R.L. Brohier, *Changing Face of Colombo* (Colombo, 1984).

657 Raven-Hart, R., 'Supplementary Notes to Heydt's Ceylon', *Journal of the Ceylon Branch of the Royal Asiatic Society*, n.s., 4 (1954).

658 Raven-Hart, R., *Germans in Dutch Ceylon* (Colombo, 1956).

659 Raven-Hart, R., *The War with the Sinhalese* (Colombo, 1961).

660 'Redoute "Van Eck" op Ceylon', *Neerlandia* (1931).

661 Reimers, E., 'Old Matara and the Rebellion of 1760-61', *Journal of the Dutch Burgher Union*, [?].

662 Reimers, E., 'De 'Burghers' van Ceylon', *Neerlandia* (1921).

663 Reimers, E., *The Coming of the Dutch* (n.p., 1924).

664 Reimers, E., *The Dutch Parish Registers (School Thombos) of Ceylon, Ambalangoda, Patabendimulla, Welitara and Kosgoda* (n.p., 1950).

665 *Report of the Repair Fund of the Wolfendahl Church. With a List of Collectors and Subscribers* (Colombo, 1904).

666 Rethaan Macaré, C.A., 'Rapport Henricus van Bijstervelt aan Raja Singa (1671)', *Berigten van het Historisch Genootschap te Utrecht*, 5, 2 (1856).

667 Sanders, G.P., 'Joan Aalwis Widjewarddene Senewiratne' en de uijtgebreidheid van een mostaardzaadje. Een beloningspenning van de Verenigde Oostindische Compagnie in 1762', *Bulletin Rijksmuseum*, 42 (1994).

668 Sannasgala, P.B., *A Study of Sinhala Vocables of Dutch Origin* (Colombo, 1976).

669 Saram, L. de, 'Naval and Military Operations off Trincomalee in 1782 and 1796, and the Ceylon Medal 1795-96', *The Ceylon Observer* (1948).

670 Schulman, A., 'Numismatische herinneringen aan Ceylon onder Hollandsch bestuur', *Jaarboek Koninklijk Nederlands Genootschap voor Munt- en Penningkunde Amsterdam*, 1 (1914).

671 Shulman, D. and S. Subrahmanyam, 'Prince of Poets and Ports: Cītakkāti, the Maraikkāyars and Ramnad, ca. 1690-1710', in A. Libera Dallapiccola and S. Zingel-Avé Lallemant (eds), *Islam and Indian Regions*, 1 (Beiträge zur Südasienforschung, Südasien-Institut, Universität Heidelberg, 145) (Stuttgart, 1993).

672 Silva, C.R. de, 'Peddling Trade, Elephants, and Gems. Some Aspects of Sri Lanka's Trading Connections in the Indian Ocean in the Sixteenth and Early-Seventeenth Century', in K.M. de Silva, S. Kiribamune and C.R. de Silva (eds), *Asian Panorama. Essays in Asian History, Past and Present* (Delhi, 1990).

673 Silva, G.P.S.H. de, 'Sri Lanka Archival Sources for a Study of the History of the Country', in K.M. de Silva, S. Kiribamune and C.R. de Silva (eds), *Asian Panorama. Essays in Asian History, Past and Present* (Delhi, 1990).

674 Silva, R.K. de, and W.G.M. Beumer, *Illustrations and Views of Dutch Ceylon, 1602-1796. A Comprehensive Work of Pictorial Reference with Related Eyewitness Accounts* (Leiden, 1988).

675 Singh, S., 'Mir Jumla's Relations with the Dutch and Portuguese in Sri Lanka in 1653', *Proceeding of the Indian History Congress* (1990).

676 Sitompul, Y.M., *Inventaris van het archief van Hendrik Becker (1661-1722)* (The Hague, 1983) [see also: *Vijf ambtenaren van de VOC en de Regering in Indie. Inventarissen van de archieven van Becker, Cnoll, Van Kal, Van Polanen en Valckenier* (The Hague, 1985) [Becker was Governor in Ceylon].

677 Stapel, F.W., 'Nederlandsche herinneringen op Ceylon', *Cultureel Indië*, 1 (1939).

678 Subrahmanyam, S., 'Noble Harvest from the Sea. Managing the Pearl Fishery of Mannar, 1500-1925', in B. Stein and S. Subrahmanyam (eds), *Institutions and Economic Change in South Asia* (Delhi, 1996).

679 Tennent, J.E., *Christianity in Ceylon* (London, 1950).

680 Terpstra, H., 'Compagniesonderwijs op Ceylon', *Tijdschrift voor Geschiedenis*, 71 (1958).

681 Terwen-de Loos, J., *Het Nederlandse koloniale meubel. Studie over meubels in de voormalige Nederlandse koloniën Indonesië en Sri Lanka* (Franeker, 1985).

682 Uragoda, C.G. and Paranavitana, K.D., 'The Seventeenth-Century Dutch Hospital in Colombo', *Medical History*, 29, 2 (1985).

683 'Vergeten geschiedenisbladen (Geschiedenis Nederlands bestuur op Ceylon in de boekerij van Colombo)', *Neerlandia* (1930).

684 Veth, P.J., 'Rapport over de papieren van Joan Gideon Loten', *Kronijk van het Historisch Genootschap gevestigd te Utrecht*, vol. 16 (1860).

685 Vink, M.P.M., 'Images and Ideologies of Dutch-South Asian Contact. Cross-Cultural Encounters between the Nayaka State of Madurai and the Dutch East India Company in the Seventeenth Century', *Itinerario*, 21, 2 (1997).

686 Vink, M.P.M., 'Encounters on the Opposite Coast: Cross-Cultural Contacts between the Dutch East India Company and the Nayaka State of Madurai' (Unpublished PhD thesis, University of Minnesota, 1998).

687 Visser, H., 'Jan Brandes, de Lutherse predikant-tekenaar', *Bulletin van het Rijksmuseum*, 34, 2 (1986).

688 Vos, C.E. de, 'The Dutch Predikants of Ceylon', *Journal of the Dutch Burgher Union*, 5 (1912), 6 (1913).

689 Vos, F.H. de, 'The Capture of Trincomalee AD 1639', *Journal of the Ceylon Branch of the Royal Asiatic Society*, 10 (1887).

690 Vos, F.H. de, 'Henricus van Bylevelt's Embassy to Kandy in 1671', *Journal of the Ceylon Branch of the Royal Asiatic Society*, 11 (1889-90).

691 Vos, F.H. de, 'Genealogische en heraldische aanteekeningen aangaande Hollandsche familiën op Ceylon', *De Navorscher*, 53 (1903).

692 Vos, F.H. de, 'Mr Isaac Augustin Rumpf', *Journal of the Ceylon Branch of the Royal Asiatic Society*, 18 (1904).

693 Vos, F.H. de, 'Three Funerals of Ceylon Dutch Officials in the Eighteenth Century', *Journal of the Ceylon Branch of the Royal Asiatic Society*, 18 (1904).

694 Vos, F.H. de, 'List of some of the Founders of Families which settled in Ceylon from Europe during the Dutch Adminitration A.D. 1640-1796', *Journal of the Dutch Burgher Union*, 1 (1908).

695 Vos, F.H. de, 'Monumental Remains of the Dutch E.I.C. in Ceylon', *Journal of the Ceylon Branch of the Royal Asiatic Society* (1898-1910).

696 Vos, F.H. de, 'The Dutch Gouvernors of Ceylon', *Journal of the Dutch Burgher Union*, 2 (1909), 3 (1910), 5 (1912).

697 Vos, F.H. de, 'Laurens Pijl en Laurens Pit', *The Ceylon Antiquary and Literary Register*, 2, 4 (1917).

698 Vries, J. de, 'Holland op Ceilon', *Eigen Haard*, 20-1 (1903).

699 Wagenaar, L., *Galle: VOC-vestiging in Ceylon* (Amsterdam, 1994).

700 Wall, E.H. van der, 'De Hollanders op Ceylon. Bewerkt en voorzien van enkele aanteekeningen door J.F.L. de Balbian Verster', *Tijdschrift Aardrijkskundig Genootschap* (1922).

701 Weenink, H.S.W., 'The Dutch Burgher Union of Ceylon', *Indië G.W.*, 5 (1921-2).

702 Wimalaratne, K.D.G., K.D. Paranavithana and S.S.K. Wickramayanake (eds), *Guide to the Sources of Asian History. Sri Lanka* (Colombo, 1996).

703 Winius, G.D., *The Fatal History of Portuguese Ceylon, Transition to Dutch Rule* (Cambridge, 1971).

704 Wittewaal van Wickerburgh, B.W., 'Uit de laatste dagen der O.I. Compagnie (oorlog op Ceylon in 1765)', *Bijdragen tot de Taal- Land- en Volkenkunde van Nederlandsch-Indië*, 47 (1897).

705 Zwier, W., *Het verdrag van 1766 tusschen de VOC en den vorst van Kandi* (Amsterdam, 1927).

5. COROMANDEL

5.1. Primary Sources

706 *Bericht van de bewinthebberen van de Nederlandsche geoctroyeerde Oost-Indische Compagnie, overgelevert aan de Hoog Mogende Heeren Staten Generael der Vereenighde Nederlanden, den 4 october, 1687, op het subject van de klaghten by den Heer Marquis d'Albyville, extraordinaris envoyé van den Konicnk van Groot Britannien, gedaen over het voorgevallene tot Masulipatnam op de kust van Chormandel en tot Batancapas op de westkust van Sumatra,* ed. Pieter van Dam (Amsterdam, 1687).

707 *Brieven gezonden van Negapatnam (1748-1750 en 1757-1758)*, ed. P. Groot (Madras, 1911).

708 Burg, Pieter van der, *Curieuse beschrijving van de gelegentheid, zeden, godsdienst en ommegang van verscheyden Oost-Indische gewesten en machtige landschappen, etc van Golconda en Pegu* (Rotterdam, 1677).

709 Coutre, Jacques de, *Aziatische omzwervingen; het leven van een Brugs diamanthandelaar. Vertaald en ingeleid door Johan Verberckmoes en Eddy Stals* (Berchem, 1988); *Como remediar o Estado da India, being the Appendices of the 'Vida de Jacques de Coutre', Biblioteca Nacional, Madrid, manuscript 2780; edited with an intoduction, notes and index by B.N. Teensma* (Leiden, 1989); Andanzas asiàticas, eds E. Stols, B. Teensma and J. Verberckmoes (Madrid, 1991).

710 Floris, Peter, *Peter Floris - His Voyage to the East Indies in the 'Globe', 1611-1615* (Hakluyt Society, 2nd Series, 74), ed. W.H. Moreland (London, 1934).

711 Havart, Daniel, *Den Persiaanschen Bogaard. Beplant met zeer uitgeleesen*

spruiten der historie, en bezaait met zeltzame voorvallen, leerzame en aardige geschiedenissen, neffens opmerkelijke spreuken. In 't Persiaansch beschreven door Siech Muslady Caädy, van Cieraas. En om zijn treffelijkheyds wille in 't Nederduits gebragt, door D.H. t'Amsterdam, By Jan ten Hoorn (Amsterdam, 1688).

712 Havart, Daniel, *Persiaansche secretaris of een nette beschryving van de stijl van de Persianen gebruiken in hare brieven en notariale stukken; als ook van de feest- en vierdagen de Muhammedanen door het gehele jaar in het Koninkryk Golkonda* (Amsterdam, n.d.).

713 Havart, Daniel, *Op- en ondergang van Cormandel*, 3 vols (Amsterdam, 1693).

714 *Relations of Golconda in the Early Seventeenth Century* (Hakluyt Society, 2nd Series, 66), ed. W.H. Moreland (London, 1931) [memoranda of Anton Schorer and Pieter Gillisz. van Ravesteyn in 1614].

715 Rogerius, Abraham, *De Open-deure tot het verborgen heydendom door Abraham Rogerius* (Leiden, 1651); ed. W. Caland (Werken Linschoten Vereniging, 10) (The Hague, 1915).

716 Schorer, Anton, 'Shorer's Account of the Coromandel Coast', trans. B. Narain, ed. S.R. Sharma, *The Indian Historical Quarterly*, 16 (1940).

717 *Selections from Old Records South Arcot. Restitution of the Dutch Settlements. Report by Mr John Hodgson, dated 28th January 1818* (Cuddalore, 1911).

718 *Verklaringen van brieven gezonden van Negapatnam*, ed. P. Groot (Selections from the Records of the Madras Government, Dutch Records, 15) (Madras, 1911).

719 Vries, David Pieterszoon de, *Korte historiael end journaels aenteykeninge van verscheyden voyagiens in de vier deelen des wereltsronde, als Europa, Africa, Asia, ende Amerika gedaen* (Hoorn, 1655); ed. H.T. Colenbrander (Werken Linschoten Vereniging, 3) (The Hague, 1911).

5.2. Secondary Sources

720 Alam, Ishrat, 'The Dutch East India Company's Version of the Putting-out System in Seventeenth-Century Coromandel', *Proceeding of the Indian History Congress* (1995).

721 Alam, M. and S. Subrahmanyam, 'Exploring the Hinterland: Trade and Politics in the Arcot Nizamat', in R. Mukherjee and L. Subramanian (eds), *Politics and Trade in the Indian Ocean World: Essays in Honour of Ashin Das Gupta* (Delhi, 1998).

722 Alam, S.M., 'Masulipatam - A Metropolitan Port in the Seventeenth Century', *Islamic Culture*, 33, 3 (1959).

723 Arasaratnam, S., 'Some Aspects relating to the Establishment and Growth of European Settlements along the Tamil Coast in the Seventeenth Century', *Tamil Culture*, 7, 4 (1958).

724 Arasaratnam, S., 'The Dutch East India Company and its Coromandel Trade 1700-1740', *Bijdragen tot de Taal-, Land- en Volkenkunde*, 123 (1967).

725 Arasaratnam, S., 'The Politics of Commerce in the Tamil Kingdoms of South Asia 1650-1700', *South Asia*, 1, 1 (1971).

726 Arasaratnam, S., 'Francois Valentijn's Description of Coromandel', in *Professor K.A. Nilakantra Sastri Felicitation Volume* (Madras, 1971).

727 Arasaratnam, S., 'Weavers, Merchants and Company. The Handloom Industry in Southeastern India 1750-1790', *Indian Economic and Social History Review*, 17, 3 (1980).

728 Arasaratnam, S., 'Indian Merchants and the Decline of Indian Mercantile Activity. The Coromandel Case', *The Calcutta Historical Journal*, 7, 2 (1983).

729 Arasaratnam, S., 'The Coromandel - Southeast Asian Trade 1650-1740. Challenges and Responses of a Commercial System', *Journal of Asian History*, 18, 2 (1984).

730 Arasaratnam, S., 'Factors in the Rise, Growth and Decline of Coromandel Ports 1650-1740', *South Asia*, 7, 2 (1984).

731 Arasaratnam, S., *Merchant Companies and Commerce on the Coromandel Coast (1650-1740)* (Oxford, 1986).

732 Arasaratnam, S., 'The Rice Trade in Eastern India 1650-1740', *Modern Asian Studies*, 22, 3 (1988).

733 Arasaratnam, S., 'European Port Settlements in the Coromandel Commercial System 1650-1740', in F. Broeze (ed.), *Brides of the Sea. Port Cities of Asia from the Sixteenth to Twentieth Centuries* (Kensington, 1989).

734 Arasaratnam, S., 'Coromandel Revisited. Issues and Problems in Indian Maritime History', *Indian Economic and Social History Review*, 26, 1 (1989).

735 Arasaratnam, S., 'Merchants of Coromandel in Trade and Entrepreneurship *c.*1650-1700', in R. Ptak and D. Rothermund (eds), *Emporia, Entrepreneurs and Commodities in Asian Maritime Trade* (Stuttgart, 1991).

736 Bhattacharya, B., 'The Dutch East India Company and the Coromandel Coast 1740-1780. A Story of its Decline' (Unpublished PhD thesis, Visva Bharati University, 1993).

737 Bhattacharya, B., 'Some Aspects of the Textile Trade of the Dutch East India Company on the Coromandel Coast, 1730-1780', in P. van der Velde (ed.), *IIAS Yearbook 1994* (Leiden, 1995).

738 Bhattacharya, B., 'The Dutch East India Company and the Trade of the Chulias in the Bay of Bengal in the Late Eighteenth Century', in K.S. Mathew (ed.), *Mariners, Merchants and Oceans: Studies in Maritime History* (New Delhi, 1995).

739 Bhattacharya, B., 'Porto Novo and the Shipping in the Bay of Bengal in the mid-18th Century', in J. Everaert and J. Parmentier (eds), *Shipping, Factories and Colonization* (Brussels, 1996).

740 Bhattacharya, B., 'The Hinterland and the Coast: The Pattern of Interaction in Coromandel in the Late Eighteenth Century', in R. Mukherjee and L. Subramanian (eds), *Politics and Trade in the Indian Ocean World: Essays in Honour of Ashin Das Gupta* (Delhi, 1998).

741 Bhattacharya, B., 'The Chulia Merchants of Southern Coromandel in the

Eighteenth Century: A Case of Continuity', in O. Prakash and D. Lombard (eds), *Commerce and Culture in the Bay of Bengal, 1500-1800* (Delhi, 1999).

742 Brennig, J.J., 'The Textile Trade of Seventeenth-Century Northern Coromandel. A Study of a Pre-Modern Asian Export Industry' (Unpublished PhD-thesis, University of Wisconsin, Madison, 1975).

743 Brennig, J.J., 'Chief Merchants and the European Enclaves of Seventeenth-Century Coromandel', *Modern Asian Studies*, 11, 3 (1977).

744 Brennig, J.J., 'Joint-stock Companies of Coromandel', in B.B. King and M.N. Pearson (eds), *The Age of Partnership. Europeans in Asia before Dominion* (Honolulu, 1979).

745 Buitenen, J.A.B. and P.C. Ganeshsundaram, 'A Seventeenth-Century Dutch Grammar of Tamil', *Bulletin of the Deccan College Research Institute (Poona)*, 14 (1952-3).

746 Dijk, L.C.D. van, *Zes jaren uit het leven van Wemmer van Berchem* (Amsterdam, 1858).

747 Fragner, B.G., 'Ein Privilegium aus Golkonda für die Niederländischen Ostindische Kompanie', in C. Fragner and K. Schwarz (eds), *Festgabe an Josef Matuz. Osmanistik- Turkologie-Diplomatik* (= *Islamkundliche Untersuchungen*, 150) (Berlin, 1992).

748 Gijsberti Hodenpijl, A.K.A., 'De Nederlandsche bezittingen op de kust van Koromandel in 1780 en 1781', *De Indische Gids*, 44 (1922).

749 Gijsberti Hodenpijl, A.K.A., 'De gouverneurs van Koromandel Christiaan van Teylingen (1761-65) en Pieter Haksteen (1765-71)', *Bijdragen voor Vaderlandsche Geschiedenis en Oudheidkunde*, 5th Series, 10; 6th Series, 2-3 (1923-6).

750 Goor, J. van, 'Een Groninger predikant op de kust van Coromandel (Joh. Ruiterus)', *Bijdragen en Mededelingen betreffende de Geschiedenis der Nederlanden*, 87 (1972).

751 Kan, J. van, 'Lijst der oude boeken van de voormalige Nederlandsche Oost-Indische Compagnie ter kuste Coromandel, 1702-1795', *Verhandelingen van het Koninklijk Bataviaasch Genootschap voor Kunsten en Wetenschappen* (1932).

752 Leupe, P.A., 'Herbert de Jager', *Bijdragen tot de Taal-, Land- en Volkenkunde*, 9 (1862), 16 (1869).

753 Lubberhuizen-Van Gelder, A.M., 'Onze voorouders op de Coromandelkust', *Cultureel Indië*, 3 (1941).

754 Matthew, K.M., 'Notes on an Important Botanical Trip (1799-1800) of J.D. Rottler on the Coromandel Coast (India) with a Translation of his Original Text, Explanatory Notes and a Map', *Botanical Journal of the Linnean Society*, 113 (1993).

755 Nilakanti Sastri, K.A., 'Two Negapatam Grants from the Batavia Museum', *Indian Historical Records Commission, Proceedings of Meetings*, 14 (1937).

756 Raychaudhuri, T., *Jan Company in Coromandel, 1605-1690. A Study in the Interrelations of European Commerce and Traditional Economics* (The Hague, 1962).

757 Rea, A., *Monumental Remains of the Dutch East India Company in the*

Presidency of Madras (= *Archaeological Survey of India*, New Series, 25) (Madras, 1897).

758 Richards, J.F., 'European City-States on the Coromandel Coast', *Studies in the Foreign Relationships of India (From the Earliest Times to 1974), Professor H.K. Sherwani Felicitation Volume* (Hyderabad, 1975).

759 Stapel, F.W., 'Nog eenige gegevens over Herbert de Jager', *Bijdragen tot de Taal-, Land- en Volkenkunde van Nederlandsch-Indië*, 88 (1931).

760 Stapel, F.W., 'A Dutch Memorial Slab in India', *Epigraphia Indica*, 24.

761 Teensma, B.N., *De politieke en economische ideeën van de Bruggeling Jacques de Coutre* (Leiden, 1994).

762 Terpstra, H., *De vestiging van de Nederlanders aan de kust van Koromandel* (Groningen, 1911).

763 Terpstra, H., 'De Nederlanders in Voor-Indië bij de stichting van het fort Geldria te Paliacatte', *De Indische Gids*, 37 (1915).

764 Terpstra, H., 'Daniël Havart en zijn 'Op- en ondergang van Coromandel'', *Tijdschrift voor Geschiedenis*, 67 (1954).

765 Victor, I.H., 'A Brief History of the Tamil Bible', *Indian Church History Review*, 18, 2 (1984).

766 Wagenvoort, M., 'De Nederlanders aan de Koromandelkust', *De Indische Gids*, 10 (1912).

767 Winius, G.D., 'The Life of Jaques de Couttre. A Prime Source emerges from the Shades', *Itinerario*, 9, 1 (1985).

768 Winius, G.D., 'A Tale of Two Coromandel Towns. Madraspatnam (Fort St. George) and Sao Thome de Meliapur', *Itinerario*, 18, 1 (1994).

6. BENGAL (including Bihar)

6.1. Primary Sources

769 Haafner, Jacob, 'Verhaal van een vreeselijken hongersnood door de Engelschen in Bengalen verwekt', *Algemeene Vaderlandsche Letteroefeningen* (1807).

770 *Dutch Records from the Dutch and British E.S.Co. Commissions of 1762-63 on the Affairs in Bengal*, ed. H. Hosten (Proceedings of the Indian Historical Records Commission, 5) (Calcutta, 1923).

771 Heiden, Frans Janszoon van der, and Willem Kunst, *Vervarelyke schipbreuk van 't oost-indisch jacht Ter schelling, onder het landt Bengale;...en voorts in 't velt-leger van den Grooten Mogol, tot in 't koningrijk van Assam landewaerts opgevoert zijn. Beneffens een bondige beschrijving der koningrijken van Arrakan, Bengale, Martavan, Tanassery, &c.* (Amsterdam, 1675); ed. C.E. Warnsinck-Delprat (Utrecht, 1944) [first part only].

772 Het Oost-Indische sacspiegeltje, 1684', ed. J. de Hullu, *Bijdragen tot de Taal-, Land-, en Volkenkunde van Nederlandsch-Indië*, 76 (1920).

773 Sunderman, Isaac, *De werken van Isaac Sunderman* (Deventer, 1711).

774 *Verhael van de schrickelycke brandt der stadt Pattana int koninghrijck Bengala [13-6-1651]* (n.p., n.d.).

775 Worm, Johann Gottlieb, *Ost-indian- und persianische Reisen* (Leipzig and Dresden, 1737).

6.2. SECONDARY SOURCES

776 Alam, Ishrat, 'Saltpetre Suppliers in Bihar and the Dutch EIC: Analysis of a Dutch Enquiry into Fraud by its Servants at Chhapra', *Proceeding of the Indian History Congress* (1993).

777 Bhattacharya, B., 'A Note on the Shipbuilding in Bengal in the Late Eighteenth Century', *Itinerario*, 19, 3 (1995).

778 Boeva, L.J.W., 'De factorij Banquibazar', *Spiegel Historiael*, 15, 7/8 (1980).

779 Bonga, 'The Dutch in India. Chinsura, the Old Dutch Emporium', *Inter-Ocean* (1927).

780 Boxer, C.R., *'The Mandarin at Chinsura'. Isaac Titsingh in Bengal, 1785-1792* (Amsterdam, 1949).

781 Chaudhury, S., 'Trade, Bullion and Conquest. Bengal in the Mid-Eighteenth Century', *Itinerario*, 15, 2 (1991).

782 Chaudhury, S., 'European Companies and the Bengal Textile Industry in the Eighteenth Century. The Pitfalls of Applying Quantitative Techniques', *Modern Asian Studies*, 27, 2 (1993).

783 Chaudhury, S., *From Prosperity to Decline. Eighteenth-Century Bengal* (Delhi, 1995).

784 Chaudhury, S., 'International Trade in Bengal, Silk, and the Comparative Role of Asians and Europeans, circa 1700-1757', *Modern Asian Studies*, 29, 2 (1995).

785 Datta, K.K., *The Dutch in Bengal and Bihar, 1740-1825* (Patna, 1948).

786 Degrijze, K., 'De Oostendse Compagnie als Horzel voor de Nederlandse Handel (1722-1731)', *Tijdschrift voor Zeegeschiedenis*, 3, 2 (1984).

787 Doorninck, J.I. van, 'Izaak Sunderman', *Bijdragen tot de Geschiedenis van Overijssel*, 2 (1875).

788 Gaastra, F.S., 'Constantijn Ranst en de corruptie onder het personeel van de VOC te Bengalen, 1669-1673', in S. Groenveld and others (eds), *Opstellen aangeboden aan Prof.dr. J.J. Woltjer bij zijn afscheid als hoogleraar van de Rijksuniversiteit te Leiden* (Amsterdam and Dieren, 1985).

789 Gaastra, F.S., 'The Role of Britisch Capital in financing the Trade of the VOC Factory in Bengal, *c.*1760-1795', in J. Everaert and J. Parmentier (eds), *Shipping, Factories and Colonization* (Brussels, 1996).

790 Gijsberti Hodenpijl, A.K.A., 'De handhaving der neutraliteit van de Nederlandsche loge te Houghly in Juni 1756', *Bijdragen tot de Taal-, Land- en Volkenkunde*, 76 (1920).

791 Klerck de Reus, G.C., 'De expeditie naar Bengale in 1759', *De Indische Gids*, 11 (1889), 12 (1890).

792 Klerck de Reus, G.C., 'De vermeestering van Chinsura in 1781 en 1795',

Verhandelingen van het Koninklijk Bataviaasch Genootschap van Kunsten en Wetenschappen (1875).

793 Lequin, F., 'A New Approach to the History of the Dutch Expansion in Asia. The Personnel of the Dutch East India Company in the XVIIIth Century', *Journal of European Economic History*, 8, 2 (1979).

794 Lequin, F., *Het personeel van de Verenigde Oost Indische Compagnie in Azië in de achttiende eeuw, meer in het bijzonder in de vestiging Bengalen*, 2 vols (Leiden, 1982).

795 McVay, P., 'Private Trade and Elite Privilege, The Trial of Nicolaas Schagen, Director of Bengal', *Itinerario*, 20, 3 (1996).

796 Parmentier, J., *De holle compagnie. Smokkel en legale handel onder Zuidnederlandse vlag in Bengalen, ca.1720-44* (Hilversum, 1992).

797 Prakash, O., 'Bullion for Goods. International Trade and the Economy of Early Eighteenth-Century Bengal', *Indian Economic and Social History Review*, 13, 2 (1976).

798 Prakash, O., 'Asian Trade and European Impact. A Study of the Trade from Bengal 1630-1720', in B.B. King and M.N. Pearson (eds), *The Age of Partnership. Europeans in Asia before Dominion* (Honolulu, 1979).

799 Prakash, O., *The Dutch East India Company and the Economy of Bengal 1630-1720* (Princeton, 1985).

800 Prakash, O., 'European Trade and the Economy of Bengal in the Seventeenth and Early Eighteenth Century', in J. van Goor (ed.), *Trading Companies in Asia 1600-1830* (Utrecht, 1986).

801 Prakash, O., 'On Estimating the Employment Implications of European Trade for the Eighteenth-Century Bengal Textile Industry - A Reply', *Modern Asian Studies*, 27, 2 (1993).

802 Prims, F., *De stichting van Banquibazar* (Antwerpen, 1930).

803 Renny, C.A., 'Falta and Barnagore. Two early Dutch Settlements in Bengal', *Inter-Ocean* (1929).

804 Saha, S. and D.N. Saha, *The European Trading Companies in Bihar* (New Delhi, 1996).

805 Wilson, C.R. (ed.), *Indian Monumental Inscriptions. Vol. I. Bengal. List of Inscriptions on Tombs or Monuments in Bengal Possessing Historical or Archaeological Interest* (Calcutta, 1896).

Author Index

Part II: Archival Guide

INTRODUCTION

This part covers all archival sources in the ARA pertaining to South Asia. Similar to the bibliography, this archival guide is divided along the lines of the five main administrative divisions of the VOC in South Asia. In addition, Chapter 1 contains general descriptions of all relevant archives, collections and series and lists pieces that contain information on more than one region. This guide is also organized on certain archival principles. As a result, the following seven-point structure is maintained in all the chapters, both general and regional. These include:

1. Documents in series and pieces from the archives created by the Gentlemen XVII and the Amsterdam Chamber.
   In the regional chapters (Chapters 2-6), this section comprises only material from the Amsterdam *OBP*-series.
2. Documents in series and pieces from the archives of the other VOC Chambers.
   In the regional chapters (Chapters 2-6), this section describes material from the archives of the Gentlemen XVII, the Amsterdam Chamber (except the *OBP*-series) and the other Chambers.
3. Archives created in Asia by the VOC and its successors, the so-called Archives transferred from Asia.
4. Archives of institutions other than the VOC.
5. Archives and collections created by individuals and families.
6. Separate acquisitions of the ARA and microfilms of external archival material.
7. Maps and drawings (this section refers to *all* maps and drawings, not only those that are kept separately by the ARA).

The descriptions in sections one to three of Chapter 1, are partly based on the introductions to the inventory of Meilink-Roelofsz by Gaastra, Van Hoof, Lequin, Pennings, Slot and Zandvliet which provide an extensive overview of the VOC archives in the larger sense, including the archives transferred from Asia and those still in Asia. The introductions to the other sections are partly based on the introductions to the inventories of the various archives. Preceding the five regional sections, brief introductions have been provided regarding the history and organization of the respective regional establishments.

Apart from those general notes, more or less detailed lists of relevant materials are given for most archives and collections. Pieces have been listed whenever they have a direct bearing on Indo-Dutch interaction or provide information on South Asian societies. The lists of relevant materials have been compiled on the basis of existing inventories and tables of contents, but often also by sifting through the material itself. Obviously, all this is a result of our own predilections and inconsistencies.

1. GENERAL

1.1. VOC Series: Archives of the Gentlemen XVII and the Amsterdam Chamber

Access no.: 1.04.02
Inv. nos: VOC 1-7231
Inventory: Meilink-Roelofsz, pp. 153-289

The archives of the Gentlemen XVII and the Amsterdam Chamber constitute the backbone of the VOC archives at The Hague. The structure of the contents of the archives is what scientists call self-similar, repeating itself over and over again on different scales. Certain pieces of information from the factories for instance are reiterated on each level of the paper hierarchy, each time in a more comprehensive manner, whereas decisions can be seen to trickle down from the Gentlemen XVII to the Governor-General and Council (GG&C) at Batavia to the regional Governors and Councils to the individual factories.

The route followed by an important piece of information from factory x would be as follows: it would be sent as a letter to the regional Governor and Council (to be found in *OBP*), who would summarize the information in their *resoluties* or proceedings (in *OBP*) as well as in a letter to the GG&C (in *OBP*). At this juncture the information would be summarized in the Batavia *dagregister* or diary, and again summarized in the *generale missive* (in *OBP*) through which the information would be passed on to the Gentlemen XVII who would make their own summary on the basis of this general report and whichever part of the appended letters from the factories they found time to read, in the *Haags verbaal*.

The trail of a decision taken by the Gentlemen XVII on the basis of this information would start from the *resoluties* of the Gentlemen XVII, then passed on to the GG&C through a letter or instruction (of which a copy would be kept in the Copybook), who would mention it in their *resoluties* and pass it on to the regional Governor in a letter to be found in their *uitgaand brievenboek* or outgoing letter book. Information on the implementation of the decision at local level can be traced in the *OBP* again.

The following is a list of the document series, relevant to South Asia with references to the locations of related material outside the archives of the Gentlemen XVII and the Amsterdam Chamber, and with short descriptions of their contents.

1.1.1. *Resoluties genomen op de ordinaris en extra-ordinaris vergaderingen van de Heeren XVII*

Proceedings of the ordinary and the extraordinary meetings of the Gentlemen XVII

Access no.: 1.04.02
Inv. nos: VOC 24-211
Size: *c.* 22 metres
Period: 1602-1796

Three series of *resoluties* of the Gentlemen XVII have been preserved in the combined archives of the Gentlemen XVII and the Amsterdam Chamber: drafts / minutes (VOC 23-98), copies (VOC 99-146) and (signed) originals (VOC 147-211). The copy series (VOC 99-146) are most useful since summaries of the topics under discussion are provided in the margin for the whole period. In some instances however documents that are appended to the series of originals are not to be found with the copy series.

The *secrete resoluties* (secret proceedings) for the years 1738-94 can be found in VOC 216-18, together with the *secrete resoluties* of the Board of Directors of the Amsterdam Chamber. In addition a partial series of *resoluties* and *secrete resoluties* of the Gentlemen XVII can be found in the archives of the Zeeland and Hoorn Chambers (see 1.2.1 and 1.2.2), a list of these is found in Meilink-Roelofsz (p. 48).

The *resoluties* of the Board of Directors of the Amsterdam Chamber are also extant. The period 1602-29 is covered by VOC 225-9, and that of 1623-1796 by VOC 230-304. The *secrete resoluties* can be found with those of the Gentlemen XVII (see above). An alphabetical index to the *resoluties* is to be found in VOC 307-10.

There are several contemporary finding aids to the *resoluties* of the Gentlemen XVII in different ARA collections. A four-volume alphabetical repertory to the *resoluties* is in the archives of the Amsterdam Chamber (VOC 221-4 for the periods 1602-1736, 1737-84, 1785-94, 1794-6 respectively). Other indices are in the Zeeland Chamber archives (see 1.2.1) and the Ghesel, Hope, Van der Heim and Radermacher collections (see 1.5.13, 1.5.17, 1.5.24 and 1.5.27). For an indication of the type of catchwords that may have been used in connection with South Asian affairs see the list of topics of Batavia *resoluties* following 1.1.4.

The Gentlemen XVII were composed of eight delegate *Bewindhebbers* (Directors) from the Amsterdam Chamber, and nine from the other Chambers. The Directors of each Chamber (there were twenty in the Amsterdam Chamber), who were appointed for life, took turns sitting with the Gentlemen XVII, though often senior rather than junior members were delegated.

The Gentlemen XVII were the highest decision-making body of the VOC. Naturally all major matters were of their concern. However, policy in Asia was for a large part delegated to the GG&C in Batavia, except when the Gentlemen XVII disagreed with the GG&C. Generally two or three sessions of the Gentlemen XVII were held yearly, in any case one in autumn and one in spring. One of the more important tasks of the Gentlemen XVII was the formulation of the *eis van retouren*, a detailed list of merchandise demanded from the different factories. A copy of the *eis* was generally appended to the *resoluties* of the autumn session, but sometimes the drafting of the *eis* was not finished until the spring session. The *eisen* were divided geographically. An overview of the extent to which the *eisen* were fulfilled in the eighteenth century can be gained from the series of *kopie-eisen* with replies of the GG&C that are in the Zeeland Chamber archives (see 1.2.1).

1.1.2. *Haags verbaal / Generaal extract*
The Hague report / General extract

Access no.: 1.04.02
Inv. nos: VOC 4455-506
Period: 1653-1793

These documents relate to the so-called *Haags Besogne* but are bound in volumes with papers of other committees. VOC 4508-15 are proposals and reflections of the *Vijfde Departement* (Fifth Department) and *Preparatoir Besogne* (Preparatory Committee) for the period 1787-94.

Since the Gentlemen XVII were not permanently in session, groups of Directors were assigned tasks to carry out in the meantime. Most important was the *Haags Besogne*, composed of ten Directors from the different Chambers, located at The Hague during the summer months to read and draft answers to the correspondence received from Asia. In the process they drew up the *Haags verbaal*, a counterpart to the *Bataviaas dagregister*, as it consists of summaries of incoming letters, and also contains notes on the intended replies. At times the *verbaal* also contains briefings of newly returned Company servants. After 1787 the tasks of the *Haags Besogne* were mainly carried out by a body successively known as the Fifth Department of the Amsterdam Chamber and as the *Preparatoir Besogne*. This body drew up a *generaal extract* or summary of the *OBP* which can be found in the archives of the Zeeland Chamber, VOC 7348-448 and 7454-66 (see 1.2.1), and noted their comments in separate volumes of *poincten van reflectie op het generaal extract* or reflections on the summary (VOC 4508-15). The *Haags verbaal* also continued over this concluding period, but consists mainly of comments on the so-called *poincten van reflectie* of the Fifth Department and the *Preparatoir Besogne*.

1.1.3. *Kopieboek van brieven, instructies en andere papieren van de Heren XVII en de Kamer Amsterdam aan de Regeringen van Indië en de Kaap*
Copybook of letters, instructions, and other papers sent by the Gentlemen XVII and the Amsterdam Chamber to the Government of the Indies and the Cape

Access no.: 1.04.02
Inv. nos: VOC 312-54
Size: 4.4 metres
Period: 1614-1795

VOC 312-44 contain the letters of the Gentlemen XVII from 1614 to 1795 as well as the letters of the Amsterdam Chamber up to 1642, after which date the Amsterdam letters are bound in separate volumes, VOC 350-3, with appendices in VOC 354.

VOC 345-9 are alphabetical indices to the letters of the Gentlemen XVII for periods 1614-1707, 1707 32 (two volumes), 1733-76 and 1777-95 respectively. The Hope archives also contain a brief index (see 1.5.17). The W.A. Alting archives contain two useful volumes of extracts from the letters (see 1.5.29). The *Hoge Regering te Batavia* archives concerning Surat, Ceylon, Coromandel and Bengal all contain volumes of extracts and indices to the letters of the Gentlemen XVII concentrating on topics relevant to their respective administrations (see 2.3, 4.3, 5.3 and 6.3).

These letters were prepared mainly on the basis of the work of the *Haags Besogne* (see 1.1.2) and held a key position in the administration of the VOC in Asia. Generally orders and reflections would be sent to GG&C and passed on to the factories. These letters to Batavia were divided into chapters on different regions, the names of which were noted in the margin of the copybook. However, at times the Gentlemen XVII corresponded directly with the main South Asian factories.

1.1.4. *Kopie-resoluties van de Gouverneur-Generaal en Raden*
Duplicate proceedings of the Governor-General and Council

Access no.: 1.04.02
Inv. nos: VOC 656-847
Size: 26 metres
Period: 1613-1791

The separate series of *kopie-resoluties* are complete only for the period December 1637-April 1791. The *resoluties* over the years 1610-36 can be found in the *OBP*; Meilink-Roelofsz (pp. 169-70) lists the locations of these documents. May-August 1791 can be found in the *Hoge Regering te Batavia* collection (see 1.3.1). The *kopie-resoluties* of 1792-93 are in the archives of the *Comité tot de Zaken van de Oost-Indische Handel en Bezittingen* (see 1.4.4). *Resoluties* of the 'combined meetings' of the GG&C and the two Commissioners General during the period 1795-1800 are in the *Raad der Aziatische Bezittingen en Etablissementen* collection (see 1.4.5), the *resoluties* of later years are extant only in the Arsip Nasional (Indonesian National Archives) at Jakarta. The appendices to the *resoluties* for the period 1738-43, are also only to be found in the Indonesian National Archives, and microfilms are available at The Hague (see 1.6.2).

The *secrete resoluties* (secret proceedings) are not always found with the separate series of *kopie-resoluties*. The *secrete resoluties* of the period 1756-91 have been bound in separate volumes (VOC 840-7). Whenever the *secrete resoluties* of other periods have been included in the *kopie-resoluties* it is indicated in the inventory. If not, they can be found in the *OBP* through the typescript tables of contents.

The only complete finding aid to the *kopie-resoluties* is the chronological table in each volume. A useful, but incomplete, subject index of the *resoluties* is the printed compilation of several manuscript 'realia' repertories: *Realia. Register op de generale resolutieën van het kasteel Batavia 1632-1805* (3 vols; Batavia and The Hague, 1882-6). Another entry is the late eighteenth-century manuscript 'personalia' repertory (VOC 828-34) which, in an alphabetical order, refers to appointments, etc., by the GG&C for the period 1610-1786.

The *resoluties* are relevant to South Asia only as far as administrative affairs are concerned. Due to a time lag of sometimes over a year decisions relating to situations arising in the subcontinent are often ill-informed. Moreover the background of the policy often does not appear from the *resoluties* themselves. For this the researcher can take recourse to *Batavia's uitgaand brievenboek* (1.1.6). The *resoluties* do however often yield valuable information on the history of individual Dutch trading posts, for decisions about the establishment or the abandonment of factories were usually taken by Batavia. For this reason references to factories and the like in the *Realia*, as well as references to other regional topics dealt with in the *resoluties*, have been recorded under 2.2.1, 3.2.1, 4.2.1, 5.2.1 and 6.2.1. We provide here a list of South Asian or relevant Asia-wide topics dealt with by the GG&C in Batavia, as referred to in the *Realia*. Through the dates given in the *Realia* the relevant *resoluties* can be located. The number and period of the entries recorded in the *Realia* noted here will give the reader an idea of what is available in the *resoluties* on different topics.

Concerning the whole of South-Asia or Hindustan:
Hindostan (king of; 1 entry 1666), *Mogol, grooten* (Great Mughal; 7 entries 1633-63), *westerse comptoiren* (western factories; 8 entries 1703-47).

Concerning diplomatic relations and rulers:
ambassadeurs (ambassadors; 141 entries 1664-1787), *besending* (diplomatic mission; 22 entries 1650-1700), *contracten* (treaties; about 150 entries 1638-1804), *expeditien* (military expeditions; 7 entries 1759-60), *gezanten* (envoys; 38 entries 1642-88), *inlandsche vorsten en grooten* (indigenous rulers; about 600 entries 1702-1804), *schenkagien* (presents; 55 entries 1643-93).

Concerning Indian Ocean shipping:
inlandsche vaart en handel (indigenous trade and shipping; about 140 entries 1741-84), *passen* (passes; about 150 entries 1638-1804), *zeerovers* (pirates; 29 entries 1701-1803).

Concerning Dutch settlements and real estate:
fortificatien (forts; about 150 entries 1656-1803), *gebouwen* (buildings; about 130 entries 1639-1805), *logie* (factory building; 5 entries 1667-97).

Concerning religion:
mooren (Muslims; about 65 entries 1646-1800), *priesters* (priests, including *ulama*; 6 entries 1779-94), *Roomse (geestelijken)* (Roman Catholics; 58 entries 1691-1783). For Syrian Christians in Malabar see 3.2.1.

Concerning coinage:
dabboesen (dabbus 3 entries 1760-1), *fanums* (fanams; 17 entries 1693-1764), *munt en muntspecien* (mint and types of coins; about 250 entries 1652-1805), *muntsaken* (mint affairs; 21 entries 1741-7), *pagoden* (pagodas; 12 entries 1651-1747), *ropias* (rupees; 48 entries 1693-1792).

Concerning South Asian products and commodities:

opium:
amphioen (56 entries 1700-1805), *amphioen societeijt* (-society; 105 entries 1745-1803), *amphioen tabak* (-tobacco; 4 entries 1671-83).

spices:
areek (areca (nut); 11 entries 1745-67), *caneel* (cinnamon; 53 entries 1658-1787), *cardamom* (26 entries 1703-1802), *peper* (pepper; about 300 entries 1617-1800).

textiles, fibres, dyes:
catoen (cotton; 17 entries 1711-67), *caijertouwen* (ropes; 11 entries 1749-84), *lijwaten* (cotton textiles; about 230 entries 1648-1767), *indigo* (68 entries 1695-1800), *patholen* (patolas; 1742-47), *zijde* (silk; 9 entries 1659-1793), *zijde-cultuure* (silk culture; 44 entries 1729-64).

shells, pearls, mined commodities:
caurus de Maldivis (12 entries 1717-81), *chiancos* (conch shells; 6 entries 1696-1745), *diamanten* (diamonds; 14 entries 1637-1784), *paarlvisserijen* (pearl fisheries; 38 entries 1645-87), *peervisserij* (pearl fishery; 2 entries 1664-79), *sal amoniac* (1 entry 1759), *salpeter* (saltpetre; about 60 entries 1659-1805).

elephants:
elephanten (18 entries 1650-1766), *elephants handelaars* (-traders; 1 entry 1703), *elephants tanden* (tusks; 8 entries 1703-59).

miscellaneous:
nelij (rice; 9 entries 1708-67), *sandelhout* (sandalwood; 9 entries 1653-1778), *lapis bezoar* (3 entries 1710-26), *tamarinde (Ceijlonse)* (3 entries 1758-93).

1.1.5. *Kopie-dagregisters van Batavia*
Duplicate diaries of Batavia

There is no separate series of the Batavia *dagregisters* in the combined archives of the Amsterdam Chamber and the Gentlemen XVII. Meilink-Roelofsz (p. 172) however gives a list of the copies extant in the *OBP* series over the years 1617-36. In the archives of the Zeeland Chamber only an incomplete series running up to 1766 is to be found (see 1.2.1). Some parts of the *dagregister* are in the Sweers, Van Vliet, Specx, Mannis collections (see 1.5.3). The most complete series, starting only from 1640 but running up to 1807, is in the Indonesian National Archives. All extant *dagregisters* up to 1682 have been edited on the basis of the series now in Jakarta, supplemented with material from The Hague, by M.J.A. van der Chijs (Batavia) and J.E. Heeres and H.T. Colenbrander (The Hague) (see Bibliography, no. 11). For the Jakarta *dagregisters*, 1683-1807, microfilms are available in the ARA (see 1.6.2).

In these *dagregisters* all incoming ships and the letters that they brought were recorded (as well as the occurrences in Batavia itself). Generally abstracts of all letters from the factories were included. These documents therefore contain extensive information on South Asia and can be used as an entry to the fuller versions of the letters from the factories in the *OBP* series as the dates of the letters are usually given.

1.1.6. *Batavia's uitgaand brievenboek*
Batavia's outgoing letterbook

Access no.: 1.04.02
Inv. nos: VOC 849-1052
Size: 30 metres
Period: 1621-1792

This series contains copies of all letters, instructions, memoirs etc. to personnel and other people in the *octrooigebied* drafted by the GG&C in Batavia between 1621 and 1792. The outgoing letters of the early years however are only to be found in the *OBP* series. A list of these is provided by Meilink-Roelofsz (p. 173). Secret letters were included separately at the back of each volume from 1747 onwards but before that date they were apparently not always included in *Batavia's uitgaande brievenboek* and should be looked for in the *OBP*. After 1792 the *uitgaande brievenboek* is continued in the archives of the *Comité tot de Zaken van de Oost-Indische Handel en Bezittingen* up to 1794 (see 1.4.4).

The only complete finding aid to the *uitgaande brievenboek* is the geographically ordered table of contents at the beginning of each volume. The *Hoge Regering te Batavia* collection contains an alphabetical repertory of subjects covered in the letters sent to Coromandel over the period 1651-1737 (inv. no. 311) and several volumes of extracts from those letters, are also ordered by subject (see 5.3).

These bundles of correspondence reflect the way in which Batavia saw and presented itself to the world. They contain interesting information on what the VOC personnel in South Asia were supposed to be doing, but were apparently not doing. In the letters addressed to South Asian rulers the art of concealment reaches heights not often reached in European diplomatic relations. For instance, if they mention cordial relationship, one should most often read open hostility. Similarly the English are usually referred to as 'our English friends', especially in times of immanent war. In short, the GG&C were always busy keeping up the appearances of the Company's monopoly. Still, in *Batavia's uitgaande brievenboek* useful references can be found to the factories' news reports that motivated the policies of the GG&C.

1.1.7. *Overgekomen brieven en papieren (OBP)*
Letters and papers received

Access no.: 1.04.02
Inv. nos: VOC 1053-3987
Size: *c.* 390 metres
Period: 1607-1794

The *overgekomen brieven en papieren* (*OBP*) sent from Asia to the Gentlemen XVII and the Amsterdam Chamber are the most voluminous, richest and, therefore, the most consulted single series of the VOC archives. Nevertheless, the bulk remains unexplored. The *OBP* are made up of three bundles (VOC 1053-5) and 2943 volumes (VOC 1056-3987). A large part of the *OBP* is available on microfilm at the open stacks in the reading room of the ARA. After 1794, the *OBP* become part of the archives of the *Comité tot de Zaken van de Oost-Indische Handel en Bezittingen* (1796-1800; see 1.4.4) and the *Raad der Aziatische Bezittingen en Etablissementen* (1800-6; see 1.4.5). The *generale missiven* there are labelled *generale verslagen*.

The main finding aid to the *OBP* consists of the 36-volume typewritten tables of contents—called *register*—which are available for consultation at the ARA reading room (access nos 1.04.16.01-1.04.16.36). The *register* has been organized chronologically and from 1625 onward we also find regional headings which mostly refer to the main administrative divisions of the VOC in Asia, although at times we find separate headings such as 'Gale', 'Tutucorijn' or 'Maldivos' which otherwise are only listed under 'Ceylon'. Incidentally, one may also trace documents that relate to South Asia under 'Batavia' or other geographical headings representing places with direct shipping links to the South Asian factories. The inv. nos of the documents are VOC-numbers provided on the top of each page of the *register*. The KA-numbers refer to the old *Koloniaal Archief* series but are not valid any more. The *register* also refers to folio numbers. The counting of folios either relates to one single volume or continues into (never more than four) consecutive volumes. At times, the counting is inconsistent and may, for example, start from folio no. 1 several times. Although the *register* gives ready access to the *OBP*, it should be consulted with care because most of the topics listed serve only as a rough indication of a document's contents which in reality may cover various other subjects as well. In addition to the *register*, Meilink-Roelofsz gives a short-list of all *OBP* numbers indicating both date and region (pp. 175-216). For the years 1690-1796 we find another seven-volume register to the *OBP* under VOC 4448-54.

Most *OBP* batches start with the so-called *generale missiven* which is the annual report of the GG&C to the Gentlemen XVII. This also serves as a summary of all important events taking place in Asia. Hence, the ten-volume published extracts of these *generale missiven* (to 1750, excluding 1737-43) may serve as another aid to find dates to be traced in the *register*, the more so since these are provided with excellent indexes (see Bibliography, no. 18). For the period 1774-94 the *generale missiven*, with registers and tables of contents, are also available in the archives of the *Stadhouderlijke Secretarie* (Secretariat to the Stadtholder; see 1.4.3, inv. nos 1827-1896). Another series for the period 1768-73 is available in the Hope collection (see 1.5.17, inv. nos 37-51).

An extensive description of the *OBP* is offered in Meilink-Roelofsz (pp. 52-6). The prime asset of the *OBP* series is the detailed information it contains about the local situation in each and every factory in Asia. Most of the *OBP* reflect the annual reporting of Batavia to the Dutch Republic. As such, they not only contain the *generale missiven* and other correspondence, including various enclosures, of the GG&C directly to the Gentlemen XVII, but also duplicates of all the letters received in Batavia from the establishments in Asia. The latter are also referred to as *Batavia's ingekomen brievenboek* (Batavia letter book of incoming documents) which includes, apart from the letters to Batavia, local correspondence with subaltern factories or with Indian rulers.

This part of the *OBP* partly overlaps with the documents, also in the *OBP*, that were sent from the more important regional establishments directly to Patria, either overland through the Levant or overseas along the Cape. Initially, there had been direct consignments to Surat and the Coromandel Coast but from 1636 to 1665 all shipping connections of the South Asian establishments had to pass through Batavia first. After 1665 Ceylon, soon followed by Bengal and again Coromandel, started direct overseas voyages to the Republic. At the start of eighteenth century only Ceylon maintained this privilege and continued to rival Batavia as an entrepôt for Indian commodities, especially those from Coromandel. Later during that century both Bengal (1734-80) and Coromandel (1771-80) were once again directly linked to the Netherlands. Together with *Batavia's ingekomen brievenboek*, the Indian documents sent directly to Patria make up the bulk of the South Asian material of the *OBP* and—since the factories' archives have mostly been lost—contain by far the most extensive and detailed VOC material on South Asia.

With regard to the arrangement of the various classes of documents, roughly from the 1660s onward each annual *OBP* batch begins with letters and papers the Gentlemen XVII received from Batavia (including the *generale missiven*). These mostly concern Batavia itself or Asia as a whole, but occasionally relate to South Asia also. These are followed by letters and papers received at Patria directly from South Asia, between 1670 and 1683 listed under the main heading 'Westerkwartieren', and thereafter under the regional headings. Last comes *Batavia's ingekomen brievenboek* where documents are also arranged under the regional headings. Despite their partial overlap, the two latter classes of documents tend to differ in tone from each other because the GG&C at Batavia as immediate superiors usually received more detailed letters from South Asia. Still the letters and papers directly sent to the Gentlemen XVII frequently include documents not to be found in *Batavia's ingekomen brievenboek*.

In order to facilitate their use, this guide provides a selection from the *OBP* which includes some of the most informative documents on South Asia. We have arranged these documents in the following six 'artificial' series:

1. *Memories van overgave* (final reports)

These reports were written by the chief-factor in order to instruct his successor upon his departure. For South Asia we find *memories* written by the chiefs of Surat, Malabar, Ceylon, Coromandel and Bengal, but occasionally also by the subordinate heads of the lesser establishments of Cannanore, Vengurla, Jaffna, Batticaloa, Tuticorin, Masulipatam, Pipli and Patna. The reports are often very extensive and relate to trade and bookkeeping, internal organization, political events in the region, relations with South Asian states, social and cultural matters, historical surveys, etc. They are excellent general introductions to the regional situation and developments during the period of the author's term in office. For these reports, see under sections 2.1.1, 3.1.1, 4.1.1, 5.1.1 and 6.1.1. Outside the *OBP* several *memories* are to be found in the *Hoge Regering te Batavia* collection. Some *memories* written by Governors of Ceylon and *Commandeurs* of Malabar have been published (see Bibliography, nos 375, 383, 471 and 472).

2. *Resoluties* (proceedings)

The *resoluties* of the meetings of the highest official and the council at a particular settlement are usually very extensive and may include (extracts of) other documents such as correspondence. The *resoluties* relate to all aspects of the VOC's presence in South Asia. In general, they concern matters much more current at the time than those dealt with in the *memories van overdracht* described above. Indices to the *resoluties* do not exist, but they regularly contain summaries in the margins. Unless indicated otherwise, the *resoluties* listed in this guide cover meetings held at the settlement where the Governor, *Commandeur* or *Directeur* had its seat. For these *resoluties*, see sections 2.1.2, 3.1.2, 4.1.2, 5.1.2 and 6.1.2. In the *register* of the *OBP* most of the South Asian proceedings from the early 1720s to the early 1730s are listed under the heading 'Batavia'. (The *resoluties* of the GG&C are included in the *OBP* up to 1636, after that year they were made into a separate series; see 1.1.4.)

3. *Dagregisters* (diaries)

The *dagregisters* may once have formed the backbone of the separate archives of all or most of the settlements in the East Indies. As diaries, they described on a day-to-day basis all important events with respect to a particular factory, covering all incoming and outgoing correspondence. Unfortunately, most of these *dagregisters* have been lost. The *OBP* contain copies of some *dagregisters*, originating from just a couple of factories and covering limited periods. When no particular factory is mentioned in our survey, the *dagregister* relates to the chief settlement of a region. For these *dagregisters*, see sections 2.1.3, 3.1.3, 4.1.3, 5.1.3 and 6.1.3. (The *OBP* also contains the *dagregisters* of Batavia from the period 1617-36; for more information, see 1.1.5.)

4. *Shipping lists*

Shipping lists appear regularly in the *OBP* from the 1680s onward. They usually include vessels of the Dutch, British, French and Portuguese, as well as Indian communities. They refer to ships that have arrived and departed or—when this is not specified—vessels docked at a particular place. When the factory is not mentioned, the lists cover either the chief settlement of a region or the region as a whole. For these lists, see sections 2.1.4, 3.1.4, 4.1.4, 5.1.4 and 6.1.4. One may also get information about vessels in the various regions in South Asia from the general shipping lists under the heading 'Batavia'.

5. *Missions to Indian states*

The documents concerning (incidental) missions to South Asian courts vary greatly in length. Whenever possible, we mention the (daily) report of a mission. If the report of a mission cannot be found in the *OBP*'s tables of contents, we list the instructions, correspondence or any other papers relating to that mission. In that case, extant reports may still be found in the *resoluties*, correspondence, etc. surrounding the mission. The reports of the missions—often referred to as *ambassades* (embassies) or *hofreizen* (court journeys)—may reveal all kinds of aspects relating to South Asian courts, from court ritual and etiquette to power struggles and military confrontations. These documents are listed in sections 2.1.5, 3.1.5, 4.1.5, 5.1.5 and 6.1.5. Treaties concluded with South Asian rulers (and sometimes merchants) are also to be found scattered throughout the *OBP*. Only a part of these is available in VOC 4777-83 (see section 1.1.8) and VOC 11193-6 (see section 1.2.1) and/or published in *CDNI*.

6. *Miscellaneous*

We have included this category to list documents that appear to be unique, rare, or remarkable. This means that the selection of these documents has been very subjective. It also serves to give a general impression of the geographical and topical scope of the *OBP*. For these documents, see sections 2.1.6, 3.1.6, 4.1.6, 5.1.6 and 6.1.6.

Not included in our list are *OBP* documents concerning bookkeeping, such as *negotieboeken* (trade books), *negotiejournalen* (trade journals), (*negotie-*) *grootboeken* (ledgers), *rendementen* (returns, profits), *cognossementen* (cargo bills) and occasionally *eisen* (orders for supplies). For maps and drawings in the *OBP*, see sections 3.7 and 4.7.

1.1.8. *Kopie-translaten van tractaten gesloten met Aziatische vorsten*

Duplicate translations of treaties concluded with Asian rulers

Access no.:	1.04.02
Inv. nos:	4777-83
Size:	0.8 metre
Period:	1596-1742

This series, which includes some originally separate volumes and folders, is far from exhaustive. Some of the volumes have a geographical index. VOC 4784 is a repertory of treaties for the period 1596-1791.

Another series of copy treaties is in the Zeeland Chamber (see 1.2.1), but the most complete series of *contract boeken* (contract books) is apparently in the Archives at Jakarta. Even more complete, but scattered, are the translations to be found in the *OBP*. Many translations of treaties and grants of privileges from various sources have been published in *CDNI*.

1.1.9. *Departement van de Equipage*

Equipage Department

Access no.:	1.04.02
Inv. nos:	4927-5164
Period:	*c.* 1603-1803

Two series in this part of the Amsterdam Chamber archives contain some information on the continental waters, coasts and ports of South Asia:

VOC 5029-48 — Reports on landfalls, descriptions of the coastline (some drawings of the coastal profile) and sea lanes, etc. The series stretches 15 centimetres. Period *c.* 1640-1794.

VOC 5049-142 — Ship's logs. Many of these contain information similar to that in the above series. The series stretches 1.4 metres. Period 1622-1793.

1.1.10. *Soldijkantoor*
Pay Office

Access no.: 1.04.02
Inv. nos: 5165-6962
Period: *c.* 1602-1811

The archives of the *Soldijkantoor* contain three series that can be very useful to those interested in the VOC personnel in South Asia. The introduction by F. Lequin in Meilink-Roelofsz (pp. 57-65, with charts on pp. 109-16) provides an excellent manual to trace the career of a particular VOC servant or to establish the number and names of personnel of a particular factory at a particular time through these series.

VOC 5168-239 — General land and sea muster rolls of VOC servants in the Indies, including South Asia. 72 volumes. The series stretches 1.2 metres. Period 1720-91. Another of the originally six series of copies that is in the Zeeland Chamber archives (see 1.2.1), encompasses a longer period but is less complete. Muster rolls (but not general muster rolls) of the years after 1794 can be found in *Comptabiliteit betreffende Oost-Indische Bezittingen* (see 1.4.9).

VOC 5240-61 — Rolls of qualified civil and military VOC servants in the Indies, including South Asia, in the service of the Amsterdam Chamber. 21 volumes, 1 piece. The series stretches 3 metres. Period 1701 through 1789. Access number 1.04.24 is a typescript index to names of places figuring in the rolls. The rolls of the qualified Zeeland Chamber servants have also been preserved (see 1.2.1).

VOC 5269-6845 — *Scheepssoldijboeken* (ship's pay ledgers) of ships sailing for the Amsterdam Chamber. 1575 volumes. The series stretches *c.* 140 metres. Period 1633-1795. For a list of the series of *scheepssoldijboeken* of the other Chambers see Meilink-Roelofsz, p. 62.

The archives of the *Soldijkantoor* also hold many of the so-called *Oostindische testamenten* (East India wills), containing information on the fortunes acquired through private trade. These are:

VOC 6847-97	*Oostindische testamenten*, copies of wills made up in the VOC establishments in Asia. The series stretches 10 metres. Period 1698-1807. 51 volumes. Access number 1.04.14 is an index to the testaments.
VOC 6899-939	Separately kept testaments, only one of which was prepared in South Asia (see 6.2.1), and other papers relating to inheritances.

1.1.11. *Departement van de Commercie* Commercial Department

Access no.: 1.04.02
Inv. nos: 6963-7015
Period: *c.* 1619-1808

The papers of this Department include some material relating to the products brought from South Asia and their reception in the Netherlands, including the perennial complaints of the silk manufacturers about the supply of Bengal raw silk (see 6.2.1).

VOC 6984-6	Papers concerning the auctions of the merchandise from Asia, etc., including the price-lists of auctions held during the period 1698 through 1791. Partly printed material, one piece and two folders.

1.1.12. *Miscellaneous*

Access no.: 1.04.02

This section lists documents relating to South Asia in general (or several of its regions) which do not belong to the series described above.

VOC 4789, 4791	Lists of settlements of the VOC in Asia, with specifications of commodities and ranks or functions of VOC servants, including sections on Bengal, Coromandel, Ceylon, Malabar and Surat, n.d. (after 1730 and *c.* 1790). Four pieces.
VOC 4790	Memorandum concerning the state of affairs in the Indies, contains several surveys of ranks and functions of VOC servants, ships, artillery etc., ff. 127-68 and 193-? deal with regions in South Asia, 1764. One folder.
VOC 4814	Memorandum containing objections against the free sailing and trade between Batavia and the *westerkwartieren*, in particular concerning the private sugar trade; contains a large section on the sugar trade of Surat, 1765. One volume.
VOC 4815	Notes concerning coins, weights and measures in South Asia, *c.* 1765. One piece.

VOC 4816	List of coins, exchange rates, weights and measures in Asia, with index, including extensive sections on a great number of factories in Bengal, Coromandel, Ceylon, Malabar and Surat (ff. 1-90 contain the actual lists; ff. 91-139 contain notes on these subjects), 1769. One volume. For more details, see also 2.2.1, 3.2.1, 4.2.1, 5.2.1 and 6.2.1.
VOC 4820	Papers concerning the strength of the military troops in the Indies, including South Asia, 1790-1. One folder.
VOC 7049-50	Papers concerning bills of exchange drawn in Ceylon, Bengal and Malabar (and other places), 1715-73. Two volumes.
VOC 7052-2 I	Bills of exchange drawn in Bengal, Ceylon, Coromandel, Malabar and Surat (and other places), 1774-94. One volume, one bundle.
VOC 7062	Papers concerning the payment by the various Chambers of bills of exchange drawn in Bengal, Ceylon and Malabar (and other places), 1795. One folder.

1.2. VOC Series: Archives of the Remaining Chambers

1.2.1. *Zeeland Chamber*

Access no.:	1.04.02.
Inv. nos:	VOC 7232-13866
Period:	1612-1794
Inventory:	Meilink-Roelofsz, pp. 291-445

Although comparable to the Amsterdam Chamber in terms of size, the archives of the Zeeland Chamber have hardly been used for historical research. Perhaps one reason for this is that they are regarded as some kind of shadow archives of the Amsterdam Chamber. Because the two archives are largely overlapping, one should always consult the Zeeland Chamber for tracing documents missing from the Amsterdam Chamber. The most important Zeeland series, which compare well with the *OBP*, are the *Ingekomen stukken van Gouverneur-Generaal en Raden bij de Heren XVII en de Kamer Zeeland* (*IGG* or documents of the GG&C received by the Gentlemen XVII and the Zeeland Chamber; VOC 7527-9191) and the *Ingekomen stukken van de kantoren in Indïe bij de Heren XVII en de Kamer Zeeland* (*IKI* or documents received from the establishments in Asia by the Gentlemen XVII and the Zeeland Chamber; VOC 9541-11024).

Another reason why the Zeeland series are underused is the lack of documentary aids. Indeed, the Zeeland archives have nothing like the easily available *register* of the *OBP* of Amsterdam. Although most of the *IGG* and *IKI* volumes contain registers that resemble the table of contents used in the *OBP*, these series are classified according to the various administrative divisions of the VOC in Asia that produced the document. Unfortunately, this has not been done consistently with the result that many volumes contain papers of various factories in an arbitrary order. The most convenient access to the Zeeland Chamber, including cross-references and extensive listings, is offered by Meilink-Roelofsz (pp. 291-447). Based on the work of Meilink-Roelofsz and the criteria used for the Amsterdam Chamber, we have made a selection of documents that relate to South Asia. The following list contains documents that relate to South Asia as a whole whereas the regional references, including those to the *IKI* (which do not cover South Asia in general), have been listed under the respective regional headings.

Ingekomen stukken van Gouverneur-Generaal en Raden bij de Heren XVII en de Kamer Zeeland (IGG)
Papers received from Governor-General and Council by the Gentlemen XVII and the Zeeland Chamber

VOC 7528-95	Letters from the GG&C to the Gentlemen XVII or the Zeeland Chamber, with appendices, 1684-1792. 68 volumes. Incomplete series (VOC 7527 contains a letter from GG&C to Zeeland from 1658. VOC 7596-9 contain letters from GG&C to the Gentlemen XVII, 1689, 1751, 1758, 1778) (see also 1.1.6).
VOC 7600-9	*Resoluties* and minutes of the GG&C, various years between 1714 and 1786. Eight volumes, two pieces (see also 1.1.4).
VOC 7610-17	*Kopie-dagregisters* of Batavia, 1647-8, 1656-7, 1663, 1724, 1737, 1738, 1746, 1766. Eight volumes (see also 1.1.5).
VOC 7618-47	Letters and instructions from GG&C to subaltern factories (including South Asia), with tables of contents, 1683-1788. 30 volumes. Incomplete series.
VOC 7648-55	Secret letters from GG&C to subaltern factories (including South Asia), with tables of contents, 1755-89. Eight volumes. Incomplete series.
VOC 9180-9	Reports of the *Visiateurs-Generaal* concerning their investigations in the trade books of the various factories in the Indies (including South Asia), 1771-86. Ten volumes.

For *IGG* relating to Surat, Malabar, Ceylon, Coromandel and Bengal, see also 2.2.2, 3.2.2, 4.2.2, 5.2.2 and 6.2.2.

Soldijkantoor
Pay Office

See Section 1.1.10

VOC 11534-705	General land muster rolls of VOC servants in the Indies, including South Asia, 1691-1791. 170 volumes.
VOC 11706-820	General sea muster rolls of VOC servants in the Indies, including South Asia, 1691-1780. 114 volumes, 2 pieces.
VOC 11821-90	Rolls of qualified civil and military VOC servants in the

	Indies, including South Asia, (1685-) 1699-1791. 70 volumes.
VOC 11891-928	Rolls of qualified military VOC servants in the Indies, including South Asia, (1685-) 1692-1792. 38 volumes.
VOC 11929	Lists of missing Company servants, (1749-) 1757 (-1779). One volume.
VOC 11930-58	Permits, lists of dismissed and exempted servants, promoted servants and *vrijburgers* (free merchants) and the needy in the Indies, with testaments, 1704-86. 29 volumes.
VOC 12166-225	Rolls of promoted Company servants, (1684-) 1701-75. 59 volumes.
VOC 12226	Muster rolls of soldiers dismissed because of their invalidity, 1788. One volume.
VOC 12322-45	Rolls of several regiments sent to the Indies on VOC ships, 1784-94. 37 volumes.
VOC 12672-13307	*Scheepssoldijboeken* of ships sailing for the Zeeland Chamber, 1644-1795. 636 volumes.

For such documents relating to Malabar, Ceylon, Coromandel and Bengal, see also 3.2.2, 4.2.2, 5.2.2 and 6.2.2.

Departement van de Koopmanschappen
Commercial Department

See section 1.1.11

VOC 13375-81	Miscellaneous papers concerning the prices, etc., of merchandise from Asia, 1684-1778. Eight volumes, ten pieces.
VOC 13398-471	*Eisen*, from the Gentlemen XVII to the GG&C, concerning merchandise demanded from the Indies, with replies of GG&C and specification of goods sent by the Gentlemen XVII, 1702-92. 74 volumes. Incomplete series (see also 5.2.1 and 6.2.1).
VOC 13472-508	*Eisen*, from the GG&C to the Gentlemen XVII, concerning goods demanded from the Dutch Republic, sometimes including demands from separate factories in South Asia, *c.* 1625-1795. Incomplete series.
VOC 13509-71	*Eisen*, from the factories to the GG&C, with notes of the GG&C, often including factory-wise indices, 1669-75, 1720-90. 63 volumes.
VOC 13572-4	*Eisen*, from the factories to the Zeeland Chamber, 1774-95. Three volumes.
VOC 13575-620	*Eisen*, from the GG&C to the factories, with notes concerning merchandise and/or goods sent to Batavia, including factory-wise indices, 1719-71. 46 volumes.

Miscellaneous

VOC 7240-79	*Resoluties* of the meetings of the Board of Directors of the Zeeland Chamber, 1601-1796, the last volume contains the *secrete resoluties* over 1642-1787. 39 volumes and 1 bundle.
VOC 7280-6	Indices (more or less alphabetical) to the *resoluties* of the Zeeland Chamber, 1783-96. Seven volumes. (Indices for the periods 1749-58 and 1770-4, 1777-82 can be found in *Losse aanwinsten* (separate acquisitions, see section 1.6.1, access no. 1.11.01.01), inv. nos 1891 19d and 1912 V 1-2 respectively.)
VOC 7287-8, 7312-13	Letters from the Zeeland Chamber to the Indies, 1603-1727, 1773-94. One folder, five pieces, one volume.
VOC 7314	Index to the letters from the Zeeland Chamber to the Indies, 1795-1796. One volume.
VOC 7343-416	*Resoluties* of the meetings of the Gentlemen XVII, 1602-1796. 74 volumes (VOC 7425-33 also contain some (extracts of) *resoluties* of the Gentlemen XVII. VOC 7342 contains a kind of agenda of the meetings, 1602-1787) (see also 1.1.1).
VOC 7417-22	Indices (more or less alphabetical) to the *resoluties* of the Gentlemen XVII, 1602-1716, 1717-51, 1752-70, 1771-84, 1785-91, 1792-96. Six volumes.
VOC 7438-48, 7454-66	*Generaal extract*, extracts from letters received from the Indies, compiled by the Fifth Department of the Amsterdam Chamber, 1787-90, and the *Preparatoir Besogne*, 1791-4 (see 1.1.2 for an explanation of these bodies). 24 volumes. The extracts are arranged per region including those in South Asia.
VOC 7449-53, 7467-70	*Consideratiën*, memoranda in response to the letters received from the Indies, compiled by the Fifth Department of the Amsterdam Chamber, 1787-90, and the *Preparatoir Besogne*, 1791-4 (see 1.1.2 for an explanation of these bodies). Nine volumes. The extracts are arranged per region including those in South Asia.
VOC 7483-4	Letters from the Gentlemen XVII to GG&C, 1614-62. One piece, one folder.
VOC 7485-523	*Kopieboek van uitgaande missiven van de Heren XVII aan de kantoren in Indië* (copybook of letters from the Gentlemen XVII to the factories in the Indies), 1644-1795. 39 volumes (see also 1.1.3).
VOC 7525	Miscellaneous papers by Prince Maurits, the States General and the Gentlemen XVII for ships (1602-4); ff.

	95-118 contain early information about countries, islands and trade in the East Indies, including Surat (Cambay), Konkan (Dabhol), Ceylon, Coromandel (Pulicat and Nagappattinam) and Bengal; ff. 136-9 also deal with Cambay. One volume.
VOC 9192-540	Papers received from the Council of Justice at Batavia by the Gentlemen XVII and the Zeeland Chamber, 1636-1787. *c.* 350 volumes.
VOC 11047	Considerations of Gustaaf Willem van Imhoff concerning the state of affairs of the VOC (with appendices); ff. 67-77, 95-133 relate to the factories in South Asia, 1741. One folder.
VOC 11193-6	Treaties with Asian rulers, 1612-1773. VOC 11193 concerns mainly Thanjavur, Madurai, Ramnad, Travancore and Coromandel, 1612-1773. Four volumes (see also 1.1.8).
VOC 11188	Miscellaneous papers, including a report by Artus Gijsels on some wars in the Indies; ff. 16-17 concern Coromandel and Surat, 1621.
VOC 11191	General trade survey of the Indies, including South Asia, 1772-3. One quire.
VOC 11192	Secret considerations and advice of the High Government concerning the change in trade in the Indies, including South Asia, with appendices, 1774. One piece.
VOC 11207-8	Two copies of a list (79 pp.) of coins, exchange rates, weights and measures at a great number of factories in the Indies, including sections on places in Surat, Malabar, Ceylon, Coromandel and Bengal, printed in 1691 (at Middelburg, Zeeland). Two volumes. See also 2.2.2, 3.2.2, 4.2.2, 5.2.2 and 6.2.2 for more details.
VOC 11209	Memorandum of the Bookkeeper General and others concerning the converting of coins in the Indies into Dutch coins; ff. 86-103, 110-17, 120-3 deal with regions in South Asia, 1767. One volume.
VOC 11407-39	Ship's logs, *dagregisters*, reports, etc., in the archives of the *Departement van de Equipage* (Equipage Department), 1649-1793 (see also 1.1.9).
VOC 13693	List of bills of exchange drawn by the GG&C and the factories in Bengal, Ceylon and Malabar (and the Cape of Good Hope), 1785. One piece.

1.2.2. *Delft, Rotterdam, Hoorn and Enkhuizen Chambers*

Access no.:	1.04.02
Inv. nos:	13867-14093 (Delft), 14094-317 (Rotterdam), 14318-625 (Enkhuizen), 14626-911 (Hoorn)
Inventory:	Meilink-Roelofsz, pp. 447-73

Only very small portions of the original archives of these Chambers have been preserved. Besides a few miscellaneous papers, only the *scheepssoldijboeken* are of some relevance with respect to South Asia (see also 1.1.10 and 1.2.1).

Delft Chamber

VOC 13867	Letters from the GG&C to the Gentlemen XVII and the Delft Chamber, 1647. One volume.
VOC 13871	*Collectanea*, a kind of manual and index containing a more or less alphabetical list (only L to Z) of notes from various sources on every imaginable subject, including topics relating to South Asia, c. 1750. One volume.
VOC 13872	Kind of manual, containing papers concerning financial matters, collected by Gerard van Vredenburgh, Director of the Delft Chamber; ff. 85-100 deal with South Asia, 1620-1760. One volume.
VOC 13873	Register containing summaries from the general ledgers, including South Asia, 1742-3, 1749. One volume.
VOC 13876-14080	*Scheepssoldijboeken* of ships sailing for the Delft Chamber, 1700-95. 205 volumes.

Rotterdam Chamber

VOC 14101 I-14296	*Scheepssoldijboeken* of ships sailing for the Rotterdam Chamber, 1665-6, 1700-95. 295 volumes, one quire.

For some papers concerning Surat, see 2.2.3.

Hoorn Chamber

VOC 14318	*Secrete resoluties* of the Hoorn Chamber, 1691-1794. One volume.
VOC 14322	Papers received and dispatched by the Hoorn Chamber, with tables of contents and appendices, 1730-96. Seven volumes. Part of this series may perhaps be compared with the *OBP*, *IGG* and *IKI* of the Amsterdam and Zeeland Chambers (see 1.1.7 and 1.2.1). The papers deal with a very wide range of topics, including South Asia.
VOC 14325	Secret letters from the GG&C to the Gentlemen XVII, 1789-90. Two pieces.
VOC 14326-7	*Resoluties* of the Gentlemen XVII (partly secret, partly of meetings held in The Hague), with appendices, 1790-5. One bundle, one folder.
VOC 14331	Private minutes of the meetings of the Gentlemen XVII, drawn up by Director A. van Stralen, with appendices, 1785-93. One bundle.

VOC 14332	Private minutes of the *Haags Besogne* (see 1.1.2), drawn up by Director A. van Stralen, 1788-92. One folder.
VOC 14348-527 I	*Scheepssoldijboeken* of ships sailing for the Hoorn Chamber, 1705-95. 295 volumes. Some volumes include muster rolls.
VOC 14532-5	Miscellaneous papers concerning the prices, etc., of merchandise from Asia, 1669-86, 1765-9, 1791-4. One bundle, one folder, six pieces.

Enkhuizen Chamber

VOC 14627-35	Muster rolls of ships sailing for the Enkhuizen Chamber, 1708-79. Nine volumes.
VOC 14638-42	*Scheepssoldijboeken* of ships sailing for the Enkhuizen Chamber, 1700-94. 205 volumes. Some volumes include muster rolls.
VOC 14844	Price-list of an auction by the Enkhuizen Chamber of merchandise from Asia, 1783. One piece.

1.3. Archives Transferred from Asia

1.3.1. *Hoge Regering te Batavia*
High Government at Batavia

Access no.: 1.04.17
Inv. nos: 1-1011
Size: 20 metres
Period: 1602-1827
Inventory: in typescript, with index and introduction

In 1862 and 1863 the papers that had been kept in the attic of grain and iron warehouses since the destruction of the Castle at Batavia around 1810, were sent to the Netherlands. These were papers that related mainly to the settlements in Asia that had been abandoned by the Dutch since the eighteenth or early nineteenth century.

Many of the documents in this collection are the same as those in the *OBP*. Some pieces are however unique, especially those concerned with the-turn-of-the nineteenth-century dealings of the Dutch in South Asia and the cession of the factories in that area to the English. A collection of Persian and Telugu language letters is also included (see Appendix I). The collection has been ordered geographically. For the Surat, Malabar, Ceylon, Coromandel and Bengal parts, see 2.3, 2.7, 3.3, 3.7, 4.3, 4.7, 5.3, 5.7 and 6.3.

1 *Resoluties* of the GG&C, 3 May-7 August 1791. Copies or minutes, one volume.

24 Commodity-wise review of the state of the Dutch East India trade, 1740s. With index, one volume.

25-6 Memorandum on the desirability of a direct shipping link from the South

Asian factories to Patria, c. 1775. With reply from the Gentlemen XVII and appendices, 2 volumes.

27-8 Memorandum on the effects of opening the South Asia-Batavia trade to private traders. Includes a missive from the Gentlemen XVII with a 23 page breakdown of the loss sustained in the sugar trade to Surat over the years 1750-60, *c.* 1767. Two copies of the same.

29 Missive of the Gentlemen XVII to Batavia about the affairs of Bengal, Coromandel, Ceylon, Malabar and Surat, 1794. One volume.

36 Letters and copies of letters sent by the Prince of Orange, Dupleix, Directors of the English East India Company (EIC) and others to Governor-General Van Imhoff, 1747-50. With index, one volume.

39 Memorandum of Mr Kraane or Crâne on the *Amfioen Sociëteit* and a report (1791) of the *Preparatoir Besogne* to the same. With appendices, one volume.

1.3.2. *Boekhouder-Generaal te Batavia*
Bookkeeper General at Batavia

Access no.: 1.04.18.02
Inv. nos: 1-123
Size: 18 metres
Period: 1652-1801
Inventory: in typescript

In the early nineteenth century the copies of the journals and ledgers of the Batavian *Boekhouder-Generaal* that had been preserved in Amsterdam were destroyed or sold as waste paper along with a large part of the financial administration of the VOC that had been kept in the Netherlands. Later in the nineteenth century this was felt to be a loss and the original archives of the *Boekhouder-Generaal* were shipped to the Netherlands from Batavia. The seven copies of general ledgers that remained in Amsterdam and Zeeland after the clean-up around 1830 have lately been incorporated into this collection. The series in this collection are roughly (gaps of two years or less not indicated) as follows:

Generaal grootboek (general ledger), 1758-64, 1771-1801. (For 1658 see below, *Losse aanwinsten*, inv. no. 639)

Generaal journaal, 1700-43, 1750-90, 1800-1.

Negotie grootboek (trade ledger), 1652-3, 1703-5, 1708-9, 1713-43, 1748-60, 1763-74, 1779-81.

Negotie journaal (trade journal), 1699-1707, 1713-14, 1720-3, 1729-33, 1736-43, 1745-84, 1786, 1795-6, 1798.

Negotie memoriaal (trade memorandum-book), 1750-7, 1760-85, 1789-90.

The volumes of the *generaal grootboek* and the *negotie grootboek* have more or less alphabetical indices in front.

Of the different types of records in this collection, the *generaal grootboek*, the *generaal journaal* and the *negotie grootboek* are the most useful to researchers of a specific region. The first two are ordered geographically, the *generaal grootboek* containing general credit and debit accounts of the individual factories, while the *generaal journal* contains detailed computations of factory expenditure and income. A section in each of the yearly *negotie grootboek* volumes is devoted to the balances of specific goods.

1.3.3. *Voormalige Nederlandse bezittingen in Voor-Indië*
Former Dutch possessions in South Asia

Access no.:	1.04.19
Inv. nos:	1-162
Size:	3.7 metres
Period:	1703-1826
Inventory:	in typescript, with introductions

In 1825 the Dutch factories of mainland South Asia were finally ceded to the British along with their archives, except the secret papers and papers relating to the accountability of the contemporary staff of the factories. The latter were sent to Batavia and in 1863 forwarded to The Hague, along with the *Hoge Regering te Batavia* collection. As in the course of the eighteenth century more and more deliberations and letters had been termed secret, a considerable part of the Bengal archives was sent to Batavia. There is not much from Surat, and from Coromandel only papers relating to the very last period of Dutch presence are in this collection (see 2.3, 5.3 and 6.3).

No Malabar papers are in this collection, since Malabar had been ceded in 1814 under different circumstances. Nor are there any papers relating to Ceylon which had been conquered by the British in 1796, not to be returned after the Napoleonic Era as were most of the other conquered or surrendered Dutch factories. There are however some papers concerning the Fishery Coast, which during the 1818-25 period was subordinate to the Coromandel headquarters, then at Sadras (see 5.3).

1.4. Archives of Other Institutions

1.4.1. *Compagnieën op Oost-Indië, 1594-1603*
Early East India Companies

Access no.:	1.04.01
Inv. nos:	1-175
Size:	1.3 metres
Period:	1592-1603
Inventory:	in R. Bijlsma, *De archieven van de Compagniën op Oost-Indië* (The Hague, 1927), with introduction; also in *VROA* (1926), pp. 173-224

At the end of the sixteenth century several ad hoc trading companies were founded in a number of towns in Holland and Zeeland which merged in 1602 to become the VOC (for which reason it was called the *United* East India Company). One of these so-called *Voorcompagnieën* (pre-companies), was the *Compagnie op Oost-Indië te Middelburg*, or *Vereenigde Zeeuwsche Compagnie* (Company for the East Indies of Middelburg, or United Company of Zeeland), founded in 1600. In 1601 it sent out an expedition to Asia, as a result of which the first Dutch settlement at Surat—and in the whole of South Asia for that matter—was established in 1602, albeit temporarily and of a very limited scale. Papers regarding this event, however, are to be found in the archives of the *Staten-Generaal* (States General, see 1.4.2 and 2.4) and of the Gentlemen XVII and the Amsterdam Chamber of the VOC (see 2.2.1, VOC 601). Shortly thereafter, some of the other *Voorcompagnieën* also briefly called at the South Asian coasts, but at the time the ships in question returned home, their respective companies had already merged with the VOC. As a consequence, the archives of the *Voorcompagnieën* contain no documents relating to South Asia.

1.4.2. *Staten-Generaal,* 1576-1796
States General

Access no.: 1.01.03
Inv. nos: 1-12697
Size: 1030 metres
Period: 1550-1796
Inventory: in typescript in several volumes, numbered 1.01.02 (table of contents) to 1.01.08

The overall supervision of the VOC and the colonies lay with the States General of the Dutch Republic. They granted the charters to the Company and appointed its high officials, such as the Governor-General at Batavia. The Gentlemen XVII, the commanders of the return fleets from the East Indies, Advocates of the Company, and other officials regularly delivered reports to the States General. As a consequence, the archives of the States General may contain unique documents with respect to South Asia, which are not easy to locate, however.

The main body of the archives is arranged on the *resolutie* system. The various bundles listed below, the so-called *liassen* (inv. nos 4862-5461, 5734-50), are annexes to the *resoluties* of the States General. They may contain all kinds of documents, including annual reports and travel accounts. Indices or other finding aids to these bundles do not exist. Therefore, the indices to the *resoluties* may serve as indirect finding aids to the *liassen*. The following inv. nos consist of various kinds of indices to the *resoluties*.

Public: 3682-726 (period 1576-1730, look for instance under *Oost-Indische Compagnie* in inv. no. 3723, ff. 177-201); 3865-8 (period 1700-49); the indices for the period 1749-96 are to be found in the volumes containing the (printed) *resoluties* themselves, inv. nos 3804-64.

Secret: 4563-797 (period 1634-1796, these are actually registers frequently including indices); 4798-801 (period 1648-1772); 4802-5 (period 1694-1789); for other periods the indices are to be found in the volumes containing the *secrete resoluties* themselves, inv. nos 3904-9 (period 1592-1652) and 4538-59 (period 1790-6).

Inv. nos 4841-3 consist of registers of some of the *resoluties* concerning the

VOC, partly with indices (period 1602-12, 1638-70, 1790-3). In addition to all these indices, the subject files in the *loketkas* and the *secrete kas* (listed below) may provide a further guide to documents in the *liassen*.

4862-5461 Miscellaneous bundles (*liassen loopende*), 1550-1796, including VOC affairs and East Indian trade up to 1623. 600 Bundles.

5734-49 Bundles (*liassen*) concerning the VOC (ordinary), 1623-1795. 25 Bundles.

5750 Bundles (*liassen*) concerning the VOC (secret), 1703-95. One Bundle.

12563 Miscellaneous papers (*loketkas*) in approx. 63 folders concerning the VOC (ordinary), mostly relating to contacts with other trading companies, c. 1602-1786. Folder no. 2 contains two reports of some voyages of ships of the United Company of Zeeland to Surat, and possibly Malabar, Ceylon, Bengal and other places, *c.* 1603.

12581 Miscellaneous papers (*secrete kas*) in approx. 31 folders concerning the VOC (secret), *c.* 1621-58

See 2.4 and 4.4 for some documents specifically relating to Surat and Ceylon.

Note: the archives of the VOC contain extracts of *resoluties* and reports of the States General concerning the Company: VOC 368-86, 413-24 (*resoluties*) and 432-6 (reports), period: 1600-1786.

1.4.3. *Stadhouderlijke Secretarie*, 1747-95
Secretariat to the Stadtholder

Access no.: 1.01.50
Inv. nos: 1-2044
Size: *c.* 48 metres
Period: 1747-95
Inventory: in typescript

In 1749 the Stadtholder, Prince William IV of Orange, became *Opperbewindhebber* (Chief Director) of the VOC. In this capacity he oversaw the elections and appointments of the Company's Directors and of the high officials in Asia. Furthermore, he was responsible for the direction of military affairs. In the assembly of the Gentlemen XVII he was represented by someone who was familiar with VOC affairs. Thomas Hope was the representative of Stadtholder William V between 1766—when this Prince became *Opperbewindhebber*—and 1770 (see 1.5.17).

The archives contain a number of documents concerning the execution of the above-mentioned functions of the Stadtholder. Papers regarding South Asia have a mixed character. Some documents relate to the conflicts with the EIC at the end of the eighteenth century and the defence of VOC establishments as a result of that. Several papers date from before 1747.

1145 Letter from L. Hooreman, former *Directeur-Generaal*, to the States General, concerning the state of affairs of the Dutch possessions in the East Indies, including all the regions in South Asia, 1766. One piece.

1146 Memorandum by J.C. Radermacher for Stadtholder William V, concerning the decline of the VOC, with ff. 127-68 relating to South Asia, 1766. One volume.

1199 Lists of the military strength in the East Indies, including South Asia, with appendices, 1784, 1785, 1789-91. One folder.

1607 Collection of various documents concerning government and trade in Asia (one volume), which contains many papers relating to specific regions in South Asia. Of the other papers in this collection it is unclear as to which region they refer to, but it is rather likely they are relevant to South Asia. The papers in question—nos 1, 2, 5, 6 ('no. 39'), 9, 11 ('no. 6'), 17, 18 and 23 ('no. 31')—consist of descriptions of the processing of indigo (1) and saltpetre (2), instructions for drawing up reports (5), signal and sail instructions (6), and various unspecified memoranda, instructions and reports, 1649-70 and n.d.

For documents concerning Surat, Malabar, Ceylon, Coromandel and Bengal, see 2.4, 3.4, 4.4, 4.7, 5.4 and 6.4.

1.4.4. *Comité tot de Zaken van de Oost-Indische Handel en Bezittingen*, 1796-1800

Committee regarding East Indian Trade and Possessions

Access no.:	2.01.27.01
Inv. nos:	1-246
Size:	21 metres
Period:	1793-1800
Inventory:	in typescript with brief introduction and index and with manuscript marginalia

The Committee was the first in a series of successors to the VOC direction in the Netherlands (Gentlemen XVII, Chambers). It functioned between 1 March 1796 and 15 May 1800. The Committee was divided into four departments (defence, management of overseas establishments, commerce and equipment, and finance). Inv. nos 1-36 may be considered a continuation of the *resoluties* and the *kopieboek van brieven* of the Gentlemen XVII (see 1.1.1 and 1.1.3). Inv. nos 66-71 are the Batavia *resoluties* of 1792 and 1793 and inv. nos 72-75 contain Batavia's *uitgaand brievenboek* of 1793 and 1794. The *OBP* are also continued in this collection (inv. nos 55-65A, 79-137, 193-8). In the regional surveys of the *OBP* of the Committee (see 2.4, 3.4, 4.4, 5.4 and 6.4), only documents falling under certain categories are listed. These are the same categories that have been selected with regard to the *OBP* of the VOC. For an explanation of those *OBP* and the categories, see 1.1.7.

Access number 2.01.32 is the typescript table of contents to the *OBP* in these archives. To other parts of the archives there are some contemporary finding aids. Inv. no. 10 is an alphabetical index to the (minutes of the) Committee *resoluties*. Inv. nos 32 and 36 are alphabetical indices to the (minutes of the) letters and secret letters sent to the Indies and China. The *Realia* (see 1.1.4) also cover the Batavia *resoluties* of this period.

Of the different parts of the archives, the part created by the *Departement tot het Huishoudelijk Bestuur in Indië en de Kaap* (Department of Household Management in the Indies and the Cape) consisting of inv. nos 139-52A, is most relevant to South Asia. Inv. nos 142-6 contain excerpts of letters of the GG&C ordered geographically.

1.4.5. *Raad der Aziatische Bezittingen en Etablissementen*, 1800-6 Council of Asian Possessions and Establishments

Access no.: 2.01.27.02
Inv. nos: 1-407
Size: 36 metres
Period: 1793-1806
Inventory: in typescript with a brief introduction and index

The Council was the second in the line of successors to the VOC direction in the Netherlands. It functioned between 19 May 1800 and 4 August 1806 and was composed of three departments: Indian affairs, commerce and shipping, finance. Inv. nos 1 to 83 are the *resoluties* and outgoing letters of the Council. Inv. nos 105 to 142 may be considered a continuation of the *OBP*, but the volume and scope of the series greatly declined over this period.

There are some contemporary finding aids to parts of the collection. Inv. nos 22-7 are alphabetical indices to names and topics of the (minutes of the) *resoluties* of the Council, inv. no. 50 is the same to some of the *secrete resoluties*. Inv. no. 63 is an index to outgoing letters of the Council. Inv. nos 68 and 69 are two distinct indices to the (minutes of) the Council's letters to Batavia up to 1806, and inv. nos 80 and 81 are the same to the secret letters up to 1801 and 1804 respectively.

In the *OBP* of this period there is not much that relates directly to South Asia, where most of the establishments had been taken over by the British. There are however references to South Asia in the letters (with appendices) of the GG&C to the Council (to which inv. no. 21 of the *Hollandse Divisie bij het Ministerie van Marine en Koloniën te Parijs* is an alphabetical finding aid (see 1.4.8)) and in the *generale verslagen* (a continuation of the *generale missiven*, see 1.1.7) over the period 1796-1801 (inv. nos 123-5c) that are in this collection. For some 'stray papers' relevant to Ceylon and Coromandel see 4.4 and 5.4.

The greater part of the archives of the Commissioners General S.H. Frijkenius and S.C. Nederburgh, who were sent to Batavia in 1792 to keep an eye on the High Government and to initiate reforms, is also in this collection. In October 1799 Nederburgh returned to the Netherlands taking along part of the archives that had been created by the *Comité-Generaal* consisting of Nederburgh, Frijkenius and the Governor-General and his adjunct, which functioned between 1795 and 1799. These include *resoluties* of the *Comité-Generaal* as well as of the so-called Combined Meeting of the *Comité-Generaal* and the Council of the Indies (see 1.1.4). Reports that had been sent previously by the Commissioners are also in this collection (inv. nos 319-35) as well as in the *Comité tot de Zaken van de Oost-Indische Handel en Bezittingen* collection (inv. nos 48-54). Miscellaneous papers brought over by Nederburgh are in a separate collection (see 1.4.7).

Papers from the archives of the *Comité-Generaal*:

229-38	Minutes of the *resoluties* of the Committee, 1793-9. Ten volumes.
240	Minutes of outgoing letters of the Committee, 1794-8 (incomplete). Loose pieces.
241-8	Copies of the common and *secrete resoluties* of the Committee. Eight volumes.
249	Alphabetical index to the *resoluties* of the Committee. One volume.
250	Minutes of the *secrete resoluties* of the Committee, 1794-8. One volume.
251-80	Appendices to the *resoluties* of the Committee (incoming as well as outgoing papers), 1793-9. With table of contents (280), 30 volumes.
281-8	(*Secrete*) *resoluties* of the Combined Meeting, 1795-9. With appendices, eight volumes.
337-8	*Resoluties* of the Combined Meeting, 1798-9. Two volumes.
346	Compilation of marginal excerpts from the *resoluties* of the Combined Meeting, 1795-9. One cover.
347-8	Alphabetical index to the *resoluties* of the Combined Meeting, 1795-9. Two volumes.
349	Tables of contents to the appendices of the *resoluties* of the Combined Meeting, 1795-7. One volume.

1.4.6. *Ministerie van Koophandel en Koloniën / Marine en Koloniën*, 1806-10 Ministry of Commercial and Colonial Affairs / Naval and Colonial Affairs

Access no.:	2.01.27.03
Inv. nos:	1-225
Size:	12 metres
Period:	1798-1813
Inventory:	in typescript with index

After the establishment of the Kingdom of Holland under Louis Napoleon, the Council of Asian Possessions and Establishments was abolished. One Ministry came to be responsible for the affairs of both the East and West Indies together with those of commerce in general. The first division of the Ministry was to deal with East Indian affairs, part of the members of the *Raad der Aziatische Bezittingen en Etablissementen* (see 1.4.5) were allowed to continue their work with this division. In 1808 the Ministry was reorganized and its name slightly changed. There was no longer a separate division for Asian affairs. Still the East Indies and the West Indies were in fact dealt with separately. Since the papers concerning the West Indies and those concerning commerce in general have largely been relocated to different archives, most papers contained in this collection relate to Asia. Papers sent over from Asia were however few, due to the war-time conditions.

Relevant papers in this collection:

156 Statement of the number, names, population and importance of Asian possessions lost to the British since 1795, 1806. Three folders.

232 Copy of the journal of the Governor-General in Batavia over 1807, 1808. One volume.

1.4.7. *Uit Engeland overgezonden stukken (Nederburgh)*
Papers sent from England (Nederburgh)

Access no.: 2.01.27.04
Inv. nos: 1-118
Size: 3 metres
Period: 1791-7
Inventory: in typescript with index

This collection contains some more material concerning the doings of Commissioners General S.C. Nederburgh and S.H. Frijkenius (see 1.4.5), though mostly pertaining to the period they spent at the Cape of Good Hope (1791-3). However, part of this collection also consists of papers concerning the outlying factories. For documents on Surat, Malabar and Coromandel see sections 2.4, 3.4 and 5.4.

Other relevant pieces:

16 *Resoluties* of the Committee General, 1795. With appendices, one volume.

1.4.8. *Hollandse Divisie bij het Ministerie van Marine en Koloniën te Parijs,* 1810-14
Dutch Division at the Ministry of Naval and Colonial Affairs in Paris

Access no.: 2.01.27.05
Inv. nos: 1-53
Size: 1.5 metres
Period: 1807-14
Inventory: in typescript with index

The Division was created after the incorporation of the Netherlands into France and was a record-keeping rather than a policy-making body. The collection comprises reports and minutes of the *Chef* of the Division and of the Commissioner in Amsterdam, and some incoming pieces. The latter include letters from the Governor-General (and Council) in Batavia dating from the period 1807-11 (inv. nos 14-16, 18-19, 23-6), with an alphabetical repertory to the same for the years 1801-11 (inv. nos 21-2), and extracts of the *resoluties* of the Governor-General in 1811 (inv. nos 54-5).

1.4.9. *Comptabiliteit betreffende Oost-Indische Bezittingen*, 1795-1813
Accountancy concerning the East Indian Possessions

Access no.: 2.01.27.06
Inv. nos: 1-275
Size: 28 metres
Period: 1736-1825
Inventory: in typescript

This institution was devised in order to centralize and reorganize the financial administration of the VOC, which had previously been left to the Chambers. The archives contain some material on the matters that had been dealt with by the *Soldijkantoren* (see 1.1.10), but this material was not as well organized as it was before.

149-64 Rolls of pay accounts of Company servants that do not have accounts in a ship's pay ledger, 1736-1825. 16 volumes.
165-6 Indices to the above series on family names and personal names. Two volumes.
170-86 Muster rolls, etc., of individual ships, 1794-1807. 15 volumes and 4 quires.

1.4.10. *Ministerie van Koloniën*, 1814-49
Ministry of Colonial Affairs

Access no.: 2.10.01
Inv. nos: 1-4713
Size: 500 metres
Period: 1705-1900
Inventory: in typescript with index and introduction

After the Napoleonic Era, in 1814, a Department of Trade and Colonial Affairs was established in The Hague. Colonial Affairs were grouped together in 1818 with Education and National Industry in one Ministry (from which education was dropped in 1824) and in 1825 with Naval Affairs. Despite the fact that Colonial Affairs were part of these larger administrative divisions, the archives were kept separately. The bulk of the archives are *verbalen*, folders containing incoming and outgoing papers on a particular matter classified only by the date that the matter was concluded. Series of the decisions of the Governor-General in Batavia with (inv. nos 2770-863, secret 4526-35) and without Council (inv. nos 2435-725, secret 4497-514) have however been kept separately, as well as the deliberations of the Commissioners General of the period 1816-19, who were sent to Batavia to take over after the British interregnum and are not to be confused with the Commissioners General of the period 1793 through 1799 (see 1.4.5). These deliberations are in inv. nos 2364-483 and 4485 (secret), with various appendices, extracts and letters sent to The Hague in inv. nos 2395-433 and the secret part of those in inv. nos 4486-8, 4491-6.

The *verbalen* series are not easy to use. To the non-secret series there are three kinds of contemporary finding aids: the *agenda* (protocol register) (inv. nos 1987-2046) in which all incoming papers were listed on a daily basis, the index (inv. nos 2047-135) in which the ministerial deliberations are ordered according to subject, and another alphabetical index, called *klapper*, to the latter (inv. nos 2136-83). The headings in the index are however very general—most relevant to South Asia would be the heading *Oost-Indische Koloniën* (East Indian Colonies)—and the *klapper* is no more specific except on personal names. To the secret *verbalen* (up to 1825) the only entry is through the *agenda* (inv. nos 4359-80).

The series of deliberations of the Commissioners General of 1816-19 have tables of contents (inv. nos 2384-8, secret 4489) as well as an alphabetical index (inv. nos 2389-94, secret 4490). To the *resoluties* of the Governor-General without and with Council there are also tables and indices, respectively in inv. nos 2726-65 (secret 4515-25) and 2864-90.

During this period the Southeast Asian Archipelago had definitively superseded South Asia in terms of attention paid to it by decision makers in the Netherlands as well as in Batavia. Specifically relevant to South Asia are only two inv. nos, which contain papers on Ceylon, Coromandel and Bengal (see 4.4, 5.4 and 6.4).

1.4.11. *Legaties*
Embassies, consulates and envoys

The term *Legaties* refers to Dutch diplomatic missions abroad. Apart from the contacts between the VOC and South Asian courts, the Dutch Republic did not maintain diplomatic relations with any of the South Asian kingdoms. The archives of some of the *Legaties* in Europe, however, contain a few documents with respect to South Asia. These mostly concern contacts in South Asia between the VOC and the trading companies of other European states. The archives of the missions in France (access no. 1.02.14), Turkey (access nos 1.02.20 and 1.02.22), Portugal (access no. 1.02.18) and Sweden (access no. 1.02.07) as well as the archives of the diplomat Coenraad van Heemskerck (access no. 1.02.01) include a couple of relevant papers. The inventories of the archives of most of the *Legaties* (access nos 1.02.01 to 1.02.18) have been published in J.C.M. Pennings and T.H.P.M. Thomassen (eds), *Archieven van Nederlandse gezanten en consuls tot 1813. Deel 1: Overgedragen brieven van gezanten en consuls in de Christelijke wereld* (The Hague, 1994) (see also 2.4, 3.4, 5.4 and 6.4).

Legatie Turkije
Embassy at Constantinople (Istanbul), Turkey

Access no.: 1.02.20
Period: 1668-1811

1125 Papers from R. van Haeften (ambassador at Constantinople between 1778 and 1784) concerning the despatch of letters from the Gentlemen XVII to Surat, Cochin, Ceylon and Batavia via Constantinople, Baghdad, Basra or Alexandria, 1781-2. One folder.

Consulaat Smyrna
Consulate at Smyrna (Izmir), Turkey

Access no.: 1.02.22
Period: 1685-1811

120 Papers concerning the trade of cotton cloths from South Asia, 1783.

1.5. Personal and Family Papers

As the distinction between private and official archives was perceived less clearly in early-modern Europe than it is now, the personal archives of people who were involved with institutions like the VOC and the Admiralty constitute a substantial addition to the institutional archives *per se*, which is precisely the reason why the ARA has been collecting them. The category of personal and family papers also includes libraries of historical documents put together by collectors such as C.A. Sypesteyn.

Except for the papers of Valckenier, Van de Graaff (and Van Angelbeek) and Moens, the present selection encompasses personal and family archives that according to Roessingh and Jacquet (see Bibliography, nos 87 and 74) contain material relevant to South Asia. Note that other such archives may still lie scattered throughout the ARA. Of the collections mentioned nearly all pieces relevant to South Asia have been listed in this guide, that is except those documents of which copies occur over and over again, especially the instructions by Commissioner Van Reede and some of the *memories van overgave*. The following list is arranged in chronological order. Note, however, that many of the late eighteenth-century private archives entered here span a large part of the VOC period, including the seventeenth century.

1.5.1. *H. de Groot (1583-1645)* (supplement)

Access no.: 1.10.35.02
Inv. no.: 40-5 (inv. no. 40 comprises 116 documents, foliated consecutively)
Size: 0.28 metres
Period: seventeenth century
Inventory: in *IRAA* I (1928), pp. 73-105; copy available at the ARA with new numbers added in manuscript

A collection of papers of the famous scholar of international law Hugo de Groot relating to East Indian affairs and his involvement with the international disputes of the VOC, was sold at an auction in 1864 and was partly acquired by the ARA. Other parts of the collection were bought by the University Library of Leiden, the Rotterdam City Archives and private persons. Most of the documents relate to Southeast Asia and to relations with the other Europeans in Asia in general. Some papers however relate to South Asia. For documents relating to Malabar and Ceylon, see also sections 3.5 and 4.5.

40, ff. 331-2	List of contents of 11 letters of the King of Spain to the 'King of Canara' and to M. Alfonso de Castro, A. Furtado Mandoça a.o. over 1606-7, revealing hostile intentions towards the Dutch in South Asia, Melaka, etc., n.d.
40, f. 429	Extracts by De Groot from works of Paulus Venetus, Thomas Lopez and Eduardus Barbosa concerning some of the kingdoms in South Asia, n.d. Partly in Latin.

1.5.2. *W. Geleynssen de Jongh(e) (1594-1674)*

Access no.:	1.10.30
Inv. nos:	1-320
Size:	2 metres
Period:	1612-48
Inventory:	in *VROA* 35 (1912), pp. 94-135; *VROA* 36 (1913) I, pp. 96-104

In 1623 Wollebrandt Geleynssen de Jongh came to Surat as a *opperkoopman*, served in Burhanpur for a while and then as chief-factor of Bharuch from 1624 to 1631. After a spell in the Republic and the Archipelago, he was appointed second-in-command at Surat in 1636 and chief of Agra in 1637 where he served until 1640. While on his way from Persia to Batavia, he was taken hostage by the Portuguese at Goa in 1643 after which he spent some time in Vengurla into the year 1644. Later that year he was appointed rear admiral to the fleet sailing against Goa but he came to be occupied in Persia again soon after.

The archives, which had been kept in a trunk since the demise of Geleynssen, were ordered more or less chronologically after it came into possession of the ARA in 1912. Some more papers belonging to Geleynssen de Jongh are in the *Losse aanwinsten* collection. Two inventory items from this collection relate to his period in South Asia (see 1.6.1 and 2.6). For documents relating to specific regions, see 2.5, 3.5, 4.5, 5.5 and 6.5.

51	Agreement with Mustafa Chelibi Haji Sultan and 'Piery Beeck', merchants in Surat, on restitution of goods from the ship 'Mahamedy' that had been captured by the VOC below Ceylon and taken to Pulicat, 1628 (1037 AH). One piece.
75	Contains a daily record of the voyage from Batavia to Surat and thence inland to Agra and Benares, 1636-7.
98	Instruction, etc., of the Governor-General to the fleet sailing to occupy the bay of Goa and to Surat and Persia, 1636. One piece.
100	This volume includes the following translations: a letter from Aurangzeb from Daulatabad (1040 AH/1638 AD) concerning the Portuguese at Daman; the contract also in inv. no. 51 (see above); a letter from the Zamorin with a receipt of goods, 1641; a letter from the King of Bijapur; a letter by C. Cornelissen (Blocq) to Mustafa Khan, *Wazir* of Bijapur; a contract between the Viceroy at Goa with Mir Muhammad Rasa, the Bijapur Governor over the Konkan, 1640. In the middle part of the volume (correspondence with the Persian King and officials) is a letter by Sahib(a) Begum, daughter of the

Mughal, wife of the Shah (?), concerning an offensive fleet on its way from Surat (1055 AH/AD 1645). The fist part of the volume has copies in Persian, with and without translations, of Mughal *farmans*, etc. (see Appendix I). One volume.

103 Contains some letters to Geleynssen from Surat by Barent Pietersen and by Asaf Khan from Kabul.

106-7 Letters received by Geleynssen in Agra from Surat, Ahmadabad, Vengurla, Raybag, Bijapur (with a short appended letter between two Bijapur nobles on a Dutch-Portuguese battle), Batticaloa, Pulicat, Masulipatam, Hooghly, Pipli, Patna and Persia, 1636-8. No. 106 includes a two-folio daily record by J. Uyttenboogaert of a *caffila* from Agra to Surat. Two bundles.

146 *Resoluties* of the Vengurla factory concerning the freight charges to be paid by the ambassadors of Persia and Golkonda, 1641. One folder.

154 Instruction of the GG&C to the commanders of the fleet sailing for Malabar, Goa, etc., 1642.

155 *Farmans* of Shah Jahan granting toll privileges to the Dutch in Agra, Ahmadabad, Vadodara, Pipli, etc., 1642 (1052 AH). One piece.

234 List of the average prices of pearls, by A. van Oostenden in Gombroon, 1641. One piece.

276A Instruction by J. Maetsuijcker to the fleet sailing from Ceylon to Persia, 1645. One folder.

278 Minutes of letters of Geleynsen to be sent from various ships lying near Goa, Panjim, Negombo, Vengurla and Daman, 1644-5. One folder.

283, 284 Letters received by Geleynsen in Gombroon (either directed to him or copies of letters to people in other locations), 1644-6. Two volumes. Including letters from VOC personnel in Bengal, Masulipatam, Pulicat, Negombo, Galle, Vengurla, Surat and Lahore (?) (many replies by Geleynssen are in inv. no. 102).

295 List of goods destined for Masulipatam transhipped in Ceylon, 1645. One piece.

1.5.3. *S. Sweers, J. van Vliet, J. Specx, F. Mannis*

Access no.: 1.10.78
Inv. nos: 1-9
Size: 0.6 metre
Period: 1620-74, 1702
Inventory: in *IRAA* I (1928), pp. 3-37, with introduction and detailed list of the contents

Papers derived from these four seventeenth-century VOC servants were put together with some additional material in nine volumes in the early eighteenth century. All of them had served in Asia but only Salomon Sweers was active in South Asia, mainly in Ahmadabad for 18 months around 1635. From *c.* 1641 till 1645 he took care of the correspondence of the GG&C with the *westerkwartieren* and hence of the entries in the *Bataviaas dagregister* concerning South Asia and the Persian Gulf. For documents relating to specific regions, see 2.5, 4.5, 5.5 and 6.5.

5, ff. 71-185	*Dagregister* of Batavia, 1632-3 and first half of 1644.*
5, ff. 186-205	Include notes on voyages from Golkonda to Aleppo, from Goa to Surat, from Surat to Hormuz, and on currencies and weights in Coromandel.
6, ff. 1-259	Minutes of the entries in the *Bataviaas dagregister* concerning South Asia (and surrounding areas) made by S. Sweers, 1641-4.*
8, ff. 43-83	Minutes of the entries in the *Bataviaas dagregister* concerning Coromandel and Bengal, 1643.*
9, ff. 189-200	Instruction to P. Boreel, on his departure to South Asia, etc., as Commissioner to announce the armistice with Portugal, 1642.

* The published edition of the *Dagregisters* of Batavia (see 1.1.5) over these years and for this region is based mainly on the copies in this collection.

1.5.4. *Van Goens*

Access no.: 1.10.32
Inv. nos: 1-105
Size: 1 metre
Period: 1619-1872
Inventory: in typescript, with introduction and genealogy

Family papers of the Van Goens family, given in custody to the archives by Mrs Van Goens-Huender in 1959. Of interest are the papers belonging to Rijklof van Goens and his son Rijklof van Goens the Younger. Van Goens the Elder started his career in the Indies in Coromandel from 1631 to 1634. Between 1653 and 1675 he served as inspecting commissioner and military commander, Admiral, etc., in various parts of South Asia, with periods as *Commandeur*, Governor, etc., in Ceylon. From 1678 to 1681 he was Governor-General. His son served in Ceylon from 1658 to 1669 in various positions and as Governor from 1675 to 1679. For documents relating to Malabar and Ceylon, see also 3.5 and 4.5.

6	Memoirs of Rijklof van Goens the Elder, continued by his son, 1619-80. With nineteenth-century transcripts, one bundle. See also *Berigten van het Historisch Genootschap te Utrecht*, 5, 2 (1856).
10, 15-17	Deeds of appointment of Van Goens the Elder to various positions in South Asia, 1653, 1657, 1664, 1672. Four charters.

1.5.5. *J. Hudde (1628-1704)*

Access no.: 1.10.48
Inv. nos: 1-51
Size: 1 metre
Period: 1602-1703
Inventory: in *VROA* 49 (1926) I, pp. 225-32, with introduction

Johannes Hudde was a Director of the Amsterdam Chamber from 1679 to 1703 and sat in the Committee that was to redress the state of Company affairs. Part of the collection however derives from his father G. Hudde who was Director between 1632 and 1647. It was donated to the ARA in 1871 by members of the related Dedel family. For documents relating to Coromandel and Bengal, see also 5.5 and 6.5.

38 Instruction of the Gentlemen XVII to H. van Rheede, Commissioner to South Asia, 1684. One piece.

1.5.6. *Sypesteyn* (supplement)

Access no.. 1.13.19.02
Inv. nos: 1-9
Size: 0.17 metres
Inventory: in typescript

Collection of historical documents of C.A. Sypesteyn sold at auction in London in the first quarter of the nineteenth century, partly acquired for the ARA by King William I some time afterwards. Contains important writings relating to Mughal India and Ceylon. See also Appendix I. For documents relating to Surat and Ceylon, see 2.5 and 4.5.

1.5.7. *H. Becker (1661-1722)*

Access no.: 1.10.05.01
Inv. nos: 1-61
Size: *c.* 1.5 metres
Period: 1708-28
Inventory: in *Vijf ambtenaren van de VOC en de regering in Indië; inventarissen van de archieven Becker, Cnoll, Van Kal, Van Polanen en Valckenier* (The Hague, 1985)

Hendrik Becker was posted as an army captain in Malabar in 1692 and in Ceylon in 1694. In 1701 he was appointed *Fiscaal* at Nagappattinam. He served as Governor of Ceylon from 1707 to 1716. The materials in the collection have come down to the ARA through various channels and have been added as late as the 1980s. Nearly all papers in the collection date from Becker's period in Ceylon (see 4.5), but two documents relate to Company personnel in Malabar (see 3.5).

60 Daily record of East India news, 1718-19. One volume.

1.5.8. *Boreel*

Access no.: 1.10.10
Inv. nos: 1-478
Size: *c.* 7 metres
Period: 1443-1931
Inventory: in typescript

Family papers. Of interest are some papers relating to Jacob Boreel Jansz (1711-78) who served as Councillor Fiscal to the Admiralty at Amsterdam. The documents concern Ceylon (see 4.5).

1.5.9. *A. Valckenier (1695-1751)*

Access no.: 1.10.05.05
Inv. nos: 1-130
Size: 1.35 metres
Period: 1703-71
Inventory: in *Vijf ambtenaren van de VOC en de regering in Indië; inventarissen van de archieven Becker, Cnoll, Van Kal, Van Polanen en Valckenier* (The Hague, 1985)

Adriaan Valckenier was a functionary of the VOC between 1714 and 1741, and served at Batavia during this entire period. From 1737 onward he was Governor-General. He never stayed in South Asia, but his collection contains a letter which he received from Patna (see 6.5).

1.5.10. *Van Hoorn van Riebeeck*

Access no.: 1.10.45
Inv. nos: 1-65
Size: 1.25 metres
Period: 1595-1780
Inventory: in typescript / manuscript

Includes papers belonging to Pieter van Hoorn (Councillor of the Indies from 1663), Joan van Hoorn (Governor-General between 1704 and 1709) and his father-in-law Abraham van Riebeeck (Governor-General between 1709 and 1713). The collection was acquired by the ARA in several instalments. For documents relating to Ceylon, see also 4.5.

45 Translations from Persian by P. Guilebaud of the will of Aurangzeb and an account of the battle at Jajau and what further transpired between Shah Alam (i.e. Muazzam, the Emperor to be Bahadur Shah) and Azam Shah, 1707.

1.5.11. *G.L. Vernet (1711-75)*

Access no.: 1.10.82
Inv. nos: 1-13
Size: 1.3 metres
Period: 1752-66
Inventory: in typescript

George Lodewijk Vernet was a functionary of the VOC between 1732 and 1769. He arrived at Cossimbazar in 1742, became chief-factor at Hooghly in 1754, to be promoted to *Opperhoofd* in Cossimbazar again one year later. From 1763 to 1769 he was *Directeur* of Bengal. For documents relating to Bengal, see 6.5.

1.5.12. *L.J. van Eck (1719-65)*

Access no.:	1.10.106
Inv. nos:	1-47
Size:	0.4 metre
Period:	1719-65
Inventory:	in typescript, with introduction and index

Lubbert Jan van Eck served the VOC in Porto Novo and Pulicat from 1747 onward, from 1758 as Governor of Coromandel. In 1761 he was appointed Governor of Ceylon. The papers in this collection were acquired by the ARA in 1853. See also 1.5.15. For documents relating to Ceylon and Coromandel, see 4.5 and 5.5.

1-7 Papers concerning Van Eck's private trade, including a contract (1761) concluded between the Tranquebar Government of the Danish East India Company, Van Eck and a Mr La Beaume in which it was agreed that the Danes would lease the ship King of Denmark for a joint commercial venture to the Nicobar Islands, Pegu and Bengal and back to Tranquebar. Van Eck would have a 50 per cent share in this venture and the Danish East India Company and La Beaume 25 per cent each. The period covered is 1756-63. Two folders and five pieces.

10-11 Papers concerning the legacy of L.J. van Eck, 1765-9.

32, 46 Contain extracts from British reports concerning the battle between the French and the British near Wandiwash, the arrival of reinforcements from Bombay, etc., and of a letter of Mr Trembly from Bengal concerning the Nawab's agitation against European establishments and the rumours of a march of Mughal troops on Patna, n.d. and 1760. In English, and French.

1.5.13. *J. van Ghesel (1707-73)*

Access no.:	1.10.31
Inv. nos:	1-209
Size:	*c.* 1 metre
Period:	1603-1773
Inventory:	in typescript with introduction

Jacob van Ghesel served as a Director to the Amsterdam Chamber of the VOC from 1757 to 1773. The collection consists of official material and some notes on various topics relating to the VOC trade by Van Ghesel himself. Included are papers left by Pieter de Witt, Director (1696-1712) and grandfather of Van Ghesel's wife. The collection was donated to the ARA by a distant relative of the family in the later part of the nineteenth century. Some papers from the collection have been published in the 1859 and 1872-5 issues of *KHGU*, without mention of the provenance of the papers however. For documents relating to Surat, Ceylon, Coromandel and Bengal, see also 2.5, 4.5, 5.5 and 6.5.

22 Extracts from the *resoluties* of the Gentlemen XVII, 1698-1772, with index to the *resoluties*, 1605-1758. One folder.

48 Extracts by Van Ghesel from letters and other papers of the East Indian factories, ordered geographically, 1752-72. One folder, partly published in *KHGU*, 29 (1873), pp. 558-96 (see Bibliography, no. 54).

156 Project of the 1772 *eis* of silk fabrics for Amsterdam. Two pieces.

162 Inventory of a cabinet belonging to the Income Department, in which South Asian coins were kept, n.d. Four pieces.

174-6, 178-82 Papers concerning the estimation of gold, silver and coin values in (South) Asia, including a note by Van Ghesel on the possibility of changing the value of the rupee and extracts by him of works on coins, measures and weights. 24 pieces and a folder. Inv. no. 176 has been published in *KHGU*, 28 (1872), p. 72 a.o. (see Bibliography, no. 16).

188 *Beknopte historie van het Mogolse keizerrijk en de zuydelijke aangrensende landen* (Batavia, 1758). An introductory description and history of the subcontinent from *c.* the ninth century AD onward, with genealogy of the Mughals and the Maratha Kings and notes on places and dynasties in Ikkeri, Malabar, Madurai, Ramnad, Thanjavur and Bengal, and copies of recent treaties of the British, French, Nadir Shah, etc. Written by Jacobus Mossel (see Bibliography, no. 39).

189 Geographical notes by Van Ghesel and others on places of the VOC trade ordered alphabetically, n.d. One folder

202 Papers concerning cinnamon, 1699-1705. Four pieces. Partly published in *KHGU*, 28 (1872), pp. 32-5 (see Bibliography, no. 16).

1.5.14. *J.C. Baud (1789-1859)*

Access no.: 2.21.007.58
Inv. nos: 1-1106
Size: *c.* 28 metres
Period: 1585-1985
Inventory: in *VROA* (1917), pp. 497-613, with introduction, supplement in typescript

Jean Chrétien Baron Baud held innumerable offices relating to the East Indies, mostly at the High Government in Batavia or at ministries in The Hague. Between 1833 and 1836 he was interim Governor-General; from 1839 to 1848 he was Minister of Colonial Affairs. Although he was never stationed in South Asia, he collected some documents relating to the subcontinent which deal mostly with coinage, exchange rates, etc., between the 1670s and 1770s. For documents relating to Surat, Ceylon, Coromandel and Bengal, see also 2.5, 4.5, 5.5 and 6.5.

1061 Considerations concerning the value of gold and silver in the East Indies with respect to the VOC, including all of the regions in South Asia (two copies), 1760. Two pieces.

1065 Considerations of Reinier de Klerk, member of the Council of Batavia, in reaction to the remarks of Schreuder, in particular concerning the calculation of rupees in Malabar, Surat, Bengal, etc., *c.* 1762-75.

1.5.15. *Panthaleon van Eck*

Access no.: 1.10.65.01
Inv. nos 1-403
Size: 5 metres
Period: 1398-1943
Inventory: in typescript; the inventory of access no. 1.10.106 (see 1.5.12) also covers the items belonging to L.J. van Eck that are in this collection

Family papers. Of interest are the papers relating to Lubbert Jan van Eck (see 1.5.12), the bulk of these, however, concern his death and funeral in Ceylon and his legacy (see below and 4.7). Also in this collection are some official papers dating from his tenure in Coromandel (see 5.5).

58-9 Notification of the demise and project for the funeral of L.J. Van Eck, 1765. Two pieces, printed.

60 Letters of the executors of the will to the heirs. With appendices, one folder.

61-7 Papers concerning Van Eck's legacy, including some relating to a legal procedure, undertaken by D.C. Vick, *opperkoopman* at Coromandel c.s. against the executors of the will, over their share in seven boxes of Bengal calicoes sent to Batavia some years before, 1765-79 (see also 1.5.12, inv. no. 11). Two folders and thirteen pieces.

1.5.16. *Cort van der Linden*

Access no.: 2.21.040
Inv. nos: 1-522
Size: 10.5 metres
Period: 1634-1934
Inventory: in typescript, with genealogy

Family papers. Of interest are documents relating to Philippus Franciscus Cort (d. 1752), *Fiscaal* and Secretary at Nagappattinam around the 1740s, and some of his close relatives. For documents relating to Coromandel, see 5.5.

1.5.17. *Th. and J. Hope*

Access no.: 1.10.46
Inv. nos: 1-120
Size: 5 metres
Period: 1602-1782
Inventory: in typescript, with introduction

Thomas Hope was a banker and representative of Stadtholder William V with the VOC from 1766 to 1770 (see 1.4.3). His son Jan or John Hope was a Director of the Amsterdam Chamber of the VOC between 1770 and 1784. The collection consists solely of papers relating to the VOC, which were probably kept at the Oostindisch Huis together with the rest of the VOC archives until the transfer to the ARA in 1856. There are some useful finding aids to parts of the VOC archives in this collection as well as papers relating to the South Asian region specifically (see also 2.5, 3.5, 4.5, 5.5 and 6.5).

3 Index to the *resoluties* of the Gentlemen XVII, 1602-1762 is only up to the letter S. One folder.

5 Index to the letters of the Gentlemen XVII to the East Indies and the Cape, 1613-92. One folder.

1.5.18. *J.A. van Plettenberg (1739-1793)*

Access no.: 1.10.67
Inv. nos: 1-43
Size: 0.34 metre
Period: 1780-8
Inventory: in typescript

Joachim Ammema van Plettenberg went to the East Indies in 1764 and served the VOC until *c.* 1783. He never stayed in South Asia, but received some letters from Coromandel while he was Governor of Cape of Good Hope (see 5.5).

1.5.19. *C.J. Wolterbeek (1766-1845), Admiraliteitscolleges* (Admiralty)

Access no.: 1.01.47.19 (papers concerning Maritime and Naval affairs in the Wolterbeek collection)
Inv. nos: 1-88
Size: 0.88 metre
Period: 1781-1853
Inventory: in J. de Hullu, *De archieven der Admiraliteitscolleges* (The Hague, 1924), pp. 353-63

C.J. Wolterbeek became a Lieutenant in 1785, and was Vice-Admiral between 1831 and 1844. The collection includes a number of drawings of South Asian seaboards (see 1.7.10).

1.5.20. *Van Slingelandt-De Vrij Temminck*

Access no.: 3.20.52
Inv. nos: 1-657
Size: 18.3 metres
Period: 1550-1813
Inventory: in *IRAA* III (1930), pp. 270-340, with introduction, genealogy and detailed list of contents

Family papers. Of interest are the papers relating to Egbert de Vrij Temminck who performed many other functions besides being a director of the VOC between 1742 and 1785. These are miscellaneous documents, most of which concern specific regions, chiefly Bengal (see also 2.5, 4.5, 5.5 and 6.5).

567 Folder no. 70 contains papers concerning the direct sailing to the western factories of the East Indies, 1773. 17 pieces.

1.5.21. *P. van Bleiswijk (1724-90)*

Access no.: 3.01.25
Inv. nos: 1-662
Size: 9 metres
Period: 1772-87
Inventory: in typescript, with introduction and index

Pieter van Bleiswijk was *Raadpensionaris* (Grand Pensionary) of the Dutch Republic between 1772 and 1787. In this capacity he was (among many other matters) involved in the VOC and foreign relations. Because of these two concerns his collection includes a number of documents regarding South Asia as well as the rest of Asia. All papers relate to specific regions (see 2.5, 3.5, 4.5, 5.5 and 6.5).

1.5.22. *J.P. van Braam (1737-1803)*

Access no.: 1.10.11.02 (inv. nos 217-18 and 225-37 (maps and drawings) have access no. 4.BRF)
Inv. nos: 1-269, 301-15
Size: 3.45 metres
Period: 1727-1806
Inventory: in *VROA* 38 (1915) I, pp. 393-421; *VROA* 39 (1916) I, pp. 478-81; *VROA* (1950), p. 18; copy available at the ARA with partly new numbers added in manuscript and an addition in typescript

Jacob Pieter van Braam entered the navy at a very young age. He served the VOC for a while from 1764 until 1773. He again entered naval service in 1782 when he was sent to the East Indies. His papers have been donated to the ARA by his great-grandson W.H. van Braam in three instalments in 1914, 1915 and 1950.

Between 1767 and 1773 Van Braam was an equipment officer to the VOC factory in Bengal, but none of the papers seem to relate to this period. The greater part of the collection dates from Van Braam's second period of navy service, during which he was sent to Ceylon in 1785 to oversee the abandonment by the British of their positions on the island as agreed in 1784 and to check the claims of the King of Kandy. For documents relating to Malabar, Ceylon and Coromandel, see also 3.7, 4.5, 4.7 and 5.5.

100 Letters received from various authorities and private persons in Ceylon, Pulicat and Batavia, 1785. One bundle.

102 Letters of private persons in Batavia, Bengal, etc., 1785-6. One bundle.

1.5.23. *J.C. van der Hoop, Admiraliteitscolleges* (Admiralty)

Access no.: 1.01.47.29 (Papers concerning maritime and naval affairs in the Van der Hoop collection)
Inv. nos: 1-319
Size: 2.77 metres
Period: 1524-1825
Inventory: in J. de Hullu, *De archieven der Admiraliteitscolleges* (The Hague, 1924), pp. 451-82

J.C. van der Hoop functioned as an officer of justice in the Admiralty of Amsterdam from 1781 till 1795, and was Minister of Naval Affairs between 1815 and 1825. A number of documents concern Ceylon (see 4.5).

1.5.24. *Van der Heim*

Access no.: 1.10.39
Inv. nos: 1-206
Size: 2.75 metres
Period: 1609-1880
Inventory: in typescript

Includes papers of Jacob van der Heim, who was Secretary to the Meuse Admiralty between 1746 and 1795 and Director of the Rotterdam Chamber of the VOC from 1770 to 1795. For documents relating to Coromandel and Bengal, see also 5.5 and 6.5.

76-7 Indices to the *resoluties* of the Gentlemen XVII, 1670-1734 and 1735-91. Two volumes.
88 Papers concerning the import of silk into the Dutch Republic, 1729-40. One folder.
122 Papers concerning the plan for a direct shipping link to the western factories, 1773. One folder.
200 Short biography of a 'son of Jean Roi de Golconda and Alexandra Princesse de Tosna', born in 1761, who took service with the Dutch navy after a tour through Europe, n.d. and anonymous. One piece.

1.5.25. *Fagel*

Access no.: 1.10.29
Inv. nos: 1-5288
Size: 62 metres
Period: 1513-1927
Inventory: in N.M. Japikse, *Het archief van de familie Fagel* (The Hague, 1964)

Archives of the Fagel family, many members of which held high offices, starting from the mid-seventeenth century. Between 1672 and 1795 members of the family served as *Griffiers* (clerks) to the States General without interruption. The inventory items fall into three basic categories: private papers, official papers and correspondence. Among the official papers few relate directly to South Asia, the correspondence however contains many letters from people in Asia, including the subcontinent. For documents relating to Surat, Malabar, Ceylon and Bengal, see also 2.5, 3.5, 4.5 and 6.5.

1771 Letters from Colombo and Cochin to Prince William V about the British military advances in the subcontinent and their enemies: the French, Haidar Ali Khan and the Marathas, 1779-80. With appended copies of the capitulation of the French in Mahé, information on William Bolts in Austrian imperial service (1775, in French), and tables on Dutch military strength in Ceylon, including sepoys and contingents under Muslim commanders. One folder.

1.5.26. *S.I. Wiselius (1769-1845)*

Access no.: 2.21.176
Inv. nos: 1-67
Size: 1.2 metres
Period: 1788-1818
Inventory: in typescript

Wiselius was member of the *Comité tot de Zaken van de Oost-Indische Handel en Bezittingen* between 1796 and 1800, and the *Raad der Aziatische Bezittingen en Etablissementen* from 1800 to 4. In this capacity he collected a few papers relating to South Asia dating from the 1790s. For documents relating to Ceylon, see also 4.5.

58 Papers collected by Wiselius concerning the possessions and colonies in the East and West Indies, including documents regarding Surat, Bengal and coinage on the Fishery Coast, 1793. One volume.

1.5.27. *Radermacher*

Access no.: 1.10.69
Inv. nos: 1-638
Size: 6.5 metres
Period: 1601-1800
Inventory: in typescript with introduction

Family papers, donated to the ARA by the heirs in 1872. Of main interest are the papers belonging to Samuel Radermacher, director in the Zeeland Chamber of the VOC between 1730 and 61, and to Daniël Radermacher, succeeding his father as director in the Zeeland Chamber. The archives include many papers concerning the VOC management in the Netherlands (see below) and a large collection of papers from Asia arranged by region (see 2.5, 3.5, 4.5, 5.5 and 6.5).

38 Repertoria to the *resoluties* of the Gentlemen XVII, 1602-1760, some with indices. Five folders.

49-57 Notes made by the Radermachers at the *Haags Besogne* sessions and other papers relating to the *Haags Besogne*, 1697-1794. Three folders and two pieces.

455-67 Papers concerning monetary values and coinage in Asia, 1726-85, and a seventeenth-century manual on weights, measures and coin values. Nine pieces, two folders and two volumes.

485 Papers concerning the military activities of R. Siersma in South Asia, 1736-42. One folder.

1.5.28. *Falck*

Access no.: 2.21.006.48
Inv. nos: 1-133
Size: 3.3 metres
Period: 1737-1850
Inventory: in *VROA* 36 (1913), pp. 187-202, with introduction; copy available at the ARA with partly new inv. nos added in manuscript

Family papers. Of interest are the papers relating to Otto Willem Falck and Iman Willem Falck. The former was a servant of the VOC between 1756 and 1775. He functioned as *Fiscaal* and chief in Chinsura and Hooghly, and as *Opperhoofd* at Patna from 1768 onward. He became one of the Gentlemen XVII in 1786. His cousin or uncle Iman Willem Falck was born at Colombo in 1736. After a stay in the Dutch Republic he returned to the East Indies in 1757. From 1765 until his death in 1785 he was Governor of Ceylon. For papers relating to Surat, Ceylon and Bengal, see 2.5, 4.5 and 6.5.

1.5.29. *W.A. Alting (1724-1800)*

Access no.: 1.10.03
Inv. nos: 1-105
Size: *c.* 3 metres
Period: 1596-1800
Inventory: in the inventories of the Van Alphen collection in *VROA* 23 (1900), pp. 29-37, and of the Engelhard collection in *VROA* (1916) I, pp. 501-2; copy available at the ARA with partly new inv. nos added in manuscript

Willem Arnold Alting served the VOC in Batavia from 1750 onward, from 1780 to 1796 as Governor-General. His papers came into possession of N. Engelhard, whose personal archives have come down to the ARA in two phases; the first part through the widow of F.E.M. van Alphen and the other part some 15 years later though J.C. Baud. The papers originally belonging to Alting have of late been sequestered from the Van Alphen / Engelhard collection and made into a separate collection.

Although Alting never served in the subcontinent, quite a few papers in this collection relate directly to South Asia (see 2.6, 3.6, 4.6, 5.6 and 6.6). The collection also contains many volumes of extracts of and tables to the correspondence and *resoluties* of the GG&C, the most useful of which have been listed below, together with some other pieces relevant to South Asia in general.

1 List of contracts (*farmans*, *cauls*, etc.) concluded with Asian rulers, etc., 1596-1758, ordered by region, with numbers referring to a series of *verbalen*, probably the contract books that are now in the archives in Jakarta (see 1.1.8). One volume.

2 Contains various instructions and letters, 1610-1791, including a draft for a memorandum on a direct shipping link to South Asia from Patria (see above *Hoge Regering Batavia*, inv. nos 25-6) and a copy of Kraane's memorandum on the *Amfioen Sociëteit* (see above *Hoge Regering Batavia*, inv. no. 39). One volume.

4-5 Extracts of the letters of the Gentlemen XVII to the GG&C, 1613-1766. Organized under different headings, including the South Asian regions in chapters 11 and 12. Two volumes.

8 List of *memories van overgave*, etc., 1620-1750, ordered by region. One volume.

20 Letters of H.A. van Rheede from Hooghly, Nagappattinam, Pulicat, Jaffna and Cochin to various persons, 1686-91, letters of Governor-General Camphuys with appendices received by Van Rheede over the same period. One volume.

60 Various memoranda, etc., relating to a revaluation, or a different method of establishing the intrinsic value of the Dutch florin relative to the currencies in Asia, as decreed by the GG&C in 1767, with many lists of relative values and a detailed discussion of the different coins in the subcontinent, 1766-9. One volume.

1.5.30. *P.A. Brugmans (1769-1851)*

Access no.: 1.10.13
Inv. nos: 1-176
Size: 1.5 metres
Period: 1613-1870
Inventory: in J. de Hullu, *Stukken, voor het meerendeel afkomstig van Mr. P.A. Brugmans en Mr. A. Brugmans* (The Hague, 1920), with introduction

P.A. Brugmans functioned as second Advocate to the VOC from 1793 till 1796. The collection also contains papers originating from his son A. Brugmans, and from various people connected to the VOC in Asia. Some papers relate to southern Coromandel and Ceylon (see 4.5 and 5.5).

1.5.31. *Besier*

Access no.: 2.21.021
Inv. nos: 167-270
Size: 0.3 metre
Period: 1601-1800
Inventory: in typescript with introduction

Family papers. Of interest is one document relating to A.G. Besier (1758-1829) who held several political positions, usually concerning naval and colonial matters. In his capacity as member of the *Staatsbewind*, section Navy and Colonies, between 1801 and 1805, he acquired one letter relating to South Asia.

205 Three letters from Jacob Kal at Delfshaven, including one concerning the value of the factories in Surat, Cochin and Pulicat (and Melaka), 1802. One folder.

1.5.32. *C.A. and C.H. Ver Huell*

Access no.: 2.21.004.04
Inv. nos: 1-493
Size: 5.8 metres
Period: 1779-1835
Inventory: in *IRAA* IV (1931), pp. 94-134, with introduction and detailed list of contents

Christiaan Anthonie Ver Huell (1760-1832) functioned between 1788 and 1793 as member of the Military Commission to the East Indies, which had to inspect the defence of the Dutch settlements in South Asia and the rest of the Indies (see also *Stadhouderlijke Secretarie* under 2.4, 3.4, 4.4 and 5.4). From 1802 to 1805 he served as a member of the Commission for East Indian Affairs, an advisory body with regard to the future trade and government of the East Indies. His brother Carel Hendrik Ver Huell (1764-1845) was Minister of Naval Affairs between 1805 and 1807. In their official positions both brothers collected a number of documents relating to South Asia. For papers concerning the defence of VOC settlements in Malabar, Ceylon and Coromandel, see 3.5, 4.5 and 5.5.

46 Agreement between the British King and the French King concerning the interpretation of Article 13 of the peace treaty concluded on 3 September 1783 at Versailles, 1787. One piece, in French.

207 Short survey of the Dutch settlements in the East Indies before and after 1780 by S.C. Nederburgh (see 1.5.33), 1806. One piece, in French.

1.5.33. *Nederburgh*

Access no.: 1.10.59
Inv. nos: 1-1619
Size: *c.* 14 metres
Period: 1431-1965
Inventory: in typescript in two parts, with two indices and with genealogies

Family papers, the greater part belonging to S.C. Nederburgh (1762-1811), who served as Advocate in the Committee of the Amsterdam Chamber for the sale of the VOC possessions on the Malabar Coast during the years 1790 to 1792, after which he was sent to the Cape and Batavia as Commissioner General (see 1.4.5 and 1.4.7). Other members of the family however served in Asia as well, mainly in the Archipelago. Much material concerning the turn of the nineteenth-century vicissitudes befalling the Dutch in South Asia can be found in the correspondence with people in the region from this collection (see also 2.5, 3.5, 4.5, 5.5 and 6.5).

104 Extracts from *resoluties* of the GG&C with notes by S.C. Nederburgh on the VOC establishments in South Asia and other regions, 1785-7. One folder.

139 Letter of H. van Stralen to S.C. Nederburgh suggesting him to withhold from the State Commission the papers concerning the sale of the Malabar establishments and the true financial situation of Ceylon, 1791. One piece.

878 Contains a description of the method of production of 'cayer' (?) ropes and fuses in Ceylon, and of the treatment and reproduction of 'sappers' (?) from Coromandel, 1784. Also some extracts from letters of the *Dissave* of 'Tangule' Van Belm and *Dissave* Van Schuler, Ceylon, 1795 and n.d.

1055 Letters, receipts, bills of exchange concerning the private trade S.C. Nederburgh was conducting from Batavia through I. Titsingh and C. Citters in Bengal, through P.H. Meppen in Pulicat and Madras, and through F.Th. Lichtenstein in Tranquebar, 1794-6. One bundle, some pieces in French, and German.

1.5.34. *W. and G.K. van Hogendorp*

Access no.: 2.21.006.49
Inv. nos: 1-205
Size: 25 metres
Period: 1766-1856
Inventory: in *VROA* 36 (1913), pp. 225-69, with supplement

Of interest are the papers relating to Gijsbert Karel van Hogendorp (1762-1834, brother of D. van Hogendorp, see 1.5.35) who held several high positions in the Netherlands. He never stayed in South Asia (or anywhere else in the East Indies) yet collected a few documents relating to the region.

42 Miscellaneous papers, including memorandum by Dirk van Hogendorp concerning the East Indies with sections on Surat, Malabar, Ceylon, Coromandel and Bengal, 1814. One bundle.

145 Papers concerning the East Indies and the sale of the VOC, including an essay on the government of the British East Indies with sections on South Asia (to be found in the folders labelled 'Inleiding' and 'Henchman'), *c.* 1800. One bundle.

1.5.35. *W. and D. van Hogendorp*

Access no.: 2.21.008.69
Inv. nos: 1-272
Size: 3.6 metres

Period: 1760-1891
Inventory: in *VROA* 45 (1922) I, pp. 177-214; with supplement in *VROA* (1927) I, pp. 117-23

Of interest are the papers relating to Dirk van Hogendorp (1761-1822, brother of G.K. van Hogendorp, see 1.5.34) who functioned at Patna in Bengal between approximately 1786 and 1789, before he was stationed in Java. He returned to the Netherlands around January 1799 and made a stopover in Bombay where he came into contact with the British Governor. In 1802 he was member of the *Commissie tot de Oostindische Zaken* (Commission for East Indian Affairs). The archives include a few documents regarding South Asia that he collected in his various functions, as well as his memoirs, which partially relate to his sojourns in South Asia. For documents concerning Surat and Bengal, see also 2.5 and 6.5.

22 Report by former Commissioner General S.C. Nederburgh (see 1.5.33) to the *Raad der Aziatische Bezittingen en Etablissementen* concerning the government and trade of the East Indies; the first part include sections on north India and its history, 1802. One folder.
42 Memoirs of Dirk van Hogendorp, including his years at Patna, *c.* 1820. One folder. Published in *Memoires du Général Dirk van Hogendorp* (see Bibliography, no. 30).
44 Record of service of Dirk van Hogendorp and notes of facts and dates from his life until 1814, compiled by himself, including his years at Patna, n.d. (possibly *c.* 1814). Two pieces.

1.5.36. *H.J. van de Graaff (and J.G. van Angelbeek)*

Access no.: 2.21.074
Inv. nos: 1-63
Size: 0.8 metre
Period: 1491-1828
Inventory: in typescript, with introduction and genealogy

Family papers, donated to the ARA by the heirs in 1924. Of interest are the papers relating to Hendrik Johan van de Graaff (1782-1827) and his maternal grandfather Johan Gerard van Angelbeek (1727-99). Van de Graaff went to the East Indies in 1816 where he held several positions, including Senior Inspector of Finance and member of the East Indies Council between 1820 and 1826. He drowned on his way to the Netherlands as he was summoned home to account for his policies. His papers were washed ashore and suffered considerable water damage. Van Angelbeek served in Bengal between 1761 and 1763, and at Colombo until 1766. He became *Opperhoofd* at Tuticorin in 1767, functioned as *Commandeur* of Malabar between 1780 and 1793, and succeeded his son-in-law Willem Jacob van de Graaff (father of Hendrik Johan) as Governor of Ceylon in 1794. He was the last to hold this office, until 1796. The archives include a few documents regarding Ceylon and Coromandel (see 4.5 and 5.5).

1.5.37. *Moens*

Access no: 1.10.100
Inv. nos: 1-39
Size: 0.23 metre
Period: 1751-1887
Inventory: in typescript with genealogical notes

Family papers. Of interest are the papers relating to Adriaan Moens (1728-92). He served at Colombo and Trincomalee from 1755 to 1770 and was Governor of Malabar between 1770 and 1780. Until his death he held several posts at Batavia including *Directeur-Generaal* and Director of the *Amfioen Sociëteit*. A number of papers concern Malabar and Ceylon (see also 3.5 and 4.5).

16 List of events in history of the Moens family, kept by Adriaan Moens, two copies, 1697-1789. Two pieces.
19 Biography of Adriaan Moens, drawn up by his son Pieter Jozias, with a copy and accompanying letter, 1837. Three pieces.
20 Essay by H.M.C. van Oosterzee on Adriaan Moens, two printed copies, probably offprints from the *Zeeuwsche Volks-Almanak*, nineteenth century (?). One folder.
21 Letters of Jan Isebree Moens to H.C.M. (*sic*) van Oosterzee concerning the biography of his grandfather Adriaan Moens, 1859. One folder.

1.6. Separate Acquisitions and Microfilms

1.6.1. *Losse aanwinsten*
Separate acquisitions

Access no.: 1.11.01.01
Inv. nos: 1-2152
Size: 45 metres
Period: up to 1800
Inventory: in typescript, with introduction and index

This collection contains separately acquired pieces that have not (yet) been relocated to any of the more substantial archives of the ARA. The items are arranged according to the year of acquisition but have recently been given sequential inv. nos. The old numbers based on the year of acquisition are mentioned between brackets. There are some similar, left-over collections (access nos 1.11.02-1.11.04) but these do not contain any material on South Asia.

72 Survey of coins, weights and measures used in Asia, especially South Asia, ordered by region, *c.* 1675. One volume (1859 A I h).
115 Contains journals of VOC ships sailing from or along several places on the South Asian coast, 1677-81. One volume (1866 A VI c).
119 Descriptions of Asian countries, etc., e.g. the Great Mughal, Surat, Gujarat, Malabar, and ship's logs, letters and instructions concerning trade and

shipping of the VOC, 1617-36. One volume (1866 A XII). See also *KHGU*, 8-10 (1852-4).

150 Descriptions of Asian plants and naturalia with pictures. Volume two also contains a Dutch translation of a Bengali text on Hindu holidays in Bengal and various notes consisting of one or two pages on: the numerical figures used by Banias, cremation and *sati* in 'the Kingdom of Carnatika' (Chandragiri?) and Bengal; Hindu priests in Coromandel (pilgrimages to Kanchipuram and Tirupati); the way oxen are bred in Bengal and Surat and elephants caught in Ceylon; pearls, bezoar stones (and a formula for its imitation Petera Cordial), diamonds (mines in Golkonda). Closed *c.* 1710. Two volumes, greater part in German (1872 A XVIII A).

151 Extracts by P.A.S. van Limburg-Brouwer taken from the letters of Coromandel (1613-29), Ceylon (1612-17), Surat (1615-29), Arabia (1614-29) and Persia (1623-9) as well as from the general correspondence regarding these factories (1612-55), c. 1860. One bundle.

172 Compendium of very brief summaries of contracts (*farmans*, *cauls* etc.) concluded with rulers in the East Indies, 1596-1610, 1688-91. Two quires.

621 Contains an extract from the daily record of the embassy of J.J. Ketelaar to the Great Mughal (1710s) with a description of the throne at the palace in Delhi, by E.C. Graeff (first clerk to the embassy), and an account of a home voyage from Bengal, consisting mostly of abstracts of letters, 1759-61. Two pieces (1893 20 k). For the published version by J.Ph. Vogel and a partial translation by D. Kuenen-Wicksteed, see Bibliography, no. 328.

628 Considerations about the possibility of opening up Batavia to shipping and trade of Muslims, Banias and others, 1705. One piece (1893 29d).

639 Appears to be a general ledger of Batavia over 1658. With index, one volume (1893 29 p).

675 Letter of Ph. Baldaeus with a request to J. van Vollenhoven to write a rhymed introduction to his *Nauwkeurige beschrijving* (see Bibliography, no. 2). One piece (1894 34z).

737 Overview of the different trading places in Asia and the goods to be bought or sold in each of these, compiled c. 1700. One piece (1896 CI).

838 Correspondence of J.W. Falck, based at Surat, with persons in Batavia, Bengal, Cochin and Ahmadabad, concerning private affairs, 1753-61 (1900 XXIX 02).

959 Journal of surgeon G. Heeck kept on different ships during his third voyage to and in the East Indies, 1654-6, with descriptions of temples and statues in India and Ceylon (1903 XV). For an abridged edition by S.P. l'Honoré Naber, see *Marineblad* (1910-11).

1553 Contains a copy of the instruction to H.A. van Rheede, Commissioner to Bengal, Coromandel, Ceylon, etc., 1684. Part of a volume (1930 I 01).

1649 Label of the box that contained H. de Jager's descriptions of plants (now missing) received from Batavia in 1694. One parchment (1934 IX).

1660 Journal of the voyage of J. Gunnaeus as ambassador to Persia and Commissioner to Surat, Ceylon, Coromandel, etc., 1651-2 (1935 III 02).

1824 Invoice for the Zeeland Chamber of calicoes and silks received from Ceylon and Bengal, 1738. One piece, printed (1953 II).

1914 Price-lists of auctions by the Zeeland, Rotterdam, Hoorn and Enkhuizen Chambers of merchandise from Asia, 1765-9 (X 13b-d).

1970 'Dutch treaties in the East'. This is a discourse on early Dutch expansion in Asia and a survey of treaties and contracts concluded with Asian rulers, 1595-6, compiled shortly after 1800, the first volume is signed J. Mc Quoid. Three volumes, in English (1968 III 1-3).

2121 Papers belonging to W. Geleynsen the Jongh (see 1.5.2). Including an order of rarities and decorative objects from the Mughal Empire by Amsterdam-based J. van Wickevoort (1634) and navigational instructions for the stretch from Galle to Nagappattinam to Masulipatam (*c.* 1621). One bundle.

For documents concerning Surat, Malabar, Ceylon, Coromandel and Bengal, see 2.6, 3.6, 4.6, 5.6 and 6.6. For maps and drawings in this collection, see 1.7.10, 3.7 and 4.7.

1.6.2. *Microfilms of external archival material*

Access no.: 1.11.06.01 to 1.11.06.07
Inventories: in typescript

Apart from the microfilms of some of its own collections (e.g. part of the *OBP*), the ARA possesses microfilms of material from other collections. Important papers include: Marcellus Bles (*c.* 1690-1760: film no. 1.1.1342, inventory in *IRAA* (1971), pp. 61-2) in a private collection at The Hague (see 3.6 and 4.6) and some papers from the Mossel family collection at Renswoude concerning the so-called *Amfioen Sociëteit* which had the exclusive right to sell the opium procured by the Company in Bengal (see 6.6). In addition, there are microfilms of the *dagregisters* of Batavia for the period 1683-1807 (access no. 1.11.06.01) and the appendices to the *resoluties* of the GG&C for the period 1738-43 (access no. 1.11.06.07) from the Indonesian National Archives, as well as microfilms of documents of the Dutch Reformed Church in Ceylon, the so-called Wolvendaal Church Archives at Colombo (access no. 1.11.06.02).

1.7. Maps and Drawings

The maps and drawings kept at the ARA have mostly been separated from the archives they originally belonged to and made into specific collections. There is no separate collection of VOC maps since most of these were transferred to the 'VEL', 'VELH' and 'MCAL' collections (and possibly others) and merged with maps of a different background. For a survey of maps in the ARA pertaining to Ceylon, see also Paranavitana, *An Inventory of Sri Lanka Maps* (see Bibliography, no. 632).

Note that apart from maps that relate to more than one region, regional maps are also listed here in case they are an integral part of a separate, original collection such as that of Vingboons (1.7.2: 619) or D'Après de Mannevilette (1.7.4: 6549, 6550).

1.7.1. *Verzameling buitenlandse kaarten, Leupe (VEL)*
Foreign map collection, Leupe

Access no.: 4.VEL
Inv. nos: A-BB, 1-2175 (2831 items)
Period: 16th-19th centuries
Inventory: P.A. Leupe, *Inventaris der verzameling kaarten berustende in het Rijksarchief*, volume 1 (The Hague, 1867); geographically arranged (inconsistent), with introduction

This collection consists of maps and drawings that mostly originate from the secretarial offices of the Amsterdam and Zeeland Chambers of the VOC and the WIC (West India Company). Some maps and drawings originate from other authorities, for instance the *Staten-Generaal* (States General), the *Staten van Holland* (States of Holland), the Society of Surinam and the Secretariat of Berbice. The inventory was compiled by Leupe, a former major of the Marine Corps. The collection includes a great number of maps on South Asia. It also contains maps originating from the 'Atlas Amsterdam' or 'Atlas de Graaff' (*c*. 1695), a mapbook compiled by Isaac de Graaff who was chief cartographer of the VOC between 1705 and 1743. The entire collection has been put on microfiche. For maps and drawings concerning one single region, see also 2.7, 3.7, 4.7, 5.7 and 6.7.

223 Map of the Kanara and the Deccan coasts, between Surat and the river Pen. Including nautical information about the ships Wijk op Zee and De Soldaat, seventeenth century (?).

226 Map of the area between Gujarat, Konkan, Bijapur and Dabhol. Map of the area between Gujarat, Konkan, Bijapur and Cranganur on the Malabar Coast, by R. Pilatus, seventeenth century (?). Originating from the 'Atlas Amsterdam' or 'Atlas de Graaff'.

227 Map of the Deccan coast, between Suvali and Rajapur. Map of Malabar Coast, between Rajapur and Cape Comorin and the islands off this Coast. With descriptions concerning the landfall on the Maleke island, eighteenth century (?). Probably published by Van Keulen.

231 Map of Kanara and Malabar, between Honavar and Cape Comorin and a part of the coasts of Coromandel and Ceylon. Originating from the 'Atlas Amsterdam' or 'Atlas de Graaff'.

234 Map of the Maldives, the coasts of Malabar, Madurai and Ceylon. Two pages, copperplate print. With legend.

250 Map of the coasts of Madurai and Coromandel, between Teganapatam and 'Naticoelanar', and a part of the west coast of Ceylon, seventeenth century. With notes. Originating from the 'Atlas Amsterdam' or 'Atlas de Graaff'.

252 Map of the Coromandel Coast, between Manapadu and Nagappattinam. Map of the west coast of Ceylon, between Colombo and Jaffna. Map of the coast near Kayalpatnam and Punneikayal. Map of Kalpitiya. Probably seventeenth century. Originating from the 'Atlas Amsterdam' or 'Atlas de Graaff'.

254 Map of the Coromandel Coast, between Tondi and 'Punt Godde Warre' (Point Calimere?). Map of the coast of Orissa.

255 Map of the Coromandel Coast, between Nagappattinam and Narasapur. Map of the coast of Orissa and a part of Bengal, between Narasapur and Pipli, seventeenth century. Originating from the 'Atlas Amsterdam' or 'Atlas de Graaff'

860 Map of the Indian Ocean and adjacent countries, by Nicolaus Blancardus, seventeenth century (?).

861 Map of India, Ceylon and the Southeast Asian Archipelago, published by Gerard van Keulen. Coloured.

862 Map of India and Ceylon, by Thomas Jeffreys, 1768. Very detailed. Coloured.

881 Map of the Malabar and Coromandel Coasts, according to de L'Isle and Bruzen La Martinière. Copperplate print.

923 Map of Ceylon, a part of the Malabar and Coromandel Coasts including Madurai and 'Inchiado' (coast between the Pamban Channel and Point Calimere), by engineer J.C. Toorzee, seventeenth century. Detailed map, with notes.

924 Map of Ceylon, a small part of the coasts of Malabar, Madurai and Coromandel, seventeenth century. Originating from the 'Atlas Amsterdam' or 'Atlas de Graaff'.

925 Map of the fortifications of Malabar, Madurai and Coromandel near the coast, seventeenth century. With notes and an indication of the depths near the coast.

1100 Map of Bengal, Bihar, Awadh and Allahabad, with a part of Delhi and Agra exhibiting the course of the Ganges, between Hardwar and the sea, by William Faden, geographer to the King, 1786.

1.7.2. *Verzameling buitenlandse kaarten, supplement, Leupe-l'Honoré Naber (VELH)*

Foreign map collection, supplement, Leupe-l'Honoré Naber

Access no.: 4.VELH
Inv. nos: 844 items
Period: 16th-19th centuries
Inventory: S.P. l'Honoré Naber, *Inventaris der verzameling kaarten berustende in het Rijksarchief*, First Supplement (The Hague, 1914); geographically arranged (inconsistent), with introduction and indices on personal and geographical names

This collection consists of foreign maps and charts that were acquired by the ARA in the years 1867-1886. Some maps that were overlooked during the compilation of the inventory of the *Verzameling buitenlandse kaarten, Leupe* (*VEL*) (see 1.7.1) were also added to this collection. The initial descriptions, made by A. Telting and J. de Hullu, were revised in 1914 by l'Honoré Naber, former Captain of the Dutch Navy. A supplement to this collection concerns the *Atlas*

Vingboons (see Bibliography, nos 61, 239 and 262). Both the main collection and the supplement include maps and drawings concerning South Asia. For maps and drawings concerning one single region, see also 2.7, 3.7, 4.7, 5.7 and 6.7.

106 Map of the coasts of the Deccan and Malabar, between Surat and Cape Comorin, after 1756. With notes.

107 Map of the coast of Malabar, Surat and Cape Comorin. Coloured drawing on parchment, seventeenth century.

110 Map of the Malabar Coast, between 'Rio Calcoulanghe' (Kayankulam) and Cape Comorin, 1667 (?). To be found in the journal of Michiel Gerritsz. Boos.

113 Map of the south coast of Malabar, Madurai and Coromandel in the East Indian Sea, from Cape Comorin to Nagappattinam. Probably eighteenth century. With detailed descriptions of the situation of factories on the southern coast of India and the northern coast of Ceylon.

114 Map of the southern corner of India, with Ceylon and the Adam's Bridge, eighteenth century (?).

115 Map of the east coast of India (Coromandel), from Palmyras Point to the area south of Nagappattinam, eighteenth century (?). Map of India, Ceylon, the Maldives and the Southeast Asian Archipelago, by Nicolaum Visscher.

153 Part of the Indian Ocean and South India, including Ceylon and the Maldives, 1778. With annotations. Copperplate print.

156 *Ligtende zeefakkel off de geheele Oost-indische Waterweereldt*, volume 2, by G.D. Haan, 1761 (i.e. nautical atlas of East Indian waters). Including various maps of Bengal, Coromandel Coast, Ceylon, Malabar, the Bengal River, the Maldives, the Bay of Galle, Malabar and the roadstead of Surat, the mud bay of Cranganur, roadstead Chetwai and Bombay.

321 Sketch map of South Asia, early seventeenth century. Originating from 'Annotatien van Buchelius' (?).

322 Map of Hindustan, 1782. Copperplate print.

619 *Verzameling van paskaarten dienende tot de vaart naar Oost- en West-Indien*, by Johannes Vingboons, *c.* 1660 (i.e. collection of compass maps, designed for the voyages to the East and West Indies). Including:

- 7 Malabar Coast between Cochin and Cape Comorin.
- 11 Surat River.
- 25 The fort of Batticaloa on Ceylon.
- 33 View of the English factory in Bombay, seen from the sea and from the land.
- 41 View of Cannanore.
- 47 Detailed plan of Cochin, bird's-eye view.
- 48 Detailed plan of Cochin.
- 49 View of Dabhol, seen from the sea.
- 50 Close view of Dabhol.
- 53 Map of Goa and the surrounding area.
- 56 Bird's-eye view of Negombo.

61 Plan of Jaffna.
90 View of Galle, seen from the sea.
95 View of Raybag.
104 View of the castle and the royal palace of Bijapur.
105 View of Bijapur on the side of the river Mandora.

1.7.3. *Departement van Marine, centraal archief, Leupe (MCAL)*
Ministry of Naval Affairs, central archives, Leupe

Access no.: 4.MCAL
Inv. nos: Inv. nos 1-6216 (*c.* 6500 items).
Period: 17th-19th centuries
Inventory: *Catalogus der verzameling van kaarten van het ministerie van Marine* (The Hague, 1872), with handwritten supplement; geographically arranged (inconsistent), with introduction and index (1979, in typescript) on personal names

This collection consists mainly of nautical charts, originating from the *Departement van Marine* (1813-72). The inventory was revised by Leupe (see 1.7.1). The collection includes many charts concerning South Asia dating from after 1825 which have not been listed here. For maps and drawings concerning one single region, see also 2.7, 3.7, 4.7, 5.7 and 6.7.

65 East India pilot of general and particular charts, on the largest scale ever published, including Bombay, Madras and Bengal, by Black, Kingsbury, Parbury and Allen, 1819.
4197 Map of Kanara Coast, Konkan, Malabar, Coromandel, Madurai and Ceylon, by Hadriano Relando. Coloured.
4220 Chart of a part of the coasts of India and Gujarat, by John Mc Cluer, 1789. With continuation of the chart to Zyghur. Copperplate print.
4229 Plan of Chaul on the Malabar Coast with 'Drake's Track', and plan of Surat River, by J. Russel, 1750.
4230 Plan of the river 'Nunsaree', by John Ringrose, 1784. With sail instructions. Copperplate print.
4231 Plan of the river 'Gundivee', by John Ringrose, 1783. Copperplate print.
4233 Plan of 'Demaon' (Daman?), surveyed by John Mc Cluer, 1788. Copperplate print.
4234 Plan of the river Dhanu, by John Ringrose, 1787. With sail instructions.
4235 Plan of the river Agashi, and plan of the island 'Arnol' on double the other scale, by John Ringrose, 1784. With a view of 'Arnol'.
4236 Plan of the river 'Manhora' on the island Salsette, by Archibald Blair, 1777.
4237 Plan of 'Vassava', by Lieutenant Edward Harvey, 1777.
4238 Plan of 'Mayham', surveyed by Lieutenant Edward Harvey, 1777. With landfall.
4257 Plan of 'Underoot Island' with 'Pattimar's Track' by John Mc Cluer, 1790.

4260 Map of Ceylon, Malabar Coast and the Maldives, 1773. With VOC trademark.
4264 Chart of the north end of Ceylon, by P. Heywood, 1802. Includes Nagappattinam Road, by George Shortland, 1803. With instruction.
4286 Map of the Bay of Bengal and the Andaman Islands, by Lieutenant Blair and Captain Moorsom, 1789-90.
5946 Map of the peninsula of India, from the river Krishna to Cape Comorin, from the latest authorities, exhibiting its political division, according to the partition treaty made at Srirangapatnam, by J. Rennell, 1792.

1.7.4. *Ministerie van Koloniën (MIKO)*
Ministry of Colonial Affairs

Access no.: 4.MIKO
Inv. nos: *c.* 3000 items
Period: 18th-20th centuries
Inventory: K. Zandvliet, G.L. Balk and F.E.Ch. Hoste, *Inventaris van de kaarten en tekeningen van het Ministerie van Koloniën (1702) 1814-1963* (The Hague, 1993); geographically arranged (inconsistent), with introduction and indices on personal names and institutions

This collection consists of maps and drawings that originate from the *Ministerie van Koloniën* (1813-1950) (see also 1.4.10) and four private collections, deposited by Loten, Engelhard, Busscher and Henrici. The collection includes some maps with respect to South Asia, most of them depicting locations in Ceylon and the Fishery Coast. It also contains a significant number of maps relating to South Asia that were produced after 1825 (not included in this guide). Virtually the entire collection has been put on microfiche. A concordance between inv. nos and microfiche nos is available. For maps and drawings concerning Ceylon, see also 4.7.

720 Map of Dutch property overseas, by A. Koot, early nineteenth century.
776 Map of Dutch property overseas, by Lastdrager, supervised by W.A. Elberts, early nineteenth century. Litho.
6549 Supplement to *Neptune Oriental*. Compilation of the work of J.B.N.D. D'Après de Mannevillette, 1781. Including:
- 29.3 Port of Bombay.
- 32 Coromandel Coast, Golkonda, Orissa and Bengal.
- 32.2d Map of the Bay of Bengal.

6550 *The complete East-India Pilot or Oriental Navigator* ... by experienced officers of the East-India Company and from the *Neptune Oriental*. Compilation of the work of J.B.N.D. D'Après de Mannevillette. Revised edition, *c.* 1800. Including:
- 42 Islands, rocks, and shoals in the Indian Ocean.
- 43 'Track of the Calcutta'.
- 46 The northern part of the Indian Ocean.

47	The coast of India.
50	Appearances of Aguada fort.
51	The coast of India, Ceylon.
52	Palk Straits and Bay.
53	Kalpitiya 'Road' and the east coast of Ceylon.
54	The harbour of Colombo.
55	Galle, and bay of Nilwala.
56	Trincomalee and Vandeloos Bay.
57	The bay and harbour of Trincomalee.
58	The Oriental seas and islands.
59	The Bay of Bengal.
60	The coast of India.
61	The road of Pulicat, and Fort St. David.
62	The coast of India.
63	The Northern Circars.
64	The bay of Coringa.
65	The northern part of the Bay of Bengal.
66	The mouths of the river Hooghly.
68	The Andaman and Nicobar Islands.
95	The coast of India.

W23 Map of Ceylon, south coast of India (Malabar and Coromandel) and the Maldives, *c.* 1752-7. Scale 1:360,000 (microfiche no. 108).

W37 Map of south coast of India, between Goa and the 'Samgam River' (Penner?) on the Coromandel Coast. Drawn by land surveyor Pieter de Bevere, *c.* 1752-7 (microfiche no. 110).

1.7.5. *Ministerie van Oorlog, buitenlandse plans van vestingen (OBPV)*
Ministry of War, foreign plans of fortifications

Access no.:	4.OBPV
Inv. nos:	708 items
Period:	17th-19th centuries
Inventory:	copied from typescript index cards, geographically arranged (inconsistent)

This collection consists of maps and drawings of fortifications abroad; the South Asian ones relate only to Ceylon (see 4.7).

1.7.6. *Topografische Dienst en rechtsvoorgangers (TOPO)*
Topographic Service and legal predecessors

Access no.:	4.TOPO
Inv. nos:	8439 items
Period:	18th-20th centuries
Inventory:	in typescript

Of interest are the collection of C.J. van de Graaff, which includes some maps and drawings relating to Ceylon, and a few separate sheets originating from atlases, which concern the Mughal Empire and Tranquebar (see also 4.7 and 5.7).

16A-423 Map of the Mughal Empire, by Matthias Seutteri, n.d.

1.7.7. *Collectie Bergsma (BMF)*
Bergsma collection

Access no.: 4.BMF
Inv. nos: 1-564 (880 items)
Period: 16th-19th centuries
Inventory: in typescript, geographically arranged (inconsistent), with introduction, concordance and indices on personal and geographical names

This collection was compiled by engineer E.H. Bergsma probably between 1830 and 1899. It consists mainly of maps originating from atlases dating from the period 1570-1890. Part of the collection is to be found in various provincial archives in the Netherlands. The collection's foreign maps are kept by the ARA and include South Asia. For maps and drawings concerning one single region, see also 3.7, 4.7, 5.7 and 6.7.

406 Map of South Asia, by Abraham Ortelius, 1597.
407 Map of India beyond the Ganges, Melaka, Siam, Cambodia, Laos, Pegu a.o. Published by Isaak Tirion, third quarter of the eighteenth century.
409 Supplement to the map of India. Page eight of the supplement to a map of India and Ceylon, consisting of eight pages, by A. Arrowsmith, 1816. With inset of Punjab.
410 Bottom half of a survey page of the map of India and Ceylon, by A. Arrowsmith, 1816. Coloured.
411 Two pages of a map of India and Ceylon, consisting of several pages, showing the southern tip of India, by A. Arrowsmith, 1822. Coloured.
412 Page 16 of a map of India and Ceylon, consisting of several pages, the mouth of the river Krishna, by A. Arrowsmith, 1822. Possibly a mackle.
413 *Philip's New Map of India, compiled from the Most Authentic Sources*, by W. Hughes, third quarter of the eighteenth century. Coloured. With inset of the east of the Bay of Bengal.
415 Newly constructed and extended map of India, from the latest surveys, printed for the use of the British army in India, by John Walker, 1825. Coloured.
419 Map of India and Ceylon, by Isaak Tirion, third quarter of the eighteenth century.
420 Map of the south of India and Ceylon, early nineteenth century.
421 Map of Hindustan, by J. Carl Ausfeld, 1805. Coloured.
423 Map of North India, mid-eighteenth century.

424 Map of the Malabar and Coromandel Coasts, by Guillaume Delisle, 1780. Coloured.

425 Map of India, including the area adjacent to the Himalayas, by Major Rennell, 1782. Coloured. With inset of Calcutta.

426 Map of North India, early nineteenth century. With inset of the mouth of the Ganges.

428 Map of North India, by F. de Wit, I. Covens and C. Mortier, 1759.

429 Historical and statistical illustration of countries, rivers, cities and towns on the eastern or Gangetic side and western or Bombay side of India, from original notes commenced in 1809.

1.7.8. *Familie Vosmaer (VMF)*
Vosmaer family

Access no.: 4.VMF
Inv. nos: *c.* 45 items (inv. no. 848 comprises *c.* 50 documents, maps and drawings, foliated consecutively)
Period: 17th-20th centuries
Inventory: in typescript, with introduction; appendix 3 lists some maps concerning South Asia

Of interest are the maps and drawings originating from Jacobus Cornelis Matheus Radermacher (1741-83), who married a stepdaughter of Governor-General Reynier de Klerck and held various posts in the East Indies during the years 1757-63 and 1767-83. During the latter period he was a member of the Council of the Indies among other positions. The collection includes some maps and drawings relating to South Asia, bound in one volume with other documents.

848, f. 3 Plan of the city of Kandy, with legend containing military information and drawings of VOC soldiers and defeated, 'indigenous' enemies, n.d. Scale *c.* 1:6000. Copperplate print.

848, f. 46 Map of the Lakhya and Banar Rivers near Dhaka and the Brahmaputra River up to Guwahati in Assam, with anchorage and landing stages, n.d. Scale *c.* 1:210,000. Coloured.

848, f. 47 Map of northwest Ceylon and the theatre of war on the southeast coast of India, framed with plans of (forts at) Bombay, Trincomalee, Nagappattinam, Tranquebar, Cuddalore, Tiruchirappalli, 'Divicote' (south of Porto Novo), Chidambaram, Pondicherry, Madras, Arcot, Chengalpattu, Karunguli, Poonamallee, Wandiwash, Gingee, Masulipatam, Vishakhapatnam and Calcutta, 1770. Scale: *c.* 1:100,000. Copperplate print.

1.7.9. *Aanwinsten (AANW)*
Acquisitions

Access no.: 4.AANW
Inv. nos: *c.* 4000 items

Period: 17th-19th centuries
Inventory: in typescript, geographically arranged (inconsistent)

This collection consists of separately acquired maps and drawings since 1888, that have not (yet) been relocated to any of the more substantial map collections of the ARA. The items are numbered according to the year of acquisition, but in the revised inventory they are arranged by region. For maps and drawings concerning Ceylon and Coromandel, see also 4.7 and 5.7.

1457 Compass map of the Indian Ocean, between the Cape of Good Hope and Sumatra, by Joan Blaeu. Parchment, 1704.
1421 Map of the Indian Ocean with adjacent countries and a part of the Pacific, drawn by J.D. Barbié du Bocage, 1800.

1.7.10. *Miscellaneous*

Ingekomen stukken van de kantoren in Indië bij de Heren XVII en de Kamer Zeeland (IKI)
Papers received from the establishments in the Indies by the Gentlemen XVII and the Zeeland Chamber

See 1.2.1
Access no.: 1.04.02

VOC 10098 II Maps and drawings relating to the tour of inspection to Cochin, Travancore and the Fishery Coast by Governor Gustaaf Willem van Imhoff of Ceylon, concerning the bay near Vilinjam between Anjengo and Tengapattanam, and on Ceylon the 'Carretchie' area and an elephant corral near the village 'Welancoelam', 1739.

Wolterbeek

See 1.5.19
Access no.: 1.01.47.19

66 Description of seaboards of Ceylon and those of Coromandel up to Bengal, with drawings (after the original) by Dirk Muller, 1780. One volume.

Losse aanwinsten
Separate acquisitions

See 1.6.1
Access no.: 1.11.01.01

150 Contains pictures of Asian plants and naturalia, and three pictures of animals (1872 A XVIII A).
809 Drawings of the coastal stretches, harbours and bays of Ceylon, the west coast of India and the Cape of Good Hope by Captains D. van Schilde en Hoogendorp, 1757. One volume (1899 XXIII 20).

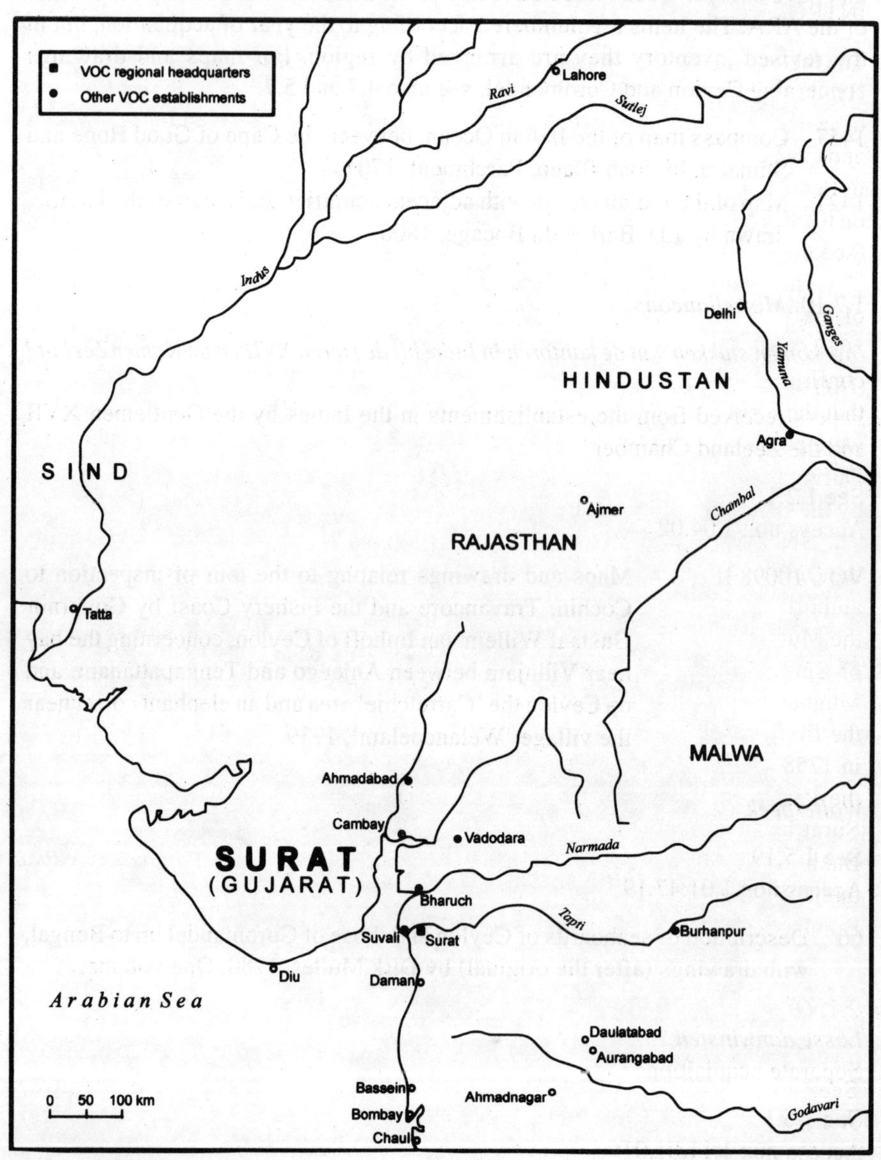

Map 2. The VOC in Surat

2. SURAT (including Sind and Hindustan)

INTRODUCTION

The factory at Surat served as the headquarters for the VOC's activities in Gujarat, Hindustan (mainly Agra), Malwa/Khandesh (mainly Burhanpur) and, occasionally, Sind. From 1620 onward this region was managed by a *Directeur* and Council seated in Surat. Initially, the Surat *Directie* also included Gombroon in Persia and Mocha in Yemen. For a short while, from 1673 to 1676, Vengurla on the Konkan Coast belonged to Surat but was afterwards transferred to Malabar (see the section on Malabar).

The earliest Dutch contacts with Surat date from 1602 following the voyage of the *Vereenigde Zeeuwsche Compagnie* (see 1.4.1). However, it was only in 1617, after obtaining the provisional permission from the Mughal governor to be confirmed by the Mughal Prince Khurram (later to become Emperor Shah Jahan), that the VOC established a permanent base in Surat. Soon after, other factories were raised at Bharuch, Ahmadabad, Vadodara, Cambay, Burhanpur and Agra. During the years 1781-4 and 1795-1818, the VOC settlements were taken over by the British, to be permanently transferred to them in 1825.

Since Surat was only a trading post under unimpaired Mughal sovereignty, the *Directie*'s local contacts were mainly with Mughal officials: the various local authorities in the city of Surat, the *Subahdar* in Ahmadabad and, occasionally, the Mughal Emperor himself. There were also irregular contacts with the rulers of Sind, Rajasthan and Malwa, the latter two regions providing access to the Mughal capitals of Agra and Delhi. While Mughal authority was waning during the first-half of the eighteenth century, the Marathas formally annexed Gujarat in 1758. But some tracts remained beyond the Maratha rule of the Gaikwar and the Peshwa and came under the authority of local Nawabs. As early as 1733, Surat became *de facto* independent under the nominal Mughal Governor Teg Bakht Khan whose family continued to rule Surat, albeit under increasing British tutelage from 1753 onward. In 1800 Surat was formally incorporated into the Bombay presidency, to be followed by the rest of Gujarat in 1817.

2.1. *Overgekomen Brieven en Papieren (OBP)*
Letters and Papers Received

See 1.1.7
Access no.: 1.04.02
Inv. nos: VOC 1053-3987

Letters and papers concerning Surat are mostly listed under headings such as 'Suratte', 'Souratta', etc. These headings occur occasionally in the volumes containing documents sent directly from South Asia to the Gentlemen XVII and the Amsterdam Chamber, but more particularly in the volumes that consist of copies of documents sent from South Asia to Batavia in the *Batavia's ingekomen brievenboek*. In a few cases, letters and papers relating to Surat may also be found under the heading 'Batavia'.

2.1.1. *Memories van overgave* (final reports)

VOC 1215, ff. 598-602	*Directeur* Gerard Pelgrim to Hendrick van Gent, April 1655.
VOC 1245, ff. 698-702	*Directeur* Leonard Winninx to Dirck van Adrichem, May 1662.
VOC 1267-8, ff. 1288-99	Interim *Directeur* Abraham Hartman to Andries Boogaart, April 1668.
VOC 1329, ff. 1468v-74	*Directeur* Willem Volgher to Sijbrant Abbema, February 1677.
VOC 1654, ff. 890-990	*Directeur* Hendrick Zwaerdecroon to Pieter de Vos, April 1702.
VOC 1797, ff. 162-78	*Directeur* Johannes Grotenhuijs to Cornelis Bezuijen, March 1710.
VOC 1885, ff. 86-160	*Directeur* Joan Josua Ketelaer to Daniel Hurgronje, January 1716.
VOC 2842, ff. 465-656	*Directeur* Johannes Pecock (to Johan de Roth), *c.* 1754.
VOC 2994-5, n.f.	*Directeur* Louis Taillefert to Jan Drabbe, *c.* 1760 (to be found at the back of the volume).
VOC 3066, ff. 284-517	*Directeur* Louis Taillefert to Jan Drabbe, March 1760.
VOC 3239, ff. 394-625	*Directeur* Christiaan Lodewijk Senff to Martinus Joan Bosman, December 1768.
VOC 3982, ff. 103-34	*Directeur* Abraham Josias Sluysken to Peter Sluysken, *c.* 1792.

2.1.2. *Resoluties* (proceedings)

VOC 1079, n.f.	1624.
VOC 1083, ff. 132-5	1623.
VOC 1094, ff. 116-17	1628.
VOC 1100, ff. 212-20	1628-30.
VOC 1109, ff. 150-5	1632-3.
VOC 1117, ff. 497-534	*c.* 1635 (among other documents).
VOC 1117, n.f.	1636.
VOC 1119, ff. 1612-31	1636-7 (among other documents).
VOC 1127, ff. 74-5	1638.
VOC 1130, ff. 1244-5	1639.
VOC 1135, ff. 440-2	1640.
VOC 1135, ff. 460, 462	Partly concerning Goa, 1640.
VOC 1135, f. 522	1641.
VOC 1135, ff. 580, 583	1641.

VOC 1203, f. 753	1654.
VOC 1215, ff. 645-56	1655-6.
VOC 1215, ff. 715-26	1655-6.
VOC 1215, f. 779	1655.
VOC 1224, ff. 122-49	1656-7.
VOC 1234, f. 316	Concerning the 'Anachoda' of a vessel of the King, 1660.
VOC 1239, ff. 1317-20	*c*. 1662.
VOC 1261, ff. 757-8	1667.
VOC 1321, ff. 978-80	1675.
VOC 1341, ff. 905-10	1679.
VOC 1349, ff. 1608-10	Concerning financial dealings with one Amin Khan, 1678.
VOC 1351, ff. 2578-9	1679.
VOC 1355, ff. 372-4	1680-1.
VOC 1364, ff. 343-6	1681.
VOC 1379, ff. 2587-8	1682.
VOC 1383, ff. 661-75	1683-4.
VOC 1398, ff. 495-8	1684-5.
VOC 1398, ff. 546-68	1685.
VOC 1398, ff. 571-3	1685.
VOC 1398, ff. 576-82	1685.
VOC 1409, ff. 1642-51	Concerning passes to sail to Malabar granted to some merchants, 1685.
VOC 1409, ff. 1708-12	1685-6.
VOC 1425, ff. 289-319	1686.
VOC 1425, ff. 415-25	1686.
VOC 1434, ff. 370-423	1686-7.
VOC 1448, ff. 408-13	1689.
VOC 1448, ff. 434-?	1689.
VOC 1459, ff. 1072-3	1690.
VOC 1459, ff. 1082-112	1690.
VOC 1475, ff. 295-377v	1689.
VOC 1476, ff. 113-211	1690.
VOC 1479, ff. 222-81	1690 (among other documents).
VOC 1507, ff. 220-47	1692-3.
VOC 1512, ff. 374-428	Principally concerning financial matters, *c*. 1692.
VOC 1529, ff. 88-395	1691-2.
VOC 1548, ff. 145-377	1692-3.
VOC 1549, ff. 282-410	1693-4.
VOC 1614, ff. 1139-40	1700.
VOC 1620, ff. 330-3	1691.
VOC 1620, ff. 426-9	1698.
VOC 1627, ff. 129-30	Concerning copper, 1698.
VOC 1635, ff. 336-71	1700.
VOC 1635, ff. 494-7	1700.
VOC 1635, ff. 988-1009	1700.

VOC 1639, ff. 212-23	1700.
VOC 1652, ff. 1034-8	1702-3.
VOC 1659, ff. 91-477	1700-1.
VOC 1671, ff. 1881-1921	1703-4.
VOC 1685, ff. 2574-81	1704.
VOC 1714, ff. 8-17	1705.
VOC 1714, ff. 20-7	1705.
VOC 1714, ff. 37-40	Concerning the confiscation of Muslim vessels, 1705.
VOC 1719, ff. 2140-2	Concerning negotiations with the local authorities, 1707.
VOC 1719, ff. 2219-35	Concerning negotiations with the local authorities, 1707.
VOC 1746, ff. 66-103	1707.
VOC 1746, ff. 359-?	1706-7.
VOC 1763, ff. 55-77	*c.* 1708.
VOC 1963, ff. 165-8	1721 (among other documents).
VOC 2020, ff. 1180-487	1724-5.
VOC 2038, ff. 1521-614	1725-6.
VOC 2054, ff. 201-13	*c.* 1726.
VOC 2060, ff. 1600-729	1726-7.
VOC 2085, ff. 1934-2054	1727-8.
VOC 2104, ff. 180-1	1728.
VOC 2116, ff. 4720-867	1728-9.
VOC 2151, ff. 7307-461	1729-30.
VOC 2168, ff. 97?-116	1729-30.
VOC 2168, ff. 221-2	1730.
VOC 2168, ff. 245?-9	1730.
VOC 2174, ff. 2429-42	*c.* 1731 (among other documents).
VOC 2202, ff. 134-63	1731.
VOC 2202, ff. 246-7	1731.
VOC 2202, ff. 257-476	1730-1.
VOC 2251, ff. 161-418	1731-2.
VOC 2251, ff. 1154-74	Concerning a Muslim merchant, *c.* 1732.
VOC 2251, ff. 18-33	1732.
VOC 2293, ff. 205-682	1732-3.
VOC 2293, ff. 683-721	In cooperation with the British and the French, concerning the Surat war, 1732-3.
VOC 2293, ff. 1341-50	*c.* 1733 (among other documents).
VOC 2321, ff. 80-440	1733-4.
VOC 2321, ff. 935-8	Concerning illegal trade, 1733.
VOC 2321, ff. 951-76	1733-4.
VOC 2355, ff. 109-402	1734-5.
VOC 2390, ff. 125-600	1735-6.
VOC 2415, ff. 113-356	1736-7.
VOC 2447, ff. 153-604	1737-8.
VOC 2475, ff. 98-500	1738-9.

VOC 2509, ff. 143-746	1739-40.
VOC 2509, ff. 1405-12	1739.
VOC 2509, ff. 24-41	1740.
VOC 2544, ff. 85-568	1741.
VOC 2544, ff. 841-1254	1740-1.
VOC 2545, ff. 2533-7	1741.
VOC 2582, ff. 281-1090	1741-2.
VOC 2582, ff. 1513-81	1741-2 (among other documents).
VOC 2582, ff. 2114-63	*c*. 1742.
VOC 2610, ff. 135-?	1742-3.
VOC 2654, ff. 207-1150	1743-4.
VOC 2679, ff. 157-?	1744-6.
VOC 2704, ff. 181-680	1746-7.
VOC 2747, ff. 167-1318	1747-9.
VOC 2740, ff. 1319-?	1749.
VOC 2786, ff. 9-540	1749-50.
VOC 2786, ff. 595-880	1750.
VOC 2786, ff. 921-1000	1750.
VOC 2786, ff. 1125-322	1750-1.
VOC 2803, ff. 135-508	1751-2.
VOC 2803, ff. 565-?	1752.
VOC 2823, ff. 175-414	1752-3.
VOC 2842, ff. 143-464	1753.
VOC 2842, ff. 739-920	1753-4.
VOC 2863, ff. 55-99	1754.
VOC 2863, ff. 235-86	1754-5.
VOC 2967, n.f.	1758-9 (at three places in the volume).
VOC 2976, ff. 583-86	1758, 1760.
VOC 2997, n.f.	1760.
VOC 3026, n.f.	1760.
VOC 3028, ff. 116-22	1761.
VOC 3028, n.f.	1761.
VOC 3063, n.f.	1761.
VOC 3068, ff. 950-80	Concerning the occupation of the factory at Surat by the Nawab, 1762-3.
VOC 3068, ff. 1130-44	Concerning conflicts with the British, 1763.
VOC 3092, ff. 32-?	1762.
VOC 3092, n.f.	1762.
VOC 3094, 69-?	*c*. 1763.
VOC 3094, ff. 127-36	1763.
VOC 3122, n.f.	1762 (?).
VOC 3154, n.f.	1763.
VOC 3155, n.f.	1763-4.
VOC 3179, ff. 98-256	1766.
VOC 3184, ff. 1-361	1765.
VOC 3238, ff. 217-393	1768.
VOC 3269, n.f.	1769.

VOC 3297, ff. 20-49	1770.
VOC 3298, n.f.	1770.
VOC 3328, 99-?	1771.
VOC 3354, ff. 87?-?	1772.
VOC 3408, ff. 315?-?	1774.
VOC 3409, n.f.	1772-3.
VOC 3438, n.f.	1774-5.
VOC 3446, ff. 402-6	1773.
VOC 3462, ff. 306-471	1775.
VOC 3490, ff. 66-71	1777.
VOC 3490, ff. 74-235	1777.
VOC 3521, ff. 118-78	1777-8.
VOC 3521, ff. 200-1	1778.
VOC 3521, ff. 223-41	1778.
VOC 3549, ff. 36-43	1779.
VOC 3549, ff. 145-301	1778-9.
VOC 3576, ff. 98-300	1779-80.
VOC 3576, ff. 339-40	Concerning the recruitment of Muslim sailors, 1780.
VOC 3594, f. 15	1776.
VOC 3670, ff. 7-32	1784.
VOC 3670, ff. 111-257	1780-1, 1782, 1785.
VOC 3696, ff. 98-100	1785.
VOC 3696, ff. 138-54	1781.
VOC 3697, n.f.	1785.
VOC 3728, n.f.	1785-6.
VOC 3804, ff. 97-9	1787.
VOC 3805, n.f.	1787.
VOC 3854, n.f.	1788-9.
VOC 3899, ff. 113-260	1789-90.
VOC 3933, ff. 67-186	1790-1.
VOC 3983, n.f.	1790-2.

2.1.3. *Dagregisters* (diaries)

VOC 1117, ff. 472-96	November 1634-April 1635.
VOC 1210, ff. 757-88	January-April 1656.
VOC 1383, ff. 617-29	January 1683-January 1684.
VOC 1398, ff. 471-84	May 1684 January 1685.
VOC 1409, ff. 1572-641	February-December 1685.
VOC 1409, ff. 1725-31	December 1685-January 1686.
VOC 1422, ff. 1607-12	Agra, *c.* 1686.
VOC 1422, ff. 1620-5	Agra, *c.* 1686.
VOC 1425, ff. 335-75	February-December 1686.
VOC 1425, ff. 434-5	December 1686-January 1687.
VOC 1434, ff. 455-87	April-November 1687.
VOC 1475, ff. 378-426	April-December 1689.

VOC 1476, ff. 212-69v	April-December 1690.
VOC 1529, ff. 396-577v	December 1691-December 1692.
VOC 1548, ff. 378-593	December 1692-December 1693.
VOC 1549, ff. 414-550	January-November 1694.
VOC 1582, ff. 14-44	January-February 1696.
VOC 1636, ff. 95-421	Kept by the *Fiscaal*, December 1698-January 1700.
VOC 2202, ff. 648-871	January-December 1731 (?).
VOC 2251, ff. 644-983	1731.

2.1.4. *Shipping lists*

VOC 1162, ff. 116-9	Vessels that passed along and departed from Suvali, 1647.
VOC 1166, ff. 797-803	Arrival and departure of English and Muslim vessels, 1647.
VOC 1208, ff. 456-60	Arrival and departure of Muslim, Bania, English and royal vessels, 1654-5.
VOC 1364, f. 350	Departed English and French vessels, *c.* 1681.
VOC 1379, ff. 2555-64	Vessels that arrived at and departed from Surat, 1681-2.
VOC 1383, ff. 630-2	Vessels that arrived at and departed from Surat, 1683-4.
VOC 1388, ff. 2173-5	Arrival and departure of English and indigenous vessels, 1683.
VOC 1416, ff. 1539v-45	Vessels that arrived at and departed from Surat, 1684-5.
VOC 1439, ff. 1551-5	Vessels that arrived at Surat, *c.* 1687.
VOC 1635, f. 816	*c.* 1700.
VOC 1660, ff. 964-6	Mughal and Surat vessels, 1701.
VOC 1660, f. 967	1700.
VOC 1666, ff. 688-96	Muslim and private vessels, 1701.
VOC 1714, ff. 41-3	*c.* 1705 (among other documents).
VOC 1746, ff. 262-80	Arrival of vessels, 1707.
VOC 1763, ff. 117-122	Departed Muslim vessels, *c.* 1708.
VOC 1779, ff. 129-33	Departed Muslim vessels, 1708-9.
VOC 1829, ff. 122-3	Muslim and other vessels that departed from Surat, 1711-12.
VOC 1843, ff. 134-5	Departed Muslim vessels, 1712-13.
VOC 1856, f. 239	Departed vessels, *c.* 1714.
VOC 1963, ff. 400-21	*c.* 1721.
VOC 1963, ff. 159-64	Arrival of foreign vessels, 1720.
VOC 1983, ff. 126-31	Arrival of foreign vessels, 1721.
VOC 1983, ff. 132-40	*c.* 1722.
VOC 1999, ff. 80-5	*c.* 1723.
VOC 2104, ff. 138-44	Arrival of vessels, 1728.
VOC 2137, ff. 209-11	Arrival of vessels, 1729.

VOC 2168, ff. 190-4	Vessels that arrived at Surat, 1729.
VOC 2251, ff. 1121-2	1731.
VOC 2293, ff. 1353-60	1732.
VOC 2321, ff. 783-4	1733.
VOC 2390, ff. 1203-7	Vessels that arrived at Surat, 1735.
VOC 2415, ff. 753-8	Vessels that arrived at Surat, 1736.
VOC 2447, ff. 1097-104	Arrival and departure of vessels, 1737.
VOC 2475, ff. 853-9	Arrival and departure of vessels, 1738.
VOC 2509, ff. 1291-4	Vessels that arrived and departed from Surat, *c.* 1740.
VOC 2545, ff. 1658-62	Vessels that arrived at Surat, *c.* 1741.
VOC 2582, ff. 1582-7	Vessels that arrived at Surat, 1741.
VOC 2885, ff. 96-?	Arrival of foreign European vessels, *c.* 1756.
VOC 2967, ff. 195-200	Arrival and departure of foreign vessels, *c.* 1759.
VOC 3179, ff. 472-4	Vessels that arrived at Bombay, 1766.
VOC 3207, ff. 144-7	Vessels that arrived at Bombay, 1767.
VOC 3354, ff. 84-6	Vessels that arrived at Bombay, *c.* 1772.
VOC 3381, ff. 20-3	Vessels that arrived at Bombay and Surat, *c.* 1773.
VOC 3408, ff. 310-14	Vessels that arrived at Surat, 1774.
VOC 3437, ff. 6-14	Vessels that arrived at Bombay and Surat, *c.* 1775 (among other documents).
VOC 3462, ff. 17-19	Vessels that arrived at Bombay and Surat, 1775-6.
VOC 3490, ff. 38-9	Vessels sailed from Batavia to Surat during the period 1756-75, *c.* 1777.
VOC 3490, ff. 40-1	Vessels that arrived at Bombay and Surat, 1776-7.
VOC 3490, ff. 62-3	Vessels that arrived at Bombay and Surat, 1777.
VOC 3521, ff. 33-6	Vessels that arrived at Bombay and Surat, 1777-8.
VOC 3549, ff. 32-5	Vessels that arrived at Bombay and Surat, 1778-9.
VOC 3576, ff. 341-4	Vessels that arrived at Bombay and Surat, 1779-80.

2.1.5. *Missions to Indian states*

VOC 1168, ff. 626-38	Mission to the Mughal by Joan Tack, June-August 1648 (report).
VOC 1168, ff. 710-20	Mission to the Mughal by Joan Tack, June-August 1648 (report).
VOC 1201, ff. 759-75	Mission to the Mughal by Joan Berckhout and Joan Tack, December 1652-March 1653 (report).
VOC 1210, ff. 1050-2	Mission to the Mughal by Joan Tack, 1656 (report).
VOC 1239, ff. 1258-1316	Mission to the Mughal by Dircq van Adrichem, 1662 (report). See also Bibliography, no. 319.
VOC 1323, ff. 629-31	Mission to the Mughal by Joannes Bacherius, September 1677 (report) (see also under Bengal, 6.1.5).
VOC 1329, ff. 1451-3	Mission to the Mughal by Joannes Bacherius, January 1677 (instructions).

VOC 1475, ff. 145-213 — Mission to the Mughal by Johannes Bacherus, 1689 (correspondence) (see also under Coromandel, 5.1.5).

VOC 1818, ff. 142-55 — Mission to the Mughal by Jan Josua Ketelaer, *c.* 1712 (report). See also Bibliography no. 328.

VOC 1829, ff. 168-231 — Mission to the Mughal by Jan Josua Ketelaer, *c.* 1712 (report).

VOC 1843, ff. 148-204 — Mission to the Mughal by Jan Josua Ketelaer, *c.* 1713 (report).

2.1.6. *Miscellaneous*

VOC 1062, ff. 87-105 — Report of Pieter Gielis van Ravesteijn concerning his journey from Masulipatam to Surat and the trade over there, May 1615-February 1616.

VOC 1113, ff. 247-55 — Report concerning the state of affairs and trade in Hindustan and Gujarat, *c.* 1634.

VOC 1246-8, ff. 745-? — Report concerning the plundering of Surat by Shivaji, January 1664.

VOC 1298, ff. 663-96 — Documents concerning conflicts with Muslims, 1673-4.

VOC 1408, ff. 763-90 — Report of Isaac Solmans concerning his visit to Surat, 1685.

VOC 1409, ff. 1680-700 — Report concerning the temporary occupation of Bharuch by peasants, 1685.

VOC 1495, ff. 57-94v — Trade survey concerning Surat between 1671 and 1687.

VOC 1559, ff. 605v-47v — Documents concerning Jewish traders at Surat, *c.* 1694.

VOC 1625, ff. 163-303 — Report by Commissioner Pieter Ketting concerning his activities in Surat, 1698.

VOC 1625, ff. 63-102 — Report of a journey from Agra to Surat, May-June 1699.

VOC 1639, ff. 178-211 — Documents concerning a visit to 'Anetchan', Governor of Surat, *c.* 1700.

VOC 1671, ff. 2016-100 — Reports concerning Muslim conflicts, 1703-4.

VOC 1682, ff. 919-1279 — Report of a voyage to, and sojourn at Surat by Captain Ad. Palesteijn, September 1703-April 1704.

VOC 1717, ff. 879-1140 — Report of an expedition to Surat in connection with conflicts with the local authorities, August 1705-June 1706.

VOC 1763, ff. 78-92 — Reports concerning developments at the Mughal court, 1707-8.

VOC 1843, ff. 217-382 — Letters, *farmans* etc. received during the mission by Jan Josua Ketelaer to the Mughal, *c.* 1712-13.

VOC 1843, ff. 405-37 — Documents concerning a revolution at the Mughal court, *c.* 1713.

VOC 1856, ff. 71-223	Documents concerning developments at the Mughal court, *c.* 1714.
VOC 1874, ff. 1305-84	Documents concerning the expenses of the mission to the Mughal by Jan Josua Ketelaer, *c.* 1716 (?).
VOC 1897, ff. 66-104	Translation of a *waqia* (news report), Delhi, *c.* 1717.
VOC 1963, ff. 169-72	Document concerning weights, measures and currencies in Surat, *c.* 1721.
VOC 2355, ff. 707-880	Documents concerning the re-establishment of the factory at Ahmadabad, *c.* 1735.
VOC 2475, ff. 860-84	Report concerning the siege of Daman and Bassein by the Marathas, and the conquest of the Mughal Empire by Persia, 1739.
VOC 2707, ff. 92-161	Report by Secretary Senf concerning Daman, 1747.
VOC 2781, ff. 1-?	Documents concerning the trade between Surat and China, 1751-2.
VOC 2911, ff. 44-107	*Radicale beschrijving* i.e. an official review of Surat, September 1758. See also Bibliography, no. 331.
VOC 2954, ff. 409-841	Correspondence between Ceylon and the Dutch Republic concerning Surat, 1742-5.
VOC 2955, ff. 842-1067	Correspondence between Ceylon and the Dutch Republic concerning Surat, 1742-5.
VOC 3117, ff. 248-55	Document concerning weights, measures and currencies in Surat, *c.* 1764.
VOC 3179, ff. 6-35	Essay by *Directeur* Christiaan Lodewijk Senff concerning the sugar trade, 1766.
VOC 3727, ff. 95-146	Essay by *Directeur* Abraham Josias Sluijsken concerning the state of affairs at Surat, 1786.

2.2. Other VOC Series

2.2.1. *Archives of the Gentlemen XVII and the Amsterdam Chamber*

See 1.1
Access no.: 1.04.02

Kopie-resoluties van de Gouverneur-Generaal en Raden
Duplicate proceedings of the Governor-General and Council

See 1.1.4
Inv. nos: VOC 656-847

In the *Realia* repertory to the *resoluties* several relevant headings are to be found, among these:

Agra (5 entries 1679-1741), *Amadabaet* (Ahmadabad; 3 entries 1673-1743), *Broodchia* (Bharuch; 4 entries 1653-1745), *Cambait* (Cambay; 2 entries 1743-5), *Dieuw* (Diu; 2 entries 1654-7), *hasbulhockums* (hasb-ul-hukums; 1 entry 1715), *Sindij* (Sind; 1 entry 1656), *Souratte* (Surat; about 550 entries 1633-1792), *stad Diuw* (Diu city; 3 entries 1653-62).

Miscellaneous

VOC 601 Letter from Hans de Wolff and Lafer, factors at Surat, to the factors of the United Company of Zeeland at Aceh (Sumatra), April 1602 (see also 1.4.1 and 2.4). Published in Unger, *De oudste reizen van de Zeeuwen*, pp. 149-50; and in De Jonge, *De opkomst van het Nederlandsch gezag*. Vol. 2, pp. 495-6 (see Bibliography, nos 13, 120).

VOC 653 Bill of the purchase of Gujarati textiles at Aceh, probably early seventeenth century. One piece.

VOC 4759 Memorandum containing a draft for a direct trade connection between the Dutch Republic and Surat and Malabar, with appendices, 1773-4. Three volumes, one piece.

VOC 4816 List of coins, exchange rates, weights and measures in Asia, with index, including sections on Surat, Ahmadabad, Bharuch and Agra (ff. 1-90 contain the actual lists; ff. 91-139 contain notes on these subjects), 1769. One volume.

VOC 4904 Description of India or the area of the Great Mughal (fragment), *c.* 1622. One piece.

VOC 4905 Description of the government of Humayun, Akbar and Jahangir, 1626. One piece. The last section is part of VOC 4906, ff. 64-73 (see below).

VOC 4906 Memorandum of Francois Pelsaert, chief-factor at Agra, concerning the VOC trade in Hindustan, and the last section of a description of the government of Humayun, Akbar and Jahangir (see VOC 4905), 1626-7. One volume. Pelsaert's memorandum has been published by Kolff and Van Santen, *Geschriften*. For an English translation, see Moreland and Geyl, *Jahangir's India* (see Bibliography, no. 330).

VOC 4907 Papers concerning the lawsuit against Pieter van Helsdingen, former *Independent Fiscaal* in Surat, 1701-3. Three pieces.

VOC 4908 Lists of profits made on sold goods at Surat, 1713-14. Two pieces.

2.2.2. *Archives of the Zeeland Chamber*

See 1.2.1
Access no.: 1.04.02

Ingekomen stukken van Gouverneur-Generaal en Raden bij de Heren XVII en de Kamer Zeeland (IGG)
Papers received from Governor-General and Council by the Gentlemen XVII and the Zeeland Chamber

VOC 9048-9088 Letters and reports received by GG&C from Surat, with appendices, (1681-) 1683-1764 (-1768). 41 volumes. Incomplete series.

Ingekomen stukken van de kantoren in Indië bij de Heren XVII en de Kamer Zeeland (IKI)
Papers received from the establishments in the Indies by the Gentlemen XVII and the Zeeland Chamber

VOC 10406-26	Letters and other papers from the *Directeur* and Council of Surat to the Gentlemen XVII, with appendices, 1687-1790. 21 volumes. Incomplete series. Including the *resoluties* of the *Directeur* and Council of Surat, 1777-9 (VOC 10419) and 1789 (VOC 10426).
VOC 10427-31	*Resoluties* of the *Directeur* and Council of Surat, 1758-9, (1777-8), 1785-6, (1789). Incomplete series.
VOC 10432-4	Letters by *Independent Fiscaal* and interim *Directeur* Pieter van Helsdingen to Gentlemen XVII and to Governor and Council at Batavia, and a memorandum by Van Helsdingen to Commissioner Paulus de Roo, 1690-7. Three volumes.

Miscellaneous

VOC 11136	Letter from the Gentlemen XVII to Pieter Gillisz. van Ravensteijn, chief-factor in Surat, concerning a treaty concluded between the VOC and EIC, 1620. One piece.
VOC 11207-8	Two copies of a list (79 pp.) of coins, exchange rates, weights and measures at a great number of factories in the Indies, including Surat, Ahmadabad, Bharuch and Agra, printed in 1691 (at Middelburg, Zeeland). Two volumes.
VOC 11314	Papers concerning the accusations against former *Directeur* Gelmer Vosburgh, 1689-5. One volume.
VOC 11315	Letter from an Asian merchant in Surat to Johannes Bacherus, former envoy to the Mughal Emperor Aurangzeb and second in the commission of Hendrik Adriaan van Reede tot Drakenstein, 1690. One piece.
VOC 11316	Secret minutes of *Directeur* Hendrik Zwaardecroon, administrator Joan Grootenhuys and *Independent Fiscaal* Jean Diodati concerning their negotiations with the Mughal court, 1700. One volume.
VOC 11317	*Dagregister* of the ship Beverwijk lying in the roadstead of Surat, 1703-4. One volume.
VOC 11318	*Dagregister* of the ship Drie Kronen, belonging to the fleet under command of Meyndert de Boer, lying in the roadstead of Surat, 1703-4. One volume.
VOC 11319	Papers concerning the case conducted by former *Fiscaal* Abraham Cornelis de la Haye against Willem van der Laan, former warehouse-master at Surat, 1741-2, 1756. One volume.

VOC 11320	*Dagregister* of the ship Ellemeet, belonging to the fleet under command of Meyndert de Boer and Willem Six, concerning a conflict between the VOC and merchants from Surat, 1705-6. One volume.
VOC 11321	List of the expenses during the mission to the Mughal in the years 1710-13 for Joan Joshua Ketelaar, and of the gifts of the VOC to the Court, 1716. One volume.
VOC 11322	Papers concerning the estate of former *Directeur* Abraham Wijns, 1728. One volume.
VOC 11323	Appendices to comments of *Directeur* Jan Schreuder on the letters from the Gentlemen XVII to the GG&C, 1742-5. One volume (see below VOC 11326).
VOC 11324	Memorandum of chief-factor Christiaan Lodewijk Senff concerning the case of Willem van der Laan, former warehouse-master at Surat, with appendices, 1752. One volume.
VOC 11325	Plea concerning the complaints about Willem van der Laan, former warehouse-master at Surat, 1752. One piece.
VOC 11326	Letters from the Gentlemen XVII to the GG&C at Batavia dating from the period 1742-7 concerning Surat, with comments on these of *Directeur* Jan Schreuder, 1756. One volume (see above VOC 11323).
VOC 11327	Papers concerning the lawsuit of the *Fiscaal* in Surat against the deserter Johan Hapke van Coxhaven and others, 1759. One volume.
VOC 11328	*Memorie van overgave* by *Directeur* Louis Taillefert to chief-factor Jan Drabbe, 1760. One volume.
VOC 11329	Appendices to the *memorie van overgave* by *Directeur* Louis Taillefert, 1760. One volume.
VOC 11330	Papers concerning the lawsuit of the *Fiscaal* in Surat against Franciscus Angelie, 1761. One volume.

2.2.3. *Archives of the Delft, Rotterdam, Enkhuizen and Hoorn Chambers and miscellaneous*

See 1.2.2
Access no.: 1.04.02

Archives of the Rotterdam Chamber

VOC 14099	Private letters from Hendrik Zwaardecroon in Surat to a Director of the Rotterdam Chamber, 1702. One folder.

2.3. Archives Transferred from Asia

Hoge Regering te Batavia
High Government at Batavia

See 1.3.1
Access no.: 1.04.17

759-65	Extracts of letters from the GG&C and from the Gentlemen XVII, 1636-1791. With repertories, six volumes and two pieces.
766-71	(Minutes) of letters from the GG&C, 1790, 1792, 1799, 1802-3. With appendices, six volumes.
772	Originals of letters received from other European factories at Surat, 1793-7. One Volume, in English, French and Portuguese.
773	Minute of a secret letter from Batavia to M. Monté, interim *Commandeur*, 1796. One volume.
774-97	Letters from Surat to Batavia, 1791-5, 1801-4. With appendices and alphabetical repertories, 24 volumes, among which some are duplicates.
798-803	Secret letters from Surat to Batavia, 1789-95. With appendices, six volumes.
804-6	Letters of the Surat Resident to Batavia, 1820-3. With appendices, three volumes.
807-23	(*Secrete*) *resoluties* of the Surat Council, 1791-5. With alphabetical repertories, 15 volumes and two pieces.
824-5	*Dagregister* of Surat, 1791-2. Two folders.
826	Several reports and memoranda concerning Surat, 1686-1750, including a report on the timber-yard by C.L. Senff, 1750, and papers concerning the Company brokers Raksika Das and Bhagwan Das, 1697-9, and textile brokers from Ahmadabad. One volume.
827-8	Instructions concerning the various duties of the Surat personnel, 1750, 1758-60 (includes some correspondence of the Surat *Directie*). Two volumes.
829-34	*Memories van overgave* by H. Zwaardecroon to P. de Vos, 1702; J. Grootenhuys to C. Besuyen, 1710; and J.J. Ketelaar to D. Hurgronje, 1716. Six volumes (of which five are identical).
835	Advice of P.L. Phoonsen to Batavia concerning the calicoe trade and types of coins in Surat, 1740. With appendices, one volume.
836-7	Memorandum on opening trade to private traders by J. Schreuder, 1746. With appendices, two identical volumes. For another copy, see 2.5, Hope, inv. no. 66.
838-42	*Memories van overgave* by *Directeur* Johan Schreuder to Johannes Pecock, 1750; *Directeur* Pecock to Johan de Roth, 1753. With appendices, five volumes (of which four are identical).
843	Report on the state of (the establishments under) the Surat *Directie* by D. van Rheeden, 1758. One volume.

844-5 Secret *memorie van overgave* by *Directeur* Louis Taillefert to Jan Drabbe, 1760. With appendices, two volumes.
846-7 Memorandum of C.L. Senff about the Surat sugar trade, 1766. With appendices, two identical volumes.
848-9 *Memorie van overgave* by *Directeur* Christiaan Lodewijk Senff to Martinus Johan Bosman, 1768. With appendices, two identical volumes.
850-3 Memorandum on the state of (the establishments under) the Surat *Directie* by A.J. Sluysken, 1786. With appendices, four copies of the same.
854 *Memorie van overgave* by *Directeur* Abraham Josias Sluysken to Peter Sluysken, 1792. With appendices, one volume.
855 Translations of *farmans* granted by the Great Mughal, 1618-1729. One volume.
856 Papers concerning the loss sustained on Bengal silk sold in Surat, 1746-54.
857 Reply of J. Schreuder to the accusations of mismanagement brought against him, 1747. With appendices, one volume.
858 Memorandum to the British in Bombay containing objections to the actions of the British factors at Surat, 1748. With appendices, one volume, contains some letters in English, and French.
859 Record kept by M.J. Bosman of the actions of Indian regents and the British that were to the detriment of the VOC and of measures taken by him, 1772-3. One volume.
860 Report by A.J. Sluysken on his negotiations with the British about the captured factory of Bharuch, 1773. With appendices, one volume.
861-3 Memoranda of A.J. Sluysken about the financial mismanagement of M.J. Bosman and in defence of his own conduct, 1777. With appendices, three volumes of which two are identical.
864 Papers concerning the renting and subsequent sale of the ship De Goede Hoop to an Englishman, 1782-90. One volume.
865 Letter of E. Meyer concerning his management of the wages, 1795. One piece.
866 Papers concerning the accusations against former *Directeur* P. Sluysken, 1800-1. With appendices, three volumes.
867 Letters of the British Government at Fort William to the British authorities in Batavia and extracts of letters from the commercial department in Batavia to Bombay, 1809-14. One volume, in English.
868-9 Appendices to letters from Surat to Batavia, including a list of papers returned to the Dutch together with the factory in 1818 and papers concerning the renovation of the factory buildings, 1818-25. Two volumes, partly in English (see also Appendix I).
870-2 Report of B.C. Verploegh on the restoration of the Surat factory to the Dutch, 1818-19. With appendices, mostly letters in English and French, three volumes.

Voormalige Nederlandse bezittingen in Voor-Indië
Former Dutch possessions in South Asia

See 1.3.3
Access no.: 1.04.19

137-41 *Resoluties* of the *Directeur* and Council at Surat, 1794-7. Four volumes, one volume appendices.
142-47 (Minutes of) *secrete resoluties* and appendices, 1784, 1787, 1792-5. Three volumes, one piece, two covers.
148-9 Daily report from Surat by Henricus Sissingh, chief surgeon and member of the Council, 1787-1803. Apparently written towards the end of the period. Two covers.
150 Incoming papers, 1795-7. Bad condition, one volume.
151 Extracts of orders of the Gentlemen XVII and of the GG&C, arranged according to subject, 1722-69. With alphabetical index, one cover.
152 Plea of *Directeur* Senff in response to the complaints raised against him by Klinkert, 1771.
153-62 Incoming and outgoing letters of the Surat Residency, 1818-26. Nine volumes and one piece.

2.4. Archives of Other Institutions

Staten-Generaal
States General

See 1.4.2
Access no.: 1.01.03

12563, folder 2 Reports concerning the voyage of some ships of the United Company of Zeeland (see 1.4.1) to Surat (among other places), *c.* 1603. Two pieces (see also 2.2.1). Published in Unger, *De oudste reizen van de Zeeuwen naar Oost-Indië*, pp. 138-48; and in De Jonge, *De opkomst van het Nederlandsch gezag*. Vol. 2, pp. 484-94 (see Bibliography, nos 13, 120).

Stadhouderlijke Secretarie
Secretariat to the Stadtholder

See 1.4.3
Access no.: 1.01.50

1180 Correspondence between the Stadtholder and Surat (incomplete), *c.* 1760. One folder.
1230 Description of the invasion in 1738-9 of the Mughal Empire by Nadir Shah of Persia, mid-eighteenth century. One bundle.
1929 Report by the so-called Military Commission (consisting of Captains

J.O. Vaillant and C.A. Ver Huell (see 1.5.32) and Lieutenant-Colonel J.F.L. Graevestein) to the Stadtholder concerning the defence in Surat (and other places), with appendices, 1792. One folder.

Comité tot de Zaken van de Oost-Indische Handel en Bezittingen
Committee regarding East Indian Trade and Possessions

See 1.4.4
Access no.: 2.01.27.01

Overgekomen brieven en papieren (OBP)
(letters and papers received)

61, ff. 148?-1629 Report concerning Surat (among other regions), *c.* 1793.
63, n.f. Report concerning Surat (among other regions), *c.* 1795.
64, n.f. Report concerning Surat (among other regions), *c.* 1796.
65, n.f. Report concerning Surat (among other regions), *c.* 1797.
65a, n.f. Report concerning Surat (among other regions), *c.* 1794.
133, ff. 19-21 *Resoluties*, 1793.
133, ff. 83-5 *Resoluties*, 1794.
133, n.f. *Resoluties*, 1792-5 (at the back of the volume?).

Uit Engeland overgezonden stukken (Nederburgh)
Papers sent from England (Nederburgh)

See 1.4.7
Access no.: 2.01.27.04

97-100 *Resoluties* of the Surat Council, 1791-3. With duplicates, four volumes and two covers.
101-4 Letters of the Council to Batavia, 1792-3. Partly with duplicates, four covers.

Legatie Turkije
Embassy at Constantinople (Istanbul), Turkey

See 1.4.11
Access no.: 1.02.20
Period: 1668-1811

168 Register of letters despatched, including letters to J. de Roth, *Directeur* at Surat, 1756-7. One volume.

2.5. PERSONAL AND FAMILY PAPERS

Geleynssen de Jongh(e)

See 1.5.2
Access no.: 1.10.30

2	Contains correspondence with English ships lying in the roadstead of Suvali, 1623-4, *resoluties* of the fleet sailing for Surat and Persia, 1627, *resoluties* taken on board ships lying at Suvali, 1633.
17	Instruction by P. van den Broecke to Geleynsen, going to Burhanpur, 1624. One piece.
14	Letters of Geleynsen to P. van den Broecke at Surat a.o., sent from the ship Schoonhoven, and from Surat, Burhanpur and Bharuch, 1623-6.
19	Letters from J. Mahieus in Surat, 1624. One folder.
20-6	Papers concerning the VOC trade in Burhanpur and Bharuch, including trade-journals and ledgers of these factories, 1623-8. Three volumes, three pieces and one folder.
27	Instruction by P. van den Broecke to Geleynssen to trace the VOC *caffila* coming from Agra, 1625. One piece.
28	Contains descriptions of trade, agriculture, manufacturing, shipping, etc., in Bharuch, Vadodara, Cambay and Ahmadabad (1628-9), the means of existence, the way wars are conducted, religion, laws, manners and customs of the inhabitants of Hindustan, and of the origins, religion, laws and customs of the Parsis in Gujarat and a discourse by Geleynssen on the most advantageous way to trade in Bharuch, 1628. One volume. For Caland's publication of this manuscript, see Bibliography, no. 325.
29A	*Resoluties* of the convoy from Batavia sailing for Surạt and Persia, including an agreement with the English at Surat concerning the indigo trade, 1631-3. One piece.
30-1	Contain letters of Geleynsen sent from Bharuch, Ahmadabad, Vadodara and Surat to various persons, 1627-31, 1636-7. Two volumes.
32-8	Letters to Geleynsen from various VOC servants in Surat, Agra, Ahmadabad, Lahore, Bharuch, Cambay and Vadodara, 1625-31.
42-50	Various invoices of goods from Bharuch, Cambay, Ahmadabad, Surat, Agra, 1624-39. Three volumes, three folders and two pieces.
52	Trade journal and ledger of the Bharuch factory, 1628-31. One volume.
53	Calculation of the toll and other expenses on some goods sent from Bharuch to Ahmadabad. One piece.
54-5	Acknowledgements of debt of P. van den Broecke and

	Geleynssen concerning loans taken from local brokers and from J. Mahieusen. One piece and one folder.
56-7	Papers concerning the balance of goods, debts and other possessions of the Bharuch factory, 1631. Two covers.
58	Deed by Surat *Directeur* J. van Hasell permitting Geleynssen to return to the Republic. One piece.
71	Review of the quality of the goods from Surat, Persia, Batavia received in Amsterdam, 1634. One piece.
97	Deed appointing Geleynssen to the position of second-in-command of Surat, 1636. One piece.
97A	Letters of Geleynssen sent from Agra, Bayana, Hindaun, Jalor, Ahmadabad and Surat to various Dutchmen and to Asaf Khan, 1639-40, also some acknowledgements of debt of the Agra factory concerning loans from local merchants, *hundies*, etc., 1637-9. One volume.
99	Papers concerning the legal *resoluties* of J. van Twist vs. "Wissendas", VOC broker, 1635-6. One folder.
101-4	Letters sent by Geleynssen from Agra, also some acknowledgements of debt of the Agra factory concerning loans from local merchants, *hundies*, etc., 1637-9. Three volumes and one piece (see also Appendix I).
105	Letters from Surat to Geleynssen with appended letters from the GG&C, 1634-9. One bundle.
109-10	Letters received from A. Barentsen in Ahmadabad and B. Pieters in Surat, 1636-9. One piece and one folder.
113-14	Invoices of goods sent from Agra, 1637-40. Two volumes.
116-18	Trade journals and ledgers of the Agra factory, including some invoices of goods, expenses etc., 1637-40. Six volumes.
122	Debt accounts of the Surat factory, 1639-40. One folder.
123	List of expenses incurred at the Agra factory, 1637-8. One volume.
124	Ledger on bills of exchange drawn on and endorsed by the Agra factory, 1637-40. One volume, in bad state.
125	Note on (denied) debts incurred by VOC personnel in Agra, 1636-40. One volume.
129	Current accounts of Geleynsen at Surat, 1637-40. One folder.
130	Inventory of the Agra factory at the departure of Geleynsen, 1640. One piece.
159, 161	Correspondence of Geleynsen with P. Croocq at Surat, 1640-3.
166A, 174	(Extracts of) letters of C. Weijlandt at Agra, 1640-1. One piece and one folder.
177	Letters of the GG&C to P. Croocq in Surat, 1641. One folder.
187	Extract of a letter of J. Sigismundus (Wurffbain) in Cambay to Surat, 1642. One piece.

199	Letter of P. Croocq in Surat to the Commander of the Dutch fleet at Goa, 1641. One piece.
217	Letter of H. Nachtegael from the ship Den Witten Oliphant just arriving at Surat, 1641. One piece.
223, 223A	Lists from Batavia of goods to be sent from Surat, etc., 1642. Two pieces.
224-5, 227	Invoices of goods from Agra and Surat, 1640-3. Two pieces and one folder.
231-232	Price-lists of goods in Ahmadabad and Surat, 1641-3. One folder and one piece.
236	List of medicines to be supplied to Batavia from Surat, etc., 1641-2. One folder.
279, 290	Letters of A. Baerenssen and C. Weijlandt in Surat, 1645. Two folders.
294	*Resoluties* of the *Directeur* and Council at Surat, 1645. One folder.
296	Invoices and price-lists of Surat and Persia and a letter of P. Croocq at Surat. One piece.
297C	List of Muslim and Bania goods laden into the warship Reijnsburch destined for Gombroon. One piece.
316	Instruction of the Surat *Directeur* to a ship sailing from Suvali to Mocha, 1642. One piece.

Sweers, Van Vliet, Specx, Mannis

See 1.5.3
Access no.: 1.10.78

1, f. 83	Testimony by J. van Twist to the good behaviour of S. Sweers as Cashier of Ahmadabad, 1636.
2, ff. 51-4	Notes by S. Sweers from the letters of Surat *Directeur* P. Croocq, 1643.
2, ff. 133-4	Letter of H. Thombergen in Surat to S. Sweers, 1658.
7, ff. 228-53	Trade journal of Surat, 1634.
9	Description of the situation of Gujarat, Persia and Arabia by A. Beckers to the GG&C, 1624.

Sypesteyn (supplement)

See 1.5.6
Access no.: 1.13.19.02

1 Daily record of the embassy of Surat *Directeur* J.J. Ketelaar to the Mughal court at Lahore and Delhi, 1711-13. One volume. For the published version by J.Ph. Vogel and a partial translation by D. Kuenen-Wicksteed, see Bibliography, no. 328.

Van Ghesel

See 1.5.13
Access no.: 1.10.31

164 Note by Van Ghesel on a claim to the inheritance of Francois du Bois, *onderkoopman* at Surat, 1756. One piece.

Baud

See 1.5.14
Access no.: 2.21.007.58

1063-4 *Resoluties* of the Gentlemen XVII and report of the Zeeland Chamber concerning the proposal of the extraordinary member of the Council at Batavia Jan Schreuder to devalue the rupee at Surat and to calculate the exchange rate of the various currencies according to European standards, 1765-6. Two pieces.

Hope

See 1.5.17
Access no.: 1.10.46

66 Considerations of J. Schreuder concerning free shipping and trade at Surat, 1746. One volume. For another copy, see 2.3, *Hoge Regering te Batavia*, inv. nos 836-7.

Van Slingelandt - De Vrij Temminck

See 1.5.20
Access no.: 3.20.52

566 Folder no. 58 contains miscellaneous papers concerning Surat, including a survey of the sugar sent to Surat, 1756-65. Six pieces.

Bleiswijk

See 1.5.21
Access no.: 3.01.25

228 Papers concerning a successful attack by the British on Bharuch, 1773-4. One folder, partly in English.

229 Letter from Abraham Jonas Sluysken in Bombay to his cousin/nephew criticizing the policies of Governor Iman Willem Falck, 1773. One piece.

Fagel

See 1.5.25
Access no.: 1.10.29

2350, 2399, 2408, 2422, 2454, 2470, 2480, 2505, 2585, 2600, 2629, 2647, 2669, 2732, 2733, 2736, 2739, 2740, 2749, 2750, 2753, 2866
Contain correspondence of members of the Fagel family with Surat-based A.J. Sluysken, a blood relative of the family, 1764-92. The letters deal with private trade and various other matters. For example, inv. no. 2749 contains a description of the different religions and peoples of Hindustan.

2500 Contains a letter to Surat *Directeur* W.J. van de Graaf in which H. Fagel the Elder recommends A.J. Sluysken, 1777.

Radermacher

See 1.5.27
Access no.: 1.10.69

536 Report on former Surat *Directeur* J. Roth, *c.* 1760. With appendices, one folder.

Falck

See 1.5.28
Access no.: 2.21.006.48

5 Papers concerning Nadir Shah of Persia and the capture of Delhi, 1739. Three pieces in one folder.

9 Memorandum concerning the infringements by the EIC on the ancient rights and privileges of the VOC in Surat (and Bengal), chiefly since the peace concluded in 1784 (incomplete), *c.* 1786. One piece.

Alting

See 1.5.29
Access no.: 1.10.03

38 Considerations about the implementation of new rules in Surat concerning free shipping and goods permitted for private trade by VOC functionaries, 1746. One volume.

59 Memorandum of *Directeur* C.L. Senff on a dispute with the British involving tolls and seals, 1767. One piece.

75 Considerations about the state of the Surat factory by A.J. Sluysken, 1786. One volume.

94 Review of the correspondence between Batavia and Surat concerning the construction of a new factory lodge, 1752-8. One piece.

Nederburgh

See 1.5.33
Access no.: 1.10.59

137 Notes on the letter sent by the Surat *Directeur* and Council to the Gentlemen XVII in 1787, n.d. One piece.
431 Considerations of M.J. Bosman and A.J. Sluysken at Surat on the utility of the Bharuch factory, 1770. One volume.
432 *Memorie van overgave by Directeur* Abraham Josias Sluysken to Peter Sluysken, 792. With appendices, one volume.

W. and D. van Hogendorp

See 1.5.35
Access no.: 2.21.008.69

53 Attestation presented by the Governor of Bombay to Dirk van Hogendorp during his stay over there, 1799. One piece, in English.

2.6. Separate Acquisitions and Microfilms

Losse aanwinsten
Separate acquisitions

See 1.6.1
Access no.: 1.11.01.01

165 Contains an account of the invasion of Nadir Shah against the Mughal Empire in 1738-9 extracted from newsletters in Persian. One folder (1876 A XXII 11).
698 Memorandum of C.L. Senff against the memorandum of L. Taillefert about Surat, 1759. One volume (1895 LXX 03).
1976 Letters of P. van den Broecke in Surat to W. Geleynsen de Jongh in Bharuch. Two folders (1969 II 3).

2.7. Maps and Drawings

Verzameling buitenlandse kaarten, Leupe (VEL)
Foreign map collection, Leupe

See 1.7.1
Access no.: 4.VEL

225 Map of Surat River, seventeenth century (?).
868 Map of the cities and villages between Surat and Ahmadabad, seventeenth century. Received from Surat, 1699.
869 Plan of factories or rental houses of the VOC in the city of Surat, seventeenth century. Received from Surat, 1699.

870 Plan of the buildings that could be built on the property of the old factory, belonging to the VOC, seventeenth century. Received from Surat, 1699.

871 Plan of the buildings that could be built on the property belonging to Muhammad Shahid, seventeenth century. Received from Surat, 1699.

872 Plan of the buildings that could be built in the yards and the surrounding grounds, bought by the VOC, seventeenth century. Received from Surat, 1699.

873 Plan of the new factory set up in the former residence of Governor Itibar Khan. The house is built against the city wall along Surat River, eighteenth century. Received from Batavia, 1714.

874 Plan of a piece of property in Surat, belonging to the VOC, eighteenth century. With explanation. Received from Batavia, 1735.

875 Map and description of the tent at the beach of Suvali, eighteenth century. Received from Batavia, 1735.

876 Plan of the factory to be built in Bharuch, 1699. With description. Received from Batavia, 1735.

877 Plan of the old factory at Bharuch and the accompanying buildings, 1699. Received from Batavia, 1735.

878 Plan of the residence and the warehouses of the VOC in Ahmadabad, 1697. Received from Batavia, 1735.

879 Drawing of the factory in Ahmadabad, 1697. Received from Batavia, 1735.

880 Drawing and plan of the factory in Agra, 1699. Received from Surat, 1699.

Verzameling buitenlandse kaarten, supplement, Leupe-l'Honoré Naber (VELH)
Foreign map collection, supplement, Leupe-l'Honoré Naber

See 1.7.2
Access no.: 4.VELH

105 Compass map of Surat River, seventeenth century. Originating from the papers left by the Commissioner General Pieter Ketting of Surat. 1695.

323 Drawing of the cities and villages between Surat and Ahmadabad, late seventeenth century. Originating from the papers left by Pieter Ketting, 1695.

Departement van Marine, centraal archief, Leupe (MCAL)
Ministry of Naval Affairs, central archives, Leupe

See 1.7.3
Access no.: 4.MCAL

4223 Map of the river Belapur, by J. Lendrum, 1793. Copperplate print.

4232 Map of the rivers Bulsar and 'Omersari', by Lieutenant John Ringrose, 1784. Originates from the collection of Governor Hornsby.

5947 Map of Hindustan, or the Mughal Empire, from the latest authorities, by J. Rennell, 1788.

Hoge Regering te Batavia
High Government at Batavia

See 1.3.1
Access no.: 1.04.17

869 Includes two plans of the Surat factory (riverside), *c.* 1822.

3. MALABAR (including Kanara and Konkan)

INTRODUCTION

The VOC administration in Malabar supervised the coastal factories of the Malabar, Kanara and Konkan Coasts, stretching from Tengapattanam in the south to Vengurla in the north. Although initially part of the Ceylon administration, Malabar became a separate *Commandement* in 1669, managed by a *Commandeur* and Council in Cochin.

The *Voorcompagnieën* first appeared in the area in 1603 (see 1.4.1). A year later the VOC signed an agreement with the Zamorin of Calicut. Apart from irregular trade, this did not result in any permanent settlements in Malabar as the Company was primarily involved in its failed efforts to conquer Portuguese Goa. In view of this, a factory was established at nearby Vengurla in 1637, initially under the direct authority of Batavia but later, from 1673 to 1676, under Surat, and, from 1676 until its demise in 1693, under Malabar. In Malabar proper a small settlement was set up at Kayankulam in 1647 but this functioned only irregularly. The Company became seriously involved in the area only as late as the 1660s. After a few unsuccessful attempts, the VOC captured Cranganur and Quilon from the Portuguese in 1661, to be followed by Cochin and Cannanore two years later. Soon after that, the VOC concluded treaties with various local rulers and established factories at Ponnani, Purakkad, Vypin, Tengapattanam and Pallippuram. In 1667 or 1668 a factory was set up at Barcelore on the Kanara Coast. Other factories established in the course of time included Mangalore, Azhikkodu, Calicut, Chetwai, Karunagappalli and various smaller stations. After the lost battle against Travancore at Colachel in 1741, the power of the Company gradually declined. Between 1770 and 1790 the forts at Cannanore, Cranganur and Pallippuram were sold to the local rulers. Cochin and Quilon were finally transferred to the British in 1795.

In Malabar the VOC maintained close relations with a host of indigenous rulers, those of Cochin, Travancore and Calicut being the most important amongst them. Other principalities in touch with the Dutch included Chirakkal, Cannanore, Tekkumkur, Vadakkumkur, Purakkad, Parur, Alangadu, Valluvanadu, Kayankulam, Karunagappalli, Karthikappalli, Desinganadu, Edappalli, Chennamangalam, Cranganur, Attingal and Badagara. There were also contacts with Mysore, especially during its expansion under Haidar Ali and Tipu Sultan. At

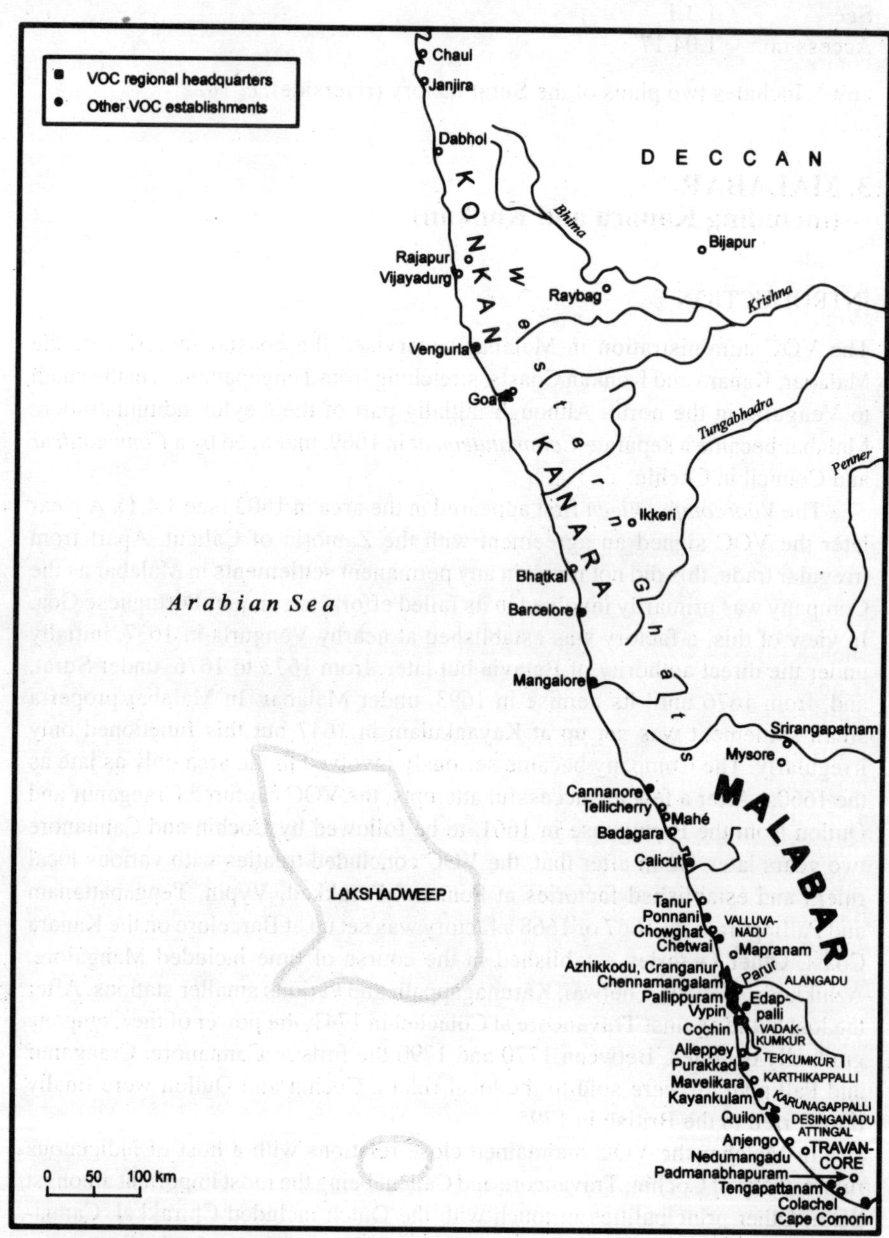

Map 3. The VOC in Malabar

the Kanara and Konkan Coasts, relations were maintained with Ikkeri (from Barcelore), Bijapur (from Vengurla) and the Marathas (the latter two also from Coromandel). In addition, the VOC occasionally had contacts with the Lakshadweep as well as with the Angria 'pirates' who were based at Vijayadurg and controlled parts of the Konkan Coast

With regard to the archives described in this guide, documents mentioned under Ceylon also include various papers regarding Malabar, especially before September 1663 when Malabar was still part of the Ceylon government. Even for documents on Travancore one should also look under Ceylon because of its close links with the VOC settlements on the adjacent Fishery Coast which was administered from Colombo. As far as possible, in each section of this chapter we have listed documents regarding Konkan separately under the heading 'Vengurla', as this factory was directly managed from Batavia during a substantial part of its existence (1637-73).

3.1. *Overgekomen Brieven en Papieren (OBP)*
Letters and Papers Received

See 1.1.7
Access no.: 1.04.02
Inv. nos: VOC 1053-3987

Letters and papers concerning Malabar are mostly to be found under headings such as 'Mallabaer', 'Cust van Mallabar' (Coast of Malabar), 'Couchin', 'Chochijn', 'Calicut', 'Cananor'. Initially, letters and papers concerning Vengurla and the Konkan are regularly listed under headings like 'Wingurla', 'Goa', 'Goas Bhare' (Goa's Billows), 'Visiapour' and 'Cust van India', but until 1676 they may also be found under Surat.

All these headings occur in the volumes containing documents sent directly from South Asia to the Gentlemen XVII and the Amsterdam Chamber, as well as the volumes that consist of copies of documents sent from South Asia to Batavia in the *Batavia's ingekomen brievenboek* (Batavia letterbook of incoming documents). In a few cases, letters and papers relating to Malabar, Kanara and Konkan may also be found under the heading 'Batavia'. In the section on *dagregisters* (see 3.1.3) many of these are labelled *inlandse* (indigenous). These documents are extensive *dagregisters* of contacts with the local rulers of Malabar.

3.1.1. *Memories van overgave* (final reports)

VOC 1256, ff. 227-39	Rijcklof van Goens to Isbrand Gosken and Ludolff van Coulster, April 1666.
VOC 1267-8, ff. 1020-41	*Commandeur* IJsbrant Goske to Lucas van der Dussen, January 1668.
VOC 1329, ff. 1336v-84	*Commandeur* Hendrick van Rheede to Jacob Lobs, March 1677 (see also 3.1.6, VOC 1370, ff. 2276-340?).

VOC 1349, ff. 1490-3	Daniel Joncktus at Cannanore to Jacob Schoors, September 1678.
VOC 1406, ff. 865-83	*Commandeur* Marten Huijsman to Gelmer Vosburgh, April 1684.
VOC 1649, ff. 68-93	*Commandeur* Magnus Wichelman to Mattheus Schenkenberg, January 1701.
VOC 2015, ff. 81-129	*Commandeur* Johannes Hertenberg to Jacob de Jong, November 1723.
VOC 2047, ff. 245-85	*Commandeur* Johannes Hertenberg to Jacob de Jong, December 1723.
VOC 2340, ff. 376-479	*Commandeur* Adriaen Maten to Julius Valentijn Stein van Gollonesse, January 1735.
VOC 2354, ff. 645-817	*Commandeur* Adriaen Maten to Julius Valentijn Stein van Gollonesse, January 1735.
VOC 2601, ff. 87-160	*Commandeur* Julius Valentijn Stein van Gollonesse to Reinerus Siersma, *c.* 1743.
VOC 2710, ff. 1083-1120	*Commandeur* Reinerus Siersma to Corijn Stevens, February 1748.
VOC 2714, ff. 189-236	*Commandeur* Reinerus Siersma to Corijn Stevens, February 1748.
VOC 3019, ff. 283-383	*Commandeur* Casparus de Jong to Godefridus Weyerman, March 1761.
VOC 3147, ff. 1109-1219	*Commandeur* Godefridus Weyerman to Cornelis Breekpot, February 1765.
VOC 3266, ff. 195-287	*Commandeur* Cornelis Breekpot to Christiaan Lodewijk Senff, February 1769.
VOC 3509, ff. 562-883	Governor Adriaan Moens to Johan Gerard van Angelbeek, April 1781.

For published translations and editions, see Bibliography, nos 375, 383.

Vengurla: *Memories van overgave* (final reports)

VOC 1275-8, ff. 1749-50	Resident Leendert Leenderts to Rombout Leser, 1670.
VOC 1321, ff. 959v-61	By factor Rombout Leser, February 1676.

3.1.2. *Resoluties* (proceedings)

VOC 1231, ff. 375-6	Quilon, 1659.
VOC 1231, f. 550	Concerning the confiscation of a Muslim vessel at Cochin, 1659.
VOC 1239, ff. 1169-78	1663.
VOC 1239, ff. 1193-9	1662.
VOC 1239, ff. 1206a-1206c	Concerning conflicts with the English at Cochin, 1663.

VOC 1245, ff. 537-8	1664.
VOC 1245, ff. 574-5	1664.
VOC 1333, ff. 479-83	1678.
VOC 1333, ff. 512-15	Partly concerning the Portuguese, *c.* 1678 (among other documents).
VOC 1343, ff. 440-3	1679.
VOC 1361, f. 314v	1680.
VOC 1361, ff. 337v-9	*c.* 1680.
VOC 1370, ff. 2110v-2	1681.
VOC 1370, ff. 2169v-75	1681.
VOC 1396, ff. 775-8	Concerning an uprising in Cochin, 1684.
VOC 1425, ff. 102-8	Concerning conflicts at the factory at Cannanore, 1686.
VOC 1528, ff. 55-7	1693.
VOC 1528, ff. 298-379	1693.
VOC 1547, ff. 216-23v	1694.
VOC 1593, ff. 222-66	1697.
VOC 1619, ff. 65-188	1699.
VOC 1627, ff. 131-221	1698.
VOC 1634, ff. 241-400	1699-1700.
VOC 1646, ff. 202-408	1700-1.
VOC 1658, ff. 164-287	1701-2.
VOC 1725, ff. 735-1008	1704-6.
VOC 1741, ff. 334-496	1706-7.
VOC 1757, ff. 46-9	Concerning a conflict between the King of Cochin and indigenous Syrian Christians, 1708.
VOC 1757, ff. 506-80	1707-8.
VOC 1762, ff. 338-45	Concerning conflicts between the King of Cochin and the Zamorin of Calicut, 1708.
VOC 1773, ff. 457-646	1708-9.
VOC 1774, ff. 1429-531	1708-9.
VOC 1778, ff. 85-90	Concerning the King of Cochin, 1708.
VOC 1778, ff. 267-73	1709.
VOC 1790, ff. 603-69	1709-10.
VOC 1797, ff. 162-83	1709.
VOC 1805, ff. 792-6	1709.
VOC 1807, ff. 394-443	1710-11.
VOC 1807, ff. 482-3	1711.
VOC 1825, ff. 93-8	1712.
VOC 1825, ff. 107-11	1712 (among other documents).
VOC 1825, f. 195	1712.
VOC 1825, ff. 201-3	1712.
VOC 1825, ff. 455-567	1711-12.
VOC 1838, ff. 259-522	1712-13.
VOC 1838, ff. 791-4	1713.
VOC 1843, ff. 1-3	1712.
VOC 1843, f. 42	Concerning pepper treaties, 1712.

VOC 1843, ff. 53-4	Concerning the Maldives (partially), 1712.
VOC 1843, ff. 57-66	1712 (among other documents).
VOC 1852, ff. 484-670	1713-14.
VOC 1866, ff. 277-542	1714-15.
VOC 1880, ff. 206-68	Concerning the Zamorin of Calicut, 1715-16.
VOC 1881, ff. 667-1001	1715-16.
VOC 1885, ff. 16-22	Partly concerning the war with the Zamorin of Calicut, 1716.
VOC 1891, ff. 94-150	1717.
VOC 1891, ff. 219-28	1717.
VOC 1905, ff. 224-32	1718.
VOC 1912, ff. 179-90	1717.
VOC 1912, ff. 245-74	1717-18.
VOC 1924, ff. 244-396	1718-19.
VOC 1942, ff. 247-409	1719-20.
VOC 1947, ff. 222-31	1719.
VOC 1958, ff. 215-382	1720-1.
VOC 1963, ff. 132-48	1720 (among other documents).
VOC 1977, ff. 182-307	1721-2.
VOC 1993, ff. 146-311	1722-3.
VOC 1994, ff. 995-1012	Concerning coffee, 1723.
VOC 2010, ff. 304-507	1723-4.
VOC 2015, ff. 43-64	Concerning coffee, *c.* 1724.
VOC 2027, ff. 315-668	1724-5.
VOC 2033, ff. 462-81	1724-5.
VOC 2033, ff. 565-66	1725.
VOC 2048, ff. 330-808	1725-6.
VOC 2054, ff. 155-7	1726.
VOC 2054, ff. 341-60	1725-6.
VOC 2054, ff. 431-5	1726.
VOC 2054, ff. 125-6	1726.
VOC 2054, ff. 131-59	1726.
VOC 2060, ff. 2037-9	1727.
VOC 2070, ff. 363-800	1726-7.
VOC 2078, ff. 286-90	1727.
VOC 2078, ff. 562?-9	1727.
VOC 2078, ff. 638-91	1727.
VOC 2086, ff. 2377-9	Concerning pepper, 1727.
VOC 2097, ff. 226-705	1727-8.
VOC 2104, ff. 4-23	1728.
VOC 2130, ff. 201-533	1728-9.
VOC 2137, ff. 76-107	*c.* 1727.
VOC 2137, ff. 207-10	Concerning conflicts between Muslims and Hindus at Cannanore, 1729.
VOC 2160, ff. 269-717	1729-30.
VOC 2167, ff. 332-3	1730.

VOC 2188, ff. 433-1013	1730-1.
VOC 2200, ff. 139-725	1730-1.
VOC 2227, ff. 424-892	1731-2.
VOC 2230, ff. 2351-7	1729.
VOC 2230, ff. 2716-9	1731.
VOC 2231, ff. 3210-11	1732.
VOC 2231, ff. 3270-3	1731 (among other documents).
VOC 2231, ff. 3299-3301	1731-2.
VOC 2234, ff. 4649-810	1731-2.
VOC 2247, ff. 48-52	1732.
VOC 2247, ff. 175-598	1731-2.
VOC 2248, ff. 3341-9	*c.* 1732.
VOC 2249, ff. 713-21	1729.
VOC 2249, ff. 1137-42	1731.
VOC 2249, ff. 1908-10	1732.
VOC 2249, f. 2047	Concerning pepper trade, 1732.
VOC 2249, ff. 2049-52	1731.
VOC 2250, ff. 2363-550	1731-2.
VOC 2282, ff. 1975-2484	1732-3.
VOC 2292, ff. 365-992	1732-3.
VOC 2301, ff. 3640-78	Concerning shipbuilding, 1734.
VOC 2309, ff. 342-6	Concerning a foreign vessel, 1734.
VOC 2309, ff. 351-3	Concerning a foreign vessel, 1734.
VOC 2309, ff. 372-81	Concerning a foreign vessel, 1734.
VOC 2311, ff. 1689-2098	1733-4.
VOC 2320, ff. 144-55	*c.* 1734.
VOC 2320, ff. 226-31	Concerning Alangadu, *c.* 1734.
VOC 2320, ff. 242-4	Concerning Alangadu, *c.* 1734.
VOC 2320, ff. 258-67	Concerning Cannanore, 1734.
VOC 2320, ff. 322-30	1734.
VOC 2320, ff. 593-1218	1733-4.
VOC 2320, ff. 1245-58	1731.
VOC 2320, ff. 1764-8	*c.* 1734.
VOC 2320, ff. 1985-90	1734.
VOC 2342, ff. 1540-2073	1734-5.
VOC 2354, ff. 987-1490	1734-5.
VOC 2378, ff. 1631-2068	1735-6.
VOC 2389, ff. 255-840	1735-6.
VOC 2407, ff. 1886-2403	1736-7.
VOC 2414, ff. 771-1469	1737.
VOC 2434, ff. 1229-2147	1737-8.
VOC 2446, ff. 52-106	Concerning the cargo of some vessels, 1737.
VOC 2446, ff. 301-868	1737-8.
VOC 2463, ff. 1321-1862	1738-9.
VOC 2474, ff. 138-47	Concerning the cargo of some vessels, 1739.
VOC 2474, ff. 155-840	1738-9.

VOC 2497, ff. 1544-2554	1739-40.
VOC 2507, ff. 323-?	1739-40.
VOC 2528, ff. 1776-2414	1740-1.
VOC 2542, ff. 511-19	Recorded by the war council at Colachel, 1741.
VOC 2542, ff. 533-1268	1740-1.
VOC 2563, ff. 1603-2494	1741-2.
VOC 2577, ff. 323-1318	1741-2.
VOC 2579, ff. 3985-4032	1741-2.
VOC 2581, ff. 6031-234	Recorded by the war council, concerning the war against Travancore, 1741-2.
VOC 2581, ff. 7339-522	Recorded by the war council at Colachel, Tuticorin, Cape Comorin and Quilon, 1741.
VOC 2604, ff. 1111-489	1742-3.
VOC 2609, ff. 271-1308	1742-3.
VOC 2626, ff. 847-1146	1743-4.
VOC 2632, ff. 153-1072	1744.
VOC 2646, ff. 231-4	1745.
VOC 2648, ff. 1165-834	1744-5.
VOC 2653, ff. 139-776	1744.
VOC 2653, ff. 785-868	1745.
VOC 2653, ff. 893-984	1745.
VOC 2653, ff. 1051-190	1745.
VOC 2670, ff. 237-722	1745-6.
VOC 2678, ff. 285-?	1746.
VOC 2678, ff. 377-?	1745-6.
VOC 2678, ff. 747-58	1746.
VOC 2678, ff. 762-78	*c.* 1746.
VOC 2678, ff. 784-916	1746.
VOC 2695, ff. 236-813	1747.
VOC 2703, ff. 9-484	1746-7.
VOC 2703, ff. 655-920	1746-7.
VOC 2703, ff. 935-?	*c.* 1747.
VOC 2715, ff. 265-803	1747-8.
VOC 2723, ff. 83-348	1747.
VOC 2723, ff. 363-776	1747.
VOC 2723, ff. 799-984	1747.
VOC 2723, ff. 1131-266	1747-8.
VOC 2723, ff. 1279-350	1748.
VOC 2724, ff. 1433-?	1748.
VOC 2737, ff. 178-474	1748-9.
VOC 2746, ff. 121-736	1748-9.
VOC 2759, ff. 136-473	1749-50.
VOC 2765, ff. 13-276	1749.
VOC 2765, ff. 383-543	1749-50.
VOC 2765, ff. 591-?	1750.
VOC 2765, ff. 12?-248	1750.

VOC 2776, ff. 182-543	1750-1.
VOC 2777, ff. 544-816	1751.
VOC 2785, ff. 139-?	1750-1.
VOC 2788, ff. 771-96	*c.* 1751.
VOC 2789, ff. 21-450	1751.
VOC 2797, ff. 137-361	1751-2.
VOC 2802, ff. 9-156	1752.
VOC 2802, ff. 257-436	1751-2.
VOC 2802, ff. 451-70	1752.
VOC 2802, ff. 479-?	1752.
VOC 2815, ff. 170-322	1752-3.
VOC 2823, ff. 8-83	1752.
VOC 2823, ff. 147-239	1752-3.
VOC 2823, ff. 252-60	1753.
VOC 2823, ff. 266-?	1753.
VOC 2834, ff. 206-341	1753-4.
VOC 2842, ff. 18-57	1753.
VOC 2842, ff. 151-250	1753-4.
VOC 2842, ff. 303-?	1754.
VOC 2857, ff. 92-101	1754.
VOC 2857, ff. 172-310	1754-5.
VOC 2863, ff. 13-29	1754.
VOC 2863, ff. 44-90	1754.
VOC 2863, ff. 157-209	1754-5.
VOC 2863, ff. 240-?	1755.
VOC 2865, ff. 173-338	1754.
VOC 2877, ff. 170-305	1755-6.
VOC 2906, n.f.	1756-7.
VOC 2929, n.f.	1757-8.
VOC 2960, ff. 160-70	1759.
VOC 2961, ff. 247-391	1758-9.
VOC 2987, ff. 226-383	1759-60.
VOC 3019, ff. 168-81	1761.
VOC 3020, ff. 409-700	1760-1.
VOC 3056, ff. 414-700	1761-2.
VOC 3086, ff. 252-60	1762-3.
VOC 3087, ff. 364-806	1762-3.
VOC 3102, ff. 3079-89	1764-5.
VOC 3115, ff. 243-79	1763-4.
VOC 3115, ff. 356-69	1764.
VOC 3116, n.f.	1763-4.
VOC 3146, ff. 420-32	1764-5.
VOC 3146, ff. 512-946	1764-5 (?).
VOC 3147, ff. 1238-44	1765.
VOC 3147, ff. 1274-8	1765.
VOC 3177, ff. 407-29	1766.

VOC 3177, ff. 506-36	1766.
VOC 3178, ff. 549-836	1765-6.
VOC 3205, ff. 179-87	1767.
VOC 3206, ff. 456-776	1766-7.
VOC 3236, ff. 183-476	1767-8.
VOC 3266, f. 366	Concerning bookkeeping, 1768.
VOC 3267, ff. 368-834	1768-9.
VOC 3296, n.f.	1769-70.
VOC 3325, ff. 317-18	Concerning debts, 1771.
VOC 3326, ff. 567-83	1771.
VOC 3327, n.f.	1770-1.
VOC 3352, ff. 186-91	Concerning a conflict with the King of Cochin, 1772.
VOC 3353, n.f.	1771-2.
VOC 3380, ff. 142-7	Concerning fortifications, 1772.
VOC 3380, ff. 157-430	1772-3.
VOC 3380, ff. 491-3	Concerning debts, *c.* 1773.
VOC 3405, ff. 122-7	1773.
VOC 3406, ff. 502-5	Concerning debts, 1773.
VOC 3407, n.f.	1773-4.
VOC 3435, ff. 264-5	Concerning debts, 1775.
VOC 3436, n.f.	1774-6.
VOC 3460, ff. 168-71	Concerning debts, 1776.
VOC 3461, ff. 340-553	1776.
VOC 3488, ff. 165-86	1777.
VOC 3489, ff. 206-392	1777.
VOC 3489, ff. 474-7	Concerning debts, 1777.
VOC 3519, ff. 45-53	1778.
VOC 3520, ff. 220-421	1778.
VOC 3520, ff. 524-6	Concerning debts, 1778.
VOC 3548, ff. 149-328	1779.
VOC 3575, ff. 185-339	1780.
VOC 3575, ff. 446-59	Concerning Haidar Ali Khan, 1780.
VOC 3617, ff. 27-65	1782.
VOC 3617, ff. 98-105	Concerning the war with the British, 1783.
VOC 3617, ff. 219-420	1781.
VOC 3618, ff. 576-633	1781.
VOC 3644, ff. 81-106	1782.
VOC 3644, ff. 170-2	Concerning debts, 1783.
VOC 3644, ff. 276-90	1783.
VOC 3644, ff. 322-7	1781.
VOC 3644, f. 376	1783.
VOC 3644, ff. 401-6	1783-4 (among other documents).
VOC 3645, ff. 262-491?	1782-4.
VOC 3668, ff. 43-6	1784.

VOC 3668, ff. 55-9	1783-4.
VOC 3668, ff. 65-9	1784.
VOC 3668, ff. 99-132	1784 (among other documents).
VOC 3668, ff. 157-8	1784.
VOC 3668, ff. 248-51	1784.
VOC 3668, ff. 381-90	1701 (?).
VOC 3669, n.f.	1784.
VOC 3695, ff. 35-69	1784-5 (among other documents).
VOC 3695, ff. 164-212	1785.
VOC 3749, f. 159	1787.
VOC 3751, ff. 150-1	Concerning debts, 1786.
VOC 3752, n.f.	1785-6.
VOC 3753, ff. 820-2	Concerning debts, 1787.
VOC 3753, ff. 947-66	1787 (among other documents).
VOC 3753, ff. 986-1002	1787-8 (among other documents).
VOC 3801, ff. 38-46	1787.
VOC 3801, ff. 95-135	1788.
VOC 3801, ff. 248-74	1788 (among other documents).
VOC 3802, ff. 388-90	Concerning debts, 1788.
VOC 3803, n.f.	1787-8.
VOC 3849, ff. 48-9	1788.
VOC 3849, ff. 171-209	1789.
VOC 3849, ff. 324-7	1789.
VOC 3850, ff. 441-9	1788-1789 (among other documents).
VOC 3850, ff. 526-41	1789.
VOC 3850, ff. 558-88	1789-1790 (among other documents).
VOC 3851, n.f.	1788-9.
VOC 3895, ff. 46-103	1790 (among other documents).
VOC 3895, ff. 258-61	Concerning debts, 1790.
VOC 3896, ff. 389-91	1790.
VOC 3896, ff. 621-3	1790.
VOC 3897, n.f.	1789-90.
VOC 3929, ff. 29-54	1790-1.
VOC 3929, ff. 78-88	1791 (among other documents).
VOC 3929, ff. 233-5	1791.
VOC 3929, ff. 350-9	1791.
VOC 3930, n.f.	1790-1.
VOC 3971, ff. 1885-94	Concerning the war between Travancore and Tipu Sultan of Mysore, 1790.
VOC 3980, ff. 74-8	Concerning the stationing of guards at the 'Kanarijnse' temple, 1791.
VOC 3980, f. 127	Concerning an assassination by the King of Cochin, 1791.
VOC 3980, ff. 144-213	1791-2 (among other documents).
VOC 3980, ff. 334-6	1792.
VOC 3980, f. 444	1792.

Vengurla: *Resoluties* (proceedings)

VOC 1129, ff. 261-325	Concerning Goa, 1638-9.
VOC 1133, ff. 490-5	1640 (among other documents).
VOC 1133, ff. 512-13	1640.
VOC 1134, n.f.	Concerning Goa, 1640.
VOC 1135, ff. 460, 462	Partly concerning Goa, 1640.
VOC 1144, ff. 221-7	Concerning Goa, *c.* 1643.
VOC 1144, ff. 303-38	Concerning Goa, 1642-3.
VOC 1157, ff. 454-5	*c.* 1645.

3.1.3. *Dagregisters* (diaries)
(for an explanation of the term *inlandse* see under 3.1)

VOC 1177, ff. 45-59	January-March 1650.
VOC 1274, ff. 171-80	'Canara' (Barcelore?), June-July 1670.
VOC 1527, ff. 640-70v	Cochin, concerning Malabar rulers, 1692.
VOC 1925, n.f.	*Inlandse*, November 1718-September 1719.
VOC 1943, ff. 410-1016	October 1719-September 1720.
VOC 1959, ff. 383-890	*Inlandse*, October 1720-September 1721.
VOC 1978, ff. 321-765	*Inlandse*, October 1721-October 1722 (?).
VOC 1993, ff. 312-572	October 1722-April 1723.
VOC 1994, ff. 573-875	May-September 1723.
VOC 2011, ff. 508-1212	*Inlandse*, October 1723-September 1724.
VOC 2028, ff. 669-1436	*Inlandse*, October 1724-September 1725.
VOC 2049, ff. 809-1332	*Inlandse*, October 1725-September 1726.
VOC 2071, ff. 801-1479	*Inlandse*, October 1726-September 1727.
VOC 2098, ff. 706-1334	*Inlandse*, October 1727-September 1728.
VOC 2131, ff. 534-1073	*Inlandse*, October 1728-September 1729.
VOC 2161, ff. 718-1227	*Inlandse*, October 1729-September 1730.
VOC 2188, ff. 1014-398	*Inlandse*, October 1730-March 1731.
VOC 2189, ff. 1391-898	*Inlandse*, April-September 1731.
VOC 2201, ff. 1775-2226	January-December 1730.
VOC 2201, ff. 2227-878	*Inlandse*, April 1730-March 1731.
VOC 2228, ff. 893-1796	*Inlandse*, October 1731-October 1732.
VOC 2248, ff. 1949-2160	1731.
VOC 2248, ff. 2161-3278	*Inlandse*, April 1731-March 1732.
VOC 2279, ff. 579-1088	Concerning Malabar rulers, October 1732-March 1733.
VOC 2280, ff. 1089-699	Concerning Malabar rulers, April-September 1733.
VOC 2292, ff. 993-?	January-December 1732.
VOC 2310, ff. 537-1688	Concerning Malabar rulers, October 1733-September 1734.
VOC 2340, ff. 485-1034	Concerning Malabar rulers, October 1734-March 1735.

VOC 2341, ff. 1053-539	Concerning Malabar rulers, April-December 1735.
VOC 2376, ff. 345-1034	Concerning Malabar rulers, October 1735-March 1736.
VOC 2377, ff. 1035-630	Concerning Malabar rulers, April-September 1736.
VOC 2405, ff. 224-1203	Concerning Malabar rulers, October 1736-March 1737.
VOC 2406, ff. 1204-1885	Concerning Malabar rulers, April-September 1737.
VOC 2433, ff. 212-1228	Concerning Malabar rulers, October 1737-November 1738.
VOC 2462, ff. 153-1320	Concerning Malabar rulers, October 1738-September 1739.
VOC 2495, ff. 230-910	*Inlandse*, October 1739-March 1740.
VOC 2496, ff. 911-1543	*Inlandse*, April-September 1740.
VOC 2507-2508, n.f.	January-December 1739.
VOC 2507-2508, n.f.	*Inlandse*, April 1739-March 1740.
VOC 2526, ff. 249-1034	*Inlandse*, October 1740-March 1741.
VOC 2527, ff. 1035-775	*Inlandse*, April-September 1741.
VOC 2561, ff. 295-885	*Inlandse*, October 1741-March 1742.
VOC 2562, ff. 886-1602	*Inlandse*, April-September 1742.
VOC 2602, ff. 269-805	*Inlandse*, October 1742-March 1743.
VOC 2603, ff. 806-1110	*Inlandse*, April-September 1743.
VOC 2624, ff. 176-530	*Inlandse*, October 1743-March 1744.
VOC 2625, ff. 531-846	*Inlandse*, April-September 1744.
VOC 2647, ff. 344-1164	*Inlandse*, October 1744-September 1745.
VOC 2671, ff. 732-1060	*Inlandse*, October 1745-September 1746.
VOC 2696, ff. 814-1334	*Inlandse*, October 1746-September 1747.
VOC 2715, ff. 804-1197	*Inlandse*, October 1747-September 1748.
VOC 2738, ff. 475-822	*Inlandse*, October 1748-September 1749 (the table of contents of this volume has accidentally been replaced by the one belonging to volume no. VOC 2737).
VOC 2759, ff. 474-786	*Inlandse*, October 1749-September 1750.
VOC 2777, ff. 817-1286	*Inlandse*, October 1750-September 1751.
VOC 2797, ff. 362-718	*Inlandse*, October 1751-September 1752.
VOC 2815, ff. 323-598	*Inlandse*, October 1752-September 1753.
VOC 2834, ff. 341-666	*Inlandse*, October 1753-September 1754.
VOC 2857, ff. 311-578	*Inlandse*, October 1754-September 1755.
VOC 2877, ff. 306-464	*Inlandse*, October 1755-September 1756.
VOC 2906, n.f.	*Inlandse*, October 1756-September 1757.
VOC 2929, n.f.	October 1757-September 1758.
VOC 2961, ff. 392-640	*Inlandse*, October 1758-September 1759.
VOC 2987, ff. 429-624	*Inlandse*, October 1759-September 1760.

VOC 3020, ff. 701-978	*Inlandse*, October 1760-September 1761.
VOC 3056, ff. 701-1117	*Inlandse*, October 1761-September 1762.
VOC 3087, ff. 807-1060	*Inlandse*, October 1762-September 1763.
VOC 3116, n.f.	*Inlandse*, October 1763-September 1764.
VOC 3145, ff. 225-388	*Inlandse*, October 1764-September 1765.
VOC 3178, ff. 876-1050	*Inlandse*, October 1765-September 1766.
VOC 3206, ff. 821-947	*Inlandse*, October 1766-September 1767.
VOC 3237, ff. 561-652	*Inlandse*, October 1767-September 1768.
VOC 3267, ff. 835-?	*Inlandse*, October 1768-September 1769.
VOC 3296, n.f.	*Inlandse*, October 1769-September 1770.
VOC 3327, n.f.	*Inlandse*, October 1770-September 1771.
VOC 3353, n.f.	*Inlandse*, October 1771-September 1772.
VOC 3380, ff. 494-574	*Inlandse*, *c.* 1773 (October 1772-September 1773?).
VOC 3407, n.f.	*Inlandse*, October-December 1773.
VOC 3436, n.f.	*Inlandse*, January-December 1775.
VOC 3460, ff. 178-230	*Inlandse*, January-December 1776.
VOC 3489, ff. 481-508	*Inlandse*, January-December 1777.
VOC 3520, ff. 527-69	*Inlandse*, 1778.
VOC 3801, ff. 136-63	*Inlandse*, January-February 1788.

Vengurla: *Dagregisters* (diaries)

VOC 1143, ff. 688-703	November 1643-February 1644.
VOC 1165, ff. 99-109	April-September 1646.
VOC 1170, ff. 699-714	April-October 1647.
VOC 1170, ff. 721-26	April-June 1648.
VOC 1178, ff. 470-87	April-December 1649.
VOC 1203, ff. 893-907	April-July, 1654.

3.1.4. *Shipping lists*

VOC 1280, ff. 497-8	*c.* 1671.
VOC 1416, ff. 1426-8	Vessels that arrived at and departed from Cochin, 1684-5.
VOC 1429, ff. 1370v-?	Vessels that arrived at and departed from Cochin, 1685.
VOC 1474, ff. 184-9v	Vessels that arrived at and departed from Cochin, 1689-90.
VOC 1474, ff. 900-9	Vessels that arrived at and departed from Cochin, 1689-91.
VOC 1638, ff. 90-103	Vessels that arrived at and departed from Cochin, 1699.
VOC 1928, ff. 14-17	Dutch and foreign vessels that arrived at Cochin, 1718-19.

VOC 1947, ff. 328-35	Dutch and foreign vessels that arrived at and departed from Cochin, 1719-20.
VOC 1999, ff. 75?-?	Vessels that arrived at and departed from Cochin, 1722-3.
VOC 2015, ff. 472-7	Arrival and departure of Dutch and other European vessels, 1723-4.
VOC 2033, ff. 446-55	Arrival and departure of Dutch and foreign vessels, 1724-5.
VOC 2054, ff. 314-19	Arrival and departure of Dutch and other vessels, 1725-6.
VOC 2078, ff. 514-19	Arrival and departure of Dutch and foreign vessels, 1726-7.
VOC 2104, ff. 421-5	Dutch and foreign vessels that arrived at and departed from Cochin, *c.* 1728.
VOC 2137, ff. 442-51	Vessels that arrived at and departed from Cochin, 1728-9.
VOC 2167, ff. 460-5	Arrival and departure of vessels, 1729-30.
VOC 2201, ff. 3268-73	Arrival and departure of vessels, 1731.
VOC 2231, f. 3302	Vessels that arrived at and departed from Cochin, 1731-2.
VOC 2248, ff. 3554-9	Vessels that arrived at and departed from Cochin, *c.* 1732
VOC 2248, f. 3560	Dutch vessels at Cochin, *c.* 1732.
VOC 2249, ff. 2053-6	Arrival and departure of British and Portuguese vessels, *c.* 1732.
VOC 2282, ff. 2491-?	Dutch vessels, 1733.
VOC 2320, ff. 1318-23	Arrival and departure of Dutch, British, French, Portuguese and Muslim vessels, *c.* 1734.
VOC 2342, f. 2074	1735.
VOC 2354, ff. 900-7	Vessels that arrived at and departed from Cochin, 1734-5.
VOC 2354, ff. 945-63	Dutch vessels, *c.* 1735.
VOC 2378, f. 2105	1736.
VOC 2389, ff. 1710-20	Dutch vessels at Cochin, 1736.
VOC 2389, ff. 1721-9	Arrival and departure of Dutch, British, French, Portuguese and Muslim vessels, 1735-6.
VOC 2407, f. 2431	1737.
VOC 2414, ff. 2176-91	Dutch vessels at Cochin, *c.* 1737.
VOC 2414, ff. 2192-7	Arrived and departed Dutch, British, French, Portuguese and Muslim vessels, 1736-7.
VOC 2435, f. 2148	1738.
VOC 2446, ff. 990-1006	Dutch vessels at Cochin, *c.* 1738.
VOC 2446, ff. 1007-9	Arrived and departed Dutch, British, French, Portuguese and Muslim vessels, 1737-8.
VOC 2446, ff. 103-4	1738.

VOC 2463, f. 1863	1739.
VOC 2474, ff. 1049-53	Arrival and departure of Dutch, British, French, Portuguese and Muslim vessels, 1738-9.
VOC 2498, f. 2555	1740.
VOC 2507-8, ff. 3449-65	Dutch vessels at Cochin, *c.* 1740.
VOC 2507-2508, ff. 3466-73	Arrival and departure of Dutch, British, French, Portuguese and Muslim vessels, *c.* 1740.
VOC 2529, f. 2415	1741.
VOC 2542, ff. 1451-62	Vessels at Cochin, *c.* 1741.
VOC 2542, ff. 1463-8?	Arrival and departure of Dutch, British, Portuguese and Muslim vessels, 1740-1.
VOC 2543, ff. 4217-?	1741.
VOC 2564, f. 2737	1742.
VOC 2580, ff. 5624-39	Vessels at Cochin, *c.* 1742.
VOC 2580, ff. 5640-5	Arrival and departure of Dutch, British, Portuguese and Muslim vessels, 1741-2.
VOC 2604, f. 1490	1743.
VOC 2626, f. 1147	1744.
VOC 2648, f. 1835	1745.
VOC 2669, f. 218	1746.
VOC 2863, ff. 210-6	Foreign vessels, 1755.
VOC 3055, ff. 350-62	Foreign vessels, 1761-2.
VOC 3086, ff. 322-30	Foreign vessels, 1762-3.
VOC 3115, ff. 381-90	Foreign vessels, 1763-4.
VOC 3145, ff. 177-86	Foreign vessels, 1764-5.
VOC 3178, ff. 847-57	Foreign vessels, 1765-6.
VOC 3206, ff. 782-808	Foreign vessels, 1766-7.
VOC 3237, ff. 492-534	Foreign vessels, 1767-8.
VOC 3548, ff. 340-96	Vessels that arrived at and departed from Cochin, 1778-9.
VOC 3575, ff. 353-408	Vessels that arrived at and departed from Cochin, 1779-80.
VOC 3644, ff. 180-253	Foreign and indigenous vessels that arrived at and departed from Cochin, 1781-2.
VOC 3668, ff. 265-342	Vessels that arrived at and departed from Cochin, 1782-3.
VOC 3695, ff. 227-331	Vessels that arrived at and departed from Cochin, 1783-4.
VOC 3849, f. 31	Vessels at Alleppey, 1788.
VOC 3895, ff. 271-345	Arrival and departure of vessels, 1788-9.
VOC 3929, ff. 243-330	Arrival and departure of vessels, 1789-90.
VOC 3980, ff. 350-423	Arrival and departure of vessels, 1790-1.

3.1.5. *Missions to Indian states*

VOC 1231, ff. 513-14	Mission to Ikkeri by Abram Carter, 1659 (instructions).

VOC 1251, ff. 723-840	Mission to Travancore, Madurai and Ramnad by Hendrick van Rede, October 1665 (report).
VOC 1267-8, ff. 1113-16	Mission to Ikkeri by Govert de Bruijn, May 1668 (report).
VOC 1275-8, ff. 1725-?	Mission to the Zamorin of Calicut and to Cranganur by Burgart, *c.* 1670 (various documents).
VOC 1349, ff. 1487-9	Mission to the Kings of Cochin and Kayankulam by Hendrick Reijns, 1679 (instructions).
VOC 1349, ff. 1587?-8?	Mission to Kayankulam by Hendrick Rijns and Marten Samson, 1679 (report).
VOC 1361, ff. 482-4	Mission to Kayankulam by Samson and Sonsbeek, 1680 (report).
VOC 1388, ff. 1962-5	Mission to Kayankulam by Arnoult Schlosser, 1683.
VOC 1406, ff. 909-33	Mission to Ikkeri by Wilkens, April-May 1684.
VOC 1454, ff. 1279v-92	Mission to Attingal by Hendrick Reijnst (and others), October 1688 (report).
VOC 1527, ff. 303-6	Mission to Ikkeri by merchant Babba Prabhu, November 1691 (various documents).
VOC 1527, ff. 525-38	Mission to Prince Kerala Varma in Travancore by Alexander Wigmans, 1691 (reports).
VOC 1547, ff. 186-97	Mission to the Zamorin of Calicut at Chowghat by Louis Taispel, 1694 (report).
VOC 1547, ff. 198-210	Mission to Kayankulam and Purakkad by Cornelis Blicklandt and others, *c.* 1694 (report).
VOC 1571, ff. 95-103	Mission to Attingal by Jan Grotenhuijs and Louis Taijspil, 1695 (instructions).
VOC 1598, ff. 168-98	Mission to the King of Cochin by Abraham Vinck and Barent Ketel, 1697 (report).
VOC 1619, ff. 189-92	Mission to Badagara by Engel Bouwman, March 1699 (report).
VOC 1627, ff. 247-50	Mission to Parur, 1698 (report).
VOC 1627, ff. 251-76	Mission to the King of Cochin, 1698 (reports).
VOC 1634, ff. 505-8	Mission to the Zamorin of Calicut, 1700 (report).
VOC 1646, ff. 447-9	Mission to the second prince of the Zamorin by Blicklant, *c.* 1701 (instructions).
VOC 1649, ff. 99-102	Mission to the Zamorin at Ponnani, 1700 (report).
VOC 1649, ff. 103-9	Mission to Quilon, Kayankulam and Purakkad by Abraham Vinck, 1700 (report).
VOC 1679, ff. 160-9	Mission to Kayankulam by Ferdinand Hanibal Groen (partly), *c.* 1703 (report).
VOC 1731, ff. 149-53	Mission to the King of Cochin, 1705 (reports).
VOC 1778, ff. 121-4	Mission to the Raja of Cranganur by Willem Moerman (partly), *c.* 1709 (report).
VOC 1928, ff. 20-64	Mission to the Zamorin of Calicut by Joannes

	Hertenberg, December 1718-January 1719 (report).
VOC 1947, ff. 354-67	Mission to the Valluvakonatiri of Valluvanadu in 'Arangolla' by Isaac Isaacsz. and Joseph de Guz, *c.* 1720 (report).
VOC 2227, ff. 310-15	Mission to the Zamorin of Calicut (partly), 1732 (correspondence).
VOC 2231, ff. 3139-76	Mission to the King of Travancore (at Quilon?), March-April 1732 (report).
VOC 2249, ff. 1815-76	Mission to the King of Travancore, *c.* 1732 (report).
VOC 2249, ff. 1911-36	Mission to the King of Cochin by Maten, *c.* 1732 (report).
VOC 2281, ff. 1905-16	Mission to the King of Cochin by Johannes Steenhuijsen and Robertus Kramer, May 1733 (report).
VOC 2320, ff. 178-218	Mission to Alangadu by Willem Feling and Arend Willem Ninaber, *c.* 1734 (report).
VOC 2320, ff. 1704-32	Mission to Alangadu by Feling and Van de Welle, 1734 (report).
VOC 2354, ff. 14-124	Mission to Travancore by Willem Feling and Ab van de Welle, *c.* 1735 (report).
VOC 2354, ff. 1491-1621	Mission to Ikkeri, et*c.*, by Crijn Stevens and Abraham Gosenson, *c.* 1735 (report).
VOC 2414, ff. 1740-2156	Mission to the Kolathiri of Cannanore and to Ikkeri, *c.* 1737 (report).
VOC 2446, ff. 246-82	Mission to Ikkeri by Reinicus Siersma and Johannes Mooijaart, *c.* 1738 (report).
VOC 2624, ff. 100-14	Mission to the King of Travancore at Mavelikara by Daniel Berger and Nicolaes Bowijn, June-July 1744 (report).
VOC 3086, ff. 294-300	Mission to Travancore by interpreter Joan Pereira, 1763 (report).
VOC 3177, ff. 436-68	Mission to Haidar Ali Khan of Mysore by S.C. Saffin and F.B. Zimmerman, April-May 1766 (report).
VOC 3177, ff. 473-81	Mission to the Kings of Travancore and Cochin by Etienne and Saffin, May 1766 (report).
VOC 3405, ff. 135-40	Mission to Travancore by Tongeren and Holsenberg, *c.* 1774 (report).
VOC 3668, ff. 133-5	Mission to Tipu Sultan of Mysore by Saffer en Vernede, *c.* 1784 (instructions).
VOC 3753, ff. 1003-8	Mission to Travancore by J.L. van Spall and J.A. Scheids, 1788 (report).
VOC 3980, ff. 56-8	Mission to the King of Cochin by Lunel and Eversdijk, 1791 (report).

Vengurla: *Missions to Indian states*

VOC 1122, ff. 469-501	Mission to Bijapur by Nicolaes van Twist, January-March 1637 (report). For a condensed published version, see Bibliography, no. 55.

3.1.6. *Miscellaneous*

VOC 1252-3, n.f.	Report concerning Pieter Vertange's journey to Tekkumkur, 1665.
VOC 1254, ff. 1098-1107	Report concerning Pieter Vertange's journey to Tekkumkur, *c.* 1665.
VOC 1261, ff. 315-47	Correspondence concerning turmoil in Malabar and especially at Cannanore, 1666-7.
VOC 1266, ff. 864-83	Report by Rijcklof van Goens concerning the state of affairs of the government of Ceylon, Malabar and the Fishery Coast, 1669.
VOC 1307, ff. 333-72	Report concerning events on the Malabar Coast, *c.* 1675.
VOC 1307, ff. 688-724	Report of a journey by Governor of Ceylon Rijclof van Goens to Malabar, 1675.
VOC 1308, ff. 799-826	Report by Gelmer Vosburgh concerning the governing of Malabar by Hendrik van Reede, June 1675.
VOC 1321, ff. 798v-823	Report by Rutgaart de Heijde concerning his visit to the Kanara Coast, December 1675-March 1676.
VOC 1351, ff. 2573-6	List of the Company's (Dutch and local) servants at Malabar, 1679.
VOC 1352, ff. 281-376	Report concerning Malabar, the Kanara Coast and Vengurla, 1680.
VOC 1352, ff. 555-75	Report concerning Malabar, *c.* 1680.
VOC 1370, ff. 2152-69	Report concerning trade in Mysore, 1681.
VOC 1370, ff. 2276-340	Reaction to the *memorie van overgave* by Hendrick van Rheede for Jacob Lobs (dating from March 1677), 1681.
VOC 1474, ff. 450-3v	Survey of the pepper trade between 1659 and 1689.
VOC 1591, ff. 783-951v	Instructions to Hendrick Zwaerdecroon at his departure as Commissioner to Malabar, 1697.
VOC 1593, ff. 76-167v	Correspondence with rulers, nobles and merchants at Malabar and on the Kanara Coast, 1697.
VOC 1593, ff. 693-977	Report of the activities of Commissioner Hendrick Zwaerdecroon in Malabar, April-November 1697.
VOC 1607, ff. 182-397	Report of the activities of Commissioner Hendrick Zwaerdecroon in Malabar, December 1697-April 1698.

VOC 1611, ff. 201-347	Correspondence with kings, nobles and merchants at Malabar, 1697.
VOC 1611, ff. 521-680	Instructions by Commissioner Hendrick Zwaerdecroon to Magnus Wichelman at Cochin, 1698.
VOC 1634, ff. 401-86	Notes of conferences with kings and nobles of Malabar, September-November 1700.
VOC 1634, ff. 509-857	Correspondence with kings and nobles of Malabar, 1699-1700.
VOC 1646, ff. 454-501	Documents concerning meetings with Malabar rulers at Cranganur and Pudikovil (near Cranganur), *c.* 1701.
VOC 1646, ff. 507-816	Correspondence with and other documents concerning Malabar kings, 1700-1.
VOC 1694, ff. 60-84	Report concerning trade in Ikkeri and on the Kanara Coast, 1703.
VOC 1694, ff. 94-128	Report concerning conflicts between the King of Cochin and the Zamorin of Calicut, *c.* 1704.
VOC 1731, ff. 489-?	Report of a meeting with the King of Cochin, 1706.
VOC 1762, ff. 374-?	Report of a meeting with the King of Cochin and other Malabar nobles, 1707-8.
VOC 1774, ff. 907-1092	Report concerning the war with the Zamorin of Calicut and the King of Parur, January-September 1709.
VOC 1790, ff. 39-96	Daily report kept during an expedition of the Dutch armed forces against Calicut and Parur, November 1709-April 1710.
VOC 1807, ff. 120-32	Report by Barent Ketel concerning his visit to the southern factories and meetings with several kings, July 1711.
VOC 1812, ff. 228-49	Report concerning the 'bandit' Kanoji Angria, 1711.
VOC 1852, ff. 329-418	Report by Barent Ketel concerning his journey to Cranganur and Chetwai, July-August 1714.
VOC 1880, ff. 138-205	Report concerning the expedition against the Zamorin of Calicut, December 1715-April 1716.
VOC 1885, ff. 257-438	Documents concerning the Malabar war, 1715-16.
VOC 1924, ff. 65-122	Documents concerning the reinstallation of 'Ittanda Wanganattoe' as Velose Nambiyar at Mapranam, *c.* 1719.
VOC 1942, ff. 224-46	Report concerning meetings with the Kings of Kayankulam and Purakkad at Cochin, 1720.
VOC 1963, ff. 149-54	Document concerning weights, measures and currencies in Malabar, *c.* 1721.
VOC 1963, ff. 155-217	Documents concerning the smuggling of pepper at Kayankulam, *c.* 1721.

VOC 1978. ff. 766-801	Correspondence concerning conflicts between Purakkad, Tekkumkur, Vadakkumkur, Kayankulam and Repolim, 1722.
VOC 1982, ff. 287-395	Documents concerning conflicts between Hindus and Muslims at Cannanore, *c.* 1722.
VOC 2015, ff. 361-422	Report concerning conflicts between the Punnathur Nambidi and the Manakkulam Nambidi, *c.* 1724.
VOC 2187, ff. 353-432	Report by Jacob de Jong concerning his journey to Cranganur to reconcile two local nobles, 1731.
VOC 2201, ff. 2897-3099	Report by Jacob de Jong concerning his journey to Alangadu, *c.* 1731.
VOC 2232, ff. 3476-905	Report by Commissioner Wouter Hendrix concerning his journey to Malabar, September 1731-March 1732 (see 3.2.2 VOC 8985-9047 and 11311).
VOC 2279, ff. 438-548	Report by Adriaan Maten concerning his journey to the southern factories in Malabar, July-August 1733.
VOC 2281, ff. 1810-72	Correspondence concerning the war between Ikkeri and the Ali Raja at Cannanore, 1733.
VOC 2309, ff. 423-94	Report by Willem Feeling and Abraham Welle concerning their mission to reconcile the rulers of Quilon, Kayankulam and Travancore, May-July 1734.
VOC 2320, ff. 298-312	Documents concerning the 'pirate' Kanoji Angria, *c.* 1734.
VOC 2320, ff. 1507-1698	Report concerning a conflict with Ikkeri, *c.* 1734.
VOC 2389, ff. 957-1125	Report concerning the peace concluded between the second and third prince of Vadakkumkur, 1735.
VOC 2389, ff. 1486-1550	Correspondence concerning the succession in 'Cartadawie', 1735.
VOC 2424, ff. 137-477	Report by Renicus Siersma and Samuel Mooijaart concerning their journey to Barcelore and Cannanore, 1736.
VOC 2456, ff. 464-711	Report by Gustaaf Willem von Imhoff concerning his journey to Malabar, the Fishery Coast and part of Ceylon, January-April 1739.
VOC 2507-8, ff. 1265-2500	Correspondence concerning the war against Travancore, 1739-40.
VOC 2543, ff. 2571-962	Report concerning the Dutch armed forces at Vadakkumkur, 1740-1.
VOC 2543, ff. 2963-3318	Report concerning the war against Travancore, 1741.
VOC 2564, ff. 2495-736	Report concerning the war against Travancore, 1741-2.

VOC 2868, ff. 809-27	*Radicale beschrijving* (i.e. an official review) of Malabar (and Ternate), December 1756.
VOC 2893, ff. 1466-1502	Document concerning the state of affairs in Malabar, 1758.
VOC 2911, ff. 108-153	Improved document concerning the state of affairs in Malabar, *c.* 1758.
VOC 3070, ff. 2047-313	Document concerning the state of affairs of the factories in Malabar, *c.* 1763.
VOC 3145, ff. 206-8	Document concerning weights, measures and currencies in Malabar, *c.* 1765.
VOC 3188, ff. 443-936	Documents concerning fraud in bookkeeping, *c.* 1767.
VOC 3189, ff. 937-84	Documents concerning the fortifications at Cochin and Cannanore, *c.* 1766.
VOC 3201, ff. 791-842	Document concerning the events in Madurai, Ramnad and Travancore, 1767.
VOC 3205, ff. 193-225	Reports concerning the reduction of the settlements at Cochin and Cannanore, 1767.
VOC 3295, ff. 189-230	Report concerning contacts with the King of Travancore, *c.* 1770.
VOC 3295, ff. 231-95	Essay by Senff concerning the state of affairs in Malabar, *c.* 1770.
VOC 3325, ff. 133-72	Report concerning negotiations with envoys from Travancore, *c.* 1771.
VOC 3326, ff. 334-482	Documents concerning conflicts with the King of Cochin, *c.* 1771.
VOC 3431, ff. 198-298	Some treaties, etc., concluded with Travancore (among other kingdoms), 1665-91.
VOC 3619, n.f.	Memorandum by Van Asbeek concerning Malabar, *c.* 1782.
VOC 3801, ff. 212-47	Notes concerning a meeting with the King of Travancore and his *Dalawa*, 1788.

Vengurla: *Miscellaneous*

VOC 1129, ff. 108-233	Report concerning the occupation of Goa, July 1638-July 1639.
VOC 1144, ff. 109-167	Report concerning Goa, August 1642-March 1643.
VOC 1144, ff. 256-302	Report concerning Goa, August 1642-January 1643.
VOC 1150, ff. 367-410	Report concerning Goa, October 1642-April 1643.
VOC 1158, ff. 401-76	Report concerning a journey to Goa and the King of Kandy, *c.* 1645.
VOC 1352, ff. 281-376	Report concerning Malabar, the Kanara Coast and Vengurla, 1680.

VOC 2389, ff. 1369-1485	Report by Jan Delille concerning his mission to Vengurla, 1736.

3.2. Other VOC Series

3.2.1. *Archives of the Gentlemen XVII and the Amsterdam Chamber*

See 1.1
Access no.: 1.04.02

Kopie-resoluties van de Gouverneur-Generaal en Raden
Duplicate proceedings of the Governor-General and Council

See 1.1.4
Inv. nos: VOC 656-847

In the *Realia* repertory to the *resoluties* several relevant headings are to be found, among these:

Aicotta (Azhikkodu; 1 entry 1702), *Bagare* (Badagara? 1 entry 1706), *Barssaloor* (Barcelore; 4 entries 1702-46), *Canara* (1 entry 1676), *Chettua* (Chetwai; 2 entries 1715-19), *Cochim* (Cochin; 34 entries 1622-1800), *Coilang* (Quilon; 3 entries 1659-1702), *Coudewaar* (1 entry 1676), *Cranganoor* (Cranganur; 1697-1732), *Innemacka* (1 entry 1732), *Lakkadivose Eilanden* (Lakshadweep; 1 entry 1787), *Mallabaar* (Malabar; about 550 entries 1652-1795), *Sammorijn* (Zamorin of Calicut; 19 entries 1662-1759), *Thomese (St., christenen)* (St. Thomas Christians; 2 entries 1665), *Travancoor* (Travancore; 14 entries 1751-9), *christenen (Lascorijns, Toepassen)* (Christians (soldiers); 2 entries 1694).

Miscellaneous

VOC 536, 538	Documents of admiral Pieter Willemsz. Verhoeff, consisting of two copies of a treaty concluded with the Zamorin of Calicut in October 1608 (published in *CDNI*, I, pp. 53-4), and a letter to VOC fleets off the coast of Calicut, 1608. Three pieces.
VOC 545	Letter of Jacob de Bitter to VOC servants on the Malabar Coast concerning the establishment of a factory at Cannanore, 1608.
VOC 4618	Papers of the so-called Committee of the Amsterdam Chamber for the sale of the VOC possessions on the Malabar Coast, concerning the contemplated cession of the establishments to the King of Travancore, 1790-2. One folder. Some documents relating to the work of this Committee (see 1.6.19 and 3.6) are also in the Nederburgh private collection.
VOC 4631	Notes of Advocate Pieter van Dam and other papers concerning the Malabar Coast and Ceylon, 1664-1702. One folder.
VOC 4654	Memorandum in reply of the Directors of the VOC to a claim by the *Westindische Compagnie* (WIC, West India Company)

	of three million guilders by way of compensation for the possession of settlements on the Malabar Coast, 1705. Printed, one piece.
VOC 4726	Memorandum of the Directors to the States General concerning the conflicts with the English about Malabar (and other places), 1686. Printed, two pieces.
VOC 4759	Memorandum containing a draft for a direct trade connection between the Dutch Republic and Malabar and Surat, with appendices, 1773-4. Three volumes, one piece.
VOC 4787	Conditions offered by Haidar Ali of Mysore toward the conclusion of a treaty with the VOC, 1780. One piece.
VOC 4816	List of coins, exchange rates, weights and measures in Asia, with index, including sections on Cochin, Kayankulam, Purakkad, Cannanore, Quilon, Tengapattanam and 'Canara' (Barcelore?) (ff. 1-90 contain the actual lists; ff. 91-139 contain notes on these subjects), 1769. One volume.
VOC 4903	Description of Malabar by Liebrecht Hooreman (*Raad van Indië*), concerning in particular the profits and losses, with proposals for improvement, 1756. One piece.
VOC 7054	Papers originating from Cochin concerning bills of exchange, 1779-92. One volume.

Vengurla

Kopie-resoluties van de Gouverneur-Generaal en Raden
Duplicate proceedings of the Governor-General and Council

See 1.1.4
Inv. nos: VOC 656-847

In the *Realia* repertory to the *resoluties* several relevant headings are to be found, among these:

Angreanen (Angria 'pirates'; 8 entries 1738-56), *Angria* (3 entries 1707-15), *Dendarajapour* (Janjira; 4 entries 1756-9), *Goa* (21 entries 1636-1702), *Vinapourse landen* (Bijapur; 1 entry1664), *Wingurla* (Vengurla; 7 entries 1648-1702).

Miscellaneous

VOC 537	Letter written by admiral Pieter Willemsz. Verhoeff off the coast of Goa to Coromandel concerning textiles to be given to Jacob de Bitter, 1608. One piece.
VOC 4816	List of coins, exchange rates, weights and measures in Asia, with index, including sections on Vengurla and Bijapur (ff. 1-90 contain the actual lists; ff. 91-139 contain notes on these subjects, 1769). One volume.

3.2.2. *Archives of the Zeeland Chamber*

See 1.2.1
Access no.: 1.04.02

Ingekomen stukken van Gouverneur-Generaal en Raden bij de Heren XVII en de Kamer Zeeland (IGG)
Papers received from Governor-General and Council by the Gentlemen XVII and the Zeeland Chamber

VOC 8985-9047	Letters and reports received by GG&C from Malabar, with appendices, 1681-1754. 68 volumes. Incomplete series. VOC 9014 contains papers belonging to the report of Wouter Hendricx, extraordinary member of the Council and Commissioner for Malabar affairs, 1732 (see VOC 11311 below and VOC 2232 (3.1.6)).
VOC 9190	Report of *Visiateur-Generaal* A.H. Dormieux and *Boekhouder-Generaal* P.J.L. de Fillietax concerning fraud in the trade books of Malabar, with appendices, 1776. One volume.
VOC 9191	List of the supply, purchase and selling prices of 'round' pepper and areca from Malabar for the years 1687-9, drawn up on the basis of the trade books of the factory at Nagappattinam, 1700. One volume.

Ingekomen stukken van de kantoren in Indië bij de Heren XVII en de Kamer Zeeland (IKI)
Papers received from the establishments in the Indies by the Gentlemen XVII and the Zeeland Chamber

VOC 10098	Daily report of a tour of inspection to Cochin, Travancore and the Fishery Coast by Governor Gustaaf Willem von Imhoff, with maps, January-April 1739. One volume.
VOC 10208-10321, 10405	Letters and other papers from the *Commandeur* (sometimes *Directeur*) and Council of Malabar to the Gentlemen XVII and the Zeeland Chamber (and others), with appendices, (1682-) 1689-1793. 115 volumes. Incomplete series. Including: VOC 10292 *Dagregister* of the negotiations and correspondence between the *Commandeur* and Malabar rulers, October 1766-September 1767 VOC 10298 Includes a *dagregister* of Malabar, October 1769-September 1770. VOC 10307 Includes a *dagregister* of Malabar, January-December 1776.

	VOC 10308	Includes a *dagregister* of Malabar, January-December 1777.
	VOC 10309	Includes a *dagregister* of Malabar, January-November 1778.
	VOC 10311	Includes a *dagregister* of Malabar, January-December 1780.
	VOC 10314	Includes *resoluties* of the *Commandeur* and Council of Malabar, 1781-2.
	VOC 10315	Includes *resoluties* of the *Commandeur* and Council of Malabar, 1783.
	VOC 10319	Includes a list of arrived and departed vessels, 1786.

VOC 10322-9	*Resoluties* of the *Commandeur* and Council of Malabar, 1756-61, (1781-) 1785-91. Eight volumes. Incomplete series.
VOC 10330-403	*Dagregisters* of Malabar, 1721-66, (1769-) 1770-5 (-1780). 74 volumes. Incomplete series.
VOC 10404	*Memorie van overgave* by *Commandeur* Julius Valentijn Stein van Gollonesse to Reinerus Siersma, 1743. One volume.

For maps and drawings in this series concerning Malabar (together with Ceylon), see 1.7.10.

Soldijkantoor
Pay Office

See 1.2.1 and 1.1.10

VOC 12453-506	General muster rolls of VOC servants in Malabar, 1772-8. 54 volumes. Including some musters rolls of qualified VOC servants in Malabar for the years 1722, 1756-8, 1765, 1767-78.
VOC 12507-23	Rolls of qualified VOC servants in Malabar, 1737-66 (-1776). Seventeen volumes.
VOC 12524-5	Rolls of the families of VOC servants in Malabar, 1728-40 (-1768).

Miscellaneous

VOC 11123	Printed memorandum of the VOC concerning a claim by the *Westindische Compagnie* (WIC, West India Company) because of the possession of Cochin and Cannanore, with appendix, 1704. One quire.
VOC 11144	Copy of a newspaper report from London concerning a defeat suffered by the EIC against Haidar Ali of Mysore and the Marathas, as a result of which the shares of this Company decreased in value, 1769. One piece.

VOC 11207-8	Two copies of a list (79 pp.) of coins, exchange rates, weights and measures at a great number of factories in the Indies, including Cochin, Kayankulam, Purakkad, Cannanore, Quilon, Tengapattanam and 'Canara' (Barcelore?), printed in 1691 (at Middelburg, Zeeland). Two volumes.
VOC 11309	Papers concerning the valuation and the use of coins in trade transactions in Malabar, 1732. One volume.
VOC 11310	*Memorie van overgave* by *Commandeur* Adriaan Maten to Julius Valentijn Stein van Gollonesse, 1735. One volume.
VOC 11311	Appendices to a report by Wouter Hendricx, Commissioner of Malabar, 1735. One volume (see above VOC 8985-9047 and 3.1.6 VOC 2232).
VOC 11312	Lists serving as a check on the trade books and ledgers for the years 1742-63 of the factory at Cochin, 1767. One volume.
VOC 11314	*Memorie van overgave* by *Commandeur* Reinerus Siersma to Corijn Stevens, 1748. One volume.

Vengurla

Ingekomen stukken van de kantoren in Indië bij de Heren XVII en de Kamer Zeeland (IKI)
Papers received from the establishments in the Indies by the Gentlemen XVII and the Zeeland Chamber

VOC 10112	Report concerning money loan of a Portuguese merchant in Goa to the VOC government of Ceylon, with appendices, 1785-6. One volume.

Miscellaneous

VOC 11207-8	Two copies of a list (79 pp.) of coins, exchange rates, weights and measures at a great number of factories in the Indies, including Vengurla and Bijapur, printed in 1691 (at Middelburg, Zeeland). Two volumes.

3.2.3. *Archives of the Delft, Rotterdam, Enkhuizen and Hoorn Chambers and miscellaneous*

Access no.: 1.04.02

Vengurla

VOC 14912	Newsletter from Goa about the Estado da India, 1595. One folder, in German. Newsletter from Goa about the Dutch and Portuguese, 1600. One folder, in German.

3.3. ARCHIVES TRANSFERRED FROM ASIA

Hoge Regering te Batavia
High Government at Batavia

See 1.3.1
Access no.: 1.04.17

599-608	Extracts of letters from Batavia to Malabar, 1662-1790. With repertoria, ten volumes.
609-15	Minutes of letters from Batavia, 1790-4, 1802-3. Seven volumes.
616-20	Letters to the Governor from subordinate factories, 1788-94. Appended to inv. no. 618 is a list of names of lepers in Pallippuram, 1791. With chronological repertories, five volumes.
621-72	(Secret) letters from Malabar to Batavia, 1789-95, 1797, 1799-1800, 1802-7. With appendices, 52 volumes and covers.
673-7	Letters of the Governor and Council to subordinate and other factories in South Asia, 1789-93. With chronological repertories, five volumes.
678-9	Letters from the Governor and Council to the Dutch Republic, 1790-1793. Two volumes.
680	Letter of *Commandeur* H.A. van Rheede tot Drakesteyn and the Council of Cochin to the Gentlemen XVII, 1675. One volume.
681	Extracts of Malabar Council *resoluties*, 1771-81. One volume.
682-9	(*Secrete*) *resoluties*, 1790-5. With alphabetical repertories. Seven volumes and one cover.
690-5	Notes of meetings and other contacts between the Governor and Indian rulers, 1789-94. Six volumes.
696-9	*Dagregister* of Cochin, 1789-92. Four volumes.
700-4	Deeds of appointment and promotion of Company servants in Malabar, 1789-93. Five volumes.
705	Papers concerning the income of individual Company servants, 1789-90. One volume.
706-11	Rolls of the white population and their servants in Cochin, 1789-94.
712-16	Papers concerning the legal *resoluties* in Malabar, 1789-95. Five volumes.
717	Instruction of Rijklof van Goens relating to Malabar, 1663 and an instruction of Ceylon Governor Jacob Hustaard to the Malabar *Commandeur*, 1664. One volume.
718	Instruction of H.A. van Rheede tot Drakensteyn to Malabar, 1691. One volume.
719-20	Memoranda of Commissioner P. de Roo to the *Commandeur* and to the head of the Cannanore fortress; daily record of the ship Spierdijk kept on a trip to Goa; record of the commercial transactions with merchant Babba Prabhu, 1695. Two volumes.

721-3 Memoranda of *Commandeur* Marten Huysman, 1684, and of Commissioner H. Zwaardecroon, 1698. Three volumes (of which two are identical).

724-6 *Memories van overgave* by *Commandeur* Magnus Wichelmann to M. Schenckenbergh, 1701; *Commandeur* Johannes Hertenberg to Jacob de Jong, 1723. With appendices, three volumes (two of which are identical).

727-8 Report by W. Blom on the condition of trade on the Coast and a refutation of this by some councillors of the High Government, 1731-2. With appendices, two volumes.

729 Additional report of ex-*Commandeur* W.H. Ramskrammer, 1733. One volume.

730 *Memorie van overgave* by *Commandeur* Frederik Cunes to Casparus de Jong, 1756. With appendices, one volume.

731-3 (Secret) memoranda about the Malabar trade by *Commandeur* C. de Jong, Governor-General J. Mossel and Councillor L. Hooreman, 1757-9. Three volumes.

734 *Memorie van overgave* by *Commandeur* Casparus de Jong to Godefridus Weyerman, 1761. With appendices, one volume.

735-6 Memoranda of J. Schreuder to the GG&C, 1763, 1766. With appendices, two volumes.

737-40 *Memories van overgave* by *Commandeur* Godefridus Weyerman to Cornelis Breekpot, 1765; *Commandeur* Breekpot to Christiaan Lodewijk Senff, 1769. Also a memorandum of Breekpot to Batavia on the importance of Malabar, 1769. Four volumes (of which two are identical).

741-5 Memorandum of C.L. Senff, 1770. With appendices and repertories. Five volumes.

746 Message of J.W. van de Graaff concerning the trade ledgers, 1774. With appendices, one volume.

747-8 *Memorie van overgave* by Governor Adriaan Moens to Johan Gerard van Angelbeek, 1781. With appendices, two identical volumes.

749 Secret memorandum of J.G. van Angelbeek containing a plan for the defence of Malabar, 1789. One volume.

750 *Memorie van overgave* by *Commandeur* Johan Gerard van Angelbeek to Jan Lamberus van Spall, 1793. One volume.

751 Memorandum of J.L. van Spall concerning events during the British take-over in Cochin, 1798. With appendices, one volume.

752 Addition to the memorandum on reduction of expenditure in Malabar, 1756-64. One volume.

753 *Memorie van overgave* by *Commandeur* Casparus de Jong to Godefridus Weyerman, 1761. One volume.

754 Papers concerning the sale of Cannanore to the Ali Raja of Cannanore by the VOC, 1766-78. One volume.

755 Papers concerning alleged frauds during the period 1746-63 by

G. Weyerman and J.A. Sweers de Landas, 1764-74. With appendices, six parts.

756 Papers concerning repairs to the Quilon fortress, 1770-2. One volume.

757 Papers concerning the pawning and sale of a three-master ship by the Ali Raja, 1771-86. One volume.

758 Papers concerning 'the Commission to the levy of the 50th penny as a liberal gift to the Company in Malabar', 1791-3. One volume.

Vengurla

719-20 Memoranda of Commissioner P. de Roo to the *Commandeur* and to the head of the Cannanore fortress; daily record of the ship Spierdijk kept on a trip to Goa; record of the commercial transactions with merchant Babba Prabhu, 1695. Two volumes.

3.4. ARCHIVES OF OTHER INSTITUTIONS

Stadhouderlijke Secretarie
Secretariat to the Stadtholder

See 1.4.3
Access no.: 1.01.50

1179 Correspondence between the Stadtholder and *Commandeur* Adriaan Moens, 1775-9. One folder.

1607 Collection of various documents concerning government and trade in Asia (one volume). Including:

- 10 Instructions to Rijklof van Goens concerning Ceylon, Malabar and Madurai, 1664.
- 19 Instructions to the chief-factors and council of Cochin ('no. 26'), 1663.
- 20 Contract, alliance and confederation concluded between the VOC, Cochin and Purakkad ('no. 27'), 1663.
- 21 Treaty between Rijckloff van Goens on behalf of the VOC and the King of Cochin and his princes, n.d. (second-half seventeenth century).
- 22 Treaty between Governor-General Johan Maetsuijker on behalf of the VOC and Prince 'Ramnesterry', the nearest successor of Cannanore on behalf of the Kolathiri (of Chirakkal) ('no. 29'), n.d. (between 1653 and 1678).

1913-14 Memorandum (with duplicate) by the so-called Military Commission (consisting of Captains J.O. Vaillant and C.A. Ver Huell (see 1.5.32) and Lieutenant-Colonel J.F.L. Graevestein) to the Stadtholder concerning the defence of Cochin, with appendices, 1790. Two folders (see also 3.5, Ver Huell).

Comié tot de Zaken van de Oost-Indische Handel en Bezittingen
Committee regarding East Indian Trade and Possessions

See	1.4.4
Access no.:	2.01.27.01

Overgekomen brieven en papieren (*OBP*)
(letters and papers received)

58, ff. 189-94	Documents concerning the capitulation at Cochin, *c.* 1797.
61, ff. 148?-1629	Report concerning Malabar (among other regions), *c.* 1793.
63, n.f.	Report concerning Malabar (among other regions), *c.* 1795.
64, n.f.	Report concerning Malabar (among other regions), *c.* 1796.
65, n.f.	Report concerning Malabar (among other regions), *c.* 1797.
65a, n.f.	Report concerning Malabar (among other regions), *c.* 1794.
131, ff. 5-6	*Resoluties*, 1792.
131, ff. 176-7	*Resoluties* concerning bookkeeping, 1793.
131, ff. 184-240	List of arrived and departed vessels, 1791-2.
131, ff. 261-79	*Resoluties*, 1793.
132, n.f.	*Resoluties*, 1792-3.

Uit Engeland overgezonden stukken (Nederburgh)
Papers sent from England (Nederburgh)

See	1.4.7
Access no.:	2.01.27.04

79 *Resoluties* of the Malabar Council, 1792-3. With duplicate, two volumes.
80 Secret letter from Malabar to Batavia, with appended *secrete resoluties* of the Council and correspondence with the King of Travancore (and some translations of *olas* granted by the latter to local 'balias') and others, 1792-3. One volume.
81 Letter to Batavia, 1793. With appendices and duplicate, two volumes.

Legatie Frankrijk
Embassy at Paris, France

See	1.4.11
Access no.:	1.02.14
Period:	1747-1810

559 Papers concerning the purchase of a house in Cochin by Francois de Sales, Bishop of Verapoli, Vicar Apostolic of Malabar, for the benefit of missionaries, 1775. One folder.

Vengurla

Legatie Portugal
Consulate General at Lisboa, Portugal

See 1.4.11
Access no.: 1.02.18
Period: 1702-1804

26 Excerpts from a Portuguese report concerning the war against the King of Bonsulo near Goa, *c.* 1782. One piece.

3.5. PERSONAL AND FAMILY PAPERS

De Groot (supplement)

See 1.5.1
Access no.: 1.10.35.02

40, ff. 300-1 Letter of S. van der Haghen and Council in Bantam, requesting the Gentlemen XVII to send some warships to drive the Portuguese out of Malabar in cooperation with the Zamorin, 1605.
40, ff. 424v-5 Concept (by De Groot) for a letter from the Gentlemen XVII to the Zamorin concerning the treaty concluded with Admiral S. van der Haegen (1606).

Geleynssen de Jongh(e)

See 1.5.2
Access no.: 1.10.30

145 Act of commitment of the Zamorin of Calicut to supply an amount of pepper, 1641. One piece.
156 Contract between P.S. Groes and the King of Kayankulam, 1643. One piece.
181 (Extract) letters of the GG&C to the Zamorin of Calicut and the King of Purakkad, around 1641. One folder
186 Contains a letter of the Zamorin of Calicut to Batavia, 1641.
323 Letter from the ship Amboyna to the King of 'Parcattij' (Purakkad?), 1644. One piece.

Van Goens

See 1.5.4
Access no.: 1.10.32

25 Letter of Huisman in Cochin to R. van Goens the Younger, 1680. One piece.

Becker

See 1.5.7
Access no.: 1.10.05.01

57-58 Verdicts of the Malabar Council of Justice on J. Hoeck van Straalsont and on the local merchant 'Janoe' (Nanu?) Prabhu, 1715. Two pieces.

Hope

See 1.5.17
Access no.: 1.10.46

102 Extracts of letters of the Gentlemen XVII concerning Malabar, *eisen* for Malabar, etc., 1669-1769; extracts from letters of the GG&C concerning Malabar, 1738-70; papers concerning the memorandum of Schreuder, 1763-5; papers concerning the discharged VOC servants G. Weyerman and J.A. Sweers de Landas, 1764-7. One folder.

Bleiswijk

1.5.21.
Access no.: 3.01.25

237 Letters concerning the threat of the Portuguese at Goa to conquer Malabar, 1774. Four pieces and two quires.

238 Excerpt from a report concerning a war between the British and the Marathas under the command of Haidar Ali (of Mysore?), in which the Marathas were threatened by the loss of Malabar, Mahé and Arcot, 1780. One piece, partly French.

Fagel

See 1.5.25
Access no.: 1.10.29

1777 Papers concerning Portuguese designs on Cochin as reported by one Mr van der Hoop, 1775. Three pieces.

Radermacher

See 1.5.27
Access no.: 1.10.69

521-2 Considerations by Van Beuningen (among others) concerning Malabar and the withdrawal of some factories, 1684. Two pieces.

523 Letter to the Batavia judiciary concerning the *Commandeur* and second-in-command of Malabar, J. de Jong and J. de Roode, 1733. One piece.

524 Profit and loss account of the Malabar factories, 1758-61. One piece.
525 Extract from Malabar letters, 1772. One piece.

Alting

See 1.5.29
Access no.: 1.10.03

17 List of names of Malabar rulers, their dynasties, nobles, *zamindars*, etc., Cochin, 1738 (ff. 51-72). One volume.
23 Letter of H. Zwaardecroon from Cochin to Batavia, 1697. One volume.

Ver Huell

See 1.5.32
Access no.: 2.21.004.04

15 Report by J.O. Vaillant, C.A. Ver Huell and J.F.L. Graevestein (i.e. the Military Commission concerned with defence) regarding their activities on the Malabar Coast, 1790. One folder (see also 3.4, *Stadhouderlijke Secretarie*).
16-17 Two memoranda (by the Military Commission?) (inv. no. 16 for Stadtholder William V) concerning the defence of the Dutch settlements on the Malabar Coast, 1790 and n.d. One bundle and one folder.
18 Letters, memoranda, reports and lists concerning the defence of Cochin, 1790. One bundle.
19 Memorandum by C.F. Reimer concerning the defence of Cochin, 1790. One folder.
20 Exposition by or concerning the King of Cochin, directed to the Military Commission and the Stadtholder, 1790. One folder.

Nederburgh

See 1.5.33
Access no.: 1.10.59

138 Secret letters of the delegates of the Amsterdam Chamber and of the Malabar Governor concerning the sale of VOC establishments to the King of Travancore, 1790-2. One folder.
140 Letter of E.J.O. Craeyvanger, 1792. One piece.
141 Letter of *Directeur* J.G. van Angelbeek requesting a transfer to Ceylon, n.d. Fragment, one piece.
430 *Memorie van overgave* by Governor Adriaan Moens to Johan Gerard van Angelbeek, with marginal notes by the GG&C, 1781. One volume.
697 Letters of J.G. van Angelbeek, 1792-3. Two pieces.

Moens

See 1.5.37
Access no.: 1.10.100

12 Letter of Pope Clemens XIV to Governor Moens of Malabar, in which the former expresses his gratitude for the protection provided by the latter to Malabar's Christians, in particular the Roman Catholics, Latin with Dutch translation, 1772. One charter, one folder.
13 Letter of Adriaan Moens to his family members concerning the conflict between the VOC and Haidar Ali Khan of Mysore, 1776. One piece.
14 *Memorie van overgave* by Governor Adriaan Moens to Johan Gerard van Angelbeek, April 1781. One volume.

Vengurla

Geleynssen de Jongh(e)

See 1.5.2
Access no.: 1.10.30

2 Contains *resoluties* of the Council of the fleet at Goa, 1623.
112 Instruction of the GG&C to the fleet sailing for the coast of the subcontinent and Goa, 1639. One piece.
142 Daily record kept by Geleynsen over the period 1640-4, which includes his captivity at Goa, his stay in Vengurla and his voyage from there via Ceylon to Batavia. One volume.
147 Instruction of the GG&C to the fleet sailing for the coast of the subcontinent and Goa, 1641. One piece.
149-50 Papers concerning an armistice with the Portuguese at Goa as well as in Europe, 1641-2. One piece and one folder.
151 Treaty between the Portuguese and Bijapur, 1641. One piece.
165 Letters to Geleynsen from C.C. Blocq and J.D. Gallen in Vengurla, 1641-3. One folder.
167 Idem from D. Bouwens, lying off Goa, 1641. One piece.
178-9 (Extracts of) letters of the GG&C to C.C. Blocq at Vengurla and M. Quast at Goa, 1641. Two folders.
186 Contains a letter of the King of Bijapur to Batavia, 1041 AH /AD 1641.
196-8 Letters (in the name) of D. Bouwens, commander of the fleet off Goa to the King of Bijapur, the Bijapuri Governor Mustafa Khan, and P. Croocq at Surat, 1640-2. Two pieces and a folder.
200-2 Letters to D. Bouwens from Mustafa Khan, the King of Bijapur and C.C. Blocq at Vengurla, *c.* 1641. One piece and two folders.
216 Letters of C. Cornelissen (Blocq) at Vengurla to P. Croocq at Surat, 1641. One folder.
219 Letter of a Dominican monk at Goa to a Jesuit priest at Surat, 1641. One piece.

228 Lists of goods sent from Vengurla to Persia, 1641. One folder.

253-5 *Resoluties* of putting the ship De Pauw into the bay of Goa, a testimony of H. van Tuinen as to the necessity of this action and the correspondence of Geleynsen and the ship's council with Portuguese officials and the Viceroy about their arrest, 1643. Three pieces and a folder.

257-8 Letters to Geleynsen at Goa from C. van Sanen at Vengurla and from H. van Thuijnen, J. Jeeles, F. Venturin and the Viceroy at Goa (some from aboard De Pauw), 1643. One piece and one folder.

260 Papers concerning negotiations with the Portuguese at Goa, 1643. Three pieces.

261-6 Invoices of goods aboard De Pauw to be left at Goa, expenses of Geleynsen in Goa, etc., 1643-4. Three pieces, two folders and one volume.

267 Instruction of the GG&C to the fleet sailing to occupy the bay of Goa, 1643. One piece.

268 Letters of C.C. Blocq from the roadstead of Goa, 1643. One folder.

268A Request of Geleynssen to be relieved of his house arrest in Batavia which was to last until he gave a satisfactory account for intruding into Goa, 1644. One piece.

271 Provisional treaty between the VOC and the Estado da India, 1644. One folder, in Portuguese with Dutch translation from Latin version (not in this folder, see 4.4, *Staten-Generaal*).

272 Publication of the Dutch-Portuguese armistice, 1644. One piece, in Portuguese.

285 Letter of Tristão de Ataide in Chaul, 1645. One piece, in Portuguese.

317 Letters of C. Cornelissen (Blocq) among others from Vengurla, Rajapur, Raybag, etc., and a *dagregister* kept at Vengurla and Raybag, 1641. One folder (originally part of a volume).

326 Instruction to M. Poortmans going to the Bijapur court with gifts for Mustafa Khan, 1644. One piece.

3.6. Separate Acquisitions and Microfilms

Losse aanwinsten
Separate acquisitions

See 1.6.1
Access no.: 1.11.01.01

108 Alphabetical repertory of kingdoms, regions, functionaries, cities, etc., in Malabar, by 'Sara Jacoba', *c.* 1740. One volume (1865 A I).

166 Contains an account of the battle of the VOC ship Vrouwe Geertruida and the Maratha fleet, 1775. Printed, seven pages. (1876 A XXII 01).

262 Letter concerning the expiry of B. van der Lely in Cochin, 1666. One piece (1882 B XIV).

829 Extract of the journal of the ship 't Huys ter Mye under the command of G.C. Hartz, concerning a pirate attack at the latitude of Bassein, 1769. One piece (1900 XXIV).

1276 Letter of J.G. van Angelbeek from Cochin with an appended description of the battle of Tipu Sultan with the King of Travancore (with small pictures of a redoubt 'Tjerapoetoemale' and rockets flying over it), a report on the political situation in South India, etc., 1790. Four pieces (1913 XLIII 24).

MICROFILMS OF EXTERNAL ARCHIVAL MATERIAL

Bles collection

See 1.6.2
Microfilm no.: 1.1.1342 M

5 Abstract translation from Malayalam or Tamil of a Hindu book entitled 'Tchira Wikkum' (mid-eighteenth century). Two pieces.

Vengurla

Losse aanwinsten
Separate acquisitions

See 1.6.1
Access no.: 1.11.01.01

2087 Contains the appointment of A. Westerholt as commander of the fleet sailing against Goa, 1637. One charter (1981 02).

3.7. MAPS AND DRAWINGS

Verzameling buitenlandse kaarten, Leupe (VEL)
Foreign map collection, Leupe

See 1.7.1
Access no.: 4.VEL

229 Portrayal of the low countries of the Malabar Coast, from the fortress of Cranganur beyond the fortress of Quilon, with an indication of the river depths, 1687, by Jan Thim. Schipper, revised by H.G. Faarant, reserve officer candidate and engineer.

230 Plan of 'Calvuetty' or shipyard, east of Cochin, by D. Zijnen, 1764. Copy with description.

232 Map of the mud bank on the coast of the land of the King of Travancore, by de Preut, eighteenth century.

251 Sketch of the bay at the 'Hoek of Brins Jan' (Vilinjam), 6 miles from Anjengo and 5 miles from Tengapattanam, 1740, received from Ceylon.

882 Map of a part of the Malabar Coast or the stretching of the rivers between Chetwai and Quilon, 1767. Private map by Joh. Wilh. de Graaf, ten pages (see also inv. nos 883 and 884).

883 Part of the Malabar Coast or the stretching of the rivers between Chetwai and Quilon, 1767. Private map by A. Heidenreich. Copy of inv. no. 882. With a view of the mountains (see also inv. no. 884).

884 Part of the Malabar Coast or the rivers stretching between Chetwai and Quilon, 1767. Private map by A. Heidenreich. With indication of agricultural lands. Copy of inv. no. 882 (see also inv. no. 883).

886 Plan of the factory on Barcelore, by Nicolaus de Graaf, seventeenth century. With notes. Originating from the 'Atlas Amsterdam' or 'Atlas de Graaff'. Including:

a Plan of the Dutch factory at Barcelore.
b Barcelore River, between the mouth and the city.

887 View of the fort at Mangalore, by Nicolaus de Graaf, seventeenth century. With notes. Originating from the 'Atlas Amsterdam' or 'Atlas de Graaff'.

888 Plan of the fort in Cannanore, by Nicolaus de Graaf, seventeenth century. With notes. Originating from the 'Atlas Amsterdam' or 'Atlas de Graaff'. Including:

a Plan of the castle Cranganur, 1678.
b Plan of the fort in Quilon, 1678.
c Drawing of the factory on Kayankulam, 1678.
d Plan of the factory on Kayankulam, 1678.

889 Plan of the fortress of Cannanore, located on a rock on the Malabar Coast, approximately 36 miles north of Cochin, by H.G. Faarant, *Vaandrig* (reserve officer candidate), 1696. With legend.

890 Plan and project for the reduction of Cannanore, by Captain E. Paravicini and Lieutenant-Engineer N. Guyard, 1767. With legend (see also inv. no. 891).

891 Plan and project for the reduction of Cannanore (see also inv. no. 890). With slight changes, by C.A. Luepken and C.P. Keller, 1767. With legend.

892 Drawing of the Cranganur castle, seen from the island 'Moschieten' (Musquiten), by Nicolaus de Graaf, 1678. Originating from the 'Atlas Amsterdam' or 'Atlas de Graaff'. Including:

a Drawing of the castle Cranganur, seen from 'Ilha de Leeti'.
b Cranganur River, between the mouth and Noordwijk.
c Sight on the redoubt at Pallippuram.

893 Plan of the fortress of Cranganur, by H.G. Faarant, reserve officer candidate and engineer, 1696. With legend.

894 Drawing of the invasion and conquest of the city of Cochin by the military force of Ryckloff van Goens, by M.E. Proot, 1663. With legend.

895 Plan of Cochin, with suggested changes of the fortifications, 1663.

896 Sight on Cochin and a part of Vypin Island, 1677. With legend. Originating from the 'Atlas Amsterdam' or 'Atlas de Graaff'.

897 Plan of Cochin with its external buildings, 1680. Including:

a Cochin as it is supposed to be fortified, shown here without external buildings.
b Cranganur River and the land of Cranganur.
c The land of Travancore.

898 Map of Cochin and surrounding territories, 1691. Originating from the 'Atlas Amsterdam' or 'Atlas de Graaff'.

899 Plan of the capital Cochin and the Malabar Coast, by Sergeant Hans George Faarant, 1696. With explanation.

900 Plan of Cochin, by Captain W.O. Massenfeld and Lieutenant-Engineer D. Zynen, February 1765. With legend. Copy.

901 Plan of the city and the fortresses of Cochin in February 1767, and part of Vypin in March 1767, by Lieutenant-Engineer D. Zynen, 1767. Including:
a Part of the uttermost corner of Vypin, showing gardens, wilderness, wasteland, and the beach.
b Profiles.

902 Plan of the city and fortresses of Cochin (see also inv. nos 901, 903 and 904), changed in April 1767 (see inv. no. 901a-b).

903 Plan of the city and fortresses of Cochin (see also inv. nos 901, 902 and 904), changed according to the orders of the GG&C, March 1767, by Captain E. Paravicini and Lieutenant-Engineer N. Guyard. Copy (see inv. no. 901a-b for the legend).

904 Plan of the city and fortresses of Cochin, March 1767 (see inv. no. 901a-b for the legend).

905 Plan of the fortress Cochin, according to surveyor Carl von Krause, 1782, by Schenk. Copy with legend (see also inv. no. 906).

906 Plan of the fortress Cochin, according to surveyor Carl von Krause, 1782, by Lieutenant-Engineer D. van Lier. With legend (see inv. no. 905).

907 Map of Cochin, by A.A. Buijskes, eighteenth century. With legend.

908 Plan of the fortresses on the western and southern half of Cochin, including suggestions for improvements. Made after the original drawing of Major-Engineer Reymer, by P. Elias, eighteenth century. Including several detailed drawings (see also inv. nos 909 and 910).

909 Plan of the fortresses of Cochin, after the suggested improvements were realized on paper (see inv. no. 908), by Heidenreich, after the original drawing of Major-Engineer Reymer. With legend (see also inv. no. 910).

910 Plan of the fortresses of Cochin, after the suggested improvements were realized on paper (see inv. no. 908), by Lieutenant B. van Lynden, after the original drawing of Major-Engineer Reymer. With legend (see also inv. no. 909).

911 Drawing of Vypin Island, by F.C. Heupner, 1793.

912 Drawing of the fortress Quilon, situated approximately 24 miles south of the capital Cochin, by Hans Georg Faarant, 1687. Remeasured by L.N. van Duyvendaal. With legend.

913 Drawing of the fortress Quilon, after a suggested reduction, 1703. With legend.

914 Plan of a projected factory in Quilon, by D. Zynen, 1766. With legend.

915 Plan of the construction on 'Padricotta Parri', 1718. Received from Malabar, 1718. Part of the report of the expedition of Sergeant-Major Hans Frederik Bergman.

916 Plan of the construction of Edaturutti, 1718. Received from Malabar, 1718. Part of the report of the expedition of Sergeant-Major Hans Frederik Bergman.

917 Plan of the fort of 'Maparany' (Mapranam?), 1718. Received from Malabar, 1718. Part of the report of the expedition of Sergeant-Major Hans Frederik Bergman.

918 Plan of the construction of Chetwai, 1718. Received from Malabar, 1718. Part of the report of the expedition of Sergeant-Major Hans Frederik Bergman.

919 Plan of the construction of 'Poedoecoenatte', 1718. Received from Malabar, 1718. Part of the report of the expedition of Sergeant-Major Hans Frederik Bergman.

920 Plan of the construction of 'Aynamaka', with the location of troops, 1718. Received from Malabar, 1718. Part of the report of the expedition of Sergeant-Major Hans Frederik Bergman.

921 Plan of the construction of 'Papenette', with location indications of troops and artillery, 1718. Received from Malabar, 1718. Part of the report of the expedition of Sergeant-Major Hans Frederik Bergman.

922 Plan of the fort of 'Poetenbare', 1718. Received from Malabar, 1718. Part of the report of the expedition of Sergeant-Major Hans Frederik Bergman.

Verzameling buitenlandse kaarten, supplement, Leupe-l'Honoré Naber (VELH)
Foreign map collection, supplement, Leupe-l'Honoré Naber

See 1.7.2
Access no.: 4.VELH

108 Map of the Malabar Coast around Cannanore, 1667 (?). Originating from the journal of Michiel Gerritsz. Boos.

109 Map of the Malabar Coast, between 'Tolle' and 'Wallemokan', 1667 (?).

Departement van Marine, centraal archief, Leupe (MCAL)
Ministry of Naval Affairs, central archives, Leupe

See 1.7.3
Access no.: 4.MCAL

4198 Map of the Malabar Coast, between Rajapur and Cape Comorin, with islands, and with scouting of the island 'Maleke'. Map of the Deccan coast, between Suvali and Rajapur, eighteenth century. Coloured.

4221 Map of a part of the Malabar Coast from a survey, by John McCluer, 1791. Copperplate print.

4222 Map of a part of the Malabar Coast and part of the Lakshadweep reduced from a survey, by John McCluer, 1791. Copperplate print.

4240 Plan and view of Janjira, commonly called Danda Rajapuri, on the Malabar Coast, by A. Werner, 1771. Copperplate print. Including:
a 'Conserah Island'.
b Janjira Fort.

4242 Plan of the bar and entrance of the river Bankot on the Malabar Coast, 1789. With landfall.

4243 Plan of 'Gariah' harbour on the Malabar Coast, by Sir William Hewett, 1756. Copperplate print, with note.

4244 Eye-draught of 'Dewgur' harbour on the Malabar Coast, by Archibald Blair, 1784. With note and view.

4245 View and plan of Sindhudurg or Melinde on the Malabar Coast, by Co. John Watson, 1765.

4248 Plan of the river Baliapatam, by John David Spaeth, 1792. With view and landfall.

4249 Plan of the island Dharmapatam on the Malabar Coast, by J. Walker, 1783.

4250 Plan of the mudbank of Cranganur on the Malabar Coast from the early editions, by Van Keulen, 1775. Copperplate print. With instruction.

4256 Chart of the Lakshadweep in the province of Malabar, surveyed by Lieutenant John Wedgebrough, 1795. Including:
a 'Kalpeni' and Minicoy.

4258 Map of 'Seuheli' Islands and reef called 'Seuheli-Par' by the natives (Suheli Par in the Lakshadweep?), by John Mc Cluer, 1790.

Overgekomen brieven en papieren (OBP)
Letters and papers received

See 1.1.7
Access no.: 1.04.02

VOC 3352 Includes an outline of the fort at Quilon, 1773.

Hoge Regering te Batavia
High Government at Batavia

See 1.3.1
Access no.: 1.04.17

756 Includes two maps of the Quilon fortress (one with projected changes), 1772-3.

Braam

See 1.5.22
Access no.: 4.BRF

229 Plan of the situation of Cochin in the river estuary, eighteenth century (?).

Losse aanwinsten
Separate acquisitions

See 1.6.1
Access no.: 1.11.01.01

1276 Includes small pictures of a redoubt 'Tjerapoetoemale' and rockets flying over it (belonging to a description of the battle of Tipu Sultan with the King of Travancore), 1790 (1913 XLIII 24).

Vengurla

Verzameling buitenlandse kaarten, Leupe (VEL)
Foreign maps collection, Leupe

See 1.7.1
Access no.: 4.VEL

224 Sea chart of the coast where 'pirate' Kanoji Angria was active, between 'Schreyershoek' and the river 'Sangisser', eighteenth century (?). Four pages.
228 Map of the bay and the coast of Goa, seventeenth century (?).
885 Drawing of the factory at Vengurla, by Nicolaus de Graaf, 1678. With explanation. Including:
  a Plan of the area between the factory and the town of Vengurla.
  b The town of Vengurla.

Departement van Marine, centraal archief, Leupe (MCAL)
Ministry of Naval Affairs, central archives, Leupe

See 1.7.3
Access no.: 4.MCAL

4239 Plan of the port of Chaul on the Konkan Coast, belonging to the Marathas, 1784. With views.
4241 Plan of Rajapur River, surveyed by John McCluer, 1791. Copperplate print.
4246 Plan of Vengurla on the Malabar Coast, and plan of the principal rocks of Vengurla, by Captain Joseph Huddart, 1784. Copperplate print, with legend.
4247 Plan of Goa harbour on the Malabar Coast, by Reeves Woodson, 1775. With landfall.

Collectie Bergsma (BMF)
Bergsma collection

See 1.7.7
Access no.: 4.BMF

433 Map of the island of Goa and the adjacent areas, mid-eighteenth century.
434 Map of Goa, by Pierre van der Aa (?), 1729. Originating from Van Linschoten, *Itinerario* (see Bibliography, nos 35, 36).

4. CEYLON (including Fishery Coast and Maldives)

INTRODUCTION

The VOC *Gouvernement* of Ceylon covered the Dutch activities on the island of Ceylon proper, the Maldives and the Fishery Coast, the latter on the Indian mainland from Cape Comorin in the south to Point Calimere in the north. Although at first the Governor and Council resided at Galle, Colombo became the regional headquarters in 1656. Apart from the Governor in Colombo, there were *Commandeurs* at Jaffna, Galle and, from 1663, at Cochin; the latter becoming independent in 1669. During most of the period, Trincomalee on the eastern coast and Tuticorin, the chief factory of the Fishery Coast, were each administered by an *Opperhoofd.* Apart from this VOC hierarchy, the Dutch also maintained the indigenous system of provincial chiefs or *Dissaves* who served as important intermediaries between the Dutch and the local population. Although the VOC *de facto* controlled large tracts of territory on Ceylon, especially in the south-western and northern parts of the island, until 1765 the Raja of Kandy remained the *de jure* sovereign over the entire island.

The first contacts between the Dutch and Ceylon date from 1602 when one of the early voyages of the *Voorcompagnieën* (see 1.4.1), headed by Joris van Spilbergen, paid a visit to Kandy. Being seen as a potential ally against the Portuguese, the VOC was granted various trading privileges by the Kandy Raja as early as 1612. It was only 26 years later that the VOC began to settle down on the island: taking Batticaloa in 1638, Trincomalee in 1639, Galle in 1640, Negombo in 1644, Kalutara in 1655, and Colombo in 1656. Finally, after conquering Jaffna and Mannar, the Portuguese were completely wiped out of Ceylon in 1658. On the Fishery Coast the Dutch established a factory at Kayalpatnam after they received a *caul* from Madurai in 1645. In 1658 the Company captured Tuticorin and concluded treaties with the regional rulers of Ramnad (1658) and Madurai (1659) to be followed by the establishment of factories at Punneikayal, Manapadu, Vembar, Baipar, Kilakkarai, Cape Comorin, Adirampatnam and Alwar Tirunagarai. On Ceylon proper, the VOC expanded deeper into the coastal hinterlands of the southwest and by 1680 had incorporated some of the most productive cinnamon areas of the island. But it was only after the 1765 war with Kandy that the VOC annexed the entire coastline of the island. In 1796 the island was surrendered to the British. Only the factories on the Fishery Coast were returned to the Dutch in 1818 and were now administered from Sadras on the Coromandel Coast. Like the other remaining VOC establishments on the mainland, they were finally abandoned in 1825.

The *Gouvernement* of Ceylon maintained relations with the Kings of Kandy and, on the Fishery Coast, with the Nayaks of Madurai and the Setupatis of Ramnad. Besides, VOC servants frequently sailed from Ceylon to the Maldives and paid visits to the islands' Sultans. To a lesser extent, there were contacts on the Indian mainland with Sivagangai, various Palaiyakkarars (Poligars) and, occasionally, with the Marathas, Arcot, Thanjavur and Travancore. Relations with these latter powers were also maintained from other regions.

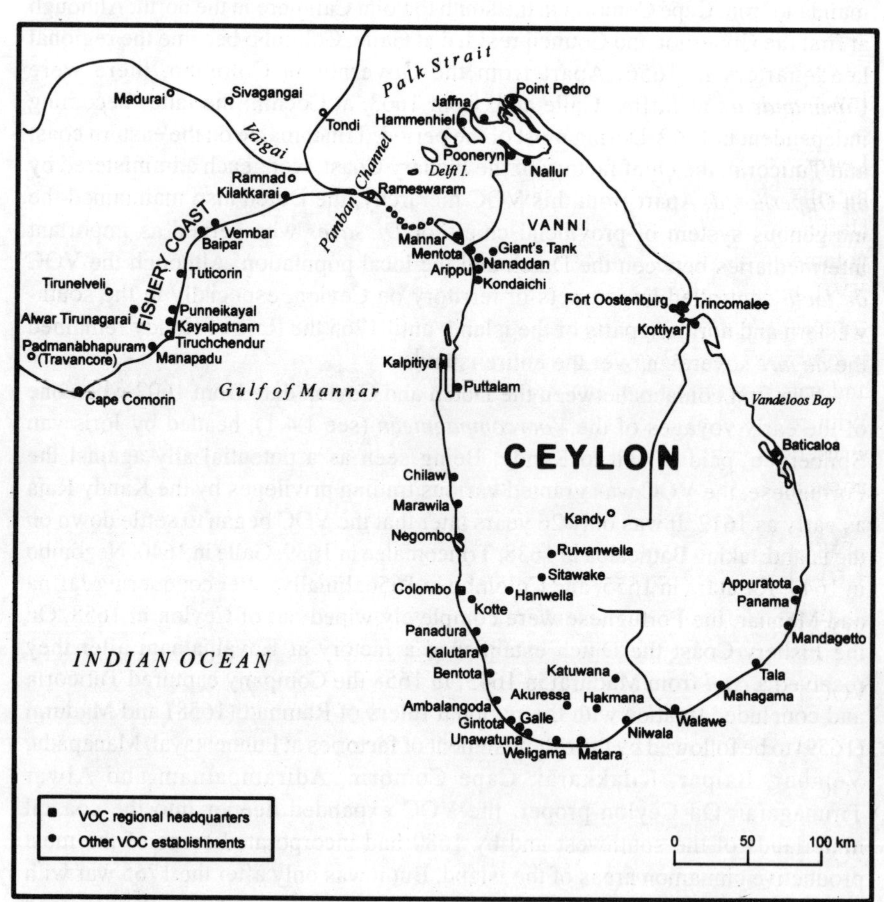

Map 4. The VOC in Ceylon

With respect to the archives kept at the ARA, information concerning the Maldives may also be found in documents relating to the Cape of Good Hope, which are, however, not listed in this guide. For papers concerning the Fishery Coast between 1818 and 1825 one should also look under Coromandel.

4.1. *Overgekomen Brieven en Papieren (OBP)*
Letters and Papers Received

See	1.1.7
Access no.:	1.04.02
Inv. nos:	VOC 1053-3987

Letters and papers concerning Ceylon, the Fishery Coast and the Maldives are mostly listed under headings such as 'Ceijlon', 'Seijlon', 'Colombo', 'Gale', 'Jaffenepatnam', 'Tutucorijn', 'Maldivos', etc. All these headings occur in the volumes containing documents sent directly from South Asia to the Gentlemen XVII and the Amsterdam Chamber, as well as in the volumes that consist of copies of documents sent from South Asia to Batavia in the *Batavia's ingekomen brievenboek* (Batavia letterbook of incoming documents). In a few cases, letters and papers relating to Ceylon may also be found under the heading 'Batavia'. With regard to missions to Kandy (see 4.1.5), we have not listed the reports written by interpreters (from the 1710s onward) since they usually follow immediately after the more regular mission reports.

4.1.1. *Memories van overgave* (final reports)

VOC 1242, ff. 966-92	Governor Rijcklof van Goens to Jacob Hustart, September 1663.
VOC 1243-4, ff. 930-4	Former *Landvoogd* (Governor) of Ceylon Adriaan van der Meijden to provisional Governor Roothaes and factor Borchorst, March 1663.
VOC 1246-8, ff. 2857-918	Governor Rijcklof van Goens to Jacob Hustaard, December 1663.
VOC 1251, ff. 627-58	By *Commandeur* Anthonij Pavilioen at Jaffna, September 1665.
VOC 1252-3, n.f.	*Commandeur* Anthonij Pavilioen (at Jaffna) to Jerefaes (Vos?), September 1665.
VOC 1254, ff. 1127-79	*Commandeur* Anthonij Paviljoen (at Jaffna) to Jerefaes (Vos?), September 1665.
VOC 1256, ff. 419-26	To *Opperhoofd* Lourens Pijl at the Fishery Coast (by Lucas van der Dussen?), April 1666 (see also VOC 1259, ff. 154A-71A? under 4.1.6).
VOC 1256, ff. 144A-53A	To *Opperhoofd* Lourens Pijl at Tuticorin (by Lucas van der Dussen), April 1666 (see also VOC 1259, ff. 154A-71A? under 4.1.6).

VOC 1313, ff. 257v-82	Governor Rijcklof van Goens Sr. to Rijcklof van Goens Jr., April 1675.
VOC 1321, ff. 846-55	By De Graeuwe at Batticaloa to Joan Blommert, April 1676.
VOC 1343, ff. 300-69	Governor Rijckloff van Goens to Laurens Pijl, December 1679.
VOC 1351, ff. 2361-87	Governor Johan Maatsuijcker to Jacob van Kittensteijn, February 1650.
VOC 1351, ff. 2388-416	Governor Rijcklof van Goens Sr. to Rijcklof van Goens Jr., April 1675.
VOC 1351, ff. 2417-515	Governor Rijckloff van Goens to Laurens Pijl, December 1679.
VOC 1491, ff. 385-545	Governor Laurens Pijl to Thomas van Rhee, January 1692.
VOC 1519, ff. 88v-201	Governor Laurens Pijl to Thomas van Rhee, January 1692.
VOC 1590, ff. 323-400v	Governor Thomas van Rhee to Gerrit de Heere, February 1697.
VOC 1597, ff. 33-128	Governor Thomas van Rhee to Gerrit de Heere, February 1697.
VOC 1605, ff. 999-1022	Chief-factor Rijckloff de Bitter at Jaffna to Pieter Petitfils, March 1698.
VOC 1610, ff. 129-43	Chief-factor Rijckloff de Bitter at Jaffna to Pieter Petitfils, March 1698.
VOC 1673, ff. 870-916	*Commandeur* Hendrick Collard at Jaffna to Adam van der Duijn, June 1703.
VOC 1707, ff. 1429-39	*Opperhoofd* Nicolaes Welter at Tuticorin to Jan Bierens, October 1705.
VOC 1731, ff. 141-61	*Opperhoofd* Nicolaes Welter at Tuticorin to Jan Bierens, September 1705.
VOC 1738, ff. 719A-69A	Governor Cornelis Jan Simons to Hendrick Bekker, December 1707.
VOC 1762, ff. 55-132	Governor Cornelis Joan Simons to Hendrik Becker, December 1707.
VOC 1878, ff. 237-375	Governor Hendrick Becker to (Isaac) Augustijn Rumph, November 1716.
VOC 1896, ff. 137-?	Governor Hendrick Becker to Isaac Augustin Rumph, November 1716.
VOC 2482, ff. 1844-2013	Governor Gustaaf Willem van Imhoff to Willem Maurits Bruijnink, *c.* 1740.
VOC 2506, ff. 329-650	Governor Gustaaf Willem van Imhoff to Willem Maurits Bruijnink, *c.* 1740.
VOC 2598, ff. 1635-1714	Governor Daniel Overbeek to Julius Valentijn Stein van Gollonesse, April 1743.
VOC 2772, ff. 394-460	Governor Julius Valentijn Stein van Gollonesse to Gerard Joan Vreland, February 1751.

VOC 2900, ff. 439-539	Governor Joan Gideon Loten (to Jan Schreuder), February 1757.
VOC 3013, ff. 1042-80	Governor Jan Schreuder to Lubbert Jan van Eck, December 1761.
VOC 3029, ff. 130-423	Governor Jan Schreuder to Lubbert Jan van Eck, December 1761.

For published translations, see Bibliography, nos 467, 471, 472.

4.1.2. *Resoluties* (proceedings)

VOC 1144, ff. 67-76	*c.* 1643 (among other documents).
VOC 1162, ff. 281-3	Extract from the *resolutie* book of Galle, *c.* 1646.
VOC 1173, ff. 446-9	Concerning the Fishery Coast, 1649.
VOC 1177, f. 345	1650.
VOC 1177, ff. 410-11	1650.
VOC 1185, ff. 408-9	Galle, 1651.
VOC 1201, ff. 579-90	1653.
VOC 1226, ff. 908-9	1658.
VOC 1226, ff. 912-17	1657.
VOC 1227, ff. 314-45	1657-8.
VOC 1231, ff. 213-31	1658-9.
VOC 1231, ff. 520-44	1659.
VOC 1231, f. 609	1659.
VOC 1239, ff. 1184-92	1662.
VOC 1251, ff. 1009-16	Concerning pastors at Jaffna, 1665.
VOC 1251, ff. 1029-1120	1665.
VOC 1252-3, n.f.	*c.* 1665.
VOC 1254, ff. 1111-21	*c.* 1665.
VOC 1256, ff. 529-48	1666.
VOC 1261, ff. 378-573	1666-8.
VOC 1266, ff. 693-4	1669.
VOC 1267-8, ff. 1211-18	Concerning the church council at Colombo, 1668.
VOC 1270, 1521-4	Tuticorin, 1669.
VOC 1271-3, ff. 1480-1	1669.
VOC 1271-3, ff. 1538-53	Partially recorded at Galle, 1669.
VOC 1274, ff. 628-9	1671.
VOC 1280, ff. 7-44	Concerning Madurai and the Setupati of Ramnad, 1671.
VOC 1280, f. 397	1671.
VOC 1281-4, ff. 995-1104	1671.
VOC 1285, ff. 121-40	Batavia, concerning the French at Ceylon, *c.* 1672 (among other documents).

VOC 1288, ff. 302-34	Concerning conflicts with the French, *c.* 1672.
VOC 1288, ff. 522-55	*c.* 1672.
VOC 1292, ff. 87-201	1673.
VOC 1295, ff. 233-4	1673.
VOC 1295, ff. 712-6	1673.
VOC 1295, ff. 719-26	1673.
VOC 1298, ff. 410-20	1674.
VOC 1299, ff. 167-82	1674.
VOC 1302-1303, ff. 619-24	1674.
VOC 1304, ff. 253-67	1674.
VOC 1308, ff. 337-57	Partly concerning the Fishery Coast, 1675.
VOC 1313, ff. 308v-9	1675.
VOC 1316, ff. 178-204	1676-7.
VOC 1322, ff. 1401v-?	1676.
VOC 1324, ff. 270-305	1677.
VOC 1324, ff. 564-79	1677-8.
VOC 1333, ff. 145-90	Partly concerning Pondicherry, 1678.
VOC 1340, ff. 1206v-8	Concerning the sending of Persian horses to Rajasinga of Kandy, 1677.
VOC 1340, ff. 1325-33	1678.
VOC 1340, ff. 1451-7	1678.
VOC 1343, ff. 149-64	1679.
VOC 1351, ff. 2516-26	1678.
VOC 1355, ff. 103-31	1680.
VOC 1370, ff. 1675-6	1681.
VOC 1373, ff. 112-66	1682.
VOC 1373, ff. 270-1	1683.
VOC 1383, ff. 181-302	1683.
VOC 1383, ff. 505-51	1683.
VOC 1383, ff. 590-602	1683.
VOC 1396, ff. 143-266	1684.
VOC 1396, ff. 407-18	Tuticorin, concerning conflicts between Paravars and Muslims, 1684.
VOC 1406, ff. 538-98	1683.
VOC 1406, ff. 654-66	*c.* 1683.
VOC 1410, ff. 174-243	1685.
VOC 1420, ff. 284-426	1685-6.
VOC 1433, ff. 443-509	1687.
VOC 1447, ff. 818-25	1682-8 (?).
VOC 1454, ff. 1143-53	Partly concerning peace negotiations with Kandy, 1688.
VOC 1470, ff. 1083-1159v	1690.
VOC 1506, ff. 1507-1728v	1692.
VOC 1524, ff. 341-532	1693.
VOC 1524, ff. 896-902	1693.

VOC 1524, ff. 1042-3	Jaffna, 1693.
VOC 1524, ff. 1115-1115v	Jaffna, 1693.
VOC 1543, ff. 518-21v	Jaffna, 1694.
VOC 1544, ff. 752-8	1694.
VOC 1570, ff. 766-?	1695.
VOC 1581, ff. 238-48	1695-6.
VOC 1581, ff. 519-21	1696.
VOC 1584, ff. 607-62	Jaffna, 1696.
VOC 1590, ff. 536-40v	Concerning cinnamon, 1697.
VOC 1590, ff. 715-48	Jaffna, concerning the elephant trade, 1697.
VOC 1597, ff. 318-23	1697.
VOC 1597, ff. 355-94	1696-7.
VOC 1597, ff. 679-733	Jaffna, concerning the elephant trade, 1697.
VOC 1604 III, ff. 752-80	1698-9.
VOC 1615 I, ff. 406-53	1699.
VOC 1615 III, ff. 515-65	1699.
VOC 1625, ff. 92-128	Concerning the Kandyan court, 1699.
VOC 1631, ff. 300-59	1700.
VOC 1632, ff. 622-49	Concerning the elephant trade, *c.* 1700 (among other documents).
VOC 1643, ff. 214-307	1701.
VOC 1644, ff. 760-1	Concerning the diving for conch shells, 1701.
VOC 1655, ff. 292-354	1702.
VOC 1656, ff. 1142-5	Galle, *c.* 1702.
VOC 1665, ff. 113-21	Concerning a gift to the King of Kandy, 1701.
VOC 1665, ff. 25-30	Concerning the funeral of Gerrit de Heere, 1702.
VOC 1665, ff. 156-62	1702.
VOC 1672, ff. 278-488	1703.
VOC 1674, ff. 187-9	*c.* 1703.
VOC 1679, ff. 404-14	1703.
VOC 1684, ff. 2236-42	1705.
VOC 1686, ff. 370-700	1703-4.
VOC 1687, ff. 1092-156	Jaffna, 1704.
VOC 1687, ff. 1224-5	Jaffna, 1704.
VOC 1688, ff. 1786-95	Concerning the French, 1705.
VOC 1693, ff. 407-12	Concerning envoys from Kandy, 1704.
VOC 1693, ff. 588-91	Jaffna, 1704.
VOC 1693, ff. 606-15	Concerning the *areca* and elephant trade, 1704.
VOC 1693, ff. 616-?	Jaffna, 1704.
VOC 1693, ff. 852-6	Concerning envoys from Kandy and the elephant trade, 1704.
VOC 1693, ff. 922-?	1704.
VOC 1693, ff. 134-42	1705.
VOC 1706, ff. 527-955	1704-5.
VOC 1707, ff. 1791-8	Galle, 1705.
VOC 1713, ff. 14-15	1705.

VOC 1713, f. 57	1690.
VOC 1713, ff. 298-336	1706.
VOC 1713, ff. 387-8	Galle, 1705.
VOC 1713, ff. 97-9	1705.
VOC 1720, ff. 255-9	Jaffna, 1705.
VOC 1720, ff. 351-3	1694.
VOC 1721, ff. 217-554	1705-6.
VOC 1722, ff. 880-8	Galle, 1706.
VOC 1723, ff. 1161-4	Galle, concerning gunpowder, 1706.
VOC 1731, ff. 171-6	Concerning the elephant trade, 1705.
VOC 1731, ff. 199-216	*c.* 1705.
VOC 1738, ff. 268-577	1706-7.
VOC 1739, ff. 1227-30	Jaffna, 1707.
VOC 1745, n.f.	1707.
VOC 1754, ff. 362-533	1707-8.
VOC 1762, ff. 415-21	*c.* 1708.
VOC 1769, ff. 376-627	1708-9.
VOC 1772, ff. 2025-8	Galle, 1709 (among other documents).
VOC 1786, ff. 434-580	1709-10.
VOC 1787, ff. 581-8	1710.
VOC 1804, ff. 302-497	1710-11.
VOC 1805, ff. 1117-19	Jaffna, 1710.
VOC 1811, ff. 273-95	1711.
VOC 1820, ff. 224-467	1711-12.
VOC 1836, ff. 366-493	1713.
VOC 1837, ff. 634-50	1712.
VOC 1842, ff. 168-70	1710.
VOC 1843, ff. 53-4	Cochin, partially concerning the Maldives, 1712.
VOC 1850, ff. 254-509	1714.
VOC 1851, ff. 1100-41	1714.
VOC 1851, ff. 1182-5	1714.
VOC 1864, ff. 223-338	1714-15.
VOC 1865, f. 1013	Concerning gifts to Kandy, 1713.
VOC 1876, ff. 2197-218	1716-17.
VOC 1878, ff. 506-638	1716.
VOC 1892, ff. 99-100	Galle, 1717.
VOC 1892, ff. 110-11	1717.
VOC 1892, ff. 380-652	1717.
VOC 1896, ff. 1-57	1717.
VOC 1907, ff. 504-770	1718.
VOC 1919, ff. 222-421	1718-19.
VOC 1939, ff. 213-467	1719-20.
VOC 1955, ff. 282-478	1720-1.
VOC 1975, ff. 466-674	1721-2.
VOC 1982, ff. 779-810	1721-2.
VOC 1991, ff. 140-403	1722-3.
VOC 1992, ff. 566-70	Jaffna, 1723 (among other documents).

VOC 1992, ff. 1048-57	1723.
VOC 1998, ff. 702-12	1723.
VOC 1998, ff. 725-39	1723.
VOC 1998, ff. 138-41	Jaffna, 1723.
VOC 2008, ff. 271-472	1723-4.
VOC 2009, ff. 974-80	Tuticorin, 1724.
VOC 2025, ff. 187-327	1724-5.
VOC 2032, ff. 507-72	1724-5.
VOC 2032, ff. 728-801	1725.
VOC 2032, ff. 929-65	1725.
VOC 2032, ff. 94-166	1725.
VOC 2045, ff. 191-582	1725-6.
VOC 2053, ff. 63-194	1726.
VOC 2053, ff. 438-590	1726.
VOC 2053, ff. 702-94	1726.
VOC 2053, ff. 287-650	*c.* 1726.
VOC 2064, ff. 4159-533	1727.
VOC 2067, ff. 324-1008	1726-7.
VOC 2068, ff. 1308-30	Tuticorin, concerning textiles and treaties with local merchants, *c.* 1727.
VOC 2069, ff. 1591-690	Concerning an uprising of VOC troops and the condition of Fort Colombo, 1727.
VOC 2077, ff. 27-73	1727.
VOC 2077, ff. 92-134	1727.
VOC 2077, ff. 889-?	1727.
VOC 2084, ff. 1439-600	1727-8.
VOC 2091, ff. 4339-498	1728.
VOC 2094, ff. 607-1168	1727-8.
VOC 2103, ff. 780-876	Concerning gunpowder, fortifications, ammunition, etc., 1728.
VOC 2109, ff. 466-570	1729.
VOC 2109, ff. 591-8	Jaffna, 1729 (among other documents).
VOC 2116, ff. 4591-719	1729.
VOC 2124, ff. 293-601	1729.
VOC 2125, ff. 602-1104	1728-9.
VOC 2136, ff. 41-72	1729.
VOC 2136, ff. 1107-26	1729 (among other documents).
VOC 2146, ff. 4735-80	1729.
VOC 2157, ff. 299-513	1729-30.
VOC 2167, ff. 457-9	1729.
VOC 2167, ff. 536?-626	1730 (among other documents).
VOC 2184, ff. 302-503	1730-1.
VOC 2199, ff. 241-341	1730-1.
VOC 2199, ff. 663-85	1731.
VOC 2199, ff. 58-62	Galle, concerning the unlawful activities of the deceased Resident at Kilakkarai Reijnier Helmondt, *c.* 1731.

VOC 2199, ff. 90-140	1731.
VOC 2222, ff. 425-913	1731-2.
VOC 2245, ff. 143-225	1731.
VOC 2245, ff. 790-3	1729 (among other documents).
VOC 2245, ff. 1103-219	1732.
VOC 2246, ff. 108-560	1731-2.
VOC 2272, ff. 555-1608	1732-3.
VOC 2290, ff. 163-217	1733.
VOC 2290, ff. 359-660	1733.
VOC 2291, ff. 11-70	*c.* 1733.
VOC 2306, ff. 552-1126	1733-4.
VOC 2308, ff. 2126-7	Concerning church matters, 1734.
VOC 2319, ff. 569-698	1734.
VOC 2319, ff. 1181-?	1734.
VOC 2319, ff. 54-134	1734.
VOC 2336, ff. 428-815	1734-5.
VOC 2337, ff. 1022-54	Galle, 1735.
VOC 2352, ff. 129-396	1734-5.
VOC 2352, ff. 887-1078	1735.
VOC 2353, ff. 1683-998	1735.
VOC 2371, ff. 707-980	1736-7.
VOC 2372, ff. 981-1127	1736.
VOC 2372, ff. 1723-37	Galle, 1736.
VOC 2388, ff. 21-53	1735.
VOC 2388, ff. 481-509	1736.
VOC 2388, ff. 536-43	Galle, 1736.
VOC 2400, ff. 537-64	Concerning Kandy, 1737.
VOC 2401, ff. 682-1224	1737-8.
VOC 2401, ff. 1225-329	1736.
VOC 2413, ff. 25-449	1736-7.
VOC 2413, ff. 745-970	1736, 1737.
VOC 2413, ff. 1646-52	1737.
VOC 2413, ff. 161-387	1737.
VOC 2429, ff. 533-898	1738.
VOC 2444, ff. 69-696	1737-8.
VOC 2444, ff. 1418-72	Concerning the Kandyan court, 1737.
VOC 2444, ff. 1678-850	1738.
VOC 2445, ff. 43-490	1738.
VOC 2445, ff. 491-514	Concerning the Kandyan court, *c.* 1738.
VOC 2445, ff. 1528-57	Tuticorin, 1738 (among other documents).
VOC 2457, ff. 712-1016	1738-9.
VOC 2457, ff. 1017-32	Concerning conflicts between Ramnad and Muslims, and the safety of the Pamban Channel, 1739.
VOC 2472, ff. 189-304	1739.
VOC 2472, ff. 850-66	1739.

VOC 2472, ff. 1313?-18 — 1739.
VOC 2473, ff. 44-62 — Concerning conflicts between Ramnad and Muslims, and the safety of Rameswaram Island, 1739.
VOC 2473, ff. 517-1146 — 1739.
VOC 2473, ff. 1291-4 — Concerning church matters, *c.* 1739.
VOC 2491, ff. 433-927 — 1739-41.
VOC 2492, ff. 928-9 — 1740.
VOC 2506, ff. 370-2 — 1740.
VOC 2506, ff. 387-9 — Concerning Kandy, 1740.
VOC 2506, ff. 573-7 — 1740.
VOC 2506, ff. 582-92 — 1740.
VOC 2506, ff. 45-328 — 1740.
VOC 2520, ff. 384-709 — 1741.
VOC 2521, ff. 710-1033 — 1741-2.
VOC 2540, ff. 39-966 — 1740-1.
VOC 2541, ff. 2141-50 — 1741.
VOC 2541, ff. 2163-72 — 1741.
VOC 2541, ff. 2247-53 — 1741.
VOC 2541, ff. 2458-93 — Recorded by the war council at Cape Comorin, *c.* 1741.
VOC 2541, ff. 2541-846 — 1741.
VOC 2541, ff. 3113-22 — Concerning church matters, 1741.
VOC 2558, ff. 438-1044 — 1742.
VOC 2559, ff. 1045-55 — Concerning church and school matters, 1742.
VOC 2576, ff. 217-668 — 1742.
VOC 2576, ff. 1991-2008 — Concerning the elephant trade at Jaffna, 1742.
VOC 2576, ff. 2024-33 — 1742.
VOC 2596, ff. 495-915 — 1742-3.
VOC 2597, ff. 916-1588 — 1743.
VOC 2598, ff. 1589-1608 — 1743.
VOC 2599, ff. 2388-94 — Concerning the textile trade, Tuticorin, 1743.
VOC 2600, ff. 2920-48 — Galle, 1743.
VOC 2618, ff. 192-617 — 1744.
VOC 2619, ff. 618-1030 — 1744.
VOC 2620, ff. 1031-1635 — 1744.
VOC 2621, ff. 1636-49 — 1744.
VOC 2622, ff. 2598-601 — 1744.
VOC 2622, ff. 2602-16 — Jaffna, 1744 (among other documents).
VOC 2622, ff. 2739-40 — Concerning church matters, 1744.
VOC 2643, ff. 381-692 — 1745.
VOC 2644, ff. 693-1402 — 1745.
VOC 2645, f. 1403 — 1745.
VOC 2663, ff. 383-1068 — 1746.
VOC 2664, ff. 1069-112 — 1746.
VOC 2691, ff. 251-? — 1746-7.

VOC 2712, ff. 185-673	1747-8.
VOC 2713, ff. 1104?-5	Concerning school matters, 1748.
VOC 2721, ff. 219-944	1747.
VOC 2722, ff. 945-1768	1747.
VOC 2722, ff. 1841-2070	1747.
VOC 2734, ff. 181-716	1748-9.
VOC 2745, ff. 129-1178	1748.
VOC 2745, ff. 1343-?	1748.
VOC 2756, ff. 298-1128	1749-50.
VOC 2757, ff. 1129-42	1750.
VOC 2757, f. 1564	Concerning the printing of a Tamil version of three Gospels, 1742.
VOC 2773, ff. 461-996	1751.
VOC 2774, ff. 997-1005	1751.
VOC 2775, ff. 1670-1	Galle, 1752.
VOC 2795, ff. 198-9	1752.
VOC 2795, ff. 650-2	1751.
VOC 2796, ff. 673-1201	1751-2.
VOC 2796, ff. 1228-37	Galle, 1752.
VOC 2813, ff. 337-739	1753.
VOC 2814, ff. 932-3	1753.
VOC 2814, ff. 1085-8	Concerning church matters, 1753.
VOC 2831, ff. 276-679	1754.
VOC 2832, ff. 680-7	1753-4.
VOC 2832, f. 912	1754.
VOC 2878, ff. 303-6	1756.
VOC 2879, ff. 326-599	1756.
VOC 2903-2904, n.f.	1757.
VOC 2926, ff. 1-892	1758.
VOC 2927, ff. 893-?	1758.
VOC 2958, n.f.	1759.
VOC 2959, n.f.	1759.
VOC 2982, ff. 382-652	1760.
VOC 2983, ff. 653-952	1760.
VOC 2984, ff. 953-1202	1760.
VOC 3011, ff. 165-6	*c.* 1761 (among other documents).
VOC 3012, ff. 524-1040	1761-2.
VOC 3016, ff. 2241-699	1761.
VOC 3048, ff. 304-679	1762.
VOC 3052, n.f.	1762.
VOC 3053, ff. 2077-260	1762.
VOC 3079, ff. 31-219	1762-3.
VOC 3083, ff. 1622-723	1763-4.
VOC 3084, ff. 1895-2196	1763.
VOC 3095, ff. 262-5	1761.
VOC 3109, ff. 131-78	Concerning disturbances on Ceylon, 1764.

VOC 3109, ff. 416-28	1764.
VOC 3111, ff. 819-1316	1764.
VOC 3112, ff. 1589-1727	1764.
VOC 3141, ff. 1671-1907	1764-5.
VOC 3141, ff. 2033-4	1766.
VOC 3143, ff. 2363-3101	1765.
VOC 3173, ff. 832-97	1766.
VOC 3174, ff. 1304-19	1766.
VOC 3174, ff. 1563-5	1767.
VOC 3175, ff. 1655-2318	1766.
VOC 3203, ff. 1204-666	1767.
VOC 3231, ff. 5-7	Galle, 1764.
VOC 3231, ff. 201-3	1768.
VOC 3233, f. 1124	Galle, concerning church matters, 1769.
VOC 3234, n.f.	1768.
VOC 3262, ff. 107-10	1769.
VOC 3262, ff. 253-5	1769.
VOC 3263, f. 579	Concerning the Muslim merchants at Kilakkarai, 1769.
VOC 3263, ff. 723-4	1769.
VOC 3264, n.f.	1769.
VOC 3293, ff. 792-?	1770.
VOC 3322, ff. 711-14	Galle, 1771.
VOC 3324, n.f.	1771.
VOC 3349, ff. 780-90	Galle, 1772.
VOC 3350, n.f.	1772.
VOC 3376, f. 51	1773.
VOC 3377, ff. 563-4	1773.
VOC 3377, ff. 613-20	Galle, 1773.
VOC 3378, n.f.	1773.
VOC 3401, ff. 57-8	1774.
VOC 3402, ff. 433-40	1774.
VOC 3402, ff. 600-1	Galle, 1774.
VOC 3402, ff. 659-74	Galle, 1774.
VOC 3403, n.f.	1774.
VOC 3431, ff. 196-7	1775.
VOC 3432, ff. 719-20	Galle, *c.* 1775.
VOC 3433, n.f.	1775.
VOC 3457, ff. 548-59	Galle. 1776.
VOC 3458, ff. 583-893	1776.
VOC 3484, f. 49	1777.
VOC 3486, n.f.	1777.
VOC 3515, f. 21	1778.
VOC 3515, ff. 65-70	1778.
VOC 3516, f. 759	Galle, 1779.
VOC 3517, n.f.	1778.

VOC 3543, ff. 251-4	1779.
VOC 3545, ff. 631-3	Concerning the diving for pearls and conch shells, 1780.
VOC 3545, ff. 652-63	Galle, 1779-80.
VOC 3545, ff. 683-95	1780.
VOC 3546, n.f.	1779.
VOC 3571, ff. 74-86	1780.
VOC 3571, ff. 269-72	1780.
VOC 3572, ff. 520-33	1780-1.
VOC 3573, n.f.	1780.
VOC 3611, ff. 77-105	1782.
VOC 3612, ff. 604-8	1781-2.
VOC 3615, n.f.	1781.
VOC 3636, ff. 17-24	1783.
VOC 3636, ff. 146-94	1783.
VOC 3639, ff. 1338-40	Galle, 1784.
VOC 3640, n.f.	1782.
VOC 3642, n.f.	1783.
VOC 3662, ff. 143-83	1783-4.
VOC 3666, n.f.	Galle (?), 1783-4.
VOC 3691, ff. 680-2	Concerning conflicts with Nawab Muhammad Ali of Arcot, 1785.
VOC 3691, ff. 859-97	1786.
VOC 3692, n.f.	1785.
VOC 3693, n.f.	1785.
VOC 3720, ff. 143-204	1786.
VOC 3722, ff. 771-4	1787.
VOC 3722, ff. 817-30	1787 (among other documents).
VOC 3724, n.f.	1786.
VOC 3725, n.f.	1786.
VOC 3726, n.f.	1786 (at the end of the volume).
VOC 3749, ff. 94-101	Galle, 1787.
VOC 3749, ff. 102-9	1787.
VOC 3749, ff. 128-80	Partially recorded at Galle, 1787 (among other documents).
VOC 3750, ff. 429-53	1787.
VOC 3750, ff. 505-10	1787.
VOC 3785, f. 32	Galle, 1788.
VOC 3785, ff. 53-63	1788.
VOC 3785, ff. 266-8	1788.
VOC 3786, ff. 423-65	1787.
VOC 3788, ff. 1243-58	Partially recorded at Galle, 1788 (among other documents).
VOC 3790, ff. 1786-9	1788.
VOC 3790, ff. 1894-1900	Partially recorded at Galle, 1788.

VOC 3790, ff. 1936-2046	Partially recorded at Galle, 1788 (among other documents).
VOC 3790, ff. 2106-7	1788.
VOC 3791, ff. 2144-5	1788.
VOC 3791, ff. 2191-233	Partially recorded at Galle, 1788-9 (among other documents).
VOC 3792, ff. 2538-636	1788.
VOC 3794, ff. 3724-34	1788-9 (among other documents).
VOC 3795, ff. 4409-20	Galle, 1789.
VOC 3796, n.f.	1787.
VOC 3797, n.f.	1787.
VOC 3798, n.f.	1788.
VOC 3799, n.f.	1788.
VOC 3836, ff. 74-182	Partially recorded at Galle, 1788-9 (among other documents).
VOC 3838, ff. 865-944	1789.
VOC 3840, ff. 1909-47	Galle, 1789-90.
VOC 3840, ff. 1965-80	Galle, 1790.
VOC 3842, ff. 2565-619	1789-90 (among other documents).
VOC 3843, f. 3244	Galle, 1789.
VOC 3844, n.f.	1788-9.
VOC 3845, n.f.	1789.
VOC 3846, n.f.	1789.
VOC 3880, ff. 10-17	Galle, 1790.
VOC 3880, ff. 216-62	1790 (among other documents).
VOC 3880, ff. 372-80	1777, 1786.
VOC 3882, ff. 737-62	1790 (among other documents)
VOC 3882, ff. 794-831	1790.
VOC 3882, ff. 879-902	1790 (among other documents).
VOC 3882, ff. 934-1035	1790 (among other documents).
VOC 3882, ff. 1103-30	1790.
VOC 3883, ff. 1276-1361	Galle, 1790.
VOC 3884, ff. 2004-110	Concerning an uprising at Matara, 1790.
VOC 3885, ff. 2397-404	1790, 1791.
VOC 3885, ff. 2449-51	1790.
VOC 3885, ff. 2471-545	1790.
VOC 3887, ff. 3568-87	Galle, 1790 (among other documents).
VOC 3888, ff. 3651-63	Partially recorded at Galle, 1790.
VOC 3888, ff. 3867-93	Galle, 1790-1 (among other documents).
VOC 3888, ff. 4083-98	1790-1 (among other documents).
VOC 3890, ff. 4729-31	1791.
VOC 3890, ff. 4750-72	1791 (among other documents).
VOC 3891, ff. 4776-808	1791 (among other documents).
VOC 3892, ff. 5110-5	1791.
VOC 3892, ff. 5128-346	1790.

VOC 3892, ff. 5428-9	Galle, 1790.
VOC 3892, ff. 5439-40	Galle, 1790.
VOC 3892, ff. 5462-5	Galle, 1790.
VOC 3893, n.f.	1790.
VOC 3894, n.f.	1790.
VOC 3921, ff. 13-35	Partially recorded at Galle, 1791 (among other documents).
VOC 3922, ff. 801-41	1791.
VOC 3923, ff. 1429-52	Partially recorded at Galle, 1791-2 (among other documents).
VOC 3924, ff. 1526-35	1791.
VOC 3924, ff. 1553-4	Galle, 1791.
VOC 3924, ff. 1946-79	Partially recorded at Galle, 1792 (among other documents).
VOC 3925, ff. 2189-241	Partially recorded at Galle, 1791-2 (among other documents).
VOC 3926, ff. 2723-8	1792.
VOC 3926, f. 2830	Galle, 1792.
VOC 3927, n.f.	1791.
VOC 3975, ff. 40-127	Partially recorded at Galle, 1792-3 (among other documents).
VOC 3975, ff. 241-4	1792.
VOC 3975, ff. 346-9	1792.
VOC 3975, ff. 379-407	1792 (among other documents).
VOC 3975, ff. 434-83	1792 (among other documents).
VOC 3975, ff. 523-34	1792 (among other documents).
VOC 3975, ff. 597-630	Concerning military matters, 1791.
VOC 3977, ff. 1688-95	1792.

4.1.3. *Dagregisters* (diaries)

VOC 1148, ff. 445-508	Negombo, May-August 1644.
VOC 1156, ff. 389-407	Negombo, February-April 1645.
VOC 1243-4, ff. 2108-73	Colombo, October 1662-March 1663.
VOC 1420, ff. 505-34	*c.* 1686.
VOC 2167, ff. 460-515	*c.* 1730.

4.1.4. *Shipping lists*

VOC 1330, ff. 932v-?	Dutch and other vessels, 1677.
VOC 1373, ff. 254-66	Vessels that arrived at and departed from Colombo, 1682-3.
VOC 1383, ff. 425-32	Vessels that arrived at and departed from Ceylon, 1683.
VOC 1396, ff. 563-75	Vessels that arrived at and departed from Ceylon, 1684.

VOC 1405, ff. 1902v-14	Vessels that arrived at and departed from Ceylon, 1683-4.
VOC 1410, ff. 333-49	Vessels that arrived at and departed from Ceylon, 1685.
VOC 1416, ff. 1170-7	Vessels that arrived at and departed from Colombo, 1684-5.
VOC 1416, f. 1237	1685.
VOC 1416, ff. 1330-2	1685.
VOC 1420, ff. 589-603	Vessels that arrived at and departed from Ceylon, 1686.
VOC 1429, ff. 1203v-7	Vessels that arrived at and departed from Colombo, 1685-6.
VOC 1429, ff. 1306-9	Vessels that arrived at and departed from Ceylon, *c.* 1686.
VOC 1433, ff. 522-9	Vessels that arrived at and departed from Colombo, 1687.
VOC 1438, f. 1306v	Vessels that arrived at and departed from Ceylon, *c.* 1687.
VOC 1438, f. 1381v	Vessels departing from Tuticorin and Galle for Bengal, *c.* 1687.
VOC 1446, ff. 317-30	Vessels that arrived at and departed from Colombo, 1688.
VOC 1447, ff. 806-7	1688.
VOC 1454, ff. 1092-3	1687.
VOC 1468, f. 434	1690.
VOC 1469, ff. 565-9	Vessels that arrived at and departed from Galle, *c.* 1690.
VOC 1470, ff. 784-91	Vessels that arrived at and departed from Colombo, 1690-1.
VOC 1470, f. 1160	1691.
VOC 1492, ff. 302-20	Vessels that arrived at and departed from Colombo and Galle, 1691-2.
VOC 1492, ff. 355-6	*c.* 1691.
VOC 1506, ff. 1435-6v	1692.
VOC 1506, ff. 1440-56v	Vessels that arrived at and departed from Colombo, 1692.
VOC 1525, ff. 1483-4v	1693.
VOC 1525, ff. 1485-1500	Vessels that arrived at and departed from Colombo, 1693.
VOC 1544, ff. 855-93v	Vessels that arrived at and departed from various places in Ceylon and the Fishery Coast, 1693-4.
VOC 1544, ff. 894-5	1694.
VOC 1585, ff. 1410-50	Vessels that arrived at and departed from Ceylon, 1696.
VOC 1585, ff. 1452-3	1696.
VOC 1590, ff. 656-7	1697.

VOC 1591, ff. 1318-19	Vessels on the Fishery Coast, 1697.
VOC 1644, ff. 939-40	1701.
VOC 1656, ff. 1101-2	1702.
VOC 1673, ff. 1022-3	1703.
VOC 1679, ff. 123-35	*c.* 1703.
VOC 1679, ff. 139-47	*c.* 1703.
VOC 1707, ff. 1740-1	*c.* 1705.
VOC 1731, ff. 315-17	*c.* 1706.
VOC 1739, ff. 1320-1	*c.* 1707.
VOC 1756, ff. 1528-9	1708.
VOC 1772, ff. 2000-5	Foreign vessels, 1708, 1709.
VOC 1772, ff. 2014-15	1709.
VOC 1778, ff. 12-14	Foreign vessels, 1708.
VOC 1789, ff. 1870-1	1710.
VOC 1789, ff. 1872-5	Arrival and departure of foreign vessels, *c.* 1710.
VOC 1806, ff. 1386-7	1711.
VOC 1806, ff. 1388-90	Vessels that arrived at and departed from Ceylon, *c.* 1711.
VOC 1824, ff. 2242-3	1712.
VOC 1824, ff. 2244-5	Arrival and departure of foreign vessels, *c.* 1712.
VOC 1837, ff. 1033-6	Vessels arrived at and departed from Ceylon, 1713
VOC 1837, ff. 1037-8	1713.
VOC 1842, ff. 113-16	1712.
VOC 1842, ff. 117-19	Arrival and departure of foreign vessels, 1712.
VOC 1851, ff. 1190-1	1714.
VOC 1851, ff. 1192-3	Arrival and departure of vessels, 1714.
VOC 1865, ff. 978-9	1715.
VOC 1865, ff. 984-6	Arrival and departure of vessels, 1715.
VOC 1869, ff. 307-9	1714.
VOC 1869, ff. 310-13	Foreign vessels, 1714.
VOC 1879, ff. 961-3	1716.
VOC 1879, ff. 964-5	Arrival and departure of vessels, 1716.
VOC 1893, ff. 1018-19	1717.
VOC 1893, ff. 1020-2	Arrival and departure of foreign vessels, 1717.
VOC 1896, ff. 99-102	*c.* 1717.
VOC 1896, f. 129	*c.* 1717.
VOC 1896, ff. 130-3	Arrival and departure of foreign vessels, *c.* 1717.
VOC 1908, ff. 1704-5	Arrived foreign vessels, *c.* 1718.
VOC 1908, f. 1706	1718.
VOC 1921, ff. 956-7	Arrival of foreign vessels, *c.* 1719.
VOC 1927, f. 235	Arrival of foreign vessels, *c.* 1719.
VOC 1927, ff. 235-9	*c.* 1719.
VOC 1941, f. 1184	Arrival and departure of foreign vessels, 1719-20.
VOC 1941, f. 1185	1720.
VOC 1946, ff. 281-3	Arrival of foreign vessels, *c.* 1720.
VOC 1946, ff. 14-15	*c.* 1720.

VOC 1957, ff. 1364-5	1721.
VOC 1957, ff. 1366-9	Arrival and departure of foreign vessels, 1721.
VOC 1963, f. 276	Arrival of foreign vessels, *c.* 1721.
VOC 1963, ff. 277-92	*c.* 1721.
VOC 1976, ff. 1578-9	1722.
VOC 1976, ff. 1580-3	Arrival and departure of foreign vessels, 1721-2.
VOC 1982, ff. 388-9	1721.
VOC 1982, ff. 390-3	Arrival and departure of foreign vessels, 1721.
VOC 1992, ff. 926-7	1723.
VOC 1992, ff. 928-30	Arrival and departure of foreign vessels, 1722-3.
VOC 1998, ff. 477-81	Arrival and departure of foreign vessels, 1721-2.
VOC 1998, ff. 690-1	1722.
VOC 1998, ff. 156-7	1723.
VOC 1998, ff. 158-61	Arrival and departure of foreign vessels, 1722-3.
VOC 2009, ff. 1170-1	1724.
VOC 2009, ff. 1172-3	Arrival and departure of foreign vessels, 1723-4.
VOC 2015, ff. 184-7	1724.
VOC 2015, ff. 188-?	Arrival and departure of foreign vessels, 1723-4.
VOC 2026, ff. 885-6	1725.
VOC 2026, ff. 887-90	Foreign vessels, 1724-5.
VOC 2032, ff. 340-2	1725.
VOC 2032, ff. 343-9	Arrival and departure of foreign vessels, 1724-5.
VOC 2046, ff. 891-2	1726.
VOC 2046, ff. 893-5	Foreign vessels, 1725-6.
VOC 2053, ff. 1070-1	1726.
VOC 2053, ff. 1072-6	Arrival and departure of foreign vessels, 1725-6.
VOC 2069, ff. 1798-9	1727.
VOC 2069, ff. 1800-2	Arrival and departure of foreign vessels, 1726-7.
VOC 2077, ff. 845?-6	1727.
VOC 2077, ff. 847-8	Arrival and departure of foreign vessels, 1726-7.
VOC 2096, ff. 2195-6	1728.
VOC 2096, ff. 2197-8	Arrival and departure of foreign vessels, 1727-8.
VOC 2103, ff. 954-6	1728.
VOC 2103, ff. 957-60	Arrival and departure of foreign vessels, 1727-8.
VOC 2127, ff. 1830-1	1729.
VOC 2127, ff. 1832-4	Arrival and departure of foreign vessels, 1728-9.
VOC 2158, ff. 1076-7	1730.
VOC 2158, ff. 1078-80	Arrival and departure of foreign vessels, 1729-30.
VOC 2167, ff. 429-31	1729.
VOC 2167, ff. 432-5	Arrival and departure of foreign vessels, 1728-9.
VOC 2186, ff. 1743-4	1731.
VOC 2186, ff. 1745-55	Arrival and departure of foreign vessels, 1730-1.
VOC 2199, ff. 538-9	*c.* 1731.
VOC 2199, ff. 540-2	Arrival and departure of foreign vessels, *c.* 1731.
VOC 2225, ff. 2287-8	1732.
VOC 2225, ff. 2289-91	Arrival and departure of foreign vessels, 1731-2.

VOC 2245, ff. 975-82	Arrival and departure of vessels, *c.* 1732.
VOC 2245, ff. 983-4	1732.
VOC 2246, ff. 1027-31	Arrival and departure of foreign vessels, *c.* 1732.
VOC 2273, ff. 2299-300	1733.
VOC 2273, ff. 2301-8	Arrival and departure of foreign vessels, 1732-3.
VOC 2308, ff. 2092-3	1734.
VOC 2308, ff. 2095-8	Arrival and departure of foreign vessels, 1733-4.
VOC 2319, ff. 275-6	1733, arrival and departure of foreign vessels, *c.* 1734.
VOC 2338, ff. 2011-12	1735.
VOC 2338, ff. 2013-16	Arrival and departure of foreign vessels, 1734-5.
VOC 2352, ff. 614-16	1734.
VOC 2352, ff. 617-20	Arrival and departure of vessels, 1733-4.
VOC 2374, ff. 2334-5	1736.
VOC 2374, ff. 2336-9	Arrival and departure of foreign vessels, 1735-6.
VOC 2388, ff. 641-5	Arrival and departure of foreign vessels, 1734-5.
VOC 2403, ff. 2143-4	1737.
VOC 2403, ff. 2145-6	Arrival and departure of foreign vessels, 1736-7.
VOC 2413, ff. 1582-3	1736.
VOC 2413, ff. 1584-6	Arrival and departure of foreign vessels, 1735-6.
VOC 2431, ff. 1964-5	1738.
VOC 2431, ff. 1966-9	Arrival and departure of foreign vessels, *c.* 1738.
VOC 2444, ff. 1361-3	Arrival and departure of foreign vessels, *c.* 1738.
VOC 2445, ff. 1402-4	1738.
VOC 2445, ff. 1405-11	Arrival and departure of foreign vessels, 1737-8.
VOC 2460, ff. 2069-70	Vessels at Colombo, 1739.
VOC 2460, ff. 2072-4	Arrival and departure of foreign vessels, 1738-9.
VOC 2493, ff. 1727-8	1740.
VOC 2493, ff. 1729-31	Arrival and departure of foreign vessels, 1739-40.
VOC 2524, ff. 1779-80	Vessels at Colombo, 1741.
VOC 2524, ff. 1781-6	Arrival and departure of foreign vessels, 1740-1.
VOC 2540, ff. 1624-8	Arrival and departure of foreign vessels, 1739-40.
VOC 2541, ff. 3223-4	Foreign vessels arriving at Colombo, Jaffna and Galle, *c.* 1741.
VOC 2560, ff. 1903-4	Vessels at Colombo, 1742.
VOC 2560, ff. 1905-10	Arrival and departure of foreign vessels, 1741-2.
VOC 2570, ff. 1783-9	Foreign vessels arriving at Colombo, Jaffna and Galle, *c.* 1742.
VOC 2600, ff. 2680-1	Vessels at Colombo, 1743 (among other documents).
VOC 2600, ff. 2682-7	Arrival and departure of foreign vessels, 1742-3.
VOC 2622, ff. 2768-71	Arrival and departure of foreign vessels, 1743-4.
VOC 2622, ff. 2772-3	1743-4.
VOC 2668, ff. 3487-93	Arrival and departure of foreign vessels, 1745-6.
VOC 2668, ff. 3494-5	1746.
VOC 2693, ff. 1450-3	Arrival and departure of foreign vessels, 1746-7.

VOC 2693, ff. 1454-5	1747.
VOC 2713, ff. 1111-16	Arrival and departure of foreign vessels, 1747-8.
VOC 2713, ff. 1117-18	1748.
VOC 2735, ff. 1037-8	1749.
VOC 2735, ff. 1039-44	Arrival and departure of foreign vessels, 1748-9.
VOC 2757, ff. 1567-8	Vessels at Colombo, 1750.
VOC 2757, ff. 1571-2	Arrival and departure of foreign vessels, 1749-50.
VOC 2775, ff. 1526-9	Arrival and departure of foreign vessels, 1750-1.
VOC 2775, ff. 1530-1	1751.
VOC 2795, ff. 603-4	1752.
VOC 2795, ff. 612-14	Arrival and departure of foreign vessels, 1751-2.
VOC 2814, ff. 1095-6	1753.
VOC 2814, ff. 1097-9	Arrival and departure of foreign vessels, 1752-3.
VOC 2833, ff. 1135-6	1754.
VOC 2833, ff. 1137-43	Arrival and departure of foreign vessels, *c.* 1753-4.
VOC 2881, ff. 1152-3	1756.
VOC 2881, ff. 1154-7	Arrival and departure of vessels, *c.* 1756.
VOC 2881, ff. 1158-67	Arrival of foreign vessels, *c.* 1755.
VOC 2902, ff. 1065-70	*c.* 1757.
VOC 2902, ff. 1071-3	Arrival and departure of vessels, 1757.
VOC 2902, ff. 1074-8	Arrival and departure of foreign vessels, 1757.
VOC 2925, ff. 998-1005	*c.* 1758.
VOC 2925, ff. 1006-10	Arrival and departure of Dutch vessels, 1758.
VOC 2925, ff. 1014-20	Arrival and departure of foreign vessels, 1757-8.
VOC 2957, ff. 1693-8	*c.* 1759.
VOC 2957, ff. 1699-1702	Arrival and departure of vessels, 1759.
VOC 2957, ff. 1703-6	Arrival and departure of foreign vessels, *c.* 1759.
VOC 2986, ff. 1822-5	*c.* 1760.
VOC 2986, ff. 1826-8	Dutch vessels that arrived at and departed from Colombo and Punneikayal, 1760.
VOC 2986, ff. 1829-34	Arrival and departure of foreign vessels, 1760.
VOC 3017, ff. 2796-9	*c.* 1761.
VOC 3017, ff. 2800-2	Arrival and departure of Dutch vessels, 1761.
VOC 3017, ff. 2803-6	Arrival and departure of foreign vessels, 1760-1.
VOC 3049, ff. 742-5	*c.* 1762.
VOC 3049, ff. 746-9	Arrival and departure of Dutch vessels, 1762.
VOC 3049, ff. 750-6	Arrival and departure of foreign vessels, 1761-2.
VOC 3082, ff. 1518b-19	*c.* 1763.
VOC 3082, ff. 1520-6	Arrival and departure of Dutch vessels, 1763.
VOC 3082, ff. 1527-37	Foreign vessels arriving and departing from Colombo, Galle and Trincomalee, *c.* 1763.
VOC 3110, ff. 782-90	Arrival and departure of Dutch vessels, 1764.
VOC 3110, ff. 791-802	Arrival and departure of foreign vessels, *c.* 1764.
VOC 3110, ff. 812-13	*c.* 1764.
VOC 3140, ff. 1529-35	Arrival and departure of vessels, 1765.

VOC 3140, ff. 1536-45	Arrival and departure of foreign vessels, *c.* 1765.
VOC 3140, ff. 1556-7	*c.* 1765.
VOC 3174, ff. 1462-7	Arrival and departure of Dutch vessels, 1766.
VOC 3174, ff. 1468-77	Arrival and departure of foreign vessels, 1766.
VOC 3174, ff. 1488-9	*c.* 1766.
VOC 3201, ff. 964-70	Arrival and departure of Dutch vessels, *c.* 1767.
VOC 3201, ff. 971-6	Arrival and departure of foreign vessels, *c.* 1767.
VOC 3202, ff. 982-3	*c.* 1767.
VOC 3233, ff. 956-61	Arrival and departure of Dutch vessels, *c.* 1768.
VOC 3233, ff. 962-8	Arrival and departure of foreign vessels, *c.* 1768.
VOC 3233, ff. 989-900	*c.* 1768.
VOC 3263, ff. 698-702	Arrival and departure of Dutch vessels, *c.* 1769.
VOC 3263, ff. 703-10	Arrival and departure of foreign vessels, *c.* 1769.
VOC 3292, ff. 597-601	Arrival and departure of Dutch vessels, *c.* 1770.
VOC 3292, ff. 602-14	Arrival and departure of foreign vessels, *c.* 1770.
VOC 3292, ff. 624-5	*c.* 1770.
VOC 3323, ff. 737-40	Arrival and departure of Dutch vessels, *c.* 1771.
VOC 3323, ff. 741-5	Arrival and departure of foreign vessels, *c.* 1771.
VOC 3323, ff. 751-2	*c.* 1771.
VOC 3349, ff. 638-43	Arrival and departure of Dutch vessels, *c.* 1772.
VOC 3349, ff. 644-51	Arrival and departure of foreign vessels, *c.* 1772.
VOC 3349, ff. 656-7	*c.* 1772.
VOC 3377, ff. 461-5	Arrival and departure of Dutch vessels, *c.* 1773.
VOC 3377, ff. 466-70	Arrival and departure of foreign vessels, *c.* 1773.
VOC 3377, ff. 476-7	*c.* 1773.
VOC 3402, ff. 516-20	Dutch vessels that arrived at and departed from Colombo, Galle and Tuticorin, *c.* 1774.
VOC 3402, ff. 521-9	Foreign vessels that arrived at and departed from Colombo, Galle and Trincomalee, *c.* 1774.
VOC 3402, ff. 533-4	*c.* 1774.
VOC 3432, ff. 547-51	Dutch vessels that arrived at and departed from Colombo, Galle and Tuticorin, 1775.
VOC 3432, ff. 552-66	Foreign vessels that arrived at and departed from Colombo, Trincomalee and Galle, 1775.
VOC 3432, ff. 571-2	*c.* 1775.
VOC 3457, ff. 463-4	Dutch vessels that arrived at and departed from Colombo, Galle and Tuticorin, 1776.
VOC 3457, ff. 468-74	Foreign vessels that arrived at and departed from Trincomalee, Galle and Colombo, 1776.
VOC 3457, f. 502	*c.* 1776.
VOC 3485, ff. 528-31	Dutch vessels that arrived at and departed from Colombo, Galle and Tuticorin, 1777.
VOC 3485, ff. 532-42	Foreign vessels that arrived at and departed from Colombo, Trincomalee and Galle, 1776-8.
VOC 3485, f. 548-9	1777.

VOC 3516, ff. 523-7	Dutch vessels that arrived at and departed from Colombo, Galle and Tuticorin, 1778.
VOC 3516, ff. 528-36	Foreign vessels that arrived at and departed from Colombo, Trincomalee and Galle, 1777-8.
VOC 3516, f. 541-2	1778.
VOC 3544, ff. 503-4	Dutch vessels that arrived at and departed from Colombo and Galle, 1779.
VOC 3544, ff. 505-11	Foreign vessels that arrived at and departed from Colombo, Trincomalee and Galle, 1778-9.
VOC 3544, f. 516-17	1779.
VOC 3572, ff. 502-4	Dutch vessels that arrived at and departed from Colombo and Galle, 1780.
VOC 3572, ff. 505-10	Foreign vessels that arrived at and departed from Colombo, Tuticorin and Galle, 1779-81.
VOC 3572, ff. 642-3	1780.
VOC 3613, ff. 2054-6	Dutch vessels that arrived at and departed from Colombo and Galle, 1781.
VOC 3613, ff. 2057-64	Foreign vessels that arrived at and departed from Colombo and Galle, 1780-2.
VOC 3614, ff. 2086-7	1782 (among other documents).
VOC 3614, f. 2088	1781.
VOC 3637, ff. 792-3	Dutch vessels that arrived at and departed from Colombo and Galle, 1782.
VOC 3637, ff. 794-802	Foreign vessels that arrived at and departed from Colombo and Galle, 1782.
VOC 3638, f. 815	1782.
VOC 3639, ff. 1216-17	Dutch vessels that arrived at and departed from Galle, 1783.
VOC 3639, ff. 1218-31	Foreign vessels that arrived at and departed from Colombo and Galle, 1783-4.
VOC 3639, f. 1294	1783.
VOC 3662, ff. 23-4	Vessels serving the French Crown, 1784.
VOC 3664, ff. 853-5	Dutch vessels that arrived at and departed from Colombo and Galle, 1784.
VOC 3664, ff. 856-71	Foreign vessels that arrived at and departed from Colombo and Galle, 1784.
VOC 3665, f. 984	1784.
VOC 3690, ff. 479-82	Dutch vessels that arrived at and departed from Colombo, Galle and Punneikayal, 1785.
VOC 3690, ff. 483-6	Foreign vessels at Colombo and Galle, 1785.
VOC 3690, f. 622	1785.
VOC 3723, ff. 1134-46	Vessels that arrived at, departed from and passed along Colombo and Galle, 1786.
VOC 3723, f. 1267	1786.
VOC 3787, f. 839	*c.* 1788.

VOC 3788, ff. 1065-8	Dutch vessels that arrived at and departed from Colombo and Galle, 1787.
VOC 3788, ff. 1069-76	Foreign vessels that arrived at and departed from Colombo and Galle, 1787.
VOC 3788, ff. 1085-6	*c.* 1788 (among other documents).
VOC 3794, ff. 3572-3	Arrival and departure of vessels, 1788.
VOC 3794, ff. 3574-5	Arrival and departure of Dutch vessels, 1788.
VOC 3794, ff. 3576-7	Vessels that arrived at and departed from Punneikayal, 1788.
VOC 3794, ff. 3578-83	Vessels that arrived at and departed from Colombo, 1788.
VOC 3794, ff. 3584-9	Foreign vessels that arrived at Galle, 1788.
VOC 3794, ff. 3596-7	1777 (?) (among other documents).
VOC 3837, f. 525	*c.* 1789.
VOC 3839, ff. 1678-83	Vessels that arrived at and departed from Colombo, Galle and Punneikayal, 1789.
VOC 3839, ff. 1684-93	Foreign vessels that arrived at and departed from Colombo and Galle, 1789.
VOC 3839, f. 1697	1789 (among other documents).
VOC 3887, ff. 3266-9	Arrival and departure of Dutch vessels, 1790.
VOC 3887, ff. 3270-4	Arrival and departure of foreign vessels, 1790.
VOC 3887, ff. 3279-80	1790 (among other documents).
VOC 3888, f. 3909	1789.
VOC 3923, ff. 1234b-40	Dutch and foreign vessels that arrived at and departed from Colombo, Galle and Tuticorin, 1791.
VOC 3923, ff. 1244-5	*c.* 1791 (among other documents).
VOC 3923, f. 1453	1790.

4.1.5. *Missions to Indian states*

VOC 1158, ff. 401-76	Mission to Kandy (and report concerning a journey to Goa), *c.* 1645 (report).
VOC 1251, ff. 723-840	Mission to Travancore, Madurai and Ramnad by Hendrick van Rede, October 1665 (report).
VOC 1267-8, ff. 1159-91	Mission to Madurai by Hendrick van Rheede, June 1668 (report).
VOC 1275-8, ff. 2064-73	Mission to Kandy by Hendrick Draeck, *c.* 1670 (report).
VOC 1280, ff. 376-96	Mission to Kandy by Hendrick Bijstervelt, *c.* 1671 (report).
VOC 1281-4, ff. 1224-36	Mission to Kandy by Hendrick Bijstervelt, *c.* 1671 (report).
VOC 1316, ff. 477-9	Mission to Kandy by Johannes de Buckoij, *c.* 1676 (instructions).
VOC 1324, ff. 306-9	Mission to Kandy by Harman Wanderpoel, 1677 (report).

VOC 1329, ff. 1218v-20	Mission to Kandy by Johannes de Bricquoij, 1677 (instructions).
VOC 1330, ff. 893-6	Mission to Madurai by Adolf Bassingh, September 1677 (instructions).
VOC 1330, ff. 922v-3	Mission to Madurai by Adolf Bassingh, November 1677 (correspondence).
VOC 1361, ff. 376-83	Mission to Kandy by Joannes de Bucquaij, *c.* 1680 (report).
VOC 1370, ff. 1679v-82	Mission to Kandy by Jacob Kuijck van Mierop, 1681 (instructions).
VOC 1373, ff. 187-223	Mission to Kandy by Jacob Cuijk van Mierop, 1682 (correspondence).
VOC 1383, ff. 552-66	Mission to Ramnad by Jan van Vlied, May-June 1683 (report).
VOC 1406, ff. 600-13	Mission to Ramnad by Joan van Vliet, May-June 1683 (report).
VOC 1406, ff. 614-33	Mission to Kandy by Van Mierop, 1683 (correspondence).
VOC 1410, ff. 276-9	Mission to Kandy by Jacob Cuijk van Mierop, December 1685 (report).
VOC 1447, ff. 540-76	Mission to Kandy by Claes Alebos, December 1687-February 1688 (report).
VOC 1447, ff. 693-729	Mission to Kandy by Claes Alebos, July-September 1688 (correspondence).
VOC 1464, ff. 192v-262	Mission to Madurai by Nicolaes Welter, 1689 (report).
VOC 1468, ff. 239-325v	Mission to Madurai by Nicolaes Welter, 1689 (report).
VOC 1470, ff. 997-1010	Mission to Kandy by Pieter van der Leeuw, 1690 (report).
VOC 1486, ff. 463-85v	Mission to Kandy by Pieter van der Leeuw, 1690 (report).
VOC 1506, ff. 1225-49	Mission to Kandy by Abraham Emans, 1692 (correspondence).
VOC 1524, ff. 975-1011	Mission to Kandy by Abraham Emans, 1693 (report).
VOC 1538, ff. 383-415v	Mission to Kandy by Abraham Emans, 1693 (report).
VOC 1581, ff. 98-138	Mission to Kandy by Abraham Emans, 1695 (report).
VOC 1590, ff. 430-66	Mission to Kandy by Thobias van Amstel and Abraham Emans, 1697 (report).
VOC 1590, ff. 467-91v	Mission to Kandy by Jeronimus Seeq, 1697 (report).
VOC 1597, ff. 83-108	Mission to Kandy by Jeronimus Seek, January-May 1697 (report).

VOC 1597, ff. 256-97	Mission to Kandy by Thobias van Amstel and Abraham Emans, 1697 (report).
VOC 1615 III, ff. 641-54	Mission to Ramnad by Adam van der Duijn and Barend Gast, 1699 (report).
VOC 1625, ff. 34-66	Mission to Ramnad by Adam van der Duijn and Barend Gast, 1698-1699 (report and other documents).
VOC 1649, ff. 63-72	Mission to Kandy by *Mudaliyar* Alphonso Perera, 1700 (report).
VOC 1655, ff. 689-701	Mission to Kandy by Captain Gregorius d'Acosta, 1702 (report).
VOC 1665, ff. 653-66	Mission to Kandy by Captain Gregorius d'Acosta, 1702 (report).
VOC 1672, ff. 511-17	Mission to Kandy by Jan Frederick Bruijs, 1704 (report).
VOC 1693, ff. 142-8	Mission to Kandy, 1704 (report).
VOC 1693, ff. 308-17	Mission to Kandy by Jan Frederick Bruijs, 1704 (report).
VOC 1706, ff. 1013-24	Mission to Kandy by Jan Frederik Bruijs, 1705 (report).
VOC 1713, ff. 144-54	Mission to Kandy by Jan Frederik Bruijs, 1705 (report).
VOC 1739, ff. 902-22	Mission to Kandy by Gregorius Dacosta, 1707 (report).
VOC 1745, n.f.	Mission to Kandy by Gregorius da Costa, 1707 (report).
VOC 1755, ff. 939-1010	Mission to Kandy by Hans Frederik Berghman and Jan Frederik Bruijs, July-September 1708 (report).
VOC 1762, ff. 868-74	Mission to Madurai by two agents of the VOC, 1708 (report).
VOC 1771, ff. 1297-1345	Mission to Kandy by Jan Frederick Bruijs, February-March 1709 (report).
VOC 1771, ff. 1470-1595	Mission to Ramnad by Taij and Barent Gast, May-July 1709 (reports).
VOC 1778, ff. 94-105	Mission to Kandy by Jan Frederick Bruijs, *c.* 1709 (report).
VOC 1778, ff. 41-8	Mission to Ramnad by Taij and Barent Gast, *c.* 1709 (report).
VOC 1787, ff. 920-97	Mission to Kandy by Jodocus Wilhelm Hillebrant, January-March 1710 (report).
VOC 1787, ff. 998-1033	Mission to Kandy by Jodocus Wilhelm Hillebrant, July-September 1710 (report).
VOC 1805, ff. 748-85	Mission to Kandy by Jodocus Wailhelm Hillebrand, January 1711 (report).
VOC 1811, ff. 94-172	Mission to Kandy by Jodocus Hiltebrand, September 1710-January 1711 (report).

VOC 1821, ff. 680-718	Mission to Kandy by Cornelis van Beaumont, November 1711-January 1712 (report).
VOC 1828, ff. 65-96	Mission to Kandy by Cornelis van Beaumont, November 1711-January 1712 (report).
VOC 1837, ff. 833-55	Mission to Kandy by Jan Frederick Bruijs, December 1712-February 1713 (report).
VOC 1855, ff. 858-61	Mission to Kandy by Willem Hendrick de Bevere, November 1713-January 1714 (report).
VOC 1865, ff. 817-52	Mission to Kandy by J.W. Hiltebrant and J.B. Vernattij, November 1714-January 1715 (report).
VOC 1876, ff. 2219-42	Mission to Kandy by Jan Jenner, November-December 1716 (report).
VOC 1879, ff. 780-818	Mission to Kandy by Daniel Schorer, November 1715-January 1716 (report).
VOC 1879, ff. 878-89	Mission to Kandy by Adriaen van Langenhoven, July 1716 (report).
VOC 1893, ff. 808-35	Mission (to Kandy?) by Jan Jenner, December 1716 (report).
VOC 1893, ff. 900-7	Mission to Kandy by Jan Jenner, November 1717 (instructions).
VOC 1893, ff. 1047-61	Mission to Madurai by Jan Janner, June-August 1717 (correspondence).
VOC 1896, ff. 65-85	Mission to Kandy by Jan Jenner, December 1716 (*sic*) (report).
VOC 1909, ff. 1116-38	Mission to Kandy by Jan Jenner, March 1718 (report).
VOC 1912, ff. 80-116	Mission to Kandy by Jan Jenner, *c.* 1718 (report).
VOC 1920, ff. 594-613	Mission to Kandy by Jacob Rijcken and Jurgen Revoet, November 1718-January 1719 (report).
VOC 1941, ff. 987-1021	Mission to Kandy by Gerrit Kalden, December 1719-January 1720 (report).
VOC 1946, ff. 138-201	Mission to Kandy by Gerrit Kalden, December 1719-January 1720 (report and correspondence).
VOC 1956, ff. 998-1042	Mission to Kandy by Dirck ter Pesel, November 1720-January 1721 (report).
VOC 1957, ff. 1170-81	Mission to Kandy by Cornelis Takel, April-May 1721 (report).
VOC 1963, ff. 345-53	Mission to Kandy by Takel in connection with the decease of the empress, *c.* 1721 (instructions).
VOC 1976, ff. 1199-1233	Mission to Kandy by Joannes Beekman, December 1721-January 1722 (report).
VOC 1982, ff. 21-83	Mission to Kandy, *c.* 1722 (reports).
VOC 1982, ff. 304-27	Mission to Kandy by Cornelis van Takel, May 1721 (report).
VOC 1982, ff. 642-731	Mission to Kandy by Joan Beekman, (October-December?) 1722 (report and correspondence).

VOC 1992, ff. 571-602	Mission to Kandy by Joan Beekman, December 1722 (report).
VOC 1992, ff. 895-909	Mission to the Maldives by Iben Isaacz. and Jacob de Koninx, May 1723 (report).
VOC 1998, ff. 327-9	Mission to Kandy by Joan Beekman, *c.* 1723 (instructions).
VOC 1998, ff. 537-643	Mission to Kandy by Johan Beekman, October-December 1722 (reports).
VOC 1998, ff. 830-60	Mission to the Maldives by Jacob de Coning, *c.* 1723 (report).
VOC 2009, ff. 700-46	Mission to Kandy by Adriaen Maten, February-April 1724 (report).
VOC 2009, ff. 1043-51	Mission to Ramnad by Huijbert Driemond and Reijnier Helmond, February-May 1724 (reports).
VOC 2015, ff. 159-276	Mission to Kandy by Adriaen Maarten, February-April 1724 (report and correspondence).
VOC 2015, ff. 544-695	Mission to Ramnad by Huijbert Driemont and Rijnier Helmond, February-May 1724 (report).
VOC 2026, ff. 533-59	Mission to Kandy by Hendrik Fredrik van Gent, December 1724-February 1725 (report).
VOC 2032, ff. 406-506	Mission to Kandy, February 1725 (reports).
VOC 2053, ff. 822-6	Mission to Kandy by Beekman, January 1726 (correspondence).
VOC 2068, ff. 1153-86	Mission to Kandy by Dirk Pieter Beekman, December 1726-February 1727 (report).
VOC 2068, ff. 1477-1500	Mission to the Maldives by Barent de Wit, Barent van Rees and Jan Tielman, May 1727 (report).
VOC 2077, ff. 303-53	Mission to Kandy by D.P. Beekman, *c.* 1727 (report).
VOC 2077, ff. 694-730	Mission to the Maldives, May 1726 (report).
VOC 2096, ff. 1919-47	Mission to the Maldives, February-May 1728 (report).
VOC 2103, ff. 903-89	Mission to Kandy by Dirk Pieter Beekman, January-March 1728 (report).
VOC 2103, ff. 775-813	Mission to the Maldives, *c.* 1728 (report).
VOC 2126, ff. 1379-1406	Mission to Kandy by Gerrit Valk, January-March 1729 (report).
VOC 2136, ff. 782-889	Mission to Kandy by Gerrit Valk, January-March 1729 (reports).
VOC 2158, ff. 728-81	Mission to Kandy by Pieter Cornelis de Patot and Gualterus 't Lam, December 1729-April 1730 (report).
VOC 2167, ff. 276-86	Mission to Kandy, *c.* 1730 (instructions).
VOC 2167, ff. 723-839	Mission to Kandy by Pieter Cornelis de Patot and Gualterus 't Lam, December 1729-April 1730 (reports).

VOC 2185, ff. 798-849	Mission to Kandy by Johan Wilhelm Schnee, December 1730-March 1731 (report).
VOC 2185, ff. 1167-85	Mission to Ramnad by Reijnier Helmondt, January-February 1731 (reports).
VOC 2199, ff. 738-844	Mission to Kandy by Schee, *c.* 1731 (reports).
VOC 2199, ff. 857-81	Mission to Ramnad (by Reijnier Helmondt?), *c.* 1731 (report).
VOC 2223, ff. 1176-1245	Mission to Kandy by Johan Wilhelm Schnee, December 1731-March 1732 (report).
VOC 2224, ff. 1728-35	Mission to the Maldives, March 1732 (instructions).
VOC 2245, ff. 1391-1472	Mission to Kandy by Joan Wilhelmus Schnee, *c.* 1732 (report).
VOC 2246, ff. 958-72	Mission to the Maldives, *c.* 1732 (instructions).
VOC 2273, ff. 2032-76	Mission to Kandy by Daniel Agreen and Harmannus Ladenius, February-April 1733 (report).
VOC 2307, ff. 1605-53	Mission to Kandy by Daniel Agreen and Marthin Weijer, February-April 1734 (report).
VOC 2308, ff. 1853-87	Mission to the Maldives by Hendrik Bosse and Martin Coenraets, March-June 1734 (report).
VOC 2319, ff. 976-1046	Mission to Kandy, February-March 1734 (report).
VOC 2337, ff. 1125-60	Mission to Kandy by Frans Willem Falk, January-March 1735 (report).
VOC 2337, ff. 1353-87	Mission to the Maldives, 1735 (report).
VOC 2352, ff. 1124-1206	Mission to Kandy by Frans Willem Falk, *c.* 1735 (report).
VOC 2372, ff. 1425-544	Mission to Kandy by Jacob de Jong, 1736 (report).
VOC 2373, ff. 1660-93	Mission to Kandy by Daniel Agreen and Arent van Broijel, November 1736-January 1737 (report).
VOC 2374, ff. 2041-76	Mission to Ramnad by Wouter Trek, 1736 (report).
VOC 2413, ff. 561-606	Mission to Kandy, *c.* 1737 (report).
VOC 2413, ff. 1491-1521	Mission to Ramnad by Wouter Trek, 1736 (report).
VOC 2430, ff. 1626-730	Mission to Kandy by Johannes Hakkert, January-May 1738 (report).
VOC 2444, ff. 2092-237	Mission to Kandy by Johannes Hackert, January-May 1738 (report).
VOC 2458, ff. 1248-1311	Mission to Kandy by Jan Christoffel Cleijbert, January-July 1739 (report).
VOC 2458, ff. 1415-44	Mission to Kandy by Cramer and Steijger, September-November 1739 (report).
VOC 2473, ff. 159-458	Mission to Kandy by Jan Christoffel Klijbert and Joannes van Santen, 1739 (reports).
VOC 2492, ff. 1178-1229	Mission to Kandy by Macquet and De Salve, February-April 1740 (report and correspondence).
VOC 2492, ff. 1243-1313	Mission to Kandy, August-October 1740 (report and correspondence).

VOC 2506, ff. 105-200	Mission to Kandy by Macquet and De Salve, February-April 1740 (report and correspondence).
VOC 2522, ff. 1271-1341	Mission to Kandy by Jacob Boon and Warnar Berghuijs, February-April 1741 (report and correspondence).
VOC 2540, ff. 1189-1306	Mission to Kandy, August-October 1740 (report and correspondence).
VOC 2541, ff. 2962-3103	Mission to Kandy by Jacob Boon and Warnar Berghuijs, February-April 1741 (report and correspondence).
VOC 2559, ff. 1317-71	Mission to Kandy by Richard van Minnen and Harmanus van Bern, 1742 (report and correspondence).
VOC 2576, ff. 1563-1668	Mission to Kandy, 1742 (report and correspondence).
VOC 2598, ff. 1919-76	Mission to Kandy by Albertus Linklaan, 1743 (report and correspondence).
VOC 2599, ff. 2074-9	Mission to Kandy by Ferdinand Anthonij Scholtsz and Jacobus Bouman, 1743 (instructions).
VOC 2599, ff. 2107-62	Mission to Ramnad by Js.Fs. Krijtsman and F. Danens, May-July 1743 (report).
VOC 2621, ff. 1907-93	Mission to Kandy by Ferdinand Anthonij Scholtsz and Jacobus Bouman, 1743 (report and correspondence).
VOC 2645, ff. 1750-1867	Mission to Kandy by Huijbert Hogerwaart, 1745 (report and correspondence).
VOC 2665, ff. 1692-1793	Mission to Kandy by R. van Minnen, 1746 (report and correspondence).
VOC 2665, ff. 1794-1801	Mission to Kandy by J. Heezer, *c.* 1745 (report).
VOC 2692, ff. 989-1148	Mission to Kandy, *c.* 1747 (report and correspondence).
VOC 2713, ff. 817-39	Mission to Kandy by Jacob van Zollen/Zoelen, *c.* 1747 (report and correspondence).
VOC 2713, ff. 853-93	Mission to Kandy by Pieter Spiering, 1748 (report and correspondence).
VOC 2735, ff. 822-64	Mission to Kandy by Ferdinand Anthon Grave van Rantzow, Jacob Hinderman and Hubert Hogerwaard, 1748-9 (report and correspondence).
VOC 2735, ff. 876-914	Mission to Kandy by Van de Hoff, March-April 1749 (report and correspondence).
VOC 2757, ff. 1313-71	Mission to Kandy by Jan Godfried Pape and Arnoldus van Sprang, 1750 (reports and correspondence).
VOC 2774, ff. 1194-1250	Mission to Kandy by Jacob van Berghem and Arnoldus van Sprang, 1751 (reports and correspondence).

VOC 2795, ff. 382-421	Mission to Kandy by Robertus Cramer and Huybert Hogerwaart, December 1752-January 1753 (report and correspondence).
VOC 2832, ff. 826-73	Missions to Kandy by Marten Rein and Jacob Castelijn, March-April and December 1754 (report and correspondences).
VOC 2880, ff. 833-70	Mission to Kandy by Frans van D'Hoorn, April-June 1756 (report and correspondence).
VOC 2900, ff. 700-28	Mission to Kandy by Huijbert Hogerwaart, December 1756-January 1757 (report).
VOC 2924, ff. 550-633	Mission to Kandy by Robertus Cramer and Anthonij Diederig, *c.* 1758 (report and correspondence).
VOC 2956, ff. 1222-69	Mission to Ramnad by J.R. Francois and J.H. Medeler, *c.* 1759 (report).
VOC 2956, ff. 1362-1412	Mission to Kandy by Anthonij Diederig, 1759 (report and correspondence).
VOC 2986, ff. 1620-57	Mission to Kandy by Antonij Diderich, 1760 (report and correspondence).
VOC 3171, ff. 283-325	Mission to Kandy by G.L. de Coste and P.L. Smid, *c.* 1766 (report).
VOC 3199, ff. 152-266	Mission to Kandy by Van Angelbeek, *c.* 1767 (report).
VOC 3231, ff. 398-405	Mission to Kandy by De Coste, *c.* 1768 (report).
VOC 3262, ff. 223-43	Mission to Kandy by Borwater, 1769 (report).
VOC 3291, ff. 126-41	Mission to Kandy by Prins, *c.* 1770 (report and correspondence).
VOC 3321, ff. 305-21	Mission to Kandy by Nassenveld, *c.* 1771 (report).
VOC 3347, ff. 257-90	Mission to Kandy by Holst, *c.* 1772 (report).
VOC 3349, ff. 733-40	Mission to Arcot-occupied Ramnad by Johan Gerard van Angelbeek, December 1772 (report).
VOC 3376, ff. 171-80	Mission to Kandy by Prins, *c.* 1773 (report).
VOC 3401, ff. 113-22	Mission to Kandy by C. de Cock, *c.* 1774 (report).
VOC 3431, ff. 161-73	Mission to Kandy by J. de Bordes, *c.* 1775 (report).
VOC 3456, ff. 96-126	Mission to Kandy by Mekern, 1776 (report).
VOC 3484, ff. 108-19	Mission to Kandy by Jacobus de Bordes, February-March 1777 (report).
VOC 3515, ff. 153-64	Mission to Kandy by Jacobus de Bordes, February-March 1778 (report).
VOC 3543, ff. 141-59	Mission to Kandy by Jacobus de Bordes, February-March 1779 (report).
VOC 3571, ff. 172-86	Mission to Kandy by Jacobus de Bordes, February-April 1780 (report).
VOC 3611, ff. 160-88	Mission to Kandy by F.J. Billing, 1782 (report).
VOC 3613, ff. 1076-90	Mission to Kandy by J.P.C. Telenius and J.F. Conradi, February-April 1781 (report).
VOC 3636, ff. 215-146	Missions to Kandy by Reintous, Potken and Da

	Fonseka, September-October 1782, March-April 1783 (3 reports).
VOC 3662, ff. 132-42	Mission to Kandy by H.D.D. da Fonseca, 1784 (report).
VOC 3720, ff. 85-133	Missions to Kandy by Fretz, Screuder and Van Angelbeek, March-April, August-September 1786 (2 reports).
VOC 3786, ff. 531-9	Mission to Kandy by M.P. Raket, March-April 1787 (report).
VOC 3794, ff. 3695-709	Mission to the regent at Tirunelveli by Franken, *c.* 1788 (report).
VOC 3838, ff. 1192-1211	Mission to Kandy by A. Samlant, March 1789 (report).
VOC 3886, ff. 2653-73	Mission to Kandy by Vollenhoven, February-March 1790 (report).

4.1.6. *Miscellaneous*

VOC 1187, ff. 509-31	Expedition to Tuticorin, January-March 1649.
VOC 1256, ff. 446-56	Report of the first pearl fishery under the Dutch, 1666.
VOC 1256, ff. 481-513	Report of Lucas van der Dussen and Isaack de St. Martin, concerning their visit to Jaffna, 1666.
VOC 1259, ff. 40A-116A	Instructions and report concerning the visit to Jaffna of Lucas van der Dussen and Isacq de St. Martin, 1666.
VOC 1259, ff. 117A-43A	Report of Lucas van der Dussen concerning his visit to the Fishery Coast, 1666.
VOC 1259, ff. 154A-71A	Reaction by *Opperhoofd* of the Fishery Coast Lourens Pijl (among others) to the memorandum and the report concerning the Fishery Coast of Lucas van der Dussen, 1666.
VOC 1266, ff. 650-80	Report concerning the occupation of Batticaloa and Kottiyar, *c.* 1668.
VOC 1266, ff. 864-83	Report by Rijcklof van Goens concerning the state of affairs of the government of Ceylon, Malabar and the Fishery Coast, 1669.
VOC 1270, ff. 150-82	Manifest by Hendrick van Rheede and Laurens Pijl concerning conflicts on the Fishery Coast with the Nayak of Madurai, *c.* 1669.
VOC 1274, ff. 187-203	Report concerning a meeting between Rijcklof van Goens and regent 'Barmiliappa Pulle' of Madurai, 1670.
VOC 1280, ff. 125-253	Report of Rijcklof van Goens jr. concerning his journey to Batticaloa, Trincomalee, Jaffna, etc., 1671.

VOC 1281-1284, ff. 1081-99	Report of Aert Coninck concerning his journey to the Maldives, *c.* 1671.
VOC 1281-1284, ff. 1174-1223	Report of Rijcklof van Goens jr. concerning the state of affairs in eastern Ceylon, 1671.
VOC 1292, ff. 357-83	Report about a journey to Colombo's uplands, 1674.
VOC 1292, ff. 544-63	Document in secret code, 1674.
VOC 1297, ff. 882-944	Documents concerning the Brahmin Timmarasa, 1674.
VOC 1302-1303, ff. 585-94	Report concerning an uprising at the Kandyan court in 1665, *c.* 1674.
VOC 1308, ff. 326-36	Report concerning the state of affairs on the Fishery Coast, *c.* 1675.
VOC 1315, ff. 262-302	Correspondence concerning uprisings at Jaffna, 1676.
VOC 1315, ff. 306-34	Documents concerning the state of affairs in Ceylon, 1676.
VOC 1315, ff. 339-54	Documents concerning the Nayak of Madurai, *c.* 1676 (among other documents).
VOC 1316, ff. 205-20	Report by Marten Huijsman concerning trade on the Fishery Coast, 1676.
VOC 1321, ff. 777v-8	Genealogical tree of the Kings of Kandy, *c.* 1676.
VOC 1321, ff. 869v-72	Documents concerning an envoy from Ramnad, *c.* 1676.
VOC 1324, ff. 313-23	Declaration by Jan Verwer about his imprisonment at Kandy, 1677.
VOC 1329, ff. 1262-86	Documents concerning Caperman's journey to 'Cottate', 'Pannagaedij', 'Callecate', etc., 1677.
VOC 1340, ff. 1401v-21	List of the Company's (Dutch and local) servants in the Ceylon government, 1678.
VOC 1351, ff. 2352-7	Report concerning the state of affairs on Ceylon, 1680.
VOC 1363, ff. 203-94	Document concerning the state of affairs on Ceylon, 1681.
VOC 1369, ff. 1381-1403	Transfer of Nagappattinam from the Ceylon government to Coromandel, *c.* 1681.
VOC 1370, ff. 1632v-63	Reports concerning Dutch and English fled from Kandy, 1681.
VOC 1370, ff. 1779-2066	Documents concerning the state of affairs in Ceylon and trade related conflicts with the King of Kandy, *c.* 1681.
VOC 1383, ff. 552-66	Report concerning the Setupati of Ramnad, 1683.
VOC 1387, ff. 1745-56	Report concerning the Fishery Coast, 1683.

VOC 1396, ff. 296-319	Correspondence concerning the Setupati of Ramnad and his envoys, *c.* 1684.
VOC 1396, ff. 514-36	Report concerning a Portuguese who fled from Kandy, *c.* 1684.
VOC 1405, ff. 1827-56	Documents concerning the Setupati of Ramnad, 1684.
VOC 1416, ff. 1346-60	Report by Nicolaes Welter concerning his visit to Kilakkarai, *c.* 1685.
VOC 1433, ff. 248-332	Report concerning Kandy, February-December 1687.
VOC 1447, ff. 599-682	Report concerning envoys from Kandy, February 1688-January 1689.
VOC 1454, ff. 1159v-1203	Report by *Dissave* Cornelis Blicklant concerning his imprisonment at Kandy and the siege and conquest of Weligama by Kandy, 1688.
VOC 1479, ff. 384-404	Documents concerning the war with Ramnad and the occupation of Rameswaram Island, 1690.
VOC 1479, ff. 530-42	Documents concerning the elephant trade, *c.* 1680-90.
VOC 1479, ff. 591-654	Trade surveys concerning the Fishery Coast between 1669 and 1690.
VOC 1506, ff. 773-870	Report of Thomas van Rhee's journey along the Fishery Coast, August-September 1692.
VOC 1524, ff. 1044-99	Report by commander Floris Blom of Jaffna concerning his visit to Vanni, 1693.
VOC 1544, ff. 982-1021v	Documents concerning a Dutch-Sinhalese-Dutch dictionary, 1694.
VOC 1570, ff. 622-50	Report of a pearl fishery at Mannar and Arippu, *c.* 1695.
VOC 1590, ff. 291-308	Documents concerning the elephant trade, 1697.
VOC 1591, ff. 718-82v	Report of a journey by Gerrit de Heere to Jaffna, 1697.
VOC 1597, ff. 180-241	Documents concerning conflicts between the pastors at Galle and Matara, 1696.
VOC 1597, ff. 245-67	Report concerning a journey by Krijn Caperman to the factories on the Fishery Coast south of Tuticorin, 1696.
VOC 1597, ff. 140-88	Documents concerning a pearl fishery at Kondaichi, 1697.
VOC 1597, ff. 191-247	Report of a journey by Gerrit de Heere to Jaffna, 1697.
VOC 1604 II, ff. 226-607	Report of a journey by Gerrit de Heere around Ceylon, March-September 1698.
VOC 1605, ff. 1083-1122	Correspondence concerning conflicts with the Muslim Citakkati Periya Tambi at the Fishery Coast, 1698.
VOC 1607, ff. 403-67	Letter concerning the elephant trade at Jaffna, 1698.

VOC 1615 II, ff. 471-514	Report of a journey by Gerrit de Heere to Tuticorin, includes several maps, September-October 1699.
VOC 1616, ff. 686-778	Documents concerning a pearl fishery at Kondaichi, 1699.
VOC 1616, ff. 1036-1118	Sinhalese grammar by Joannes Ruell, *c.* 1699 (see also Appendix I).
VOC 1629, ff. 665-836	Document concerning Rajasinga and the Kandyan court, 1700.
VOC 1632, ff. 672-713	Documents concerning a pearl fishery at Tuticorin, 1700.
VOC 1632, ff. 714-44	Report of a journey by Crijn Caperman along the Fishery Coast, January-February 1700.
VOC 1656, ff. 884-933	Report of a journey by Nicolaes Welters along the southern Fishery Coast, September-October 1702.
VOC 1682, ff. 751-839	Report of a journey by C.J. Simons to Jaffna, March-June 1704.
VOC 1706, ff. 1040-51	Report concerning a meeting with the Queen of Madurai, 1705.
VOC 1722, ff. 1059-77	Correspondence with and concerning the King of the Maldives, 1706.
VOC 1731, ff. 472-92	Reports concerning a mission by envoys from Kandy to Madurai, March 1706.
VOC 1756, ff. 1194-1210	Report concerning a visit by the Nayak of Madurai to Tuticorin, 1708.
VOC 1756, ff. 1280-1319	Correspondence with and concerning the Setupati of Ramnad, 1708.
VOC 1772, ff. 1818-47	Reports concerning indigenous churches and schools in Ceylon, 1708-9.
VOC 1788, ff. 1366-1415	Report of journey by Hendrik Becker to the coast of Madurai, September-October 1710.
VOC 1788, ff. 1423-55	Documents concerning the fight against 'Totteas' (Tottiyars?) and 'Marruos' (Maravars?) 'bandits' at 'Arrescherij', 1710.
VOC 1789, ff. 1778-1842	*Wetboek der Bramines of eerste goddelijke boek derselve* (i.e. lawbook of the Brahmins being their first divine book), edited by Pastor Petrus Sinjeu, *c.* 1710.
VOC 1805, ff. 1039-48	Report concerning envoys from Ramnad, February-April 1711.
VOC 1851, ff. 1239-1315	Documents concerning the Hindu 'priest' Timmarasa, *c.* 1714.
VOC 1865, ff. 867-97	Documents concerning a war between Ramnad and Thanjavur and the Danish involvement in it, *c.* 1715.
VOC 1896, ff. 24-44	Correspondence concerning a visit of the King of Kandy to some temples in connection with his ill health, *c.* 1717.
VOC 1921, ff. 776-832	Correspondence concerning conflicts between

	Paravars and the 'Armaneesen' around 'Tale' and 'Coertale', 1719.
VOC 1941, ff. 919-42	Documents concerning a meeting with the Nayak of Madurai at Tuticorin, 1720.
VOC 1946, ff. 221-70	Documents regarding cinnamon, *c.* 1720.
VOC 1957, ff. 1215-62	Documents concerning the journey of an envoy from Thanjavur to Jaffna, *c.* 1721.
VOC 1963, ff. 156-232	Documents concerning coffee-growing in Ceylon, *c.* 1721.
VOC 1975, ff. 853-1032	Documents concerning a pearl fishery at Kondaichi, 1722.
VOC 1982, ff. 86-94	Document concerning weights, measures and currencies in Ceylon, *c.* 1722.
VOC 1992, ff. 665-745	Documents concerning conflicts with indigenous servants of the VOC, *c.* 1723.
VOC 1992, ff. 829-83	Documents concerning tollage at the Pamban Channel by Ramnad, *c.* 1723.
VOC 2026, ff. 659-833	Documents concerning conflicts between Paravars and the *Maniyakkarar* of the village 'Mehoer', 1724.
VOC 2068, ff. 1343-71	Report concerning the misbehaviour of the former Tuticorin *Opperhoofd* Jan Driemond, 1727.
VOC 2077, ff. 523-72	Document concerning the treaty concluded with textile merchants in the Fishery Coast, 1726.
VOC 2185, ff. 955-94	Report by Versluijs about his journey to Galle, 1731.
VOC 2185, ff. 1007-23	Report concerning a meeting with the Nayak of Madurai at Tuticorin, 1731.
VOC 2246, ff. 75-107	Documents concerning the private trade conducted by the *huijsvrouw* (housewife) of Van Domburg, *c.* 1732.
VOC 2246, ff. 114-213	Documents concerning the debt of the factory at Kilakkarai, *c.* 1732.
VOC 2260, ff. 166-420	Report by Commissioner Jacob Christiaan Pielat concerning his journey to Ceylon, 1733.
VOC 2290, ff. 825-50	Report concerning the damage suffered by the VOC because of the activities of the former Governor Pieter Vuijst, *c.* 1733.
VOC 2308, ff. 1987-2032	Correspondence concerning textile trade on the Fishery Coast, *c.* 1734.
VOC 2353, ff. 2149-578	Documents concerning cinnamon workers unwilling to serve the Dutch and moving to Kandy, *c.* 1735.
VOC 2402, ff. 1717-1894	Report by Gustaaf Willem van Imhoff concerning his journey to Galle and Matara, 1737.
VOC 2428, ff. 317-418	Essay by Gustaaf Willem van Imhoff concerning

	the trade on the Fishery Coast (ff. 435-532: annexes), *c.* 1738.
VOC 2430, ff. 1103-1389	Report by Gustaaf Willem van Imhoff concerning his journey around Ceylon, *c.* 1738.
VOC 2456, ff. 464-711	Report by Gustaaf Willem von Imhoff concerning his journey to Malabar, the Fishery Coast and part of Ceylon, January-April 1739.
VOC 2459, ff. 1617-30	Report concerning envoys from Ramnad, *c.* 1739.
VOC 2493, ff. 1910-34	Reports concerning the fortifications of the trading stations in Ceylon, *c.* 1740.
VOC 2541, ff. 2335-77	Report concerning the declining textile trade at Manapadu, *c.* 1741.
VOC 2600, ff. 2571-636	Reports concerning Dutch buildings at Jaffna, Galle, Tuticorin, Trincomalee and Batticaloa, 1743.
VOC 2665, ff. 1995-2005	Report concerning envoys from Thanjavur, 1746.
VOC 2666, ff. 2053-354	Documents concerning the war against Ramnad, 1746.
VOC 2666, ff. 2055-406	Report by Tuticorin *Opperhoofd* A. Domburg concerning his journey to Rameswaram Island, 1746.
VOC 2667, ff. 2978-3272	Documents concerning an uproar at Matara, *c.* 1746.
VOC 2812, ff. 92-133	Reports concerning a mission of Siamese monks to Kandy, 1753.
VOC 2855-6, ff. 678-3064	Various unspecified documents concerning Ceylon and the Fishery Coast, 1755-6.
VOC 3013, ff. 1097-1507	Document concerning an uprising (supposedly instigated by Kandy) in the Dutch controlled territories in Ceylon, *c.* 1761.
VOC 3013, ff. 1508-1649	Document concerning the history of the Dutch presence in Ceylon from 1602 to 1757, 1760 (see also 4.3, *Hoge Regering te Batavia*, inv. no. 572). For a published version, see Bibliography, no. 452.
VOC 3014, ff. 1685-2031	Report by Schreuder concerning his journey around the Ceylon government, 1760.
VOC 3052, n.f.	Description of Madurai, *c.* 1762.
VOC 3112, ff. 1340-1587	Report concerning the war against Kandy, *c.* 1764.
VOC 3138, ff. 674-814	Report concerning the occupation of and withdrawal from Kandy, 1765.
VOC 3171, f. 384	Document concerning weights, measures and currencies in Ceylon, *c.* 1766.
VOC 3232, ff. 745-854	Document concerning events in Madurai, Ramnad and Travancore, 1768.
VOC 3402, ff. 602-3	Exchange rates of the *pagoda* in Madurai between 1745 and 1774, *c.* 1774.

VOC 3431, ff. 198-298	Some treaties etc. concluded with Madurai (1659-1711), Kandy (1649-1766) and Ramnad (1658-1769) (among other kingdoms).
VOC 3485, ff. 631-714	Inventory and state of affairs of the artillery etc. in Ceylon, *c.* 1777.
VOC 3837, ff. 664-7	Seven treaties concluded with the Nayak of Madurai between 1659 and 1711.
VOC 3883, ff. 1604-806	Report concerning an uprising at Matara, 1790.
VOC 3891, ff. 4823-981	Documents concerning Kandy, 1790-1.
VOC 3915, ff. 1015-1265	Documents concerning the coinage at Tuticorin, *c.* 1791.
VOC 3976, ff. 1331-71	Report concerning a pearl fishery at Tuticorin, 1792.

4.2. Other VOC Series

4.2.1. *Archives of the Gentlemen XVII and the Amsterdam Chamber*

See 1.1
Access no.: 1.04.02

Kopie-resoluties van de Gouverneur-Generaal en Raden
Duplicate proceedings of the Governor-General and Council

See 1.1.4
Inv. nos: VOC 656-847

In the *Realia* repertory to the *resoluties* several relevant headings are to be found, among these:

Batticaloa (4 entries 1665-1700), *Caab Comerijn* (Cape Comorin; 3 entries 1740-4), *Calpatijn en Chilan* (Kalpitiya and Chilaw; 1 entry 1658), *Candia* (Kandy; 29 entries 1703-78), *Ceijlon* (about 1500 entries 1639-1797), *Cingalees* (Sinhalese; 2 entries 1670-5), *Cotiaar* (Kottiyar; 2 entries 1665-93), *Cottate* (1 entry 1692), *Dwars in de Weg* (in the Bay of Trincomalee; 1 entry 1698), *Gale* (3 entries 1640-3), *havenen en baaijen* (harbours and bays; 3 entries 1701-12), *Jaffanapatnam* (Jaffna; 4 entries 1658-1701), *Kalpetty* (Kalpitiya; 1 entry 1700), *Krijgsraad van Colombo* (court-martial in Colombo; 29 entries 1731-7), *Maldivos* (9 entries 1732-51), *Manaar* (Mannar; 1 entry 1658), *marale* (kind of law; 1 entry 1699), *Nigombo* (5 entries 1644-96), *Ponnecail* (Punneikayal; 1 entry 1679), *Putuancare* (1 entry 1685), *Rammenacoil* (Rameswaram; 1 entry 1665), *Seminarium op Colombo* (Colombo seminary; 2 entries 1722), *Teuverheer* (Setupati of Ramnad or Raja of Sivagangai; 2 entries 1665-96), *Theuver* (Setupati of Ramnad or Raja of Sivagangai; 5 entries 1755-60), *Trinquonomale* (Trincomalee; 6 entries 1672-1702), *Tutucorijn* (Tuticorin; 7 entries 1658-1795).

Under the heading *ambassadeurs* references can be found to the Kandyan envoys to Batavia (15 entries 1741-67).

Miscellaneous

VOC 447	*Resoluties* recorded at the ship Zierikzee off the coast near Batticaloa, concerning the inconvenience caused by the ship's crew to the local inhabitants, 1603. One piece.
VOC 4631	Notes of Advocate Pieter van Dam and other papers concerning the Ceylon and Malabar Coast, 1664-1702. One folder.
VOC 4816	List of coins, exchange rates, weights and measures in Asia, with index, including sections on Colombo, Galle, Jaffna, Mannar and Tuticorin (ff. 1-90 contain the actual lists; ff. 91-139 contain notes on these subjects), 1769. One volume.
VOC 4893	Letter by Frederik de Vries in Elseneur (Helsingør), accompanying a treaty concluded in August 1618 between Denmark and Kandy, 1649. Two pieces.
VOC 4894	Daily report by Joannes Leeuwenson (Secretary of Rijklof van Goens) of his journey overland from Ceylon to the Dutch Republic, 1675. One volume. Published in *Bijdragen* (1863), pp. 89-144 (see Bibliography, no. 33).
VOC 4895	Memorandum of Joost Segenaer at Amsterdam to Director Le Sage concerning the state of affairs in Ceylon, criticizing the policies of Rijklof van Goens, 1676. One piece.
VOC 4896	Papers concerning the accusations against Laurens Pijl, Governor of Ceylon, about his mismanagement, with notes of Advocate Pieter van Dam, 1676-85. One folder.
VOC 4897	Notes of a faithful servant of the VOC with critical remarks about the policies concerning Ceylon of father and son Rijklof van Goens, with proposals to economize on administration, and with notes of Advocate Pieter van Dam, 1678. One piece.
VOC 4898	Report by Anthony Caldere, born at Colombo, concerning his stay at the court of Kandy, 1697. One piece.
VOC 4899	Papers concerning a Ceylonese herb, 'achmella', serving as a medication against kidney stones, 1688-97. One folder.
VOC 4900	Memorandum with critical remarks about a treaty to be concluded with the King of Kandy, 1693. One folder.
VOC 4901	Secret letter of the Gentlemen XVII to the Governor and Council of Ceylon, urging to take precautions with respect to foreign warships, and a treaty of November 1785 between the Dutch Republic and France, 1787. Two pieces.
VOC 4902	Papers concerning troubles of VOC servants in Ceylon, caused by the instruction that half of the amount of bills of exchange to the Republic had to be deposited as gold and silver coins in the VOC fund, 1790-3. One folder.
VOC 7057	Papers originating from Colombo concerning bills of exchange, 1780-95. One volume.

4.2.2. *Archives of the Zeeland Chamber*

See 1.2.1
Access no.: 1.04.02

Ingekomen stukken van Gouverneur-Generaal en Raden bij de Heren XVII en de Kamer Zeeland (IGG)
Papers received from Governor-General and Council by the Gentlemen XVII and the Zeeland Chamber

VOC 8901-84 Letters and reports received by GG&C from Ceylon, with appendices, 1681-1749 (-1786). 84 Volumes. Incomplete series.

Ingekomen stukken van de kantoren in Indië bij de Heren XVII en de Kamer Zeeland (IKI)
Papers received from the establishments in the Indies by the Gentlemen XVII and the Zeeland Chamber

VOC 9735-10030 Letters and other papers from the Governor and Council of Ceylon to the Gentlemen XVII (and others), with appendices, 1681-1793. 296 volumes. Incomplete series. Including:

- VOC 9748 Letters from Pieter Macaré, *Independent Fiscaal* of Ceylon, to the Gentlemen XVII, 1703-4.
- VOC 9755 Includes *resoluties* of the Governor and Council of Ceylon, 1705.
- VOC 9782 Papers concerning accusations against Johannes de Krouse, head and *Dissave* of the Colombo district, 1712.
- VOC 9794 Includes orders and instructions of the Governor concerning various locations in his district, 1707-15.
- VOC 9804-5 Includes papers concerning the sale of lands and gardens on Ceylon during the government of Governor Hendrik Becker, 1719.
- VOC 9841 Papers concerning the trial against former Petrus Vuyst, 1730.
- VOC 9846-51 Include correspondence and other papers of Jacob Christiaan Pielat, Commissioner of Ceylon, 1732-3.
- VOC 9868 Includes the prayer of Our Father translated into Tamil, 1739.

<table>
<tr><td></td><td>VOC 9922</td><td colspan="2">Includes a *memorie van overgave* by Governor Joan Gideon Loten to Jan Schreuder, February 1757.</td></tr>
<tr><td></td><td>VOC 10011</td><td colspan="2">Includes papers concerning the Luxemburg Regiment, 1788.</td></tr>
<tr><td></td><td>VOC 10012</td><td colspan="2">Includes a general description of Ceylon, 1788.</td></tr>
<tr><td></td><td>VOC 10022-4</td><td colspan="2">Include papers concerning the Military Commission of Ceylon, and the Meuron Regiment, 1791.</td></tr>
<tr><td></td><td>VOC 10030</td><td colspan="2">Includes letters concerning the Military Department of Ceylon, 1792.</td></tr>
<tr><td>VOC 10031-51</td><td colspan="3">Letters and other papers from the Governor and Council of Ceylon to the Zeeland Chamber, with appendices, (1681) 1693-1795. Eighteen volumes. Incomplete series.</td></tr>
<tr><td>VOC 10052</td><td colspan="3">Minutes of a meeting concerning considerations of Gustaaf Willem van Imhoff, departing Governor, 1740. One volume.</td></tr>
<tr><td>VOC 10053-68</td><td colspan="3">*Resoluties* of the Governor and Council of Ceylon, 1740, 1757-61, 1786 (-1787). Sixteen volumes.</td></tr>
<tr><td>VOC 10069-78</td><td colspan="3">Letters from the Governor and Council of Ceylon to the GG&C, 1707-83. Ten volumes. Incomplete series.</td></tr>
<tr><td>VOC 10079-80</td><td colspan="3">Correspondence of the Governor and Council, 1687-8, 1722. Incomplete series.</td></tr>
<tr><td>VOC 10081-3</td><td colspan="3">Papers relating to Jacob Christiaan Pielat, Commissioner of Ceylon, 1732-4. Three volumes.</td></tr>
<tr><td>VOC 10084-6</td><td colspan="3">*Dagregisters* of Ceylon, January-December 1688, December 1746-September 1747, March-November 1757. Three volumes. VOC 10085 contains information concerning a mission by the King of Kandy to the Governor of Ceylon.</td></tr>
<tr><td>VOC 10087-105</td><td colspan="3">Daily reports of tours of inspection by Governors and others, 1698-1760. Twenty volumes.</td></tr>
<tr><td></td><td>VOC 10087</td><td colspan="2">Galle, Matara, Jaffna and Colombo district, by Governor Gerrit de Heere, with appendices, March-September 1698.</td></tr>
<tr><td></td><td>VOC 10088</td><td colspan="2">Jaffna, by Governor Cornelis Jan Simons, with appendices, March-June 1704.</td></tr>
<tr><td></td><td>VOC 10089</td><td colspan="2">Fishery Coast, by factor Cornelis Jaay and Bookkeeper Barend Gast, May-July 1709.</td></tr>
<tr><td></td><td>VOC 10090</td><td colspan="2">Ceylon, by Governor Isaac Augustijn Rumpf, with maps and drawings, April-October 1717.</td></tr>
<tr><td></td><td>VOC 10091</td><td colspan="2">Mannar and Jaffna, by Governor Stephanus Versluys, January-April 1730.</td></tr>
</table>

	VOC 10092	Jaffna, by Governor Stephanus Versluys, January-April 1730.
	VOC 10093	Fishery Coast, by Governor Stephanus Versluys, January-February 1731.
	VOC 10094	Galle, by Governor Stephanus Versluys, July 1731.
	VOC 10095	Fishery Coast, by Governor Stephanus Versluys, February 1732.
	VOC 10096	Galle and Matara, by Governor Gustaaf Willem van Imhoff, March-April 1737.
	VOC 10097	Ceylon, by Governor Gustaaf Willem van Imhoff, May-August 1738.
	VOC 10098	Cochin, Travancore and the Fishery Coast, by Governor Gustaaf Willem van Imhoff, with maps, January-April 1739.
	VOC 10099	Galle and Matara, by Governor Gustaaf Willem van Imhoff, February-March 1745.
	VOC 10100	Jaffna, by Governor Julius Valentijn Stein van Gollonesse, February-May 1746 (see also VOC 10101).
	VOC 10101	Appendices to VOC 10100, with a map.
	VOC 10102	Manapadu and Punneikayal on the Fishery Coast, by Albertus Domburg, *Opperhoofd* of the Fishery Coast, April-May 1746.
	VOC 10103	Rameswaram Island, by Albertus Domburg, *Opperhoofd* of the Fishery Coast, August 1746.
	VOC 10104	Appendices to VOC 10105.
	VOC 10105	Ceylon, by Governor Jan Schreuder, June-September 1760 (see also VOC 10104).
VOC 10106-8	Missions by VOC servants to the court of Kandy. Three volumes (see also VOC 10085 above).	
	VOC 10106	By J. Hackert, January-May 1738.
	VOC 10107	By Johan Christoph Klijbert, *Fiscaal* of Jaffna, January-June 1739; by Johan Christoph Klijbert and Johannes van Sanden, July 1739.
	VOC 10108	By Richard Minnen, Bookkeeper at Colombo, January-April 1746.
VOC 10109-10	Daily reports concerning the pearl fishery, March-May 1728 and February-May 1746. Two volumes.	
VOC 10112	Report concerning a money loan of a Portuguese merchant in Goa to the VOC government of Ceylon, with appendices, 1785-6. One volume.	
VOC 10113-15	Papers concerning the trial against officers of the	

	Luxemburg Regiment on Ceylon, 1784-7. Three volumes.
VOC 10116-22	Papers concerning the trial against former Governor Petrus Vuyst, 1729-32. Ten volumes.
VOC 10123	Papers concerning the trial against *Dissave* Claas Isaacqs, 1712. One volume.
VOC 10124-6	Papers concerning the trial against Governor Stephanus Versluys, 1732-3. Three volumes.
VOC 10127-32	Papers concerning the trial against Joan de Mauregnault, *Fiscaal* of Colombo, 1742-40. Six volumes.
VOC 10133	Papers concerning disturbances in Ceylon during the years 1732-3, 1736. One volume.
VOC 10134	Appendices to the report of Jacob Christiaan Pielat, Commissioner of Ceylon, 1732-3. One volume
VOC 10135-7	Papers concerning the trial against Gerrit Verschragen, factor and former *Dissave* of Matara, 1733. Three volumes.
VOC 10138-40	Papers concerning the trial against Governor Diderik van Domburg, 1733-4. Three volumes.
VOC 10141-7	Accounts of the court-martials in Colombo, 1729. Eight volumes.
VOC 10148	List of lands in the district 'Tennamaravadi' in Ceylon, 1721. One volume.
VOC 10149	List of lands, drawn up during a description of territories sold by the VOC, n.d. Three volumes.
VOC 10150	Survey of guns etc. on the city walls, in outposts and warehouses in Colombo and in other stations on Ceylon, 1779. One volume.
VOC 10151-206	Letters from the *Commandeur* and Council of Galle to the Gentlemen XVII (and others), with appendices, (1683-) 1716-92. 56 volumes.
VOC 10207	Letters from the *Commandeur* and Council of Galle to the Zeeland Chamber, (1688-) 1703 (-1788). One volume.

For maps and drawings in this series concerning Ceylon, see 4.7 and 1.7.10.

Soldijkantoor
Pay Office

See 1.2.1 and 1.1.10

VOC 12372-443	General muster rolls of the VOC servants in Ceylon, 1694-1778, with rolls of the crew members of VOC vessels stationed on Ceylon, 1707-78. 72 volumes.
VOC 12443 I	Survey of soldiers in Ceylon, 1784. One piece.
VOC 12444	Ledger concerning the pay bills of the disabled, drawn up at Colombo, 1790-2. One volume.

VOC 12455	Pay rolls of the crew members of VOC vessels in the harbours of Ceylon, 1696. One volume.
VOC 12446-52	Rolls of VOC servants at Colombo who have become *vrijburgers*, 1759-2. Seven volumes. VOC 12448 contains a testament of Wilhelmus Philipus van Keuylenburg and Maria Rebecca Ebert, drawn at Colombo, 1761.

Miscellaneous

VOC 7325	Letters from the Amsterdam Chamber to the Zeeland Chamber concerning the sending of ships and crew to Ceylon (and other matters), 1763. One piece.
VOC 9523-5	Papers concerning the trial against Petrus Vuyst, former Governor of Ceylon, 1729-32. Five volumes.
VOC 11067	Papers concerning factor Marten van Domburgh, departed in 1604 on board of the ship Zeelandia, and his imprisonment by the Portuguese, after a shipwreck on the Maldives, 1612-13. One folder.
VOC 11165	Letters from the church council at Colombo to the classis of Walcheren (in Zeeland), with appendices, 1738-55. One folder.
VOC 11194	Includes a trade journal of Trincomalee, 1700-1.
VOC 11207-8	Two copies of a list (79 pp.) of coins, exchange rates, weights and measures at a great number of factories in the Indies, including Colombo, Galle, Jaffna, Mannar and Tuticorin, printed in 1691 (at Middelburg, Zeeland). Two volumes.
VOC 11291	Papers concerning the complaints of Governor Hendrik Becker about Nicolaas van Heuvel, member of the Council of Jaffna, 1708-9. One volume.
VOC 11292	Correspondence between Colombo and Jaffna concerning the mismanagement in the latter place, 1712. One volume.
VOC 11293	Papers concerning the tenures on Ceylon, 1717-20. One volume.
VOC 11294	Notes of the VOC interpreters made during the mission with envoy Gerrit Kalden to the court of Kandy, trans-lation from Sinhalese, 1719-20. One volume.
VOC 11295	Papers concerning the depopulation of the 'Pitigal Korale' by order of the King of Kandy, 1722. One volume.
VOC 11296	Papers drawn up in Colombo and Galle concerning the bad condition of the ship Blijdorp, 1728. One volume.
VOC 11297	Memorandum of Governor Gustaaf Willem van Imhoff concerning the trade on the Fishery Coast, with appendices, 1738. Two volumes.

VOC 11298	Report concerning the visitation of church and school in Galle and Matara by pastors and *scholarchen*, One volume.
VOC 11299	Papers concerning the tender of linen by Albertus Domburg, *Opperhoofd* of the Fishery Coast, 1746. One volume.
VOC 11300	An appeal by former Governor Willem Maurits Bruyninck dating from 1746, concerning miscalculations of *fanams* on the Fishery Coast during the period 1740-4, with appendices, 1755. One volume.
VOC 11301	Letter of the Directors of the Amsterdam Chamber to the Zeeland Chamber concerning reinforcements to be sent to Ceylon, 1761. One piece.
VOC 11302	Papers concerning the revolt of the Sinhalese against the government of the VOC, 1761. One folder.
VOC 11302 I	*Resoluties* of the GG&C concerning the appointment of Lubbert Jan van Eck as Governor of Ceylon, 1761. One quire.
VOC 11303	*Memorie van overgave* by Governor Jan Schreuder to Lubbert Jan van Eck, 1762. One folder. Some pages are missing.
VOC 11304	*Memorie van overgave* by Governor Jan Schreuder to Lubbert Jan van Eck, with marginal *secrete resoluties* of the Governor-General and Council at Batavia concerning this *memorie*, 1762. One volume.
VOC 11305	*Memorie van overgave* by Governor Jan Schreuder to Lubbert Jan van Eck, 1762. One volume.
VOC 11306	Description of the Kingdom of Madurai by G.E. Holst, with table of contents and appendices, 1762. One volume.
VOC 11307	Memorandum of Andreas Jacobus de Lij, chief administrator at Colombo, to the Gentlemen XVII concerning damages to the cargo of ships that arrived from the Dutch Republic, with appendices, 1763. One volume.
VOC 11308	Papers concerning the conflict between the VOC and the Portuguese merchant Joseph Ribeiro, concerning his money loan to the VOC government in Ceylon, 1788-94. One folder.
VOC 13670	Expense claims for the Zeeland Chamber concerning requirements provided to VOC ships during their stay in Ceylon, 1697. One volume.

4.2.3. *Archives of the Delft, Rotterdam, Enkhuizen and Hoorn Chambers and miscellaneous*

No relevant documents found in inventories.

4.3. Archives Transferred from Asia

Hoge Regering te Batavia
High Government at Batavia

See 1.3.1
Access no.: 1.04.17

496-7 Papers (originating from Coromandel) regarding complaints and trials concerning Dirk Bronnekam, son of Pieter van Spall (theft from Paravars in Tuticorin), 1819-27. Two covers.

505-17 Extracts from letters and *resoluties* of the Gentlemen XVII and the GG&C, 1680-1785, one volume concerning ecclesiastical affairs, 1643-1760, one concerning trade, 1680-1747. With repertories, 13 volumes.

518-31 (Secret) correspondence from and to Colombo, 1789-1808, including list of papers sent by R. Prediger during his mission to collect the Company personnel from Ceylon, 1807. Incomplete. With appendices, 11 volumes.

532 *Secrete resoluties* of the Ceylon Council, concerning the Military Department, 1791. One volume.

533-5 Daily record kept by Governor Jan Schreuder during the General Inspection, 1760-61. With appendices, three volumes.

536 Daily record kept by J.G. van Angelbeek, ambassador to the court of Kandy, 1767. One volume.

537 Daily record of a tour of inspection in the areas of Kottiyar, 'Jambligam' and 'Kaltokolampattoe' by the Second of Trincomalee Jaques Fabrice van Senden in 1786, and some letters from Trincomalee, 1785-9. One volume.

538 Provisional regulations and records of the number of Company servants and their fees, 1757-8. One volume.

539 Printed regulations for the Ceylon garrisons, 1767, handwritten copy of a treatise by the King of Prussia on the art of war, 1762 (in German), and a treatise on warfare against the Sinhalese by C. C. Wohlfahrt for Governor I.W. Falck. One volume.

540 Minutes of secret letters from Batavia to Ceylon, 1759. One volume.

541 Memorandum of A. Pavilioen reflecting on the instruction of Rijkloff van Goens concerning the governance of the country of Jaffna and Mannar. One volume.

542 Description of the state of Ceylon, Madurai, Southern Coromandel, Malabar and Kanara with administrative advice by R. van Goens, 1675-80. One volume.

543-4 Memoranda of H.A. van Rheede and R. van Goens the Younger concerning the state of the Company in Ceylon, 1677-80. With appendices, two volumes.

545 Memorandum of P. de Graauwe, Commander of Batticaloa, Panama, Kottiyar and Trincomalee, to his successor J. Bloemert, containing a description of those lands and their population, 1676. One volume.

546 Speculative reflections on the state of the Company in Ceylon, 1681. One volume.

547-9 Instruction of Commissary H. Zwaardecroon to the Political Council at Jaffna, with marginal notes by Governor G. de Heere, 1697. Three copies of the same.

550-6 *Memories van overgave* and other memoranda by Governor Cornelis Jan Simons to Hendrik Becker, 1707; Governor Becker to Isaak Augustijn Rumpf, 1716; Commissary J.C. Pielat to Governor Diederik van Domburg, 1734; Governor Daniel Overbeek to Julius Valentijn Stein van Gollenesse, 1743; Governor Stein van Golenesse to Gerard Johan Vreelandt, 1751; *Commandeur* G. Woutersz of Jaffna to the Political Council of Jaffna, 1732; G. Woutersz. to Iman de Jonge, 1737; *Commandeur* of Jaffna and Council to G.W. van Imhoff, 1738. Seven volumes, some with appendices.

557-61 Memorandum concerning the calicoe trade and assessment of the currency on the coast of Madurai by G.W. van Imhoff, 1738, and remarks of Bengal *Directeur* J.A. Sichterman and *Commandeur* of Malabar J.V. Stein van Golenesse to the same, 1739-40. With appendices, five volumes.

562-5 *Memorie van overgave* by Governor Gustaaf Willem van Imhoff to Willem Maurits Bruyninck, 1740. With appendices and repertories. Four copies of the same, two with commentary by the GG&C.

566 Considerations concerning (the above?) memorandum of G.W. van Imhoff by the Governor and Council, with notes by the GG&C, 1740. One volume.

567-70 *Memories van overgave* by Governor Daniel Overbeek to Julius Valentijn Stein van Golenesse, 1743; Governor Stein van Golenesse to Gerard Johan Vreelandt, 1751. Four volumes (of which three are identical).

571 Secret description of the Ceylon government by J. Schreuder, 1756. One volume.

572 Short history of the main events in Ceylon since the advent of the Dutch in 1602 until 1757, 1660. One volume (see also 4.1.6, VOC 3013, ff. 1508-1649). For a published version, see Bibliography, no. 452.

573-9 *Memories van overgave* by Governor Joan Gideon Loten to Jan Schreuder, 1757; Governor Schreuder to Lubbert Jan van Eck, 1761, 1762. The latter with appendices and repertory, seven volumes.

580 History of the revolts in Company lands instigated by the Kandyans at the end of 1760, by P. Blanckert, *c.* 1762. One volume.

581 Memorandum concerning the events in 1762 in the countries of the Maravars (Ramnad), Madurai and Travancore, by G. Sweepe, 1762. One volume.

582 Reports on the provinces Chilaw and Puttalam by C. Rose, A. Moens and C.C. Wolfarth, 1765-6. One volume.

583-4 Memoranda by the Captain-Engineer C.F. Reimer and the Director of fortifications of Pondicherry concerning the defence and fortification of Colombo, Galle, Trincomalee, Oostenburg, Jaffna and Mannar, with explanations of plans and maps that are not (anymore) in this volume, 1787. One volume.

585 Memorandum on the state of the area of Vanni by Th. Nagel, 1793. One volume.

586 Memorandum of W.J. van der Graaff accompanying the transfer of government to J.G. van Angelbeek, with marginalia by the GG&C, 1794. One volume.

587 *Resoluties* of the Colombo court-martial, 1729. One volume.

588 Advise to the GG&C by W. Blom at the request of ex-members of the Colombo court-martial, 1736. Also papers concerning the *eis* of porcelain for Colombo. One volume.

589 Papers concerning the Mannar pearl fisheries and the Malabar conquests of Nawab Haidar Ali Khan, 1766, and copies of treaties concluded with south Indian rulers by the Company, 1688-1753. One volume.

590 Papers belonging to the mission to Colombo of James Buchanan, envoy of Muhammad Ali Khan Walajah, the Nawab of Arcot, concerning the Tuticorin and Mannar pearl fisheries, 1788. One volume, in French, English, Dutch.

591 Papers belonging to the embassy to Kandy of A. Samlant, including a daily register of the trip, 1789. Also some letters of Governor Van der Graaff to his brother, 1789. One volume.

592 Printed peace treaty between the Company and Rajasinga, Emperor of Kandy, 1766. One piece.

593 Treaty with the Nawab of Arcot (represented by I. Dott), 1786. One piece, in French.

594-7 Papers concerning the second-in-command of Galle and *Dissave* of Matara C. van Angelbeek and the revolt in the *dissavany* of Matara, 1790-1. With appendices, four volumes.

598 Reports on the surrender of Colombo and Galle to the British, 1796-9. One volume.

4.4. Archives of Other Institutions

Staten-Generaal
States General

See 1.4.2
Access no.: 1.01.03

12581, folders 20-1A Contain the armistice between the VOC and Portugal principally concerning Ceylon, November 1644, and the treaty between the States General and the King of Portugal concerning Galle, March 1645. Five pieces, partly in Portuguese and Latin.

Stadhouderlijke Secretarie
Secretariat to the Stadtholder

See 1.4.3
Access no.: 1.01.50

1181-4 Correspondence between the Stadtholder and Governors J.M. With Falck and W.J. de Graaff and factors J.F. Conradi and P.D. van Ranzow, 1775-6, 1780, 1784-6, 1789-93. Four folders.

1223 Excerpt from a letter of the Governor and Council of Ceylon to the Gentlemen XVII concerning the state of affairs of the seminary in Ceylon, 1739, with appendices, mid-eighteenth century. One quire.

1224 Printed letters of the Gentlemen XVII to the States General concerning conflicts with the British on Ceylon, 1763. One folder.

1225 Minutes of the GG&C and a verbatim report of I. Falck concerning the events with regard to Falck's appointment as Governor of Ceylon, 1765. One folder.

1227 Explanations of De La Lustrière concerning proposals to strengthen the Company's establishments in Ceylon, with notes regarding these proposals, 1787. One folder.

1228 Papers concerning the military situation in Ceylon, 1790. One bundle.

1229 Letter of a Major in the artillery in Ceylon, E. Paravicini de Capelli, to his brother, B.E. Paravicini de Capelli, concerning objections against his promotion to the rank of a Colonel and accusations made against him by the GG&C, with appendices, 1791. One folder.

1607 Collection of various documents concerning government and trade in Asia (one volume). Including:

- 3 Papers by chief-factor François de Haase concerning coinage on Ceylon, 1666.
- 10 Instructions to Rijklof van Goens concerning Ceylon, Malabar and Madurai, 1664.
- 13 Instructions to Commander Jan van der Laen departing from Jaffna for the occupation of Nagappattinam, 1658.
- 25 Instructions concerning the sailing from Gombroon to the Bay of Galle ('no. 32'), 1663.
- 26 Order concerning the sailing to Galle ('no. 33'), 1664.
- 27 Order and memorandum concerning the sailing from Coromandel to Batavia via Ceylon ('no. 39'), 1666.

1915-18 Memorandum (with duplicate) by the so-called Military Commission (consisting of Captains J.O. Vaillant and C.A. Ver Huell (see 1.5.32) and Lieutenant-Colonel J.F.L. Graevestein) to the Stadtholder concerning the defence of Ceylon, with appendices; report concerning the Commission's activities on Ceylon (and Coromandel and Melaka), 1790 (among other documents). Four folders (see also 4.5, Ver Huell).

Comité tot de Zaken van de Oost-Indische Handel en Bezittingen
Committee regarding East Indian Trade and Possessions

See	1.4.4
Access no.:	2.01.27.01

Overgekomen brieven en papieren (OBP)
(letters and papers received)

57, ff. 219-49	*Resoluties*, concerning the surrender of Ceylon to the British, 1796 (among other documents).
61, ff. 148?-1629	Report concerning Ceylon (among other regions), *c.* 1793.
62, n.f.	Report concerning Ceylon (among other regions), *c.* 1794.
63, n.f.	Report concerning Ceylon (among other regions), *c.* 1795.
64, n.f.	Report concerning Ceylon (among other regions), *c.* 1796.
65a, n.f.	Report concerning Ceylon (among other regions), *c.* 1794.
126, ff. 75-7	*Resoluties*, concerning the transfer of the vessels of Tuticorin to Galle, 1793.
126, f. 85-235	*Resoluties*, partially recorded at Galle, 1793-5 (among other documents).
126, ff. 275-88	*Resoluties*, 1794.
127, ff. 431-3	Shipping list, 1791-2.
128, ff. 790-1191	Reports concerning Ceylon, 1794.
130, n.f.	*Resoluties*, 1796.
130, n.f.	Documents concerning the surrender of settlements on Ceylon to the British, *c.* 1795-6 (at two places in the volume).

Miscellaneous

237h	Papers concerning trade of the factory in Galle, 1795. Seventeen pieces.
241e	Letter of P. Kuntz concerning the British take-over of Colombo, with appendices (including a *Madras Courier* of 8 March 1796). Four pieces.
241j	Memoranda and a letter by Th. Contamine concerning the fall of Ceylon (and how it could have been avoided), 1799-1800. Four pieces, in French.

Raad der Aziatische Bezittingen en Etablissementen
Council of Asian Possessions and Establishments

See 1.4.5
Access no.: 2.01.27.02

340 Major Vaugine's account concerning the surrender of Colombo to the British, 1798. With appendix, one bundle.

394b Memorandum of Th. Contamine concerning the defence of Ceylon. With letters of the same, 1800, 1803. Three pieces (see also above, *Comité tot de Zaken van de Oost-Indische Handel en Bezittingen, Miscellaneous* 241j).

404j Statement of the shipping space used for private trade to Ceylon, Batavia and the Cape since 1791, 1802. One piece.

Ministerie van Koloniën
Ministry of Colonial Affairs

See 1.4.10
Access no.: 2.10.01

3090 Contains a bundle (of which the first folio is marked Litt. A) of copies of Colombo and Tuticorin correspondence of 1794, including letters to the Nawab of Arcot and Nawab 'Neysam Mulk Hedeimadoe Dowla Mahomet Abdul Khan Bahader Heja Bazgan' (Nizam Ali Khan?). One bundle.

4.5. Personal and Family Papers

De Groot (supplement)

See 1.5.1
Access no.: 1.10.35.02

40, ff. 457-60 Include an extract of a report by S. de Weert on his experiences in Ceylon, between 1602 and 1604.

Geleynssen

See 1.5.2
Access no.: 1.10.30

135 Letters of the King of Kandy to A. Westerwolt. Two pieces, in Portuguese with translations.

163, 188-9, 192-3 (Extracts of) letters of J. Thijssen from Galle and Colombo to Geleynssen and various VOC personnel in the subcontinent, 1640-3. Two folders and three pieces.

260 Contains papers passed between Dutch and Portuguese negotiators at Goa concerning a dispute over Ceylon, 1643.

271 Provisional treaty between the VOC and the Estado da India, 1644. One folder, in Portuguese with Dutch translation from the Latin version (not in this folder, see 4.4, *Staten-Generaal*).

272 Publication of the Dutch-Portuguese armistice, 1644. One piece, in Portuguese.

273 Protest of the GG&C to the Goan Viceroy about the hostile acts of P. de Mascarenhas on Ceylon, 1643. One piece.

274 Instruction to ships sailing for Ceylon from the area of Goa, 1644. One piece.

275 Agreement between the VOC and the Goan Viceroy to partition Ceylon, 1645. One folder, in Portuguese with translation.

Sweers, Van Vliet, Specx, Mannis

See 1.5.3
Access no.: 1.10.78

2, ff. 183 Commission letter to J. van Vliet (nephew of S. Sweers), Colombo, 1670.

2, ff. 186-7, 192, 193-202, 231-3 Letters from Colombo by J. van Vliet and A. Sweers, R. van Goens the Younger and R. van Goens the Elder (all relatives of S. Sweers) to Sweers and private persons in the Republic, 1670-3.

4, ff. 176-8 Instruction for the fleet sailing for Ceylon from Batavia, 1641.

7, ff. 183-99 Description of Ceylon concerning its fertility, richness, condition and humours of the inhabitants, their religion and attitude toward strangers, further which parts of the island the Portuguese have since some years conquered and taken from the natives, with an attestation of the murder of Commander W. J. Coster by Sinhalese in 1640. Probably written by J. Coster who took part in the embassies of 1638-40 to Kandy mentioned in the piece.

Van Goens

See 1.5.4
Access no.: 1.10.32

18 Report on Ceylon and the measures taken by Van Goens, *c.* 1676. Fragment, one quire.

22-3 Deeds of appointment of R. van Goens the Younger as *Dissave* of Colombo, 1665, and as Governor, 1670. One piece and one charter.

Sypesteyn (supplement)

See 1.5.6
Access no.: 1.13.19.02

3 Considerations of R. van Goens about Ceylon and subordinate factories etc., 1658. One volume.

Becker

See 1.5.7
Access no.: 1.10.05.01

1-2 Letters of Becker to Batavia, 1716-17. Five pieces.
3-5 Letters of Governor Becker to Galle and Matara, 1715, and n.d. Three pieces.
6-9 Letters from Colombo to the Gentlemen XVII, 1713-14, 1716. Four volumes.
10-16 Letters from Batavia to the Governor etc. in Colombo, 1708-16. 15 pieces.
17-30 Letters to Becker from VOC servants and church ministers in Colombo, Jaffna, Galle, Tuticorin and one from Maria Moor in Galle, 1709-19. 22 pieces.
31-2 Letters from unnamed persons, one of them located in 'Maoye', 1715 and n.d. Two pieces.
36-7 Extracts from letters of the Gentlemen XVII concerning Becker's career and the VOC in Ceylon, 1711-15. Three pieces.
38 Concept instruction by Becker to VOC-merchant J. Idema in Colombo. One piece.
39-41 (Concept and minute of) the *memorie van overgave* by Governor Hendrik Becker to Isaak Augustijn Rumpf, 1716. Three volumes.
42-4 Papers concerning some irregularities at the seminary of Matara and the consequent legal procedures against teachers. 15 pieces.
45 Concept instruction to the seminaries on Ceylon, 1716. One piece.
46-9 Papers concerning legal *resoluties* of the Muslim 'Wawoepulle' vs the indigenous physician 'Michiel Sonny Ondatje'; the Judiciary vs 'Abouker' and 'Coenje Tamby' (theft); Becker vs I.A. Rumpf; the Judiciary vs interpreter Domingo Foneca, 1710-16. Six pieces.
54 Secret letter from the GG&C to Governor L. Pijl, 1689. One piece.
59 Comparison of expenses and profits of the Ceylon *Gouvernement*, 1716-17. Two pieces.

Boreel

See 1.5.8
Access no.: 1.10.10

124 Papers relating to G.W. von Imhoff, mostly letters to his representatives in the Republic J. Boreel and D. Armenault, including some dating from Von Imhoff's period in Ceylon concerning private trade and remittances, 1738-40. One bundle.

Van Hoorn van Riebeeck

See 1.5.10
Access no.: 1.10.45

44 Includes a report about the court at Kandy by the French mestizo François Mazotin, 1707.

57 Papers concerning the war in Ceylon, 1764-5. One folder.

Van Eck

See 1.5.12
Access no.: 1.10.106

20 Copybook of letters of Van Eck, sent mainly from Colombo, 1758-65. One volume.

33-7 Letters received by Van Eck in Ceylon, 1761-5. Five folders.

38 Letters of L.J. van Eck to Europe, the Cape, Batavia, 1764. One volume.

Van Ghesel

See 1.5.13
Access no.: 1.10.31

152 Note on the prices of non-assorted cowrie shells stored at Enkhuizen and Amsterdam, 1742-55. One piece.

177 Notes of J. van Ghesel on a memorandum of Van Imhoff and the considerations (1740) to the same of J. Sichterman concerning the Fishery Coast (1760). One piece.

194 Extract from the *Haags verbaal* on a letter of Ceylon Governor G. de Heere concerning the pearl fisheries, 1701. One piece.

Baud

See 1.5.14
Access no.: 2.21.007.58

1058 Comments by *Directeur* Johan Albert Sichterman of Bengal on the considerations of Governor Gustaaf Willem van Imhoff of Ceylon concerning the trade and valuation of the money on the Fishery Coast, 1739. One piece.

Hope

See 1.5.17
Access no.: 1.10.46

65 *Memorie van overgave* by Governor Gustaaf Willem van Imhoff to Willem Maurits Bruyninck, 1740. One volume.

69 Volume with appendices, containing a 108-folio historical description of Madurai since the middle of the sixteenth century by G.E. Holtz (or Holst), an inventory by A. Homoet of all recent repairs to the VOC fortifications in Ceylon, glossaries of words used in the cinnamon production and in relation to the land revenue, some notes on cinnamon production (number of people employed, amounts exported since 1700) and detailed tables on the land revenues since 1740 in the districts under VOC control, 1762. One volume.

70 *Memorie van overgave* by Governor Jan Schreuder to Lubbert Jan van Eck, 1762. One volume.

72 *Secrete resoluties* concerning the Governor and Council of Ceylon, 1764-5. One volume.

88 Papers concerning: the expedition against and treaty with the King of Kandy (1765-6); the appointment of Governor L.J. van Eck and the memorandum his predecessor J. Schreuder left him (with notes); the appointment of Governor J.W. Falck; trade ledgers of Ceylon; slaves, rulers, nobles and VOC personnel, the Colombo trade; the legal *resoluties* against P. Ferrand accused of fraud; samples of cinnamon (with notes), 1761-70. One folder.

89 Papers concerning: the cinnamon trade, 1769-70, salaries and other financial affairs of Ceylon, 1675-1767; an instruction to J. van Sanem appointed as apothecary on Ceylon, 1680, summary of the *memorie van overgave* by Governor Gustaaf Willem van Imhoff to Willem Maurits Bruining (1740); A.J. and A. de Lij in Colombo and Galle, 1748-69; military affairs of Ceylon, 1766-80. One folder.

102 Contains a request by C. de Jonge to be reimbursed for the cost of laying out a pepper plantation at Galle.

Van Slingelandt - De Vrij Temminck

See 1.5.20
Access no.: 3.20.52

566 Folder no. 47 contains miscellaneous papers concerning Ceylon, including documents regarding the war against Kandy, 1765, and a list of vessels that had departed, 1750-60. Twelve pieces.

Bleiswijk

See 1.5.21
Access no.: 3.01.25

229 Letter from Abraham Jonas Sluysken in Bombay to his cousin/nephew criticizing on the policies of Governor Iman Willem Falck, 1773. One piece.

230 Letters from Governor Iman Willem Falck to Stadtholder Prince William V and the Gentlemen XVII concerning an impending attack by Nawab Muhammad Ali of Tuticorin (*sic*, i.e. Arcot), 1773. Four pieces.

231 List of the military troops, engineers and artillerists on Ceylon, 1774. One piece.
240 Correspondence between the Zeeland Chamber and Pieter van Bleiswijk concerning the return of Trincomalee by the British, 1784-5. Five pieces and one quire.
393 Letter from Count de Castries, Minister of Colonial Affairs of France, to Gerard Brantsen, accompanying De Castries' transfer to Brantsen of the correspondence between Governor Iman Willem Falck and Macartney of Fort St. George, mostly concerning Trincomalee and/or Kandy, with appendices in French, 1784-5. One piece and one quire.
513 Letters from Mattheus Lestevenon and Gerard Brantsen to the Gentlemen XVII regarding the consequences for the VOC of the peace treaty with Great Britain, mostly concerning Trincomalee, 1783. Two pieces.

Van Braam

See 1.5.22
Access no.: 1.10.11.02

64 Letters received from the GG&C in Batavia and the Governor and Council in Ceylon, 1784-5. One bundle.
65 Letters received from the Governor and Council of Ceylon, 1784-6. One bundle.
98 Journal kept by Van Braam during his stay in Galle, 1785. One volume.
99A-D Correspondence (mainly incoming) of Van Braam with the Governor-General (and Council), Rear-Admiral J.H. van Kinsbergen and the Governor of Ceylon, 1784-6. Four bundles.
101 Letters received from the Governor of Ceylon, 1785-6. One bundle.
104 Notes of Van Braam on the dispute of the Company with the King of Kandy over the coastal fortresses and the beaches. One folder.
105 Relation of the conspiracy against the King of Kandy in 1760, the Kandyan administrative system etc., 1786. One volume.
106 Peace-treaty between the VOC and the King of Kandy, 1766. One piece.
107 Report of J.G. van Angelbeek on his embassy to the King of Kandy, 1767. One volume.
108 Instruction of Ceylon Governor W.J. van de Graaff to the envoys to the Kandyan court, 1785. One piece.
109 Relations of the elephant fights in honour of the Dutch envoys in 1785 and the training of elephants, n.d. One folder.
110 Extract letter of W.J. van de Graaff on the dispute with the King of Kandy over the Mannar and Kalpitiya beaches, 1785. One piece.
111 Letter of the Kandyan envoys to the Ceylon Governor demanding retrocession of the western coastal stretches, 1785. One piece.
115 Memoranda on the state of the Company in Ceylon and suggestions for improvement, by P. Sluysken, 1785. One bundle.

116 Memoranda on the Trincomalee and Oostenburg fortifications by C.F. Reimer, 1785. One folder.

117 Extract of a letter by W.J. de Graaf on the Colombo and Galle fortifications, 1785. One piece.

120 Relation of the trip from Trincomalee to Colombo by military men Hamele and Van Schuler, 1785. One piece.

123 Relation by J.F. van Senden of events that occurred in Trincomalee and Jaffna during the Anglo-Dutch hostilities over the years, 1781-5, 1785. One volume.

199 Daily record kept by Trincomalee Commander J.F. van Senden on his tour of inspection through Kottiyar, Thampalakamam and 'Kattoekolompattoe', 1786. One volume.

200 Report by the same on a hurricane, 1786. One piece.

Van der Hoop

See 1.5.23
Access no.: 1.01.47.29

78 Letters of J. P. van Braam, 1783-8. One folder.

127 Report of A.W. Willinck on his voyage to Ceylon, 1783-5. One piece.

Fagel

See 1.5.25
Access no.: 1.10.29

2408, 2429, 2669, 2747 Contain correspondence of members of the Fagel family with P. Sluysken, VOC merchant at Colombo, 1770-3, 1788.

2536, 2600 Contain correspondence with Governor I.W. Falck, 1780, 1784.

2866 Contains a letter from Governor W.J. van de Graaf, 1792.

Wiselius

See 1.5.26
Access no.: 2.21.176

56 Papers collected by S.I. Wiselius in his capacity as member of the *Comité tot de Zaken van de Oost-Indische Handel en Bezittingen*, with table of contents; document no. 4 consists of a memorandum by Wiselius concerning Ceylon (and the Cape of Good Hope), n.d. (possibly *c.* 1794). One piece, in French.

58 Papers collected by Wiselius concerning the possessions and colonies in the East and West Indies, includes documents regarding coinage on the Fishery Coast (and Surat and Bengal), 1793. One volume.

Radermacher

See 1.5.27
Access no.: 1.10.69

487 Extract from secret letters of Governor H. Becker to the Gentlemen XVII concerning H. Zwaardecroon and H. Pijl, 1713. One piece.
488 Papers concerning the financial condition of Ceylon, 1715, 1763-6. One folder.
489 Extract from a letter of Governor Vuyst and Council concerning a drought and an island that had not been recorded on the map, 1728. One piece.
490 Papers concerning Governor Vuyst, 1729-30. One folder.
491 Descriptions of Ceylon, 1730. Two pieces.
492 Letters of I.V. Stein van Golenesse to S. Radermacher concerning the situation in Ceylon.

Falck

See 1.5.28
Access no.: 2.21.006.48

132 Translation (two copies) of a Sinhalese letter from court-nobles in Kandy to Governor I.W. Falck, 1772. One folder.

Alting

See 1.5.29
Access no.: 1.10.03

17 Report on the origin of the Nayaks of Madurai by A. Bassing, resident at the Nayak Court in Tiruchirappalli, 1677 (ff. 1-32); report on the (non-Company) trade in pepper and areca nut at Tiruchirappalli by A. Bassing, n.d. (ff. 33-9); project of the Tuticorin trade by the Governor and Council at Colombo, 1667 (ff. 40-5); notes on customary law of the Jaffna area concerning succession, purchase, sale, etc., with a copy of the *resoluties* of the Jaffna Council of 1658 (ff. 45v-50). One volume.
50 Extracts from the *olas* of complaint deposed at the *thombo* charging local officials, *zamindars* and some VOC functionaries with various kinds of maltreatment, *c.* 1760. One volume.
51 *Memorie van overgave* by Governor Jan Schreuder to Lubbert Jan van Eck, 1761. One volume. First pages missing.
72 Letters of Jaffna's *Commandeur* B.J. Raket, 1784-95. One volume.
73 Papers of *Commandeurs* Van Senden in Trincomalee and Krayendorff in Galle, 1785-6. One volume.
82-3 Letters and other writings of P. Sluysken, *Commandeur* at Galle, 1788-96. Two volumes.
93 An account of recent events in Ceylon by J.G. van Angelbeek, 1796. One piece.

Brugmans

See 1.5.30
Access no.: 1.10.13

118 Report to the *Directoire* of the French Republic on Ceylon and the Cape of Good Hope by Louis Manneron, former agent of France to those regions, 1797. One piece.

Ver Huell

See 1.5.32
Access no.: 2.21.004.04

21 Report by J.O. Vaillant, C.A. Ver Huell and J.F.L. Graevestein (of the Military Commission) concerning their activities in Ceylon (and Coromandel and Melaka), 1790. One folder (see also 4.4, *Stadhouderlijke Secretarie*).

22 Memorandum by J.O. Vaillant (and the Military Commission?) for Stadtholder William V concerning the defence of Ceylon, with appendices, 1790. One bundle.

23 Letters from Governor W.J. de Graaff to the Military Commission concerning the defence on Ceylon, 1790. One folder.

24 Papers concerning the local and European troops in Ceylon, 1790. One folder.

25 Papers concerning the Swiss regiment of Colonel O.J. de Meuron, 1790. One folder.

26 Papers concerning the artillery at Galle, Colombo, Jaffna and Trincomalee, 1790. One bundle.

27 Papers concerning the maritime affairs of Ceylon, 1790. One folder.

28 Papers concerning the warehouses, factories, shops, VOC servants and slaves in Ceylon, 1790. One bundle.

29 Papers concerning the hospitals at Colombo and other settlements in Ceylon, 1790. One folder.

30 *Resoluties* concerning the artillery in Ceylon, recorded at Colombo, 1787-8. One volume.

31 Letter from Iman W. Talen to Governor-General Reinier de Klerk concerning the defence of the forts in Ceylon, 1779. One piece.

32 Letter from J.G. Fornbauer to Governor W.J. de Graaff concerning the proposals of J.O. Vaillant with regard to the keelhauling of large ships in the Bay of Trincomalee, 1791. One piece.

Nederburgh

See 1.5.33
Access no.: 1.10.59

117-26 Papers concerning the Luxemburg and De Meuron Regiments serving in Ceylon, etc., 1785-94. Two volumes, six pieces and two folders.

151 Extracts from the *resoluties* of the Gentlemen XVII on expenses incurred on Ceylon, etc., to be paid by France, 1786. One piece.

267 Memorandum by A.J. Sluysken on the inflation of paper and copper money, by fault of the VOC policy, and the hardships suffered by the people getting paid copper money in Ceylon, n.d. One piece.

433 Estimate of the income of a Ceylon Governor, taking the income of Versluys as an example, 1729. One piece.

434 Secrete memorandum of Governor Van Eck to M. Rein to be used in case of demise of the former, 1765. One piece.

435 Letters of F.H. Billink to Van der Perre, 1786. Two pieces.

436 Abstracts of letters from Galle and Colombo, 1786-7. One folder.

437 Extract *resoluties* of the Gentlemen XVII concerning plans of redoubts on Ceylon, 1787. One piece.

438 Notes from the *Haags verbaal*, 1770-89 concerning the Ceylon pearl fisheries. One piece.

439 Letter of Governor W.J. van de Graaff to the Commissioners General, then at the Cape, 1792. One folder.

440 Memorandum containing complaints concerning the management of Governor W.J. van de Graaff, 1794. With appendices, one folder.

441 Letter of W.J. van de Graaff concerning the *Dissave* of Vanni, Nagel, 1793. One piece.

442 *Memorie van overgave* by Governor Willem Jacob van de Graaff to Johan Gerard van Angelbeek, 1794. One volume.

443 Letter of army captain Schede at Galle with a copy of his daily record of the war against Kandy, 1764-6 appended, 1794. One folder.

444 Letters of Governor W.J. de Graaff to the Commissioner General, 1795. Two pieces.

445 Letter of C.F. Reimer to Batavia on digging canals in Ceylon, 1795. One piece.

446 Memorandum of C. Francken concerning the British take-over of Ceylon, 1797. One piece.

447 Letter of C.F. Reimer concerning cinnamon plantations in Ceylon, n.d. Two pieces (minute and copy of the same).

448 Memorandum on Ceylon, n.d. One piece.

727 Letter of D.Th. Fretz at Galle, 1799. One piece.

731 Letters of Governor W.J. van de Graaff, 1788-9. Some only in part, one folder.

757 Letters of P. Sluysken concerning Ceylon, 1804, with additions by S.C. Nederburgh. Two pieces.

790 Paper on the value of the *pagoda* at Tuticorin, *c.* 1788. Fragment, one piece.

816 Note on the payment of the Ceylon bills as resolved by the Gentlemen XVII in 1794, n.d. One piece.

818 Letter of S.C. Nederburgh criticizing a letter of Governor-General W.A. Alting to Ceylon, 1795. One piece.

824 Letter of the Gentlemen XVII with orders for the defence of Ceylon and the Cape in case of a war with France, 1793. One piece.

Van de Graaff (and Van Angelbeek)

See 1.5.36
Access no.: 2.21.074

6 Letters of H.J. van de Graaff to various people, including one to Gibson and Co. on Ceylon (no. d), 1825. Eleven pieces, one folder.

58 Peace treaty concluded between the States General and the King of Kandy, signed on behalf of the States General by Johan Gerard van Angelbeek, chief-factor at Colombo, February 1766. One piece.

Moens

See 1.5.37
Access no.: 1.10.100

11 Certificate of baptism of the Dutch congregation at Colombo concerning the children of Adriaan Moens and Sara Maria Ra(c)ket over the period 1764-8, 1783. One piece.

15 Drafts of the tombstones of Susanna Adriana Moens and Sara Maria Racket (both passed away at Colombo, respectively in 1761 and 1768), buried with some of their children in the Wolvendaal Church at Colombo, 1786-8. One folder.

22 Certificate of baptism of the Dutch congregation at Colombo concerning Jacob Matthias Moens in 1768, 1819. One piece.

4.6. Separate Acquisitions and Microfilms

Losse aanwinsten
Separate acquisitions

See 1.6.1
Access no.: 1.11.01.01

51 Contains a treaty with Portugal about Ceylon, 1644. One volume (1853 B II 01).

61 Daily record kept on the voyage to Ceylon under the command of G. Hulft and on the subsequent mission to Kandy, with appendices, 1655-6. One volume (1857 B V).

166 Contains an instruction to the new Governor S. Versluys by the GG&C, 1729. 45 ff. (1876 A XXII 01).

168 Correspondence of Governor S. Versluys with Reverend J.W. Marininus in Galle concerning the affairs of churches and schools in Galle, Matara, etc., 1730-2. One folder (1876 A XXII 03).

170 Description of customary law governing civil affairs such as inheritance, adoption, gifts, confiscation, purchase, sale, mortgage and redemption of agricultural lands in the Jaffna area, 1707. 70 ff. (1876 A XXII 05). Another copy is in the Royal Institute for the Tropics, Amsterdam, no. S 363.3, I-II.

171 Treatise on the condition of the Ceylon Government by R. van Goens the Younger, 1680. One cover (1876 A XXII 06).

186 *Memorie van overgave* by Governor Hendrik Becker to Isaak Augustijn Rumpf, 1716. One piece (1879 A XVI a).

425 Papers of J.G. Loten. The covers marked E-G and K belong to his period as Governor of Ceylon, 1752-7, which include: a letter to the Gentlemen XVII, a volume of incoming letters from the outposts on Ceylon, etc., a volume of rules applying in case of an emergency in Colombo, a protocol for the departure of Van Loten, an advise on how to reach Europe overland by the Basra-Aleppo caravan. One bundle (1888 09w).

456 Sentence passed by the Batavia Council on Ceylon Governor P. Vuist, 1732. One piece (1889 17a).

598 Daily record of Governor I.A. Rumpf's trip to Hanwella, Galle, Matara and Negombo, 1717. With drawings and plans. One volume (1892 32a).

599 Idem of Rumpf's tour of Jaffna, Mannar and Kalutara, 1719-20. With map, drawings and plans (1892 32b).

600 Notes made by I.A. Rumpf on his journey to Negombo, 1720-1. With drawings and plans. One volume (1892 32c).

695 *Resoluties*, daily records and other papers concerning the war in Ceylon, 1656. One volume (1895 LXVIII).

909 Relation of the installation ceremony of G.W. Imhoff as Governor, 1736. Six pieces (1902 XX 04).

1001 Note on the state of the Company (trade) in Ceylon by H.A. van Rheede, 1677. One volume (1905 LII).

1522 Another copy of inv. no. 598. One volume (1926 I 08).

1523 Another copy of inv. no. 599. One volume (1926 I 09).

1878 Papers concerning slave trade and slave ownership in Ceylon, eighteenth century. One folder (1960 VI).

2049 Deeds done by Dutch notaries and the judiciary in Ceylon, 1687, 1750-1808. One bundle (1974 I).

2092 Modern English translations and summaries of the *resoluties* of the Church Council of Colombo, 1735-97. Four bundles, in typescript (1981 07).

Microfilms of external archival material

Bles collection

See 1.6.2
Microfilm no.: 1.1.1342 M

1 Letters and reports concerning the embassy to the King of Kandy, with annex, 1747. One volume.

4.7. Maps and Drawings

Verzameling buitenlandse kaarten, Leupe (VEL)
Foreign map collection, Leupe

See 1.7.1
Access no.: 4.VEL

233 Map of the ledge of 'Insignore' and 'Tutancoli', part of the coast of Madurai, by Captain A.J. Dalhoff, 1775. With explanatory notes.
235 Map of Ceylon and the coast of Madurai, seventeenth century. Two pages.
236 Map of Ceylon and the coast of Madurai, seventeenth century, copperplate print.
237 Map of the eastern part of Ceylon. Map of the Vandeloos Bay. Map of the Batticaloa River, seventeenth century. With notes. Originating from the 'Atlas Amsterdam' or 'Atlas de Graaff'.
238 Map of the big river of Matara named Nilwala Ganga by C.P. Keller, 1743. With explanation.
239 Map of the big river of Matara named Nilwala Ganga, by C.P. Keller, 1743. With explanation.
240 Plan of the shipyard of Colombo, according to Sublieutenant A.A. Buyskens, 1790, by P. Elias.
241 Map of the Bay of Trincomalee, eighteenth century. Copy of the plan of d'Après de Manivillette.
242 Map of Trincomalee, Bay of Trincomalee and its surroundings, eighteenth century. Four pages.
243 Map of Trincomalee and its surroundings, eighteenth century. With indication of the landing point of the British and the French.
244 Map of the Bay of Trincomalee, by J.A. Sommer, eighteenth century. With notes.
245 Map of the mouth of the Bay of Trincomalee, by C.F. Reimer, 1787.
246 Chart of the passage west of the Compagnie Eiland and of a suitable keelhaul location, both in the Bay of Trincomalee, by Sub-lieutenant J.F. Reitz, 1790. With notes.
247 Plan of the port or the Bay of Galle, eighteenth century.
248 Plan of the port of Galle, by Sub-lieutenant A.A. Buiskes, 1790. Two pages.
249 Plan of the port of Galle, by P. Elias, 1790. Copy.
253 Plan of the factory of Punneikayal, after it was damaged by the great flood of November 1720. With notes, 1722. Received from Ceylon.
926 Map of Ceylon, eighteenth century.
927 Map of Ceylon, concerning the possessions of the VOC, in particular the beaches ceded to the VOC after the peace of 1776, by Du Perron, 1789.
928 Description and maps of Ceylon, 1606. The original was written by

the General of Ceylon, on demand of the King of Portugal. Including plans of:

a Colombo.
b 'Planta da Courassa que esta na ponta St. Lourenso'.
c Negombo.
d Fortification of Negombo.
e Chilaw.
f Puttalam.
g 'Mapar Island' (Mannar Island?).
h Jaffna.
i Trincomalee.
k Fortification of Trincomalee.
l 'Arcos Bay'.
m Batticaloa.
n 'Tanavare'.
o Matara.
p 'Beligao'.
q Fortification of Galle.
r 'Alicao'.
s Kalutara.
t Fort of Kalutara.
u Fort of 'Sofragam'.
v Fort of 'Malvana'.
w 'Manieravare'.

929 Plan of Giant's Tank or 'Catte Carré' and surrounding areas, by C.P. Keller. Received from Ceylon, 1742.

930 Detail of Giant's Tank or 'Catte Carré', by C.P. Keller. Received from Ceylon, 1742.

931 Detail of Giant's Tank or 'Catte Carré', by surveyor B. van Lier. Received from Ceylon, 1747.

932 Plan of Giant's Tank, with the surrounding areas, by D. Matthysz., 1790. Copy. Original map made by P. Toenander (Foenander?).

933 Plan of Giant's Tank, by D. Matthysz., 1790. Copy. Original map made by P. Toenander (Foenander?). This tank or pond had the size of 3121 *Morgen*.

934 Plan of the part of Mantota and Nanaddan that was to be irrigated by Giant's Tank, eighteenth century. With legend, 27 pages of different sizes.

935 Plan of the cinnamon gardens and their main roads, located in the district of Kalutara, eighteenth century.

936 Plan of the Salpiti Korale cinnamon gardens near 'Nawelle', with their main roads, by D. Matthysz. With notes.

937 Plan of the Alutkuru Korale cinnamon gardens, with their main roads, by D. Matthysz.

938 Plan of the cinnamon gardens, located in the district of Panadura and along the road behind Kalutara River, by C. van Houten. Copy.

939 Piece of land of the natives of 'Chena' called 'Cattoegalawille',

located in the village 'Degambedde' in the Hewagam Korale, approximately a half an hour walk from the fortress of Hanwella, by Boomgart, Colombo, 1720. With notes about the different kinds of trees. Received from Ceylon, 1721. Consisting of three parts:

1 The trees before being cut down.
2 After the cutting down and the burning of the trees, the land ready to be sown.
3 The growing of several kinds of new trees, especially cinnamon trees.

940 Plan of the elephants corral, situated in the village 'Welancoelaan', under the church 'Ilpecarwe', 1740. With legend.

941 Map of the bay, the city and the fortifications of Colombo, seventeenth century. Received from Ceylon, 1655.

942 Map of the main parts of the besieged city of Colombo, with an indication of its fortifications, by George Schedel, 1656. Very detailed.

943 Little map, showing the castle and the city of Colombo, indicating changes and improvements according to the GG&C, by Adriaen de Leeuw, 1659. Includes a legend, signed up by Ryckloff van Goens and Adriaen van de Meyde and the weapon of Colombo, on which the trademark of the VOC is shown.

944 Plan of the castle, the city of Colombo and its surrounding areas, by surveyor Stevens, 1681. With detailed notes. Originating from the 'Atlas Amsterdam' or 'Atlas de Graaff'.

945 Plan of the castle Colombo in 1692, by engineer J.C. Toorzee, 1697. With legend.

946 Plan of the castle Colombo, by engineer J.C. Toorzee, 1697. With legend.

947 Plan of the castle Colombo with complementary parts, by J.C. Toorzee, 1698. With legend.

948 Plan of the castle Colombo with additional buildings, constructed between October 1697 and January 1698, by J.C. Toorzee, 1698. With legend.

949 Project to find out how to construct a fortification with minimum costs, by J.C. Toorzee, 1698. With legend.

950 Plan of the castle, the city of Colombo and its surrounding areas, seventeenth century. With explanation. Originating from the 'Atlas Amsterdam' or 'Atlas de Graaff'.

951 Plan of the castle of Colombo, showing the gunpowder cellars, by C.P. Boomgart, 1722.

952 Plan of the city and the castle of Colombo, after the changes concerning the fortification, 1733. Received from Ceylon, 1733. With detailed legend.

953 Plan of the area outside of the castle, the suburb of Colombo with its waters, roads, heights, gardens and sowing fields, by Lieutenant and Surveyor Carel David Wentzel, 1762. With register.

954 Map of the fortress, the old city of Colombo with its surrounding

areas, the sea, the inner roadstead, the banks and ledges, the main external buildings, gardens, roads and heights, by Lieutenant and Surveyor P. Toenander (Foenander?), 1785. With legend.

955 Situation map, showing profiles of the roads and heights around the castle of Colombo and outside the old city gate, by Lieutenant and Surveyor P. Toenander (Foenander?), 1785. With legend.

956 Plan of the castle and the external works of Colombo, by P. Brosette, Colombo, 1785. With legend.

957 Profiles of the fortifications around Colombo, with the Kaffersveld and the roads surrounding the old city, belonging to the situation map, by Lieutenant and surveyor P. Toenander (Foenander?), 1785. With legend.

958 Plan of the castle of Colombo, with the suburb, the island, the 'Gaalsche Vlakte', and the 'Wassers Kwartier', 1786. With legend.

959 Plan of the castle of Colombo, by Captain of Artillery, Regiment of Luxembourg De Tiniels, 1786. With French notes.

960 Plan for the reinforcement of the castle of Colombo, 1787 (?). With notes.

961 Plan and project for the reinforcement of the castle of Colombo, by Parivicini di Capelli, Colombo 1787. With legend.

962 Plan and project for the reinforcement of the castle of Colombo, by Parivicini di Capelli, Colombo 1787. With legend.

963 Plan of Colombo, by La Goupilliére, 1787. With explanation. Copy. Signed by De La Lustiére, president of the fortification of Pondicherry.

964 Plan of Colombo and its surrounding areas, with its fortifications, after the project of 1787, by La Groupilliére. With explanation. Copy. Signed by De La Lustiére, president of the fortification of Pondicherry.

965 Draft version of the plan for the project concerning the reinforcements of the buttresses on Colombo, from the bulwark Leiden to Klippenburgh, by C.F. Reimer, 1787 (?).

966 Main plan belonging to the evaluation of the project for reinforcing Colombo, by C.F. Reimer, 1787.

967 Plan of the polygon of Rotterdam (Analaitivu?) and Middelburg (Punkudutivu?), with the projected external works, by C.F. Reimer, 1787. With profile (see also inv. no. 969).

969 Profiles belonging to the plan of the polygon of Rotterdam (Analaitivu?) and Middelburg (Punkudutivu?) (see also inv. no. 967).

970 Plans and profiles of the different bastions, by C.F. Reimer, 1787.

971 Design of a project to reinforce Colombo, without its external works, 1787.

972 Design of the third project to reinforce Colombo and its works, 1787.

973 Design of a third project to reinforce Colombo, with several changes, 1787.

974 Main plan for the improvements on the castle of Colombo, as suggested by H.H. Vaillant, Ver Huell and Grevensteyn, Military-

Commissioner, by D. Matthysz. Copy after a drawing by Major-Engineer Reymer (see inv. no. 977).

975 Main plan for the improvements on the castle of Colombo (see inv. no. 974), by G.E. Schenk. Copy after a drawing by Major-Engineer Reymer.

976 Main plan for the improvements on the castle of Colombo (see inv. no. 974), by P. Elias. Copy after a drawing by Major-Engineer Reymer.

977 Profiles belonging to the main plan for the improvements of Colombo (see inv. no. 974), by D. Matthysz., P. Elias, C.F. Reitz. Copy after the original by Major-Engineer Reymer.

978 Plan of the fortification of Colombo, remeasured by Major-Engineer Reymer, showing the recently developed dam cracks, by G.E. Schenk, 1790 (?). With legend.

979 Plan of the fortification of Colombo, remeasured by Major-Engineer Reymer, showing the recently developed dam cracks, by Sub-lieutenant A.A. Buyskes, 1790. With legend.

980 Situation-plan of the castle, suburb, and surrounding areas of Colombo, concerning a possible siege, by P. Elias. Copy after the plan of Schenk.

981 Situation-plan of the village of Kotte, an hour and a half's walk from Colombo, by P. Elias, 1790 (?). Copy.

982 Plan of the new gunpowder mill, on which the millstones and the radar are shown, by P. Toenander (Foenander?), Colombo, 1792.

983 Plan and profile of the gunpowder mill, built in Hulfsdorp after the example of the mills the British used in Bengal, by P. Toenander (Foenander?), Colombo, 1792.

984 Plans and profiles of some military buildings of different sizes, eighteenth century.

985 Plan of the front and back of the Governor's residence in Colombo, 1687. With explanation. Originating from the 'Atlas Amsterdam' or 'Atlas de Graaff'.

986 Plan of the Governor's residence in Colombo, 1687. With explanation. Originating from the 'Atlas Amsterdam' or 'Atlas de Graaff'.

987 Plan for the restoration of the church of Colombo, by La Goupilliére. Including:

a Front view.
b Widthwise.
c Lengthwise.
d Main plan.

988 Drawing of the fort and the city of Negombo, seventeenth century. Received from Ceylon, 1658.

989 Plan of the city and the fort of Negombo, the island 'Pittuancarre', Walcheren and the lake, seventeenth century. With depiction of a Vyfhoek (fort with five corners) on the island Texel, and legend. Originating from the 'Atlas Amsterdam' or 'Atlas de Graaff'.

990 Little map of the irregular fort of Negombo, after the recent reparations, 1720. With legend.

991 Drawing of the fort at Mannar, as it was improved after the conquest, seventeenth century. With explanation.

992 The fort at Mannar on the southeast corner of Mannar Island, 1672. With explanation. Originating from the 'Atlas Amsterdam' or 'Atlas de Graaff'. Including:

- a The stone bulwark Arippu, located on the seaside opposite the pearl banks of Mannar.
- b The fort at Kalpitiya on the northeast corner of Kalpitiya island.

993 Plan of the little fort Mannar, with indication of the damaged bulwark, eighteenth century. Received from Ceylon, 1740. With explanation.

994 Plan of the fort at Mannar, by La Goupilliére, 1787. With legend. Copied after De La Lustiére.

995 Map of Jaffna and the surrounding areas, including the islands, seventeenth century. Originating from the 'Atlas Amsterdam' or 'Atlas de Graaff'.

996 Map of the landscape 'Carretchie' on the border of Vanni, governed from Jaffna, by J.H. Steyn. Received from Ceylon, 1740. Copy.

997 Drawing of the city and the castle of Jaffna, after the conquest by the VOC, by J. Nessel. Received from Ceylon, 1658.

998 Plan of the castle of Jaffna, 1693. Received from Batavia. With legend.

999 Plan of the fort at Jaffna, 1693. Originating from the 'Atlas Amsterdam' or 'Atlas de Graaff'. Including:

- a Point Pedro on the most northern seaside of Jaffna.
- b Hammenhiel on the southwest of the island Amsterdam (Karaitivu), west of Jaffna.
- c The stone bulwark De Pijl.

1000 Plan of the castle of Jaffna, with projected canals and covered road, eighteenth century. With legend.

1001 Plan of the fort of Jaffna with different scales, by La Goupilliére. Copied after De La Lustiére.

1002 Map of Jaffna, 1787.

1003 Design of a Jaffna gunpowder mill, eighteenth century.

1004 Plan of the projected buildings on the square outside the castle of Jaffna, eighteenth century. With legend.

1005 Plan of the granaries in Jaffna, 1722. Received from Ceylon, 1722. Including:

- a Same plan in a different size.

1006 Outline from the seminary at Nallur, 1691.

1007 Outline from the seminary at Nallur, in the region of Jaffna, 1691. With legend and copy, sent by H.A. van Reede to Commander Blom, in charge of the building activities, signed by H. Zwaardecroon. Indicated as secret, 1690.

1008 Map of the region of Trincomalee, 1691. The scale of this map got lost during the conquest of Trincomalee in 1795.

1009 Map of Trincomalee as it was during the Portuguese period, seventeenth century. With notes and explanation. Originating from the 'Atlas Amsterdam' or 'Atlas de Graaff'. Including:
a Plan of Trincomalee.
b The Bay of Trincomalee.
c Fort Oostenburg on the 'winterbay' of Trincomalee.

1010 Plan of Trincomalee concerning the improvements that are to be made without delay, eighteenth century. With legend.

1011 Plan of Trincomalee, eighteenth century. With profile.

1012-26 Plan and revised plan concerning the reinforcement of the fortifications of Trincomalee, by C.F. Reimer, De La Lustiére, G.E. Schenk, D. Matthysz. and P.J. Tency, between 1785 and 1795.

1027-9 Plan of Fort Oostenburg, eighteenth century.

1030 Plan of Fort Oostenburg and the projected lower works, by W. Löwe, 1779. Received from Ceylon, 1780. With detailed legend.

1031 Plan of Fort Oostenburg, 1786. With profiles.

1032 Plan of Fort Oostenburg, as it was in 1785 and a plan, concerning the necessary changes and reinforcements of the fort, by C.F. Reimer, 1787 (?). With legend.

1033 Plan of the improved *waterpas* in front of Fort Oostenburg, by C.F. Reimer.

1034 Plan and profiles of some batteries and their basements, by C.F. Reimer.

1035 Plans and profiles of the levels and the batteries, by C.F. Reimer.

1036 Plan of Fort Oostenburg, by De La Lustiére, 1787. Copy, by La Goupillière. With legend. For profiles see inv. no. 1037 (see also inv. no. 1038).

1037 Profiles of the plan of Fort Oostenburg (see inv. no. 1036).

1038 Map of the mouth of the inner Bay of Trincomalee, showing Fort Oostenburg and the island Dwars in de Weg, by C.F. Reimer, 1787. Contradicting inv. no. 1036.

1039 Plan of Fort Oostenburg, by C.F. Reimer, 1788 (?).

1040 General plan concerning the reinforcements on the fortifications of Fort Oostenburg, designed by H.H. Vaillant, Ver Huell and Graevesteyn, by G.E. Schenk. Copy after C.F. Reimer.

1041 General plan concerning the reinforcements on the fortifications of Fort Oostenburg, designed by H.H. Vaillant, Ver Huell and Graevesteyn, by D. Matthysz.

1042 Special plans and profiles concerning Fort Oostenburg, by P. Elias.

1043 Plan of a possible way of cutting the Kaalen Berg, by G.E. Schenk, drawn after the original of C.F. Reimer.

1044 Situation-plan of Fort Oostenburg, drawn up from two different plans, by surveyor D.C. Belcke. With legend.

1045 Plan of the island Dwars in de Weg in the Bay of Trincomalee, eighteenth century. With profiles and instruction. Including:
a The island Old Dwars in den Weg.

1046-7 Map of the Nilwala, the great river of Matara, by C.P. Keller. Received from Ceylon, 1742. With explanation.

1048 Plan concerning the improvement of Matara, eighteenth century. With profile and legend.

1049 Plan and profiles of the redoubt Van Eck (Matara), by J.J. Entink. With legend.

1050 Plan of the port of the redoubt Van Eck (Matara), by J.J. Entink.

1051 Map of the land on the western side of the fortress Matara.

1052 Plan of the fortress Batticaloa, seventeenth century. With legend. Originating from the 'Atlas Amsterdam' or 'Atlas de Graaff'. Including:
- a Plan of the fortress Batticaloa.
- b The 'cat' within Batticaloa.
- c Drawing of the fortress Kalutara, as is was in 1681.

1053 Outline of Galle, with project concerning the reinforcement of the city, by Adriaen de Leeuw, 1659. With legend and notes by H.H. Ryckloff van Goens and Adriaen van der Meyden.

1054 Plan of Galle, showing adverse heights and risky rocks, seventeenth century. With sailing instructions. Originating from the 'Atlas Amsterdam' or 'Atlas de Graaff'. Including:
- a View of Galle.
- b The Bay of Galle.

1055 Little map of a part of Galle, between the bulwarks Uytrecht and Vlagge Klip, by J.C. Toorze(e), 1694.

1056 Plan of Galle to the Kraalbaai, eighteenth century. With legend. Including:
- a The projecting corner of Unawatuna (enlarged).

1057 Project concerning the reinforcements of Galle, showing the canal, road and redoubt in front of the city gate, and the enlargement of the Punte der Ster, eighteenth century. With legend and profiles.

1058 Plan of Galle, by A. Johannes, 1784.

1059 Plan of Galle, by De La Lustière, 1787. Copied by La Goupillière. With legend (see inv. no. 1060).

1060 Profiles concerning Plan of Galle, inv. no. 1059.

1061 Plan of the fort of Galle and its fortifications, by De La Lustière, 1787. Copied by La Goupillière (see inv. no. 1062).

1062 Main project plan concerning the renewal of the main front of the fortification of Galle, by C.F. Reimer, 1787. Contradicting the plan of De La Lustiére, inv. no. 1061.

1063 Plan of Galle, by C.F. Reimer, 1780s (?) (see inv. no. 1064 for profiles).

1064 Profiles concerning the Plan of Galle (see inv. no. 1063).

1065 Main plan concerning the strengthening of the land front of Galle, made by H.H. Vaillant, Ver Huell and Gravesteyn, by P. Elias, copied after Reimer (see inv. no. 1068 for profiles).

1066 Main plan concerning the strengthening of the land front of Galle, made by H.H. Vaillant, Ver Huell and Gravesteyn, by D. Matthysz., copied after Reimer.

1067 Plan and coupe of the projected improvements of the level of Galle, by D. Matthysz., copied after Reimer.

1068 Profiles concerning the main plan (see inv. no. 1065), by P. Elias, copied after Reimer.

1069-70 Plan concerning the reinforcements on the outer corner of Unawatuna, taking the possibilities of the defence of the Bay of Galle from the opposite side into consideration, copied after Reimer.

1071 Plan of the fort at Galle and its surroundings, by Reimer and G.E. Schenk, 1790. With legend.

1072 Plan of Kalutara, eighteenth century, with legend.

1073 Plan of the bulwark of Hanwella, seventeenth century, with profiles and legend. Including:
- a Drawing of the bulwark of Hanwella.
- b Plan of the bulwark of 'Maltuane'.
- c Drawing of the bulwark of 'Maltuane'.

1074 Plan of 'Arandere', ten miles east of Negombo, seventeenth century. With legend. Originating from the 'Atlas Amsterdam' or 'Atlas de Graaff'. Including:
- a Drawing of 'Tontotte', 9 to 10 miles east, a little north of Negombo.
- b Plan of Ruwanwella, 9 miles east, a little south of Negombo.
- c Plan of Sitwaka, 8 miles east, a little north of Colombo.

1075 Plan of Hakmana, 4 to 5 miles north-east of Matara. Originating from the 'Atlas Amsterdam' or 'Atlas de Graaff'. Including:
- a Plan of Katuwana, approximately 8 miles northeast of Matara.
- b Plan of the bulwark of 'Chinnecallette Delle', 4 to 5 miles south of the Batticaloa river.
- c Plan of the bulwark of 'Erckelenchene', approximately 1 mile south of the Bay of Trincomalee.

1076 Plan of 'Pittuancarre', 1 to 2 miles northeast of Kalutara. Plan of the *pagger* 'Mapulegam', 6 to 7 miles north-northeast of Galle. Plan of 'Pittugelle', 6 miles east of Galle. Plan of Akuressa, 5 miles north-northwest of Matara, seventeenth century. Originating from the 'Atlas Amsterdam' or 'Atlas de Graaff'.

1085 Outline of the collapsed part of the warehouse in Punneikayal, 1720.

Verzameling buitenlandse kaarten, supplement, Leupe-l'Honoré Naber (VELH)
Foreign map collection, supplement, Leupe-l'Honoré Naber

See 1.7.2
Access no.: 4.VELH

111 Map of the west coast, between 'Manarbel' (Mannar?) and Galle, 1667 (?). To be found in the journal of Michiel Gerritsz. Boos.

112 Map of the west coast, between Mannar and Negombo, eighteenth century.

326 Map of Ceylon, with Adam's Bridge, probably seventeenth century. Coloured drawing.

327 Ceylon (*Insula Ceylon olim Taprobana*), eighteenth century, copperplate print.

328 Collection of various maps, by Johannes van Campen and Martinus Leusecam, 1719. Including:

1 General depiction.
2 The island Leijden.
3 The island Delft.
5 Map of Ceylon, showing the twelve provinces in the south-west.
6 The province 'Pannengammo'.
7 The province 'Waddemoxatie', including three churches.
8 The province 'Patchepalle', including four churches.
9 The province 'Kaxxicatoemoele'.
10 The province 'Caxxetchie'.
11 The island Eluvativu or 't Woest Eijland.
12 Mantota.
13 Map of the four provinces of Jaffna.
14 The province 'Belligammo', including four churches.
15 The island Nainativu or Haarlem.
16 The province 'Carnawelpattoe'.
17 The province 'Heelpattoe' (Wilpattu?).
18 The church 'Pringallie'.
19 The church 'Illipecarne'.
20 The church 'Polverainkattoe'.
21 The church 'Ponnoxyn'.
22 The island Karaitivu or Amsterdam.
23 The landscape 'Parengichitticoelam'.
24 The province 'Moeliawalle'.
25 The village 'Poedoekoedi-iripoe'.
26 The province 'Tinnamarawadie'.
27 The province 'Timmoraatie', including five churches.
28 'Wanathan'.
29 The island Punkudutivu or Middelburg.
30 The island Anailativu, being Rotterdam or 'Donneklara'.
31 Mannar.
32 'Moesellipattoe'.

329 Map-book of Ceylon, 1753. Offered to the department of Colonial Affairs by J.P.S. Farrod de Fellens, 1834.

330 Map of the Pasdum and Walallwiti Korale, 1771, by J.L. Guiara, commissioned by Iman Willem Falck, Governor of Ceylon. Coloured drawing.

331 Map of the hinterland of the west coast of Ceylon between Kalutara and Chilaw to the borders of Kandy. Probably late-eighteenth century. Coloured drawing.

332 General map of the borders and main roads, and the 'Hina' Korale plantations of cinnamon, coffee, pepper, areca and *kijaten*, 1794, by P.L. Herman, commissioned by Willem Jacob van de Graaff, Governor and *Directeur* of Ceylon. Coloured drawing.

333 General map of the borders and main roads, and the Happittigam Korale plantations of cinnamon, coffee, pepper, areca and *kijaten*, 1794, by P.L. Herman, commissioned by Willem Jacob van de Graaff, Governor and *Directeur* of Ceylon. Coloured.

334 General map of the borders and main roads, and the Alutkuru Korale plantations of cinnamon, coffee, pepper, areca and *kijaten*, 1794, by P.L. Herman, commissioned by Willem Jacob van de Graaff, Governor and *Directeur* of Ceylon. Coloured.

335 Plan and map of the situation outside the castle, de suburb and the *gravetten* (closed off areas) of Colombo, including the waters, roads, heights, gardens and sowing fields, eighteenth century, by C.C. Wohlfarth, Coloured.

336-8 Plans and profiles of the castle of Colombo and its fortifications, 1787 (?) (see also inv. no. 339).

339 Profiles of the projected fortifications of the castle of Colombo, 1787 (?) (see also inv. nos 336-338).

340-3 Plans and profiles of the fortifications of Colombo, 1787 (?).

344 Exposition concerning the condition of the fortifications of Negombo, Batticaloa and Trincomalee, including drawings of plans and views of these works, 1720. Apparently belonging to the papers received in 1720 or 1721.

345 Plan of the withdrawal from Ruwanwella to Sitwaka, in 1764, by Major Bischoff. Coloured.

346 Plan of Kandy, near the encampment of Governor Van Eck, 1765 (?). Coloured.

347 Plan of the royal palace of Kandy, 1765 (?).

348 Design for a mast- and sailmaker's proposed to be built in the naval arsenal Trincomalee, 1814. Drawing, by S. Wood.

349 Plan of a store and canvas room proposed to be built in Trincomalee. Drawing, copied by J. Brosst at the Vepery Academy.

350 Plan of the naval arsenal and adjoining bay with soundings at Trincomalee, surveyed by S. Wood, 1814. Coloured.

351 Design for a porter's lodge proposed to be built in the naval arsenal Trincomalee, by S. Wood, 1815.

352 Design for an iron store proposed to be built in the naval arsenal Trincomalee, by S. Wood, 1815.

353 Design for a military guardhouse proposed to be built in the naval yard Trincomalee, 1815.

354 Plan of eight sawpits proposed to be built in the naval arsenal Trincomalee, by S. Wood, 1814. Coloured.

355 Plan of a wharf and jetty with careenages proposed to be built at Trincomalee, 1813. Coloured.

356 Plan of a careenage proposed to be built at Trincomalee, 1813. Coloured.

357 Probably a plan for a hospital proposed to be built at Trincomalee, by W.P. Breslerfecit. Coloured.

Departement van Marine, centraal archief, Leupe (MCAL)
Ministry of Naval Affairs, central archives, Leupe

See 1.7.3
Access no.: 4.MCAL

4251 Chart of the Maldives, by Commander R. Moresby and Lieutenant F.J. Powell, 1814. Copperplate print.

4253 Map of the islands near the Maldives, by John van Keulen, 1813. Copperplate print.

4254 Plan of 'Atil Maldiva' or Kings Island Atoll, and 'Aria' Atoll on the west side of the Maldives. From Van Keulen by Captain Antonio Klink, 1811.

4255 Plan of Kings Island Road, and view of Kingstown, Maldives. Taken on board the sloop Columbo, Peter Sandelyn, 1727.

4259 Map of the island Ceylon and the coast of Madurai. Coloured edition.

4261 Chart of the island Ceylon with the adjacent coast of India, by Captain Heywood and Mast. Wedgeburgh of the Bombay Marine, 1822. Copperplate print.

4262 Chart from Colombo, round by south and east to Point Pedro on Ceylon and from Point Pedro to Tranquebar, by Captain P. Heywood, 1806. Copperplate print.

4263 Plan of Vandeloos Bay on the east coast of Ceylon by P. Heywood, 1802. Copperplate print.

4265 Plan of 'Nyle' or Nilwala Bay on the south coast of Ceylon, 1783. With note.

4266 Plan of Batticaloa Road on Ceylon with a survey of the rock 'B', discovered in 1802 by H.M.S. Intreped, 1805. Copperplate print.

4267 Chart of the harbour of Galle, surveyed by Captain David Inverarity, 1800. Copperplate print.

Ministerie van Koloniën (MIKO)
Ministry of Colonial Affairs

See 1.7.4
Access no.: 4.MIKO

W24 Plan of the castle and the city of Colombo and its surroundings, drawn by B. van Lier, *c.* 1753. Scale 1:14,500 (microfiche no. 108).

W25 Plan of the castle and the city of Colombo. Street map indicating military and non-military buildings. Presented to Joan Gideon Loten by B. van Lier, 1756. Scale 1:2,100 (microfiche 110).

W27 Map of the Bay of Trincomalee, *c.* 1752-7. Scale 1:36,500 (microfiche 108).

W28 Plan of the fort of Trincomalee. Inset: bird's-eye view of the fort. Including legend of the buildings, *c.* 1753. Scale 1:1,400 (microfiche no. 108).

W29 Plan of the fort of Trincomalee, including legend of the buildings, *c.* 1752-7. Scale 1:1,650 (microfiche no. 109).

W30 Plan of the Fort Oostenburg, east of the Bay of Trincomalee, *c.* 1752-7. Scale 1:635 (microfiche no. 109).

W31 Plan of the fort of Trincomalee, the Bay, Fort Oostenburg and the island Dwars in de Weg, *c.* 1752-7. Scale 1:7,500 (microfiche no. 109).

W32 Map of the east coast of Ceylon between fort of Batticaloa and the river 'Palvakeaar', with the distance between Batticaloa and Trincomalee, *c.* 1752-7. Scale 1:195,000 (microfiche no. 109).

W33-4 Map of the Bay and the city of Galle. Two slightly different maps of the same area, *c.* 1752-7 (microfiche no. 109).

W35 Map of the Fishery Coast, between Manapadu and Rameswaram Island, *c.* 1752-7. Scale 1:270,000 (microfiche no. 110).

W42 Map of Ceylon, presented to Governor Gerrard Joan Vreeland of Ceylon. Includes maps of the fortifications of Pooneryn, Arippu, 'Jlipkarwe', Mannar, Batticaloa, Oostenburg, Trincomalee, Katuwana, Matara, Galle, Kalpitiya, Hanwella, Negombo, Kalutara, Colombo, Jaffna, Point Pedro, Hammenhiel, Pijl, Beschutter, Eliphant and De Leeuw on the border of the map. Drawn by B. van Lier, 1753. Scale 1:175,000 (microfiche no. 111).

Ministerie van Oorlog, buitenlandse plans van vestingen (OBPV)
Ministry of War, foreign plans of fortifications

See 1.7.5
Access no.: 4.OBPV

1.110 Drawing of the fortification of Galle, by C.J. v.d. Graaff, 1787. Coloured (see also *Topografische Dienst en rechtsvoorgangers* (*TOPO*), inv. no. 15.111).

1.111 Plan of Fort Oostenburg, originating from the report concerning the present state of the fortification, 1786. Coloured.

1.112 Plan and profiles of the redoubt Van Eck, 200 *toises* from Matara, by J.J. Entink, 1766. Coloured.

1.113 View of the gate of the redoubt Van Eck (Matara), by J.J. Entink, *c.* 1775. Coloured.

1.117 Profile to the project of Colombo, 1787, by Paravicini, Forenbauer and La Goupillière, 1787 (?) (see also *Topografische Dienst en rechtsvoorgangers* (*TOPO*), inv. no. 15.109).

4.413 Plan of Trincomalee concerning the improvements that are to be made without delay on the coast of Ceylon. One map by Linazow (?), 1786; the other maps by C.J. v.d. Graaff, 1787. Coloured.

Topografische Dienst en rechtsvoorgangers (TOPO)
Topographic Service and legal predecessors

See 1.7.6
Access no.: 4.TOPO

15.109 Profile that is part of a project to improve the fortifications of Colombo, drafts by Paravicini, J.G. Fornbauer and De la Goupillière, 1787. Scale *c.* 1:150 (belongs to a set of ten sheets, see *Ministerie van Oorlog, buitenlandse plans van vestingen* (*OBPV*), inv. no. 1.117).

15.110 Plan of the fort at Trincomalee, indicating fortifications built by the French, by Von Lutzow, 1786. Scale *c.* 1:1000.

15.111 Harbour or Bay of Galle, 1786 (belongs to a set of six sheets, see *Ministerie van Oorlog, buitenlandse plans van vestingen* (*OBPV*), inv. no. 1.110).

Collectie Bergsma (BMF)
Bergsma collection

See 1.7.7
Access no.: 4.BMF

435 Compass map of Ceylon, by Gerard van Keulen, 1753. Coloured. With depth indication.

436 New map of Ceylon, published by Isaak Tirion, mid-eighteenth century.

437 Map of Ceylon, by Tobiae Conradi Lotteri, third-quarter of the eighteenth century. Coloured. With description.

Aanwinsten
Acquisitions

See 1.7.9
Access no.: 4.AANW

1213 Map of the district situated between the 'Kaymettse' River and the province Puttalam including the district of Chilaw, by C.C. Wohlfarth, 1766. Originating from *Hoge Regering Batavia*, inv. no. 582.

1148 Map of Giant's Tank and surroundings, drawn by P. Foenander (Toenander?) 1790. Copied by D. Matthysz (see also *Verzameling buitenlandse kaarten, Leupe* (*VEL*), inv. nos 932-3).

1615 Floor plan of a drying house (on Ceylon?), n.d. Originating from *OBP*.

1616 Floor plan of wooden sheds (on Ceylon?), 1788. Originating from *OBP*.

1620 Sketch of a fortification on the seaside, without geographical indication, possibly Ceylon, n.d.

1598 Drawing of a casemate with basement, possibly in Ceylon, n.d.

1597 Floor plan of a new forge, possibly in Ceylon, eighteenth century.

Overgekomen brieven en papieren (OBP)
Letters and papers received

See 1.1.7
Access no.: 1.04.02

VOC 1470, ff. 798-9	Dried specimen, water colour and description of the medicinal Ceylonese herb 'Acmella' by the chief chirurgeon at Colombo, *c.* 1691.
VOC 1544, ff. 1021-?	Plans of a projected seminary and a projected leper house in Ceylon and of the council hall at Galle, 1694.
VOC 1615 II, ff. 471-514	Includes land chart of the coast of Madurai and 'Inchiado' (Coromandel Coast between the Pamban Channel and Point Calimere) and several maps depicting the fortress, inner roadstead and carpenter's yard at Tuticorin and surroundings, by engineer Toorzee. Coloured. Originating from the report by Governor Gerrit de Heere on his trip to Tuticorin, 1699.
VOC 1921, ff. 767-9	Includes drawing of the fortifications in Ceylon, *c.* 1719. Coloured.

Ingekomen stukken van de kantoren in Indië bij de Heren XVII en de Kamer Zeeland (IKI)
Papers received from the establishments in the Indies by the Gentlemen XVII and the Zeeland Chamber

See 1.2.1
Access no.: 1.04.02

VOC 9714	Includes maps and plans of the seminary at Nallur, 1690 (part of papers concerning the activities of Commissioner General Hendrik Adriaan van Reede tot Drakenstein).
VOC 10090	Maps and drawings relating to the tour of inspection around Ceylon by Governor Isaac Augustijn Rumpf, concerning forts and warehouses (e.g. for cinnamon) at Colombo, Hanwella, Kalutara, Galle, Katuwana, Matara and Negombo, as well as elephant hunting, 1717.
VOC 10101	Map belonging to a report of Ferdinand Anton van Ranzow, *Dissave* of Jaffna, concerning the borders between Kandy and VOC territory in the Mantota region, showing the area around Arippu and Kondaichi, 1746.

Hoge Regering te Batavia
High Government at Batavia

See 1.3.1
Access no.: 1.04.17

582 Includes a map of Chilaw, 1765-6.

Stadhouderlijke Secretarie
Secretariat to the Stadtholder

See 1.4.3
Access no.: 1.01.50

1226 Map of the fort at Trincomalee, *c.* 1770.

Panthaleon van Eck

See 1.5.15
Access no.: 1.10.65.01

60 Contains drawings of the tombstone of L.J. van Eck and the 'board of mourning' hung in the Dutch church of Colombo, 1765.

Braam

See 1.5.22
Access no.: 4.BRF

230 View of the coastal profile of Ceylon from the clip Den Olyphant, eighteenth century (?).
231 Map of the stretch of beach on the island in the Bay of Trincomalee that ships used to be pulled into, with an instruction for the use of the pulling installations, eighteenth century (?).
232 Plan of the Bay of Galle, eighteenth century (?).

Moens

See 1.5.37
Access no.: 1.10.100

15 Drafts of the tombstones of Susanna Adriana Moens and Sara Maria Raket (both passed away at Colombo, respectively in 1761 and 1768), buried with some of their children in the Wolvendaal Church at Colombo, 1786-8. One folder.

Losse aanwinsten
Separate acquisitions

See 1.6.1
Access no.: 1.11.01.01

112 Contains a map of the west coast of Ceylon, 1667 (1886 A IV KA 58).
215 Detailed maps of northern (Jaffna, Mannar area) and southwestern (Negombo, Colombo, Galle, Matara area) Ceylon, made between 1753 and 1780. 38 maps in two volumes (1880 A II). For more details, see Paranavitana, *An Inventory of Sri Lanka Maps*, pp. 5-7 (see Bibliography, no. 632).

425	Contains, in cover F, a plan of the fortress of Colombo in which the houses and names of the inhabitants are indicated for the period 1756-7.
598	Contains plans and drawings of VOC forts and buildings in Hanwella, Galle, Matara, Colombo and Negombo and a drawing of elephants in an enclosure, 1717.
599	Contains a large general map of the Jaffna peninsula and plans and drawings of VOC objects in Jaffna, Mannar and Kalutara and a drawing of the coats of arms of the VOC establishments in Ceylon, 1719-20 (see also inv. no. 598).
600	Contains plans and drawings of VOC objects in the Negombo area, 1720-1.
1522-3	Contain some other copies of the plans and drawings that are in inv. nos 598 and 599.

5. COROMANDEL

INTRODUCTION

The VOC administration in Coromandel stretched along India's east coast from Nagappattinam in the south to Bimlipatam in the north. It also included a few factories in the interior such as at Nagulvancha and Golkonda (*c.* 1660-90). The Coromandel headquarters at Pulicat also supervised early Dutch activities in Arakan as well as the factories in Bengal until 1655, and Pegu until their closure around 1680. In 1690, the Governor and Council shifted from Pulicat to Nagappattinam. Pulicat was henceforward administered by an *Opperhoofd*, as were often the other main stations at Sadras, Masulipatam, Palakollu, Bimlipatam and Jagannathapuram. Masulipatam served as the chief establishment for the northern Coromandel Coast. After Nagappattinam was transferred to the British in 1784, the VOC headquarters shifted back to Pulicat.

Only two years after one of the *Voorcompagnieën* (see 1.4.1) had briefly engaged itself in the region in 1603, the first VOC factory was established at Masulipatam legalized by a *farman* from the Sultan of Golkonda, to be followed by another one at nearby Petapoli in 1606. In the south, the Nayak of Gingee allowed the Dutch to settle at Teganapatam and Thiruppapuliyar in 1608. Two years later, the King of Vijayanagara, now seated at Chandragiri, granted the VOC a factory at Pulicat. From this time onward, the Dutch established various other factories on the Coast such as at Golkonda, Golepallem, Gondewarom, Narasapur, Palakollu, Draksharama, Porto Novo, St. Thome, Sadras, Alambaram, Nagulvancha, Jagannathapuram, Bimlipatam, Tirumullaivaisal, Cuddalore, Karikal and Nagore. Nagappattinam was captured from the Portuguese in 1658 and Pondicherry from the French in 1693 (the latter to be returned in 1699). From the late seventeenth century onward, the VOC more and more focused its activities on the south. In the eighteenth century, the Dutch factories became increasingly squeezed by the ongoing political conflicts in the interior, involving the states of

Map 5: The VOC in Coromandel

Hyderabad, Arcot and the Marathas, and also by the increasing pressure from the British and French. Most conspicuous were the loss of Masulipatam to the French in 1750 and Nagappattinam to the British in 1781. As elsewhere in India, the remaining Dutch factories were seized by the British during the Napoleonic wars. These were partly restored in 1818 (with the headquarters at Sadras also administering the Fishery Coast), only to be finally handed over in 1825.

During the seventeenth century, the VOC at Coromandel primarily maintained relations with the sultanate of Golkonda and with the various successor states of Vijayanagara in Chandragiri/Vellore, Gingee and Thanjavur. As the political situation changed after about 1650, the Dutch came in regular contact with the southeasterly expanding polities of Bijapur, the Mughals and the Marathas. Their expansion gave birth to the increasingly autonomous states of Hyderabad, Arcot and Thanjavur (now under Maratha rule).

Documents concerning the Andaman and Nicobar Islands (only a few) are included in this chapter. Information regarding Coromandel may also be found in documents mentioned under Ceylon, especially during the earlier period. Documents concerning the Fishery Coast (see Ceylon) between 1818 and 1825 are also to be found under Coromandel.

5.1. *Overgekomen Brieven en Papieren (OBP)*
Letters and Papers Received

See	1.1.7
Access no.:	1.04.02
Inv. nos:	VOC 1053-3987

Letters and papers concerning Coromandel are mostly to be found under headings such as 'Chormandel', 'Cust van Cormandela' (Coast of Coromandel), 'Nagapatnam', 'Masulipatnam', 'Sadraspatnam', 'Sadragapatnam', 'Tegenepatnam', etc. These headings occur in the volumes containing documents sent directly from South Asia to the Gentlemen XVII and the Amsterdam Chamber, as well as the volumes that consist of copies of documents sent from South Asia to Batavia in the *Batavia's ingekomen brievenboek* (Batavia letterbook of incoming documents). In a few cases, letters and papers relating to Coromandel may also be found under the heading 'Batavia'.

5.1.1. *Memories van overgave* (final reports)

VOC 1242, ff. 791-818	Governor Laurens Pith to Cornelis Speelman, *c.* 1663.
VOC 1243-1244, ff. 2174-?	Governor Laurens Pith to Cornelis Speelman, July 1663.
VOC 1252-1253, n.f.	Governor Cornelis Speelman to Anthonij Paviljoen, October 1665.
VOC 1254, ff. 650-712	Governor Cornelis Speelman to Anthonij Paviljoen, October 1665.

VOC 1348, ff. 1189-209	*Opperhoofd* Wilhelm Hartsuijcker at Masulipatam to Hendrick van Outhoorn, February 1679.
VOC 1638, ff. 120-36	*Opperhoofd* Bruijning Wildelant at Masulipatam to Theodorus de Hase, March 1700.
VOC 1664, ff. 411-49	By *Opperhoofd* Theodorus de Haese at Masulipatam, May 1702.
VOC 1712, ff. 457-86	Governor Dirck Comans to Joannes van Steelant, September 1705.
VOC 1761, ff. 484-520	*Opperhoofd* Hendrik van Outshoorn van Sonnevelt at Masulipatam to Hendrik Grousius, August 1708.
VOC 1796, ff. 1-27	Governor Johannes van Steelant to Daniel Bernard (Guilliams), September 1710.
VOC 1811, ff. 27-43	*Opperhoofd* Hendrick Grousius at Masulipatam to Gerrit Westrenen, September 1711.
VOC 1884, ff. 115-60	Governor Daniel Bernard (Guilliams) to Adriaen de Visser, *c.* 1716.
VOC 2166, ff. 103-246	Governor Dirk van Cloon to Adriaen Pla, *c.* 1730.
VOC 2166, ff. 247-56	By *Opperhoofd* Adriaen Pla at Masulipatam, January 1730.
VOC 2317, ff. 291-341	Governor Adriaen Pla to Elias Guillot, *c.* 1734.
VOC 2442-3, ff. 2667-821	Governor Elias Guillot to Jacob Mossel, *c.* 1638.
VOC 2631, ff. 405-525	Governor Jacob Mossel to Galenus Mersen, *c.* 1744.
VOC 2720, ff. 745-890	Governor Galenus Mersen to Mr. Libregt Horeman, *c.* 1748.
VOC 3125, ff. 288-98	Governor Lubbert Jan van Eck to Christiaan van Teylingen, October 1761.
VOC 3312, ff. 2002-99	Governor Pieter Haksteen to Reynier van Vlissingen, September 1771.

5.1.2. *Resoluties* (proceedings)

VOC 1055, n.f.	1610.
VOC 1061, f. 173	Masulipatam, 1616.
VOC 1061, ff. 193-218?	1615 (?)-1616.
VOC 1062, ff. 52-66	Petapoli/Nizampatnam, 1615-16.
VOC 1063, ff. 405-6	Masulipatam, 1616.
VOC 1065, ff. 83-9	1616-17.
VOC 1085, ff. 222-7	1624.
VOC 1097, ff. 468-70	1629.
VOC 1098, f. 495	Masulipatam, 1629.
VOC 1100, ff. 63-4	1629.
VOC 1109, ff. 288-96	1632.
VOC 1109, ff. 324-5	1633.

VOC 1127, ff. 194, 203	1637-8.
VOC 1132, ff. 197-235	1638-9.
VOC 1138, ff. 768-9	1642.
VOC 1152, ff. 173-81	Concerning Chinanna (broker), 1644.
VOC 1161, ff. 841-86	1645-6.
VOC 1177, ff. 306-12	1650.
VOC 1208, ff. 345-6	1654.
VOC 1210, ff. 971-4	1656.
VOC 1234, ff. 177-8	Masulipatam, 1661.
VOC 1242, ff. 760-2	Concerning a request of the King of Golkonda, 1663.
VOC 1242, ff. 784-6	Concerning gifts to commander-in-chief Neknam Khan, 1663.
VOC 1242, ff. 830-2	1663.
VOC 1295, ff. 121-4	Concerning the siege of St. Thome, 1673.
VOC 1295, ff. 235-42	1673.
VOC 1295, ff. 692-7	Concerning St. Thome, 1673.
VOC 1295, ff. 700-2	Concerning St. Thome, 1673.
VOC 1298, ff. 274-84	Concerning St. Thome and Thanjavur, 1674.
VOC 1304, ff. 290-300	1674.
VOC 1313, ff. 187-8	Concerning Golkonda and Pulicat, 1675.
VOC 1315, ff. 512-26	Concerning St. Thome, 1676.
VOC 1351, ff. 2304-6	1679.
VOC 1369, ff. 1441-4	1681.
VOC 1369, f. 1469	1681.
VOC 1378, ff. 1633v-6	1682.
VOC 1382, ff. 641-50	Concerning the fortifications of Nagappattinam, 1665.
VOC 1384, f. 392c	1684.
VOC 1398, ff. 362-70	1684.
VOC 1411, ff. 435-6, 456	Concerning cargo, 1685.
VOC 1411, ff. 486-7	Concerning merchant Chirum Chodanda, *c.* 1685.
VOC 1411, ff. 549-66	Concerning Golkonda, 1685-6.
VOC 1414, ff. 402v-12	Concerning a new fortress at Nagappattinam, 1685.
VOC 1423, ff. 298-309	1686.
VOC 1450, ff. 932-44	Concerning gifts to the Mughal at Golkonda, 1687.
VOC 1450, ff. 1241-3	1688.
VOC 1472, ff. 1014-52v	1689.
VOC 1473, ff. 693-714	1690.
VOC 1473, ff. 750-4v	Teganapatam, 1690.
VOC 1508, ff. 364-531v	1691-2.
VOC 1511, ff. 1302-3v	Masulipatam, 1692.
VOC 1526, ff. 633-769v	1693.
VOC 1546, ff. 455-503v	1693-4.
VOC 1546, ff. 962-74v	Partly concerning Pondicherry, 1693.
VOC 1586, ff. 186-8	Masulipatam, 1696.
VOC 1617, ff. 106-354	1699.

VOC 1617, ff. 493-9	Masulipatam, 1699.
VOC 1618, ff. 1222-47	*c.* 1699 (among other documents).
VOC 1657, ff. 105-14	Partly concerning the Danes, 1699.
VOC 1664, ff. 495-8	1699.
VOC 1678, ff. 468-78	Pulicat, 1703.
VOC 1684, ff. 2368-74	Masulipatam, 1704 (among other documents).
VOC 1688, ff. 1834-6	1705.
VOC 1730, ff. 438-47	1706.
VOC 1819, ff. 215-302	1712.
VOC 1927, ff. 34-46	1719.
VOC 1954, ff. 177-205	1721.
VOC 1962, ff. 185-215	1721 (among other documents).
VOC 2014, ff. 74-6	1724.
VOC 2031, ff. 189-93	1725.
VOC 2031, ff. 245-59	1725.
VOC 2041, f. 3135	Masulipatam, 1726.
VOC 2064, ff. 4605-722	1727.
VOC 2076, ff. 92-292	1726-7.
VOC 2076, ff. 954-8	1726-7.
VOC 2076, ff. 1014-43	1727.
VOC 2076, ff. 658-702	Pulicat, concerning the coinage of rupees, 1727.
VOC 2084, ff. 1252-1438	1727-8.
VOC 2087, ff. 2763-863	1728.
VOC 2090, ff. 4287-338	1728.
VOC 2102, ff. 53-78	Pulicat, 1727-8.
VOC 2115, ff. 3902-4164	1728-9.
VOC 2135, ff. 430-86	1729 (among other documents).
VOC 2147, ff. 4782-844	1729-30.
VOC 2151, ff. 7208-306	1730.
VOC 2197, ff. 62-230	1730.
VOC 2197, ff. 231-43	Masulipatam, 1730.
VOC 2197, ff. 798-980	1730-1.
VOC 2197, ff. 981-1024	Masulipatam, 1730-1.
VOC 2197, ff. 1705-14	Masulipatam, *c.* 1731.
VOC 2198, ff. 73-218	1731.
VOC 2198, ff. 26-88	1731.
VOC 2243, ff. 67-151	1731.
VOC 2243, ff. 152-6	Masulipatam, 1731.
VOC 2243, ff. 646-8	1731.
VOC 2243, ff. 781-966	1731-2.
VOC 2243, ff. 967-1002	Masulipatam, 1731.
VOC 2243, ff. 1987-96	Nagappattinam and Pulicat, *c.* 1732.
VOC 2244, ff. 109-455	1732.
VOC 2244, ff. 456-88	Masulipatam, 1732.
VOC 2244, ff. 1333-1555	1732.
VOC 2244, ff. 43-65	Masulipatam, 1732.
VOC 2244, ff. 336-99	1732.

VOC 2244, ff. 400-12	Masulipatam, 1732.
VOC 2289, ff. 131-369	1732-3.
VOC 2289, ff. 395-440	Masulipatam, 1732-3.
VOC 2289, ff. 959-60	1733.
VOC 2289, ff. 45-75	Masulipatam, 1733.
VOC 2289, ff. 759-802	1733.
VOC 2289, ff. 803-30	Masulipatam, 1733.
VOC 2317, ff. 342-534	1733-4.
VOC 2317, ff. 535-618	Masulipatam, 1733-4.
VOC 2317, ff. 1361-?	1734.
VOC 2318, ff. 1577-88	Masulipatam, 1734.
VOC 2318, ff. 2709-870	1734.
VOC 2318, ff. 2871-916	Masulipatam, 1734.
VOC 2318, ff. 3356-60	Pulicat, 1734.
VOC 2349, ff. 79-152	*c.* 1735.
VOC 2349, ff. 153-65	Masulipatam, *c.* 1735.
VOC 2350, ff. 179-868	1734-5.
VOC 2350, ff. 869-1152	Masulipatam, 1734-5.
VOC 2351, ff. 3263-94	1735.
VOC 2351, ff. 3559-96	Masulipatam, 1735.
VOC 2351, ff. 3939-4022	1735.
VOC 2351, ff. 4023-52	Masulipatam, 1735.
VOC 2386, ff. 61-260	1735-6.
VOC 2386, ff. 261-308	Masulipatam, 1735-6.
VOC 2386, ff. 1037-82	1736.
VOC 2386, ff. 1083-6	Masulipatam, 1736.
VOC 2387, ff. 148-440	1736.
VOC 2387, ff. 441-509	Masulipatam, 1736.
VOC 2387, ff. 1587-1600	Masulipatam, 1736.
VOC 2412, ff. 56-128	1736.
VOC 2412, ff. 129-44	Masulipatam, *c.* 1737.
VOC 2412, ff. 103-295	1736-7.
VOC 2412, ff. 296-340	Masulipatam, 1736-7.
VOC 2412, ff. 1547-1654	1737.
VOC 2412, ff. 1655-72	Masulipatam, 1737.
VOC 2427, ff. 425-34	1738.
VOC 2427, ff. 441-2	1738.
VOC 2427, ff. 449-55	1738.
VOC 2427, ff. 465-6	1738.
VOC 2427, ff. 471-6	1738.
VOC 2427, ff. 490-500	1738.
VOC 2427, ff. 517-8	1738.
VOC 2427, ff. 528-9	1738.
VOC 2442, ff. 57-77	1737.
VOC 2442, ff. 78-100	Masulipatam, 1737.
VOC 2442, ff. 477-515	1737.
VOC 2442, ff. 639-910	1737-8.

VOC 2442, ff. 911-58	Masulipatam, 1737-8.
VOC 2442-3, ff. 2073-228	1738.
VOC 2442-3, ff. 2229-38	Masulipatam, 1738.
VOC 2442-3, ff. 2941-57	Masulipatam, 1738.
VOC 2442-3, ff. 33-44	1738.
VOC 2442-3, ff. 45-59	Masulipatam, 1738.
VOC 2442-3, ff. 383-447	1738.
VOC 2442-3, ff. 448-59	Masulipatam, 1738.
VOC 2455, ff. 449-59	1739.
VOC 2455, ff. 471-4	1739.
VOC 2470, ff. 161-442	1738-9.
VOC 2470, ff. 443-83	Masulipatam, 1738-9.
VOC 2470, ff. 1876-?	1739.
VOC 2471, ff. 107-58	1739.
VOC 2471, ff. 449-52	1739.
VOC 2471, ff. 507-25	Masulipatam, 1739.
VOC 2471, f. 839	Bimlipatam, 1739.
VOC 2471, ff. 848-9	Masulipatam or Bimlipatam, *c.* 1739.
VOC 2471, ff. 893-940	1739.
VOC 2471, ff. 1335-48	*c.* 1739.
VOC 2505, ff. 125-618	1739-1740.
VOC 2505, ff. 619-82	Masulipatam, 1739-40.
VOC 2505, ff. 1827-63	1739-40.
VOC 2505, ff. 1951-4	1740.
VOC 2506, ff. 1-86	1740.
VOC 2506, ff. 87-96	Masulipatam, 1740.
VOC 2506, ff. 515-16	1740.
VOC 2506, ff. 533-40	Masulipatam, 1740 (among other documents).
VOC 2538, ff. 93-280	1740-1.
VOC 2538, ff. 281-92	Masulipatam, 1740-1.
VOC 2538, ff. 819-72	1740.
VOC 2538, ff. 873-86	Masulipatam, 1740.
VOC 2538, ff. 1465-1724	1741.
VOC 2538, ff. 1725-70	Masulipatam, 1741.
VOC 2539, ff. 2467-75	Concerning Dutch fortifications at Nagappattinam, 1741.
VOC 2539, ff. 2611-76	1741.
VOC 2539, ff. 2677-736	Masulipatam, 1741.
VOC 2539, ff. 3405-12	Masulipatam, 1741 (among other documents).
VOC 2539, ff. 3471-566	1741.
VOC 2539, ff. 3567-75	Masulipatam, 1741.
VOC 2573, ff. 39-219	1741-2

VOC 2573, ff. 220-36	Masulipatam, 1741.
VOC 2574, ff. 101-618	1742 (among other documents).
VOC 2574, ff. 619-22	Masulipatam, 1742.
VOC 2608, ff. 28-56	*c.* 1742.
VOC 2608, ff. 57-69	Masulipatam, 1742.
VOC 2608, ff. 129-361	1742-3.
VOC 2608, ff. 362-76	Masulipatam, 1742-3.
VOC 2608, ff. 51-332	1743.
VOC 2608, ff. 333-93	Masulipatam, 1743.
VOC 2631, ff. 23-85	1743.
VOC 2631, ff. 161-404	1743-4.
VOC 2631, ff. 673-?	1744.
VOC 2652, ff. 33-106	1744.
VOC 2652, ff. 107-16	Masulipatam, 1744.
VOC 2652, ff. 136-45	Masulipatam, 1744.
VOC 2652, ff. 155-8	Masulipatam, 1745.
VOC 2652, ff. 278-656	1744-5.
VOC 2652, ff. 657-733	Masulipatam, 1745.
VOC 2652, ff. 837-980	1745.
VOC 2652, ff. 981-96	Masulipatam, 1745.
VOC 2652, ff. 1010-?	Masulipatam, 1745.
VOC 2677, ff. 39-124	Masulipatam, *c.* 1746.
VOC 2677, ff. 150-5	Masulipatam (?), 1746.
VOC 2677, ff. 1-425	1746.
VOC 2702, ff. 34-114	1746.
VOC 2702, ff. 323-506	1746-7.
VOC 2702, ff. 633-910	1747.
VOC 2720, ff. 49-122	1747.
VOC 2720, ff. 217-368	1747-8.
VOC 2720, ff. 493-744	1748.
VOC 2744, ff. 35-96	1748.
VOC 2744, ff. 197-442	1748-9.
VOC 2744, ff. 559-642	1749.
VOC 2750, ff. 190-218	1749.
VOC 2750, ff. 223-9	1749.
VOC 2750, ff. 249-314	1749.
VOC 2764, ff. 39-158	1749.
VOC 2764, ff. 241-576	1749-50.
VOC 2764, ff. 37-187	1750.
VOC 2767, ff. 173-8	1749.
VOC 2784, ff. 119-354	1750-1.
VOC 2784, ff. 391-458	1751.
VOC 2784, ff. 653-928	1751.
VOC 2784, ff. 69-?	Masulipatam, 1751.
VOC 2801, ff. 69-266	1751-2.
VOC 2801, ff. 367-?	1752.
VOC 2822, ff. 45-116	1752.

VOC 2822, ff. 137-72	1752.
VOC 2822, ff. 259-406	1752-3.
VOC 2822, ff. 535-796	1753.
VOC 2841, ff. 93-172	1753.
VOC 2841, ff. 313-696	1753-4.
VOC 2841, ff. 809-906	1754.
VOC 2852, ff. 1-701	1754-5.
VOC 2863, ff. 59-120	1754.
VOC 2863, n.f.	1755.
VOC 2876, ff. 183-644	1755-6.
VOC 2898, n.f.	1756-7.
VOC 2922, n.f.	1757-8.
VOC 2952, ff. 1-403	1758-9.
VOC 2980, ff. 177-390	1759-60.
VOC 3010, ff. 213-474	1760-1.
VOC 3044, ff. 200-487	1761-2.
VOC 3077, ff. 81-3	1763.
VOC 3078, n.f.	1762-3.
VOC 3107, ff. 57-64	1764.
VOC 3108, n.f.	1763-4.
VOC 3134, ff. 37-146	1765.
VOC 3136, n.f.	1764-5.
VOC 3164, ff. 534-46	1766.
VOC 3165, ff. 1-700	1765-6.
VOC 3166, ff. 701-1765?	1766.
VOC 3197, ff. 63-91	1767.
VOC 3198, n.f.	1766-7.
VOC 3229, ff. 164-236	1768.
VOC 3230, n.f.	1767-8.
VOC 3261, n.f.	1768-9.
VOC 3289, ff. 304-29	1770.
VOC 3290, n.f.	1769-70.
VOC 3320, ff. 311-15	1771.
VOC 3345, ff. 8-15?	1772 (among other documents).
VOC 3345, ff. 275-329	1772.
VOC 3346, n.f.	1771-2.
VOC 3373, ff. 126-556	1773.
VOC 3375, n.f.	1772-3.
VOC 3399, ff. 112-22	1774.
VOC 3400, n.f.	1773-4.
VOC 3420, ff. 419-21	1774.
VOC 3430, n.f.	1774-5.
VOC 3455, ff. 462-888	1775-6.
VOC 3483, n.f.	1777.
VOC 3512, ff. 95-247	1778.
VOC 3513, ff. 448-500	1778.

VOC 3514, n.f.	1778.
VOC 3540, ff. 33-8	1779.
VOC 3540, ff. 152-227	1778-9.
VOC 3542, n.f.	1778-9.
VOC 3568, ff. 37, 41-2	1780.
VOC 3569, ff. 255-460	1780.
VOC 3570, n.f.	1780.
VOC 3691, ff. 680-2	Colombo, concerning conflicts with Nawab Muhammad Ali of Arcot, 1785.
VOC 3718, ff. 234-60	1785-6.
VOC 3719, n.f.	1785-6.
VOC 3773, f. 3284	Batavia, concerning a map of the fort at Pulicat, 1788.
VOC 3783, ff. 34-81	1786-8.
VOC 3784, n.f.	1786-8.
VOC 3834, n.f.	1788-9.
VOC 3835, n.f.	1789-90.
VOC 3876, ff. 50-383	1790-1.
VOC 3878, n.f.	Pulicat, 1790.
VOC 3879, n.f.	1790-1.
VOC 3892, ff. 5441-2	1790.

5.1.3. *Dagregisters* (diaries)

VOC 1087, n.f.	Pulicat, November 1623-November 1625.
VOC 1092, n.f.	Masulipatam, January-November 1627.
VOC 1095, ff. 28-47	Pulicat, April-September 1628.
VOC 1095, ff. 48-77	Masulipatam, March 1626-September 1628.
VOC 1109, ff. 271-87	Pulicat, June-December 1632.
VOC 1117, ff. 674-80	July-November 1635.
VOC 1134, n.f.	Pulicat, *c.* 1640.
VOC 1161, ff. 887-975	Pulicat, September 1645-September 1646.
VOC 1191, ff. 773-994	June 1651-March 1652.
VOC 1316, ff. 530-46	January-February, *c.* 1676.
VOC 1692, ff. 353-400	Kept by Commissioner Bernard Phoonsen, May-October 1704.
VOC 1778, ff. 60-80	Golkonda, January-February 1709.
VOC 2505, ff. 1655-80	May-July 1740.

5.1.4. *Shipping lists*

VOC 1369, f. 1419	Private vessels that arrived at and departed from Porto Novo, Cuddalore and Pondicherry, 1680-1.
VOC 1378, ff. 1801-5	Vessels that arrived at and departed from Masulipatam, 1681-2.
VOC 1378, ff. 2083v-3100	Arrival and departure of private vessels, 1681-2.

VOC 1398, ff. 371-86, 441	1683-4.
VOC 1405, ff. 1354v-68	Private vessels arrived at and departed from Pulicat, 1682-3.
VOC 1405, ff. 1804v-16	1683-4.
VOC 1414, ff. 558-75	1684-5.
VOC 1423, ff. 806-30	1686.
VOC 1429, ff. 1175-7	Vessels that arrived at and departed from Masulipatam, *c.* 1686.
VOC 1596, ff. 182-?	Foreign vessels that arrived at and departed from Masulipatam, 1696-7.
VOC 1610, ff. 269-73	Foreign vessels that arrived at and departed from Masulipatam, 1697-8.
VOC 1624, ff. 247-54	Vessels that arrived at and departed from Masulipatam, 1698-9.
VOC 1649, ff. 185-95	Foreign vessels that arrived at and departed from Masulipatam, 1700-1.
VOC 1664, ff. 647-?	Vessels that arrived at and departed from Masulipatam, 1701-2.
VOC 1678, ff. 291-9	Vessels that arrived at and departed from Masulipatam, 1702-3.
VOC 1730, ff. 452-6	Arrival and departure of vessels, 1706.
VOC 1761, ff. 428-33	Vessels that arrived at and departed from Masulipatam, 1707-8.
VOC 1796, ff. 28-38	Vessels that arrived at and departed from Masulipatam, 1709-10.
VOC 1855, ff. 53-6	Vessels that arrived at and departed from Masulipatam, 1713-14.
VOC 1869, ff. 56-61	Arrival and departure of private vessels, 1714-15.
VOC 1896, ff. 29-?	Vessels that arrived at and departed from Masulipatam, 1716-17.
VOC 1912, ff. 132-8	Vessels that arrived at and departed from Masulipatam, 1717-18.
VOC 1946, ff. 42-8	Vessels that arrived at and departed from Masulipatam, 1718-19.
VOC 1962, ff. 334-?	Vessels that arrived at and departed from Masulipatam, 1719-20.
VOC 1962, ff. 549-56	Private vessels that arrived at Masulipatam, 1720-1.
VOC 1981, ff. 143-9	Private vessels that arrived at and departed from Masulipatam, 1721-2.
VOC 1997, ff. 100-4	Private vessels that arrived at and departed from Masulipatam, *c.* 1723.
VOC 2014, ff. 1596-1603	Private vessels that arrived at and departed from Masulipatam, *c.* 1724.
VOC 2031, ff. 451-8	Arrival and departure of private and small vessels, *c.* 1725.

VOC 2076, ff. 1084-92	Arrival of private vessels, *c.* 1727.
VOC 2102, ff. 137-42	Foreign and other vessels that arrived at Masulipatam, 1728.
VOC 2135, ff. 119-27	Vessels at Masulipatam and Porto Novo, *c.* 1729.
VOC 2146, ff. 4643-7	Vessels that arrived at and departed from Masulipatam and Porto Novo, 1728-9.
VOC 2181, ff. 5599-603	Foreign vessels that arrived at and departed from Porto Novo and Pulicat, 1731.
VOC 2197, ff. 511-13	Porto Novo, *c.* 1731.
VOC 2197, ff. 691-6	Masulipatam, 1730.
VOC 2197, ff. 1920-5	Arrival and departure of vessels, *c.* 1731.
VOC 2197, ff. 1930-?	Arrival and departure of vessels, *c.* 1731.
VOC 2244, ff. 184-90	Private vessels that arrived at and departed from Masulipatam, 1731-2.
VOC 2244, ff. 688-96	Private vessels that arrived at and departed from Porto Novo, *c.* 1732.
VOC 2289, f. 898	Vessels that arrived at and departed from Pulicat, 1731-2.
VOC 2289, ff. 959-?	Private vessels at Porto Novo, 1732-3.
VOC 2318, f. 2611	Indigenous vessels arrived at and departed from Bimlipatam, *c.* 1734.
VOC 2349, ff. 590-5	Foreign vessels at Porto Novo and Pulicat, *c.* 1735.
VOC 2349, ff. 700-20	Vessels at Nagappattinam, *c.* 1735.
VOC 2351, ff. 3780-5	Vessels that arrived at and departed from Masulipatam, 1734-5.
VOC 2351, f. 3857	Indigenous vessels that arrived at and departed from Bimlipatam, 1734-5.
VOC 2351, ff. 4409-15	Private vessels at Pulicat and Porto Novo, *c.* 1735.
VOC 2351, ff. 4469-?	*c.* 1735.
VOC 2387, ff. 1602-8	Vessels that arrived at and departed from Masulipatam, 1735-6.
VOC 2387, f. 1617	Vessels that arrived at and departed from Bimlipatam, *c.* 1736.
VOC 2412, ff. 334-9	Private vessels arrived at Porto Novo and Pulicat, *c.* 1737.
VOC 2412, ff. 366-71	*c.* 1737.
VOC 2442, ff. 354-9	Private vessels at Porto Novo, 1736-7.
VOC 2442, ff. 386-99	*c.* 1738.
VOC 2442-2443, ff. 2964-74	Vessels that arrived at and departed from Masulipatam, *c.* 1738.
VOC 2442-3, f. 2998	Vessels that arrived at and departed from Bimlipatam, *c.* 1738.
VOC 2442-3, ff. 235-9	Private vessels at Porto Novo, 1737-8.

VOC 2471, ff. 802-11	Vessels that arrived and departed from Masulipatam, *c.* 1739.
VOC 2471, ff. 846-7	Indigenous vessels that arrived at Masulipatam and/or Bimlipatam, *c.* 1739.
VOC 2471, ff. 1178-83	Vessels that arrived and departed from Porto Novo, *c.* 1739.
VOC 2538, ff. 1185-98	Private vessels at Masulipatam and Porto Novo, 1739-40.
VOC 2538, ff. 1294-1302	Dutch vessels, *c.* 1741.
VOC 2539, ff. 3791-804	Private vessels at Masulipatam, 1740-1.
VOC 3043, f. 199	Arrival and departure of foreign and private vessels, 1762.
VOC 3077, f. 439	Arrival and departure of foreign and private vessels, 1763.
VOC 3107, f. 397	Arrival and departure of foreign and private vessels, 1764.
VOC 3164, ff. 607-8	Arrival and departure of foreign and private vessels, 1766.
VOC 3197, ff. 41-2	Arrival and departure of foreign and private vessels, 1767.
VOC 3260, ff. 669-70	Arrival and departure of foreign vessels, *c.* 1769.
VOC 3289, ff. 11-12	Arrival and departure of foreign and private vessels, *c.* 1770.
VOC 3320, ff. 346-50	Arrival and departure of foreign and private vessels, *c.* 1771.
VOC 3345, ff. 48-9	Foreign and private vessels that arrived at and departed from Nagappattinam, *c.* 1772.
VOC 3374, ff. 832-3	Arrival and departure of foreign and private vessels, *c.* 1773.
VOC 3399, ff. 509-10	Arrival and departure of foreign and private vessels, *c.* 1774.
VOC 3429, ff. 252-4	Arrival and departure of foreign and private vessels, *c.* 1775.
VOC 3454, ff. 250-1	Vessels that arrived at and departed from Nagappattinam, 1776.
VOC 3541, ff. 449-50	Arrival and departure of vessels, 1779.

5.1.5. *Missions to Indian states*

VOC 1100, ff. 77-84	Mission to King Venkata III of Vijayanagara, *c.* 1630 (report).
VOC 1231, ff. 329-30	Mission to Bijapur by Dom Pedro Henricques, December 1658 (instructions).
VOC 1302-3, ff. 457-525?	Mission to Golkonda by Pieter Smith, November 1671 (report).

VOC 1328, ff. 617-22	Mission to Shivaji by Herbert de Jager, *c.* 1677 (report).
VOC 1418, ff. 799-904	Mission to Golkonda by Laurens Pith, March-May 1686 (report).
VOC 1423, ff. 435-594	Mission to Golkonda by Laurens Pith, March-July 1686 (report).
VOC 1450, ff. 947-73	Mission to the Mughal (i.e. Aurangzeb in the Bhima valley) by Joannes Bacherus, 1688 (instructions) (see also VOC 1510, ff. 354-410, and under Surat, 2.1.5) (among other documents).
VOC 1463, ff. 205-15	Mission to Thanjavur by Arnoldus Soolmans, December 1688 (report).
VOC 1486, ff. 285v-8v	Mission to Gingee by Lanius, 1690 (instructions).
VOC 1510, ff. 354-410	Mission to the Mughal by Johannes Bacherus, *c.* 1689 (various documents) (see also VOC 1450, ff. 947-73).
VOC 1581, ff. 212-68	Mission to the Mughal court by the Company's broker and interpreter 'Annamontoe', 1695 (report).
VOC 2166, ff. 391-401	Mission to Thanjavur, *c.* 1730 (report).
VOC 2318, ff. 2312-23	Mission to Nawab Haji Husain of Pithapuram and Prince Timma Raghu of Peddapuram by Vrijmoet, June 1734 (report).
VOC 3292, ff. 705-38	Mission to Arcot by Huijsken, September-December 1770 (report).
VOC 3349, ff. 733-40	Mission to the Nawab of Arcot in Ramnad by Johan Gerard van Angelbeek, December 1772 (report).

5.1.6. *Miscellaneous*

VOC 1061, ff. 90-1	Document concerning the diamond trade at Gingee, 1615. See also Pieter van Dam, *Beschryvinge*, Vol. 2, Part 2, pp. 174-6 (see Bibliography, no. 12).
VOC 1062, ff. 87-105	Report by Pieter Gielis van Ravesteijn concerning his journey from Masulipatam to Surat and the trade over there, May 1615-February 1616.
VOC 1231, ff. 773-4	Report by Nathaniel Freder concerning his meeting with the General of Bijapur, 1659.
VOC 1242, ff. 859-66	Report concerning a journey to a diamond mine by Pieter de Lange, 1663. See also Pieter van Dam, *Beschryvinge*, Vol. 2, Part 2, pp. 176-81 (see Bibliography, no. 12).
VOC 1243-4, ff. 906-?	Report concerning a journey to a diamond mine by Pieter de Lange, 1663 (see above).

VOC 1243-4, ff. 961-?	Report by Pieter de Lange concerning his visit to the army of Neknam Khan, *c.* 1663.
VOC 1254, ff. 553-76	Treaties with dyers in and around Nagappattinam, *c.* 1665.
VOC 1275-8, ff. 1502-21	Report by Francois Tivart concerning his journey to Draksharama, Golkonda, etc., January 1670.
VOC 1308, ff. 296-325	Report concerning the state of affairs at Nagappattinam, *c.* 1675.
VOC 1321, ff. 888-91	Document concerning negotiations with envoys from Thanjavur, 1676.
VOC 1322, ff. 1384-91	Document concerning negotiations with envoys from Thanjavur, 1676.
VOC 1323, ff. 326-34v	Correspondence between the factory at Teganapatam and Herbert de Jagher staying with the army of Shivaji, 1677.
VOC 1329, ff. 1162-82	Documents concerning peace negotiations with Bijapur, 1676-7.
VOC 1339, ff. 1033v-71	Report by Floris Bolwercq concerning his sojourn in Orissa and Bimlipatam, *c.* 1678.
VOC 1369, ff. 1381-1403	Transfer of Nagappattinam from the Ceylon government to Coromandel, *c.* 1681.
VOC 1373, ff. 602-860	Report by Jacob Jorisz. Pits concerning his visit to northern Coromandel, *c.* 1682.
VOC 1378, ff. 1852v-2046	Report by Jacob Jorisz. Pits concerning his visit to northern Coromandel, 1682.
VOC 1450, ff. 789-824	Report concerning the factory at Golkonda, 1688.
VOC 1473, ff. 782-930	Reports concerning the factory at Golkonda, 1691.
VOC 1509, ff. 815-916v	Letters from the Company's Brahmins in the Mughal army at Gingee and other places, *c.* 1692.
VOC 1522, ff. 1236-1309	Report by Theodore Telghuijs concerning his journey to the Coromandel Coast, 1693.
VOC 1523, ff. 615-90	Report by Theodore Telghuijs concerning his journey to the Coromandel Coast, 1693.
VOC 1581, ff. 89-165	Reports concerning weavers' villages in Thanjavur, 1695.
VOC 1610, ff. 332-70	Documents concerning a visit by Pieter Calandrini and Willem Oosterharen to Aurangzeb's general Zulfiqar Ali Khan, 1698.
VOC 1617, ff. 586-695	Correspondence with the French concerning the transfer of Pondicherry, *c.* 1699.
VOC 1624, ff. 227-64	Advices of Laurens Pit concerning the *Visiadoor*, the *Adigar*, interpreters, etc., *c.* 1699.
VOC 1640, ff. 317-92	Report by Dirck Comans concerning the factories on the southern Coromandel Coast, September 1700-January 1701.

VOC 1657, ff. 394-744	Documents concerning the high prices of textiles, 1696-1701.
VOC 1678, ff. 358-99	Report by J. van Steland concerning his visit to the factories at Palakollu and Draksharama, 1703.
VOC 1730, ff. 75-203	Documents concerning debtors and the desolate state of the factory at Sadras, 1706.
VOC 1751, ff. 1384-1424	Report concerning the condition of Fort Geldria at Pulicat, 1708.
VOC 1865, ff. 867-97	Documents concerning a war between Thanjavur and Ramnad and the Danish involvement in it, *c.* 1715.
VOC 1957, ff. 1215-62	Documents concerning the journey of an envoy from Thanjavur to Jaffna, *c.* 1721.
VOC 2076, ff. 805-47	Document concerning weights, measures and currencies in Coromandel, *c.* 1727.
VOC 2076, ff. 710-20	Letter concerning the advance of Nizam-ul-Mulk to Aurangabad and a Maratha general, *c.* 1727.
VOC 2198, ff. 195-231	Correspondence concerning Arcot, *c.* 1731.
VOC 2575, ff. 2061-100	Report concerning the troubles caused by the invasion of the Marathas, *c.* 1742.
VOC 2665, ff. 1995-2005	Report concerning envoys from Thanjavur, 1746.
VOC 2752, ff. 648-86	Report concerning the Nicobar Islands (among other places), *c.* 1750.
VOC 2891, ff. 924-60	*Radicale beschrijving* (i.e. an official review) of Coromandel, November 1757.
VOC 3045, ff. 490-819	Document concerning conflicts with the British and the French, 1762.
VOC 3046, ff. 820-991	Document concerning conflicts with the British and the French, 1762.
VOC 3134, ff. 271-337	Documents concerning the behaviour of *Opperhoofd* F.J. Lovenaar of Jagannathapuram, *c.* 1765.
VOC 3164, ff. 496-532	Documents concerning the debts of merchants at Sadras, Pulicat and Jagannathapuram, *c.* 1766.
VOC 3197, ff. 367-462	Report by Pieter Haksteen concerning his journey to Bimlipatam, Jagannathapuram, etc., 1767.
VOC 3281, ff. 1769-1992	Documents concerning the repatriated former Nagappattinam Secretary J. Haselcamp, *c.* 1770.
VOC 3399, ff. 123-296	All treaties and privileges concerning Coromandel rulers and the Dutch from 1612 onward, *c.* 1774.
VOC 3429, ff. 299-353	Treaties, *cauls* and other privileges enjoyed by the Dutch in Thanjavur, *c.* 1775.
VOC 3431, ff. 198-298	Some treaties, etc. concluded with Thanjavur (among other kingdoms), 1676-91.
VOC 3662, ff. 84-131	Documents concerning the losses suffered at the surrender of Pulicat and Jagannathapuram, 1784.

5.2. Other VOC Series

5.2.1. Archives of the Gentlemen XVII and the Amsterdam Chamber

See 1.1
Access no.: 1.04.02

Kopie-resoluties van de Gouverneur-Generaal en Raden
Duplicate proceedings of the Governor-General and Council

See 1.1.4
Inv. nos: VOC 656-847

In the *Realia* repertory to the *resoluties* several relevant headings are to be found, among these:

Alemperwe (Alambaram; 5 entries 1701-33), *Andoman* (Andaman Islands; 1 entry 1656), *Bimilipatnam* (Bimlipatam; 2 entries 1664-5), *Clavera* (1 entry 1663), *Conjemeere* (Kunimedu; 2 entries 1701-2), *Cormandel* (about 900 entries 1611-1795), *Daatcheron* (Draksharama; 3 entries 1654-1731), *firman* (1 entry 1651), *Golconda* (5 entries 1650-1708), *nabab* (of the Golkonda Carnatic; 6 entries 1652-64), *Nagapatnam* (Nagappattinam; 11 entries 1653-1703), *Narsapour* (Narasapur; 1 entry 1656), *neijk* (Nayak of Thanjavur; 1 entry 1653), Nicobaarsche eijlanden (Nicobar Islands; 2 entries 1753-5), *Palliacatta* (Pulicat; 16 entries 1616-1791), *Palicol* (Palakollu; 3 entries 1666-1731), *Petapoulij* (Petapoli; 1 entry 1654), *Pondicherij* (6 entries 1694-1700), *Sadraspatnam* (Sadras; 5 entries up to 1744), *Tansjouwer (Naijk van)* ((Nayak of) Thanjavur; 2 entries 1653-1705), *Tegenapatnam* (3 entries 1665-1702).

Miscellaneous

VOC 542 Letter from VOC factors at Petapoli to Admiral Pieter Willemsz. Verhoeff, 1608. One piece.
VOC 544 Letter from Jacob de Bitter to VOC servants at Coromandel concerning the establishment of a factory at Teganapatam, 1608. One piece.
VOC 546 *Caul* of the Nayak of Gingee concerning the establishment of a factory at Teganapatam, 1608. One piece. Published in *CDNI*, I, p. 55.
VOC 547 Memorandum of Jacob de Bitter concerning his activities in Coromandel and the establishment of a factory at Teganapatam, 1608. One piece. Published in De Jonge, *De opkomst van het Nederlandsch gezag*. Vol. III, pp. 281-2 (see Bibliography, no. 120).
VOC 548 Memorandum of Lodewijck Isacksz. concerning the trade on the Coromandel Coast, 1608.
VOC 590 Letter from Wemmer van Berchen, chief-factor in Coromandel, at Masulipatam to Adolf Thomasz., factor at Pulicat, 1612. One piece.

VOC 637-52	Various financial documents concerning Coromandel (and Aceh on Sumatra), including papers concerning the purchase of textiles, cinnamon, steel, cotton and indigo at Masulipatam, Petapoli and Teganapatam, and the purchase of two horses at Golkonda for the King of Aceh, 1607-12. Seventeen pieces.
VOC 4733	Papers concerning the complaints of the VOC about the French East India Company concerning the capture of ships and the behaviour of the French in Masulipatam, with appendices, 1760. One folder.
VOC 4816	List of coins, exchange rates, weights and measures in Asia, with index, including sections on Pulicat, Masulipatam, Teganapatam, Nagappattinam, Golkonda, Palakollu, Draksharama, Bimlipatam, Nagulvancha, Sadras, Petapoli and Jamshedpet (ff. 1-90 contain the actual lists; ff. 91-139 contain notes on these subjects), 1769. One volume.
VOC 4886	Extracts of letters, reports, treaties and other papers concerning the VOC trade in Coromandel, 1682. One volume.
VOC 4887	Ordinance of the Persian *Diwan* Muhammad Shafi concerning the VOC trade at Masulipatam (Portuguese translation), 1690. One piece.
VOC 4888	Letter from G. Ploos van Amstel, *Independent Fiscaal* of Coromandel, to the Gentlemen XVII, with appendix, 1690. Two pieces.
VOC 4889	Notes concerning coinage in Nagappattinam, 1695-6. One folder.
VOC 4890	Extract of the *resoluties* of the GG&C concerning the appointment of Pieter Haksteen as Governor of Coromandel, 1765. One piece.
VOC 4891	Petitions of the former Secretary and Cashier at Nagappattinam to Directors, concerning the restitution of an amount of money wrongfully confiscated, with appendices, 1765-9. One quire.
VOC 4892	Papers concerning the lawsuit against Johannes Haselkamp, former factor in Coromandel, 1780. One folder.
VOC 7015	*Eisen van retouren* (see 1.1.1) from the Directors to Coromandel, Bengal and Batavia, 1700. One piece.

5.2.2. *Archives of the Zeeland Chamber*

See 1.2.1
Access no.: 1.04.02

Ingekomen stukken van Gouverneur-Generaal en Raden bij de Heren XVII en de Kamer Zeeland (IGG)
Papers received from Governor-General and Council by the Gentlemen XVII and the Zeeland Chamber

VOC 8808-900	Letters and reports received by GG&C from Coromandel, with appendices, 1681-1779 (-1784). 93 Volumes. Incomplete series.

VOC 9191 List of the supply, purchase and selling prices of round pepper and areca from Malabar over the years 1687-9, drawn up on the base of the trade books of the factory at Nagappattinam, 1700. One volume.

Ingekomen stukken van de kantoren in Indië bij de Heren XVII en de Kamer Zeeland (IKI)

Papers received from the establishments in the Indies by the Gentlemen XVII and the Zeeland Chamber

VOC 9625-708 Letters and other papers from the Governor and Council of Coromandel to the Gentlemen XVII (and others), with appendices, 1687-1792. 84 volumes. Incomplete series. Including:

- VOC 9626 Letter and other papers from Bernard Phoonsen, extraordinary member of the Council, to the Gentlemen XVII, concerning his inspections as Commissioner of Coromandel, 1704.
- VOC 9662 Includes secret letters to the GG&C at Batavia concerning conflicts with the French and British on the Coromandel Coast, 1757-62.

VOC 9709-14 Papers concerning the activities of Commissioner General Hendrik Adriaan van Reede tot Drakenstein, 1686-90. Six volumes.

VOC 9715-19 *Resoluties* of the Governor and Council of Coromandel, 1756-86. Five volumes. Incomplete series.

VOC 9720 *Dagregister* of Laurens Pit, Governor of Coromandel and Commissioner of Golkonda, staying at Masulipatam, October-December 1686. One volume.

VOC 9721-31 Correspondence dating from various periods between the Governor and Council of Coromandel and subaltern factories (Golkonda, Masulipatam, Teganapatam, Pulicat, Sadras, Nagappattinam and Porto Novo), 1687-1730. Eleven volumes. Incomplete series.

VOC 9732 Letter from the *Independent Fiscaal* Hendrik Becker to the Gentlemen XVII, with appendices, 1703. One volume.

VOC 9734 Case files of the Council of Justice in Coromandel concerning deserters, 1759-60. One volume.

VOC 9735 Papers concerning the extortion of Frederik Jan Lovenaar, *Opperhoofd* at Jagannathapuram, 1765. One volume.

Soldijkantoor

Pay Office

See 1.2.1 and 1.1.10

VOC 12384 Includes a muster roll of the VOC servants in Coromandel, 1712. One volume.

Miscellaneous

VOC 11207-8	Two copies of a list (79 pp.) of coins, exchange rates, weights and measures at a great number of factories in the Indies, including Nagappattinam, Pulicat, Masulipatam, Teganapatam, Golkonda, Palakollu, Draksharama, Bimlipatam, Nagulvancha, Sadras and Petapoli, printed in 1691 (at Middelburg, Zeeland). Two volumes.
VOC 11284	Memorandum of the GG&C for Gelmer Vosburgh, appointed as Governor and Commissioner of Coromandel, 1696. One volume.
VOC 11285	Papers concerning matters between *Independent Fiscaal* Hendrick Becker and former Governor Dirk Comans (with map of part of the southern Coromandel Coast and its hinterland, see also 5.7), 1706. One volume.
VOC 11286	Letter from acting Governor Pieter Haksteen to GG&C concerning the escape of Governor Christiaan van Teylingen, with appendices, 1765. One volume.
VOC 11287	Papers concerning the estate of C.L. Hagemeyster, former second in command at Bimlipatam, about which a lawsuit was started between the executor of the estate and the British Court of Justice at Madras, 1761-9. One volume.
VOC 11288	Papers concerning a petition of Johannes Hazelkamp, former Secretary and Cashier at Nagappattinam, for the restitution of a sum of money that he had paid from his estate to the VOC, 1769-71. Two volumes.
VOC 11289	Papers concerning the case of Johannes Hazelkamp, former Secretary of the Council of Police and Cashier at Nagappattinam, 1770. One volume.
VOC 11290	Report by J.E. Kuhn concerning the condition of the fort at Bimlipatam, 1771. One volume.

5.2.3. *Archives of the Delft, Rotterdam, Enkhuizen and Hoorn Chambers and miscellaneous*

No relevant documents found in inventories.

5.3. Archives Transferred from Asia

Hoge Regering te Batavia
High Government at Batavia

See 1.3.1
Access no.: 1.04.17

300-20 Several collections of extracts from and repertories to letters dispatched from Batavia and by the Gentlemen XVII to Coromandel, 1651-1775.

321-34 Minutes of letters from Batavia to Coromandel, 1790-1805, secret letters, 1784-96.

335 Secret letters received in Batavia from Coromandel, 1779. With tables of contents, appendices, one volume.

336 Extracts from letters of the Coromandel Governor and Council to Batavia, 1758-71. One volume.

337 Correspondence between Batavia, Ceylon and Coromandel concerning a dispute with Thanjavur, 1778-80. One volume.

340 *Memorie van overgave* by Governor Adriaan Pla to Elias Guillot, 1734. One volume.

341 Description of the Company's trade and general situation in Coromandel, by J. van der Wayen. Two copies of the same in one volume.

342 *Memorie van overgave* by Governor Steven Vermont to Lubbert Jan van Eck, 1759. With appendices, one volume.

343 Miscellaneous papers among which some concerning the consolidation of the Nagappattinam castle and the *memorie van overgave* by Governor Lubbert Jan van Eck to Christiaan van Teylingen, 1760-2. One volume.

344 *Memorie van overgave* by Governor Pieter Haksteen to Reynier van Vlissingen, 1771. One volume.

345 Papers concerning the textile trade, including lists of prices, weights and measures, coins, shiploads, etc., over the years 1629-1760 and 1765-71. Two parts in one volume.

346 Orders and instructions by the Governor of Coromandel to Nagappattinam and dependent villages, 1665-74. One volume.

347 Extract *resoluties* and letters of the High Government concerning gold supply and coinage, 1744-66. One volume.

348 Instruction to Lieutenant-Colonel J.B. Roussel leading an expedition to Bengal and Coromandel, 1759. With appendices, one volume.

349-54 Papers regarding personal disputes and suspected malfunctioning concerning Haselkamp, Maudave, Van Teylingen, Paulus Loman, C.P. Keller, 1760-9. Five volumes.

354 Letter of D.C. Vick to Batavia about the indebtedness of Porto Novo merchants, 1768. With appendices, one volume.

355 Reports on the Coromandel trade, 1778. One volume.

356 Documents concerning the complaints by citizens of Nagappattinam about the *Adigar*, being Willem van Duynevelt, 1779. With appendices, two parts in one volume.

357 Papers documenting complaints by the Hindu, 'Naga Maloe Wengeda Soepa Rayaloe' concerning injustices to his father, the former interpreter, 'Naga Waloe Chinaya Wayker', including complaints of Nagappattinam citizens about the interpreters. With appendices, seven parts in one volume.

358 Papers concerning the complaints lodged against W.H.G. van Byland, 1790-1. Seven pieces in one cover.

359 Dutch and English translations of complaints by two merchants of Jagannathapuram, 1790-1. One volume.

360-2 Papers concerning a possible retreat of the VOC from the Coast, 1792. Three volumes.

363 Papers concerning debts to the Company of Captain Meyer and the Harrop and Stevenson firm in Tranquebar, 1802-4. One volume.

364-79 General report of the recovery of the Dutch possessions in Coromandel from the British in 1818 by J.A. van Braam. With appendices, 17 volumes.

380 Table of contents to the *verbalen* of the head of Coromandel and Madurai, 1820. With appendices, one volume (see also below, *Voormalige Nederlandse bezittingen in Voor-Indië*, inv. nos 117-21).

381-407 Letters from the head of Coromandel to the GG&C and the Commissioners General, 1818-24. With appendices, 27 volumes.

408-80 *Verbalen* of the head of Coromandel and Madurai, 1818-25. 74 volumes. For copies and finding aid, see below, *Voormalige Nederlandse bezittingen in Voor-Indië*, inv. nos 71-116 and 117-21.

481-95 General reports on the Jagannathapuram, Palakollu, Pulicat, Sadras and Tuticorin residences, 1823. In triplicate, 14 volumes / covers.

496-97 Papers regarding complaints and trials concerning Dirk Bronnekam, sons of Pieter van Spall (theft from Paravars in Tuticorin), 1819-27. Two covers.

498 Financial reckoning between the Coromandel and Batavia orphanages over 1766-1807, made in 1820. With appendices, one volume.

499-500 Papers concerning measurement of the uncultivated lands in Palakollu, 1823. One volume, one cover.

501-4 Papers concerning the transfer of the Dutch settlements to the British, 1825. Four volumes (two identical).

Voormalige Nederlandse bezittingen in Voor-Indië
Former Dutch possessions in South Asia

See 1.3.3
Access no.: 1.04.19

71-116 Minute *verbalen* of the head of Coromandel and Madurai, 1818-25. 46 volumes. For a more complete series, see above, *Hoge Regering Batavia*, inv. nos 408-80.

117-21 Table of contents to the above, 1821-5. Five volumes. The table of 1820 is in *Hoge Regering Batavia*, inv. no. 380.

122-4 Correspondence of the Sadras residency with Batavia, 1818-24. Incomplete, three volumes.

125-35 Correspondence of the head in Sadras with Palakollu, Pulicat, and Tuticorin, 1819-25. Incomplete, 11 volumes.

136 Instructions of the head to the civil servants, 1818, 1822, 1824. One volume.

5.4. ARCHIVES OF OTHER INSTITUTIONS

Stadhouderlijke Secretarie
Secretariat to the Stadtholder

See 1.4.3
Access no.: 1.01.50

1222 Excerpt from a letter from the GG&C to the Gentlemen XVII concerning the desertion of the former Governor of Coromandel Christiaan van Teylingen, Shipmaster Jolle and Bookkeeper Hasz to Madras, and the attitude of the British toward this case, 1766. One piece.

1607 Collection of various documents concerning government and trade in Asia (one volume). Including:

- 4 Transfer of the Coromandel government, n.d.
- 7 Instructions to Captain Peter Wasch and the council of Nagappattinam during the absence of Governor Laurens Pit ('no. 15'), 1658.
- 8 Memorandum from Governor Antonio Pavilioen to chief-factor Pieter Smith and council of Fort Geldria at Pulicat.
- 12 Explanations concerning the order given to factor Pieter van den Broecke to capture the English ship at Masulipatam, 1667.
- 13 Instructions to Jan van der Laen leaving Jaffna as *Commandeur* for the occupation of Nagappattinam, 1658.
- 14 Report by Pieter de Lange and François Thivert to Governor Laurens Pit concerning their journey to Teganapatam and Sadras, 1663 (see inv. no. 14a below).
- 16 *Memorie van overgave* by Governor Laurens Pit to Cornelis Speelman ('no. 16'), 1663.
- 24 Instructions to steersman Thomas Fredericksz. and corporal Baey Sacx to sail and watch the coast and sea between Tranquebar and 'Colchow' ('no. 31'), 1665.
- 27 Order and memorandum concerning the sailing from Coromandel to Batavia via Ceylon ('no. 39'), 1666.
- 28 Excerpt from a letter to Governor Cornelis Speelman at Nagappattinam ('no. 35'), n.d. (between 1663 and 1665).
- 14a Report by chief-factor Pieter d'Lange to Governor Laurens Pit concerning the diamond mines in Golkonda ('no. 2'), 1663.

1610 Instructions to Bernard Phoonsen, Commissioner to Coromandel, 1703; his memorandum in this capacity to Governor Johannes van Steelant, 1705; *memorie van overgave* by Governor Dirk Comans to Johannes van Steelant, 1705; instructions and oath for *Fiscaals*, 1688-9. One volume.

1611 Instructions of Hendrik Adriaen van Reede tot Drakensteyn, Commissioner General of the Gentlemen XVII, to Governor Laurens Pit and council, 1689. One volume.

1612 Report by Johannes van Steelant, chief-factor of northern Coromandel, concerning his journey to Pulicat and Draksharama, with appendices, 1703. One volume.

1915 Report by the so-called Military Commission (consisting of Captains J.O. Vaillant and C.A. Ver Huell (see 1.5.32) and Lieutenant-Colonel J.F.L. Graevestein) concerning its activities in Coromandel (and Ceylon and Melaka); report of the military state of affairs in Coromandel, 1790 (among other documents). One folder.

Comité tot de Zaken van de Oost-Indische Handel en Bezittingen
Committee regarding East Indian Trade and Possessions

See 1.4.4
Access no.: 2.01.27.01

Overgekomen brieven en papieren (OBP)
(letters and papers received)

61, ff. 148?-1629	Report concerning Coromandel (among other regions), *c.* 1793.
62, n.f.	Report concerning Coromandel (among other regions), *c.* 1794.
63, n.f.	Report concerning Coromandel (among other regions), *c.* 1795.
64, n.f.	Report concerning Coromandel (among other regions), *c.* 1796.
65a, n.f.	Report concerning Coromandel (among other regions), *c.* 1794.
125, n.f.	Report concerning Coromandel, 1793.
125, n.f.	Various documents concerning Coromandel, *c.* 1795-7.

Raad der Aziatische Bezittingen en Etablissementen
Council of Asian Possessions and Establishments

See 1.4.5
Access no.: 2.01.27.02

394f, 397b Papers concerning the former chief-factor of Coromandel J. Eilbracht, 1800-2. 30 pieces.

Uit Engeland overgezonden stukken (Nederburgh)
Papers sent from England (Nederburgh)

See 1.4.7
Access no.: 2.01.27.04

47 General report on Coromandel over the year 1794, 1795.

Ministerie van Koloniën
Ministry of Colonial Affairs

See 1.4.10
Access no.: 2.10.01

3090 Contains appendices to the *generaal verslag* (general report) on Coromandel of 1818, mostly correspondence of J.A. Braam and some of 1794. Appendix 14 is a volume of annotated extracts and translations of all the contracts (*farmans*, *cauls* etc.) concluded by Coromandel rulers and *zamindars* with the VOC, with an extensive index. Three folders, parts in French, and English.

Ambassadeur Coenraad van Heemskerck
Envoy Coenraad van Heemskerck

See 1.4.11
Access no.: 1.02.01
Period: 1672-1701

434 Request to the King (of France?) to return two ships lent in 1674 to the French after the capitulation of St. Thome, 1698. One piece.

Legatie Frankrijk
Embassy at Paris, France

See 1.4.11
Access no.: 1.02.14
Period: 1747-1810

443 Papers concerning mutual claims of the VOC and the French East India Company concerning several ships, and hostilities at Masulipatam, Sadras and Nagappattinam, 1750-68. One bundle.

464 Papers concerning claims of the VOC on the French East India Company, because of payments made to the council of Pondicherry, 1763. One folder.

469 Papers concerning claims of Governor Christiaan van Teylingen and Bookkeeper Jan Marcus Scheepen on the French East India Company, for unpaid supplies, 1765-70. One folder.

5.5. Personal and Family Papers

Geleynssen

See 1.5.2
Access no.: 1.10.30

39 Letters received by Governor M. Isbrantsen from Batavia, 1628-30. Three pieces.

108	Letters of C. Reijniersz, J. de Meere and A. Heussen from Masulipatam, 1637-9.
144	Letter of commission by A. Heussen and B. de Gruijter in Masulipatam to R. Maertensz in charge of the Dutch sailors aboard the ship belonging to the Golkonda *Sar-khail* Muhammad Said Ardistani (from 1643: Mir Jumla) destined for Persia, 1640.
152	Extracts from the *dagregister* of Pulicat, 1642. One folder.
153	Agreement between the Commanders of the offensive fleet and the Portuguese at Nagappattinam. With a report on the agreement by C. de Potter, 1642. One piece.
160, 162	Letters to Geleynssen by A. Gardenijs in Pulicat and A. Heussen and B. de Gruijter in Masulipatam, 1640-3. Two folders.
175	(Extract) letters by the GG (&C) to Pulicat, 1641-2. One folder.
184-5	Letters to Batavia from A. Heussen and B. de Gruijter in Masulipatam and A. Gardenijs in Pulicat, 1642. Two folders.
204	Letter of A. Gardenijs in Pulicat to J.D. Gale off Goa, 1642. One piece.
207-11	Letters of A. Heussen and B. de Gruijter and A. Gardenijs from Masulipatam to Vengurla, Surat and Pulicat, 1640-2. Four pieces and a folder.
212-13	Letters of A. Gardenijs from Pulicat to Surat and Vengurla, 1641-2. Two pieces.
214	Letter to the Governor by C.L. Blaeu and D. Bouwens lying off Nagappattinam, 1642. One piece.
215	Correspondence of the Coromandel Governor with the Viceroy at Goa and the Portuguese Captain General at St. Thome, 1642. One piece.
230	Lists of prices of merchandise at Masulipatam, 1640-2. One folder.
256	Letter of A. Heussen and B. de Gruijter in Masulipatam to Geleynsen at Goa, 1643. One piece.
301	Letter of P. Sijme at Masulipatam to Geleynssen, 1647. One piece.

Sweers, Van Vliet, Specx, Mannis

See	1.5.3
Access no.:	1.10.78

1, ff. 81-2	Letter of A. Gardenijs in Pulicat to Governor-General Specx, 1632.
2, ff. 21-3	Letter of Governor A. Gardenijs to the GG&C, 1641.
2, ff. 135-6	Letter of Governor L. Pit to S. Sweers, 1661.
3, ff. 163-90	Report (by former Governor C. Reyniersz.) to the Gentlemen XVII on the state of Coromandel, 1639.
4, ff. 73-89	Remonstrance by former Governor A. Gardenijs to the Gentlemen XVII, 1635.
4, ff. 184	Remonstrance by J. Specx and P. Lucasz. in defence of their brother-in-law A. Gardenijs, 1634.

Hudde

See 1.5.5
Access no.: 1.10.48

39 Message of the Gentlemen XVII to the States General in response to the questions asked by the English envoy d'Albyville on events at Masulipatam and in Sumatra, 1687. Printed, one volume.

Van Eck

See 1.5.12
Access no.: 1.10.106

12 Letters received at Porto Novo, 1749, 1751-4. One folder.
13-19 Letters received at Pulicat, 1754-8. Two folders and five pieces.
20 Contains letters sent by L.J. van Eck during his term as Governor of Coromandel, 1758-61.
21 Letter of L.J. van Eck, 1758. One piece.
22, 24 (Extracts of) letters to Governor S. Vermont on facilitating the promotion of Van Eck and on the calicoe trade, 1755-6. Two pieces.
25-8 Letters received by Van Eck at Pulicat, 1758-61. Two folders and two bundles.
29 Letters of J. Visscher in Palakollu and J. Theodorick in Masulipatam, 1760 and n.d. Two pieces.
45 Translation of a letter sent to 'Soukaar Letjeme Daassoe' by someone with the army of Rasu (Raja) Ananda, on the siege of the 'Pettapoeram' fortress (Peddapuram or Pithapuram?) in the vicinity of Vijayawada, with a PS (by Van Eck?) concerning gifts to be presented to himself and to Hagemeister by Appanna, the *Diwan* of Rasu Ananda, n.d. One piece.

Van Ghesel

See 1.5.13
Access no.: 1.10.31

191 Report on the flight of the discharged Governor Van Teylingen, 1764. Two pieces, identical copies.

Baud

See 1.5.14
Access no.: 2.21.007.58

1048 Letter from the Gentlemen XVII to the GG&C concerning the damage inflicted on the textile trade of the VOC by the different calculations of the *pagoda* by the servants of the VOC and the EIC at Coromandel, 1678. One piece.

Pantaleon van Eck

See 1.5.15
Access no.: 1.10.65.01

54 Deed appointing L.J. van Eck to the position of *opperkoopman* in Pulicat 1755. One piece.
55 Letter book of Governor L.J. van Eck, 1758-61. With appendices, one portfolio.
56 Deed appointing L.J. van Eck to the position of Governor. One piece.

Cort van der Linden

See 1.5.16
Access no.: 2.21.040

429 Letters from Ph.F. Cort and his wife Adriana Catharina Engelbert van Bevervoorde, to their father (and father-in-law) Gijsbert Cort, sent from Nagappattinam, Batavia and the Cape of Good Hope, with a death announcement, dated 25 August 1752, of Ph.F. Cort at Nagappattinam, 1745-52. 23 pieces in one folder.
453 Letters from Ph.F. Cort to his parents and brother, with birth certificate of his wife Adriana Catharina Engelbert van Bevervoorde (who was baptised and passed away at Nagappattinam in June 1731 and December 1750 respectively) and a list of goods taken along in 1744 from the Dutch Republic, 1731-51. Fourteen pieces in one folder.
454 Letters from Ph.F. Cort, with an excerpt from the *resoluties* of 24 August 1750 of the Council of Coromandel (with Cort as President) concerning a civil dispute with Pieter van Son, President of the Council of Justice, 1747-51. Seven pieces in one folder.
455-64 Papers of and concerning Anna Euphemia Cort (baptised at Nagappattinam November 1750, daughter of Ph.F. Cort and Adriana Catharina Engelbert van Bevervoorde), mostly regarding her becoming an orphan (1952 in Coromandel), her possessions and her education, 1750-79. Five pieces, four folders, one volume.

Hope

See 1.5.17
Access no.: 1.10.46

92 Notes and excerpts concerning Coromandel for the *Haags verbaal*, 1755-70, and extracts from letters of the Gentlemen XVII to Coromandel, 1765-8. One folder.
94 Relation of the arrival of Governor P. Haksteen in Coromandel and the flight of C. van Teylingen, with some papers concerning the latter, 1765-7. One folder.

Van Plettenberg

See 1.5.18
Access no.: 1.10.67

15 Letters received from E. Hughes in Nagappattinam and Madras, 1780. Two pieces.

Van Slingelandt - De Vrij Temminck

See 1.5.20
Access no.: 3.20.52

566 Folder no. 57 contains a letter from the Gentlemen XVII to Governor Christiaan van Teylingen, 1763. One piece.
567 Folder no. 90 contains papers concerning Nagappattinam and the demand of the British for free sailing in the eastern seas, 1783-5. Eight pieces.

Bleiswijk

See 1.5.21
Access no.: 3.01.25

238 Excerpt from a report concerning a war between the British and the Marathas under the command of Haidar Ali (Khan of Mysore?), in which the Marathas were threatened by the loss of Arcot and Malabar, 1780. One piece, partly in French.
239 Papers concerning agreements entered into by the VOC about the trade with and the use of Nagore and 'Kiwalore', 1773. Seven pieces.
511 Excerpts from the *secrete resoluties* of the States General and the States of various provinces concerning the demands of Great Britain with respect to the possession of Nagappattinam (remarks which the States feel should be rejected lest the VOC perish), with appendices partly in French, 1783. One folder.
512 Excerpt from the *secrete resoluties* of the States of Holland and West-Friesland, consisting of the decision not to transfer Nagappattinam to Great Britain but to make other concessions, 1783. One piece.

Van Braam

See 1.5.22
Access no.: 1.10.11.02

119 Report of A. Kuvel on the restoration to the VOC of the factories captured by the British on the Coromandel Coast, 1785. One piece.
121 Report of J.S. Stavorius, Commander of the warship Goes, on his voyage from Trincomalee and his actions in Coromandel, 1785. One folder.
314 An eyewitness account of the battle of 13 June 1783 near Cuddalore

between the British under General Stuardt and the French under De Bussy, both with their local allies. One piece, in French.

Van der Heim

See 1.5.24
Access no.: 1.10.39

94 Papers concerning the case against J. Hazelkamp, former VOC servant at Nagappattinam, 1780. One folder.

Radermacher

See 1.5.27
Access no.: 1.10.69

499 Calculation of the profits made under Governor D. van Cloon, 1724-8. One piece.

Alting

See 1.5.29
Access no.: 1.10.03

31 Judicial roll of Nagappattinam, 1738-40. One volume.
48 Questioning on the pillage and burning of the VOC lodge at Bimlipatam, 1756. Fifteen folios.

Brugmans

See 1.5.30
Access no.: 1.10.13

103 Papers concerning the trial of J. Haselkamp, former Cashier of the Nagappattinam factory, 1765-80. One folder.

Ver Huell

See 1.5.32
Access no.: 2.21.004.04

21 Report by J.O. Vaillant, C.A. Ver Huell and J.F.L. Graevestein (the Military Commission) concerning their activities in Coromandel (and Ceylon and Melaka), 1790. One folder (see also 5.4, *Stadhouderlijke Secretarie*).
33 Report by J.O. Vaillant, C.A. Ver Huell and J.F.L. Graevestein for Stadtholder William V concerning the defence on the Coromandel Coast, 1790. One folder.
34 Memoranda, reports and lists concerning the defence of Coromandel, 1790. One folder.

Nederburgh

See 1.5.33
Access no.: 1.10.59

428 Instruction of H.A. van Rheede to the Governor and Council of Coromandel, 1689. One volume.
429 *Memorie van overgave* by Governor Pieter Håksteen to Reynier van Vlissingen, 1771. One volume.
481 Extract from the *Madras Courrier* concerning the military operations of a French battalion under Mouson, 1804. One piece.
528 Extracts from letters of A. Couperus, prisoner of war of the British at Tranquebar, 1796-1807, on the situation of the British in South Asia (among other subjects), 1805. One piece.
634 Memorandum of the Directors of the VOC to the Supreme Court in the case of J. Hazelkamp, former Cashier at Nagappattinam, 1777-8. One piece.
716 Letter of J. Bourgoigne at Tranquebar, 1797. One piece.
724 Contains a letter of C.L. Eilbracht at Pulicat, 1798.

Van de Graaff (and Van Angelbeek)

See 1.5.36
Access no.: 2.21.074

61 An account by the commander of the ship Rotterdam concerning the events on that ship during the flight of Christiaan van Teylingen, former Governor of Coromandel, 1765. One piece.

5.6. Separate Acquisitions and Microfilms

Losse aanwinsten
Separate acquisitions

See 1.6.1
Access no.: 1.11.01.01

147 Instructions of the Gentlemen XVII (?) to the GG&C concerning Coromandel, 1652-1733. Three volumes (1870 A II).
1512 Letter of Nagappattinam clerk B. Brouwer thanking Governor R. van Vlissingen for his kind recommendation, 1773. One piece (1925 IV 17).
2045 Letter of Nagappattinam merchant R. van Vlissingen to P.C. Hasselaar about the VOC's wartime misfortunes in Coromandel with appended translations of various deeds done by the Nawab of Arcot and the Raja of 'Tansjanagaram' (Thanjavur?), including a letter of the Maratha chief Raghunath Rao, etc., 1771-3. Two thin volumes.

5.7. Maps and Drawings

Verzameling buitenlandse kaarten, Leupe (VEL)
Foreign map collection, Leupe

See 1.7.1
Access no.: 4.VEL

1077 Map of the voyage of Pieter Smith, from Pulicat via Masulipatam to Golkonda, from where he travelled overland through the Carnatic, 1671-2. Detailed map with notes (see also inv. no. 1078).

1078 Copy of inv. no. 1077, seventeenth century. Map of the realm of Thanjavur. Originating from the 'Atlas Amsterdam' or 'Atlas de Graaff'.

1079 Little map of the land between Pondicherry and Madras, 1698. Received from Batavia, 1699.

1080 Plan of the outline of the new Fort De Vijf Sinnen, Nagappattinam, 1705. With detailed legend. Plan of the old Portuguese city, 1705.

1081 Plan of the bulwarks of Nagappattinam, 1705, with detailed legend.

1082 Plan of Nagappattinam, eighteenth century, with legend accompanying the different works, for example mosques. Originating from the 'Atlas Amsterdam' or 'Atlas de Graaff'.

1083 Plan of Fort De Vijf Sinnen at Nagappattinam, eighteenth century, with detailed explanations. Originating from the 'Atlas Amsterdam' or 'Atlas de Graaff'.

1084 Profile of Fort De Vijf Zinnen, 1720. Originating from the 'Atlas Amsterdam' or 'Atlas de Graaff'.

1086 Plan of a fort, designed by the French in Karikal, eighteenth century. Received from Coromandel, 1740.

1087 Plan of the factory at Sadras, seventeenth century. With legend. Drawing of the factory, mentioned above. Plan from the factory to Porto Novo. Drawing of the factory, mentioned above. Originating from the 'Atlas Amsterdam' or 'Atlas de Graaff'.

1088 Plan of Tiruchirappalli and surroundings, with the encampments of the British (commanded by Colonel Stringer Lawrence) and the French army, in the years 1753-4, by John Roque, 1757. Copperplate print.

1089 Plan of Pulicat, showing Fort Geldria and the adjacent fisherman's village 'De Coepangh', seventeenth century, with profile and legend. Originating from the 'Atlas Amsterdam' or 'Atlas de Graaff'.

1090 Plan of Fort Geldria at Pulicat, 1708. With profile and legend.

1091 Plan of Pulicat and surroundings, eighteenth century. With legend.

1092 Plan of the fortress of Pulicat, eighteenth century.

1093 Plan of Pulicat, by H.C. van der Hoff, eighteenth century. With profile.

1094 Map of the district of Pondicherry, seventeenth century. With legend. Map of the siege of Pondicherry. Plan of the fort in Pondicherry. Originating from the 'Atlas Amsterdam' or 'Atlas de Graaff'.

1095 Map of the siege of the city and the fort of Pondicherry, seventeenth century. With detailed legend. Originating from the 'Atlas Amsterdam' or 'Atlas de Graaff'.

1096 Situation-plan of the city and the fort of Pondicherry, seventeenth century. With detailed legend. Originating from the 'Atlas Amsterdam' or 'Atlas de Graaff'.

1097 Plan of the fortress and the city of Pondicherry, with its surrounding villages and rivers, by surveyor Jacob Verbergmoes, 1694. With legend.

1098 Plan of the city and the fortress of Pondicherry, 1694. With instructions on how to renovate the city.

1099 Plan of the fortress Pondicherry without the external works, as it was in the period of the conquests, 1694 (?).

Verzameling buitenlandse kaarten, supplement, Leupe-l'Honoré Naber (VELH)
Foreign map collection, supplement, Leupe-l'Honoré Naber

See 1.7.2
Access no.: 4.VELH

116 Map of the Coromandel Coast, between 'Octacar' and Masulipatam, 1666 (?). Originating from the journal of Michiel Gerritsz. Boos.

117 Map of the Coromandel Coast, between 'Calbelon' and 'Calletoere' (Caliatur, i.e. Krishnapatnam?), 1666 (?). Originating from the journal of Michiel Gerritsz. Boos.

325 Map of the road from the Coromandel Coast to the interior, by Colin Mackenzie, 1788. Copperplate print.

Departement van Marine, centraal archief, Leupe (MCAL)
Ministry of Naval Affairs, central archives, Leupe

See 1.7.3
Access no.: 4.MCAL

4224 Plan of Nancowry harbour (Nicobar Islands) from a survey, by Captain Alexander Kyd, 1792.

4307 Survey of the Pulicat shoals, by John Goldingham, 1792. With views.

4310 Correct chart of the river and bay of Nagore, by Thomas Dibdin, 1779. With legend.

4318 Plan of the Bay of Bengal, Andaman Islands, surveyed by Lieutenant Blair and Captain Moorsom, 1790.

4319 Plan of Port Campbell on the Andaman Islands, by Lieutenant Blair, 1789. With views by J. Wales. Including:
- a Old Port Cornwallis on the Andaman Islands.
- b The south-west part of the port from 'Mask I'.
- c The north-west part of the port from 'Mask I'.

4320 Plan of Port Meadows on the Andaman Islands, by Edward Cooke, 1792. With instruction.

4321 Plan of a strait through the great Andaman Islands, by John Wales, 1795.

4322 Plan of the north-east harbour on the great Andaman Islands, surveyed by Archibald Blair, 1791. Including:

Plan of the coast of the great Andaman Islands.

4330 Plan of the island Car Nicobar, by Phineas Hunt, 1769.

Topografische Dienst en rechtsvoorgangers (TOPO)
Topographic Service and legal predecessors

See 1.7.6
Access no.: 4.TOPO

16A-421 Outline relating to Tranquebar, by Matthias Seutter, n.d.

16A-422 Plan and view of Fort Dansborg at Tranquebar, by Matthaeus Seutter, n.d.

Collectie Bergsma (BMF)
Bergsma collection

See 1.7.7
Access no.: 4.BMF

431 Map of the Coromandel Coast, early nineteenth century. With legend.

440 Map of the environs of Madras, surveyed by W. Faden, 1814.

441 Map of Pondicherry, third-quarter of the eighteenth century. With legend.

Aanwinsten
Acquisitions

See 1.7.9
Access no.: 4.AANW

221 Drawing of Gerrit van Westrenen, Governor of Coromandel, and his family, going on a trip accompanied by a military escort. Offered as a new-year's greeting by the drummers in the garrison of Nagappattinam, 1724.

1418 Fort Geldria in Pulicat, seventeenth century. See also Schouten, *Oost-Indische voyagie*, p. 289 (see Bibliography, no. 48 and *Verzameling buitenlandse kaarten, Leupe* (*VEL*), inv. nos 1089-93).

Zeeland Chamber; miscellaneous

See 5.2.2
Access no.: 1.04.02

VOC 11285 Includes a map of part of the southern Coromandel Coast and its hinterland, facing f. 116, 1706.

Hoge Regering te Batavia
High Government at Batavia

See 1.3.1
Access no.: 1.04.17

361 Includes a map of the Coromandel Coast, 1792.

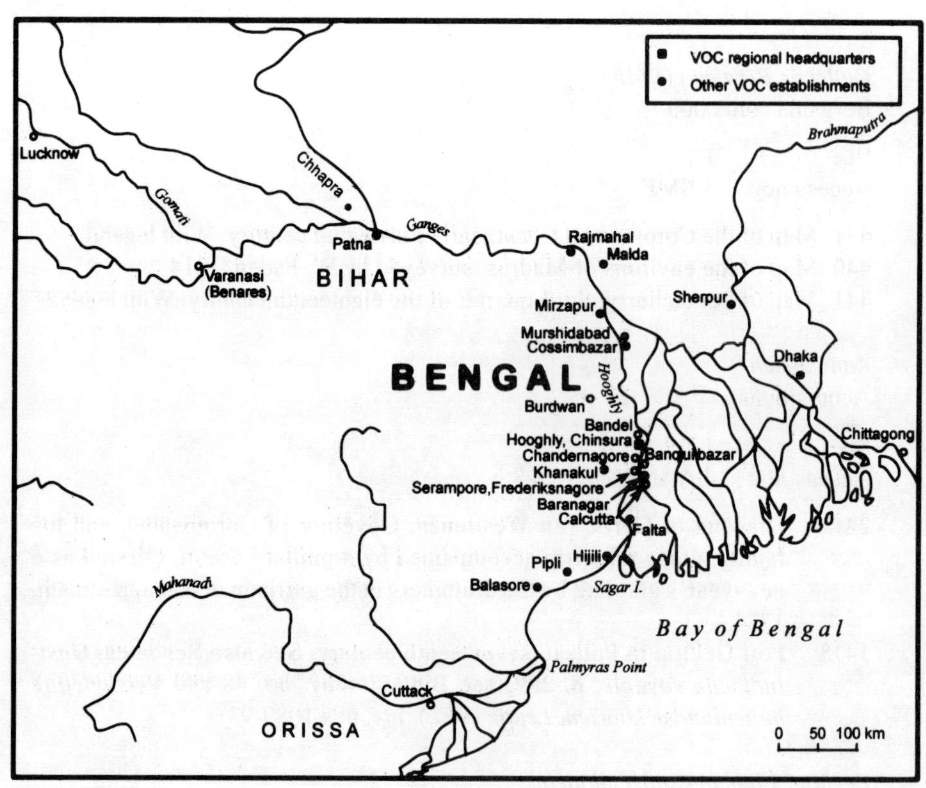

Map 6. The VOC in Bengal

6. BENGAL (including Bihar)

INTRODUCTION

The VOC administration in Bengal stretched from Balasore in Orissa to Dhaka in eastern Bengal. It also maintained factories in the interior, mainly along the river Hooghly and as far as Patna in Bihar. At first, the Bengal factories were managed from Coromandel with Pipli and Hooghly as the main local centres. In 1655 Bengal was made a separate division under a *Directeur*, based (from 1656) at the village of Chinsura near Hooghly.

The Dutch started to explore the region in 1607 but only settled down in the late 1620s when they acquired a *caul* for a factory at Pipli from the local *Faujdar* in the name of the Nawab of Orissa. A few years later, the Dutch received a *caul* from the Mughal *Subahdar* of Bengal, later to be confirmed by an imperial *farman*, which led to the establishment of the factories at Hooghly (1635) and Patna (1638). After a temporary withdrawal to Pipli and Balasore on the coast of Orissa, the Company returned to Bengal after 1645, reopening its factories at Hooghly and Patna and setting up new ones at Cossimbazar, Dhaka and Udaiganj. Later the VOC established, often temporary, stations at places like Khanakul, Malda, Baranagar, Rajmahal, Karimabad (in Murshidabad), Chhapra, Sherpur, Mirzapur, Hijili and Falta. After about 1750 the trading activities of the VOC in Bengal came under the ever tightening supervision of the British. As with many of their other South Asian establishments, the Dutch had to abandon their Bengal factories between 1781 and 1784, again between 1795 and 1817, and finally after 1825.

The Dutch in Bengal maintained close relations with the various levels of the Mughal state: mainly the local authorities near the various factories or the increasingly autonomous provincial *Subahdars* based at Dhaka or Murshidabad. There were also occasional contacts with the Rajas of Burdwan and the Nawabs of Awadh.

6.1. *Overgekomen Brieven en Papieren (OBP)*
Letters and Papers Received

See 1.1.7
Access no.: 1.04.02
Inv. nos: VOC 1053-3987

Letters and papers concerning Bengal are mostly to be found under the heading 'Bengale' or 'Bengalen'. These headings occur in the volumes containing documents sent directly from South Asia to the Gentlemen XVII and the Amsterdam Chamber, as well as the volumes that consist of copies of documents sent from South Asia to Batavia in *Batavia's ingekomen brievenboek* (Batavia letterbook of incoming documents). In a few cases, letters and papers relating to Bengal may also be found under the heading 'Batavia'.

6.1.1. *Memories van overgave* (final reports)

VOC 1212, ff. 211-25	Commissioner Joan Verpoorten to *Directeur* Pieter Sterthemius, October 1655.
VOC 1271-3, ff. 2029-180	*Opperhoofd* Pieter Hoffmeester at Pipli to Abraham Wijns, August 1669.
VOC 1275-8, ff. 1421-7	Chief-factor Jacobus Verburgh at Patna to Jacobus Salderus, December 1669.
VOC 1569, ff. 44-53	*Directeur* Arnoldus Muijkens to Pieter van Dijxhoek, February 1695.
VOC 1796, ff. 123-48	*Directeur* Willem de Roo to Anthonij Huijsman, *c.* 1710.
VOC 1889, ff. 1356-71	*Directeur* Anthonij Huijsman to Ewout van Dieshoeck, November 1717.
VOC 1896, ff. 176-?	*Directeur* Anthonij Huijsman to Ewout van Dishoek, November 1717.
VOC 1981, ff. 188?-206	*Directeur* Ewout van Dishoek to Petrus Vuijst, *c.* 1722.
VOC 2196, ff. 419-32	*Directeur* Jacob Sadelijn to Rogier Berenaart, January 1732.
VOC 2763, ff. 447-70	*Directeur* Jan Huijgens to Jan Kerseboom, *c.* 1750.
VOC 2849, ff. 89-138	*Directeur* Jan Kersseboom to Louis Taillefert, February 1755.
VOC 2849, ff. 139-275	*Directeur* Louis Taillefert to Adriaan Bisdom, *c.* 1755.
VOC 2862, n.f.	*Directeur* Jan Kersseboom to Louis Taillefert, February 1755.
VOC 2977, ff. 784-814	*Directeur* Adriaan Bisdom to Louis Taillefert, November 1760.
VOC 3075, ff. 1316-1478	*Directeur* Louis Taillefert to George Lodewijk Vernet, November 1763.
VOC 3284, ff. 610-713	*Directeur* George Lodewijk Vernet to Boudewijn Versewel Faure, March 1770.
VOC 3473, ff. 557-679	*Directeur* Johannes Bacheracht to Johannes Mattheus Ross, July 1776 (with appendices, 1777).

6.1.2. *Resoluties* (proceedings)

VOC 1242, ff. 886-90	1663.
VOC 1242, ff. 913-19	1663.
VOC 1251, ff. 1475-6	1665.
VOC 1251, ff. 1798-9	1665.
VOC 1256, ff. 655-6	1666.
VOC 1279, ff. 658-9	1671.
VOC 1281-1284, ff. 951-4	Concerning the journey of Commissioner Willem Volger, 1671.

VOC 1288, ff. 125-46	Concerning the conflict with Malik Qasim, 1672.
VOC 1299, ff. 617-29	*c.* 1674.
VOC 1302-1303, ff. 354-5	1674.
VOC 1304, ff. 178-9	1674.
VOC 1307, ff. 586-95	Concerning Cossimbazar, *c.* 1675
VOC 1313, ff. 104-5	1675.
VOC 1315, f. 579	1676.
VOC 1315, f. 654	1676.
VOC 1316, f. 576	1676.
VOC 1322, f. 1343	1676.
VOC 1324, ff. 455-6	1677.
VOC 1328, ff. 485v-7	Concerning Nawab Shaista Khan, 1677.
VOC 1330, ff. 856-8	1677.
VOC 1378, ff. 1305-9	1682.
VOC 1378, ff. 1409-14	1681-2.
VOC 1384, ff. 603-5	1683.
VOC 1384, ff. 826-43	1683.
VOC 1387, ff. 1185v-6	1683.
VOC 1397, ff. 86-117	1684.
VOC 1397, f. 209	1684.
VOC 1448, ff. 200-2	1688.
VOC 1459, ff. 810-18	1689-90.
VOC 1463, ff. 98v-9	Concerning the English at Dhaka, 1689.
VOC 1471, ff. 183-4v	1689.
VOC 1471, ff. 465-82	Concerning the French, *c.* 1690 (among other documents).
VOC 1493, f. 197	1690.
VOC 1518, ff. 558-9v	Concerning the factory at Patna, 1692.
VOC 1545, ff. 175-249	1693-4.
VOC 1569, ff. 63-4	1695.
VOC 1581, ff. 98-102	Concerning war vessels, 1696.
VOC 1581, ff. 54-6	Concerning enemy vessels, 1696.
VOC 1586, ff. 481-4	1696.
VOC 1656, ff. 1379-83	1702.
VOC 1664, ff. 112-18	1702.
VOC 1674, ff. 19-28	1703.
VOC 1678, ff. 75-8	Cossimbazar, 1703.
VOC 1692, ff. 16-24	1704.
VOC 1712, ff. 73-86	*c.* 1705.
VOC 1753, f. 259	1708.
VOC 1849, ff. 193-6	1714.
VOC 1962, ff. 191-5	1721.
VOC 2022, ff. 2543-4	1725.
VOC 2022, ff. 2551-64	1725.
VOC 2022, ff. 2568-9	1725.

VOC 2022, ff. 2649-54	1725.
VOC 2023, f. 3039	1725.
VOC 2030, ff. 96-101	1725.
VOC 2030, ff. 13-18	1725.
VOC 2039, ff. 1915-27	1725.
VOC 2041, ff. 2969-3014	1726.
VOC 2041, ff. 3158-9	Concerning Japanese copper, 1726.
VOC 2052, ff. 93-103	Hooghly and Cossimbazar, 1726.
VOC 2052, ff. 225-9	Patna, 1726.
VOC 2052, ff. 301-8	1726.
VOC 2052, ff. 261-308	1726.
VOC 2052, ff. 479-94	1726.
VOC 2062, ff. 3067-108	1726-7.
VOC 2062, ff. 3375-544	1727.
VOC 2063, ff. 4052-133	1727-8.
VOC 2075, ff. 201-16	1727.
VOC 2075, ff. 304-6	1727.
VOC 2075, ff. 535-43	1727.
VOC 2085, ff. 1842-1933	1727-8.
VOC 2089, ff. 3865-986	1728.
VOC 2090, ff. 4258-86	1728.
VOC 2114, ff. 3359-452	1728-9.
VOC 2122, ff. 6949-7203	1729-30 (among other documents).
VOC 2147, ff. 5269-373	1729-30.
VOC 2165, ff. 181-452	1729.
VOC 2166, ff. 45-122	1729.
VOC 2195, ff. 97-210	1730-1.
VOC 2195, ff. 654-714	1730-1.
VOC 2196, ff. 211-446	1731.
VOC 2196, ff. 1051-65	*c.* 1731.
VOC 2196, ff. 39-72	1731-2.
VOC 2196, ff. 19-32	1731.
VOC 2196, ff. 49-100	1731.
VOC 2214, ff. 5409-633	1732 (among other documents).
VOC 2241, ff. 121-702?	1732.
VOC 2241, ff. 1281-1306	1732.
VOC 2242, ff. 273-796	1732.
VOC 2288, ff. 165-361	1732-3.
VOC 2288, ff. 39-77	1733.
VOC 2288, ff. 43-110	1733-4.
VOC 2316, ff. 206-384	1734.
VOC 2316, ff. 611-780	1734.
VOC 2316, ff. 314-688	1734.
VOC 2348, ff. 262-586	1734-5.
VOC 2348, ff. 798-882	1735.
VOC 2348, ff. 153-424	*c.* 1735.

VOC 2348, ff. 571-4	Concerning conch shells, 1735.
VOC 2385, ff. 173-432	1735-6.
VOC 2385, ff. 250-600	1736.
VOC 2411, ff. 197-462	Partially recorded at Cossimbazar and Patna, 1736-7.
VOC 2440, ff. 123-674	1737-8.
VOC 2440, ff. 1004-1214	1738.
VOC 2440, ff. 1396-1412	Concerning vessels, *c.* 1738.
VOC 2441, ff. 239-648	1738.
VOC 2455, ff. 344-6	1739.
VOC 2469, ff. 21-96	1738.
VOC 2469, ff. 291-438	1738-9.
VOC 2469, ff. 53-274	1739.
VOC 2469, ff. 516-686	1739.
VOC 2489, ff. 35-9	Concerning saltpetre, 1740.
VOC 2489, ff. 269-86	1740.
VOC 2504, ff. 131?-389	1739-40.
VOC 2504, ff. 66-75	1740.
VOC 2504, ff. 185-424	1740.
VOC 2504, ff. 697-1005	1740.
VOC 2504, ff. 1091-5	1740.
VOC 2518, ff. 346-510	*c.* 1741 (among other documents).
VOC 2537, ff. 54-173	1740-1.
VOC 2537, ff. 421-576	1741.
VOC 2537, ff. 1171-1806	1741.
VOC 2556, ff. 249-332	1742 (among other documents).
VOC 2556, ff. 643-4	*c.* 1742.
VOC 2556, ff. 658-62	*c.* 1742.
VOC 2571, ff. 19-23	1741.
VOC 2571, ff. 187-392	1741-2.
VOC 2572, ff. 275-904	1742.
VOC 2594, ff. 15-17	1743.
VOC 2594, ff. 345-477	1742-3 (among other documents).
VOC 2608, ff. 217-?	1742-3.
VOC 2608, ff. 117-?	1743.
VOC 2629, ff. 189-698	1743.
VOC 2629, ff. 787-908	1743-4.
VOC 2629, ff. 1034-46	1744.
VOC 2641, ff. 142-7	1745-6.
VOC 2651, ff. 403-1150	1744-5.
VOC 2651, ff. 1223-?	1745.
VOC 2661, ff. 11-33	1746 (among other documents).
VOC 2661, ff. 181-4	Concerning the condition of a vessel, *c.* 1746.
VOC 2676, ff. 189-658	1745.
VOC 2676, ff. 907-?	1746.
VOC 2689, ff. 130-4	1747.

VOC 2689, ff. 164-5	*c.* 1747.
VOC 2689, f. 178	*c.* 1747.
VOC 2701, ff. 97-453	1747.
VOC 2701, ff. 488-692	1746-7.
VOC 2701, ff. 813-?	1747.
VOC 2707, ff. 13-20	1746.
VOC 2707, ff. 230-1	1747.
VOC 2711, ff. 144-6	*c.* 1748.
VOC 2719, ff. 183-782	1747.
VOC 2719, ff. 909-?	1747-8.
VOC 2726, ff. 25-67	1747.
VOC 2732, ff. 132-7	*c.* 1749.
VOC 2743, ff. 105-394	1748.
VOC 2743, ff. 593-?	1748-9.
VOC 2750, ff. 23-66	1748.
VOC 2750, ff. 364-82	1749.
VOC 2750, ff. 397-407	1749.
VOC 2754, ff. 29-32	*c.* 1750.
VOC 2763, ff. 119-398	1749-50.
VOC 2763, ff. 471-585	1750.
VOC 2767, ff. 377-464	1749-50.
VOC 2767, ff. 472-?	1750.
VOC 2771, ff. 34-39	1751.
VOC 2771, ff. 171-7	1751.
VOC 2783, ff. 185-574	1750-1.
VOC 2783, ff. 717-?	1751.
VOC 2783, ff. 49-320	1751.
VOC 2788, ff. 23-228	*c.* 1751.
VOC 2788, ff. 237-?	*c.* 1751.
VOC 2794, ff. 9-16	1752.
VOC 2800, ff. 97-212	1751-2.
VOC 2800, ff. 259-342	1752.
VOC 2811, ff. 26-8	*c.* 1753.
VOC 2811, ff. 48-54	*c.* 1753.
VOC 2821, ff. 37-376	1752.
VOC 2821, ff. 461-602	1753.
VOC 2829, ff. 119-24	1754.
VOC 2829, ff. 138-41	*c.* 1754.
VOC 2829, ff. 282-4	*c.* 1754.
VOC 2840, ff. 41-390	1753.
VOC 2840, ff. 539-734	1753-4.
VOC 2844, ff. 351-?	*c.* 1753-4.
VOC 2849, ff. 389-92	*c.* 1755.
VOC 2849, ff. 418-23	*c.* 1755.
VOC 2850, ff. 560-982	1755.
VOC 2850, ff. 985-1023	1755 (among other documents).

VOC 2862, ff. 169-568	1754.
VOC 2862, ff. 649-834	1754.
VOC 2862, ff. 921-1078	1755.
VOC 2862, n.f.	1755.
VOC 2865, ff. 13-134	1754.
VOC 2871, ff. 35-41	1756.
VOC 2872, n.f.	1756.
VOC 2873, n.f.	Concerning bookkeeping, *c.* 1756.
VOC 2874, ff. 333-6	*c.* 1756.
VOC 2874, ff. 368-71	*c.* 1756.
VOC 2894, ff. 8-12	*c.* 1757.
VOC 2894, ff. 174-201	*c.* 1757 (among other documents).
VOC 2894, ff. 211-15	*c.* 1757.
VOC 2895, ff. 1?-877	1757.
VOC 2917, ff. 11-14	1758.
VOC 2917, ff. 146-58	*c.* 1758.
VOC 2918, ff. 1-673	1758.
VOC 2920, ff. 1104-97	Partially concerning the British, 1757-8.
VOC 2950, n.f.	1759-60.
VOC 2975, ff. 16-26	1760.
VOC 2975, ff. 191-7	*c.* 1760.
VOC 2975, ff. 202-440	1760.
VOC 2976, ff. 587-603	Concerning textiles, 1760.
VOC 2976, ff. 654-7	1760.
VOC 2977, ff. 666-701	1760.
VOC 2977, ff. 821-943	1760.
VOC 3004, ff. 1-4	1761 (among other documents).
VOC 3004, ff. 17-34	1761.
VOC 3004, ff. 70-9	1761.
VOC 3004, ff. 336-536	1760.
VOC 3005, ff. 537-1432	1761.
VOC 3006, ff. 1840-9	Concerning textiles, 1761-2.
VOC 3008, ff. 2590-7	Concerning bookkeeping, *c.* 1761.
VOC 3009, ff. 2759-918	1760-1.
VOC 3036, ff. 16-38	1762.
VOC 3037, ff. 386-821	1761-3.
VOC 3039, ff. 977-1117	1761-2.
VOC 3040, ff. 1326-7	Patna, 1762.
VOC 3040, f. 1368	1762.
VOC 3041, ff. 1758-63	Concerning bookkeeping, 1762.
VOC 3067, ff. 605-25	Concerning textiles, *c.* 1763 (among other documents).
VOC 3071, ff. 14-22	1763.
VOC 3071, ff. 152-222	1763.
VOC 3072, ff. 402-22	1763.
VOC 3072, ff. 431-42	1763.

VOC 3072, ff. 576B-620	Concerning bookkeeping, 1763.
VOC 3073, ff. 662-?	1762-3.
VOC 3074, ff. 766-1083	1763.
VOC 3075, ff. 1246-1315	1762-3.
VOC 3103, ff. 11-19	1764.
VOC 3103, ff. 74-102	1763-4.
VOC 3104, ff. 321-831	1763-4.
VOC 3105, ff. 832-5	Concerning creditors, 1764.
VOC 3106, ff. 1327-8	1764.
VOC 3106, ff. 1365-1409	1764-5.
VOC 3106, ff. 1566-72	Concerning bookkeeping, 1763-4.
VOC 3130, ff. 13-19	1765.
VOC 3130, ff. 225-8	Concerning debtors, 1765.
VOC 3130, ff. 300-8	1765.
VOC 3130, ff. 311-50	1764-5.
VOC 3131, ff. 401-874	1764-5.
VOC 3132, ff. 1199-1203	Concerning bookkeeping, 1765.
VOC 3133, f. 1261	1765.
VOC 3133, ff. 1310-14	1765.
VOC 3167, ff. 57-99	1766.
VOC 3167, ff. 270-302	1766.
VOC 3167, ff. 422-34	1766.
VOC 3168, ff. 437-955	1765-6.
VOC 3169, ff. 1204-9	Concerning bookkeeping, 1766.
VOC 3170, ff. 1412-85	1766-7.
VOC 3192, ff. 100-18	1767.
VOC 3193, ff. 371-81	1767.
VOC 3193, ff. 402-7	1767.
VOC 3193, ff. 606-12	1767-8.
VOC 3194, ff. 694-835	1767.
VOC 3195, ff. 883-1037	1766.
VOC 3195, ff. 1176-1245	1767.
VOC 3196, ff. 1246-?	1767.
VOC 3226, ff. 38-51	1768.
VOC 3226, ff. 108-38	1768.
VOC 3226, ff. 327-79	1768.
VOC 3226, ff. 531-6	1768-9.
VOC 3227, ff. 567-75	1768.
VOC 3227, ff. 611-14	1768-9.
VOC 3228, ff. 1-?	1768.
VOC 3255, ff. 9-14	Concerning debtors, 1769.
VOC 3255, ff. 103-82	1769.
VOC 3256, ff. 634-43	1770.
VOC 3257, ff. 788a-824	1769-70.
VOC 3258, n.f.	1769.
VOC 3279, ff. 632-4	1770.

VOC 3283, ff. 43-53	1770.
VOC 3283, ff. 138-258	1769-70.
VOC 3284, ff. 583-611	1770.
VOC 3285, n.f.	1770.
VOC 3286, n.f.	Concerning bookkeeping, 1769-71.
VOC 3288, ff. 1209-25	1770-1.
VOC 3316, ff. 10-17	1771.
VOC 3316, ff. 79-102	1771.
VOC 3316, ff. 457-60	1771.
VOC 3316, ff. 465-75	1771.
VOC 3317, n.f.	1770-1.
VOC 3319, ff. 544-602	1771.
VOC 3319, ff. 607-21	1771-2.
VOC 3319, ff. 624-34	1771.
VOC 3341, ff. 9-17	1772.
VOC 3342, ff. 353-79	*c.* 1772, 1773 (among other documents).
VOC 3342, ff. 469-647	1771-2.
VOC 3343, n.f.	1771.
VOC 3370, ff. 12-33	1773.
VOC 3370, ff. 90-149	1773.
VOC 3370, ff. 446-55	Concerning bookkeeping, 1774.
VOC 3371, n.f.	1773.
VOC 3395, ff. 18-41	1774-5.
VOC 3395, ff. 133-8	1774.
VOC 3395, ff. 208-10	1775.
VOC 3396, ff. 516-66	1774.
VOC 3396, ff. 592-846	1774.
VOC 3396, f. 855	Concerning bookkeeping, 1775.
VOC 3397, n.f.	1774.
VOC 3425, ff. 26-80	1775.
VOC 3426, ff. 381-451	1775.
VOC 3426, ff. 504-23	1775-6 (among other documents).
VOC 3426, ff. 624-41	1775-6.
VOC 3427, n.f.	1775.
VOC 3451, ff. 171-233	1776.
VOC 3451, ff. 243-51	1776.
VOC 3451, ff. 278-93	1776-7 (among other documents).
VOC 3451, ff. 457-69	1776-7.
VOC 3452, ff. 534-1010	1776.
VOC 3453, n.f.	Concerning bookkeeping, *c.* 1776.
VOC 3478, ff. 11-27	1777.
VOC 3478, ff. 335-443	1777.
VOC 3478, ff. 454-8	1777.
VOC 3479, ff. 579-606	1777.
VOC 3479, ff. 629-72	*c.* 1777 (among other documents).
VOC 3480, ff. 832-79	1777-8.

VOC 3481, n.f.	1777.
VOC 3509, ff. 13-45	1778.
VOC 3509, ff. 184-258	1778.
VOC 3509, ff. 273-4	1778.
VOC 3509, ff. 277-82	Concerning the prevention of diseases on vessels, 1778.
VOC 3509, ff. 350-70	1778.
VOC 3510, n.f.	1778.
VOC 3536, ff. 35-75	1779 (among other documents).
VOC 3536, ff. 322-37	1779.
VOC 3537, ff. 356-70	1779 (among other documents).
VOC 3537, ff. 425-36	1779-80.
VOC 3537, ff. 445-71	1777-9 (among other documents).
VOC 3538, n.f.	1778-9.
VOC 3564, ff. 17-32	1780 (among other documents).
VOC 3564, ff. 90-142	1780.
VOC 3565, ff. 332-557	1780.
VOC 3566, ff. 579-751	1779.
VOC 3610, ff. 36-42	1781.
VOC 3610, ff. 48-9	1781.
VOC 3610, ff. 56-7	1781.
VOC 3610, ff. 65-6	1780.
VOC 3610, ff. 79-104	1781, 1782 (among other documents).
VOC 3659, ff. 230-314	1781, 1782, 1784.
VOC 3659, f. 379	1785.
VOC 3659, ff. 394-5	1785.
VOC 3659, ff. 411-26	1784-5 (among other documents).
VOC 3660, n.f.	1781, 1784.
VOC 3686, ff. 41-176	1785.
VOC 3686, ff. 497-501	1786.
VOC 3687, ff. 594-7	1786.
VOC 3687, ff. 629-42	1785-6.
VOC 3688, n.f.	1785.
VOC 3714, ff. 73-156	1786.
VOC 3715, f. 595	1787.
VOC 3715, ff. 629-44	1786.
VOC 3715, f. 677	1786.
VOC 3716, n.f.	1786.
VOC 3745, ff. 19-34	1785, 1787.
VOC 3745, ff. 99-180	1787.
VOC 3747, n.f.	1787.
VOC 3828, ff. 385-465	1789.
VOC 3829, n.f.	1787.
VOC 3830, n.f.	1787.
VOC 3918, ff. 276-340	1790.
VOC 3918, ff. 378-86	1792 (among other documents).

VOC 3919, n.f.	1790.
VOC 3946, ff. 1646-7	1786.
VOC 3953, n.f.	1791.

6.1.3. *Dagregisters* (diaries)

VOC 1200, ff. 476-83	January 1653.
VOC 1411, ff. 799-811	Dhaka, November-December 1685.
VOC 2153, ff. 8674-819	January-August 1730.
VOC 2165, ff. 959-1016	January-August 1730.
VOC 2195, ff. 379-479	September-December 1731.
VOC 2196, ff. 857-1050	January-August 1731.
VOC 2241, ff. 889-1031	September-December 1731.
VOC 2288, ff. 701-1219	1732.
VOC 2556, ff. 333-571	Hooghly, 1742.
VOC 2920, ff. 1472-1616	Hooghly, January 1757-August 1758.
VOC 3509, ff. 434-49	Hooghly, July-December 1778.

6.1.4. *Shipping lists*

VOC 1261, ff. 723-5	Departure of vessels, *c.* 1667.
VOC 1279, ff. 660-2	Muslim and other vessels that arrived at Balasore, 1671.
VOC 1369, ff. 1285-90	Foreign vessels that departed from Balasore, 1681.
VOC 1378, ff. 1337v-42	Muslim and English vessels that departed from Balasore and Hooghly, 1681-2.
VOC 1378, ff. 1398-1403	Vessels that arrived at and departed from Balasore, 1682.
VOC 1387, ff. 1175v-80	Vessels that departed from Balasore, 1682-3.
VOC 1387, ff. 1263v-6	Vessels that arrived at Balasore, *c.* 1683.
VOC 1403, f. 498	Vessels that arrived at and departed from Balasore, 1683-4.
VOC 1403, ff. 532v-6	Vessels that departed from Balasore, 1683-4.
VOC 1414, ff. 309-12	Vessels that arrived at and departed from Balasore, 1684-5.
VOC 1429, f. 944	Vessels that arrived at and departed from Balasore, *c.* 1686.
VOC 1438, f. 1381v	Vessels that departed from Tuticorin and Galle for Bengal, *c.* 1687.
VOC 1596, ff. 69-71	Vessels that arrived at and departed from Hooghly, 1696-7.
VOC 1596, f. 11	Arrival of foreign vessels, 1697.
VOC 1610, ff. 71-3	Foreign vessels that arrived at and departed from Balasore, 1697-1698.
VOC 1610, ff. 140-?	Foreign vessels that arrived at and departed from Hooghly and Balasore, *c.* 1698.

VOC 1624, ff. 119-24	Arrival and departure of foreign and private vessels, *c.* 1699.
VOC 1624, ff. 88-?	Foreign vessels that arrived at and departed from Hooghly and Balasore, *c.* 1699.
VOC 1638, ff. 89-92	Private vessels that arrived at and departed from Hooghly and Balasore, *c.* 1700.
VOC 1638, ff. 93-?	*c.* 1700.
VOC 1638, f. 16	Private vessels that arrived at Balasore, 1700.
VOC 1645, ff. 52-6	Arrival of various kinds of vessels, 1701.
VOC 1648, ff. 165-?	Private vessels departed from Hooghly and Balasore, 1700-1701.
VOC 1648, ff. 153-4	Arrived English vessels, *c.* 1701.
VOC 1648, ff. 156-61	Indigenous vessels that arrived at and departed from Hooghly and Balasore, 1701.
VOC 1656, ff. 1263-6	Arrival of various kinds of vessels, 1701-2.
VOC 1664, ff. 211-12	Private vessels that departed from Balasore, 1701-2.
VOC 1664, ff. 108-10	Private vessels that arrived at Hooghly, 1702.
VOC 1664, f. 111	Small vessels, 1702.
VOC 1664, ff. 196-?	Arrival of foreign vessels, 1701-2.
VOC 1678, f. 82	1703.
VOC 1689, ff. 59-61	Arrival of private vessels, 1704.
VOC 1692, ff. 80-?	*c.* 1704.
VOC 1704, ff. 66-9	Arrival of various kinds of vessels, 1704-5.
VOC 1712, ff. 66-70	Muslim and other vessels that arrived at Hooghly, 1705.
VOC 1712, ff. 80-5	Departed private vessels, 1704-5.
VOC 1712, ff. 88-9	*c.* 1705.
VOC 1720, ff. 100-1	Foreign vessels, 1705-6.
VOC 1730, f. 112	Indigenous vessels that arrived at Balasore, 1705.
VOC 1730, ff. 184-7	Foreign vessels that arrived at and departed from Hooghly, 1705.
VOC 1730, ff. 70-?	*c.* 1706.
VOC 1730, ff. 56-?	Arrival and departure of vessels, 1706.
VOC 1737, ff. 237-9	Arrival of foreign vessels, *c.* 1707.
VOC 1744, ff. 149-51	Departure of indigenous vessels, 1706.
VOC 1744, ff. 98-9	*c.* 1707.
VOC 1744, ff. 100-5	Arrival of indigenous, foreign and English vessels, 1707.
VOC 1753, ff. 78-80	Arrival and departure of foreign vessels, 1707-8.
VOC 1761, ff. 269-70	Departure of indigenous vessels, 1707-8.
VOC 1761, ff. 153-6	Arrival and departure of indigenous and foreign vessels, 1708.
VOC 1761, ff. 212-?	*c.* 1708.
VOC 1768, ff. 1719-26	Arrival and departure of indigenous and foreign vessels, 1708-9.

VOC 1777, ff. 395-9	Arrival and departure of vessels, 1708-9.
VOC 1777, ff. 286-93	Arrival and departure of indigenous and foreign vessels, 1709.
VOC 1777, ff. 297-?	*c*. 1709.
VOC 1785, ff. 289-92	Arrival and departure of private and sailing vessels, 1709-10.
VOC 1796, ff. 90-6	Departure of vessels, 1709-10.
VOC 1796, ff. 278-83	Arrival and departure of foreign vessels, 1710.
VOC 1803, ff. 681-5	Arrival and departure of indigenous and foreign vessels, 1710-11.
VOC 1818, ff. 126-8	Arrival and departure of indigenous and foreign vessels, *c*. 1712.
VOC 1828, ff. 72-8	Dutch and other foreign vessels that arrived and departed, *c*. 1712.
VOC 1828, ff. 233-5	Indigenous vessels that departed from Hooghly, 1711-12.
VOC 1828, ff. 218-19	Indigenous vessels that arrived from the river Ganges, 1712.
VOC 1835, ff. 212-15	Vessels that arrived at and departed from Hooghly, 1712-13.
VOC 1842, ff. 220-1	Indigenous private vessels that departed from Hooghly, 1712-13.
VOC 1842, ff. 412-?	Private vessels that arrived at Hooghly, 1713.
VOC 1849, ff. 172-5	Vessels that arrived at and departed from Hooghly, 1713-14.
VOC 1854, ff. 158-60	Departure of indigenous vessels, 1713-14.
VOC 1863, ff. 194-7	Arrival and departure of indigenous vessels, *c*. 1715.
VOC 1868, ff. 179-82	Private vessels that arrived at Hooghly, *c*. 1715.
VOC 1868, ff. 183-?	*c*. 1715.
VOC 1877, ff. 202-12	Arrival and departure of vessels, 1716.
VOC 1884, ff. 233-5	Indigenous vessels that arrived at Hooghly, 1716.
VOC 1884, ff. 296-7	*c*. 1716.
VOC 1891, ff. 91-2	Arrival of foreign vessels, 1717.
VOC 1896, f. 137	1717.
VOC 1896, ff. 138-41	Foreign vessels that arrived in the river Ganges, 1717.
VOC 1905, ff. 3-4	Arrival and departure of vessels, 1718.
VOC 1912, ff. 197-200	*c*. 1718.
VOC 1912, f. 201	Foreign indigenous vessels that arrived in the Bengal River, 1718.
VOC 1924, ff. 97-100	Arrival and departure of indigenous vessels, *c*. 1719.
VOC 1938, ff. 103-4	Arrival of foreign vessels, 1720.
VOC 1946, ff. 84-6	Foreign vessels that arrived at Hooghly, 1719.
VOC 1954, ff. 127-9	Arrival of private vessels, 1721.
VOC 1962, f. 34	*c*. 1721.

VOC 1962, ff. 36-41	Arrival and departure of Muslim and other indigenous vessels, *c.* 1721.
VOC 1962, ff. 187-90	Departure of Muslim vessels, 1720-1.
VOC 1972, ff. 135-7	Arrival of foreign vessels, 1722.
VOC 1981, ff. 108-14	Arrival of indigenous vessels, 1721.
VOC 1981, f. 118	1721.
VOC 1981, ff. 324-?	Departure of indigenous vessels, 1721-2.
VOC 1981, ff. 148-9	Arrival of indigenous vessels, 1722.
VOC 1981, f. 187	1722.
VOC 1990, ff. 128-9	Indigenous vessels on the river Ganges, 1723.
VOC 1997, ff. 157-65	Departure of Muslim vessels, 1722-3.
VOC 2007, ff. 284-5	Indigenous vessels on the river Ganges, 1723-4.
VOC 2013, ff. 58-69	Departure of Muslim vessels, 1723-4.
VOC 2024, ff. 157-9	Indigenous vessels on the river Ganges, 1725.
VOC 2030, ff. 108-13	Muslim vessels that departed from the river Ganges, *c.* 1725.
VOC 2030, ff. 170-5	Foreign vessels that arrived on the river Ganges, 1725.
VOC 2043, ff. 104-5	Indigenous vessels on the river Ganges, 1726.
VOC 2052, ff. 127-34	Departure of Muslim vessels, *c.* 1726.
VOC 2052, ff. 213-19	Muslim and other vessels on the river Ganges during the 'southern season', *c.* 1726.
VOC 2065, ff. 193-4	Indigenous vessels on the river Ganges, 1727.
VOC 2075, ff. 513-14	Muslim and other foreign vessels that arrived on the river Ganges, *c.* 1727.
VOC 2075, f. 515	*c.* 1727.
VOC 2101, ff. 137-43	Muslim vessels that departed from the river Ganges, 1727-8.
VOC 2101, ff. 381-5	Muslim and other foreign vessels that arrived on and departed from the river Ganges, *c.* 1728.
VOC 2101, f. 386	*c.* 1728.
VOC 2123, ff. 93-5	Muslim and other indigenous vessels on the river Ganges, 1729.
VOC 2134, ff. 253-5	Muslim vessels that departed during the northern monsoon, *c.* 1729.
VOC 2134, ff. 279-81	Muslim and other foreign vessels that arrived on the river Ganges, *c.* 1729.
VOC 2156, ff. 174-5	Muslim and other indigenous vessels on the river Ganges, 1730.
VOC 2165, ff. 296-300	Muslim vessels that departed from the river Ganges during the northern monsoon, *c.* 1730.
VOC 2165, f. 1131	Muslim and other indigenous vessels on the river Ganges during the 'southern season', *c.* 1730.
VOC 2183, ff. 185-6	Muslim and other indigenous vessels, 1731.
VOC 2195, ff. 625-31	Muslim vessels that departed from the river Ganges, *c.* 1731.

VOC 2196, ff. 1181-3	Muslim and other indigenous vessels on the river Ganges during the 'southern season', *c.* 1731.
VOC 2220, ff. 211-14	Muslim and other indigenous vessels, 1732.
VOC 2241, ff. 1255-63	Muslim vessels that departed from the river Ganges during the northern monsoon, *c.* 1732.
VOC 2242, ff. 1734-60	Muslim and other indigenous vessels on the river Ganges during the 'southern season', *c.* 1732.
VOC 2288, ff. 187-94	Muslim vessels that departed from the Bengal River during the northern monsoon, *c.* 1733.
VOC 2304, f. 211	British vessels departed from Calcutta, 1734.
VOC 2304, f. 212	French and private vessels that arrived at Chandernagore, *c.* 1734.
VOC 2304, ff. 213-14	Muslim and other foreign vessels that arrived on the river Ganges, *c.* 1734.
VOC 2316, ff. 1040-6	Muslim and other vessels that arrived on the river Ganges, 1734.
VOC 2316, ff. 933-40	British, French and Muslim vessels, *c.* 1734 (among other documents).
VOC 2348, ff. 762-9	Indigenous vessels that departed from the river Ganges during the northern monsoon, *c.* 1735.
VOC 2348, ff. 508-9	Vessels that sailed from Calcutta to Hooghly, *c.* 1735.
VOC 2348, f. 510	French and private vessels that arrived at Chandernagore, 1735.
VOC 2348, ff. 511-12	Muslim and other foreign vessels that arrived on the river Ganges during the southern monsoon, 1735.
VOC 2385, ff. 640-1	Indigenous vessels that departed from the river Ganges, *c.* 1736.
VOC 2399, ff. 254-60	British, French, Muslim and other indigenous vessels that arrived or lost on the river Ganges, *c.* 1737.
VOC 2411, n.f.	British, French and Muslim vessels that arrived or were lost on the river Ganges, *c.* 1737.
VOC 2427, ff. 303-7	British, French and indigenous vessels on the river Ganges, *c.* 1738.
VOC 2441, ff. 917?-24	British, French and indigenous vessels, *c.* 1738.
VOC 2455, ff. 294-7	British, French and indigenous vessels on the river Ganges, *c.* 1739.
VOC 2469, ff. 1007-12	British, French and indigenous vessels, *c.* 1739.
VOC 2489, ff. 291-304	British, French and indigenous vessels on the river Ganges, *c.* 1740.
VOC 2504, ff. 1065-70	Arrival and departure of British, French, Muslim and other vessels, *c.* 1740.
VOC 2518, ff. 515-25	British, French and indigenous vessels on the river Ganges, *c.* 1741.

VOC 2537, ff. 2058-63	Arrival and departure of British, French, Muslim and other vessels, *c.* 1741.
VOC 2556, ff. 574-82	British, French and indigenous vessels on the river Ganges, *c.* 1742.
VOC 2572, ff. 1108-11	Arrival and departure of British, French, Muslim and other vessels, *c.* 1742.
VOC 2594, ff. 478-9	British, French and indigenous vessels, *c.* 1743.
VOC 2617, ff. 178-82	British, French and indigenous vessels, *c.* 1744.
VOC 2641, ff. 121-4	British, French and indigenous vessels, *c.* 1745.
VOC 2661, ff. 158-64	British and indigenous vessels, *c.* 1746.
VOC 2689, ff. 135-42	British and indigenous vessels, *c.* 1747.
VOC 2711, ff. 122-4	British and indigenous vessels, *c.* 1748.
VOC 2754, f. 227	Departure of British vessels, 1750-1.
VOC 2829, ff. 294-7	Arrival and departure of foreign vessels, *c.* 1754.
VOC 2862, ff. 835-8	Arrival of indigenous and other foreign vessels, *c.* 1755.
VOC 2862, ff. 1079-82	Departure of indigenous and foreign vessels during the northern monsoon, *c.* 1755.
VOC 2874, f. 431	Arrival and departure of foreign vessels, *c.* 1756.
VOC 3426, ff. 572-3	Arrival and departure of private vessels, 1775.
VOC 3451, ff. 502-3	Arrival and departure of private vessels, 1776.
VOC 3479, f. 700	British vessels that sailed from Europe to the Indies, 1777.
VOC 3479, f. 704	Arrival and departure of foreign vessels, 1777.
VOC 3509, f. 474	Private vessels that arrived on and departed from the river Ganges, 1778.
VOC 3537, f. 527	Private vessels that arrived on and departed from the river Ganges with Dutch passes, 1779.
VOC 3565, f. 572	British vessels that arrived on and departed from the river Ganges, 1779-80.
VOC 3687, f. 702	Arrival and departure of Danish vessels, 1778-85.

6.1.5. *Missions to Indian states*

VOC 1270, ff. 346-88	Mission to Raja Udai Singh of Burdwan by Joan van Leene, October-November 1669 (various documents).
VOC 1288, ff. 74-80	Mission to Dhaka by Pieter Hofmeester, 1672 (report)
VOC 1323, ff. 336-70	Mission to Dhaka, March-August 1677 (report) (among other documents).
VOC 1328, ff. 512v-15	Mission to the Mughal by Joannes Bacherius, 1677 (instructions) (see also under Surat, 2.1.5).
VOC 1610, ff. 49-50	Mission to Prince Muhammad Azim by Jacob Pelgrom and Anthonij Huijsman, 1698 (report).

6.1.6. *Miscellaneous*

VOC 1232, ff. 597-617	Report and other documents concerning Arnold van Wachtendonck's journey to Patna, 1660.
VOC 1281-4, ff. 916-39	Report concerning a journey of Commissioner Willem Volger, June-December 1671.
VOC 1305, ff. 2-1993	Documents concerning conflicts with Muslim Governor Malik Qasim and the Nawab at Dhaka, 1672-3.
VOC 1408, ff. 701-62	Report of Isaac Solmans concerning his visit to Bengal, 1685.
VOC 1831, ff. 975-95	Report concerning the state of affairs at the factory in Patna as a consequence of the aggression of Prince Farrukh Siyar, 1712.
VOC 1842, ff. 188-272	Report by Jacob Dijkhov and Bartholomeus de Wit concerning their activities at Patna, 1713.
VOC 1842, ff. 346-411	Report by Jacob Dijkhov and Bartholomeus de Wit concerning their journey to Patna, *c.* 1713.
VOC 1962, ff. 162-84	Document concerning weights, measures and currencies in Bengal, *c.* 1721.
VOC 1981, ff. 150-85	Correspondence between the factory at Patna and the VOC's broker 'de Khiram' and the Armenian merchant 'Costa Pedroes', *c.* 1722.
VOC 2038, ff. 1615-1718	Report by Jacob Christiaen Pielat concerning his journey to Patna, September-December 1725.
VOC 2052, ff. 374-432	Documents concerning conflicts with the Ostend/ Company, 1726.
VOC 2075, ff. 370-483	Documents concerning conflicts with the British at Patna, *c.* 1727.
VOC 2195, ff. 715-925	Documents concerning conflicts with the Ostend/ Company, *c.* 1731.
VOC 2455, ff. 236-88	Essay concerning the invasion of the Mughal Empire by Nadir Shah of Persia, *c.* 1739.
VOC 2870, ff. 1303-1468	*Radicale beschrijving* (i.e. an official review) of Bengal (and Persia), *c.* 1756 (see also *resoluties* of the GG&C of 23 December 1756 and 22 April 1757).
VOC 2871, ff. 242-314	Report concerning conflicts between Nawab Siraj-ud-Daula and the British at Calcutta, April-August 1756.
VOC 2948-9, n.f.	Various unspecified documents concerning Bengal, *c.* 1759.
VOC 2978, ff. 1086-1557	Trade journal, 1757-8.
VOC 3167, ff. 313-404	Documents concerning conflicts with other European merchants, November 1765-August 1766.
VOC 3170, ff. 1486-1564	Documents concerning conflicts with other European merchants, August-December 1766.

VOC 3686, ff. 207-496	Report and appendices concerning the Company's state of affairs at Calcutta, 1785.
VOC 3987, n.f.	Secret correspondence, 1779.

6.2. Other VOC Series

6.2.1. *Archives of the Gentlemen XVII and the Amsterdam Chamber*

See 1.1
Access: 1.04.02

Kopie-resoluties van de Gouverneur-Generaal en Raden
Duplicate proceedings of the Governor-General and Council

See 1.1.4
Inv. nos: VOC 656-847

In the *Realia* repertory to the *resoluties* several relevant headings are to be found, among these:

Bellasoor (Balasore; 1 entry 1667), *Bengale* (about 1000 entries 1655-1795), *Ceerpour* (Sherpur; 1 entry 1664), *Ganges* (2 entries 1721), *Ouglij* (Hooghly; 1 entry 1685), *Pattena* (Patna; 8 entries 1664-1705).

Miscellaneous

VOC 4641	Papers originating from advocate P.J. Guépin concerning the case conducted for the VOC in England against the EIC for restitution of the damage suffered during the war in Bengal, 1790-4. One bundle.
VOC 4786	Secret letter of *Directeur* J.M. Ross concerning an alliance against the British proposed by the Mughal Emperor, 1779. With appendices, including copies in Persian of documents presented by the Mughal envoy (see Appendix I), one folder.
VOC 4816	List of coins, exchange rates, weights and measures in Asia, with index, including sections on Hooghly, Cossimbazar, Patna, Pipli, Dhaka, Rajmahal, Sherpur, Balasore and Khanakul (ff. 1-90 contain the actual lists; ff. 91-139 contain notes on these subjects), 1769. One volume.
VOC 4832	Papers concerning the sale of opium over the period 1736-55 by the *Amfioen Sociëteit*. One folder.
VOC 4881	Letter to Governor-General Jacob Mossel concerning the decline in the textile trade in Bengal, 1757. One piece.
VOC 4882	Memorandum concerning the value of gold and silver, and the exchange rates between the Dutch and various Asian currencies, with notes regarding coinage in Bengal in particular, 1760, 1761. Two pieces.

VOC 4883	Printed memorandum from the Gentlemen XVII to the States General concerning complaints by the British envoy J. Yorke about the hostile behaviour of VOC servants against the British in Bengal, 1761. One piece.
VOC 4884	Partially printed papers concerning the confiscation by the VOC of the private vessel Antonetta, equipped by Robert Charnock in Vlissingen (Flushing) and arrived at Calcutta under the Dutch flag, 1789-91. One folder.
VOC 4885	Memorandum by Isaac Titsingh concerning the economy measures with regard to the VOC establishments in Bengal, with appendices, 1794. One folder.
VOC 6904	Will of J. Sadelijn, widower of A.F. Pelgrom, Hooghly, 1731. One folder.
VOC 7012-14	Papers concerning complaints of Dutch silk manufacturers, based mainly in Haarlem, over the supply of Bengal raw silk and their requests for a reduction of the import of manufactured silks from China, 1642, 1740, 1770. Partly printed, three pieces and a folder.
VOC 7015	*Eisen van retouren* (see 1.1.1) from the Gentlemen XVII to Bengal, Coromandel and Batavia, 1700. One piece.
VOC 7051	Deeds of agreement concerning bill transactions for the benefit of the factories in Bengal, 1773-85. One volume.
VOC 7053, 7058	Papers originating from Hooghly concerning bills of exchange, 1779-90. Two volumes.

6.2.2. *Archives of the Zeeland Chamber*

See 1.2.1
Access 1.04.02

Ingekomen stukken van Gouverneur-Generaal en Raden bij de Heren XVII en de Kamer Zeeland (IGG)
Papers received from Governor-General and Council by the Gentlemen XVII and the Zeeland Chamber

VOC 8730-807	Letters and reports received by the GG&C from Bengal, with appendices, (1683-) 1688-1784. 78 volumes. Incomplete series.

Ingekomen stukken van de kantoren in Indië bij de Heren XVII en de Kamer Zeeland (IKI)
Papers received from the establishments in the Indies by the Gentlemen XVII and the Zeeland Chamber

VOC 9541-97	Letters and other papers from the *Directeur* and Council of Bengal to the Gentlemen XVII (and others), with appendices,

	(1682-) 1687-1794. 57 volumes. Incomplete series. It includes *resoluties* of the *Directeur* and Council of Bengal, 1785 (VOC 9592).
VOC 9598	Secret letter from the *Directeur* and Council of Bengal to the Gentlemen XVII concerning complaints about the British frustrating Dutch trade in Bengal, 1759. One volume.
VOC 9599-614	Letters and other papers from the *Directeur* and Council of Bengal to the Zeeland Chamber (and others), with appendices, 1734-1780 (-1787). 16 volumes. Incomplete series.
VOC 9615	Letter from Isaack Soolmans, Commissioner of Bengal, to the Gentlemen XVII, with appendices, 1684. One volume.
VOC 9615 I	Report by Captain Jacob Christiaan Pielat of his journey from Hooghly to Patna, September-December 1725. One volume.
VOC 9616	*Dagregister* of Bengal, January-August 1730. One volume.
VOC 9617-22	Cashbooks and ledgers of the factories in Bengal, 1751-79. Six volumes.
VOC 9623-4	Papers concerning the accusations by 'Damoeder', VOC broker at Hooghly, against *Directeur* Jan Kersseboom, 1756-7. Two volumes.

Soldijkantoor

Pay Office

See 1.2.1 and 1.1.10

VOC 11890	Includes a roll of qualified civil and military VOC servants in Bengal, 1789. One volume.

Miscellaneous

VOC 9521	Papers concerning the case conducted by the Council of Justice at Batavia against Nicolaas van Schagen, former *Directeur* of Bengal, who has been accused of conducting private trade, 1686-1688. One volume.
VOC 9522	Papers concerning the dismissal of the factor Abraham Wijns and the legal *resoluties* conducted against him, 1692-1717. One volume.
VOC 11207-8	Two copies of a list (79 pp.) of coins, exchange rates, weights and measures at a great number of factories in the Indies, including Hooghly, Cossimbazar, Patna, Dhaka, Rajmahal, Sherpur, Balasore and Khanakul, printed in 1691 (at Middelburg, Zeeland). Two volumes.
VOC 11277	Papers concerning the conflicts between former *Directeur* Jacob Pelgrom and some VOC servants in Bengal, 1704-7. One volume.
VOC 11278	Letter of the *Directeur* and Council of Bengal to GG&C, 1722. One volume.

VOC 11279	Pleading by *Fiscaal* Jan Albert Sichterman to the *Directeur* and Council of Bengal concerning the behaviour of Shipmaster Pieter van Genegten, with appendices, 1726. One volume.
VOC 11280	Report by officer-engineer Claude Ogerdias concerning investigations in Fort Gustavus and surroundings in the Bengal region of Banquibazar, with corrections by a commission appointed by the *Directeur*, 1758. One folder.
VOC 11281	Papers concerning hostilities by VOC servants against British settlements in Bengal, 1760. One folder.
VOC 11282	Secret papers concerning thefts from the 'small' cash box in the factory at Hooghly, 1761. One volume.
VOC 11283	Papers concerning the deficit in the 'large' cash box in the factory at Hooghly, 1763. One volume.
VOC 13686	Papers concerning three bills of exchange drawn by the *Directeur* of Bengal on the VOC, without the approval of the Gentlemen XVII, 1759. Three pieces.
VOC 13690	Bills of exchange drawn in London for the payment of *sicca* rupees in Bengal, 1780. One piece.
VOC 13697	Draft of an act of agreement concerning the transfer of money to Bengal, n.d. One piece.
VOC 13698	Draft of an act of agreement concluded between the Directors of the Zeeland Chamber and an unnamed merchant concerning the payment of bills of exchange in Bengal to the *Directeur*, n.d. One piece.

6.2.3. *Archives of the Delft, Rotterdam, Enkhuizen and Hoorn Chambers and miscellaneous*

No relevant documents found in inventories.

6.3. Archives Transferred from Asia

Hoge Regering te Batavia
High Government at Batavia

See 1.3.1
Access no.: 1.04.17

163-71	Extracts from letters and *resoluties* of Gentlemen XVII and the GG&C concerning the *Westerkwartieren* and especially Bengal, 1617-1774. With repertories, Nine volumes.
172	Extracts from letters of superior bodies concerning Banquibazar, 1745-53. One cover.
172 a I-172 a II	Secret letters sent and received by the Bengal *Directie*, 1757-9. Includes copies and originals of French and English letters, among

those originals by Sir Robert Clive and Council. Also some copies in Persian of letters to the Nawab, etc., and of a *parwana* (see Appendix I). Two volumes.

173-9 Minutes of letters of the GG&C to Bengal, 1790-94, 1797, 1803. With appendices, Seven volumes.

180-205 Letters from the *Directeur* and Council of Bengal to Batavia, 1777-80, 1790-5, 1802, and secret letters, 1790-5. With appendices and repertories to some of the volumes, 26 volumes.

206 Letters of Warren Hastings (English, with translation) to *Directeur* Ross about the surrender of the Dutch factories in Bengal to the British, 1781-2. With appendices, one volume.

207-10 Letters from *Directeur* I. Titsingh to Batavia and the Gentlemen XVII, 1788-91, and to him from the GG&C, 1785-6. With appendices, four volumes.

211-12 Correspondence between the British and the Dutch in Bengal and some internal correspondence of the Dutch, 1785-94. Two volumes.

213 Extracts of the correspondence between Batavia and the Bengal *Directie* concerning a projected reduction of the costs in Bengal, 1786-91. One volume.

214-32 Minutes, extracts and copies of (*secrete*) *resoluties* of the Bengal *Directie*, 1760-95. Incomplete series (see also below, *Voormalige Nederlandse bezittingen in Voor-Indië*, inv. nos 1-16). 20 volumes, some with appendices, repertories.

233 *Resoluties* of the Bengal *Directie* concerning cuts in their budget by the GG&C, 1791-2. One volume.

234-6 *Dagregister* of Hooghly, 1790-2. Three volumes.

237 Regulations for Bengal personnel conceived by L. Taillefert, 1755. One volume.

238-40 Collection of deeds of appointment of Company personnel, 1791-5. Three covers.

241 Instruction of Commissioner H.A. van Rheede tot Drakestein to the *Directeur* and Council of Bengal, 1687, and some considerations to the same of N. Schagen, 1691. One volume.

241* Another copy of the considerations by N. Schagen and considerations by Van Riemsdijk about the bad state of the Bengal Directory, 1763, and separate memorandum of J. Bacheracht to J.M. Ross, 1777. One volume.

242 Reply by the Bengal *Directie* to the secret memorandum concerning a reduction of expenses from Batavia, 1756. With appendices, one volume.

243 Treatise by the Governor-General on Bengal coinage and interest rates and amounts of precious metal shipped throughout the *octrooigebied*, after 1756. One volume.

244 Description of Bengal (trade) with suggestions by P. van den Velde, 1757. One volume.

245 *Memorie van overgave* by *Directeur* Adriaan Bisdom to Louis

Taillefert accompanying the transfer of the *Directie*, 1760. One volume.

246 *Memorie van overgave* by *Directeur* Louis Taillefert to George Lodewijk Vernet, 1763. With appendices, one volume.

247 Memorandum of G.L. Vernet to the British Governor in Calcutta concerning complaints about obstructions of the VOC trade by the British, 1768. With appendices, one volume.

248 Memorandum on different grievances held against the British by the other European nations in Bengal, n.d. One volume, in French.

249-50 *Memorie van overgave* by *Directeur* George Lodewijk Vernet to Boudewijn Verselewel Faure, 1770. Two copies of the same.

251 Plan for the reduction of the cost of the Bengal Directory by J. Bacheracht, 1773. With appendices, one volume.

252-6 *Memorie van overgave* by *Directeur* Johannes Bacheracht to Johannes Mattheus Ross, 1776-7. Two copies of the same, with appendices, 1757-76. Five volumes.

257 Memoranda of Bengal *Directeur* J.M. Ross concerning the calicoe trade and the *eisen*, 1777. One volume.

258 Letters of a *vrijkoopman* (free-merchant) of Bengal to the Governor-General of the EIC about the decline of the Bengal trade with suggestions, 1782. One volume.

259 Papers concerning joint actions of Dutch and British ships against the Ostend Company, 1728-31. One folder.

260 Extracts from secret instructions to Ceylon, Coromandel, Bengal and Malabar and from (*secrete*) *resoluties* concerning an expedition against the British in Bengal, 1759-60. One volume.

261 Letter of the Gentlemen XVII to Batavia responding to the complaints of the British about hostilities in Bengal, 1759-60. One volume.

262-6 Papers concerning private persons (trials, financial claims, disputes), namely L. Taillefert, A.J. de Wilde, A. Bisdom, L. de Saumaise, J.C. Hoen, 1760-72. Five volumes.

267 Papers concerning Bengal *Directeur* Ross' charge to ship rice to Ceylon, 1777-9. One volume.

268 Papers concerning charges of extortion brought against the collector of Baranagar W. Danckelmann in connection with the village Bania 'Parbotti Tsjern Raay', 1780-1. Four pieces in one folder.

269 Letter concerning the riots in Baranagar by J.M. Ross, 1781. With appendices and repertory. One volume.

270 Papers concerning the dispute between *Directeur* Ross, Von Dankelmann and J. Eilbracht and the latter's alleged fraud with goods from the shipwreck of De Jonge Hellingman, 1780-1. Five pieces in one folder.

271 Response of the Bengal *Directie* to the examination of the Bengal financial ledgers of 1785-9, 1793. With appendices, one volume.

272 Papers sent to Batavia by C.L. Eilbracht in defence to accusations

of having disgraced the Dutch during the British hostilities in Bengal, 1787. With appendices, one volume. Partly in English.

273 Translations of (printed) British regulations concerning the administration of justice and revenue collection in Bengal and of an agreement concluded on this point with the *zamindars* and the Nawab, 1787-91. One volume.

274-8 Papers of the Hooghly Council of Justice concerning insubordination of J.C. Piasky on board the Vrouw Agatha, 1790, and concerning desertions from ships, 1790-4. With repertories, five volumes.

279 (Daily) reports of the ships Spaarne, Vrouw Agatha, Nieuwstad and Schagen to the Bengal *Directeur*, 1790-4. Three parts in one cover.

280 Letter of G.F.J. de Ravallet in Pondicherry in defence to accusations by J. Eilbracht, 1791. With appendices, one volume.

281-2 Papers concerning the ship Schagen, sent to Mauritius, 1794-5. One volume.

283 Notes of the meetings of the Council in Chinsura, 1795. One volume.

284 Minutes of papers sent from Batavia to Bengal, etc., 1808-9. One volume.

285 Correspondence between the British (Minto, Foote, Bertie, Drury) and the Governor-General, 1808-9. With appendices, one volume. Partly English (originals), printed notifications, 1809, in Portuguese, Dutch, Persian (see Appendix I).

286-91 General report on the recovery of the Dutch possessions in Bengal from the British in 1817-18 by J.A. van Braam. With appendices, six volumes.

292-6 *Resoluties* of the Chinsura Resident D.A. Overbeek, 1818, 1822-5. With appendices, five volumes (1819-22 are listed in this section under *Voormalige Nederlandse bezittingen in Voor-Indië*, inv. nos 67-70).

297 British *ains* or regulations concerning administration in Bengal, 1793-1825. One volume. English, partly printed, with accompanying letters in Dutch, 1823, 1825.

298-9 General report of Chinsura Resident D.A. Overbeek, partly concerning the organization of the judiciary, 1824. With appendices, three pieces and one volume.

Voormalige Nederlandse bezittingen in Voor-Indië

Former Dutch possessions in South Asia

See 1.3.3

Access no.: 1.04.19

1-16 (Minutes of) *secrete resoluties* of the *Directeur* and Council, 1757-95. Incomplete (see also above in *Hoge Regering Batavia*, inv. nos 214-32). One folder, 15 volumes.

17-36 (Minutes of) secret correspondence, incoming and outgoing, 1703-15, 1728-30, 1760-94, with intermissions. Twenty volumes.

37 Letters from the Gentlemen XVII and GG&C, 1787-91. One volume.

38-50 Secret letters from the same senders, 1728-31, 1760-90, with intermissions. 13 volumes.

51-60 Correspondence between the Hooghly factory and the Cossimbazar and Patna factories, 1790-4. Ten volumes.

61-5 Correspondence, mainly with Coromandel, Malabar, Surat, Ceylon and Melaka, 1789-94. Five volumes.

66 Report of J.M. Ross on the different locations of textile production ('arrengs'), 1767. With appendices, one volume.

67-70 *Resoluties* of the Resident and Council in Chinsura, 1819-22. Four volumes. (1818, 1822-5 are listed in this section under *Hoge Regering Batavia*, inv. nos 292-6.)

6.4. Archives of Other Institutions

Stadhouderlijke Secretarie
Secretariat to the Stadtholder

See 1.4.3
Access no.: 1.01.50

1212 *Resoluties* of the States General concerning the British attack of the VOC's properties in Bengal, 1761. One piece.

1213 Papers concerning the relations with the French in Bengal, 1780, 1783. One folder.

1217 Correspondence of T.I. de Larrey with Nicolaas Hartman, VOC advocate at Amsterdam, and the Directors of the French East India Company concerning the transfer of some land near Chandernagore from the VOC to the French East India Company, 1754. One folder.

1218 Protest note of the *Directeur* and Council at Bengal and a letter of Commissioner Vernet to the Zeeland Chamber concerning the obstruction of the free passage on the river Ganges by the British, 1759. One folder.

1219 Letter from the Gentlemen XVII to the States General with appendix, concerning conflicts with the British in Bengal, 1760. One folder.

1220 Letters from J.W. Count van Welderen, Dutch envoy in England, and the registrar H. Fagel to the *Raadpensionaris* (Grand Pensionary) Pieter Steyn, concerning conflicts with the EIC in Bengal, 1763.

1221 Memorandum of De Chevalier, former French Governor of Bengal, and letters from C. Sittig, *Predikant* of the States General at Paris and M. Lestevenon van Berkenrode, Dutch envoy in France, all concerning proposals to recruit troops and improve the defence of the East Indian possessions, 1781. One folder.

1607 Collection of various documents concerning government and trade in Asia (one volume). Including:

   15 Report by *Directeur* Mattheus van der Brouck concerning the VOC's 'reversal' in Bengal, 1664.

Comité tot de Zaken van de Oost-Indische Handel en Bezittingen
Committee regarding East Indian Trade and Possessions

See 1.4.4
Access no.: 2.01.27.01

Overgekomen brieven en papieren (OBP)
(letters and papers received)

59, ff. 330-5	Report concerning the surrender of settlements in Bengal to the British in 1795, *c.* 1797 (among other documents).
60, n.f.	*Memorie van overgave* by *Directeur* Isaac Titsingh to Cornelis van Citters Aarnoutszoon, *c.* 1792.
61, ff. 148?-1629	Report concerning Bengal (among other regions), *c.* 1793.
62, n.f.	Report concerning Bengal (among other regions), *c.* 1794.
63, n.f.	Report concerning Bengal (among other regions), *c.* 1795.
64, n.f.	Report concerning Bengal (among other regions), *c.* 1796.
65, n.f.	Report concerning Bengal (among other regions), *c.* 1797.
65a, n.f.	Report concerning Bengal (among other regions), *c.* 1794.
124, n.f.	*Resoluties*, 1792.
124, ff. 10-38	*Resoluties*, 1794.
124, ff. 62-77	*Resoluties*, 1795.
137, ff. 1-107	*Memorie van overgave* by *Gezaghebber* Cornelis van Citters Arnoutszoon to Johan Wilhelm van Haugwitz, February 1796.
137, ff. 108-208	*Resoluties*, 1795.

Miscellaneous

223	Letter of Bengal chief-factor C. van Citters to the Gentlemen XVII, 1795. One piece.

Ministerie van Koloniën
Ministry of Colonial Affairs

See 1.4.10
Access no.: 2.10.01

3090 Contains correspondence from and to Chinsura, 817-1818. Two bundles, some letters in English, and French.

3196 Report on the trade situation in Bengal, 1819. One folder.

Legatie Frankrijk
Embassy at Paris, France

See 1.4.11
Access no.: 1.02.14
Period: 1747-1810

486 Papers concerning a claim by Jaen Gijsbert Decker, Councillor and *Schepen* (Sheriff) at Haarlem (whose wife was the widow of *Opperhoofd* Jacques la Tour at Jaffna), on Law de Lauriston, commander of the French troops in Bengal, 1781. One folder.

Legatie Zweden
Mission in Sweden

See 1.4.11
Access no.: 1.02.07
Period: 1675-1810

142 Treatise on a conflict with the EIC originated in 1759 in Bengal, *c.* 1765. One folder.

6.5. PERSONAL AND FAMILY PAPERS

Geleynssen

See 1.5.2
Access no.: 1.10.30

111 Letter of J. Mahieusen in Pipli to Geleynssen, 1639. One piece.

Sweers, Van Vliet, Specx, Mannis

See 1.5.3
Access no.: 1.10.78

2, f. 179 Letter from Bengal by C. Ranst, 1671 (?).
2, ff. 228-9 Notes on M. van den Broeck and (fraud in) Cossimbazar, *c.* 1673.

Hudde

See 1.5.5
Access no.: 1.10.48

36 Letter of C. Ranst to J. Hudde in which he lays the blame for a missing sum of 196,000 rupees on Muslim officials, 1682. With appendices, one folder.

Valckenier

See 1.5.9
Access no.: 1.10.05.05

3 Letter from J. Drabbe at Patna concerning his appointment as *Opperhoofd* of that factory, 1741. One piece.

Vernet

See 1.5.11
Access no.: 1.10.82

1-3 Letters, partly written by G.L. Vernet, chiefly sent from Cossimbazar to the Council at Hooghly, 1755-63.
4 Letters, possibly from Cossimbazar, notes concerning textiles, minutes of the Council at Hooghly, miscellaneous letters, and bills, 1746-63, 1766.
5 Correspondence with and between Cossimbazar, Hooghly, other VOC settlements in Bengal, the British and the French, 1762-5.
6-12 Miscellaneous correspondence, partly to and from G.L. Vernet, mostly sent to and from Cossimbazar and Hooghly, 1750-3, 1755-66.

Van Ghesel

See 1.5.13
Access no.: 1.10.31

7 Papers concerning the trouble to the VOC brought on by the EIC in Bengal, 1757-70. One folder, partly published in *KHGU*, 28 (1872), pp. 97-102; 29 (1873), pp. 529-45, 597-8 and 30 (1874), pp. 630-2, 638-47, 729-31 (see Bibliography, nos 16, 54).
80 Letter of J.G. Decker requesting Van Ghesel to represent the interests of former Bengal *Directeur* G.L. Vernet, 1772. One piece, published in *KHGU*, 28 (1872), pp. 194-6 (see Bibliography, no. 16).

Baud

See 1.5.14
Access no.: 2.21.007.58

1042 Description (40 pp.) of events in Bengal between 1757 and 1763. One piece, in French.
1060 Considerations of Governor-General Jacob Mossel and *resoluties* of the Council at Batavia concerning coinage, interest and other financial matters in Bengal, textile trade and return goods for the Dutch Republic, 1757. One piece.

Hope

See 1.5.17
Access no.: 1.10.46

11 Notes on matters concerning Bengal, extracted from the *Haags verbaal*, 1711-40. One volume.

12 Extract from the *memorie van overgave* by *Directeur* Louis Taillefert, 1755. One volume.

84-5 Papers concerning trade and Company affairs in Bengal, 1756-66. Mainly notes, extracts for use at the *Haags Besogne*. Two folders.

86 Idem, 1754-70. With *eisen* of silk, 1665; papers concerning the calicoe trade, 1694-1768; extracts concerning criminal *resoluties* in Bengal, 1768.

Van Slingelandt - De Vrij Temminck

See 1.5.20
Access no.: 3.20.52

563 Folder no. 17 contains notes concerning the return goods from Bengal, 1750-9. Seven pieces.

564 Folder no. 34 contains printed considerations of Governor-General Jacob Mossel on coinage in Bengal, 1757. One piece.

565 Folder no. 41 contains papers (some printed) concerning complications between the VOC and EIC in Bengal, 1759-65. Hundred pieces, partly in French.

567 Folder no. 68 contains correspondence of Egbert de Vrij Temminck concerning financial matters of former *Directeur* George Lodewijk Vernet (see above), 1772. Three pieces. Folder no. 73 contains papers concerning bills of exchange of Bengal, 1773. Four pieces. Folder no. 88 contains a letter from advocate Boers to Egbert de Vrij Temminck concerning complaints of the French about the VOC's *Directeur*, with appendices, 1780. Three pieces.

Bleiswijk

See 1.5.21
Access no.: 3.01.25

232 Letter from *Directeur* Johannes Mattheus Ross to the Gentlemen XVII concerning the possibility of having Shah Alam II enter into an agreement with the VOC instead of the EIC, according to which the *subahs* of 'Matteh' on the Bay of Bengal would be transferred to the VOC, with appendices, 1779. Five pieces.

233 List of the papers sent by Casper Leon Eilbracht to Pieter van Bleiswijk to avoid their destruction by the VOC, includes a petition to release his unlawfully imprisoned brother Jacob, memoranda about the mismanagement of *Directeur* Johannes Mattheus Ross, and about insults uttered by the government to him, with appendices, 1781, 1783-6. One bundle.

Van der Heim

See 1.5.24
Access no.: 1.10.39

126, 144 Papers concerning private trade in Bengal, in particular an affair involving the ship Antoinetta, belonging to R. Charnock, citizen of Vlissingen (Flushing), 1789. One volume. and a folder.

Fagel

See 1.5.25
Access no.: 1.10.29

2399, 2422, 2687 Contain correspondence of H. Fagel the Elder with R.R. Keyser, warehouse-keeper at Cossimbazar, 1771, 1773, 1789.

Radermacher

See 1.5.27
Access no.: 1.10.69

166 Extract from a French memorandum on Bengal, 1768. One piece.
436 Papers concerning the *Amfioen Sociëteit* at Batavia, 1766. One folder.
484 Notes by S. Radermacher on Bengal, 1753. One piece.
486 Noteş taken from a report by the commander of the military expedition in Bengal Roussel, 1759. One piece.

Falck

See 1.5.28
Access no.: 2.21.006.48

1 Documents concerning the appointment of O.W. Falck at the VOC, and the bill of the proceeds of the goods brought along with the return to the Dutch Republic, 1756-75. Eight pieces in one folder.
2 Papers concerning the conflict at Chinsura between O.W. Falck, *Fiscaal* and *Dorpmeester* (Village-head) at that place, and officer Saumaise, 1766. Three pieces in one folder.
3 Letter of *Directeur* George Lodewijk Vernet and Council at Hooghly to the factor O.W. Falck, 1768. One piece.
4 List of British, French and Dutch vessels wrecked on the Bengal River during the storm of 11 October 1737.
7 Papers concerning the occupation of Chinsura and the rest of Bengal by the British and the confiscation of goods belonging to the Dutch, including a letter from J. Goutvorst at Cossimbazar to O.W. Falck, 1789. One folder.
8 Letter (from O.W. Falck?) from Hindustan to a cousin in Europe, unsigned and n.d., (*c.* 1781?). One piece.
9 Memorandum concerning the infringements by the EIC on the ancient rights and privileges of the VOC in Bengal (and Surat), chiefly since the piece concluded in 1784 (incomplete), *c.* 1786. One piece.
10 Essay concerning the unsatisfactory manner in which the VOC's interests

in Bengal have been looked after since 1757, with appendices, 1789. One volume.

15 Letter from J.C.L. Blume at Hooghly to O.W. Falck, accompanying his memorandum concerning considerations about the VOC's general state of affairs in the East Indies and proposals for improvement, and a letter accompanying the same memorandum when sent to Governor-General W.A. Alting, 1792-4. One folder.

Alting

See 1.5.29
Access no.: 1.10.03

7 Extracts of contracts (*farmans, hasb-ul-hukums,* etc.) granted to the VOC in Bengal, 1619-1752. Bad condition, one volume.

21 Instruction to the Bengal *Directeur* and Council by Van Rheede, 1687. One volume.

65 Letters and other writings of under merchant Blume at Hooghly, 1781-92. One volume.

68 Letters of a Bengal *vrijkoopman* (free-merchant) to Warren Hastings on the decline of exports from Bengal, the political situation in South Asia, the VOC, etc., 1782 (Dutch translations). Two volumes.

Nederburgh

See 1.5.33
Access no.: 1.10.59

97 Correspondence of S.C. Nederburgh with W. Dunkin of the EIC and with J. Stuart, representing the VOC in the case against the EIC over the losses suffered in Bengal during the Anglo-Dutch war, 1790-1. One folder.

111 Notes on opening Asia to private trade and the possibility of thus reviving the Bengal trade, *c.* 1780. One folder.

136 Request of W.J. Werkman to S.C. Nederburgh concerning the inheritance of his father Willem Kerkman, Resident at Dhaka, 1791. One piece.

268 Part of a letter (of I. Titsingh?) concerning the coining of silver in Calcutta, n.d. One piece.

421 Secret and non-secret *memories van overgave* by *Directeur* Johannes Bacheracht to Johannes Mattheus Ross, 1777, with marginal notes of the GG&C. Two volumes.

422 Papers concerning the British conquest of VOC possessions in Bengal and demands of the VOC to be reimbursed over the period of occupation (1781-9). One volume.

423 Reports of J. Eilbracht and Patna chief-factor C. Citters on the rights and privileges of the VOC in Bengal, 1785. One volume.

424-5 Letter and notes of I. Titsingh, concerning Company affairs in Bengal, 1788, 1792. Two pieces.
426 Letters of C. Citters from Bengal, 1792-3. One folder.
427 Lists and bills concerning the warehouses in Bengal in connection with the British take-over, 1796-7. One folder.
709 Letter of C. Bie from Frederiksnagore, 1796. Damaged, one piece.

W. and D. van Hogendorp

See 1.5.35
Access no.: 2.21.008.69

10 Note by Dirk van Hogendorp concerning the financial management in Bengal, with excerpt from a letter from Bengal, 1788. Two pieces.

6.6. Separate Acquisitions and Microfilms

Losse aanwinsten
Separate acquisitions

See 1.6.1
Access no.: 1.11.01.01

540 Extracts from letters of the Gentlemen XVII to the GG&C concerning Bengal, 1700, 1762. Two pieces (1891 08h).
1084 Deed of appointment of F. de Haze as *Directeur* of Bengal, Batavia, 1673. One charter (1906 XLV 24).
1247 Letters of Governor-General W. Alting to William V, Prince of Orange, and his treasurer, with appendices concerning the account of the Prince at the *Amfioen Societeit* in Batavia, 1770-91. One bundle (1913, I 36).
1693 Draft of a letter of Governor I. Titsingh to W. Jones, concerning Jones' discourse on the origin of the Chinese, Bengal, 1790. One piece, in English (1936 I 27).
1703 Papers of the Amsterdam based H. Nieulandt, caretaker of the affairs of J.C. Kist, who passed away in 1766 at Hooghly, 1765-77.

Microfilms of External Archival Material

Mossel collection

See 1.6.2
Access no.: 1.11.06.03

Film 3697, Mossel family archives, nos 12-20 Deeds and financial papers concerning the participants of the *Amfioen Societeit* at Batavia, 1764-1801. Nine pieces and two folders.

6.7. Maps and Drawings

Verzameling buitenlandse kaarten, Leupe (VEL)
Foreign map collection, Leupe

See 1.7.1
Access no.: 4.VEL

256 Map of the coast of Bengal, between Palmyras Point and the river Arakan (Burma), seventeenth century. Originating from the 'Atlas Amsterdam' or 'Atlas de Graaff'.

257 Map of the coast of Bengal, between Palmyras Point and Martaban (Pegu, Burma), seventeenth century. Originating from the 'Atlas Amsterdam' or 'Atlas de Graaff'.

258 Map of the Bengal River, between the mouth and the VOC factory in Hooghly, seventeenth century. Originating from the 'Atlas Amsterdam' or 'Atlas de Graaff'.

259 Map of the river Ganges, copied after a Muslim map, seventeenth century. Originating from the 'Atlas Amsterdam' or 'Atlas de Graaff'.

1101 Plan of the factory in Bengal, as it was on the moment of arrival of the commissioner Adriaen van Reede, seventeenth century. With legend. Plan of the factory, corrected by the commissioner. Originating from the 'Atlas Amsterdam' or 'Atlas de Graaff'.

1102 Plan of the factory garden and its surrounding areas in Hooghly, seventeenth century. With legend. Originating from the 'Atlas Amsterdam' or 'Atlas de Graaff'.

1103 Plan of the factory, like it used to be, 1743 (?). Received from Bengal, 1743 (?).

1104 Plan of Fort Gustavus, 1743 (?). Received from Bengal, with legend.

1105 Profile of the fausse-braye, 1743 (?). Received from Bengal.

1106 Plan of the Patna factory (house), with three new yards, 1734 (?). Received from Bengal, 1734. With legend.

1107 Drawing of a machine used for the winding of silk, the so-called Reel of Pouchon, 1775. Received from Bengal. With explanation.

Verzameling buitenlandse kaarten, supplement, Leupe-l'Honoré Naber (VELH)
Foreign map collection, supplement, Leupe-l'Honoré Naber

See 1.7.2
Access no.: 4.VELH

118 Map of the coast of Bengal, between 'Rio... (?)' and 'Garnegan', 1667 (?). Originating from the journal of Michiel Gerritsz. Boos.

119 New compass maps of the roadstead Balasore and the river Ganges, showing the river upstream and the delta on the mouth. Presented to Abraham Alewijn Abrahamsz., member of the Secret Commission of the VOC, 1722 (?). Bought by J.W. van Leeuwen, 1882.

120 Map of the Ganges, showing the river upstream and the delta at its mouth, probably eighteenth century. Bought by J.W. van Leeuwen, 1882.

121 Map of the Ganges, between Benares, 'Mouw' (Mau?) and 'Ponnarak', by Jan de Waal. Coloured.

122 Map of the origin and the continuation of the river Ganges or Hooghly, from Palmyras Point and Sagar Island to Chandernagore and Bandel, by Joannes van Keulen. Received from the Schneither collection, 1876. To be found in Part 5 of *De Zeefakkel*. Coloured copperplate print.

Departement van Marine, centraal archief, Leupe (MCAL)
Ministry of Naval Affairs, central archives, Leupe

See 1.7.3
Access no.: 4.MCAL

4287 Map of the northern part of the Bay of Bengal, laid down chiefly from the surveys of Bartholomew Plaisted and John Ritchie, 1772. With legend.

4291 Map of the mouth of the river Ganges or Hooghly, from Palmyras Point and Sagar Island to Chandernagore and Bandel.

4292 Map of the mouth of the river Hooghly from Palmyras Point to Sagar Island, map of the river Hooghly from Sagar Island to Chandernagore, by Captain W. Maxfield, 1817.

Collectie Bergsma (BMF)
Bergsma collection

See 1.7.7
Access no.: 4.BMF

432 Map of the mouth of the Ganges, by Henri Frix, 1726. With legend.

Appendices

APPENDIX I: DUTCH SOURCES IN INDIAN LANGUAGES

1. *Overgekomen Brieven en Papieren* (*OBP*)
Letters and Papers Received

See	1.1.7
Access no.:	1.04.02
Inv. nos:	VOC 1053-3987

The *OBP* contain little material in Indian languages. An important piece is however:

VOC 1616, ff. 1036-1118 Sinhalese grammar by J. Ruëll, vicar and rector of the seminary at Colombo. With instructions in Dutch but all tables of verb endings, declensions, etc., in Sinhalese, in its proper script, with a guide to the pronunciation of the Sinhalese alphabet, *c.* 1699.

2. Other VOC Series

Access no.: 1.04.02

VOC 4778 Contains a copy in Tamil of a letter (pencil marked 23) by the Nayak of 'Tundamandalam' (i.e. Tundira, in casu Gingee) Krishnappa to the Prince of Orange expressing his friendship toward the Dutch in Teganapatam, with a Dutch translation dated 22 April 1620.

VOC 4786 Contains Persian copies in *shekasta nastaliq* script of some documents presented to Bengal Governor J.M. Ross in March 1779 by Mirza Abul-Husain Khan, envoy of the Mughal Emperor. Responses to these documents are also available in Persian. The Persian documents are appended, all in twofold, to a letter of Ross to the Gentlemen XVII. Dutch translations are enclosed separately. The documents are as follows:

- a statement of the objectives of the mission by the Mirza himself, being a proposal to jointly fight the British in Bengal and reduce them to their former status, n.d.
- a *shuqqa-i khas* (note personally written by the Emperor) of Shah Alam II, containing an instruction to negotiate with the Mirza about the proposal, dated AH 2 Shaban 1192.
- a *parwana* of Majid-ud-Daula Abdul-Ahad Khan Bahadur

Bahram Jang stating the proposal in broad terms, dated 6 Shaban 1192.
- a *parwana* of Zulfiqar-ud-Daula Mirza Najaf Khan Bahadur Ghalib Jang of similar content, dated 22 Shaban 1192.
- an *arzi* (petition) in answer to the *shuqqa-i khas*, n.d.
- an *arzi* in answer to the *parwanas* of Zulfiqar-ud-Daula and Majid-ud-Daula, n.d.

Ingekomen stukken van de kantoren in Indië bij de Heren XVII en de Kamer Zeeland (IKI)

Papers received from the establishments in the Indies by the Gentlemen XVII and the Zeeland Chamber

See 1.2.1
Access no.: 1.04.02

VOC 9868 Includes the prayer of Our Father translated into Tamil, 1739.

3. Archives Transferred from Asia

Hoge Regering te Batavia

High Government at Batavia

See 1.3.1
Access no.: 1.04.17

The archives of the *Hoge Regering* contain relatively substantial material in Indian languages.

40-3 These documents appear to derive from archives created by Johannes Bacherus during the period 1684-93 when he served as Commissioner to the Coromandel Coast. Some 65 per cent of the documents are in Persian, while 26 per cent are in Telugu. Four of the Persian documents also carry a short line in Hindi. Of one document we have not been able to identify the language.

Back in the Netherlands after having served in Surat from *c.* 1665 to 1679, Johannes Bacherus was again sent to the Indies in 1684 as the third member of the inspecting commission that was to be led by Hendrik Adriaan van Reede tot Drakestein. After having inspected some of the establishments on the Coromandel Coast, he was sent as an ambassador to Aurangzeb who had just claimed authority over the coastal stretch between Bimlipatam and Pulicat following his conquest of Golkonda in 1687. Leaving Masulipatam on 24 December 1688 he found the Emperor encamped in the Bhima valley in the Deccan in May the following year. All in all, the mission was to last over a year. During the period spent in the imperial camp Bacherus was awarded the title of Gulzar Khan, 'the flourishing Khan'. After his return to Masulipatam Bacherus went on to inspect the VOC establishments in the northern part of the Coromandel Coast.[1]

At his death in 1693 he left a trunk full of papers. This trunk was consequently sent to Batavia where H. Zwaardecroon and W. Witmont, both of whom had been part of the team of Van Reede and Bacherus, were commissioned to make an inventory of the papers. The papers were split into those relating to Bacherus' work in southern Coromandel and those relating to northern Coromandel. Witmont was to inventory the South Coromandel papers, while Zwaardecroon took charge of the remainder.

Zwaardecroon kept the papers in Indian languages separate, bound as they were in a 'Cimendaek'. It appears that the papers in inv. nos 40-43 are exactly these papers, belonging to the embassy and the period spent by Bacherus in the Telugu speaking part of Coromandel. Unfortunately the parts of Zwaardecroon's inventory dealing with these papers and their translations no longer exist, even though the greater part of the Zwaardecroon and Witmont inventory survives.[2]

Since no inventory is available, we have chosen to give a full inventory of these documents. Because of lack of language skills the Telugu documents have been described only on the basis of the short notes scribbled onto them in Dutch. The documents in inv. nos 40-1 are divided over 168 folders, each containing one or several documents, some of these only envelopes or small scraps of paper. Inv. nos 42-3 contain a total of five documents. All documents are arranged, firstly, according to their epistolary style (*insha*) and, secondly, according to their date. In some cases we have added numbers in brackets to distinguish various documents in one folder or case.

The Mughal documents often carry various dates: the date of the decision, the date on which the document was written, the date on which it was processed at some level of the bureaucracy, etc. An attempt has been made to follow the preferential system laid down by M.A. Nayeem in the catalogue of documents dating from the reign of Aurangzeb that are in the archives at Hyderabad.[3] The documents are generally dated in the reckoning starting from the accession (*julus*) of Aurangzeb. From the fourth year of the reign which starts from the first Ramazan, beginning

[1] Van Dam, *Beschryvinge* (see Bibliography, no. 12), Vol. 2, Part 2, pp. 134-5, 172-4; Heniger, *Hendrik Adriaan van Reede* (see Bibliography, no. 403), pp. 65-7, 78; Niccolao Manucci, *Storio do Mogor, or Mogul India 1653-1703*, ed. and trans. William Irvine (London, 1907), pp. 383-8.

[2] *ARA*, VOC 1542, ff. 944-5, 'Rapport over de bevindinge der papieren naegelaten bij den Commandeur Joh. Bacherus Zaliger wegens sijne visite en commissie ter Custe Coromandel'. For the inventory, see ff. 946-1035.

[3] P. Sitapati and M.A. Nayeem eds, *Mughal Documents Catalogue of Aurangzeb's Reign*, Vol. 1: AD 1658-63, Part 1 (Hyderabad, 1980), pp. vii-xvi.

in AH 1071.[4] The dates on the documents range between the 30th and the 36th year of Aurangzeb's reign, that is between July 1686 and May 1693. Christian dates are only given here when they appear on the document.

The *farmans* and *parwanas* (A and B series) are copies written in the Mughal shorthand form of *shekasta nastaliq*, except for the *geautheuriseerde copieën* or endorsed copies which Bacherus ordered from Hyderabad. The latter are facsimile copies of the original documents, written in a clearer *shekasta nastaliq* that was the standard in South Asia for documents that were to be read by people other than clerks.

A. *Farmans* (royal orders, in Persian)

41, folder 99	Copy of a *farman* awarded to the French, dated 29 Rajab 31 Julus, with a few words in Hindi.
41, folder 100	(6) Copy of (a draft for) a *farman* granting exemption from tolls, drafted by 'Mier Haddij', dated 11 Zul-Qaada 33 Julus.
42	Endorsed copy of the *farman* of Aurangzeb in which most of the privileges enjoyed by the Company under the Sultans of Golkonda are restated: the villages held in *inam* (exempt from revenue payment) under the Sultans are again given to the Company,[5] special rates or exemptions from tolls and dues determined etc. The *farman* is dated 12 Muharram 33 Julus, this copy endorsed by the *Khadim Shar* (teacher/prescriber of Quranic law) Nur-ud-Din with his seal on AD 21 March 1690. A contemporary translation has been published in *CDNI*, III, pp. 516-23.
40, folder 40	Copy of a *farman* (in four parts).

B. *Parwanas* (official orders, in Persian)

40, folder 9	Copy of a *parwana* of Mustafa Quli Khan, *Sar-lashkar* (head of the cavalry / Governor) of Srikakulam, dated 19 Rajab 30 Julus.
41, folder 100	(1) Copy of the *parwana* of Asad Khan, *Wazir* of Aurangzeb,[6]

[4] Ibid. The reckoning of Aurangzeb's era is controversial, but Nayeem's system is consistent with the conversions of dates by VOC personnel.

30th year after the *julus*	:	1 Ramazan 1097-end of Shaban 1098	/ 22 July 1686-10 July 1687
31st	:	1098	1099 / 11 July 1687-29 June 1688
32nd	:	1099	1100 / 30 June 1688-18 June 1689
33rd	:	1000	1101 / 19 June 1689-7 June 1690
34th	:	1101	1102 / 8 June 1690-28 May 1691
35th	:	1102	1103 / 29 May 1691-16 May 1692
36th	:	1103	1104 / 17 May 1692-5 May 1693

[5] Cf. the *farman* of Abdullah Qutb Shah published in Fragner, 'Ein Privilegium aus Golkonda' (see Bibliography, no. 747), pp. 57-76.

[6] Shah Nawaz Khan and Abdul Hayy, *Maathir-ul-Umara, Biographies of the*

	in the name of Bisharat Khan, *Diwan* (overseer of the revenue collection) at Hyderabad, on exemption from tolls in the former Kingdom of Golkonda, to bridge the period in which the final *farman* would be prepared, dated 12 Zul-Qaada 33 Julus. A contemporary translation is in *CDNI*, III pp. 509-10. (5) Copy of a *parwana* of Asad Khan, granted in the name of Bisharat Khan concerning temporary exemption from the *jiziya*, dated 22 Zul-Qaada 33 Julus, received AD 22 September 1689. A contemporary translation is in *CDNI*, III, pp. 511-12.
43	(1) Endorsed copy of the *parwana* of Asad Khan concerning measures to be taken in case of desertion of Dutchmen and non-payment by debtors, and the hiring of personnel by the VOC, dated 7 Zul-Hija 33 Julus, endorsed by the *Khadim Shar* Nur-ud-Din, AD 21 March 1690. A contemporary translation is in *CDNI*, III, pp. 512-13.
40, folder 37	Endorsed copy of the *parwana* of Asad Khan, granting exemption from the *jiziya* to all VOC personnel, both Dutch and Indian, dated AH 11 (granted on 26) Zul-Hija 33 Julus /1100, endorsed by Nur-ud-Din, AD 21 March 1690. A contemporary copy is in *CDNI*, III, pp. 514-16.
43	(2) Idem, dated (6?) Zul-Hija 33 Julus, endorsed by Nur-ud-Din in AD February 1690.
41, folder 100	(4) Copy of a *parwana* in the name of Khanazad Khan, son of the *Mir Bakhshi* (officer in charge of military pay, etc.) Ruhullah Khan,[7] received AD 9 October 1689.
43	(3) Endorsed copy of a *parwana* of Asad Khan, dated 27 Muharram 33 Julus, providing a confirmation as well as an exegesis of the *farman* granted earlier that month by Aurangzeb, endorsed by the *Khadim Shar* Nur-ud-Din, AD 21 March 1690.
40, folder 42	Three identical endorsed copies of the *parwana* of Jan Sipar Khan, *Nazim,* or *Subahdar* (provincial governor) at Hyderabad, confirming the Imperial *farman* and the three *parwanas* of Asad Khan, dated AH 6 Rajab 1101, issued AD 5 May 1690, endorsed by Nur-ud-Din AD 19 May 1690. A contemporary translation is in *CDNI*, III, pp. 525-6.
40, folder 41	Copy of a *parwana* of the *Diwan* at Hyderabad Bisharat Khan, confirming the *parwana* of Asad Khan concerning the *jiziya* and that concerning the collection of debts, the desertion of Dutchmen and the hiring of Indian personnel (in inv. no. 43), issued AD 11 August 1690, endorsed by Nur-ud-Din, 9 Zul-Qaada 34 Julus / AD 16 August 1690.

Muhammadan and Hindu Officers of the Timurid sovereigns of India from 1500 to about 1780 A.D., trans. H. Beveridge; ed. Baini Prashad (reprint New Delhi, 1979) I, p. 271.

[7] Ibid., II, pp. 616-17.

41, folder 76	Endorsed copy of the *parwana* concerning freedom of tolls on the Masulipatam to Hyderabad road, given by Muhammad Shafi, *Diwan* at Hyderabad, 29 Rabi' I 34 Julus/AD 31 December 1690, endorsed AD 2 January 1691.
41, folder 68	Copy of a *parwana* awarded to the Portuguese with a short line in Hindi.

C. *Cauls* (South Indian style orders or grants)

41 (no number)	Part of an *ola* (inscribed palm leaf) in Telugu received, according to the Dutch text on the envelope in the same folder, from Mustafa Quli Khan, *Sar-lashkar* of Srikakulam on AD 8 August 1691 (folder kept separately).

D. *Other Mughal documents* (in Persian)

These are all originals, except for one draft, carrying the seals of Mughal officials, but written in Mughal shorthand, being transcripts of internal memoranda rather than public documents.

41, folder 96	Document dated 23 Jamadi I 32 Julus, with seal (of Ruhullah Khan?).
41, folder 102	*Yaddasht-i wusul* (receipt) for the 100 gold mohurs presented by Bacherus on first admission to the Emperor, dated 5 Shaban 32 Julus, with seals of Khuda Beg and Muhammad Yasin, *Khuzanchi-khazana* (officer of the treasury).[8] A short line in Hindi added on the back relates to *daroga* Mahe Mad.
43	(4) Receipt with a long list of gifts presented to the Emperor, dated 8 Shaban 32 Julus.
41, folder 101	Receipt for a golden saucer with 100 gold mohurs'presented to Aurangzeb with a brief note in Telugu.
41, folder 67	Receipt for the six elephants and six horses presented to Aurangzeb, dated 32 Julus (in Hindi: *hath(i) 6 aur ghora 6*)
41, folder 100	(2) *Yaddasht* (memorandum) notifying the *dagh* (branding) of a horse (to be) presented to the *Mir Bakhshi* Ruhullah Khan[9] with the seal of Ruhullah Khan. (3) *Yaddasht-i suwar sih-j(ada)* (memorandum concerning a horse or horseman) (to be) presented to Aurangzeb, dated 27 Rajab 30 and 23 Safar 33 Julus.
41, folder 91	Documents relating to the members of the embassy: De Haan, Witmont, Andries, Bijlevelt, Caulier, Marinus, Paulus and others.

[8] Zareena Parveen of the Andhra Pradesh State Archives at Hyderabad has translated this document for us.

[9] *Maathir-ul-Umara*, II, pp. 611-15.

41, folder 97	*Dastak* permitting departure from the imperial camp, given by Asad Khan.
40, folder 10	*Tumar* (fiscal paper) to certify the *mutaallaqan* (dependants) of the Dutch, including a list of Hindu and Muslim names (probably relating to the exemption of Dutch personnel from the *jiziya*), dated AH 1103/AD December 1793 (*sic*).
41, folder 56	*Yaddasht-i mutaallaqan . . . valandiz,* list of the Dutch dependents, probably a draft for the above document, drawn up at Draksharama in AH 1103.
41, folder 66	Document carrying the seal of Asad Khan.

E. *Incoming letters*

Most of these letters are originals, some on very fine paper. Often the name and seal of the senders are only to be found on the envelopes. Some of the envelopes are however in separate folders or have become mixed up with letters that they do not belong to, thus complicating identification. Hence a list of stray envelopes is also given below. All letters date from the period 1688-93 and are directed to Johannes Bacherus who was generally addressed as Gulzar Khan, unless otherwise indicated. Most of the correspondence seems to be dealing with business though not necessarily VOC business. For instance Bacherus was asked to mediate and to be a guarantor in a financial dispute between the Siamese ambassador and the Mughal noble Maasum Khan.

IN PERSIAN

From Maasum Khan, a Mughal noble with the rank of 2000,[10] apparently stationed at Hyderabad: inv. no. 41, folders 2, 3, 4, 53, 62 (envelope in folder 61), 104. Inv. no. 40, folder 53 and inv. no. 41, folder 79 are copies of letters sent by Kankul Venkanna, *Desai* (i.e. Persian for *Deshmukh* or local chief/official) of Masulipatam to Maasum Khan.

From Ali Akbar, Ambassador of Siam: inv. no. 40, folders 1, 2; inv. no. 41, folder 54.

From Mustafa Quli Khan, *Sar-lashkar* of Srikakulam: inv. no. 40, folder 56 (?); inv. no. 41, folders 57, 58, 60, 105, 108.

From Jan Sipar Khan, *Subahdar* at Hyderabad: inv. no. 41, folder 1.

From Mir Muhammad al-Abidin (i.e. Mir Jafar), *Sar-simt* (a kind of officer peculiar to the former Kingdom of Golkonda) of Kassimkota: inv. no. 41, folder 85.

From Mir 'Zeydh' Muhammad, *Diwan* at Masulipatam: inv. no. 41, folder 95.

From Muhammad Khan, *Qazi* at Narasapur: inv. no. 41, folder 107.

From Maulana Sahib (addressed to the 'Kapitan' of Masulipatam): inv. no. 40, folder 25.

From Aqa Mumin in Draksharama: inv. no. 40, folder 39.

From unidentified senders: inv. no. 40, folders 5, 14, 26, 43, 45, 54 and inv. no. 41, folders 55, 59, 63, 64, 69, 71, 80, 82, 84, 89-90, 93, 106, 109.

[10] Ibid., II, p. 771.

IN TELUGU

From 'Deedsjioe', Company *saraf* (banker): inv. no. 41, folder 5.
From Sidi Abdul-Nur in Ichchapuram: inv. no. 41, folder 21.
From 'Hadaij Fulha': inv. no. 41, folder 28.
From Reka Pillay Egappa Chitty, Company merchant at Masulipatam: inv. no. 41, folder 28 (envelope in folder 37).
From unidentified senders: inv. no. 41, folders 6, 7, 9-10, 12-20, 23, 25-27, 31, 33, 35, 39-40, 42, 70.

STRAY ENVELOPES

From Mir Abu Talib, *Faujdar* at Draksharama: inv. no. 40, folder 49; inv. no. 41, folder 8.
From the Company merchants belonging to the circle of 'Vepillij Narsoe', Company interpreter at Pulicat: inv. no. 41, folder 44.
From Sitaram: inv. no. 41, folder 50.
From Maasum Khan: inv. no. 40, folders 46, 58.
From Shaikh Abd-ur-Rahman, *Muhtahsib* (market superintendent): inv. no. 41, folder 74.
From Aqa Mumin in Draksharama: inv. no. 40, folder 39; inv. no. 41, folder 86.
From 'Miersijn' al-Abidin: inv. no. 41, folder 87.
From Mustafa Quli Khan: inv. no. 40, folders 38, 57; inv. no. 41, folder 88.
From Ali Akbar: inv. no. 40, folders 4, 17.
From 'Zeijd' Muhammad, *Diwan* at Masulipatam: inv. no. 40, folder 36.
From 'Deedsjioe', Company *saraf*: inv. no. 40, folder 51.
From Muhammad 'Achanbeeq' in Madapallam: inv. no. 40, folder 55.

F. *Minutes of outgoing letters*

Many translations of letters sent by Bacherus to Indians are to be found in the *OBP*, VOC 1511, ff. 1042-90v. The minutes of letters in Persian border on the illegible.

IN TELUGU

To Margal Bhupalli: inv. no. 41, folder 11.
To Mukheshwaram Rasu (Raja): inv. no. 41, folder 41.
To 'Miersia' Muhammad, *Havaldar* (caretaker, revenue farmer) of 'Conara': inv. no. 41, folder 41.
To Sitaram in Ichchapuram: inv. no. 41, folders 32, 41, 43.
To Vishvambar Dev: inv. no. 41, folders 41, 43.
To Nandepel at Srikakulam: inv. no. 41, folder 32.
To Sumerapala in 'Margol': inv. no. 41, folder 32.
To Sidi Abdul-Husain: inv. no. 41, folder 46.

IN PERSIAN

To Saru Khan Beg, *Tarafdar* (local official) at Petapoli: inv. no. 40, folder 35; inv. no. 41, folder 72.
To Shaikh Abd-ur-Rahman: inv. no. 40, folder 26.
To Maasum Khan: inv. no. 40, folders 19, 20, 28, 48.
To Mustafa Quli Khan, *Sar-lashkar* of Srikakulam: inv. no. 40, folders 24, 33.

G. *Unidentified documents*

Copies and minutes of documents in Persian
40, folders 6-8, 11-16, 18, 21-23, 27, 29-32, 34.
41, folders 29-30, 52, 65, 73, 75, 78, 81, 83, 93, 94, 98, 103.

Copies and minutes of documents in Telugu
41, folders 22, 36, 38, 45, 47-49, 51.

In an unidentified language
41, folder 92 A fragment of an *ola* inscribed with a script bearing close resemblance to Malayalam.

H. *Lists of contents*

40, folder 57 Large smudged envelope with legend: *minute in't persiaans van geschreve brieve aen verscheijde moorse grooten* (minutes in Persian of letters written to Muslim grandees).
41, folder 34 Table of contents to the originals of the four most important documents acquired as a result of the embassy to the Mughal court.

I. Documents of which the relation to the archives is unclear:

40, folder 3 Letter in Malay from a Siamese person, AD 1608.
40, folder 44 Letter from Bengal, AD 1723 (in Dutch).
40, folder 47 Document, AD 1605 (in Dutch).
40, folder 50 Acknowledgements of debt, AD 1606; letter from Surat, AD 1690 (in Dutch).
41, folder 24 Acknowledgement of debt, AD 1604 (in Dutch).

Isolated pieces can be found in some of the volumes of original correspondence of the factories that are also in the archives of the *Hoge Regering*. The following list is a selection:

172 a I, ff. 141, 153, 159, 261 Persian copies in *shekasta nastaliq* of a *parwana* of the new Bengal Nawab Muhammad Jafar and petitions (*arzi*, *arz-dasht*) to the Nawab of Bengal 1757-8, with Dutch translations.

172 a II, ff. 63, 66, 67, 119v, 129, 133, 247 — Copies in Persian of petitions by Governor A. Bisdom and the chief-factor of Cossimbazar Vernet to the Nawab of Bengal and letters (*khat*) to his *Ray-rayan* (in charge of the *khalisa* and the tolls) and the in-charge of requests, mostly with Dutch translations.

285, n.f. — Contains printed Persian translations of the notifications by the British Admiralty of the blockade of the Isles of France & Bourbon (dated 24 March, 1809) and of Java and the Moluccas (dated 10 June 1809).

868-869, n.f. — Contain a pledge to pay duties on textile by 'baupi Sorobjer', dated 1819, and three statements about the necessity of repairs of the Surat factory buildings by masons and carpenters of around the same date, all in Gujarati.

4. Archives of Other Institutions

No relevant documents found in inventories.

5. Personal and Family Papers

Van Eck

See 1.5.12
Access no.: 1.10.106

30 Contains some documents relating to Van Eck's period in Coromandel in Persian and Telugu and a document in what appears to be Burmese, possibly related to the expedition of the ship The King of Denmark (see 1.5.12):

(1) Minute of a letter in Persian to his most gracious and kind lordship (the Nizam of Hyderabad?) about the war season, date missing from page.
(2) Document in Burmese.
(3) Copies of two documents in Telugu, with Dutch translations:
- a *caul* granted by the Gajapatti Maharasu of Jeypur to the factors of Bimlipatam, 1759.
- a pledge by the factors C.L. Hagemeister and P.A. Bronsveld to pay the above Raja 2000 *pagodas* per annum, 1759.

(4) Translation of an *ola* of the King of Travancore.
(5-7) Documents in Telugu.
(8) Copy of a receipt in Telugu of Van Eck's *dubash* (interpreter), with a line in French.
(9) Document in Telugu with a postscript in Tamil by the son of the Marayappan.
(10) Document in Telugu.

44 Letter or statement in Armenian, in the dialect and script of the trading community originating from the New Julfa settlement at Isfahan, about the

keys to a certain box (with books?), drawn up in Rangoon in AD 1757, signed by Haruthiun Ter-Khatchatrènts, Grigor Evrazènts in Armenian script, Paulo Sardijnssen and Verqueth in Latin script and two others in Telugu script.[11] It is not clear how this document came into the possession of Van Eck.

Geleynssen de Jongh(e)

See 1.5.2
Access no.: 1.10.30

100 The first part of this volume contains copies in Persian (in Mughal shorthand) of the following documents, dating from the first 16 years of the reign of Shah Jahan whose era starts from his accession to the throne (*julus*) on 8 Jumada II 1037 AH.[12] Hence all the documents date from the years between AD 1628 and 1642. The documents are represented below in the order of the unfoliated volume:

(1) A *farman* (royal decree) of Shah Jahan, dated 9 Farwardi (*Fasli* calendar),[13] 1 Julus.
(2) Idem, dated 2 Khurdad 4 Julus.
(3) Idem, dated AH 29 Isfandar 7 Julus/ 29 Ramazan 1044.
(4) Idem, dated AH 19 Mihr 6 Julus / 7 Rabi II 1044.
(5) Idem, dated AH 19 Amardad 6 Julus / Muharram 1044.
(6) A *parwancha* (diminutive of *parwana*, order; authoritative letter) of Afzal Khan and Asaf Khan, dated 29 Dai 4 Julus. This *parwancha* refers to the *farman* dated 2 Khurdad 4 Julus (see 2).
(7) A *farman*, dated AH 22 Isfandar 8 Julus / 2 Shauwal 1045.
(8) Idem, dated AH 4 Aban 9 Julus / 23 Jumada I 1046, with an attached list of rates at which the tolls are set for different products in Bengal (Hooghly etc.). A contemporary Dutch translation of this *farman* is published in *CDNI*, I, pp. 286-9.
(9) A *yaddasht-i waqia* (memorandum on events), dated AH 31 Shahriwar 10 Julus / 2 Jumada II 1047 concerning a royal order.
(10) A *farman* of Shah Jahan, dated AH 24 Jamadi al-sani 11 Julus / 1047.
(11) Idem, dated AH 20 Safar 11 Julus / 1048 with a Dutch translation dated AD 17 July 1638. Another, rather different, translation of this *farman* is in *CDNI*, I, pp. 325-6.
(12, 13) Two Persian copies and two translations of a *farman*, dated AH 21 Safar 11 Julus / 1048/ AD 18 July (*sic*) 1638, with attached lists of toll rates in Bengal. Another contemporary translation has been published in *CDNI*, I, pp. 327-9.

[11] Mr Armén Joseph has determined the nature and broad contents of this piece for us.

[12] For a table of the regnal year of Shah Jahan see: S.A.I. Tirmizi, *Mughal Documents (A.D. 1628-59)*, Vol. 2 (Delhi, 1995).

[13] The months of the Fasli calendar are (in South Asian vocalization): Azur, Dai, Bahman, Isfandar, Farwardi, Ardibihist, Khurdad, Tir, Amardad, Shahriwar, Mihr and Aban (Sitapati and Nayeem, *Mughal Documents Catalogue*, Vol. 1, Part 1, p. 335).

(14) A letter (styled *parwancha*) of Asaf Khan in Lahore to his *Wakil* (representative) Hakim Muhammad Salah in Agra, dated 2 Zul-Qaada 12 Julus, about goods belonging to merchants from Quetta (in Sind) that were on board a Portuguese ship that was captured by the VOC. With a translation dated AD 7 March 1639.

(15) Minute of a letter (styled *arz-dasht*, petition) of the *Kapitan-i Valandez* (Geleynssen) to Asaf Khan, n.d. Refers to the *parwana* issued in the name of Hakim Muhammad Salah received in Zul-Qaada 29 Julus.

(16) *Parwancha* of Asaf Khan in Kabul to the chief-factor at Agra, dated 11 Muharram 12 Julus, with translation AD 13 May 1639. On the same topic as (14).

(17) *Arz-dasht* of Geleynssen to Asaf Khan, dated 14 Safar 12 Julus, with translation AD 22 June 1639; in response to (16).

(18) Minute of *arz-dasht* of Geleynssen to Asaf Khan, n.d.

(19) *Parwancha* of Asaf Khan in the name of the Emperor with translation, dated 11 Rajab 13 Julus / AD 6 November 1639.

(20) Minute of an *arz-dasht* of Geleynsen in response to (19) with translation, dated AD 29 November 1639.

(21, 22, 23) Dutch translations of *farmans*, dated AH 14 and 25 Shaban 16 Julus / 1052. Another copy of (23) has been published in *CDNI*, I, pp. 390-1.

103 Contains other copies in Persian (*shekasta nastaliq*) of the documents (14), (15), (16) and (17) that are contained in inv. no. 100 and listed above.

Sypesteyn (supplement)

See 1.5.6
Access: 1.13.19.02

2 Grammar of Hindustani and Persian by J.J. Ketelaar copied by Isaacq van der Hoeve van Uijtreght at Lucknow in 1698. With lists of declensions of nouns and adjectives and conjugations of verbs and word lists, all in Latin alphabet transcription. Also with a list of Muslim names, a list of weights and measures with their equivalents, and a short treatise on Indian 'liberation theology'. One volume. See also Bibliography, no. 327.

6. Separate Acquisitions and Microfilms

Losse aanwinsten (separate acquisitions)

See 1.6.1
Access no.: 1.11.01.01

659 Letter in Arabic script (*naskh*) from Ḳhalfan ibn Abdullah-al-Busaidi, Governor of Muscat, to the VOC Governor of Malabar, requesting permission to load timber in a ship from Muscat, 6 September 1779. One piece.

1661 Consists of a substantial amount of copies of incoming, and copies or minutes of outgoing correspondence of Hendrik van Gent, *Directeur* of the Surat factory from 1654 till his demise on 16 July 1657.[14] The bulk of the documents are concerned with the mission to Shahjahanabad (Delhi) by Joan Tack who was to bring to the attention of the Court various complaints of the VOC concerning greedy toll officials, goods stolen by a 'pirate' operating from the Kathiawar peninsula called Akiraji Varel (i.e. the Gohil ruler of Sihor?), financial claims by the merchant Virji Vohra[15] on a Company merchant called Mohan Das (who is not to be confused with the *wakil* (representative) of Akiraji Varel of the same name), etc.[16]

Leaving Agra on 10 July 1656 and arriving at Delhi eight days later, Tack was not received by Shah Jahan but he did have some audiences with Muhammad Said Ardistani,[17] the former Mir Jumla of Golkonda who had joined the Mughal ranks less than three months before receiving the title Muazzam Khan, and who had established a good relationship with the Dutch during his period in Golkonda. Tack was also received by Khalilullah Khan. There were also requests made to Jahanara Begam, better known as Begam Sahib (or Sahiba), the eldest daughter of Shah Jahan who held *jagirs* along the road from Agra to Lucknow.[18]

All these copies are written in Persian (*shekasta nastaliq*) on polished paper. About half the documents carry some Dutch notes on the contents. The pieces have been numbered with pencil in a random order and have therefore been arranged according to form and chronology, in the same way as those listed in the collection of the *Hoge Regering Batavia*. Nearly all of the documents, at least those that are dated, fall within the 30th regnal year of Shah Jahan, that is between 1 Jumada II 1066 and 30 Jumada I 1077 AH, corresponding to AD 27 March 1656 and 16 March 1657. Only three of the documents date from the period after this.

A. *Farmans*

doc. 2 *Farman* ordering Shams-ud-Din to help restore the goods stolen by Akiraji Varel to the Dutch, dated AH 14 Zul-Hija 30 Julus / 1066.

doc. 44 *Farman* issued to Roshan Zamir, concerning Virji Vohra and Mohan Das 'Naan', dated AH 14 Zul-Hija 30 Julus / 1066.

doc. 6 *Farman* written to Shaikh Muhammad Amin, 'Governor' of Surat, concerning the irregularities at the tolls and the mint, in response to letter doc. 5.

doc. 38 *Farman*, dated (?) Jumada I 30 Julus.

[14] Wijnaendts van Resandt, *Gezaghebbers* (see Bibliography, no. 131), pp. 277-8.

[15] Tirmizi, *Mughal Documents*, p. 27.

[16] *ARA*, VOC 1210, ff. 1050-2, excerpts from the daily record of the mission.

[17] *Maathir-ul-Umara*, II, pp. 188-204.

[18] Ibid., II, pp. 701, 1021. The exact location of her *jagirs* is unclear, but from the passage referring to them on p. 701 it is evident that they must be on the road to Lucknow.

B. *Nishans* (royal or princely letters)

doc. 51 *Nishan* of Dara Shukoh, the heir apparent to the Mughal throne, sent with a *sarapa* (robe of honour), dated 16 Zul-Qaada 1066, received 25 November 1656.
doc. 42 *Nishan* to Ali Quli Beg, dated 9 Safar 30 Julus.
doc. 36 *Nishan* of Murad Bakhsh, son of Shah Jahan, dated AH 14 Rabi I 30 Julus / 1067.
doc. 41 *Nishan*, dated 14 Rabi I 30 Julus.
doc. 17 *Nishan*, dated AH 16 Rabi II 30 Julus / 1067.

C. *Parwanas*

doc. 3 *Parwana* of the *Ray-rayan* concerning freedom from tolls on the road from Bengal to Agra, dated 4 Shaban 30 Julus.
doc. 8 *Parwana* of Mirak Shaikh (Haravi), the *Diwan* of Begam Sahib,[19] reminding the toll freedom enjoyed by the Dutch on the road from Delhi to Lucknow and beyond, dated 10 Shaban 30 Julus.
doc. 52 *Parwana* of Muazzam Khan concerning the arranged *farmans* (docs 2 and 44) and concerning some goods that his agent in Isfahan would like to send to Surat by a VOC ship, dated 24 Zul-Hija 30 Julus, received AD 10 December 1656.
doc. (no number) *Parwana* of Muazzam Khan, dated 10 Safar 30 Julus.
doc. 40 *Parwana* of Mutamad Khan, *Diwan* of prince Dara Shukoh,[20] dated 7 Zul-Qaada 30 Julus
doc. 43 *Parwana* of Itimad Khan (Mutamad Khan?), 22 Safar 30 Julus.
doc. 9 *Parwana* of Mirak Shaikh to Roshan Zamir, concerning accusations against the Dutch over fraud with the tolls, dated AH 14 Rabi II 30 Julus / 1066 (*sic*).
doc. 34 *Parwana* of Muazzam Khan, dated AH 29 Rabi II 1067.
doc. 35 *Parwana* of Mirak Shaikh, dated 3 Jumada I 1067.
doc. 53 *Parwana* of Muazzam Khan addressed to the Governor-General at Batavia, professing his friendship and requesting that his agent in Makassar might be taken on board a VOC ship along with some goods.

D. *Dastak* (pass)

(10) *Dastak* issued by Mirza Muzaffar Husain, containing a warning to toll collectors, dated 9 Shaban 30.

[19] Ibid., II, pp. 77-8.
[20] Ibid., II, pp. 343-4.

E. *Incoming letters*

doc. 59 Letter of Hafiz Nasr, former 'governor' of Surat, about his handing some presents to the Emperor in name of the VOC, received on 10 December 1656.

doc. 29 Letter of (or to) Ali Quli Beg, dated 26 Rabi II 1067.

doc. 37 *Kamayat* (?) of Ali Quli Beg, dated Rabi II 1067.

doc. 16 *Arz-dasht* of Mohan Das son of Uttam Chand and *wakil* of Akiraji Varel, dated 9 Zul-Qaada 1067.

doc. 27 Letter of 'Seki' Ramji (the uncle of?) Akiraji Varel, concerning 'Rajahai Maharaji'.

doc. 30 Letter of 'Seki' Ramji, n.d.

doc. 1 *Arz-dasht* of Mohan Das Uttam

doc. 39 *Arz-dasht* of Roshan Zamir.

F. *Copies of letters forwarded to Van Gent*

doc. 4 Letter of Mirak Shaikh, *Diwan* of Begam Sahib, to Shaikh Muhammad Amin, 'Governor' of Surat, warning him of the possibility of smuggling by the Dutch, dated 8 Rajab 30 Julus.

doc. 5 Letter of Rahmat Khan, *Diwan* of Ahmadabad, to Fazil Khan, concerning the tricks pulled by 'Aga Arabia', overseer of the mint, dated 12 Rajab 30 Julus.

doc. 58 Letter of Mirza (Ali) Quli Beg in response to a letter of Mohan Das, dated AH 7 Jumada I 1067.

doc. 46 Letter of Roshan Zamir to Mirak Shaikh, in response to doc. 9.

doc. 33 Letter of Sundar Das to Ali Quli Beg.

G. *Waqia* (newsreport)

doc. 15 *Waqia* reported from memory, dated 30 Safar 30 Julus.

H. *Outgoing correspondence (mainly styled arz-dasht)*

doc. 56 To Khalil Khan, with a request concerning the return of goods stolen from the VOC by the 'pirate' Akiraji Varel around Sind, as well as various other complaints over cases in which the VOC had been wronged and announcing the mission of Joan Tack to the Mughal court, dated 2 June 1656.

doc. 55 To Huri Khanam,[21] wet nurse of Begam Sahib, concerning Akiraji Varel, the claim laid on Mohan Das and other Company merchants at Surat by Virji Vohra and recommending Roshan Zamir, dated 2 June 1656.

doc. 14 To Begam Sahib, concerning the same, dated 2 June 1656.

[21] Ibid., II, p. 1021.

doc. 48	To Qutb Khan and (?) Khan, *Faujdars* (*sic*) of Junagadh, requesting the arrest of Akiraji Varel, dated 3 June 1656.
doc. 54	To Shah Jahan, concerning some of the complaints also mentioned in docs 56 and 55, dated 6 June 1656.
doc. 49	To Muazzam Khan, thanking him for the kindness shown to the envoy Joan Tack and to the Dutch at Pulicat and concerning the accusations against the Dutch voiced in doc. 9, dated 18 October 1656.
doc. 50	To Muazzam Khan, notifying him of the arrival from Basra of the horses promised to him and the Emperor in doc. 49, dated 29 Muharram 1067, 18 November 1656.
doc. 21	To Murad Bakhsh, son of Shah Jahan, in Ahmadabad, dated 5 Rabi II 1067.
doc. 20	To Murad Bakhsh, dated 6 Rabi II 1067.
doc. 23	To Murad Bakhsh, dated 12 Rabi II 1067.
doc. 25	To Ali Quli Beg, dated 19 Rabi II 1067.
doc. 32	To Muazzam Khan, dated 29 Rabi II 1067.
doc. 60	To 'Raja-i Ratmahal Jan', dated AH 16 Jumada I 1067.
doc. 61	To *nakhuda* (ship's captain) Shaikh Shahab-ar-Rab, 3 Jumada II 1067.
doc. 57	To Shah Jahan, dated 15 Jumada II 1067.
doc. 13	To Ali Quli Beg, *Faujdar* of Junagadh, dated 23 Jumada II 1067.
doc. 22	To Mir Ali Naqi, *Diwan* of Ahmadabad.
doc. 24	To Mir Ali Naqi, *Diwan* of Ahmadabad.
doc. 19	To Muazzam Khan.
doc. 7	To Namaz Khan, concerning Akiraji Varel.
doc. 11	To Begam Sahib.
doc. 47	To Khalil Khan, containing a proposal to forego the toll freedom and again pay tolls on the old footage because of misuse of the Dutch privilege by third persons, n.d.
doc. 45	To Shah Jahan, concerning the same.
doc. 12	To Mohan Das.
doc. 18	To 'Daja Kaja' about 'Raja Maharaji'.

I. *Miscellaneous*

Docs 26 (relating to Ali Quli Beg), 28 (to Mohan Das) and 31 are copies or minutes abandoned after a few words.

APPENDIX II: DUTCH CHIEFS IN BATAVIA AND SOUTH ASIA

1. BATAVIA

1610-14	Pieter Both
1614-15	Gerard Reynst
1616-19	Laurens Reael
1619-23	Jan Pietersz. Coen
1623-7	Pieter de Carpentier

1627-9	Jan Pietersz. Coen
1629-32	Jacques Specx
1632-6	Henrick Brouwer
1636-45	Antonio van Diemen
1645-50	Cornelis van der Lijn
1650-3	Carel Reniers (*see also* Coromandel)
1653-78	Joan Maetsuyker (*see also* Ceylon)
1678-81	Rijcklof van Goens Senior (*see also* Ceylon)
1681-4	Cornelis Janszoon Speelman (*see also* Coromandel)
1684-91	Joannes Camphuys
1691-1704	Willem van Oudthoorn
1704-9	Joan van Hoorn
1709-13	Abraham van Riebeeck
1713-18	Christoffel van Zwoll
1718-25	Hendrik Zwaardecroon (*see also* Surat)
1725-9	Mattheus de Haan
1729-31	Diederik Durven
1731-5	Dirck van Cloon (*see also* Coromandel)
1735-7	Abraham Patras (*see also* Bengal)
1737-41	Adriaan Valckenier
1741-3	Johannes Thedens
1743-50	Gustaaf Willem (Baron) van Imhoff (*see also* Ceylon)
1750-61	Jacob Mossel (*see also* Coromandel)
1761-75	Petrus Albertus van der Parra
1775-7	Jeremias van Riemsdijk
1777-80	Reynier de Klerck
1780-96	Willem Arnold Alting
1796-1801	Petrus Gerardus van Overstraten

2. SURAT

1620-8	Pieter van den Broecke
1628-33	Johan van Hasel
1633-4	Jacob van der Graeff
1634-40	Barend Pietersz
1640-4	Paulus Croocq
1644-8	Arent Barents (Muyskens)
1648-51	Johan van Teylingen
1651-4	Gerard Pelgrim
1654-7	Hendrik van Gent
1657-8	Isaac Coedijck
1657-61	Leonard Winnincx
1661-5	Dirk van Adrichem
1665-6	Abraham Hartman
1666-7	Huybert de Lairesse
1667-73	Andries Boogaert

1673-6	Willem Volger (*see also* Bengal)
1676-8	Sybrand Abbema
1678-9	Daniël Parvé
1680-5	Jacques de Bucquoy
1685-91	Gelmer Vosburgh (*see also* Malabar)
1691-2	Pieter van Helsdingen and Adriaan van Ommen (*see also* Malabar)
1692-?	Louis de Keizer
1695-8	Pieter Ketting
1699-1701	Hendrik Zwaardecroon (*see also* Batavia)
1701-56	Pieter de Vos
1707-8	Johan Grotenhuys
1708-10	Cornelis Besuyen
1711-15	Johan Joshua Ketelaar
1715-19	Daniel Hurgronje
1719-22	Philip Zaal
1722-6	Abraham Weijns
1726-8	Herman Bruyning
1729-40	Pieter Lourens Phoonsen
1740-9	Jan Schreuder (*see also* Ceylon)
1749-53	Johannes Pecock
1753-5	Johan de Roth
1755-9	Louis Taillefert (*see also* Bengal)
1759-63	Jan Drabbe
1763-8	Christiaan Lodewijk Senff (*see also* Malabar)
1768-76	Martinus Joan Boschman
1776-81	Willem Jacob van de Graaff (*see also* Ceylon and Coromandel)
1784-92	Abraham Josias Sluysken
1792-5	Peter Sluysken
1818-?	B.C. Verploegh

3. Malabar

1663	Pieter de Bitter and Cornelis Valkenburg
1663-6	Ludolph van Coulster
1666-8	Isbrand Godske
1668-70	Lucas van der Dussen
1670-7	Hendrik Adriaan van Reede
1677-8	Jacob Lobs
1678-84	Marten Huysman (*see also* Bengal)
1684-7	Gelmer Vosburgh (*see also* Surat)
1687-93	Isaack van Dielen
1693-4	Alexander Wigmans (*see also* Vengurla)
1694-6	Adriaan van Ommen (*see also* Surat)
1696-8	Pieter Coesaart
1698-1701	Magnus Wichelman
1701-4	Abraham Vink

1704-8	Willem Moerman
1708-9	Adam van der Duijn
1709-16	Barend Ketel
1716-23	Johannes Hertenberg (*see also* Ceylon)
1723-31	Jacob de Jong Senior
1731-4	Adriaan Maten
1734-42	Julius Valentijn Stein van Gollonesse (*see also* Ceylon)
1742-7	Reinerus Siersma
1747-51	Corijn Stevens
1751	Abraham Cornelis de la Haye
1751-6	Frederik Cunes
1756-60	Casparus de Jong
1760-4	Godefridus Weyerman
1764-8	Cornelis Breekpot
1768-70	Christiaan Lodewijk Senff (*see also* Surat)
1770-80	Adriaan Moens
1780-93	Johan Gerard van Angelbeek (*see also* Ceylon)
1793-5	Jan Lambertus van Spall

Vengurla

1637-41	Pieter (Petrus) Paets
1641-3	Nicolaes (Claes) Corneliszoon Blocq
1643-5	Cornelis van Sanen
1645-6	Martijn Poortmans
1646-8	Pieter Sterthemius (*see also* Bengal)
1648-51	Otto Hoeckgeest
1651-3	Jacob Bacheragt
1653-4	Leendert Jamon
1654-8	Leendert Janszoon
1658-64	Peter van Santvliet
1664-9	Craan Leendertszoon
1669-73	Rombout Lefer
1673-5	Alexander Wigmans (*see also* Malabar)
1675-81	Abraham Lefebre and Alexander Wigmans (*see also* Malabar)
1681-3	Robbert Lindzaij
1683-7	Daniel Jongktijs
1687-90?	Abraham Lefebre
1690?-3	Jacob Trogh

4. Ceylon

1640	Willem Jacobsz Coster
1640-6	Jan Thijssen (Payart)
1646-50	Joan Maetsuyker (*see also* Batavia)
1650-3	Jacob van Kittensteyn

1653-62	Adriaan van der Meijden
1662-3	Rijcklof van Goens Senior (*see also* Batavia)
1663-4	Jacob Hustaert (*see also* Coromandel)
1664-5	Adriaan Roothaes
1665-75	Rijcklof van Goens Senior (*see also* Batavia)
1675-9	Rijcklof van Goens Junior
1679-92	Laurens Pijl
1692-7	Thomas van Rhee
1696-1702	Gerrit de Heere
1702-7	Cornelis Jan Simonsz
1707-16	Hendrik Bekker
1716-23	Isaak Augustijn Rumph
1723-5	Johannes Hertenberg (*see also* Malabar)
1725-6	Johan Paul Schagen
1726-9	Petrus Vuyst (*see also* Bengal)
1729-32	Stephanus Versluys
1732-6	Diederik van Domburgh
1736-40	Gustaaf Willem (Baron) van Imhoff (*see also* Batavia)
1740-2	Willem Maurits Bruininck
1742-3	Daniel Overbeek
1743-51	Julius Valentijn Stein van Gollonesse (*see also* Malabar)
1751-2	Gerard Johan van Vreelandt
1752	Jacob de Jong Junior
1752-7	Joan Gideon Loten
1757-61	Jan Schreuder (*see also* Surat)
1761-5	Lubbert Jan van Eck (*see also* Coromandel)
1765-85	Iman Willem Falck
1785-94	Willem Jacob van de Graaff (*see also* Surat and Coromandel)
1794-6	Johan Gerard van Angelbeek (*see also* Malabar)

5. Coromandel

1608-10	Pieter Isaacx Eyloff
1610-12	Johan van Wesicke
1612-15	Wemmer van Berchem
1616	Hans de Haze
1616-17	Samuel Kint
1617-19	Adolf Thomassen
1619-20	Hans de Haze
1620-2	Andries Soury
1622-4	Abraham van Uffelen
1625-6	Andries Soury
1626-30	Maerten IJsbrantsz
1632	Arent Gardenijs
1632-3	David Pietersz

1633-6	Maerten IJsbrantsz
1636-8	Carel Reniers (*see also* Batavia)
1638-43	Arent Gardenijs
1643-50	Arnold Heussen
1650-1	Laurens Pit Senior
1651	Jacob de With
1652-63	Laurens Pit Senior
1663-5	Cornelis Janszoon Speelman (*see also* Batavia)
1665-76	Antony Paviljoen
1676-9	Jacques Caulier
1679-81	Willem Carel Hartsinck
1681-6	Jacob Joriszn Pits
1686-98	Laurens Pit Junior
1698-1705	Dirk Coomans
1705-10	Johannes van Steelandt
1710-16	Daniel Bernard Guilliams
1716-19	Adriaan de Visscher
1719-23	Gerrit van Westrenen
1723-30	Dirck van Cloon (*see also* Batavia)
1730-3	Adriaan Pla
1733-7	Elias Guillot
1738-43	Jacob Mossel (*see also* Batavia)
1743-7	Galenus Mersen
1747-53	Librecht Hooreman
1753-8	Steven Vermont
1758-61	Lubbert Jan van Eck (*see also* Ceylon)
1761-5	Christiaan van Teylingen
1765-71	Pieter Haksteen
1771-80	Reynier van Vlissingen
1784-5	Willem Jacob van de Graaff (*see also* Surat and Ceylon)
1785-9	Willem Blauwkamer
1789-90	Tadema
1790-5	Jacob Eilbracht
1818-24	F.C. Regel
1824-5	Henry François von Söhsten

6. BENGAL

1655-8	Pieter Sterthemius (*see also* Vengurla)
1658-63	Mattheus van den Broucke
1663-5	Rogier van Heyningen
1665-8	Arnoldus van Wachtendonck
1668-9	Joan Velters
1669-73	Constantijn Ranst Junior
1673-4	Jacob Verburgh, Pieter Hofmeester and Herman Fentzel

1674-6	François de Haze
1677-8	Willem Volger (*see also* Surat)
1678-80	Jacob Verburgh
1681-3	Nicolaas Baukes
1683-5	Marten Huysman (*see also* Malabar)
1685-8	Nicolaas Schagen
1688	Pieter Willeboorts
1688-96	Arnoldus Muyskens
1696-1701	Pieter van Dishoeck
1701-5	Jacob Pelgrom
1705-10	Willem de Roo
1710-16	Anthony Huysman
1717-22	Ewout van Dishoeck
1722-4	Petrus Vuyst (*see also* Ceylon)
1724-7	Abraham Patras (*see also* Batavia)
1727-31	Jacob Sadelijn
1731-3	Rogier Beernards
1734-44	Jan Albert Sichterman
1744-50	Jan Huygens
1750-5	Jan Kersseboom
1755	Louis Taillefert (*see also* Surat)
1755-60	Adriaan Bisdom
1760-3	Louis Taillefert (*see also* Surat)
1763-9	George Lodewijk Vernet
1769-70	Boudewijn Versewel Faure
1771-6	Johannes Bacheracht
1776-81	Johannes Mattheus Ross
1784-5	Gregorius Herklots
1785-92	Isaac Titsingh
1792-5	Cornelis van Citters Aarnoutszoon
1795	Johan Willem Salomon von Haugwitz
1817-18	Jan Andries van Braam
1818-25	Daniel Antonie Overbeek

APPENDIX III: INDO-DUTCH SPELLING LIST

This list is far from exhaustive and only serves as a rough guideline for understanding Indo-Dutch spelling. The Dutch made various, and at times hardly recognizable, versions of each Indian term they encountered. Therefore, this list attempts to compensate this inconsistency by presenting various Dutch spellings of some of the most eye-catching Indian terms: geographical and personal names, official and dynastic terms, and group names. For a glossary of VOC terms, see the on-line *VOC glossarium. Verklaring van termen, verzameld uit de RGP-publicaties die betrekking hebben op de Verenigde Oost-Indische Compagnie*, compiled by M. Kooijmans and J.E. Schooneveld-Oosterling (http://www.kb.nl/ing/).

1. Place Names

Surat (including Sind and Hindustan)

Agra	Agra
Ahmadabad	Amed Abaad, Amedabaet, Ametabad, Ammadabath
Ajmer	Asmeer
Aurangabad	Aurangabadda, Orangabath, Ourangabaad
Awadh	see Oudh
Baroda	Brodera, Brodra
Bassein	Basaijn, Bassin, Bazijn
Bayana	Bayana
Benares	Benaris, Binares
Bharuch	see Broach
Bombay	Bombaij, Bombaim, Bombaja, Bombaria
Broach	Brochia, Broot Chia, Brootschia, Brotchia
Burhanpur	Barampoer, Berhampour, Boerampoer, Brampoer
Cambay	Cambaija
Daman	Daman, Domon
Daulatabad	Dolhabat
Delhi	Dilli, Dillij; see also Shahjahanabad
Diu	Dieuw
Gujarat	Gezaratta, Gouzeratta, Guseratte
Hindaun	Hindoon
Hindustan	Hindostan, Industan
Jalor	Jaloor
Khambhat	see Cambay
Lahore	Lahoor, Lahor
Malwa	Malva
Mumbai	see Bombay
Narmada	Narwadda
Oudh	Oude
Shahjahanabad	Sahiahanabad, Sasiahanabath, Zayahamabaet; see also Delhi
Sind	Sinda, Sindhij, Sindij
Surat	Souratte, Suratten, Zouratta, Zuratte
Suvali	Soualij, Suahely, Sualij, Suhaly
Tatta	Tetta
Vadodara	see Baroda
Varanasi	see Benares
Yamuna	Djemna

Malabar (including Kanara and Konkan)

Aguada	Agoada
Alangadu	syn. Mangattij
Alappuzha	see Alleppey

Alleppey	Alepe, Allepee
Anjengo	Ansjenga
Attingal	Atingen
Azhikkodu	Aicotte
Badagara	Bargaree, Berregare
Baliapatam	Billiapattam
Bankot	Bancoot
Barcelore	Barsaloor; see also Coondapoor, Kanara, Karnatika
Basrur	see Barcelore, Coondapoor, Kanara, Karnatika
Bedrur	Bidloer, Bidroer; see also Ikkeri, Kanara, Karnatika
Bhatkal	Batacala, Batacalo
Bijapur	Visiapoer, Visiapour
Bonsulo	Bonsuelo
Calicut	Calacoute, Calicoet, Kalikut; see also Zamorin (under Malabar)
Cannanore	Cananaar, Connanoor, Kananoor; see also Ali Raja and Kolathiri (under Malabar)
Chaul	Chaul
Chavakkadu	see Chowghat
Chennamangalam	Cheremangalam, Cheremgalam, Sjeremangelan; also Chenotij, Chenotta; see also Paliyath Achan (under Malabar)
Chetwai	Chettuwa, Chitua
Chowghat	Chauwelecattoe, Sjawelcattoe
Cochin	Cochijn, Couchim, Coutheim, Coxijn, Koetsjen, Koetsjiem
Colachel	Colletje
Coondapoor	Coondapoór; see also Barcelore, Kanara, Karnatika
Cranganur	Cranganoor
Dabhol	Dabul
Danda Rajapuri	Dendarajapour
Deccan	Decan, Deccan
Desinganadu	see Quilon
Edappalli	Repelin, Repolim, Tripolin
Edaturutti	Edatouritti
Goa	Goa
Honavar	Onor
Ikkeri	Ikari, Ikeri; see also Bedrur, Kanara, Karnatika
Janjira	Gingerah
Kanara	Canara, Cannara; see also Arcot (under Coromandel), Barcelore, Bedrur, Coondapoor, Ikkeri, Karnatika, Madurai (under Ceylon), Mysore, Vijayanagara (under Coromandel) Note: it mainly refers to the area of the Kanara Coast e.g. the Dutch factory at Barcelore or its hinterland states of Ikkeri and, possibly, Mysore.
Kannur	see Cannanore

Karnatika	Carnatica, Karnatika; see also Arcot (under Coromandel), Barcelore, Bedrur, Coondapoor, Ikkeri, Kanara, Madurai (under Ceylon), Mysore, Vijayanagara (under Coromandel) Note: it generally refers to the territory of the old Kingdom of Vijayanagara. More specifically it refers to its main successor state of Chandragiri/Vellore and, occasionally, to Ikkeri or, in the eighteenth century, to Arcot and its dependencies.
Karthikappalli	syn. Betemene, Bethimenij, Carembalie
Karunagappalli	Carnapolie; also Martapoura, Martha, Martingal, Martingalcour, Pannapolie
Kayankulam	Calcoijlang, Calicoylan, Kalicoilan
Keladi	see Bedrur, Ikkeri, Kanara, Karnatika
Kochi	see Cochin
Kodungallur	see Cranganur
Kollam	see Quilon
Konkan	Concan, Cuncan
Kozhikode	see Calicut
Laccadive Islands	Lakkadivose eilanden
Lakshadweep	see Laccadive Islands
Mah~	Mahe
Malabar	Mallabaer
Mangalore	Mangeloor
Mapranam	Mapera Nette, Maperane, Maprana
Mavelikara	Mavelicarre
Mysore	Maijsoer, Massour; see also Kanara, Karnatika
Nedumangadu	syn. Peretalie, Perittallij
Pallippuram	Paliporte, Paliporto
Parur	Paroe, Parou
Ponnani	Pananay, Pannanij
Pudikovil	Poedia Calottoe, Poedicoilotte
Purakkad	Porca, Porka
Quilon	Coilan, Coylan, Koijlang
Rajapur	Raghiapour
Raybag	Ragiabaech, Ragiebaagh
Srirangapatnam	Sirengepatnam
Taingapatam	see Tengapattanam
Tanur	syn. Betette
Tekkumkur	Teckencore, Teckencour, Tekkencoer
Tellicherry	Tallicherij
Tengapattanam	Tegenepatnam, Tengapatnam, Tengepatnam Note: not to be confused with Teganapatam in Coromandel.
Thalasseri	see Tellicherry
Travancore	Trevancoor

Vadakkumkur	Berckencore, Berckencouw, Berkencour
Vaipin	Baipin, Baypin, Vaijpien
Valluvanadu	Ballanaden
Velosenadu	see Mapranam
Vengurla	Wingurla
Vilinjam	Brins Jan
Vypin	see Vaipin

Ceylon (including Fishery Coast and Maldives)

Akuressa	Accuras
Alutkuru Korale	AlloetkoerKorls
Alwar Tirunagarai	Allwatiennegary
Ambalangoda	Amblangodde
Analaitivu	Annelletivoe; syn. Rotterdam Island
Appuratota	Appoeretotte
Arippu	Aripa, Aripo, Aripoe
Baipar	Baijpaar
Batticaloa	Batacala, Batecalou, Battacaloa, Batticalo
Bentota	Bentotte
Cape Comorin	Caab Commorijn, Kaap Comorijn
Ceylon	Ceijlon, Cheijlon; see also Kandy
Chilaw	Chilau, Chilouw, Schilauw, Silauw
Colombo	Calamba, Colombo, Columbo, Kolombo
Eluvativu	Ellewativo; syn. Woest Eijland
Fishery Coast	syn. Madurese kust
Galle	Gaalen, Gale, Galen; also Puncto Gaele
Giant's Tank	syn. Reuzentank
Gintota	Gindure
Hakmana	Hakman
Hammenhiel	Hammenhiel, Hammerhiel
Hanwella	Hangwelle
Happittigam Korale	Happitagam Corle
Hewagam Korale	Hewegam Corla
Jaffna	Jaffanapatnam, Jaffenepatnaem, Jeftenapatnam
Kalpitiya	Calpentijn, Calpeti, Calpetty, Kalpettij
Kalutara	Calitura, Caliture, Calture
Kandy	Candia; see also Ceylon
Kanyakumari	see Cape Comorin
Karaitivu	Caretivo; syn. Amsterdam Island
Katuwana	Catoene, Katoene
Kayalpatnam	Cailpatnam, Kalipatnam
Kilakkarai	Cilcare, Kalkare, Kilkare
Kondaichi	Condaatje, Condaitje, Condatje
Kotte	Kotta
Kottiyar	Cotjaer, Koetjaar

Madurai	Madure, Mature; also Madurese rijk; see also Kanara, Karnatika (under Malabar) Note: after Madurai had been annexed by Arcot it was often referred to as Karnatika, 'Carnaticase benedenlanden'. Not to be confused with Matara on Ceylon or Madura near Java.
Mahagama	Mahagamme
Maldives	Maldivos, Maldiwas
Manapadu	Mannapaer
Mandagetto	Mandagetto
Mannar	Manaer
Mantota	Mantotte
Marawila	Maravile
Matara	Mature Note: not to be confused with Madurai near the Fishery Coast or Madura near Java.
Matturai	see Matara
Musal Tivu	Moesjeltieve
Nainativu	Naynativo; syn. Haarlem Island
Nallatanni Tivu	syn. Soetwaters Eyland, Vers Water Eyland
Nallur	Nalloer
Nanaddan	Nanatan
Negombo	Negumba, Nigombo
Nilwala	Nielwelle
Nilwala River	Nielvalle Gange, Nieuwallegange
Pamban	Pambe, Pembenaer
Pamban Channel	see Pamban
Panadura	Paneture
Panama	Panneme
Point Calimere	Calimeere, Caymeer, Corimorie, Kaljemere
Point Pedro	Punt Pedro; also Pedre
Pooneryn	Ponerij, Ponnerijn
Pudukkottai	see Tondaiman (under Malabar)
Punkudutivu	Poengertivol; syn. Middelburg Island
Punneikayal	Ponnecail
Puttalam	Putulang
Rameswaram	syn. Ramanecoil
Rameswaram Island	syn. Pambe eiland, Pembenaer eiland
Ramnad	see Ramanathapuram
Ramanathapuram	Rammenadewaram; also "Marruasse rijk"; see also Setupati (under Malabar)
Ruwanwella	Roeanella, Ruanelle
Salpiti Korale	Salpittie Korls
Sitwaka	Sitavaque
Sivagangai	Sewaginga; see also Udaya Tevar (under Malabar)
Sri Lanka	see Ceylon

Tala	Tale
Thampalakamam	Tamblegam
Tiruchchendur	Trisenadour, Trisinadoura
Tiruchirappalli	Tieroesirapally, Tresjenapalij, Trickenapaly, Trissenapoli, Tritchenepalij, Tritje Napalli
Tirunelveli	Ternevelho, Tirnelvelha, Tirneville
Tondi	Tondy
Trincomalee	Trincomali, Trinconomale, Trincquenemale, Trinquemale
Tuticorin	Tutucorijn
Unawatuna	Oenewatte
Vembar	Bempaar
Vandeloos Bay	Venlos baai
Vanni	Wannij
Walawe	Waluwe
Walallwiti Korale	Wallawitti Corle
Weligama	Bellegam, Billigam

Coromandel

Alambaram	Alambrue, Alemperwe, Elenbrue
Andaman Islands	Andoman
Arcot	Arcaroe, Arkadoe, Arkatte; see also Kanara, Karnatika (under Malabar) Note: its southern part around Madurai is often referred to as 'Carnaticase benedenlanden'.
Bimlipatam	Bimelepatnam, Bimilipatnam
Chennai	see Madras
Coleroon	Colderon
Cocanada	see Kakinada
Coringa	Coringa
Coromandel	Chormandel, Chormandela, Cormandel
Covelong	Couwelang
Cuddalore	Coedeloer, Coereloer
Cuddapah	Caddappa
Deccan	Decan, Deccan
Draksharama	Daatcheron
Gingee	Chensier, Chingier, Gingij, Singier, Singij, Sinsy
Golkonda	Golconda, Golkonda; see also Hyderabad
Hyderabad	Heiterabaad; see also Golkonda
Ichchapuram	Itsapoer, Itsapoeram
Irikam	Erikan
Jagannathapuram	Jaggernaijkpoeram
Jamshedpet	Samsoetepeent, Zamsoetepeet
Jinji	see Gingee
Kakinada	Kakienara
Kanchipuram	Cansjewaron, Conjewaram

Karikal	Carcal, Carical
Kassimkota	Casiemcote
Katira	Contera, Contira
Krishna	Kristna
Kunimedu	Conjemere
Machilipatnam	see Masulipatam
Madapallam	Madepalem
Madras	Madraspatnam
Masulipatam	Masilepetan, Maslipatam, Maslupatnam, Mazulipatnam
Motupalli	Moetoe Pilly
Nagappattinam	Nagapatnam, Negapatnam
Nagulvancha	Nagelwance, Nagelwanoe, Nauglauwanse, Negelewanse
Nagore	Nagore
Narasapur	Naersipoer, Narospour, Narsapour, Narsepoer
Nicobar Islands	Nicobaarsche eijlanden, Nicobares
Nizampatnam	Nysampatnam
Northern Circars	see Srikakulam
Palakollu	Paliacol, Palicol
Parangipettai	see Porto Novo
Peddapuram	Peddapour
Petapoli	Patapoely, Petapoullij, Pettapouilly, Pitijpoely
Pithapuram	Pitthapour
Pondicherry	see Puducherry
Porto Novo	Portonovo
Puducherry	Podecheri, Poedcherij, Pollicere, Poudecherij
Pulicat	Paleacatta, Paliakatten, Palliacatta; also Casteel Geldria, Geldria
Sadras	Sadrangatam, Sadrapatnam, Sadraspatnam, Sadrempatam, Sandragapatnam, Zadraspatnam
Srikakulam	Chikakol, Cicacole, Sicacol
St. Thomas	see St. Thome
St. Thome	St. Thom, St. Thomee
Tanjore	see Thanjavur
Thanjavur	Tansjour, Tansjouwer, Transjaour
Teganapatam	Tegenapatnam, Tegenepatnam Note: not to be confused with Tengapattanam in Malabar.
Thiruppapuliyar	Tierepopelier, Tierepopely
Thiruvarur	Trivaloer
Tirumalapatnam	Trimelepatnam
Tirumullaivaisal	Trimelevaes, Trimelewaas
Tirupati	Tripatij
Tranquebar	Trangabaere, Trankebaar, Tranquebaar
Tuni	Thuny
Vellore	Velour, Wiloer

Vijayanagara	Bisnagar, Visnagar; syn. Narsinga; see also Kanara, Karnatika (under Malabar)
Vishakhapatnam	Vijsagepatnam, Vijsiagapatan, Visagapatnam
Yanam	Ennam, Janam

Bengal (including Bihar)

Assam	Asam, Asem, Assam
Balasore	Bellazoor, Bellesoor
Baleshwar	see Balasore
Banar	Bonnaer
Banquibazar	Banquibasar
Baranagar	Barnagoor, Barrenger, Bernagoor
Benares	Benaris, Binares
Bengal	Bengale, Bengalen, Benghaelen
Bihar	Behaar
Burdwan	Bharda
Calcutta	Calcatte, Kalkaṭta
Chandernagore	Chanderaagoor, Sandernagoor
Chhapra	Sjappra
Chinsura	Chinsura, Cintsura, Sinsera, Sinsura, Tsunsiora
Cossimbazar	Cassembasaer, Cassima-basaer, Cassumabasar
Cuttack	Catteck
Dhaka	Decca, Dhecca
Falta	Valta, Volta
Frederiksnagore	see Serampore
Ganga	see Ganges
Ganges	Ganges
Guwahati	Koehatti
Hijili	Hinsele, Ingeli, Inselij
Hooghly	Houglij, Ougli, Ougly
Hugli	see Hooghly
Karimabad	Cariemabaath, Cariemo Abath
Khanakul	Canacoul, Channakoel
Kolkata	see Calcutta
Lakhya	Lokkia
Malda	Malda, Maldouw
Mirzapur	Miersapour
Murshidabad	Morchidabaad, Moxudabath
Orissa	Orixa, Orixoe
Palmyras Point	Puncto Palmeris
Patna	Pattana, Pattena, Puttena
Phalta	see Falta
Pipli	Pepely, Piepelij, Pipeli, Piplij
Rajmahal	Ragiamahal, Ragiemahol, Ragimahal
Sagar Island	Sagor, Sangor, Zaagor
Serampore	Seraampoer

Sherpur	Ceerpour
Udaiganj	Oudagijns
Varanasi	see Benares

2. Personal Names

Abdullah Qutb Shah (Golkonda)	Abdulla Kotb Sjah
Abul-Hasan Qutb Shah (Golkonda)	Abdul Hassen Kotubsjah, Aboe il Hassan Kotubsjah
Akbar (Mughal)	Ekbar
Akiraji Varel (Kathiawar)	Ackeraas Vareel
Ali Adil Shah (Bijapur)	Alie Adelsia
Alivardi Khan (Bengal)	Aliwerdi Khan
Asad Khan (Mughal)	Assetchan
Aurangzeb (Mughal)	Eurangseeb, Oranghseeffber, Orangzeeph
Azam Khan (Mughal)	Hasemchan
Azam Shah (Mughal)	Assem Tarra
Babba Prabhu (Malabar)	Babbaporbou
Bahadur Shah (Mughal)	Bhadur Sjah
Basavappa (Ikkeri)	Bassapa; also Ghelada Bassapa
Bhavani Sankara (Ramnad)	Bawana Singoe, Pawana Sangoe
Chanda Sahib (Arcot, Madurai)	Sanda Sahib
Chennamaji (Ikkeri)	Tsina Amasi
Chokkanatha Nayak (Madurai)	Sjoekenade Naijk, Sjokkenade Nayker
Dara Shukoh (Mughal)	Dara Secoer, Dara Shekoeh
Daud Khan (Arcot)	Daved Khan
Dost Ali Khan (Arcot)	Alidoost Khan
Ekoji (Thanjavur)	Egosie
Farrukh Siyar (Mughal)	Farog Sjeer, Farrochier
Goda Varma (Cochin)	Godormo, Kedorma
Haji Husain (Pithapuram)	Hagie Housseen
Haidar Ali Khan (Mysore)	Aider Allij Chan, Haider Alikan
Islam Khan (Mughal)	Eslingan
Itibar Khan (Surat)	Ette Baarchan
Jahangir (Mughal)	Djihaan Gier
Kankul Venkanna (Masulipatam)	Caalcolij Aukena
Kanoji Angria (Kanara)	Canage Angrea, Cangie Angria
Kattaya Tevar (Ramnad)	Catta Teuver
Kerala Varma (Travancore)	Kelorma, Kelormo
Kilavan (Ramnad)	Kelewe
Malik Qasim (Mughal)	Melccassum, Melckcassum
Mangammal (Madurai)	Mangamma
Minakshi (Madurai)	Minaatje
Mir Jafar (Bengal)	Mier Jaffer
Mir Jumla (Golkonda, Mughal)	Miersamela, Misumla; also Mosemchan; see also Muhammad Said

Muhammad Adil Shahi (Bijapur)	Mohamed Adilsja
Muhammad Ali (Arcot)	Mamoed Ali; also Machmet Alichan, Soebamachmet Alikan
Muhammad Azim (Bengal)	Mahomet a Zim
Muhammad Said Ardistani (Golkonda, Mughal)	syn. Miermamed Sahy, Mir Mameth, Mosemchan; see also Mir Jumla
Murshid Quli Khan (Bengal)	Morcied Coeli Khan
Mustafa Khan (Bijapur)	Moestafchan
Muthu Virappa Nayak (Madurai)	Moedoe Wierappa
Nadir Shah (Persia)	Nader Sjah; also Thamas Coulichan
Neknam Khan (Mughal)	Nichnamchan; also Vrichnamchon
Nizam-ul-Mulk (Hyderabad)	Nisam Moelmolk, Nisamanmolk, Nisan Melmolk
Peda Venkata (Vijayanagara)	Wenketepatie; also Wenketepatie Railoe
Pratap Singh (Thanjavur)	Pretappa Singaja
Raghuji Bhonsle (Maratha)	Ragosie Bhonsale
Raghunath Rao (Maratha)	Ragoenadarouw
Rajasinga (Kandy)	Radia Singa, Ragia Singa
Rajaram (Maratha)	Ramaragie, Ramarasja, Ramarasoe
Raksika Das (Surat)	Ritsigdas
Rama Varma (Cochin, Travancore, Cranganur)	Ramorma
Ramadeva Raya (Vijayanagara)	Rama Deur, Rama Deuwarya, Ramadewe
Saadatullah Khan (Arcot)	Sadoelachan, Sadoulachan
Safdar Ali Khan (Arcot)	Saphteralichan
Sarfaraz Khan (Bengal)	Serferaar Chan
Sarfoji (Thanjavur)	Sarbogie, Sarboji
Sengamala Das (Thanjavur)	Singamandasj; also Singe Malle. Sjangamalanaijk
Serfoji (Thanjavur)	see Sarfoji (Thanjavur)
Shah Alam II (Mughal)	Sjah Alam; also Sjah Alam Gaadsjah Gazie
Shah Jahan (Mughal)	Chasjaen, Chiasiaen, Sadogaen, Sasiahaen, Sazijachaen, Scha Jehaan, Sjah Djihaan
Shahji (Maratha, Thanjavur)	Sahagie, Sahasie; also Sagoe Rasia
Shahu (Maratha)	Sagoerasie
Shaista Khan (Bengal)	Cha Estachan, Chaestachan
Shambhuji (Maratha)	Sambosie
Shivaji (Maratha)	Sawagie, Seva Gi, Sieuwagie, Siwage, Suwagie, Suwasie; also Siva Ragia
Shivappa Nayak (Ikkeri)	Sivapa Neijck
Shuja-ud-Daula (Awadh)	Souja ud Doula
Sikandar Adil Shah (Bijapur)	Sikandaar Adilsja

Siraj-ud-Daula (Bengal)	Seraad Juddoula, Sirrayud Doella
Somashekhara (Ikkeri)	Somma Sequera, Somsecra
Sriranga (Vijayanagara)	Serangarije; also Srie Rangcrail, Srie Rangerait
Timma Raghu (Peddapuram)	Timmeragoe
Timmarasa (Jaffna)	Timmersa
Tipu Sultan (Mysore)	Tipoe Sultan; also Bahadoer Tipoe Sultan
Tirumalai Nayak (Madurai)	Tirimela Naijck
Tirumalai Setupati (Ramnad)	Tiroe Mala Chedy Paddy
Tukaji (Thanjavur)	see Tukkoji (Thanjavur)
Tukkoji (Thanjavur)	Toecoegie, Toekosie, Tokogie
Udai Singh (Burdwan)	Oudasingh
Venkaji (Thanjavur)	see Ekoji (Thanjavur)
Venkata (Vijayanagara)	Wenkete; also Vincata Patriaja Lau, Winkela Railoe
Vijaya Raghunatha (Ramnad)	Wiesie Regenaden, Wijeje Regoenade
Vijayaraghava Nayak (Thanjavur)	Visia Ragunaijk, Wiesia Ragua Nayker; also Visiagaragie
Vijayaranga Chokkanatha Nayak (Madurai)	Wisia Renga Sjokkenaden Nayk
Zulfiqar Ali Khan (Mughal)	syn. Julfacaar Chan, Julfacaerchan

3. Official and Dynastic Terms

Ali Raja (Cannanore)	Adaragia, Adersia, Adincha, Adiragia
Bhonsle (Maratha)	Bhonsale, Bonseloe
Chazhur Tavazhi (Cochin)	Chialour, Sjalour
Dalavay	Tallewaij, Talwaij
Dalawa	Dalawa
Desai	Dessaij
Dissave	Dessave
Diwan	Deuvan, Duan, Duwan
Faujdar	Fausdaar, Pausdaer
Hawaldar	Auweldaer, Haweldaar
Kanakkuppillai	Cannecappul
Karutta Tavazhi (Alangadu)	Cartadavile
Khan-i Khanan	Chan Channa
Kolathiri (Chirakkal)	Colastri, Collastrij, Kollatrij
Laskar	Lascorijn
Maharaja	Mageragie
Manakkulam Nambidi (Malabar)	Manacolottoe Nambedij, Mannecoelam
Maniyakkarar	Mannigaar
Mansabdar	Mancepdaer
Mudaliyar	Modeljaer
Mughal (Groot-)	Mogol
Mutta Tavazhi (Cochin)	Moetadavier, Moetadawille
Nawab	Nabab, Nabob

Nayak	Naijqui, Nayker, Neijck
Nayinar	Neijna
Paliyath Achan (Chennamangalam)	Palietter, Paljetter
Periya Tambi (Kilakkarai)	Peria Tambij, Perietambi
Pradani	Pardanij
Punnathur Nambidi (Malabar)	Poenatoer Nambeddij
Quilon's Raja (Desinganadu)	syn. Signatij, Signatti
Raja	Ragia, Ragie, Raija
Rani	Rani
Sar-khail (Shahi)	(Sahy) Sercheijl
Servaikkarar	Cheerwegaren
Setupati (Ramnad)	syn. Teuver, Catta Theuver, Theuverheer
Shahbandar	Sabandaer
Subahdar	Soubedaar
Tondaiman (Pudukkottai)	Thondeman, Tondeman
Udaya Tevar (Sivagangai)	Oedea Theuver
Valluvakonatiri (Valluvanadu)	Balloenade Conaderie; also Walluanattij Nambeddij
Valunnavar (Badagara)	Ballenoer, Balnoor; also Neallady Oddij
Vattattu Tavazhi (Cochin)	Bettette
Velose Nambiyar (Mapranam)	Belloaste Nambiaer, Nambeddijs Balonatu, Nambraar Balosoa
Zamorin (Calicut)	Sammorijn

4. Groups

Afghans	syn. Patanders
Banias	Benjaenen
Brahmins	Bramineesen
Chulias	Sjoliassen
Eunuchs	syn. Capados, Gelubden
Hindus	syn. Gentieven, Heydenen, Jentiefen, Jentijven
Labbai	Lebbe
Maraikkayar	Marcair, Marka
Marathas	Maratters, Marattijs, Marettys
Maravars	Marruassen, Marwas
Mughals	Mogolders
Muslims	syn. Mooren
Nayars (Malabar)	Naijros
Palaiyakkarars	Palleagaaren
Paravars	Parruassen, Paruas, Parwas
Poligars	see Palaiyakkarars
Rajputs	Radjepoeten, Rasjepoeters
Ravutan	see Rowther
Rowther	Rauten

Index to Part II and Appendices

Following Dutch rule, personal names with a prefix such as 'van' or 'de' are to be found under their full, second name.